SHAKESPEARE SURVEY

63

Shakespeare's English Histories and their Afterlives

EDITED BY

PETER HOLLAND

CAMBRIDGE UNIVERSITY PRESS
Cambridge, New York, Melbourne, Madrid, Cape Town, Singapore,
São Paulo, Delhi, Dubai, Tokyo, Mexico City

Cambridge University Press
The Edinburgh Building, Cambridge CB2 8RU, UK

Published in the United States of America by Cambridge University Press, New York

www.cambridge.org
Information on this title: www.cambridge.org/9780521769150

First published 2010

Printed in the United Kingdom at the University Press, Cambridge

A catalogue record for this publication is available from the British Library

ISBN 978-0-521-76915-0 Hardback

EDITOR'S NOTE

Volume 64, on 'Shakespeare as Cultural Catalyst', will be at press by the time this volume appears. The theme of Volume 65 will be '*A Midsummer Night's Dream*'.

Submissions should be addressed to the Editor at The Shakespeare Institute, Church Street, Stratford-upon-Avon, Warwickshire CV37 6HP, to arrive at the latest by 1 September 2011 for Volume 65. Pressures on space are heavy and priority is given to articles related to the theme of a particular volume. Please send a copy you do not wish to be returned. Submissions may also be made as attachments to e-mail to pholland@nd.edu. All articles submitted are read by the Editor and at least one member of the Advisory Board, whose indispensable assistance the Editor gratefully acknowledges.

Unless otherwise indicated, Shakespeare quotations and references are keyed to *The Complete Works*, ed. Stanley Wells, Gary Taylor, John Jowett and William Montgomery, 2nd edition (Oxford, 2005).

Review copies should be addressed to the Editor as above. In attempting to survey the ever-increasing bulk of Shakespeare publications our reviewers inevitably have to exercise some selection. We are pleased to receive offprints of articles which help to draw our reviewers' attention to relevant material.

P.D.H.

CONTRIBUTORS

PASCALE AEBISCHER, *University of Exeter*
N.W. BAWCUTT, *University of Liverpool*
JAMES C. BULMAN, *Allegheny College*
CLARA CALVO, *University of Murcia*
DERMOT CAVANAGH, *University of Edinburgh*
JANET CLARE, *University of Hull*
ALICE DAILEY, *Villanova University*
CHRISTY DESMET, *University of Georgia*
JANETTE DILLON, *University of Nottingham*
LARS ENGLE, *University of Tulsa*
ALISON FINDLAY, *Lancaster University*
CHARLES R. FORKER, *Indiana University*
RALF HERTEL, *University of Hamburg*
ANNA KAMARALLI, *Trinity College, Dublin*
ISABEL KARREMANN, *Ludwig-Maximilians-University, Munich*
VANASAY KHAMPHOMMALA, *University of Paris-Sorbonne*
ARTHUR F. KINNEY, *University of Massachussetts, Amherst*
BARBARA KREPS, *University of Pisa*
NAOMI CONN LIEBLER, *Montclair State University*
JOHN McGEE, *University of Geneva*
RANDALL MARTIN, *University of New Brunswick*
JEAN-CHRISTOPHE MAYER, *University of Montpellier 3 Paul-Valéry*
ERIC RASMUSSEN, *University of Nevada, Reno*
CAROL CHILLINGTON RUTTER, *University of Warwick*
JULIE SANDERS, *University of Nottingham*
KATHERINE SCHEIL, *University of Minnesota*
SABINE SCHÜLTING, *Freie Universität, Berlin*
ROBERT SHAUGHNESSY, *University of Kent*
JAMES SHAW, *University of Oxford*
MEREDITH SKURA, *Rice University*
EMMA SMITH, *University of Oxford*
JESÚS TRONCH-PÉREZ, *University of Valencia*

SHAKESPEARE SURVEY

ADVISORY BOARD

CONTENTS

CONTENTS

ILLUSTRATIONS

ILLUSTRATIONS

SHAKESPEARE THE HISTORIAN

CHRISTY DESMET

Nearly thirty years after the emergence of new historicism and cultural materialism in Shakespeare studies, we have had ample time to make and lose the acquaintance of a figure who quietly underwrote these literary-historical labours: Shakespeare the Historian. In a book of that name published in 1996, Paola Pugliatti imagined a Shakespeare who showed an active interest in not only the past and historical events unfolding around him, but also emerging forms of historiography.[1] But this Shakespeare, a theorist as well as a chronicler of the past, has not found a permanent place in the scholarly, much less the popular, imagination. Certainly, the failure of Shakespeare the Historian to make his mark in literary studies has something to do with new historicist methodology, in which social energies 'circulate' and there can be a 'Textuality of History' without the explicit intervention of a reading-writing subject – that is, an Author.[2] Another factor might be the resurgence, among writers ranging from William Kerrigan to Harold Bloom, of Shakespeare as an avatar for a Romantic or modern sensibility.[3] The rise and fall of Shakespeare the Historian cannot be attributed solely to the vagaries of critical orientation, however. The history of Shakespearian biography has its own story to tell about Shakespeare's interests and intellectual habits. In this essay, I consider how the figure of Shakespeare the Historian gradually takes shape in a dialectic among critical, biographical and editorial discourse, suggesting that the phenomenon offers an evocative case of what Kenneth Burke would call 'impure motives' – a working out of different agendas, not necessarily even fully formed,

that coalesces loosely into a consensus story about Shakespeare as a particular kind of cultural icon. At the same time, the fading of Shakespeare the Historian as an authoritative figure in recent times suggests how entrenched biographical traditions can be. This excursion into meta-biography will, I hope, suggest not only why the concept of Shakespeare as a historian is so difficult to sustain, but also how the figure might be re-imagined for a different Shakespearian historiography.

For better or worse, the most enduring paradigm for Shakespeare as a thinker and writer remains the post-Romantic image of Shakespeare as a literary icon – lunatic, lover, poet, and philosopher – that was firmly in place by the end of the nineteenth century. This is the image that informs Edward Dowden's widely disseminated mini-biography, in which Shakespeare begins in the theatre workshop but, as he matures, turns inward to draw on his own emotional experience, descending into

---

[1] Paola Pugliatti, *Shakespeare the Historian* (New York, 1996), p. 7.

[2] The first phrase comes from Stephen Greenblatt, *Shakespearean Negotiations: The Circulation of Social Energy in Renaissance England* (Berkeley, 1988); the second comes from Louis A. Montrose, 'Professing the Renaissance: The Poetics and Politics of Culture', in H. Aram Veeser, ed., *The New Historicism* (New York and London, 1989), pp. 15–36; p. 23.

[3] William Kerrigan, *Hamlet's Perfection* (Baltimore, 1994); Harold Bloom, *Shakespeare: The Invention of the Human* (New York, 1997). On Shakespeare and the 'birth' of modernity, see the analysis of Margreta de Grazia, '*Hamlet* before Its Time', *Modern Language Quarterly*, 62 (2001), 355–75; and Hugh Grady, ed., *Shakespeare and Modernity: Early Modern to Millennium* (London, 2000).

the emotional 'depths' after the death of his son Hamnet to produce the 'great tragedies' and ascending gradually to the philosophical 'heights' of *The Tempest* after his retirement to Stratford.[4] Shakespeare's stint as a writer of history plays, in this narrative, is merely a stage in his steady progress towards heightened intellect and emotion – in short, towards becoming a genius.

While this image of Shakespeare has persisted through popular and school culture and has been rehabilitated by retro-Romantics such as Kerrigan and Bloom in scholarly discussion during the twentieth century, Shakespeare the Man became bifurcated into Shakespeare the Man of the Theatre and Shakespeare the Author, a philosophical split aptly emblematized by those twinned institutions of high culture – the theatre and library – that sustain what Barbara Hodgdon has called the Shakespeare Trade.[5] Shakespeare the Man of the Theatre generally agrees with Sir Philip Sidney about the value of the historian's 'mouse-eaten records'.[6] Irving Ribner's venerable history of *The English History Play in the Age of Shakespeare*, the ur-text for that large run of books on Shakespeare's histories that were published in the 1970s and 1980s, defines Shakespeare's superiority to other writers of history plays by his ability to shake free from the chronological constraints of chronicle and to avoid the frivolous tales of less pure, romance histories. Shakespeare does history well by resisting the conventions of medieval and early modern historical discourse. Even Phyllis Rackin's judicious account of Shakespeare's history plays valorizes the drama at the expense of its prose sources. Rackin writes that

a major impetus for the Tudor fascination with history was to defend against the forces of modernity, to deny change, and to rationalize a bewildering world in fictions of hereditary privilege. The public commercial theater, by contrast, was a totally new phenomenon, a disreputable place where common players draped in the discarded clothes of aristocrats impersonated their betters for the entertainment (and the pennies) of a disorderly, socially heterogeneous audience.[7]

On this view, historical writing is 'univocal' and conservative, while Shakespeare's theatrical scripts are 'polyvocal' and subversive. The theatre, as an institution and a site for performative activity, thus has an invigorating effect on history and even acts as a corrective to the 'voice of official history': historiography itself 'is re-presented as a dubious construct, always provisional, subject to erasure and reconstruction, and never adequate to recover the past in full presence'.[8] In this way Shakespeare becomes something of an 'anti-historian'.

While Shakespeare the Man of the Theatre works with historical materials but remains aloof from their conservative politics and positively resists their plodding narrative method, Shakespeare the Author is by inclination more scholarly. Hodgdon describes the iconic image of the bard at his books that can be found on exhibit at the Shakespeare Centre in Stratford-upon-Avon:

A life-size mannequin of Shakespeare sits in a sturdy armchair, eyes cast down to the book he holds in his lap, a pewter tankard beside him on the rush-mat floor covering, a cup and a large leather-bound volume on a nearby joint stool. His desk, tucked into a corner lit by a lattice-paned window and covered with a small turkey carpet or tapestry fragment, holds a writing stand, inkwell, book stand, and vase of flowers; just above it are several shelves stacked with books, a pocket portfolio, and a candlestick. Looking much like an upscale early modern version of today's computer desks, this setting imagines a Shakespeare who is not a theatre man but an author, even an academic.[9]

Shakespeare the Author may have a debatable amount of Latin and Greek, but he has ample means and leisure to delve into his nicely bound

---

[4] Edward Dowden, *Shakspere* (London, 1877), pp. 58–60; discussed by Samuel Schoenbaum, *Shakespeare's Lives* (Oxford, 1991), pp. 357–8.

[5] Barbara Hodgdon, *The Shakespeare Trade: Performances and Appropriations* (Philadelphia, 1998).

[6] *Sir Philip Sidney's Defense of Poesy*, ed. by Lewis Soens (Lincoln, 1970), p. 15.

[7] Irving Ribner, *The English History Play in the Age of Shakespeare* (Princeton, 1957); Phyllis Rackin, *Stages of History* (Philadelphia, 1990), p. 22.

[8] Jean E. Howard and Phyllis Rackin, *Engendering a Nation: A Feminist Account of Shakespeare's English Histories* (London and New York, 1997), p. 59.

[9] Hodgdon, *The Shakespeare Trade*, p. 200.

Holinshed and Plutarch for dramatic material. A more nuanced image of this same Shakespeare can be found in Stanley Wells's *Shakespeare for All Time*, which describes Shakespeare's Stratford home, New Place, as providing him with 'a comfortable, book-lined study situated in the quietest part of the house to which Shakespeare retreated from London at every possible opportunity, and which members of the household approached at their peril when the master was at work'.[10]

The twentieth-century master narrative of Shakespeare's ideological leanings and intellectual habits, where the theatre is invariably at odds with the study, continues to be reinforced by such popular productions as *Shakespeare in Love*, where, immured in his study, Shakespeare can only write his signature over and over again; he seeks in vain for inspiration until he finds it out-of-doors at the theatre – first in the person of sensuous Rosalind and then in the lovely Viola who, not surprisingly, moonlights as Thomas Kent the actor.[11] The story of Shakespeare the Historian, by contrast, is strongly focused on debating the scholarly credentials of Shakespeare as Author. It is this single focus that has sustained investigations of Shakespeare's historiography well into the twentieth century but that eventually undermines Shakespeare's credibility as a historian when, in a new biographical trend, the Man of Theatre crowds out his scholarly *doppelgänger*. As I will suggest, however, healing imaginatively the rift between stage and study may offer new ways of thinking about Shakespearian history in the making.

SCHOLARLY SHAKESPEARE

That Shakespeare probably attended the Stratford Free School was first established by Nicholas Rowe,[12] and most recent biographies accept that Shakespeare probably left school at least by the age of fifteen. As Samuel Schoenbaum demonstrates, however, the notion that Shakespeare was a scholar as well as a poet – if not specifically a historian – was part of the popular tradition that fuelled his canonization. According to Schoenbaum, 'In 1877 the master of the free school, like others before

him, proudly displayed Shakespeare's desk to visitors: "William was a studious lad", he pointed out, "& selected that corner of the room so that he might not be disturbed by the other boys".' Phoebe Dighton's *Relics of Shakespeare* (1835) also included a lithograph of Shakespeare's schoolboy desk as one of its sacred icons.[13] The sentimental view of Shakespeare as a good student, however, did not go uncontested in the establishment of Shakespeare's biography.

The tradition that Shakespeare was no scholar goes back as far as Nicholas Rowe's biography (1709), where 'learning' means knowledge of the classical poets and is linked to the notion that Shakespeare had only the 'little' Latin that he had acquired at school.[14] Furthermore, the issue of Shakespeare's learning was deemed irrelevant to his portrayal of English history in his plays. Rowe, who thought the term Histories a misnomer in Shakespeare's case (most of those labelled as histories in the Folio should properly be considered tragedies), also considered that Shakespeare mined such historical texts as Holinshed and Plutarch not for historical fact or even moral lessons, but for characters:

What can be more agreeable to the Idea our Historians give of *Henry* the Sixth, than the Picture *Shakespear* has drawn of him! His Manners are every where exactly the same with the Story; one finds him describ'd with Simplicity, passive Sincerity, want of Courage, weakness of Mind, and easie Submission to the Governance of

---

[10] Stanley Wells, *Shakespeare for All Time* (Basingstoke and Oxford, 2002), p. 38.

[11] *Shakespeare in Love*, written by Marc Norman and Tom Stoppard, dir. John Madden, perf. Joseph Fiennes, Gwyneth Paltrow, Judi Dench (US, 1998).

[12] Nicholas Rowe, *Some Account of the Life of Mr. William Shakespear* (1709), with an introduction by Samuel Holt Monk, Augustan Reprint Society, 17 (Ann Arbor, 1948), pp. ii–iii; see also Schoenbaum, *Shakespeare's Lives*, p. 67.

[13] Schoenbaum, *Shakespeare's Lives*, p. 47; Phoebe Dighton, *Relics of Shakespeare* (Stratford-upon-Avon, 1835), cited by Schoenbaum, *Shakespeare's Lives*, p. 47. See also Curtis Guild, *Over the Ocean: Or, Sights and Scenes in Foreign Lands* (Boston, 1884), p. 120.

[14] Rowe, *Some Account of the Life of Mr. William Shakespear*, p. ii.

an Imperious Wife, or prevailing Faction: Tho' at the same time the Poet do's Justice to his good Qualities, and moves the Pity of the Audience for him, by showing him Pious, Disinterested, a Contemner of the Things of this World, and wholly resign'd to the severest Dispositions of God's Providence.[15]

The 'Characters' of Cardinal Beaufort's death, Wolsey and Henry VIII, and Coriolanus are also singled out for praise. The shape of Rowe's mini-encomium to Henry VI reflects the character portraiture prominent in history writing after Clarendon, a form that would also be incorporated into a wider range of commentary on Shakespeare's literary characters and would also be mercilessly satirized in Jane Austen's send-up of such character-driven histories – in her case, Oliver Goldsmith's *History of England* – in *The History of England, from the Reign of Henry the 4th to the Death of Charles the 1st*.[16] Thus, the argument that Shakespeare lacked learning undermines Shakespeare's claim to the status of scholar even as it places him within a certain tradition of history writing.

For Rowe, Shakespeare's lack of learning is evident in both his reliance on vulgate sources and his careful adherence to those source texts for both his English and Roman histories. As Shakespeare criticism developed in the eighteenth century, a lack of facility with foreign languages and literature became the focus of arguments about Shakespeare's learning. Richard Farmer's *An Essay on the Learning of Shakspeare* (2nd edition, 1767) argues that Shakespeare lacks foreign languages, having gathered all his references to classical authors from '*Excerpta, Sententiae,* and *Flores*'.[17] Although, as Schoenbaum points out, Farmer's analysis rests on his own library and prodigious reading in the texts of Shakespeare's day and, although he meant to praise Shakespeare's native wit by dismissing the possibility of classical imitation, Farmer comes across as disdainful of Shakespeare's reliance not merely on Plutarch for his Greek and Roman history, but on North's English translation.[18] What Greek expressions Shakespeare sets down, according to Farmer, were available through sources ranging from John Davies to Samuel Daniel. Holinshed

is mentioned, but only in the context of showing that Shakespeare relied on the *Chronicle* as a derivative source, not directly on Greek sources, as Upton had speculated.[19]

Alone among the early biographers who relied primarily on Rowe but appreciated Shakespeare's learning was Alexander Pope, who not only omitted Rowe's comments about Shakespeare's lack of scholarly acumen in his version of Rowe's *Life*,[20] but also, in his own Preface to the *Works of Shakespeare*, suggested that Shakespeare's familiarity with English historical writings constituted in itself evidence of learning: 'But as to his *Want of Learning*, it may be necessary to say something more: There is certainly a vast difference between *Learning* and *Languages*. How far he was ignorant of the latter, I cannot determine; but 'tis plain he had much Reading at least, if they will not call it Learning.' As Pope continues, however, it becomes clear that the evidence of learning, Shakespeare's observance of ancient 'spirit' and 'manners', is part of the Bard's ability to draw 'whatever object or nature, or branch of Science' he addresses.[21] Thus, Shakespeare's reading serves the instincts of Shakespeare the poet of Nature rather than the scholar who might be interested in history.

---

[15] Rowe, *Some Account of the Life of Mr. William Shakespear*, pp. xxviii–xxix.

[16] Jane Austen, *The History of England, from the Reign of Henry the 4th to the Death of Charles the 1st* (Chapel Hill, 1993), p. 2; Oliver Goldsmith, *Abridgement of the History of England, from the Invasion of Julius Caesar to the Death of George the Second*, from the 12th edition, Early American Imprints, second series, No. 15127 (Philadelphia, 1808).

[17] Richard Farmer, *An Essay on the Learning of Shakspeare* (1821; repr., New York, 1966), p. 17.

[18] Schoenbaum, *Shakespeare's Lives*, p. 102; Farmer, *An Essay on the Learning of Shakspeare*, pp. 18, 22.

[19] Farmer, *An Essay on the Learning of Shakspeare*, pp. 27–9.

[20] Samuel Holt Monk notes that Pope's more orderly rewriting of Rowe's biography (which even Malone accepted as Rowe's own revision) eliminated the references to Shakespeare's lack of learning (Introduction to Rowe, *Some Account of the Life of Mr. William Shakespear*, p. 10, n. 6).

[21] Alexander Pope, ed., *The Works of Mr. William Shakespear*, 6 vols. (London, 1723–5; repr., New York, 1969), vol. 1, pp. ix–x.

But Pope's was a minority voice, and to a great extent Shakespeare's ostensible lack of learning led critics to see the histories in the context of a broader, and less elevated, concept of literature. Farmer's exegesis of Shakespeare's learning makes little distinction between what we would think of as proto-novels and more 'serious' history and literature, such as Chaucer's *Book of Fame* and the *Mirror for Magistrates*; as sources, all demonstrate equally that Shakespeare was no scholar. Although he gives her only the most cursory of acknowledgements, Farmer's notion of the histories (like Rowe's) is consistent with the way in which Holinshed was packaged by the early collection of source materials, Charlotte Lennox's *Shakespear Illustrated*. Lennox's redaction of the *Macbeth* portion of Holinshed's *Chronicle*, for instance, prefigures many of the narrative techniques of the Lambs in their proto-novelistic *Tales from Shakespear*. The opening sets the scene and introduces Macdonwald in a way that is much more regular than either Shakespeare or Holinshed. Within a kind of romance plot, Lady Macbeth and Macbeth take on folkloric characters. Macbeth is a villain waiting for his chance to make mischief, a cousin to the King who is 'of a Disposition as haughty, cruel, and revengeful, as *Duncan's* was mild and peaceable'. Lady Macbeth, 'a proud, ambitious, and cruel Woman, urges on her Husband to the Murder of the King'.[22] In Lennox's narrative summary, it is difficult to separate a historical ethos from the romantic tone of other, more popular 'stories' upon which Shakespeare drew. Her sourcebook retains the very old sense that 'history' and 'story' are etymologically the same thing.

AUTHENTICATING
SHAKESPEARIAN HISTORY

As Shakespeare gradually was canonized, the status of his history writing grew proportionately, and Shakespeare became, himself, a 'source' for English readers' knowledge about English history. The kind of edifying history that was written by Goldsmith and satirized by Austen often spawned pedagogical abridgements, complete with study and essay questions that easily allowed for slippage between history writing proper and Shakespearian drama. This slippage made its way as well into quasi-scholarly discourse about the histories. Bolstered by Coleridge's remark that 'the great Duke of Marlborough acknowledged that his principal acquaintance with English history was derived from the historical plays', for instance, Thomas Peregrine Courtenay, politician and author, begins his two-volume *Commentaries on the Historical Plays of Shakspeare* with the adage that 'the youth of England take their religion from Milton, and their history from Shakspeare'.[23] The question that Courtenay sets himself is: '*what were Shakespeare's authorities for his history, and how far has he departed from them?*', combined with a pedagogical concern to know '*whether the plays may be given to our youth, as "properly historical?"*'.[24] His answer rests upon a body of historical sources ranging from the sixteenth through the nineteenth centuries. While Courtenay decides that Shakespeare's history is not accurate enough to substitute for other, more authentic historical texts, he too takes up arms in defence of the bard as Author.

The very possibility of Courtenay's amateur project – to assess the 'authenticity' of Shakespeare's history – depends on a complex of factors establishing an 'authentic' Shakespeare. As Margreta de Grazia has shown in her extensive analysis of Edmond Malone's 1790 Apparatus, the emergence of 'Shakespeare' as Foucault's sovereign subject rests upon the notion of Shakespeare as an authentic biographical and textual subject.[25] First, there is Malone's establishment of Shakespeare's earliest

---

[22] Charlotte Lennox, *Shakespear Illustrated: or the Novels and Histories on which the Plays of Shakespear are Founded* (London, 1753; repr., New York, 1973), vol. 1, pp. 252, italics in original; 270.

[23] Coleridge, *Literary Remains*, cited by Thomas Peregrine Courtenay, *Commentaries on the Historical Plays of Shakspear*, 2 vols. (London: Henry Colburn, 1840; repr., New York, 1972), vol. 1, p. iv.

[24] Courtenay, *Commentaries*, vol. 1, p. xii, italics in original.

[25] Margreta de Grazia, *Shakespeare Verbatim: The Reproduction of Authenticity and the 1790 Apparatus* (Oxford, 1991), p. 9.

printed texts as primary for the editor. As de Grazia writes, 'The new criterion of authenticity converted the Shakespearian texts into a new kind of object: one lodged in the past rather than integral to current cultural concerns.' Thanks to Malone's 'cooler model of research', which allowed for 'the gradual accumulation of the information he identified with the bygone past',[26] the text of 'Shakespeare' could now be placed next to that of such historical chroniclers as 'Holinshed', in a conceptual form of Hinman collator. (The completion of this textual project would have to wait, however, for the antiquarian revival of Holinshed's 'text' by Sir Henry Ellis – the singular number of 'text' here being this editor's contribution.) Malone's second project, establishing an 'authentic' biography for Shakespeare, in conjunction with Ellis's similar project for Holinshed and other chroniclers, made possible the notion that Shakespeare, Holinshed and such figures as Edward Hall were fellow travellers through the fields of English national history.

SHAKESPEARE AMONG THE CHRONICLES

The Keeper of Printed Books in the British Museum, Ellis was an antiquary and a librarian, but not so distinguished as to draw much enthusiasm from his biographer in the *Dictionary of National Biography*. While Ellis's post gave him privileged access to old texts and manuscripts, to a large extent his *Holinshed* manifested on a grand scale the kind of antiquarian interest that fuelled the popular collections of British antiquities, which aristocratic travellers excerpted for their tours through the countryside. (Ellis himself edited and published Brand's *Popular Antiquities* in 1813.)[27] Snippets of *Holinshed* showed up, for instance, in such venues as the periodical *The Antiquarian Repertory* (first volume 1775).[28] *Holinshed* also continued to be disseminated through collections of Shakespeare source materials in the tradition of Lennox; John Payne Collier's six-volume edition of *Shakespeare's Library* included some *Holinshed*, although, when possible, he preferred popular drama – such as *The*

Famous Victories of Henry V – and other romances to chronicle sources.[29] Framed by popular literature and romance, *Holinshed* became detached from the tradition of history writing; in Ellis's ponderous edition, by contrast, Holinshed conferred on Shakespeare new credentials as a student of history.

Ellis's large Folio of *Holinshed's Chronicle*, published by Richard Lan in 1807–8, was part of a larger project to recover and print 'significant histories and chronicles from the sixteenth century'.[30] Ellis reprints the 1587 edition, but pieces in censored portions that had been kept in circulation in eighteenth-century volumes. (This is Ellis's method as well with his edition of John Hardyng's *Chronicle*, where he combines the version printed by Richard Grafton in 1543 with additions from the Selden and Harley manuscripts available to him.) Thus, although Ellis manages to achieve a certain kind of completeness with his volume, he does so at a price, creating a *Holinshed* that readers of neither the 1577 nor 1587 editions would have read. In de Grazia's lexicon, he suppresses textual *copia* in the service of establishing a stable, unitary textual 'copy'.[31] Ellis, in other words, does to Holinshed what Malone did to Shakespeare.

Their texts stabilized, their personae individualized, the newly allied figures of Shakespeare and Holinshed stood poised to authenticate the project of Shakespearian historiography, which would achieve its most powerful form in the totalizing mechanics of E. M. W. Tillyard's version of Shakespeare as an apologist for the Tudor Myth. Ellis's foray into editing the chronicles was followed by a spate of single-volume compendia of 'Shakespeare's Holinshed' that made Holinshed more or

---

[26] De Grazia, *Shakespeare Verbatim*, p. 71.

[27] Rosemary Sweet, *Antiquaries: The Discovery of the Past in Eighteenth-Century Britain* (London and New York, 2004), p. 337.

[28] Sweet, *Antiquaries*, pp. 321–2.

[29] *Shakespeare's Library: A Collection of the Plays, Romances, Novels, Poems, and Histories Employed by Shakespeare in the Composition of his Works*, 2nd edn, 6 vols. (London, 1875).

[30] Alison Taufer, *Holinshed's Chronicle*, Twayne's English Authors Series (New York, 1999), p. 138.

[31] De Grazia, *Shakespeare Verbatim*, p. 92.

less available to teachers and students. Some gathered together excerpts from *Holinshed* under the rubric of individual plays (Boswell-Stone), while others presented the materials relevant to Shakespeare's plays in the order they appear in *Holinshed* (Hosley).[32] From here, snippets of *Holinshed* made their way into editions of Shakespeare ranging from the magisterial Arden series to the inexpensive paperback Signet editions. While the Holinshed-for-students industry was to some extent just a by-product of the larger project of establishing Shakespeare as a historian, it provides crucial material for Tillyard's own project, which was itself as much pedagogical as scholarly in its goals.

Terence Hawkes, among others, has shown that Shakespeare was gradually drawn into the long, durable project of establishing English national identity by way of English letters. The idea that Shakespeare spoke for the English nation and its values, although implicit in much nineteenth-century discourse about Shakespeare after Carlyle, took on renewed urgency in the twentieth century, particularly between the World Wars. Figures from Arthur Quiller-Couch to Walter Raleigh are prominent as scholar-ideologues in the creation of a sense of Englishness through the figure of Shakespeare.[33] E. M. W. Tillyard, as Graham Holderness and Hugh Grady have both argued, was another important player in the modernist appropriation of Shakespeare as an English Man of Letters and apologist for English nationalism.[34] As part of this national project, Tillyard also completed the apotheosis of Shakespeare the Historian.

Eustace Mandeville Wetenhall Tillyard was a classicist and a Fellow in English and then Master of Jesus College, Cambridge. Tillyard's influence on the study of Renaissance literature and on Anglo-American literary education generally rests on his pedagogical blockbuster, *The Elizabethan World Picture*, which situated Elizabethan intellectual culture within a medieval tradition that was, at heart, theological and – most importantly – largely stable and uniform. *The Elizabethan World Picture*, wide-ranging in the sources it cites, is simple in its methodology but epic in vision. Shakespeare's most memorable contribution was Ulysses's

speech on degree from *Troilus and Cressida* which, although it is given pride of place near the front of the book, is absorbed into a tapestry of references so that the Elizabethan World Picture does not, ultimately, have a strongly Shakespearian flavour. Rather, the book promotes a view of Renaissance thought whose public face is a Milton who, despite his adherence to no fewer than three heresies, was 'normal' for his age in his belief in a theological world order and who, through the intermediary of Tillyard's criticism, comes to have a normative role in English intellectual history.

According to Tillyard's preface to *The Elizabethan World Picture*, however, that little book was a by-product of a weightier project, *Shakespeare's History Plays*, which takes on more directly the task of describing a Shakespeare who believed in and represented a national politics grounded in cosmic order.[35] Tillyard's familiar account of Shakespeare's two English tetralogies – a dramatic structure largely of his own making – traces the political disorder that follows Henry IV's usurpation of the crown from Richard II through the successive upheavals marking each subsequent reign until the accession of Henry VII, by unifying the warring Houses of Lancaster and York, ushers in and fulfils the Tudor Myth. Tillyard's vision of medieval English politics and of literature's social function, as critics have pointed out repeatedly, are both ideologically conservative; and it was this conservatism that made him a prime target for cultural

---

32 See W. G. Boswell-Stone, *Shakespeare's Holinshed: The Chronicle and the Historical Plays Compared* (1896; repr., New York, 1966); Stephen Booth, *The Book Called Holinshed's Chronicles* (San Francisco, 1968); Richard Hosley, *Shakespeare's Holinshed* (New York, 1968).

33 See, for instance, Terence Hawkes, 'Entry on Q', in *Shakespeare and Appropriation*, ed. Christy Desmet and Robert Sawyer (London, 1999), pp. 33–46; 'Swisser Swatter: Making a Man of English Letters', in *That Shakespeherian Rag: Essays on a Critical Process* (London and New York, 1986), pp. 26–47.

34 Graham Holderness, *Shakespeare: The Histories* (New York, 2000); Hugh Grady, *The Modernist Shakespeare: Critical Texts in a Material World* (Oxford, 1991).

35 E. M. W. Tillyard, *The Elizabethan World Picture* (New York, 1943), p. vii.

materialist critics in Britain during the 1980s.[36] But, as Hugh Grady has argued, the reception of Tillyard's work in the United States as well as Britain suggests a less uniform ideology at work than the focus on his work's expression of a hegemonic wartime politics might allow.

A strongly pedagogical, more than a political, motive underlies Tillyard's work, according to Grady. Tillyard, he argues, steered an ameliorating path between the nineteenth-century philology of Cambridge's heritage and the 'new professionalism', the concept of education as a preparation for economic life that was being promoted by F. R. Leavis.[37] Tillyard grounded his own educational programme in that most venerable of literary activities, source study. Thus, he parades before readers authorities ranging from Polydore Virgil to William Warner, but organizes them under the banner of the most ideologically consistent of Tudor chroniclers, Edward Hall, who is *fons et origo* of Tillyard's 'Tudor myth'.[38] 'What raised Tillyard's study above the level of ordinary "source hunting"', according to Grady, 'was the attempt to synthesize the sources with a general cultural pattern that appeared, in a phrase Engels once used in a flight of hubristic fantasy, to explain almost everything'.[39] The Tudor Myth, by offering a nostalgically modernist view of English monarchical hegemony as organic medieval culture, thus gains a loose kinship with T. S. Eliot's notion of literary tradition and, methodologically, with the American New Critics. (Parenthetically, Henry Ansgar Kelly has made the complementary argument that Renaissance notions of Providence were less monolithic than Tillyard acknowledges: instead of a uniform concept of divine Providence, we find in the body of chronicles a 'series of simpler providential patterns, mainly short-range ad hoc judgments in favor of each new line of kings and against the immediate predecessor, or vice versa'.)[40]

By assimilating Tillyard's project to modernism, however, Grady underemphasizes his affinity with the older historicist tradition that promotes an 'authentic' Shakespeare from whose world the reader is estranged. Grady himself notes that 'his book is so necessary, Tillyard keeps telling us, precisely because *we* are now so different in our historical suppositions'.[41] As de Grazia also emphasizes, the reproduction of texts, both Shakespearian and historical, makes the alien past accessible, fixable, present and capable of being possessed. Thus Tillyard, like Malone before him, fixes the text by placing it in the distant past. This move, in turn, authenticates both author and work and allows Shakespeare to be seen as a historian.[42] Tillyard also sees Shakespeare as a historiographer or theorist of history. The first chapter to *Shakespeare's History Plays* suggests that 'if Shakespeare went to Holinshed for many of his facts, he had meditated on the political philosophy of Hall and of his own day'.[43] *Henry VIII*, a belated history play, also reaches back to Hall, whose *Chronicle* 'Shakespeare had read and digested in his early years' and from whom he had derived his 'philosophy of history'.[44] By his own account, Tillyard (and Shakespeare) are drawn to Hall not only for the elegant shape of his chronicle – superior, in Tillyard's view, to Holinshed's baggy collections of facts and anecdotes – but also for its philosophical depth. Tillyard thus refashions Shakespeare as an epic dramatist – in effect, another Milton. He concludes: 'I hope this book has served to strengthen the ideas of an educated Shakespeare, and of a poet more rather than less like Dante and Milton in massiveness of intellect

---

36 See Holderness, *Shakespeare's History* (New York 1985).
37 Hugh Grady, 'Instituting Shakespeare: Hegemony and Tillyard's Historical Criticism', *Assays: Critical Approaches to Medieval and Renaissance Texts*, 5 (Pittsburgh, 1989), 37–61; Grady, *The Modernist Shakespeare*, p. 169 and *passim*.
38 Edward Hall, *Union of the Two Noble and Illustre Fameles of Lancastre and Yorke* (London, 1548).
39 Grady, *The Modernist Shakespeare*, p. 171.
40 Henry Ansgar Kelly, 'Tillyard and History: Comment and Response', *Clio: A Journal of Literature, History, and the Philosophy of History*, 10 (1980), 85–8.
41 Grady, *The Modernist Shakespeare*, p. 174.
42 De Grazia, *Shakespeare Verbatim*, p. 11.
43 E. M. W. Tillyard, *Shakespeare's History Plays* (New York, 1944), p. 3.
44 E. M. W. Tillyard, 'Why Did Shakespeare Write "Henry VIII"', in *Essays: Literary and Educational* (New York, 1962), p. 48.

and powers of reflection.'[45] Educated Shakespeare, scholarly Shakespeare, a superior mind musing on historical patterns and philosophies: Tillyard's author is another manifestation of Shakespeare the Historian who stands tall in the company of the philosophical Hall and intellectual Milton.

Grady and Holderness both couple Tillyard with Lily Bess Campbell, the American historicist whose work on *A Mirror for Magistrates* likewise produced an influential account of Shakespeare's history plays as 'mirrors' of Elizabethan policy. Tillyard praised Campbell's edition of the *Mirror* as an indispensable aid to teachers and students.[46] But Campbell, unlike Tillyard (whose thematic machine is primarily pedagogical and critical) and unlike Ellis (whose impulse is primarily antiquarian and whose method is homogenizing), was a modern literary editor whose labours in the Huntington Library's pastoral vineyards produced a judiciously edited selection of the *Mirror for Magistrates* (1938), complete with the kind of editorial apparatus that Ellis's *Holinshed* lacked and that Tillyard's totalizing framework rendered unnecessary.[47] From her edition, we can tell what entered the *Mirror* when, and we can imagine, if not experience first-hand, the mutation of this text through successive editions. This editorial drive and experience, I suggest, not only tie Campbell to the long-standing project of validating Shakespeare's historiography, but also point forward to more contemporary developments in the study of English chronicles.

Holderness proposes that any attempt to demonstrate the 'organic unity' of Shakespeare's histories entails its opposite, the idea that Shakespeare's plays were, from the outset, 'discontinuous' and 'fragmentary', 'each individually and independently shaped by contemporary cultural pressures'.[48] With the figure of Shakespeare the Historian finally installed in the library and classroom, we can see the subsequent process of fragmentation in not only the number of critical books on the histories produced between the 1970s and 1990s, but even more specifically in historiographic projects aimed at dismantling the monolithic figure that the success of Tillyard's paradigm had reified. These works range from Henry Ansgar Kelly's careful study of Shake-

speare's multitudinous sources (1970), which incidentally provides scholars with a priceless bibliography, to Annabel Patterson's (1994) liberation of Holinshed from the confining aura of Shakespeare. Each of these writers is at heart something between an editor, a teacher and an antiquarian in the best sense of that word, pointing readers of different moods and capacities to primary texts that will let them play, for however long and intensely they choose, the role of historiographer.[49] But while the textual work begun in the name of Shakespeare the Historian may continue unabated, the figure himself is, sadly and ironically, being written out of the story by the most recent biographies of Shakespeare – in particular, by that paradigmatic champion of textual mutability, Stephen Greenblatt.

WILL BACK IN THE WORLD

Greenblatt's biography, the most popular and probably the most reviewed of the new spate of books on Shakespeare's life, distances the Bard from the early modern texts that sustained not only Tillyard's 'old historicism', but also Greenblatt's and many others' new historicism. In *Will in the World*, Greenblatt mentions Holinshed only three times and Hall not many more. Holinshed becomes merely the lens through which Shakespeare perceives his new home, London, and thereafter a crib to which he turns for material to trump Marlowe's *Tamburlaine* with an English epic.[50] In the *Henry VI* plays, for instance, Shakespeare takes John Cade from Holinshed and mixes his rebellion with elements of the even more distant 1381 Peasants'

[45] Tillyard, *Shakespeare's History Plays*, p. 321.

[46] E. M. W. Tillyard, '"A Mirror for Magistrates" Revisited', in *Essays: Literary and Educational*, p. 165.

[47] Lily B. Campbell, ed., *Mirror for Magistrates, Edited from Original Texts in the Huntington Library* (Cambridge, 1938).

[48] Holderness, *Shakespeare: The Histories*, p. 8.

[49] Henry Ansgar Kelly, *Divine Providence in the England of Shakespeare's Histories* (Cambridge, MA, 1970); Annabel Patterson, *Reading Holinshed's Chronicles* (Chicago, 1994).

[50] Stephen Greenblatt, *Will in the World: How Shakespeare Became Shakespeare* (New York, 2004), p. 195 and *passim*.

Revolt, but Cade's London is 'really' a portrait of Shakespeare's contemporary London: 'And it is the London crowd – the unprecedented concentration of bodies jostling through the narrow streets, crossing and recrossing the great bridge, pressing into taverns and churches and theaters – that is the key to the whole spectacle.'[51] *Will in the World* reflects back to us Shakespeare as a spectator of the local scene – not interested in the vexed Bermoothes any more than in Jack Cade's family life – a spectator who revels in the 'everyday': 'Throughout his career Shakespeare was fascinated by exotic locations, archaic cultures, and larger-than-life figures, but his imagination was closely bound to the familiar and the intimate. Or rather, he loved to reveal the presence of ordinariness in the midst of the extraordinary.'[52] Greenblatt's Shakespeare is finally less a historian than an ethnographer, enjoying the same intense immersion in his new culture that Greenblatt perceives in the writing of cultural anthropologist Clifford Geertz.[53] The sense that Shakespeare is completely caught up in the scene at hand becomes clear from the most discussed anecdote in Greenblatt's speculative biography, a hypothetical meeting between Shakespeare and the fugitive priest Thomas Campion:

Let us imagine the two of them sitting together then, the sixteen-year-old fledgling poet and actor and the forty-year-old Jesuit. Shakespeare would have found Campion fascinating – even his mortal enemies conceded that he had charisma – and might even have recognized in him something of a kindred spirit. Not in piety, for though Will (in this version of events) was a staunch enough Catholic at this point in his life to be trusted with dangerous secrets, there is no sign in his voluminous later work of a frustrated religious vocation. But Campion – a quarter century older than Will – was someone who came from a comparably modest family; who attracted attention to himself by his eloquence, intelligence, and quickness; who loved books yet at the same time was drawn to life in the world.[54]

As Greenblatt implicitly acknowledges, Campion is an older mirror image of Shakespeare, the poet of Sonnet 3 who might recognize an heir in Shakespeare as genealogical glass. But while in his anecdote Shakespeare and Campion are attracted to one another as members of some exotic species that somehow seems familiar, the two finally pass as icons in the night, neither of them aware of their mutual roles in English history. Greenblatt's new-found aesthetics of the 'everyday' in *Will in the World*, which he bestows in turn on Shakespeare, effectively prevents any historical actor from achieving the status of Historian.

Sidney's prejudice against 'mouse-eaten records' and Greenblatt's neo-romanticism aside, we have at this moment a wealth of information that would allow scholars and readers to raise Shakespeare the Historian out of the ashes of post-new historicist apostasy. Patterson's book, which has already encouraged a number of articles on Holinshed's 'others', coupled with the primary texts made available (and, more importantly, readable) by the technology of Early English Books Online, make it possible now to reconsider Shakespeare's engagement with the more remote historical texts that Tillyard wished for and Ellis's and Campbell's editions sought to provide. What is lacking is an alternative view of Shakespeare at work that complements this scholarly recovery of English history as a textual palimpsest constructed by many hands and voices over time. For Greenblatt's influential biography, by putting Will back in the world, has only hardened the distinction between scholarly Shakespeare, immured in his study with his bulky folios, and Shakespeare the theatre professional living London life to its fullest. What we need is a Will not returned to the library but a figure whose sense of texts, history and the situated self can bear up and thrive under multiplicity and indeterminacy and who can move gracefully between the Book and the World. Such a Shakespeare would be a natural collaborator and a product and practitioner of the rhetorical arts.

In his entry for Shakespeare in the *Dictionary of National Biography*, Peter Holland writes that

---

[51] Greenblatt, *Will in the World*, p. 169.
[52] Greenblatt, *Will in the World*, p. 388.
[53] Stephen Greenblatt, 'The Crowd Parts', *Common Knowledge*, 13 (2007), 211–13.
[54] Greenblatt, *Will in the World*, pp. 108–9.

At the King's New School, Stratford's splendid grammar school, William would have learned an immense amount of Latin literature and history, perhaps using the Latin–English dictionary left to the school by John Bretchgirdle who had baptized him. Among the works that Shakespeare later used as sources for his plays are a number that he would have read as part of his grammar-school education: the history of Livy, the speeches of Cicero, the comedies of Plautus and Terence, the tragedies of Seneca, and the poetry of Virgil and, above all, Ovid, who remained his favourite poet. The range of Latin writing that formed the curriculum was, by modern standards, vast. The mode of teaching, by a good teacher assisted by an usher, was one calculated to ensure the arts of memory.

The art of rhetoric, which was the goal of such an educational programme and which trained both invention and memory, was part of Shakespeare's intellectual heritage and his profession; this rhetorical heritage thus linked Warwickshire with London, the author and the theatre. Among the recent biographers, Russell Fraser speaks most persuasively about how Shakespeare's youthful memories of Warwickshire might have found voice in his history plays. Fraser depicts a child who not only was attuned to the historical events playing out before him, but also stored up in his memory names, places and events that later would attach themselves to persons and actions of a far rarer nature later in the playwright's working life.[55] In other words, Shakespeare saw both Latin literature and Warwickshire history through the same lens, a classical rhetoric that helped him merge personal memory with exotic fictions.

Shakespeare the rhetorician, with his balance of local experience and ancient literature, is also no scholarly recluse. Katherine Duncan-Jones offers a complementary vision of Shakespeare as a sociable intellectual and reader. She remarks on how the relatively open intellectual and religious atmosphere of Warwickshire during Shakespeare's youth, away from the tightly controlled court of Elizabeth, produced an unusual number of creative individuals and writers, not all of whom had the benefit of a university education. Duncan-Jones's list of the sons of the 'bookish midlands' includes George Peele, Richard Barnfield, the translator Edwin Sandys, comic actor Richard Tarlton, travel writer Richard Hakluyt, John Davies of Hereford, John Marston, John Heminge, Michael Drayton, and Fulk Greville (the last two being from Warwickshire itself). Drayton, as author of *Poly-Olbion*, especially could have shared with Shakespeare a taste for local and national history. Another, even more suggestive connection raised by Duncan-Jones is Richard Field, who probably studied at the Stratford Grammar School and went on to become a prominent London printer: 'Field's printing house may have provided Shakespeare with his first lodging in London, as well as functioning as a kind of library in which he was able to carry out wide reading without having to purchase such hugely expensive volumes as (for instance) Thomas North's translation of Plutarch's *Lives of the Noble Grecians and Romans*.'[56]

This Shakespeare is neither an Author nor a Man of the Theatre, exclusively solitary or sociable. In Warwickshire as in London, he is connected with a loose network of people and books, memories and historical 'mirrors'. Will in the Library and Will in the World are therefore two faces of one person, who interacts easily with both books and people. In search of this new rhetor-historian, it would be useful to reconsider Shakespeare's intertextual relations with the already dialogized chronicles and their authors; to extend imaginatively our sense of his collaborative interactions with other playwrights to other collaborations – perhaps more indirect – with history writers ranging from Samuel Daniel to Michael Drayton; and to think of him as sharing and debating ideas, however obliquely, with other intellectuals in the public sphere from Warwick to London. This is how Shakespeare could become once again Shakespeare the Historian.

---

55 Russell Fraser, *Young Shakespeare* (New York, 1988), p. 4.

56 Katherine Duncan-Jones, *Ungentle Shakespeare: Scenes from His Life* (London, 2001), pp. 5–6, 3–7; see also Greenblatt, *Will in the World*, pp. 193–4.

THE DECLINE OF THE CHRONICLE AND SHAKESPEARE'S HISTORY PLAYS

JEAN-CHRISTOPHE MAYER

I

Almost one-third of Shakespeare's production as a dramatist consists of plays whose themes are clearly historical.[1] His apparently keen interest in history has often been explained by the fact that he was influenced by the main ideological trends of his time (Tudor political theory, humanist civic history, Machiavellianism, Tacitism, Republicanism) or indeed that he was particularly sensitive to political events around him (Elizabethan and Jacobean politics and/or contemporary continental history).[2] However, strangely, the fact that Shakespeare turned to history in the early 1590s (and returned to it regularly for a decade or so) is rarely set in the context of the significant changes taking place on the 'market of history' during the same period, when the manner in which history was produced and consumed – and eventually conceived – was shifting.

It is not perhaps entirely fortuitous that the chronicle, which had been (since the late middle ages) the dominant historical genre of printed history, was in decline by the late 1580s, at a time when the production of histories on the Elizabethan stages was especially prolific and successful. In the 1590s the chronicle was commercially on the wane, even if, paradoxically, its cultural influence on other genres remained strong, as we shall see. The peak years for the publication of chronicles had been between 1550 and 1579, but the number of reprints and of new editions fell sharply in the next decade and then dwindled gradually until 1640 when the figures picked up very slightly.[3]

The Elizabethan chronicle was costly to produce and, while the interest in it had been great, the market for such works was pretty much glutted by 1600. The 1577 copy of Raphael Holinshed's *Chronicles* (STC 13568) retailed at 26s bound and 20s unbound. Comparatively, a copy of John Hayward's *The First Part of the Life and Raigne of King Henrie IV* (published 1599; S. T. C. 12995) could be purchased (unbound) at the more affordable

An earlier version of this essay was presented at a seminar on 'Near Misses with History' at the Stratford-upon-Avon International Shakespeare Conference (August 2008). I wish to thank the organizers of this seminar – Jeremy Lopez and Atsuhiko Hirota – as well as all the colleagues who took part in the conversations and helped me improve this essay.

[1] Plays which deal broadly with the history of the British Isles but also with continental, ancient or even legendary history.

[2] The critical literature is too vast to cite in full. To mention but a few examples: E. M. W. Tillyard, *Shakespeare's History Plays* (London, 1944); L. B. Campbell, *Shakespeare's 'Histories': Mirrors of Elizabethan Policy* (San Marino, CA, 1947); David Bevington, *Tudor Drama and Politics: A Critical Approach to Topical Meaning* (Cambridge, MA, 1968); Marie Axton, *The Queen's Two Bodies: Drama and the Elizabethan Succession* (London, 1977); Richard Hillman, *Shakespeare, Marlowe and the Politics of France* (Basingstoke, 2002); Andrew Hadfield, *Shakespeare and Republicanism* (Cambridge, 2005); Jean-Christophe Mayer, ed., *Representing France and the French in Early Modern English Drama* (Newark, 2008).

[3] Between 1550 and 1564 a total of 26 chronicles (6 new; 20 reprints of new editions) had been published, and between 1565 and 1579 the total is 36 (12 new and 24 reprints of new editions). The figures slide from 1580 for the next four decades: 1580–1594: 15; 1595–1609: 16; 1610–1624: 11; 1625–1639: 10. See: D. R. Woolf, *Reading History in Early Modern England* (Cambridge, 2000), p. 21. On the decline of the chronicle, see also Woolf, pp. 11–78.

price of 2s.[4] During the same period, an industrious artisan made about 6s a week, while an agricultural labourer earned only half as much (3s). Food was notoriously expensive and could cost up to 6d a day (the equivalent of an agricultural labourer's daily earnings).[5] It is not hard to see that the market for the chronicle was not easily expandable, as these volumes were well beyond the means of many Elizabethans. The English chronicle also suffered badly from the competition of other genres which attracted the attention of a larger fringe of the Elizabethan public, whose cultural habits were changing. History was becoming a commodity and while the chronicle could appeal to only a fairly restricted market of well-to-do buyers, shorter political histories, biographies, books of commonplaces on history, historical ballads, topical pamphlets, newsbooks as well as history plays (also marketed as playbooks) would gradually appeal to an increasingly wide spectrum of the population.

Religious books dominated the market during this period, but buyers interested in history were offered a greater variety of choice between genres over the years. Even if their market share remained relatively limited, playbooks also seemed to stir some interest, judging by their high reprint rates.[6] Interestingly, Peter Blayney's list of playbook best-sellers for the period 1583–1642 reveals that history plays sold well. Of the eleven plays on Blayney's list, seven were closely inspired by historical events and four were directly concerned with British history: Shakespeare's three plays published by Andrew Wise in the years 1597–8 – *1 Henry IV* (seven editions), *Richard III* (five editions), *Richard II* (five editions) – and Thomas Heywood's *If You Know Not Me, Part I* (five editions).[7] The approximate retail price for these playbooks was 6d, considerably less than chronicles or shorter historical works such as Hayward's *King Henry IV*. The only recorded prices paid for Shakespeare playbooks before 1623 are 5d for the 1600 quarto of *2 Henry IV* and 8d for the 1595 octavo of *Richard Duke of York (3 Henry VI)*.[8] Depending on their expectations (whether they read history for their own improvement and/or for their entertainment), readers had a wide array of choices but it seems that

at the beginning of the seventeenth century fewer people turned to chronicles to indulge themselves. Chronicles were bought more by collectors and they were increasingly used as reference books.[9] History was also available in much cheaper formats offering elements which had been conveniently recycled from the chronicles. This is why the chronicle's decline was paradoxical – despite its commercial difficulties it continued to have an

---

4 Woolf, *Reading History*, p. 45.
5 On these estimates, see Andrew Gurr, *The Shakespearean Stage 1574–1642*, 3rd edn (Cambridge, 1992), p. 12; Jean-Marie and Angela Maguin, *William Shakespeare* (Paris, 1996), p. 161.
6 The popularity of playbooks is still a contentious issue even if Peter Blayney's opinion that playbooks were not very profitable to produce and not that popular during the Shakespearian period has recently been challenged, fairly convincingly, by Alan B. Farmer and Zachary Lesser: 'The Popularity of Playbooks Revisited', *Shakespeare Quarterly* 56 (2005), 1–32. Blayney expounded his thesis in an essay which proved influential: 'The Publication of Playbooks', in *A New History of Early English Drama*, ed. John D. Cox and David Scott Kastan (New York, 1997), pp. 383–422. Farmer and Lesser argue that there was a 'boom' in the publication of printed professional plays between 1598 and 1613 ('The Popularity of Playbooks Revisited', p. 7) and found that the reprint rate of playbooks was higher than that of other works: 'about 40 percent of playbooks first published from 1576 to 1625 were reprinted within twenty years, compared to about 19 percent of sermon-books during that period and about 18 percent of all speculative books' ('Structures of Popularity in the Early Modern Book Trade', *Shakespeare Quarterly* 56 (2005), 206–13; p. 208). In his response, Blayney noted that the market share of playbooks never exceeded 2.77% for the period 1583–1642, but his figures also show a relatively sharp increase in the market share of playbooks for two crucial decades: 1593–1602 (4.18%) and 1603–1612 (3.99%). See Peter W. M. Blayney, 'The Alleged Popularity of Playbooks', *Shakespeare Quarterly* 56 (2005), 33–50; p. 48. Blayney's argument that popularity should only be judged by market share is not entirely convincing.
7 So-called closet and academic plays are not included in the list. Had they been included, another play closely related to history – Samuel Daniel's *Cleopatra* (first published 1594) – would have ranked second with eight editions. See Blayney, 'The Publication of Playbooks', p. 388.
8 Eric Rasmussen, 'Printing and Publishing', in *The Oxford Companion to Shakespeare*, ed. Michael Dobson and Stanley Wells (Oxford, 2001), pp. 353–56; p. 356.
9 Indeed, over the course of the seventeenth century 'the chronicle paradoxically regained some authority as a primary source of information for administrative and political, as well as historical purposes' (Woolf, *Reading History*, p. 49).

indirect cultural and communal impact through a variety of other genres which could reach out to a wider audience. Broadside ballads on historical subjects were sold for a penny (a halfpenny for a half-sheet) and the public amphitheatres gave access to plays staging ancient, medieval, Tudor or even contemporary history (British or foreign) for equally moderate prices (1d to 6d).[10]

Moreover, the chronicles were gradually falling into disrepute, as an increasing number of writers denounced chroniclers' supposedly dubious methods of assembling facts, criticized chronicles' alleged ill-adaptedness to the everyday needs and expectations of their readers and made fun of the sheer bulk of the volumes. Of course, such criticism often came from authors who had themselves ruthlessly pillaged the chronicles. Almost unwittingly, Shakespeare scholars have continued to fan the flames of these Elizabethan critiques. Recognition of Shakespeare's debt to the chronicles is almost invariably to the detriment of the latter, the playwright having transformed the chroniclers' so-called base matter into something rich and strange. My argument is not with the chronicles *per se* and I shall not be disputing the integral value of one of Shakespeare's main sources for his histories, Holinshed's *Chronicles*.[11] My point is that the market for history was changing, that other (often cheaper) forms of history were available, that this in turn created a climate of competition between the different formats and finally that the theatre in particular sought to carve a 'historical niche' for itself. Yet the theatre was not only concerned with securing financial gains – it too had something to say about history.

First it is crucial to try to determine *where* this criticism of the chronicles came from in order to assess its implications and to avoid taking it at face value. Some of the disapproval stemmed from scholars such as Gabriel Harvey, who raged in the margins of his copy of Livy's *Romanae Historiae Principis* against the 'many asses who dare to compile histories, chronicles, annals, commentaries' and went on to cite most of the main chroniclers of his time: 'Grafton, Stow, Holinshed, and a few others like them who are not cognizant of law

or politics, nor of the art of depicting character, nor are they in any way learned.'[12] Harvey's rage was fuelled as much by his own personal sense of superiority as by his opinion of what should constitute history. He clearly had a disregard for what we now call social history. A similar vein of criticism can be detected in the writings of his otherwise arch-opponent, Thomas Nashe, who praised the values of the poet above those of the historian. The poet was better suited to singing the great deeds of the nobility according to Nashe, who advised: 'Gentles, it is not your lay Chro-nigraphers, that write of nothing but of Mayors and Sheriefs, and the deare yeere, and the great Frost, that can endowe your names with neuer dated glory.'[13] John Donne – another poet – compared the chroniclers to gossipers in his satire of a courtier: 'More then ten Hollensheads, or Halls, or Stowes, / Of triviall houshold trash, he knowes . . .'[14] Likewise, chroniclers were easy targets for satirists like John Davies, whose works were not only cheaper but purported to be more *relevant* to the times than these mammoth volumes, Davies argued, filled with

---

[10] With a price range from 6d to 2s 6d the halls were socially more exclusive, but still accessible. See Gurr, *The Shakespearean Stage*, p. 12.

[11] Annabel Patterson has done much to transform our perceptions on these matters in her *Reading Holinshed's Chronicles* (Chicago, 1994). See also the extremely valuable Holinshed Project (headed by Paulina Kewes) at www.cems.ox.ac.uk/holinshed/. Patterson is right to point out that Holinshed's chronicles are plurivocal and socially inclusive, yet she also overstates her case slightly by idealizing the social role played by its middle-class contributors and by suggesting that the book had a very wide readership, particularly in her much cited article 'Rethinking Tudor Historiography', *The South Atlantic Quarterly* 92 (1993), 185–208; pp. 205–6.

[12] Quoted by Virginia F. Stern in: *Gabriel Harvey: His Life, Marginalia and Library* (Oxford, 1979), p. 152.

[13] Thomas Nashe, *Pierce Penilesse his Supplication to the Divell* [1592], in *The Works of Thomas Nashe*, ed. Ronald B. McKerrow (Oxford, 1966), vol. I, pp. 137–245; 194. This stance is of course redolent of Philip Sidney's who had made fun of the 'historian . . . laden with old mouse-eaten records' (*A Defence of Poetry*, ed. J. A. Van Dorsten [Oxford, 1966], p. 30).

[14] John Donne, 'Satyre IV' in *The Complete English Poems*, ed. C. A. Patrides, rev. Robin Hamilton (London, 1994), p. 167.

worthless remnants of the past, like so many dead butterflies pressed inside them: 'All these, and thousand such like toyes as These / They clapp in *Chronicles*, like *Butterflees* / Of which there is no use . . .'[15] In his aptly named 'Paper's Complaint', Davies dealt a final death blow to the chronicle by reminding would-be readers that these works 'put the Buyer to a needlesse Cost' (23) and that buyers would end up with ill-adapted, cumbersome volumes: 'the *Chronicle* as great / As some old Church-booke (that would make one sweat / To turne it twice)' (239).

Dramatists, like poets, sought to make the most of the chronicle's gradual repositioning on the Elizabethan cultural market of the past. As the chronicle's marketability was in question, the theatre (which thrived on its spoils) also sought to distinguish itself from the genre in order to promote its own relevance to the times and its capacity to speak about the past. Dramatists sought to chronicle their times in ways which – they felt – were more accurate and more in tune not only with the market of the past, but also with what they thought their audiences wanted. Some, like Thomas Tomkis, author of the academic play *Lingua* (1607), seemed to think that their audiences or their readers deserved better accounts of the past. In this play, Mendacio (Untruth) claims he had something to do with the writing of Stow's and Holinshed's chronicles: 'I must confesse I would faine have logged Stow and great Hollings-head on their elbowes, when they were about their Chronicles.'[16] Later in the play, Memory complains about the mass of facts he must remember now that every trivial event has to be recorded. His contemporaries' passion for the past is such that chroniclers record everything: 'but now every trifle must be wrapped up in the volume of eternitie. A rich pudding-wife, or a Cobler canot die but I must immortalize his name with an Epitaph: A dog cannot pisse in a Noblemans shoe, but it must be sprinkled into the Chronicles' (Act 2, scene 4).[17] Again it is the question of what should be the *proper* subject of history which is at stake here. Such questions are never devoid of a measure of social prejudice, as in Ben Jonson's *Newes from the New World Dis-*

cover'd in the Moone, a masque played before James I's court in 1620. Such prejudice stems from the theatres' will to cater for a more educated audience in the case of Jonson's masque, but the question of what constitutes history and how it should be represented was part of the larger concerns of the increasingly numerous media that claimed to speak about the past and to record the passing of time.[18] The theatre in particular felt the need to define its place and thus dramatists were naturally inclined to set down their differences with the chroniclers and impose – sometimes quite abruptly – the limits between their art and that of historiographers. Jonson's chronicler is therefore shown to be misguided in his sense of what constitutes 'posteritie' and it is precisely the way the past is recorded which is in question here beyond the familiar (if not hackneyed) criticism of the chronicles:

And I am for matter of State, Gentlemen, by consequence, story, my Chronicle, to fill up my greatbooke, which must bee three Reame of paper at least; I have agreed with my Stationer aforehand to make it so big, and I want for ten quire yet. I ha' beene here ever since seven a clocke i'the morning to get matter for one page, and I thinke I have it compleate; for I have both noted the number, and the capacity of the degrees here; and told twice over how many candles there are i'th' roome lighted, which I will set you downe to a snuffe precisely,

---

[15] John Davies, 'Papers Complaint, compild in ruthfull Rimes', in *The Scourge of Folly* (London, 1611), p. 237. Further references will be given in the text.

[16] Thomas Tomkis, *Lingua, or the Combat of the Tongue, And the five Senses for Superiority. A pleasant Comoedie* (London, 1607), Act 2, scene 1. Further references will be given in the text.

[17] In *Two wise men & all the rest fooles*, an anonymous play published in 1619, the word 'historiographer' undergoes a series of satirical transformations: 'O Histornoggerfers. a braue word. Ile make a knot of these letters' (*Two wise men & all the rest fooles* [London, 1619], p. 21; Act 2, scene 2).

[18] Another Jonson play springs to mind immediately: *The Staple of News* (1625), where the news of past and current events has become a commodity – which can be bought and sold, but also fabricated and even manufactured.

because I love to give light to posteritie in the truth of things.[19]

Shakespeare for his part had not derided the chronicler but rather the avid undiscerning reader of chronicles. In *Henry V* (1599), Captain Fluellen's endless dilatory discussions on the art of warfare and on the illustrious history of the king's ancestors in the midst of a conflict with France are the results of the Welsh Captain's bookish passion for history. His (phonetically) distorted restitutions of the chronicles are an all too obvious source of comedy: 'Your grandfather of famous memory, an't please your majesty, and your great-uncle Edward the Plack Prince of Wales, as I have read in the chronicles, fought a most prave pattle here in France' (4.7.82–5). Nonetheless, in the choruses of the play Shakespeare mimics the high style of the chronicle in an effort to lend a measure of solemnity to his story. These are moments when the play openly wishes to bring together those who had not read the chronicles and those who already had knowledge of them. Shakespeare's excuses to the latter are a way of justifying the necessarily metonymic and selective nature of drama:[20]

> Vouchsafe to those that have not read the story
> That I may prompt them, and of such as have,
> I humbly pray them to admit th'excuse
> Of time, of numbers, and due course of things
> Which cannot in their huge and proper life
> Be here presented.   (5.0.1–6)

Indeed, Elizabethan theatre had helped popularize the chronicle. This is something that Thomas Heywood – someone who earned much of his living by transforming the chronicles into popular formats – would later point out. Drama, as Heywood would have it, acquired in the process some of the didactic and virtuous qualities commonly attributed to historiography: 'playes have made the ignorant more apprehensive, taught the unlearned the knowledge of many famous histories, instructed such as cannot read in the discovery of all our *English* Chronicles'.[21] As Shakespeare's prologue suggests, drama claimed a *communal* role for itself in the sense that it tried to appeal *both* to the readers of chronicles and to those who

either could not afford to buy them, could not borrow or get access to them, or simply could not read. There were also signs that the playbook market and

---

[19] Ben Jonson, *Newes from the New World Discover'd in the Moone. A Masque, As it was presented at Court before King James 1620*, in *Ben Jonson*, ed. C. H. Herford, Percy and Evelyn Simpson (Oxford, 1952), vol. 7, p. 514, ll. 21–31.

[20] In the play's Prologue, Shakespeare had established the fact that much rested on his audiences' imagination: 'And let us, ciphers to this great account, / On your imaginary forces work' (Prologue, 17–18). All references to this play are taken from: William Shakespeare, *King Henry V*, ed. Andrew Gurr, New Cambridge Shakespeare (Cambridge, 1992). Spenser had already remarked that 'the Methode of a Poet historical is not such, as of an Historiographer. For an Historiographer discourseth of affayres orderly as they were donne, accounting as well the times as the actions, but a Poet thrusteth into the middest, even where it most concerneth him, and there recoursing to the thinges forepaste, and divining of things to come, maketh a pleasing Analysis of all' (Edmund Spenser, 'A Letter of the Authors expounding his whole intention in the course of this worke', in *The Faerie Queene* [London, 1590], p. 593).

[21] Thomas Heywood, *An Apology for Actors* (1612), intro. and notes J. W. Binns (New York, 1972), sig. F3ʳ. Others complained that the theatre had overstepped the mark in these matters and that it was trivializing history. See the refutation of Heywood's argument by I. G. [John Greene?] in *A refutation of the apology for actors* (1615), intro. J. W. Binns (New York, 1972), esp. p. 42. Heywood built part of his career thanks to the chronicles, which he pillaged to produce plays, historical verse, or historical digests. He wrote two-part plays on the reign of Edward IV (*The First and Second Partes of King Edward the Fourth* [1599]) and on Elizabeth I's reign (*If You Know Not Me, You Know No Bodie* [1605, 1606]). He later published a prose version of *If You Know Not Me*, which appeared under the title *Englands Elizabeth; Her Life and troubles* (1631). In 1608 he included part of Jean Bodin's *Methodus* in his translation of Sallust's *Histories*, but did not seem to take on board any aspects of Bodin's theory of history in his works. The following year he published a verse history of Great Britain, from Brutus to the reign of James I (*Troia Britannica, or Great Britaines Troy*), elements of which he recycled in *The Life of Merlin* (1641). The latter volume was presented to his readers as a handy digest of a series of otherwise bulky chronicles: 'In this small compendium or abstract thou hast Holinshed, Polychronicon, Fabian, Speed, or any of the rest, of more giantlike bulke or binding': Thomas Heywood, *Life of Merlin* (1641), 'To the Reader', quoted by Woolf, *The Idea of History in Early Stuart England* (Toronto, 1990), p. 245. See also L. B. Wright, 'Heywood and the Popularizing of History', *Modern Language Notes*, 43 (1928), 287–93.

that of history books overlapped, to some extent. For instance, Richard Jones, who printed the 1590 edition of Marlowe's *Tamburlaine*, had attempted to market the playbook as a work of history in his dedication 'To the Gentlemen Readers and others that take pleasure in reading Histories'.[22] There is reason to believe that such strategies bore fruit. Jonson's comedy *The Devil is an Ass* (1616) testifies in a satirical manner that the theatre (performed and printed) had penetrated the field of history and that it had begun to find a place alongside more traditional forms of history such as the chronicle:

Meercraft. By m'faith you are cunning i'the *Chronicle*, Sir.
Fitzdottrel. No, I confesse I ha't from the *Play-bookes*,
   And thinke they'are more *authentique*.[23]

The field of history was expanding and part of the humour of Jonson's jokes relies on the fact that, as the cultural market for history was growing exponentially, a hierarchy between the different genres of history (imposing a classification between fictional and more serious forms of history) had not yet been established. Indeed, these distinctions would be more firmly in place only by the end of the seventeenth century.[24] While this hierarchy was slowly becoming recognized, the theatre could make the most of its position as an intermediary between oral and written forms of history which it helped to circulate and which it also influenced directly or indirectly.[25] History in the hands of the dramatists became a source of entertainment, but the theatre also sought to appropriate its more serious aspects, which it transformed. Tudor history had not been able to perform fully the roles which it claimed for itself, because it could not yet reach out to a large enough community. These were precisely responsibilities which the theatre took on and purported to be better able to fulfil, as we shall see shortly.

II

Throughout the sixteenth century historians claimed that their writing had the power to triumph over death, jump over time and push back the limits of the visible world, *as if* the dead could be made *visibly present* again to the living. Thus, Edward Halle wrote that 'memorie maketh menne ded many a thousande yere still *to live as though thei wer present*: Thus fame triumpheth upon death, and renoune upon Oblivion, all by reason of writyng and historie.'[26] In the preface to his translation of Plutarch's *The Lives of the Noble Grecians and Romanes* (which Shakespeare consulted), Thomas North concurred and went even further, claiming that history's defining characteristic was that it

---

[22] Quoted in: Robert Weimann, *Author's Pen and Actor's Voice, Playing and Writing in Shakespeare's Theatre* (Cambridge, 2000), p. 59. Jones was probably referring to works of history rather than to history plays. The latter represented a very small part of the publishing market in and around 1590. See Farmer and Lesser, 'The Popularity of Playbooks Revisited', p. 7.

[23] Ben Jonson, *The Devil is an Ass*, in *The workes of Benjamin Jonson* (London, 1640), vol. 2, p. 120 (Act 2, scene 4).

[24] Woolf, *The Idea of History*, p. 273.

[25] George Puttenham describes for instance the way written historiography was circulated by singers and story-tellers: 'blind harpers or such like taverne minstrels that give a fit of mirth for a groat, & their matters being for the most part stories of old time, as the tale of Sir *Topas*, the reportes of *Bevis of Southampton*, *Guy of Warwicke*, *Adam Bell*, and *Clymme* of the *Clough* & such other old Romances or historicall rimes, made purposely for recreation of the common people at Christmasse diners & brideales, and in tavernes & alehouses and such other places of base resort, also they be used in Carols and rounds and such light or lascivious Poemes, which are commonly more commodiously uttered by these buffons or vices in playes then by any other person' (George Puttenham, *The Arte of English Poesie* [London, 1589; Menston, 1968], p. 64). Of course some of this folklore made its way back into the chronicle, which sometimes fed on oral history as well as on ballads. This chronicled material was then appropriated and recirculated by the theatre. The recycling continued, as, for instance, Shakespeare's plays in turn inspired balladists whose ballads were again incorporated in the later work of historiographers. Plays like *Titus Andronicus*, *The Taming of the Shrew*, *The Jew of Venice* or *King Lear* seem to have inspired balladists. See Thomas Percy, *Reliques of Ancient English Poetry*, 3 vols. (London, 1846), vol. 1, pp. 166–72, 176–81, 182–8, 189–92; Bruce R. Smith, 'Shakespeare's Residuals: The Circulation of Ballads in Cultural Memory', in *Shakespeare and Elizabethan Popular Culture*, ed. Stuart Gillespie and Neil Rhodes (London, 2006), pp. 193–217.

[26] Edward Hall, *The Union of the Two Noble and Illustre Fameles of Lancastre & Yorke* (London, 1548), 'Preface', p. ii, quoted in: Paola Pugliatti, *Shakespeare the Historian* (Basingstoke, 1996), p. 29 (italics mine).

instructed the living by reviving the dead: 'Whereas stories are fit for every place, reache to all persons, serve for all tymes, teache the living, revive the dead, so farre excelling all other bookes.'[27] That history could 'reache to all persons' was somewhat of an exaggeration on the part of North – this was one role, however, which the theatre could more appropriately claim for itself. North's translation did manage to 'reache to all persons' eventually, as it was used and transformed by dramatists. John Brende, another translator of ancient historical chronicles, had equally high hopes for history. He asserted that history turned the past into a spectacle which one could observe in the present: 'For in them [chronicles] men *may beholde, as it were before there eies*, both the whole worlde, and the goverment therof, with the policies and lawes, the discipline customes & manners of al people from the begynnyng.'[28] As for Walter Ralegh, history marked human beings' victory over time and oblivion. He noted in his *History of the World* (1614) that history was a concrete expression of the generational transmission of knowledge, a process which thus created a *tie* between the living and the dead. History, argued Ralegh, was even able to make the past present through the vision it conjured up: 'it hath carried our knowledge over the vast & devouring space of so many thousands of yeares, and given so faire and peircing eies to our minde; that we plainely behould living now, as we had lived then, that great World.'[29]

Translated into contemporary terms, it appears that what these early modern historians were trying to do was to define and establish history's scope and social role. Indeed, in the words of Michel de Certeau, it is thanks to historiography 'that a group is able to communicate with itself, by reference to that *absent third party* which is its past'.[30] Death is the subject of history and in a sense death is *subjected* to the discourse of history – this is the way the living attempt to exorcise death. Absence becomes, as it were, a common currency which the living can exchange with each other. History regulates this practice – it seeks to define the roles which readers have to play so that history can fulfil its communal purpose. History's purpose is to mend 'ceaselessly the broken threads between the past and the present'. Indeed, history 'establishes a "meaning" which overcomes the violence and the divisions imposed by time. It creates a common space of references and values which enable the group to feel united and to communicate symbolically... It is a discourse of connection which fights the disconnections brought about by competition, work, time and death.'[31] While de Certeau's definition can be useful to shed light on history's relation to the past, its communal aspects do not apply entirely to early modern historiography, whose direct influence was limited to a fairly small portion of society. These communal purposes were better served by the theatre, as we shall see.

However thought-provoking it might be, de Certeau's definition does not really help us to make sense of early modern historians' claims to be able to make the past present. Should we consider these claims to be a form of naivety, expressions of what critics have been calling since deconstruction a 'metaphysics of presence'? Or should we rethink the way we envisage the question of presence? After all, post-structuralists like Roland Barthes, Jacques Derrida, Michel Foucault or Hayden White (in the field of history) have often been criticized for their refusal to take on board the real or indeed the existence of the past. More

---

27 Plutarque, *The Lives of the Noble Grecians and Romanes*, translated from the Greek by Jacques Amyot, translated from the French by Thomas North (London, 1579), 'To the Reader', sig. *3. STC 20066.

28 John Brende, trans., *The Historie of Quintus Curcious, conteyning the Actes of the great Alexander translated out of the Latine in to Englishe* (London, 1553), sig. A3ʳ. STC 6142 (my italics).

29 Walter Ralegh, *The History of the World* [1614], ed. C. A. Patrides (London, 1971), p. 48.

30 'la communication d'un groupe avec lui-même par ce *renvoi au tiers absent* qu'est son passé' (Michel de Certeau, *L'Ecriture de l'histoire* [Paris, 1975], p. 73. My translation).

31 'elle assure un "sens" qui surmonte les violences et les divisions du temps. Elle crée un théâtre de références et de valeurs communes qui garantissent au groupe une unité et une communicabilité symboliques... C'est un discours de la conjonction, qui lutte contre les disjonctions produites par la compétition, le labeur, le temps et la mort.' Michel de Certeau, *Histoire et psychanalyse entre science et fiction* (Paris, 2002 [1987]), p. 60. My translation.

recently New Historicists have made obvious the fact that the real for them is a construct that is represented.[32] Yet if history feeds partly on fiction to mend 'ceaselessly the broken threads between the past and the present', as de Certeau would have it, New Historicism's concept of 'representation' is not fully capable of *also* acknowledging that the past *did once exist*.[33] This can be a problem as New Historicism is equally ill-prepared to account for the seemingly paradoxical claims that an absent past can be made present. While there is no denying that the past has to be reconstructed, its represented image is perhaps more complex than we had thought. Paul Ricœur suggests that we should consider that representations 'stand for' a past which is gone but which did once exist and which is preserved in the traces it has left. This 'standing for' the past is aptly summed up in Ricœur's French coinage of the term *représentance*. Ricœur coins another term – *lieutenance* – to describe the way the present image of the past constructed by historians, or indeed by playwrights (as will be clear in a moment), 'takes the place of' a past that is both absent and lost and yet did once exist and to which we are thus indebted.[34] The image, or representation, created stands for the absent past and this 'standing for' in turn produces a sense of 'further existence' and of 'added life'. However, the flip side of this sense of 'added life' is always that the past is also gone, even while we acknowledge that it did once exist.

It is, I argue, with this more ambivalent notion of representation in mind that one should reconsider early modern historians' claims to 'revive the dead'. Likewise, it is in this light that one should reread Thomas Nashe's famous praise of history plays in his *Pierce Penilesse* (1592). Interestingly, in this passage Nashe suggests that the theatre is particularly suited to performing purposes which the chronicles were not able to fulfil – by its very nature drama conveys a sense of 'added life' to the image of the past it seeks to represent. What is more, Elizabethan theatre was a truly communal art form and one which had a social role to play. Indeed, as Nashe pointed out, it was capable not only of attracting soldiers (who would otherwise have been wandering the city streets dangerously), but also of offering these soldiers and the audience at large an image of the past worth living up to:

Nay, what if I proove Playes to be no extreame; but a rare exercise of vertue? First, for the subject of them (for the most part) it is borrowed out of our English Chronicles, wherein our forefathers valiant acts (that have line long buried in rustie brasse and worm-eaten bookes) are revived, and they themselves raised from the Grave of Oblivion, and brought to pleade their aged Honours in open presence: than which, what can be a sharper reproofe to these degenerate effeminate dayes of ours? How would it have joyed brave *Talbot* (the terror of the French) to thinke that after he had lyne two hundred yeares in his Tombe, hee shold triumphe againe on the Stage, and have his bones newe embalmed with the teares of ten thousand spectators at least (at severall times), who, in the Tragedian that represents his person, imagine they behold him fresh bleeding.

I will defend it against any Collian, or clubfisted Usurer of them all, there is no immortalitie can be given a man on earth like unto Playes.[35]

---

32 Stephen Greenblatt's quest for 'the touch of the real' and his praise of 'thick description' are really sophisticated expressions of a textualism which has trouble defining its relation to the real. See Stephen Greenblatt, *Practicing New Historicism* (Chicago, 2000), esp. p. 31.

33 What François Hartog calls 'l'effectivité du passé', the fact that the past did once exist. See François Hartog, *Évidence de l'histoire, ce que voient les historiens* (Paris, 2005), p. 173.

34 Ralegh made it clear that human beings were indebted to history because historiographers constructed a present image of an absent past: 'And it is not the least debt which we owe unto History, that it hath made us acquainted with our dead Ancestors; and, out of the depth and darknesse of the earth, delivered us their memory and fame' (Ralegh, *The History of the World*, p. 48). On the two terms (*lieutenance* and *représentance*) put forward by Ricœur, see his *Temps et récit* (Paris, 1985), vol. 3, pp. 204–5 and his *La Mémoire, l'histoire, l'oubli* (Paris, 2000), p. 367.

35 Nashe, *Pierce Penilesse*, p. 212. George Puttenham had also sung the praises of 'historical Poesie' because of the present image of the past it could conjure up: 'No one thing in the world with more delectation reviving our spirits then *to behold as it were in a glasse the lively image of our forefathers*, their noble and vertuous maner of life, with other things autentike, which because we are not able otherwise to attaine to the knowledge of, by any of our sences, we apprehend them by memory' (Puttenham, *The Arte of English Poesie*, p. 31. Italics mine).

Compared to the decaying chronicles ('worm-eaten bookes'), drama had one serious advantage – it did not resurrect the dead as such, but lent physical life to their *actions* ('our forefathers valiant acts . . . are revived'). Nashe expresses the whole ambivalence of a form of representation which does not deny the absence of a past that is gone, but which lends 'further existence' to that lost past by 'standing for it' through dramatic action. It is precisely this ambivalent reconstructed image of the past which is represented in the living presence of the community ('in open presence'). If the dead Talbot returns in Nashe's implicit homage to Shakespeare's *1 Henry VI*, it is not so much to live as to bleed again ('fresh bleeding') like the sacrificial hero that Nashe turns him into, one to whom the community as a whole is indebted. To repay the community's debt to a past that did once exist but is now gone, the group, Nashe suggests, has to lay the dead hero's bones to rest again ('have his bones newe embalmed') through a dramatic ritual which enables the group to commune emotionally ('with the teares of ten thousand spectators at least'). Nashe also underlines the fact that society has to repeat this process of exhumation and reburial of the past and that this repetition is made easy, for actors are capable of almost endlessly *rehearsing* the past ('ten thousand spectators at least (at severall times)'). The audience's imagination ('imagine they behold him') naturally has a crucial role to play, as it is the community itself which creates, through the agency of drama, the present image of an absence which is at once synonymous with a lost past and with a past which existed empirically. Through the spectators' imagination, the past comes back to confront the present. The return of the absent to the present also foregrounds what *is lacking* in the present – that is to say, in this instance, and according to Nashe, an exemplary heroic figure like Talbot's, who could transform the present.

In passing, Nashe attributes a truly significant role to the history play. In his view, the historiographers were not in a position to accomplish the social purposes which they claimed they could perform. Shakespeare seems to have been equally aware of the possibilities offered by the genre. In *Henry V* (1599) the Bishop of Ely encourages the king to 'Awake remembrance of these valiant dead, / And with your puissant arm renew their feats' (1.2.115–16). Again, it is not so much a case of literally awaking the dead – the bishop's words are an invitation to make the dead *present* through remembrance and to renew the *acts* of the dead by *action*.

It is also through analogy that the dead come back on Elizabethan and Jacobean stages. *As if* is a figure of style which 'stands for' a past which is gone and yet existed formerly in the real. Thus, *Henry VIII*'s Prologue warns his audience that the dead will be visible on one condition only – that spectators understand the ambivalent value of analogy ('as if'): 'Think ye see / The very persons of our noble story / As they were living' (25–7).[36] In his *Apology for Actors* (1612), Thomas Heywood had tried to show how audiences became emotionally involved with history plays. According to Heywood, an audience was won over precisely because of the analogy which united the actor/character. The Same (an actor of flesh and blood like the audience) was coupled with the Other (an absent person): '*as if* the Personater were the man Personated', wrote Heywood.[37] The analogy produced a sense of 'further existence' which was almost true to life: 'so bewitching a thing is lively and well spirited action'. Heywood seems to concur with Nashe and Shakespeare in his analysis. Indeed, the past comes back in the present (is *represented*) only because the *acts* of the dead are played by the actor/character. In this way, it is only because the on-stage actions of the actor/character refer back to a past which is gone and yet did exist that the spectators will be transformed emotionally and will want to *further the acts of the dead* by their actions in the present:

---

[36] Emphasis added. All references are to the following edition: William Shakespeare and John Fletcher, *King Henry VIII*, ed. Gordon McMullan (London, 2000).

[37] Heywood, *An Apology for Actors*, sig. B4ʳ. Emphasis in this excerpt and in the next added. The subsequent quotations of Heywood in this paragraph are taken from the same passage.

'so bewitching a thing is lively and well spirited action, that it hath power to new mold the harts of the spectators and fashion them to the shape of any noble and notable attempt'. However, the spectators' present actions are not solely the result of the illusion produced by the actor/character – an audience is set in motion when it is also aware of the distance between the image of the past produced on stage and its present: 'What coward to see his contryman valiant would not bee ashamed of his owne cowardice?', asks Heywood. These extracts show the paradox but also the power of analogy, a mode which, as Paul Ricœur observes, 'powerfully recalls the past but also sets it at a distance, because to "be like" is both to exist and not to exist'.[38]

Heywood knew what he was talking about – he had earned part of his living by making history more accessible to readers and theatre-goers alike. Shakespeare had played a similar part and had made a significant contribution to the history play. But Shakespeare, like Heywood, also had something to say about history. 'On Worthy Master Shakespeare and his Poems', a commendatory poem published in the 1632 folio edition of Shakespeare's works, suggests that Shakespeare was particularly interested in history and that he let his readers and audiences entertain a fruitful dialogue with the past.[39] Of all his different sources of inspiration, Shakespeare, according to the author of this poem, was most attracted to Clio, the Muse of History, the source of his epic style: 'the grand / And louder tone of Clio' (44–5). There could well be an allusion to the 'muse of fire' of Henry V's Prologue in the reference to the 'heavenly fire', used by Shakespeare to transform his audiences: 'by heavenly fire / Mould us anew' (38–9). But how did Shakespeare bring about these transformations? According to the poet, Shakespeare had a paradoxical fashion of emphasizing the distance between the past and the present and yet of producing an image of the past which was garbed in the colours of the present. The following lines throw some interesting light on the ambivalent processes we mentioned previously, the fact that the representation of the past 'powerfully recalls the past but

also sets it at a distance' (in Ricœur's words cited earlier):

> A mind reflecting ages past, whose clear
> And equal surface can make things appear
> Distant a thousand years, and represent
> Them in their lively colours' just extent;
>
> (1–4)

Moreover, what characterized Shakespeare was his will to represent what *is lacking* in the present. He made death emerge among the living, he fought against amnesia, so much so that what first came up from the depths of time were violent and confused images. This is what happens when one 'blow[s] ope the iron gates / Of death and Lethe, where confusèd lie / Great heaps of ruinous mortality' (6–8). But then, the poet writes, Shakespeare learnt the art of lending a 'further existence' to the lost past: 'by art to learn / The physiognomy of shades, and give / Them sudden birth' (10–12). Shakespeare was not alone in practising this art and one can be reminded of the prologue of *The True Tragedie of Richard the third* (1594). In the prologue of this anonymous history play, Truth (that is to say, historical truth) also wishes to bring 'added life' to 'Poetrie': 'Then will I adde bodies to the shadowes'.[40] Of course 'Shadow' also meant 'actor' in Elizabethan English and one is

---

[38] '[le mode analogique] retient en lui la force de la réeffectuation et de la mise à distance, dans la mesure où être-comme, c'est être et n'être pas'. Ricœur, *Temps et récit*, vol. 3, p. 226. My translation.

[39] I. M. S., 'On Worthy Master Shakespeare and his Poems', in *William Shakespeare: The Complete Works*, ed. Stanley Wells and Gary Taylor, Compact Edition (Oxford, 1988), p. xlvii. Further references will be given in the text. The poem (whose authorship remains uncertain) was tentatively attributed to John Milton (Iohn Milton Student), but the initials could well be those of the expression 'In Memoriam Scriptoris'. The latter recalls Ben Jonson's eulogy of Shakespeare in the 1623 folio: 'To the Memory of My Beloved, the Author...'. On this poem, see also: Graham Holderness, '*Mots d'escalier*: Clio, Eurydice, Orpheus', in *Shakespeare's Histories and Counter-Histories*, ed. Dermot Cavanagh, Stuart Hampton-Reeves *et al.* (Manchester, 2006), pp. 219–40; pp. 234–7.

[40] Anonymous, *The True Tragedie of Richard the third* (London, 1594). Source: Literature Online.

immediately aware of the significance of such a pun, which called to mind that paradoxical couple (the actor/character), where one was of flesh and blood and the other an image of an absent being.

There are scenes in Shakespeare in which the ghosts of history come back to haunt the living,[41] but there are also moments when the living try to make the dead of history speak through them. In *Richard III* (1593) and *Julius Caesar* (1599), Shakespeare opens up the scars left by history and some of his characters try to make these wounds speak. Lady Anne manages to conjure up the paradoxical image of Henry VI (her father-in-law), whose wounds bleed again in the present (thus repeating the moment of his murder) and speak in the present: 'O gentlemen, see, see dead Henry's wounds / Open their congealed mouths and bleed afresh' (*Richard III*, 1.2.53–4).[42] In *Julius Caesar*, Shakespeare has Caesar's death re-enacted and places his assassination at the very heart of his play (Act 3). He lets this death permeate the rest of the play like an absent presence and shows how the living try to make their dead speak and how, like Mark Antony, they write history in the process: 'I tell you that which you yourselves do know, / Show you sweet Caesar's wounds, poor poor dumb mouths, / And bid them speak for me' (3.2.217–19).[43]

According to the author of 'On Worthy Master Shakespeare and his Poems', Shakespeare made history a 'pastime' for his contemporaries. Yet his history plays were not just a source of entertainment – his theatre was also a place where one came to reflect on the passing of time: 'Time past made pastime, and in ugly sort / Disgorging up his ravin for our sport' (31–2). The dominant image here is of a bird of prey (another common pastime for Elizabethans) regurgitating ('disgorging up') in the present a half-digested kill ('his ravin'), for public entertainment ('for our sport'). Indeed, the past returns in Shakespearian drama in shapeless, 'half-digested' forms, which are often unsavoury. Shakespeare's first tetralogy in particular depicts a nation embroiled in a series of brutal, sometimes cruel, often bloody feuds. Nonetheless, Shakespeare's art also consisted in giving, if not meaning, at the

very least some form to what the past spewed up. This is a task he assigns to some of his characters: 'Be of good comfort, Prince, for you are born / To set a form upon that indigest / Which he hath left so shapeless and so rude' (5.7.25–7), were Salisbury's words in *King John* (1596?) to the future king Henry III.[44] Nevertheless, sometimes, the return of the dead of history appears incomprehensible or indeed absurd. Hamlet, for instance, sees this return as a weight which is too burdensome for someone who feels desperately indebted to the lost past.[45] The traces that the great figures of history (Alexander the Great, Julius Caesar) have left are reduced to an absurd materiality, which in turn reminds the living of their own vanity. For Hamlet, the return of the absent of history is of no great use to the living: 'To what base uses we may return, Horatio! Why may not imagination trace the noble dust of Alexander till 'a find it stopping a bung-hole?' (5.1.192–4). The reason for this is that Hamlet's dialogue with the dead is painful, that his memory of a past that truly existed does not appease him because he has not been able to separate the lost past from the present. Only on the brink of death will Hamlet realize that his mourning process is left unfinished. The living need to tell stories of the dead for they have a debt towards a past that *existed* and yet they also have to detach their present from the lost past to live their lives. Elizabethan theatre, and particularly Shakespearian

---

41 These scenes are beyond the scope of this article. For further details, see Jean-Christophe Mayer, *Shakespeare's Hybrid Faith: History, Religion and the Stage* (Basingstoke, 2006), pp. 40–58.

42 *The Tragedy of King Richard III*, ed. J. Jowett, Oxford World Classics (Oxford, 2000).

43 *Julius Caesar*, ed. David Daniell, Arden Shakespeare Third Series (Walton-on-Thames, 1998).

44 *King John*, ed. A. R. Braunmuller (Oxford, 1989).

45 Hamlet partly considers this return as a violent imposition on his present: 'O answer me, / Let me not burst in ignorance but tell / Why thy canonized bones hearsed in death / Have burst their cerements, why the sepulchre / Wherein we saw thee quietly interred / Hath oped his ponderous and marble jaws / To cast thee up again' (*Hamlet*, ed. Ann Thompson and Neil Taylor, Arden Shakespeare [London, 2006], 1.4.45–51. All subsequent references will be given in the text).

theatre, helped the living accomplish this task —
more effectively, as Nashe and Heywood argued,
than history books ever could. Indeed, the theatre
is, to some extent, a 'memory machine', which
recycles the past, transforms it, memorizes it,
re-rehearses it, and lets audiences build connections to their past.[46] As Hamlet finally suggests, it
is by repeatedly acting out the story of the dead, by
retelling their story, that the living manage to shape
their present. This is a task that only the survivors
of history can perform:

> O God, Horatio, what a wounded name,
> Things standing thus unknown, shall I leave behind me!
> If thou didst ever hold me in thy heart
> Absent thee from felicity awhile
> And in this harsh world draw thy breath in pain
> To tell my story.   (5.2.328–33)

---

[46] See Marvin Carlson's seminal book: *The Haunted Stage: The Theatre as a Memory Machine* (Ann Arbor, 2001).

RITES OF OBLIVION IN SHAKESPEARIAN HISTORY PLAYS

ISABEL KARREMANN

This article is about rites of oblivion in Shakespearian history plays and Elizabethan culture. The conjunction of ritual and forgetting might well seem paradoxical at first sight. After all, ritual is both formally and functionally associated with memory: rehearsing highly conventionalized topoi, gestures and acts, ritual is built on repetition and recognition. It works effectively only as a formalized act that recalls a social frame of reference which asserts the validity of the ritual and in turn is asserted by it. By the same token, cultural memory depends on rites of commemoration that 'invite, rehearse or enforce social modes of recollection'.[1] The words 're-collection' and 're-member' point to both the repetitive form and the social function of ritual: turning individual members of society into an imagined community, it serves to establish continuity and collective identity. Given this mutually constitutive relation between ritual and memory, can there also be rites of oblivion? If so, what form would such ritual forgetting take, and what would be its social function? What cultural work does oblivion perform? Is there, in short, an *ars oblivionalis* just as there is an *ars memorativa*?

In a seminal essay of 1988, Umberto Eco addresses this last question and negates it categorically. From his semiological perspective, forgetting is the reverse of memory and, by extension, of the use of signs as 'a means of making present, never absent'.[2] He deduces from this that neither the acts of oblivion nor their effects can ever be represented, that forgetting is *a priori* excluded from the cultural economy of signs and meanings. Likewise, whereas he sees remembrance as a constitutive

force of culture and society, Eco dismisses forgetting as a destructive force of nature beyond human control and intentionality. I would like to suggest here that memory and oblivion are in fact complementary rather than mutually exclusive forces and that forgetting can indeed be purposeful and deliberate. Based on this premise, I will explore how the relation between mnemonic rites and oblivion is represented on the early modern stage. As we will see, it ranges from opposition to appropriation: forgetting can be induced through interrupting ritual but also through employing the very rites of commemoration in order to effect the obverse. This changed pragmatics does not necessarily invalidate the social function of ritual, though: rites of oblivion, too, can forge imagined communities.

Such a complementary understanding of remembrance and forgetting is particularly informative in regard to mnemonic rites in post-Reformation England, where many ritual practices

This article has its origin in a seminar on 'Dramatic Uses of Complaint' held at the Shakespeare Association of America 2009 conference in Washington. I am grateful to seminar leader William Kerwin for his generous support and to the seminar members, in particular Joanne Diaz and Dustin Stegner, for their incisive and helpful responses to my paper.

[1] Tobias Döring, 'Shadows to the unseen grief? Rituals of Memory and Forgetting in the History Plays', paper delivered at the International Shakespeare Conference, Brisbane, July 2006, Panel Session Cultural Memory in Shakespeare – Shakespeare in the Cultural Memory, p. 2. I am deeply obliged to Tobias Döring for so generously sharing his manuscript and his ideas with me.

[2] Umberto Eco, 'An Ars Oblivionalis? Forget It!', *PMLA*, 103 (1988), 254–61; p. 258.

were officially abolished without, however, being entirely eradicated from popular consciousness. It is by now a commonplace of early modern studies that the Reformation in England had a 'profoundly traumatic' effect on 'the meaning and conduct of life-cycle rituals'. Especially, the abolishment of the doctrine of Purgatory and of the traditional rites of mourning and commemorating the dead disrupted, as the landmark studies by Michael Neill, David Cressy and Stephen Greenblatt demonstrate, the communication between the living and the dead, as well as causing a rift among the living.[3]

In this context, the representation of mourning practices in texts and on stage takes on topical resonance. Epitaphs and elegies, deathbed and funerary speeches, scenes of grief and lament both perform and comment on the ways of commemorating the dead which were permissible in Elizabethan England. The issue of commemoration became particularly prominent in history plays because of their double perspective: looking back to the time before the Reformation, they also invited spectators to look at post-Reformation memories.[4] The historical scenes of grief, then, lent themselves to a topical reading of contemporary grievances. These grievances included not only the reformed mourning practices (and the loss of consolation they meant) but also the memory politics of the Church of England under Elizabeth.

Part of these memory politics was a strategic use of *forgetting*. The Reformation had officially consigned certain rites of commemoration to oblivion: the iconoclasm in churches, the erasure of saints' holidays from the calendar and the ban on prayers and petitions for the dead can all be seen as a concerted attempt to make a formerly Catholic population forget their traditional beliefs. This is what Eamon Duffy means when he claims that 'iconoclasm was the central sacrament of the reform'.[5] Yet apart from the fact that the destruction of material signs does not automatically erase the discarded memories,[6] this claim establishes a faulty dichotomy that too rigidly aligns Catholic practices with memory and Protestant reforms with oblivion. It does not, for example, allow for the possibility that rites of commemoration might survive in transformed and displaced practices, such as the emergent medium of the theatre.[7]

In order to appraise the mnemonic economy of early modern culture more comprehensively, a more dynamic model is needed which takes into account the interplay of remembrance and forgetting rather than seeing them as opposites; which recognizes oblivion as a force that can be constitutive, rather than destructive, of culture and society; and which makes visible the cultural devices available for consigning things to oblivion. I will attempt to put such a model to work on scenes of mourning and commemoration in three Shakespearian history plays, paying attention to the ways in which ritual lament functions as a vehicle for the equivocal memory politics in the plays as well as for the analysis and critique of Elizabethan memory politics.

If ritual in general performs a work of stabilizing, of upholding and reintegrating social groups, this is especially true for funeral rites: they aim at resolving the social and psychic disruption caused by death through a symbolic enactment of continuity and community, thereby offering consolation. In post-Reformation England, however, funerals were often sites of discord, sources of anxiety rather than solace. This tension between community-building rites of commemoration and their official elimination, between remembrance and oblivion, informs *The Tragedy of King Richard the Third*. In Katherine Goodland's terms, the play enacts a struggle between 'Richard's will to forget the dead,

---

[3] David Cressy, *Birth, Marriage, and Death: Ritual, Religion, and the Life-Cycle in Tudor and Stuart England* (Oxford, 1997), pp. 476–7. See also Michael Neill, *Issues of Death: Mortality and Identity in English Renaissance Tragedy* (Oxford, 1997) and Stephen Greenblatt, *Hamlet in Purgatory* (Princeton, 2001).

[4] Tobias Döring, *Performances of Mourning in Shakespearean Theatre and Early Modern Culture* (Houndmills, Basingstoke, 2006), p. 38.

[5] Eamon Duffy, *The Stripping of the Altars: Traditional Religion in England 1400–1580* (New Haven, 1992), p. 408.

[6] The phenomenon that an empty space formerly occupied by a monument can intensify the memorial effect is described by Adrian Forty and Suzanne Küchler in *The Art of Forgetting* (Oxford, 1999), pp. 10–11.

[7] See Döring, *Performances of Mourning*, p. 37.

to effect political amnesia by a perpetual orientation toward the future, and the mourning women who embody the past, the insistence and intrusion of memory upon human action'.[8] While Richard takes the reformed, anti-ceremonial attitude to an extreme, the ritualistic nature of their lament, enacted through speech, gestures and emotionally charged interjections, reveals patterns of actual mourning practices that were viewed as increasingly problematic after the Reformation.[9] Take, for example, the first lines of Lady Anne in Act 1, scene 2, where she weeps over the corpse of King Henry VI:

> Poor key-cold figure of a holy king,
> Pale ashes of the house of Lancaster,
> Thou bloodless remnant of that royal blood,
> Be it lawful that I invoke thy ghost
> To hear the lamentations of poor Anne,
> Wife to thy Edward, to thy slaughtered son,
> Stabbed by the selfsame hands that made these wounds.
> Lo, in these windows that let forth thy life,
> I pour the helpless balm of my poor eyes.
> O cursèd be the hand that made these holes,
> Cursèd the blood that let this blood from hence,
> Cursèd be heart that had the heart to do it.   (1.2.5–16)

The rhetorical devices of this speech – the apostrophe of the dead, the establishment of kinship between mourner and deceased, a narrative of loss, the call for vengeance and cursing of the enemy – together with non-verbal gestures like inarticulate shrieks, tears, dishevelled hair or sitting on the ground in later scenes, establish the traditional poetics of lament. To this poetics the play adds a politics of mourning: the ritual account of woe establishes the mourner's relation to the dead and authorizes her particular and partial story of the past. Expressions of grief thus also reveal, even bring about, claims of allegiance and inheritance.[10] When Lady Anne laments the death of her father-in-law, the last Lancastrian king, her position as chief mourner also denotes her royal lineage and claim to the throne, underscoring the illegitimacy of his Yorkist successor. Like another Antigone, she transgresses the strict class and gender rules of the College of Arms, which demanded that mourners must be of the same sex and near in degree to the deceased,[11] and resists the new official orders that violate the traditional laws of mourning and kinship. 'Be it lawful that I invoke thy ghost' is not so much a gesture of self-conscious uncertainty,[12] but one of defiance, and as such it strikes a double note: on the level of historical reference, it affirms her and her family's rights in the face of a new ruler's laws; on the level of topical reference, it challenges the new laws of mourning under the reformed Church.

Throughout the play, the 'weeping queens' – exiled Queen Margaret, Queen Elizabeth, the Duchess of York and Lady Anne – enact this political dimension of mourning in that they act as obstacles on Richard Gloucester's way to power, which is literally strewn with the corpses of his rivals. Their laments call him to account for his crimes. This potential of traditional expressions of grief to address contemporary civic grievances is illustrated by the report about a funeral in Lancashire in 1590 where, as an outraged reformer notes,

> some by kissing the dead corpse, others by wailing the dead with more than heathenish outcries, others with open invocations for the dead, and another sort with jangling bells, so disturb the whole action, that the minister is oft compelled to let pass that part of the service appointed for the burial of the dead and to withdraw himself from their tumultuous assembly.[13]

Richard III was staged within two years of the riotous Lancashire incident and enacts a similar Lancastrian uprising with its weeping queens. The

---

[8] Katherine Goodland, *Female Mourning and Tragedy in Medieval and Renaissance Drama* (Aldershot, 2005), p. 141.

[9] Goodland, *Female Mourning*, pp. 135–6.

[10] Döring, *Performances of Mourning*, p. 25.

[11] Goodland, *Female Mourning*, p. 143.

[12] Patricia Philippy reads this line as an 'ambivalent gesture toward intercessory prayer' in keeping with 'the play's self-conscious deployment and scrutiny of ritual lamentation throughout'. *Women, Death and Literature in Post-Reformation England* (Cambridge, 2002), p. 132. However, the efficacy of female lament (although not necessarily Lady Anne's) and the return to traditional funeral practices at the end seem to me to tip the scale towards defiance.

[13] Quoted in Cressy, *Birth, Marriage, and Death*, p. 401.

conjunction between ecclesiastical record and play, Goodland suggests, establishes the ritual 'wailing for the dead' as a matter of some concern for the official powers in Elizabethan England, just as it is a matter of concern for the patriarchal powers in the play.[14]

Yet mourning ceremonies not only interrupt Richard's will to power but are also interrupted by it. In scene after scene, ritual laments and ritual curses are cut short by Richard's entrances or interjections.[15] If the keening queens embody a memorial as well as moral force, ruthless Richard is the prince of forgetting. His actions are wholly oriented towards the present, dismissing the past and his responsibility for it out of hand: 'Harp not on that string, madam. That is past' (4.4.295). While female lament may interrupt the workings of patriarchal power and thus enable an oppositional stance,[16] its ritualistic character as well as its memorializing impetus mark it as a deeply conservative force.[17] From this perspective, the wailing women are far less subversive than Gloucester's strategic forgetfulness, as John Jowett points out: 'His spirit is revolutionary, in that his emphasis on the destroying moment of here and now crumples up and eradicates the past . . . he attempts to expunge memory as an active force in the present.'[18] Always the Machiavellian, he even charges other figures with ingrate forgetfulness while employing it himself as his chosen technique of domination. His seductive rhetoric aims at making Lady Anne and Queen Elizabeth literally forget moral propriety and their hatred of him. Richard seduces Anne into accepting his hand even over the dead body of her father-in-law and against the knowledge that he has murdered her husband, Prince Edward. Gloating over his successful performance – 'Was ever woman in this humour wooed? / Was ever woman in this humour won?' (1.2.215–16) – he prides himself in his ability to manipulate, even obliterate her memory: 'Hath she forgot already that brave prince?' (226). When he later tries to persuade Queen Elizabeth to give him her daughter in marriage, he makes her willingness to forget the precondition for his protection: 'So in the Lethe of thy angry soul / Thou drown the sad remembrance

of those wrongs' (4.4.237–8). Her final submission to Gloucester's demand for oblivion is couched in the same terms: 'Shall I forget myself to be myself?' (351). Since she is an embodiment of memory, such oblivion would indeed mean to forget her own nature.

Gloucester's bravura performances aim at erasing the memory of his misdeeds and substitute his version of events as historical truth. This strategy of manipulative theatricality becomes most explicit in scenes 3.5 and 3.7, in which his and Buckingham's charade serves to obscure their part in the murder of Hastings and to make Richard's usurpation of the crown look like a reluctant submission to duty. But Gloucester's 'struggle to outperform history, to outtalk the determinations of the past', as Stephen Marche observes, 'is undone by the arrival of the ghosts. They remove his confidence in his ability to shape events to his own liking.'[19] While in the first four acts Richard's interruptions of ritual lament effectively severed the communication between the living and the dead, he cannot suppress this communication, mediated through ceremonial commemoration, entirely. When the ghosts of those he murdered appear on the eve of the Battle of Bosworth on All Souls' Day to tell their stories and curse their murderer, they reinstate ritual

---

[14] Goodland, *Female Mourning*, p. 136.

[15] As when Richard turns the mourning scene into a play of courtship with Lady Anne (1.2) and Queen Elizabeth (4.4) respectively; when he interrupts with business of royal succession the communal lament for his brothers in 2.2 and for the young princes in 4.1; or when his interjection cuts short Queen Margaret's curse and turns it against her (1.3). For a detailed analysis of these scenes of female mourning, see Goodland, *Female Mourning*, pp. 143–53.

[16] This view is supported by Philippy, *Women, Death and Literature*, and Susanne Scholz, '"Alas! I am the Mother of these griefs": Mütterliche Trauer und weiblicher Exzess bei Shakespeares Königinnen', *Trauer tragen – Trauer zeigen: Inszenierungen der Geschlechter*, ed. Gisela Ecker (Munich, 1999), pp. 97–108.

[17] Döring, *Performances of Mourning*, p. 56.

[18] John Jowett, 'Introduction' to *Richard III*, The Oxford Shakespeare (Oxford, 2000), pp. 37–8.

[19] Stephen Marche, 'Mocking Dead Bones: Historical Memory and the Theatre of the Dead in *Richard III*', *Comparative Drama*, 37 (2003), 37–57; p. 54.

lament and, with it, historical truth.[20] It seems as if Richard's disregard for the rites of commemoration ultimately does not efface memory but brings it back with a vengeance. As a Vice-figure, he acts as 'a highly transgressive master of ceremonies';[21] yet it is his disruption of ceremony, and of commemorative ceremonies in particular, I would argue, that eventually undoes his attempts at controlling memory.

But the dichotomous opposition between ritual commemoration and its oblivionizing disturbance does not quite hold. The final scene offers a different outlook. Read as a centrepiece of the Tudor Myth, it presents the victorious Richmond, now Henry VII, as the new ruler who ends the bloody Wars of the Roses and promises England a time of 'smooth-faced peace' and 'fair prosperous days' (5.8.33–4). Significantly, this time is ushered in by the king's command for a decorous burial: all fallen soldiers are to be interred 'as becomes their births' (15). He reinstates the performance of traditional funeral rites, which had fallen into neglect under Richard. However, this is not only an act of cultural remembrance but also an act of oblivion which aims at burying the divisions of civil war (as well as obscuring the fact that Richmond is not Richard's rightful successor, but has usurped the throne).[22] That this is part of a strategic memory policy is made explicit when Richmond decrees an amnesty, an officially commanded forgetting, in the very next line: 'Proclaim a pardon to the soldiers fled' (16). The penultimate line announces the beneficent result that 'Now civil wounds are stopped, peace lives again' (40), referring back directly to Lady Anne's lament over the open, bleeding wounds of Henry VI in the presence of his murderer Gloucester: 'O gentlemen, see, see! Dead Henry's wounds / Ope their congealèd mouths and bleed afresh' (1.2.55–6). The play begins with the maimed rites of burial and the bleeding body of the king, both signalling a disrupted body politic; it ends with the dead properly buried and the 'civil wounds' closed. Peace and national unity are shown to be premised just as much on rites of memory as on rites of oblivion.

The promise of peace and unity is framed ironically, however, both on the level of historical and of topical reference. First, this scene uncannily echoes an earlier one in which peace and unity had been declared in almost the same terms and with the same ceremonial gestures. In 2.1, the antagonists, who just before had outbid each other with curses and insults, are now addressed as 'this united league' (2) by the sickly king, Edward IV. Expecting his demise, he wishes to make 'my friends at peace on earth' and enjoins them to 'make me happy in your unity' (6, 31). This unification of the factious court is performed through ceremonious oaths which are couched in terms of oblivion: 'my soul is purged from grudging hate', Rivers swears, followed by Queen Elizabeth's oath to Hastings that 'I will never more remember / Our former hatred: so thrive I, and mine' (9, 23–4). To all purposes and intents, this is a scene of communal forgetting, an amnesty to be sealed with a day of communal commemoration: 'A holy day shall this be kept hereafter' (74). Yet even before the play is over, unity has given way to the 'dire division' Richmond seeks to bury anew in the final scene (5.8.28). Remembering this earlier scene, the Elizabethan audience may well have wondered to what extent peace and unity had been achieved in their time, and at what cost.

For when *Richard III* was first performed, the promise of 'smooth-faced peace' to the heirs of

---

[20] This coincidence, spelled out by Buckingham (5.1.12), is due to Shakespeare's own manipulation of historical fact for theatrical effect: historically, the death of Buckingham and the Battle of Bosworth were separated by twenty-one months. Traditional superstition held that on All Souls' Day the murdered could return out of purgatory to haunt those who had killed them; though officially suppressed in the calendar in the Elizabethan Prayer Book, All Souls was still remembered as the day when the dead communicate with the living; see Marche, *Mocking Dead Bones*, p. 52.

[21] Robert Weimann, 'Performance, Game, and Representation in *Richard III*', in Robert Weimann and Douglas Bruster, *Shakespeare and the Power of Performance: Stage and Page in the Elizabethan Theatre* (Cambridge, 2008), pp. 42–56; p. 48.

[22] See William C. Carroll, '"The Form of Law": Ritual and Succession in *Richard III*', in *True Rites and Maimed Rites: Ritual and Anti-Ritual in Shakespeare and His Age*, ed. Linda Woodbridge (Urbana, 1992), pp. 203–19.

Richmond and the Lady Elizabeth, 'the true succeeders of each royal house' (30) had to all appearances been fulfilled in the reign of Elizabeth I. Richmond's final speech 'is, as it were, remembering the future, resonating with the inflections of Elizabethan polity'.[23] As such it can surely be read as a compliment to Elizabeth's governmental skills; but it is also a pertinent analysis of them. For it was under the very house of Tudor that England saw another 'dire division' of the country, not dynastic but religious. Confessional conflicts boiled underneath the calm and stable surface: a merely *smooth-faced* peace' indeed. As in the play, it was achieved through a complementary strategy of remembrance and oblivion. The year 1559, the first of Elizabeth's reign, for example, saw two official acts which demonstrate this double strategy: the pageant celebrating her coronation explicitly looked back to the nation's pacification under Henry VII; its theme, 'Unity', referred specifically to a concord aimed at healing the strife between church reformers and Catholics.[24] This was at least temporarily achieved in the Elizabethan Act of Uniformity of the same year, a highly tenuous attempt at hybridization. The necessary adjustments of cultural memory could only be achieved through a strategic deployment of forgetting the most contentious issues and of removing their representatives.

The opposition between memory and forgetting, between ritual and its disruption in *Richard III* thus gives way to an analysis of their complementary dynamics that were at work in Elizabethan England as well. Richmond's revivification of ceremony, which effects an erasure of unwanted memories, moreover raises the urgent question to what extent ceremony itself might be involved in processes of forgetting. Can ritual bring about oblivion, just as it enacts remembrance? This question is explored in *The Tragedy of King Richard the Second*, whose many scenes of lament demonstrate how ceremony can be employed to efface one memory while at the same time embracing another one in its stead. Oblivion is thus not brought about through a rejection or failure of ritual; rather, ritual becomes a vehicle for erasing memory.

Let us enter the play at a pivotal moment: after his return from Ireland, King Richard learns that Bolingbroke has returned from exile to lead a rebellion against him; one catastrophic message after the other arrives and Richard momentarily succumbs to despair. Instead of charging into action, he laments his losses, ultimately anticipating even the loss of his crown. His speech literally rehearses the traditional poetics of lament, its topoi and gestures, signalling that it is quoting a well-established tradition: 'Let's talk of graves, of worms and epitaphs, / . . . let us sit upon the ground / And tell sad stories of the death of kings' (3.2.141, 151–2). These ritual accounts of 'the death of kings' also evoke the political uses of lament, the authorization of the mourner's particular story of the past as well as his or her alliance with the dead: remembering the sad stories of kings that have come before him, Richard inscribes himself into a royal lineage, thereby affirming his status as anointed king, and anticipates his fate. This policy will culminate in his charge to Queen Isabel to tell 'the lamentable fall of me' as the story of 'the deposing of a rightful king' (5.1.44, 50), turning himself and his losses into a narrative that will memorialize his version of the event.

More specifically, Richard remembers here the *stories* of these kings as they had been enacted on the Elizabethan stage over the previous decade; the audience would probably recognize in the various manners of death the plots of contemporary history plays and tragedies. Richard's lament thus functions as a double act of communal remembrance that unites historical *locus* and Elizabethan *platea*: the ritual lament establishes a community of mourners on stage while also reaching out to include those among the audience who remember the traditional rites of mourning, which to them, however, are not available any more as ritual practice but only as dramatized quotations, as performance.[25]

---

[23] Jowett, 'Introduction', p. 70.
[24] Jowett, 'Introduction', p. 70.
[25] Döring discusses Richard's lament in terms of 'various poses drawn from the *theatrical* repertoire of acting and articulating mournful passions'. *Performances of Mourning*, pp. 61–3.

So far, this scene of lament functions quite conventionally, down to the appropriate gestures, in particular the sitting on the ground and the shedding of tears: 'Make dust our paper, and with rainy eyes / Write sorrow on the bosom of the earth' (142–3). These gestures of mourning implicitly perform another staple of lament, the *sic transit gloria mundi* topos. Writing with tears in dust serves as a powerful image for the vanity of the world, 'for within the hollow crown / That rounds the mortal temples of a king / Keeps Death his court' (156–8). Death conquers all, and the state and pomp of kings are no more than theatrical trappings, 'a little scene / To monarchize' (160–1). Realizing this, Richard rejects the very ceremonies that make him a king: 'Cover your heads, and mock not flesh and blood / With solemn reverence. Throw away respect, / Tradition, form and ceremonious duty, / For you have mistook me all this while' (167–70). This sounds like a downright renunciation of ceremony along with tradition. Yet as the two abdication scenes will show, while Richard does indeed divest himself of his royal prerogatives, he does so through a ritual performance which in effect re-invests his person and his story with new authority. Ritual lament allows him to do so by naming what is lost and then discarding it; by dissociating his person from 'the name of King' (3.3.145) in order to attach another name and meaning to his life; and finally by substituting the popular 'lamentable tale of me' for the 'grievous crimes' that are on historical record.

The ritual discarding of one set of symbolic props and substituting another for it is enacted by scene 3.3, in which Richard 'rehearses' his abdication speech in the circle of his supporters. He laments his predicament ('O God, O God', 13) and anticipates his forced submission to the rebel Bolingbroke. Interestingly, he prays not for strength or dignity but for oblivion: 'Oh that I were as great / As is my grief, or lesser than my name, / Or that I could forget what I have been, / Or not remember what I must be now!' (135–8). Here begins the separation of Richard as person and his 'name', of the body natural and the body politic. This separation is explicitly linked with the

desire to forget what he had been – a king in name and person – and what he is now – a king in danger of becoming a subject. As the following lines make clear, the aim of this ritual divestiture is not to leave Richard as a mere person of 'flesh and blood' (167) but rather to transform him into another state where he is secure from subjection. His speech performs an inverse coronation ceremony which at the same time doubles as a ritual of saintly investiture:

> I'll give my jewels for a set of beads,
> My gorgeous palace for a hermitage,
> My gay apparel for an almsman's gown,
> My figured goblets for a dish of wood,
> My sceptre for a palmer's walking staff,
> My subjects for a pair of carvèd saints,
> And my large kingdom for a little grave,
> A little, little grave, an obscure grave.
>
> (3.3.146–53)

The ritual character of this speech is highlighted by its anaphoric repetitions and syntactic parallelism. It enumerates the signs and rites of kingship about to be discarded, from the royal regalia to the subjects whose 'ceremonious duty' ritually affirms his kingship. Yet these signs of royal authority are not merely rejected (as in the previous scene), but rather substituted with signs of a different sacred authority: the beads and hermitage, poor gown and wooden dish, walking staff and carved saints of a hermit. He even envisions for himself an 'obscure grave' without an epitaph; all he will have is a lamentable tale written with tears into dust.[26] Yet as we will see, Richard's lament brings about his erasure from official history only to reinstate his memory on a mythical scale.

This speech, then, sets into motion the process of Richard's 'self-iconisation as Christ-like figure where Christological metaphors and allusions to sacrifice and martyrdom are painfully embodied in the act of performance itself'.[27] Richard's initial

---

[26] It is one of the ironies of history that the actual burial place of the historical Richard remains uncertain to this day, an 'obscure grave' indeed.

[27] John J. Joughin, 'Shakespeare's Memorial Aesthetics', *Shakespeare, Memory and Performance*, ed. Peter Holland

desire to renounce the ceremonies of kingship and be only 'flesh and blood' thus takes on a different meaning in retrospect: through ceremony, he transforms himself into the sacrificial flesh and blood of Christ, evoking the performative speech act of the Eucharist: 'this is my flesh and blood'. With lament providing the ritual frame, his abdication speech performs complementary acts of obliterating his memory as subjected worldly king and of re-membering him as heavenly king, subject to no one.

This dynamic of forgetting and remembering, along with ritual as its vehicle, also undergirds Richard's public abdication in 4.1. The whole scene has a highly ceremonial setting: as the stage direction indicates, the lords and commons 'Enter as to Parliament', carrying the royal regalia before them that Richard has already renounced and will officially forswear in the second half of the scene. The first half mirrors the play's opening scene with its examination of 'noble Gloucester's death' (4.1.2) and the ritual challenge between several nobles, though this time it is Bolingbroke who presides over the ceremonies of chivalry. This ceremonial setup does not change when Richard, about to be officially excluded from the 'pomp and majesty' of kingship, is brought before Parliament. On the contrary, the speech through which Richard himself enacts the ceremony of decoronation echoes the one rehearsed in 3.3, with its anaphoric repetitions and syntactic parallelisms as well as its insistence on the first person and possessive pronouns:

> With mine own tears I wash away my balm,
> With mine own hands I give away my crown,
> With my own tongue deny my sacred state,
> With mine own breath release all duteous oaths.
> All pomp and majesty I do forswear.
> My manors, rents, revenues I forgo.
> My acts, decrees, and statutes I deny. (4.1.197–203)

With this speech, Richard imaginatively erases the material and symbolic signs of his kingship from his own person – the anointment balm, his crown and sacred state that commands absolute loyalty – as well as from history: the palpable effects of his reign, grounded in 'acts, decrees and statutes', are

effaced. While this ceremonial erasure of Richard as king spells an absolute loss of political authority, the *performance* of this ceremony itself invests him with power, as he points out to his audience both on and before the stage: 'Now mark me how I will undo myself' (4.1.193). Richard becomes the beginning and end of himself, not in terms of interiorized subjectivity but rather in terms of a self-perpetuating power of performance.

The inverted coronation ceremony is often cited as evidence of Richard's unfitness as a ruler, based on his disregard for ritual and tradition. Yet Naomi Liebler reads it also as evidence of his care for the proper formalities of his civilization's rites and points out Richard's capability of turning them into rites of oblivion:

The speech is both pitiable and dangerous. Richard undoes *himself*, as well as his kingship. In denying his acts, decrees, and statutes he erases all records of his existence and occupation of the throne. This is more than the passage of control; it widens the hole in the historical record, the breach in the 'fair sequence and succession' of the Plantagenet dynasty.[28]

The power inherent in ritual spectacle, then, is not only the ability to shape the perception of the present moment, but also of how it will be perceived in historical memory, as the following contest between Richard and the Earl of Northumberland shows. Northumberland tries to force Richard to perform yet another ritual, that of public confession and penitence. By having the official accusations against him read out, Richard is to submit himself to a specific version of the history of his reign, to be memorialized in legal records. Richard of course refuses to conform, knowing full well the power of performance, as does his opponent: 'That by confessing them [his crimes] the souls of men /

(Cambridge, 2006), pp. 43–62; p. 54; for Richard as saint-like figure, specifically the parallels to Thomas Beckett, see A. G. Harmon, 'Shakespeare's Carved Saints', *SEL*, 45 (2005), 315–31.

[28] Naomi Conn Liebler, 'The Mockery King of Snow: Richard II and the Sacrifice of Ritual', in *True Rites and Maimed Rites*, ed. Woodbridge, pp. 220–239; p. 231.

May deem that you are worthily deposed' (216–17). Against this attempt at erecting in the empty place of discarded kingship the monumental image of Richard as criminal and thus 'worthily deposed' king, Richard sets the performance of himself as a Christ-like martyr: 'Nay, all of you that stand and look upon … / Though some of you, with Pilate, wash your hands, / Showing an outward pity, yet you Pilates / Have here delivered me to my sour cross, / And water cannot wash away your sin' (4.1.227, 229–32). His counter-performance is again framed by ritual lament, as when Richard pleads that he cannot read the incriminating articles because his 'eyes are full of tears; I cannot see' (234) and, despite his own consent to 'undeck the pompous body of a king' (240), keeps harping on the erasure of his title and name that leaves him only as a 'mockery king' (250). This expression recalls the cruel jokes played on Christ at the crucifixion, when he was mocked as the king of Judaea, and it sets up an alternative image of Richard as martyr against that on record in the official indictment.

Part of this struggle over the validity of images is, perhaps unsurprisingly, an act of iconoclasm. Pressed by Northumberland to read out his 'grievous crimes', Richard calls for a mirror and substitutes his own face as the truthful record of his sins:

> I'll read enough
> When I do see the very book indeed
> Where all my sins are writ, and that's my self.
> *Enter one with a glass.*
> Give me that glass, and therein will I read.
>
> (4.1.262–5)

Richard interprets his mirror image not as a guilty countenance but as the 'flattering' portrait of a youthful prince beguiled by the 'brittle glory' of splendour, of admiration and prosperity. Yet this image, while more favourable than the one Northumberland holds up, is not how Richard wishes to be remembered either, and he goes on to demolish it, rhetorically as well as materially. Similar to Richard's previous separation of his person from 'the name of king', he calls into question

whether this mirror image really represents him. A series of rhetorical questions beginning with 'Was this the face … ?' (271, 273, 275) culminates in a wordplay on the meanings of 'face' that obliterates any clear reference between image, person and word:

> Is this the face which faced so many follies,
> That was at last outfaced by Bolingbroke?
> A brittle glory shineth in this face,
> As brittle as the glory is the face. (275–8)

The verb formation 'to face' points to Richard's habitual countenancing all kinds of follies during his reign, and in the particular meaning of 'to put a new face on [something] (as in a cloth facing)'[29] it recalls York's harangue on novel fashions that distract Richard from his duties (2.1). This behaviour is now 'outfaced' by Bolingbroke, in the sense of 'silenced or defeated' or 'defied, confronted fearlessly' – or, with an ironic twist, in the sense of 'outdone, brazened out', implying that Bolingbroke's 'follies' will prove as costly for the realm as his own.[30] Finally, the meaning of 'face' oscillates between the visage, metonymically standing for the person; the representation of the person in the mirror; and the surface, or outward appearance, which is all that 'glory', and a brittle glory at that, can amount to. The erasure of stable reference is enhanced by the close syntactic parallelism amounting to almost identical repetition. The overall effect is to rhetorically efface the image of Richard that his enemies would like to monumentalize in legal documents.

Richard completes this rhetorical obliteration with the material destruction of the mirror. This act of iconoclasm, I would argue, is not so much directed against images *per se*, but against an unfavourable one that represents him as a criminal or

---

[29] See note to line 284 in *Richard II*, ed. Andrew Gurr, The New Cambridge Shakespeare, p. 158.

[30] *OED* 'to outface' = 1.a. To disconcert, silence, or defeat (a person) by face-to-face confrontation or a display of confidence, arrogance, etc.; to stare down; 2. To face boldly or defiantly, to confront fearlessly or shamelessly; to brave, defy, stand up to; 3.a. To maintain (something false or shameful) with boldness or effrontery; to brazen out.

foolish king. He symbolically destroys this image and sets up another one in its place, that of 'a rightful king' deposed and a Christ-like martyr. Iconoclasm functions here not as a stop to image-making and ceremony; on the contrary, it is an important part of the ritualized process of remaking them with a political difference, thereby shaping the semiotic and mnemonic economy of Elizabethan culture.[31]

Images, just like coins, gain currency only through circulation. Richard's vehicle for circulating his image as martyr-saint is again ritual lament. In the very next scene, which enacts his tearful parting from his wife, Richard enjoins Queen Isabel to take his story back with her to France and there to spread it according to the traditional poetics of lament:

In winter's tedious nights, sit by the fire
With good old folks, and let them tell thee tales
Of woeful ages long ago betid:
And ere thou bid good night, to quit their griefs
Tell thou the lamentable fall of me
And send the hearers weeping to their beds; . . .
For the deposing of a rightful king.   (5.1.40–50)

The ritual of mourning creates a community of grievers that sit together, narrate their losses, weep and sympathize with each other. Interestingly, this community is emphatically different from Richard's audience in the previous scene. Where, before, the members of Parliament, led by Northumberland and Bolingbroke, sought to implement an official, negative memory of his reign, Richard now imagines a non-elite group of sympathetic listeners for his lamentable tale. Anticipating his being mourned and remembered as a martyr by 'good old folks', Richard turns his story into folklore, history into myth. The way he achieves this transubstantiation is through ritual lament as a tool of effacing one image and embracing another one.

While geographic and temporal distance might support the myth-making politics of lament, they also work at home, as the final scene of the play suggests. Bolingbroke – now King Henry IV – has

just received the news of Richard's murder, condoned if not explicitly commanded by the new ruler. Henry rejects responsibility for this heinous act, along with the image of Richard as a criminal king which he had so staunchly supported before. Instead, he takes up the image of Richard as a Christ-like figure as well as Richard's chosen conduit of ritual lament:

Come mourn with me for what I do lament,
And put on sullen black incontinent.
I'll make a voyage to the Holy Land
To wash this blood off from my guilty hand.
                                    (5.6.47–50)

Accepting Richard's mythical self-image, Henry accordingly figures himself as Pilate. Despite Richard's factual lack of authority since his deposition, he has succeeded in effacing the official memory of his reign, recorded in legal documents. Graham Holderness concludes that 'history is not written by the victors, but unforgettably formulated by the dispossessed, in a poignant poetry of defeat and inconsolable loss . . . [so that] the myth of the deposed king will live far longer than the practical achievements of his enemies'.[32] In the case of *Richard II*, this assessment holds true – at least for the duration of the play's performance. As Manfred Pfister has pointed out for the history plays in general, each staging becomes a ritual commemoration of the historical figures, which increasingly sacralizes them as mythical figures.[33] This process of mythologizing history is staged by Richard's performative transformation from historical king into

---

[31] In this respect, iconoclasm functions indeed as a rite of oblivion, yet not in the destructive, anti-ceremonial sense Eamon Duffy seems to have had in mind when he called it the 'central sacrament of the reform'. For an overview of the iconoclastic debate and its implications for theatrical practice in Elizabethan England, see Anthony B. Dawson, 'The Arithmetic of Memory: Shakespeare's Theatre and the National Past', *Shakespeare Survey 52* (Cambridge, 1999), 54–67; pp. 59–61.

[32] Graham Holderness, *Shakespeare: The Histories* (Houndmills, Basingstoke, 2000), p. 196.

[33] Manfred Pfister, 'Shakespeare's Memory: Texte – Bilder – Monumente – Performances', *Germanisch-Romanische Monatsschrift*, 56 (2006), 289–306; pp. 304–5.

mythical saint. The erasure of unwanted memories is enacted not though disrupting lament, as was the case with Richard Gloucester, but on the contrary through employing it.

How do these scenes engage with the post-Reformation conflict about the making and remaking of images, a conflict, moreover, with which the theatre, because of its professional commitment to image and spectacle, was necessarily concerned?[34] On the one hand, Richard's reliance on ritual lament in order to create a memorable image of himself suggests not only that ritual remains an actively powerful force in post-Reformation England, but also that the Reformation itself, instead of abolishing ceremony and images, appropriated them for its own purposes. As Gordon McMullan instructively comments, 'We tend to think of early modern reformers as iconoclasts *par excellence*, yet the protagonists of reform knew an effective ideological weapon when they saw one, and despite their reputation as enemies of the visual image, they often preferred to reform, rather than eradicate, Catholic iconography.'[35] *Richard II*, I would argue, stages the appropriative politics behind as well as the reforming properties pertaining to ritual commemoration that were at work in Elizabethan culture.

More specifically, the figure of Richard could be read as a comment on Elizabeth's use of ceremony to fashion and circulate her own image. The topical link between Richard and Elizabeth, unforgettably forged by herself in a remark to the royal antiquary William Lambarde, has often been explored in the political context of rebellion and usurpation.[36] It is seldom if ever examined in regard to their use of ceremony and their shared skill in image-making: just as Richard turns himself into a Christ-like figure, mythologizing himself in the process, Elizabeth turned herself into the Virgin Queen by appropriating the Catholic cult of the Virgin Mary and effectively turning the forms of ritual to her own advantage.[37] From this perspective, the usual valences of iconoclasm are changed: iconoclasm is not necessarily opposed to image-making and its circulation through ceremony, but itself becomes part of this process.

On the other hand, the act of iconoclasm also gestures towards a certain anti-theatrical scepticism which is voiced most prominently by Bolingbroke. Commenting on Richard's spectacular iconoclastic gesture, he points out that Richard's complaint exaggerates his actual cause for grief: 'The shadow of your sorrow hath destroyed / The shadow of your face' (4.1.282–3), he remarks, thereby dismissing Richard's lament as precisely what it is, a performance. Richard sarcastically thanks him for not only giving him 'cause to wail but teach[ing him] the way / How to lament the cause' (291–2). This struggle over the right manner of lament lays open that it is precisely the *manner*, the performance of grief that determines how its cause will be remembered. Likewise, the Abbot of Westminster highlights the histrionic character of the pivotal scene and thereby introduces, albeit unwittingly, an ironic distance to the sacred spectacle: 'A woeful pageant have we here beheld' (311).

This irony, which would be more or less pronounced in performance, also inflects how we read the final words of the play. While we could take Henry's evocation of traditional mourning rites to indicate that his acts as king are subjected to the rule of Richard's poetics of lament, we should be alert to the possibility that he might employ it to his own political ends. 'Bolingbroke's general invitation

---

34 Dawson, 'Arithmetic of Memory', p. 58.

35 Gordon McMullan, ed., *King Henry VIII*, Arden Shakespeare 3rd Series (London, 2000), pp. 67–8.

36 For a detailed account of the Essex rebellion and analogies that contemporaries drew between Elizabeth and Richard II, see Paul Hammer, 'Shakespeare's *Richard II*, the Play of 7 February 1601, and the Essex Rising', *Shakespeare Quarterly*, 59 (2008), 1–35, and Chris Fitter, 'Historicising Shakespeare's *Richard II*: Current Events, Dating, and the Sabotage of Essex', *Early Modern Literary Studies: A Journal of Sixteenth- and Seventeenth-Century English Literature*, 11:2 (2005), p. 47.

37 An example of this is a verse register which commemorates the English Protestant martyrs who had died under her sister's reign; the last line of each stanza invokes Queen Elizabeth's name in the vein of a patron saint. This register of martyrs aims at conditioning and constructing social memory in Protestant England, yet in doing so it appropriates old Catholic rituals. See Döring, *Performances of Mourning*, pp. 58–9.

to participate in the official rites of collective mourning'[38] goes hand in hand with an attempt at erasing the memory of his own guilt in Richard's murder: he imaginatively washes Richard's blood off his hands and projects a pilgrimage to the Holy Land as a rite of atonement that is to wash his sin from the heavenly book as well (5.6.49–50). That this crusade also serves to distract his nobles' heads from the possibility of rebellion and thereby to secure his rule highlights Henry's political use of lament in retrospect.[39] Indeed, even the poetics of lament Bolingbroke employs here become suspect: while Henry commands his nobles to display immediately all the 'external manner of lament' (4.1.286), such as dressing in 'sullen black' mourning garb and marching 'weeping after this untimely bier', and emphasizes twice the sincerity of his sorrow ('*I protest* my soul is full of woe / . . . / Come mourn with me for what *I do* lament', 5.6.45, 47), the attentive audience, alerted by now to the theatricality of ceremony, may well have called his sincerity into doubt: the lord protests too much. What Joughin perceptively has described as the 'monumental overkill'[40] of Henry's final lament is thus informed by a dynamics of remembering and forgetting, as it erects a rhetorical monument to the memory of King Richard in the obscure shadow of which Henry can more securely carry out his own political interests. Viewed as an ironic quotation of Richard's ritual lament, then, this moment serves to demystify the workings of image-making and ceremony even while it at the same time proclaims the continuing power of spectacle, theatrical as well as religious and political.

This tension, only hinted at in the final scene of *Richard II*, increasingly comes to preoccupy the other plays of the second tetralogy. I will concentrate on one pivotal scene from *The History of Henry the Fourth, Part One*, which explores the memory politics of lament most explicitly. Whereas in *Richard II* traditional lament mainly served as a vehicle for the erasure of Richard's image as wicked king, in the following play the rites of commemoration become rites of oblivion proper.

The scene I have in mind occurs towards the end of *1 Henry IV*, on the battlefield of Shrewsbury.

Henry, then Prince Harry, has just slain his rival and namesake Harry Hotspur, who dies with his last words unspoken. The victorious prince finishes the sentence for him and adds this funeral speech:

> For worms, brave Percy. Fare thee well, great heart.
> Ill-weaved ambition, how much art thou shrunk!
> When that this body did contain a spirit,
> A kingdom for it was too small a bound,
> But now two paces of the vilest earth
> Is room enough. This earth that bears thee dead
> Bears not alive so stout a gentleman.
> If thou wert sensible of courtesy,
> I should not make so dear a show of zeal;
> But let my favours hide thy mangled face,
> [*He covers Hotspur's face*]
> And even in thy behalf I'll thank myself
> For doing these fair rites of tenderness.
> Adieu, and take thy praise with thee to heaven.
> Thy ignominy sleep with thee in the grave,
> But not remembered in thy epitaph. (5.4.86–100)

The poetics and politics of these obsequies seem conventional enough: Harry calls on the ghost of Hotspur, recognizing both the dead man's merit and his own position as chief mourner as well as successor to Percy's status as chivalric hero. Note, however, how literally the poetic conventions are fulfilled and, by the same token, subverted. The central speech act performed here is, in Paul de Man's terms, that of prosopopeia, the 'fiction of an apostrophe to an absent, deceased or voiceless entity, which posits the possibility of the latter's reply and confers upon him the power of speech'.[41] When Prince Harry identifies the deceased and sets up his spoken obituary in lieu of a carved monument that is to guarantee future recognition, he seems to enact the rites of commemoration to

---

[38] Joughin, 'Shakespeare's Memorial Aesthetics', p. 60.

[39] Over the two parts of *Henry IV*, this purpose becomes increasingly clear, culminating in the explicit advice Henry IV gives his son on his death-bed: 'Therefore, my Harry, / Be it thy course to busy their giddy minds / With foreign quarrels, that action hence borne out / May waste the memory of the former days' (*2 Henry IV*, 4.2.340–3).

[40] Joughin, 'Shakespeare's Memorial Aesthetics', p. 60.

[41] This is Paul de Man's definition in 'Autobiography as Defacement', *Modern Language Notes*, 94 (1979), 919–30.

the letter. By covering Hotspur's now unrecognizable face with his own 'favours', usually a glove carrying the heraldic emblem, he adds a material sign of recognition. Yet this sign tellingly serves to commemorate the victor's identity rather than that of the deceased. This gesture, I would argue, is an emblem of what Harry's obituary does: rather than conferring upon Hotspur's ghost the power of speech, it effectively takes this power from him and sets itself up instead of the latter's reply: 'in thy behalf, I'll thank myself'. What Hotspur might have found memorable about his life and death is explicitly 'not remembered in [his] epitaph': his rebellion against a usurping king, carried out in the name of honour. Throughout the play, the rebels' challenge to Henry's kingship is underpinned by memorial discourse;[42] in this scene, memorial discourse itself is appropriated to erase the spirit of rebellion. Just as Harry's glove conceals his opponent's mangled face, his speech covers the story rebellious Hotspur could have told. As Tobias Döring succinctly puts it, 'facing this noble victim, the Prince effectively effaces him'.[43] Lament as a rite of commemoration has become a rite of oblivion.

What exactly is being laid into the grave of oblivion here, not only on the stage but also in the playhouse? Christopher Ivic has suggested that this scene enacts a communal forgetting of England's 'dire divisions' by reducing it to a 'reassuring fratricide'. He argues that the play 'at once remembers and forgets the Wars of the Roses by representing them as wars between English brothers'. The scene thus elides the historical differences between the protagonists of the Wars of the Roses and 'in the process anglicizes [the] fifteenth-century Anglo-Scottish-Welsh conflict as "civil war" – that is, as, ultimately a war between English[men]'.[44] Hal's speech enacts and at the same time makes visible the dynamics of ritual remembrance/forgetting at work in this as well as the following plays: his rite of commemoration erases the knowledge of regional and class antagonism and, in keeping with the social function of ritual, establishes an imagined community: that of the English nation. While the nascent discourse of nationalism is never coherent either in the two parts of *Henry IV* or in *Henry V*, what does develop as a coherent pattern is Hal's memory politics: his strategic employment of ritual that aims at dis-remembering the divisions of the past in order to forge a shared national identity in the present and for the future.[45] Forgetting thus becomes visible as 'a formative force in the production of history and culture that participates in the cultural imaginary not merely as a counter memory waiting to be retrieved but as an active yet suppressed part of the process of identity formation itself'.[46]

This project of a unified sense of Englishness was, of course, an emphatically Elizabethan concern that the plays project onto their historical protagonist. Ironically, the mnemonic practice *in* the plays is doubled by the mnemonic practice *of* the plays: they enact a unified Elizabethan sense of nationhood that effaces the actual, regional and feudal affiliations of the early fifteenth-century protagonists it purports to remember. In this sense the history plays themselves, while performing a ritual commemoration of historical figures, at the same time also perform rites of oblivion.

---

[42] Christopher Ivic, 'Reassuring Fratricide in *1 Henry IV*', in *Forgetting in Early Modern English Literature and Culture. Lethe's Legacies*, ed. Christopher Ivic and Grant Williams (London, 2004), pp. 99–109.

[43] My analysis of this scene, including the reference to de Man, is indebted to Döring, 'Shadows to the unseen grief?'.

[44] Ivic, 'Reassuring Fratricide', p. 102.

[45] How this strategy informs Henry's acts and especially his famous Crispin's Day speech in *Henry V* is explored in detail by Jonathan Baldo in 'Wars of Memory in *Henry V*', *Shakespeare Quarterly*, 47 (1996), 132–59, and Dawson, 'Arithmetic of Memory', pp. 55–8.

[46] Ivic, 'Reassuring Fratricide', p. 100.

RICHARD II'S YORKIST EDITORS

EMMA SMITH

The possibility that Shakespeare's *Richard II* was the play described as 'the play of the deposing and killing of King Richard II' and performed on the eve of the Earl of Essex's rebellion in February 1601 has assured its status as New Historicism's poster boy.[1] The association with Essex makes the play into a perfect exemplar of the Elizabethan theatre's doomed gestures towards subversion; if it didn't exist, we would have to invent it (which, of course, perhaps we have).[2] But even as criticism has emphasized the radical energies of a play in which a lawful king is deposed without any immediate consequence for his enemies, the editorial tradition has sought to neutralize its political challenge. As this article will show, we read *Richard II* in texts that are much less comfortable with the fact of the transfer of sovereigns dramatized in the play than its earliest printed versions. Furthermore, in always preferring to reprint the 1608 text (Q4) over the popular Elizabethan editions, recent editors have tended to sacralize Richard's kingship, and to neutralize those aspects of the early texts that most challenge a mystificatory myth of unitary monarchical authority. In this delicate play of shifting allegiances and changing sides, few editors have easily followed Shakespeare's own examples of York, Northumberland and even roan Barbary, in accommodating themselves to the Lancastrian rule of Bullingbrook as Henry IV. Rather than seeking the play's political charge in putative early modern performances, therefore, this article describes a Ricardian tradition of editing *Richard II* in the late twentieth century, an uninvestigated editorial con-

sensus silently complicit in minimizing the play's political charge.

Richard II was a substantial success in print. Of the dramatic works, only *1 Henry IV*, with its crowd-puller Falstaff, equals its five quarto editions in the playwright's lifetime. It was printed in 1597 (Q1) and twice in 1598 (Q2 and Q3), a frequency suggesting that it was the most popular and marketable play of Shakespeare's early career in print. Q1 also has a long history of bibliographic endorsement. The editors of the nineteenth-century

---

I am grateful to Helen Barr, Thea Crapper, Margreta de Grazia, Laurie Maguire, Tiffany Stern and Holger Schott Syme for their comments and insight, and to seminar audiences in Bristol, Oxford, Pennsylvania, Sheffield Hallam, the Shakespeare Institute and Jadavpur University Kolkata, for the chance to rehearse some of my ideas.

[1] Augustine Philips's examination by Lord Justice Popham and Edward Fenner, 18 February 1601, *Calendar of State Papers, Domestic, 1598–1601*, pp. 435–6; Stephen Greenblatt, ed., *The Power of Forms in the English Renaissance* (Oklahoma, 1982), pp. 3–4; Jonathan Dollimore, 'Shakespeare, Cultural Materialism and the New Historicism', in Jonathan Dollimore and Alan Sinfield, eds., *Political Shakespeare: New Essays in Cultural Materialism* (Ithaca, 1985), p. 8.

[2] For the idea that scholarship has wilfully distorted the documentary evidence about the performance for its own ideological purposes, see Blair Worden, 'Which Play Was Performed at the Globe Theatre on 7 February 1601?', in *London Review of Books*, 25.13 (10 July 2003). Paul J. Hammer's 'Shakespeare's *Richard II*, the Play of 7 February 1601, and the Essex Rising', *Shakespeare Quarterly*, 59 (2008) 1–35, reassesses the evidence, and agrees with Worden's claim about Shakespearians' overreading of the incident while arguing that the play performed was indeed Shakespeare's *Richard II*.

Cambridge Shakespeare, the dominant scholarly edition of the period, stated unequivocally that 'the first quarto affords the best text'.[3] Their successor John Dover Wilson, inspired by the scholarship of the New Bibliography, was the first editor to use Q1 sustainedly as copy-text, and most modern editors have followed suit.[4] There is general agreement that Q1 represents a remarkably good text, described variously as probably 'set from well-ordered authorial papers',[5] 'the text closest to Shakespeare's holograph',[6] 'authoritative',[7] 'a generally satisfactory witness to what may be supposed to have stood in Shakespeare's autograph'.[8] Yet despite this consensus, no modern edition follows its logic: Q1 *Richard II* is never considered a recoverable, integral text in the way that recent revisionist bibliography has unconflated *King Lear* and *Hamlet*. Even the recent interest in early editions of Shakespeare's plays has not identified Q1 *Richard II* as an autonomous text, and it is the only one of the quartos which diverges significantly from F not to be included as a separate text in The New Cambridge Shakespeare: the Early Quartos series.

All modern editions of *Richard II*, and indeed all editions since 1608, import some 160 lines, first printed in Q4 of 1608, but generally thought to appear in a reliable text for the first time in the Folio of 1623, into Act 4. Two imprints of Q4 were printed in 1608. One makes no mention on the title-page of the new material, and identifies the acting company anachronistically as the Lord Chamberlain's Men, a title abandoned when they became the King's Men shortly after James's accession. The other presents 'The Tragedy of King Richard the Second: With new additions of the Parliament Scene, and the deposing of King Richard, As it hath been lately acted by the Kinges Maiesties servants, at the Globe. By William Shakes-peare'.

Q1, therefore, has widely acknowledged claims to an authenticity derived from a holograph manuscript, and its text, as attested by the fact of the first three quartos, is exceptionally popular and successful in the late Elizabethan market. Nevertheless, the structure of that text is consistently overlooked by editors in favour of Q4's 'new additions', a phrase in early modern play publication which has usually led editors to favour the earlier text instead (as in the case of, for example, *The Spanish Tragedy*, advertised with new additions in editions from 1602 onwards but almost always edited now from the undated text of *c.*1592; and, further, seen in the editorial preference until recently for the 1604 text of *Dr Faustus* rather than those later texts also advertising 'new additions'). Editors have treated what Q4 claims as 'additions' instead as 'omissions' from Qq1–3 and, although they have tended to take Q1 as copy-text, they have always also included the Q4-only lines. Even Charlton Hinman in the context of reproducing Q1 for a facsimile series dedicated to the integrity of early editions does not see Q1 as a complete text, and, uniquely for that series, includes an appendix of the facsimile pages from Q4 for the additional passages. The ideological effects of the thoroughgoing editorial preference of the 1608 text over the earlier texts in regard to the conduct of the play's Act 4 tend to be obscured by discussions about whether Qq1–3 were censored; or, to put it another way, we have substituted an interest in the

---

[3] *The Works of William Shakespeare: 'The Cambridge Shakespeare'*, ed. William George Clark, William Aldis Wright and John Glover (Cambridge, 1864), pp. 4, ix. On the scholarly and market significance of the Cambridge edition until the mid-twentieth century, see Andrew Murphy, *Shakespeare in Print* (Cambridge, 2003), pp. 202–6.

[4] John Dover Wilson, ed., *King Richard II* (Cambridge, 1939). In the section on 'The copy for *Richard II*, 1597 and 1623', Wilson asserts that Q1 'has never, I think, been accepted without qualification as a basic text before the present edition' (p. 108).

[5] Stanley Wells and Gary Taylor with John Jowett and William Montgomery, *William Shakespeare: A Textual Companion* (Oxford, 1987), p. 306.

[6] Charles R. Forker, ed., *King Richard II*, The Arden Shakespeare (London, 2002), p. 506.

[7] Andrew Gurr, ed., *King Richard II* (Cambridge, 1984), p. 175.

[8] Charlton Hinman, ed., *Richard the Second 1597: Shakespeare Quarto Facsimiles* (Oxford, 1966), p. xvi. A postscript dated a year later suggests that compositorial studies have suggested that perhaps 'the quarto provides an even less "generally satisfactory" text than we have heretofore thought': here the term 'generally satisfactory' seems to suggest something already actually rather *unsatisfactory*.

early modern production of these texts on stage and page for a reflective investigation of our contemporary editorial practice.

First, the matter of those contested lines, present for the first time in Q4. In the passage in Act 4, Richard is summoned by Bullingbrook, 'that in common view / He may surrender. So we shall proceed / Without suspicion' (4.1.155–7).[9] No location for this meeting is given in Q4 – the scene in Q1, without Richard, is located in the stage direction: '*Enter Bullingbrooke with the Lords to parliament*' (Q1 sig. G4). Richard enters, lecturing the noblemen for their fickle allegiance, offering the crown to Bullingbrook. Bullingbrook asks bluntly, 'Are you contented to resign the crown?', and Richard's contradictory answer, 'Aye – no. No – aye' (200) encapsulates his fluctuation between resignation, self-pity, *hauteur*, and misery. Richard then lists the symbols of his office as if handing them over to Bullingbrook, and proclaims 'God save King Henry' (219). Northumberland attempts to get Richard to read aloud a list of his crimes, but Richard accuses him of a betrayal for which 'water cannot wash away your sin' (241). Richard continues to temporise, and calls for a looking glass, into which he gazes, asking 'Was this the face / That like the sun did make beholders wink?' (282–3). The stage direction indicates that he smashes the glass, in this highly verbal play's most striking physical action, and he is sent from Bullingbrook's presence to the Tower.

There have been a number of bibliographic explanations for the divergence between Q1 and Q4, mostly arguing that the texts offer us 'a representative event in a narrative of control and subversion'.[10] The standard editorial position has been that the lines in Act 4 were cut because they were, in Andrew Gurr's words, 'politically sensitive'. For Gurr, 'it seems likely that some authority censored the deposition scene from the published text';[11] Charles Forker agrees that 'it seems probable that the "woeful pageant" of Richard's dethronement was considered too dangerous to print in 1597';[12] Wells and Taylor suggest that 'the actors themselves, the Bishop of London as licenser, or the printers and publishers may have

cut the original version of the abdication scene from the papers which served as copy for Q1', offering us a choice of agents but not of causes for the variation in the texts.[13] This consensus is nuanced but not substantially altered by Annabel Patterson's view that the censorship may not be attributable to direct governmental intervention in the printed play but rather to a climate of 'public surveillance' by which 'the cultural forms of late Elizabethanism took the form they did because the queen and her ministers were watching', and by Cyndia Clegg's argument that, rather than the play's representation of usurpation or deposition being the problem, it is the particular prominence of Parliament which 'corroborated late-sixteenth-century resistance theories'.[14]

The implicit argument that Q4 represents a more complete – 'original', in the terms of Wells and Taylor and Forker above – and thus textually preferable version of Q1 creates a standard modern text that is considered to be more politically radical than that of Q1 (since 'uncensored'). In fact the resulting text is more politically conservative than Q1. Theories of censorship have often been implicitly predicated on an assumption that Richard's presence in Act 4, unique to Q4 and not part of the earlier texts, makes that text more challenging to monarchical authority in depicting the shocking overthrow of a lawful monarch. Here the tendency is for bibliographic and political interpretations to become mutually reinforcing, so that the near consensus that the lines present only in Q4 are in some sense radical is generated by the repeated speculation that they were previously censored, and the idea that they had to be censored

---

[9] Quotations from the play, unless identified as Q1, Q4 or F, are taken from Gurr's Cambridge edition.

[10] Cyndia Clegg, '"By the Choise and Inuitation of al the Realme": *Richard II* and Elizabethan Press Censorship', *Shakespeare Quarterly*, 48 (1997), 432–48; p. 432.

[11] Gurr, *Richard II*, pp. 10, 175.

[12] Forker, *Richard II*, p. 165.

[13] *Textual Companion*, p. 307.

[14] Annabel Patterson, *Shakespeare and the Popular Voice* (Oxford, 1989), p. 78; Clegg, '"By the Choise and Inuitation"', p. 433.

gathers apparent corroboration from the interpretation of the scene as politically radical.

It is, however, at least possible that Richard's entry makes the scene not more transgressive but more orthodox, suggesting that only a king can 'unking' a king and that the act of usurpation should be figured as willed abdication rather than unwilled conquest. Q4 endorses Richard's kingly authority even at the moment when that authority is most under threat. The centrality the additional lines give to Richard is particularly noticeable in comparison to the scene in Qq1–3, where York's rallying cry to crown 'Henry, of that name the fourth' (4.1.112) does not require Richard's tacit, albeit reluctant, agreement, nor even his presence. When Richard is present in Act 4 in Q4, he may give up his crown and sceptre but he decisively seizes the stage and the audience, speaking 131 lines in stark contrast to Bullingbrook's eleven.[15] In Q1 Bullingbrook's 'We solemnly proclaime our Coronation' (Q1: sig. H2) is decisive, following on from Northumberland's dispatch of the renegade Bishop of Carlisle to the Tower; the version in Q4 – 'we solemnely set downe / Our Coronation' (Q4: H3v), its metrics dissipated across the line break, is an anticlimactic response to Richard's own sardonic couplet as he exits the scene he has decisively dominated: 'O good convey, conveyors are you all, / That rise thus numbly by a true Kings fall'. It is the dethroned king Richard, not his rival Bullingbrook, who triumphs theatrically in this scene.[16] This basic problem with the censorship theory was noted in 1890 by P. A. Daniel: 'it seems highly improbable that [the censor] should have contented himself with striking out a passage the only possible effect of which would be to excite the sympathy of the audience on behalf of the deposed monarch.'[17] The corollary of this observation is that the editorial tradition that so consistently prefers Q4 over Q1 in the representation of Act 4 is similarly sympathetically disposed to its martyr Richard.

Without those additional lines, the play as printed in 1597 and 1598 throws particular dramatic emphasis instead onto the scene in 3.3, when Richard and Bullingbrook meet face to face at Flint Castle. Richard's rhetoric in this scene stands in for the rhetoric of abdication in Act 4 in Q4, and employs a similar catalogue of renunciation:

> I'll give my jewels for a set of beads,
> My gorgeous palace for a hermitage,
> My gay apparel for an almsman's gown,
> My figured goblets for a dish of wood,
> My sceptre for a palmer's walking staff,
> My subjects for a pair of carvèd saints,
> And my large kingdom for a little grave.
>
> (3.3.147–52)

While Richard may attempt to assert a moral superiority through these religious substitutes, the one prop prominently missing from this list is the crown. Abdication is thus deferred, lexically and syntactically. The imagery of renouncing the costly symbols of office is repeated when Richard enters

---

[15] Few commentators on the Q4 material have followed A.W. Pollard's contention that the lines were cut not primarily for political but for dramaturgical reasons, in his suggestion that the 'Lord Chamberlain's servants in 1597 may not impossibly have thought that there was a danger of "too much Richard" and cut the lines out in the acting version from which Q1 was printed' (A. W. Pollard, intr., *King Richard II: A New Quarto* [London, 1916], p. 63). The *Complete Works* [the *RSC Shakespeare*], ed. Jonathan Bate and Eric Rasmussen (London, 2007), offers valuable statistical information on the distribution of lines/number of speeches/scenes on stage. Their Folio text gives Richard 27%/98/9 and Bullingbrook 15%/90/8 (p. 831): a similar calculation for Q1 would rebalance by taking 131 lines from Richard (around 6% of the total), 16 speeches and one scene. The reduction in the numbers for Bullingbrook would be 11 lines and 11 speeches.

[16] The evidence of the early chronicles, diverging on partisan lines, also bears this out: it is in pro-Ricardian accounts that the suggestion that the king himself be called to Parliament is found, although his resignation is usually described as taking place in the Tower of London, with the document of abdication later read out in Parliament in his absence. Jean Froissart's late fourteenth-century account, sympathetic to Richard, has Richard passing the sceptre and crown to Bullingbrook as in Q4 4.1; anti-Ricardian chroniclers do not include such a meeting. See Louisa D. Duls, *Richard II in the Early Chronicles* (The Hague and Paris, 1975), pp. 112–54 and Geoffrey Bullough, *Narrative and Dramatic Sources of Shakespeare* III (London, 1966), pp. 430–1.

[17] Daniel is quoted in *A New Variorum Edition of Shakespeare: The Life and Death of King Richard The Second*, ed. Matthew W. Black (Philadelphia, 1955), p. 373.

in 4.1 in Q4, or pre-empted when he doesn't in Q1. In 3.3 Richard descends from the walls to meet Bullingbrook, and finally to receive the appropriate tribute of subject to sovereign: '*he knee-les downe*' (Q1: sig. G2), but the end of the scene seems to register Richard's capitulation: 'what you will have I'll give, and willing too, / For do we must what force will have us do. / Set on towards London, cousin, is it so?' (3.3.204–6). Richard recognizes that he must submit, like a subject, to 'what force will have us do', and he addresses Bullingbrook here with the horizontal term of kinship, 'cousin'. The transition at this point in the play is not a formal one marked by the physical props of office as in Act 4, but rather a political conversion signalled linguistically – as has been characteristic of a play beginning with a deferred duel and continuing to structure itself around the anticlimaxes of postponed or occluded single combat. The scene, at the structural midpoint of the play, anatomizes the definitive shift of power from Richard towards Bullingbrook: in Q1 it is the last time they are on stage together. Although all the quarto texts carry the generic designation of 'tragedy' on their title-pages, Q1 seems particularly to emphasize the historical transition from one sovereign to the next in placing the tipping point in the centre of the play. Q4, and the editorial tradition that so decisively favours that text, prefer an emphasis on Richard's own tragic fall by bringing him back on stage in Act 4 for a further encounter with his political nemesis. Like Richard himself, that is to say, the editorial preference for Q4 seems unwilling to submit to the rise of Bullingbrook without one last rhetorical encounter.

That the additional lines in Q4 may actually enforce Richard's sovereign authority rather than, as has been assumed, that they are the apogee of the play's dangerous politics, is further suggested, if not explicitly owned, by the editorial language used to describe them. The title of Q4 published by William Whyte in 1608 which alludes to the textual difference from previous editions describes that new material as the 'parliament scene' – it is, as critics have identified, thus labelled a scene of parliamentary authority in which, effectively, a

constitutionally sanctioned part of the state enacts a particular legal judgement on a monarch.[18] Editors have, however, tended to prefer a different designation, referring to the extended 4.1 as a 'deposition scene' – a term which cannot be readily traced to the early modern context since it is a description that appears in neither the play nor its known sources. Malone uses the word 'deposition' twice in his account of the play's textual history, but none of the eighteenth-century editors, either Rowe, Pope, Theobald, Johnson or Malone, uses the term 'deposition scene'.[19] By the time of A. W. Pollard's facsimile of Q3 in 1916, the 'so-called Deposition Scene' is identified, and this terminology is corroborated through New Bibliographic work during the early twentieth century, including E. K. Chambers's *William Shakespeare: Facts and Problems* of 1930.[20] John Dover Wilson's 1939 edition, where the suggestion that 'Shakespeare may have fallen in love with, and lingered over, Act 4' sounds strangely like a projection of editorial rather than authorial fascination, discusses 'the so-called "Deposition" scene' and continues to place the word in quotation marks, without ever identifying what is being quoted.[21] The term is used without question or explanation but sometimes preceded by the shrug 'so-called' by the editors of Arden 2 and 3, by Andrew Gurr for the New Cambridge edition, by Herschel Baker in *The Riverside Shakespeare*, Jonathan Bate in *The RSC Shakespeare* and Katharine Eisaman Maus in the *Norton Shakespeare*. It seems that 'deposition scene' is a term which solidifies under the auspices of New Bibliography, and one which, like other of that movement's terms including 'bad quarto' and 'foul papers', has a moralistic edge beneath its aspirations to descriptive neutrality.

---

[18] Clegg '"By the Choise and Inuitation"', p. 433.

[19] Edmund Malone, *The plays and poems of William Shakspeare, in ten volumes* (London, 1790), vol. 1, p. 315.

[20] Pollard, *Richard II*, p. 32; E. K. Chambers, *William Shakespeare: A Study of Facts and Problems* (Oxford, 1930), vol. 1, p. 355.

[21] Wilson, *Richard II*, pp. xiv, 207.

The noun 'deposition' as a noun does not appear in the play nor anywhere in the Shakespeare canon. The verb 'depose' is used ten times in *Richard II*. Three occurrences do not directly connote Richard's dethronement but may be proleptic references to it (1.3.30; 2.1.107–8). Two are used in the conversation between the Gardener and the others in 3.4, for which the Queen rebukes them in strongly religious terms: 'What Eve, what serpent hath suggested thee / To make a second fall of cursèd man? / Why dost thou say King Richard is deposed?' (3.4.75–7). The other four are all used by Richard to describe what has been done to him. Initially he defiantly resists Bullingbrook's ambitions, in a speech excerpted by Robert Allott for the section 'Kings' in his 1600 anthology *Englands Parnassus* ('The breath of worldly men cannot depose / The deputy elected by the Lord', 3.2.56–7).[22] Then, in lines unique to Q4, Richard quibbles on the impossibility of taking 'griefs' along with the crown: 'You may my glories and my state depose, / But not my griefs' (4.1.191–2), and warns the noblemen pressing him to read out the accusations against him that they might read in the book of their own sins 'one heinous Article / Containing the deposing of a king' (4.1.232–3). Finally, the same phrase with a significant adjective creeps into his farewell to his queen, predicting mourning 'For the deposing of a *rightful* king' (5.1.50, emphasis added).

This last connection of the verb 'to depose' with the implication of 'a rightful king' is embedded throughout Richard's usage of the word. It is more associated with his vocabulary than with any other character, and thus 'deposing', we might say, registers the action of the play as seen from Richard's perspective. It figures the play's action as something happening to him, rather than something happening to, or being done by, Bullingbrook. Walter Pater's remark that 'Richard "deposes" himself' in the course of his appearance in 4.1 captures this paradox of self-assertion.[23] In its connotations for 'depose' the play follows the usage in Holinshed's *Chronicles*, one of its major sources, where sympathetic counsellors suggest that Richard 'willinglie . . . suffer himselfe to be deposed, and to

resigne his right of his own accord'.[24] This repeated association with Richard himself in the play and its immediate sources makes evident that 'depose' and 'deposition' are not neutral terms available for bibliographic adoption. Rather, they are already significantly ideologically committed, and committed to Richard's own cause.

To emphasize this implicit bias we can see that other meanings of the noun 'deposition' are immanent in its widespread bibliographic use as a term for the contested material in *Richard II*. The *OED*'s first meaning, dating from the early sixteenth century onwards, is 'the taking down of the body of Christ from the cross; a representation of this in art' (*OED* deposition 1). In echoing this sense of the word the editorial tradition is complicit in Richard's own Christology which figures his opponents as Judases (4.1.170) and Pilates (4.1.238–9) bringing him to a 'sour cross' (4.1.240). The *OED*'s second meaning, 'The action of laying down, laying aside, or putting away (e.g. a burden)' (*OED* deposition 2) is also implicitly sympathetic to Richard's own rhetoric of grief and burden: 'down and full of tears am I'; 'your cares set up do not pluck my cares down'; 'I give this heavy weight from off my head' (4.1.187, 194, 203). In imposing the term 'deposition' on the textually contested material, and in choosing always to reprint that material, the editing of *Richard II* tacitly sides with Richard's perspective on events and with Richard's own topos of martyrdom.

Part of the theatrical attraction of the Q4 passage is that in visualizing the transfer of sovereignty as a transfer of kingly props, the scene promises a distilled ritual tableau of its theme of shifting authority. It seems to be the moment when kingship is reassigned. But when Richard enters in Q4, he is already acknowledging Bullingbrook as king: 'Alack, why am I sent for to a king / Before I have shook off the regal thoughts / Wherewith I reigned?' (4.1.162–4). This apparent admission – although the pointed use of the indefinite

[22] Robert Allott, *Englands Parnassus* (London, 1600), p. 156.

[23] Walter Pater, *Appreciations* (London, 1910), p. 198.

[24] Bullough, *Narrative and Dramatic Sources*, p. 406.

article '*a king*' undermines Richard's ostensible deference – obscures a question rarely directly addressed in criticism of this play: when does Richard actually cease to be king and Bullingbrook begin to be king? Are these necessarily at the same moment? The shifting power balance between two rivals who never actually fight for the throne is registered throughout the play in linguistic nuance, by acknowledging, or withholding acknowledgement of, the status of the other. Does power change hands when Bullingbrook condemns Bushy and Green to execution and repeals his own banishment in 3.1? Or is it when Richard admits himself 'subjected' (3.2.176), and Bullingbrook quibbles that the castle 'contains no king' (3.3.23), or when Richard ironically names 'King Bullingbrook' (3.3.173), or when York proclaims Bullingbrook 'Henry, of that name the fourth' to which Bullingbrook replies 'In God's name I'll ascend the regal throne' (4.1.112–3), or when Richard notes 'God save the king, although I be not he' (4.1.174), or when he is taken to the Tower, or when Bullingbrook arranges his own coronation, or when – off-stage and reported by York – the people of London greet Bullingbrook with acclaim and snub Richard, when in 5.3 Bullingbrook enters as crowned king, or when Richard is murdered in 5.5? The cumulative suggestion is that it is all of these – or rather that the process by which the play dethrones one king and crowns another is just that, a process, rather than an event. Rather than dramatizing the ineffable moment by which a subject becomes a king and a king becomes a subject, the play inscribes a serial effect by which Richard's moral and material hold on the throne is weakened and Bullingbrook's grows stronger.

This shift is registered by, and conveyed in, serial verbal processes. When Richard haughtily enquires at Flint Castle 'how dare thy joints forget / To pay their awful duty to our presence?' (3.3.75–6), his words are an implicit stage direction: Northumberland has remained standing in front of his king. Such meaningful physical gestures of resistance or obeisance on the stage have their parallel in the apparatus of the play on the page. The apparatus of different texts of *Richard II* participates in, and

mystifies, the questions of the ontology of kingship enacted by the events of the play: the play, and its texts, recognize that naming is the corollary of and demonstration of sovereign authority. The early texts deploy their ability to name or proclaim a king in ways that are materially, and ideologically, distinct. What modern editors have done, as will be shown, is to ignore these nuances. As Random Cloud has noted, the supposition that the unspoken text of the printed play as reported by its speech prefixes and stage directions is 'centrifugal from the aesthetic vision of a play', or 'mere epiphenomena of the play, scaffolding to be dismantled when it could stand on its own' is problematic.[25] In *Richard II* we see a remarkably interconnected narrative of spoken and unspoken text which is obscured when editors take down that paratextual scaffolding.

To trace this narrative, I want to take Q1's naming of Richard and Bullingbrook.[26] The opening of Q1 gives us a typographical version of a flourish: 'Enter King Richard, John of Gaunt, with other Nobles and attendants'. The first speech prefix, centred like a heading or stage direction rather than the usually left-aligned type, is '*King Richard*'. Subsequent speech prefixes on this page are '*King*', and this designation continues in prefixes and stage directions through the next three acts, with

---

[25] Random Cloud, 'The Psychopathology of Everyday Art', *The Elizabethan Theatre IX*, ed. G. R. Hibbard (Ontario, 1981), pp. 100–68; p. 102. Parts of Cloud's essay – which has a much broader compass than *Richard II* – overlap with my concerns here, in some of his comments on naming in Q1 and on equivocation around the naming of Richard and Bullingbrook. Cloud's analysis is characteristically provocative and playful rather than exhaustive: I have extended his analysis to look more sustainedly at the editorial tradition and at the implications of our discussions of and preference for Q4, which he does not address. My argument suggests a more ideologically purposive collocation of editorial decisions rather than Cloud's suggestive anatomy of textual equivocation.

[26] Forker's *Appendix I* (pp. 506–41) analyses compositorial studies of Q1: the agreed allocation of copy between Hinman's Compositor A and Compositor S does not parallel the speech prefixes analysed in this essay (so it is not possible to demonstrate that one compositor prefers to call Richard king and the other does not, for example).

Bullingbrook usually called 'Duke of Hereford' in stage directions and '*Bull.*' or '*Bulling*' in speech prefixes. The Flint Castle scene (3.3) in the middle of the play might be thought to be its political fulcrum: the first encounter between the illegally returned exile and his king is the moment at which Richard's kingship first comes under most direct nominal pressure, a pressure echoed and verbalized in Bullingbrook's contemptuous repetition of the phrase 'King Richard' (3.3.36, 47, 54, 61). It is here that Bullingbrook's own attack on Richard's kingly authority begins to interweave with the play's paratextual apparatus: having heard the mocking echo of that phrase 'King Richard' we get the play's first stage direction to strip Richard of his royal prefix: '*The trumpets sound, Richard appeareth on the walls*' (F4v). The royal trumpets may still be flourishing as the king steps onto the battlements, and as York says, 'yet looks he like a king' (3.3.68; perhaps *like* here could signify mere resemblance to, rather than identity with, kingship), but the stage direction no longer calls him king. This is a potentially significant textual moment in registering the diminution of Richard's authority, a movement which is amplified in subsequent scenes.

In Q1, Bullingbrook ends 4.1 with the preparations for his coronation. When in Q4 Richard is brought in he enters as '*king Richard*', but his speech prefix is, for the first time in the play, '*Rich.*' (Q4: sig. H1v). This naming manages to suggest a tailing off of his claim to the apparently absolute title of 'King'. This curious effect may echo one of Richard's own most striking conceits:

> Now is this golden crown like a deep well
> That owes two buckets, filling one another,
> The emptier ever dancing in the air,
> The other down, unseen and full of water.
> That bucket, down and full of tears, am I,
> Drinking my griefs whilst you mount up on high.
>
> (4.1.183–8)

Richard's conceit here suggests that kingship, a well with two buckets, is both a binary – one bucket or antagonist, is high in the air while the other is down in the depths – *and* a continuum – the movement depends on the interconnectedness of the two buckets and their mutually dependent vertical traverse. The image serves to metonymize the play's own complicated inscription of the quality of kingship: *Richard II* simultaneously upholds kingship as an absolute qualitative difference between persons in a hierarchy which has only two categories: king, and not-king, but also suggests it is a relative condition, in which the king/not-king binary may be complicated by a continuum of stages in between. One of these stages is indicated by, or even inheres in, the speech prefix '*Rich.*' rather than the previously held '*King*'. In Q1 the first appearance of the speech prefix '*Rich.*' is at his next appearance in which he bids the queen farewell, but here the speech prefixes waver: the new diminutive '*Rich.*' is attached to a speech of considerable marital tenderness – 'Learn, good soul, / To think our former state a happy dream' (5.1.17–18) – but the rest of his speeches in this scene are attached to '*King*'. The Yorks discuss the shift in popularity between Richard and Bullingbrook, but by the next time Bullingbrook enters the play the stage direction is uncompromising: '*Enter the King with his nobles*' (Q1: sig. I1v). Somewhere, off-stage, the play has registered a political change. The word 'King' is now attached to Bullingbrook.

The speech prefix following this stage direction is less assured. Bullingbrook's first speech prefix as king in this play carries the speech prefix '*King H.*' (Q1: sig. I1v). In this qualifying initial, the paratextual apparatus of the quarto text registers something crucial. What has happened in this *Richard II* is not just a political reshuffle, not merely the substitution of one scion of the Black Prince for another. Rather, something has happened to relativize a former absolute. 'King' now has an initial to qualify it: it is provisional, circumstantial. '*King H.*' is a formulation which connotes, embodies, and remembers its implicit shadow '*King R.*' even at the moment when it seeks to consign him to history. It is not Bullingbrook's individual claim to the throne that is placed under suspicion by the formulation, but rather the sustaining myth of autonomous kingship. Or, to use the terms of Ernst Kantorowicz's *The King's Two Bodies*, an influential theory which derives from, as well as illuminates,

Richard II: in '*King H.*' the troubling fact of the body natural refuses to accede to the fiction of the body politic.[27]

The significance of this designation can be seen by comparing it to other playtexts. This label of '*King*' plus initial does not appear anywhere else in the early texts of Shakespeare's plays where new or contesting kings appear in the printed text. In *Henry V*, for example, Q1 (1600) and the Folio text each designates both the King of France and Henry as '*King*' in speech prefixes and stage directions. In the last scene of *Henry V*, where the two kings meet, there is a shift in the speech prefixes. The Folio opts for '*France*' and '*England*', reverting to '*King*' for Henry's speech prefixes in dialogue with Katherine when the French king has exited. In Q1 the French king is prefixed '*Fran.*' and the new and familiar '*Harry*' is introduced for Henry, a speech prefix he retains for the remainder of the play. Even where there are two kings simultaneously of different realms each called '*King*' in earlier speech prefixes the denominator '*king*' does not take on a modifier. Q1 of *3 Henry VI*, *The True Tragedy of Richard Duke of York* (1595) uses forenames as speech prefixes for the male protagonists throughout its story of the changing fortunes of Henry VI, Edward IV and the Richard Duke of Gloucester. In Q1 of *Richard III* (1597), Richard is originally called '*Glo.*' and the speech prefix '*Kin.*' is given to Edward. When Richard takes over the throne the textual acknowledgement is immediate: at 4.2 the stage direction is '*Enter Richard crownd*' (sig. H4v) and the speech prefixes follow as '*King*'. The political impact of the paratexual references in the Folio text of *Richard III* is rather different: here Richard is called '*Rich*' or '*Richard*' throughout, and the equivalent stage direction when he enters crowned observes more sceptically, '*Enter Richard in pompe*' (194). He is only elevated with an honorific speech prefix in a (failed) paratextual attempt to avoid confusion when, in the Folio's final battle, '*Rich.*' meets his nemesis and paratextual near-*doppelgänger* '*Richm.*'. Similarly, the Folio *Macbeth* calls Duncan '*King*' in speech prefixes and stage directions, but never acknowledges Macbeth's violent and illegitimate rule. At 3.1 we have '*Enter Macbeth as king*'

(139), but '*Macb.*' is stoutly retained as the speech prefix throughout. Thus, while there are precedents and parallels for the paratextual management of two kings or a transfer of sovereignty within a play, none of these uses the semantics of qualified sovereignty '*King H.*' seen in Q1 *Richard II*.

'*King H.*' is the speech prefix formulation for Bullingbrook's first entrance as Henry IV in all the quartos. The majority of speech prefixes in 5.3 are '*King*', but there are a couple of further appearances of the more nervous '*King H.*'. The point here is not about a preference for Q1 or Q4, but, as I go on to show, about what editors choose to do with these paratexual signals in *Richard II*. And if a new king has been proclaimed, the old one must, logically, have been demoted. The quartos have Richard's soliloquy in Act 5 introduced with the stage direction '*Enter Richard alone*' (Q1: sig. 13v°; Q4: sig. K) and adopt that prefix '*Rich*' for the rest of his scene, and thus it is '*Richard*', not '*King Richard*', whom Exton kills, even as he calls him 'this dead king' (5.5.117). But the quartos all do something interesting after this. In the stage direction immediately following Exton's exit with the body of Richard – the moment when it might be anticipated that the death of the previous king actually corroborates and legitimates, albeit belatedly, Bullingbrook's own kingship – the text withdraws its ostensible support. His next entrance in 5.6 is '*Enter Bullingbrooke with the Duke of Yorke*' (Q1: sig. K; Q4: sig. K3), although the speech prefixes reassert '*King*' throughout this final scene.

A brief comparison with the Folio text clarifies what is at stake, ideologically, in the quartos' naming. F uses '*Rich.*' as speech prefix throughout, and

---

27 Ernst H. Kantorowicz, *The King's Two Bodies: A Study in Medieval Political Theology* (Princeton, NJ, 1957): Kantorowicz's influential account of Shakespeare's *Richard II* as 'the tragedy of the King's Two Bodies' (p. 26) is at pp. 24–41. David Norbrook discusses Kantorowicz's study in 'The Emperor's New Body? *Richard II*, Ernst Kantorowicz, and the Politics of Shakespeare Criticism', *Textual Practice*, 10 (1996), 329–57. Margaret Shewring gives an account of John Barton's innovative 1973 RSC production and its use of the 'two bodies' concept in her *Shakespeare in Performance: King Richard II* (Manchester, 1996).

tends in the first half of the play to call Richard 'King' in stage directions. It never calls Bulling-brook king. Aumerle's question at 5.3.23, 'Where is the King?' is thus moot, for in the Folio text the stage direction entrance does not name one: '*Enter Bullingbrooke, Percie, and other Lords*' (43). In this it iterates Richard's own refusal to acknowledge his successor, naming him 'Bullingbrook' twice in his soliloquy in 5.4 (37, 59). There are many implications in this difference. F *Richard II* more closely anticipates moralized critical arguments about the dethroning of Richard as the tragic catalyst for a cycle of history plays in which rightful authority is ultimately restored in the union of York and Lancaster and the accession of Henry VII at the end of *Richard III*, what E. M. W. Tillyard influentially described as an 'epic of England', 'beginning in prosperity, the distortion of prosperity by a crime, civil war, and ultimate renewal of prosperity'.[28] By not calling Bullingbrook 'King' the Folio text suggests that his rule is illegitimate and focuses tragic attention on Richard's demise. By contrast the quartos accede to the inevitable transfer of power crucial to the succession dynamic of the history play, naming a new king without demur. (The differences between Q and F *Richard III*, discussed above, share this politics, with Q ratifying Richard's coronation and F largely withholding that support.) Ultimately, the most significant aspect of the quarto texts is not that they acknowledge Bullingbrook as sovereign but that their version of compromised kingship in the prefix '*King H.*' registers an assault on the mystified ontology of monarchy. The difference between F and Qq, that is to say, is not that one endorses Richard and the other Bullingbrook but rather that F corroborates an essentialist notion of kingship and Q1 compromises that fiction.

Discussing the importance of consolidating nominal character identities which early playtexts represent under different headings in his *Re-editing Shakespeare for the Modern Reader*, Stanley Wells suggests that it is 'proper . . . to call Bolingbroke "King Henry" after his accession, a change normally made by editors (following the First Quarto, in which however it occurs at a later point in the action than in edited texts)'.[29] Wells does not make

clear whether the notion of propriety from which he draws authority is an editorial matter or one of royal etiquette, but the sequential confusion of his parenthesis – following, however, later – is telling. Where do editors place the change from surname to royal forename? At what point does the editor, too, declare himself, willingly or pragmatically, a Lancastrian, or kneel down in textual obeisance before a new sovereign? The ways in which editors handle the transition of power between Richard and Bullingbrook shapes the kind of political sympathies they allow the play, and, as I will outline, the majority of the editorial tradition endorses Richard as king throughout his play and does not acknowledge Bullingbrook's coronation.

No edition until the twentieth century registers, following the quartos, the change in denominating Richard and Bullingbrook. Significantly, the first to do so is that of Dover Wilson, published in 1939 and prepared under the pressure of the abdication crisis of 1936, in which Edward VIII abdicated in favour of his brother. Wilson uses the speech prefixes '*K. Richard*' and '*Bolingbroke*' for the first three acts.[30] In Act 4 Richard speaks in the Parliament scene as '*K. Richard*': the stage direction has, in a faint version of the novelistic stage direction interpolation for which Dover Wilson's editions have been so roundly criticized: 'York returns with King Richard, guarded and stripped of his royal robes' but not, clearly, of his royal title.[31] Two hundred lines later, however, he is led off: '[certain lords conduct Richard guarded from the hall]', and from then onwards, Richard's changed

[28] E. M. W. Tillyard, *Shakespeare's History Plays* (London, 1944), 313, pp. 261.

[29] Stanley Wells, *Re-Editing Shakespeare for the Modern Reader* (Oxford, 1984), p. 65.

[30] The history of how the standard form in Qq and F – Bullingbrook – became the long-standard 'Bolingbroke' could be the subject of another parallel investigation into the politics of editing *Richard II* – in that case starting with Alexander Pope's edition of 1725 which introduced the now common spelling, in homage to his political and intellectual friendship with the first Viscount Bolingbroke, then in exile for his Jacobite sympathies. In this article I call the character 'Bullingbrook' except in quotations.

[31] Wilson, *Richard II*, p. 73.

status is marked by the dropping of '*King*' from stage direction and speech prefix.[32] Interestingly, however, there is no corresponding change in the denotation of Bolingbroke, who continues to be referred to in speech prefixes as '*Bolingbroke*' for the remainder of the play. Dover Wilson's *Richard II* strips one king of sovereignty but does not quite like to crown another in his place. Richard's decline is registered, but the attendant rise of Bullingbrook is unremarked.

Peter Ure's policy for the Arden 2 edition (1956) is 'based on Q1',[33] but registers no change at all in the way the textual apparatus refers to the central protagonists. Ure retains throughout the speech prefixes '*Rich.*' and '*Bol.*'. His opening stage direction in 5.3, the point at which the quartos recognize Bullingbrook as king, also has no truck with his ambition, following the Folio to remark severely '*Enter Bolingbroke, Percy, and other Lords*'.[34] This edition resolutely does not cooperate with the transfer of power that the play enacts. Throughout his New Cambridge Shakespeare edition (1984, revised edn 2003), Andrew Gurr also keeps constant speech prefixes: '*Richard*' and '*Bullingbrook*', even while arguing that 'the Q headings reflect the author's sense of the changes produced by the events of the play while F's consistency reflects the needs of the playhouse'.[35] Gurr's recognition that Bullingbrook has assumed the crown is grudging. He suspends, or even ironizes, Bullingbrook's aspiration in parentheses – '*Enter Bullingbrook [as king], Percy and other Lords*' – rather than Q1's '*Enter the King with his nobles*' at the beginning of 5.3. This designation is interesting, not least since square brackets within stage directions are conventionally used for editorial additions, rather than to make suspect those stage directions which are part of the earliest texts. No explanation for this emendation is offered by Gurr's own statement of policy on stage directions: 'In general for this edition the more elaborate stage direction, whether from Q or F, is given in the text, though where the variations are unimportant Q has been preferred.'[36]

The Folger text, edited by Barbara Mowat and Paul Werstine (1996), takes up the issue with declarative simplicity. '*King Richard*' and '*Boling-broke*' are employed as speech prefixes until 5.3, when '*King Henry*' and '*Richard*' are adopted. The logic here suggests that the same (off-stage) moment transforms '*King Richard*' into '*Richard*' and '*Bolingbroke*' into '*King Henry*'. In the New Penguin edition (1969), Stanley Wells opts for a different strategy, calling Richard '*King Richard*' to the end of Act 3, then '*Richard*' from 4.1 onwards. '*Bolingbroke*' is used until 5.3, when he enters '*now King Henry*', and this shift is recorded in the speech prefixes of the rest of the play. Richard steps down, nominally, that is to say, some time before Bullingbrook steps up; this does not dramatize a moment, but rather a period, of regal changeover, and Act 4 and the early scenes of Act 5 seem to take place in a textual interregnum.[37] The same solution is adopted by Wells and Taylor's complete Oxford edition (1986), and in the Norton text which follows it: Richard is named as '*King Richard*' in speech prefixes and stage directions until Act 4. On his entry into the Parliament scene the text calls him '*Richard*', but continues to name '*Bolingbroke*'. Some nifty editorial stage directions in 4.1 focus in and clarify the moment of the transfer of power. Bullingbrook's question 'Are you contented to resign the crown?' (4.1.190) elicits Richard's contorted reply 'Ay, no; no, ay' and a long, rhetorical speech which is at once self-abnegating and aggrandizing. Richard's 'I give this heavy weight from off my head, / And this unwieldy sceptre from my hand' is fixed as indicative of action (rather than, as might be thought characteristic, substitutive for it) by Oxford's interpolated stage directions '*Bolingbroke accepts the crown*' and '*Bolingbroke accepts the sceptre*' (4.1.191–5). Strikingly these added stage directions construct as the grammatical agent of this speech of decoronation – the subject – not Richard but Bullingbrook, intervening in the text

---

[32] Wilson, *Richard II*, p. 78.

[33] Peter Ure, ed., *King Richard II* (London, 1956), p. xxvii.

[34] Ure, *Richard II*, p. 159.

[35] Gurr, *Richard II*, p. 188.

[36] Gurr, *Richard II*, p. 177.

[37] Stanley Wells, ed., *Richard II*, New Penguin Shakespeare (Harmondsworth, 1969).

to give Bullingbrook a more active role.[38] In 5.3 Bullingbrook enters *'crowned King Henry'* in the stage direction, and his speech prefixes endorse this newly royal identity, denoting him *'King Henry'*. Richard's soliloquy in Act 5 is given by *'Richard'*, and it is *'Richard's body'* that Exton carts off-stage at the end of 5.5.

All of these versions, except Ure's, work to manage both promotion and attendant demotion. The Riverside edition (1974), by contrast, uses consistent *'K. Rich.'* and *'Bull.'* speech prefixes until 5.3, when the stage direction's deployment of both Q1's definite article and the reminder that this king is not Richard creates a syntactically uneasy amalgam: *'Enter the* KING [HENRY] *with his nobles'*.[39] Henry retains this title for the rest of the play in the speech prefix *'K. Hen'*, although Richard, too, continues to be called *'K. Rich.'* up to his death. Both, that is to say, are kings simultaneously: Bullingbrook's accession does not have to mean that Richard has necessarily forfeited the crown. The king in this edition really does have two bodies. This doubling of kings is the route followed by Charles Forker's Arden 3 edition (2002), which is the only edition to discuss in detail the difficulties of this naming issue.[40] The Arden names Richard *'King Richard'* in the speech prefixes throughout the play, pitting him against *'Bolingbroke'* for the first four acts. Forker's policy of recording Folio stage directions results in a palimpsest of names for his stage direction at 5.3: *'Enter* [F]Bolingbroke,[F] [*as*] KING [HENRY,] *with* [HARRY][F] PERCY *and other Lords*[F]*'*. Bullingbrook is thence given the speech prefix *'King Henry'*.[41] Scenes 5.3, 5.5. and 5.6 thus alternate between two kings and two courts: the logic of the speech prefixes is that Richard and Henry are both king at the same time.

The editors here deal with the early texts' dilated transfers of power between Richard and Bullingbrook in different ways, but almost none of these editions seems to subscribe to the dramatic, constitutional or material possibility that Richard has ceased to be king and Bullingbrook has become king in his place. None can quite ratify the strangeness of the process Richard calls 'unking[ing]', or its unspoken corollary, 'kinging'. Only Wells and Wells-Taylor enact without apparent fuss that proper, Polonius-like switch from old king to new, evincing no political discomfort with the structure of deposition and coronation the play depicts. Even these two editions, however, introduce a period of effective interregnum in which neither Richard nor Bullingbrook is king. No editor preserves the speech prefix that is most significant in revealing the ontological and political disturbance of the play's events: *'King H.'*. Thus we now read *Richard II* in texts evincing a sustained ideological discomfort with the transfer of power the play dramatizes, even while their editorial apparatus tends to reiterate the claims for the play's political topicality and its probable performance in Essex's rebellion. The unexamined preference for Q4 and its dramatic sympathy for Richard reveals an editorial bias towards the incumbent king rather than his challenger, and the general unwillingness both to demote Richard from the office of king and to promote Bullingbrook seems to indicate that the historical fact of the change of sovereign is paradoxically more difficult for twentieth-century readers than it was for late sixteenth-century ones. The current critical preoccupation with the possible censorship of the Elizabethan quartos and their significance to early modern monarchical politics seems curiously to have distracted modern scholars and editors from investigating their ongoing power to disturb political and editorial hierarchies: the result is that it is more difficult now than it was four hundred years ago for readers of Shakespeare's *Richard II* to avoid Richard's own martyrology and to acknowledge Henry Bullingbrook as Henry IV.

---

[38] Stanley Wells and Gary Taylor, *William Shakespeare: The Complete Works* (Oxford, 1985), p. 388.

[39] G. Blakemore Evans and J. J. M. Tobin (eds.), *The Riverside Shakespeare: Second Edition* (Boston and New York, 1997), p. 875.

[40] Forker, *Richard II*, pp. 510–12.

[41] Forker, *Richard II*, p. 442.

MAPPING THE GLOBE: THE CARTOGRAPHIC GAZE AND SHAKESPEARE'S *HENRY IV PART 1*

RALF HERTEL

Throughout much of the 1570s, Christopher Saxton must have had terrible muscle aches. Day after day, week after week, he marched through the English countryside and climbed the steepest hills; yet he was not seeking personal pleasure but was on a mission: Saxton was the first map-maker in a modern sense to be sent out by an English monarch to measure the extent of the kingdom. His project – a collection of detailed maps created with the help of the latest technology available – was intended to contribute to the aggrandizement, or cult, of Queen Elizabeth, and his maps were supposed to show the vast spatial extent of her power. Thus, it was for political reasons that Saxton grew blisters on his feet – and, indeed, map-making turned out to be political, albeit with the result, at least in the long run, not quite hoped for by Elizabeth. We do not know how content she was with Saxton's maps when they were published in 1579; we do know, however, that neither Elizabeth nor her successor James I funded any of the great cartographic projects that were to follow. None of the major map-makers of late sixteenth-century England, such as William Camden, John Speed or John Norden, received royal funding as Saxton had. Obviously at some point in the late sixteenth century, map-making had gone wrong in the eyes of English monarchy. But where exactly?

An answer emerges when we take a closer look at some of these projects, following for a moment Richard Helgerson's illuminating discussion of them.[1] My first images show the frontispiece and one sheet of Saxton's ground-breaking *Atlas of England and Wales* (Illustrations 1 and 2).

As Helgerson forcefully reminds us, the fact that this project was funded by the government and designed as a survey of the queen's property shows in the map itself.[2] The monarchic claim to the country is clearly visible: each sheet is dominated by the royal arms, reminding readers, as they turn the pages and move from county to county, that each belongs to the queen. It is as if she had printed her name all over England: Somerset is the queen's, Dorset is the queen's, Cornwall is the queen's and so on. Her claim to the country is shown even more clearly in the frontispiece that mentions neither the author of the work nor its subject. From the frontispiece alone it is not clear what this book is about – but then again, maybe it is: the drawing is dominated by the queen, and it is very much her that the work is concerned with. Saxton's map is not only about England as territory but also about England as the property of the queen. What the arms constantly remind us of, and what the frontispiece implies, is that there is no England without Elizabeth; Elizabeth *is* England. Interestingly, however, the royal arms displayed so prominently here make a tardy entry. They are absent on the first sheet, appearing only from the second sheet onwards, as if added as an afterthought. They are then crowded into narrow corners, wherever the shape of the territory leaves enough space. In other words, the royal claim over the territory seems somewhat alien to the medium

---

[1] Richard Helgerson, *Forms of Nationhood: The Elizabethan Writing of England* (Chicago, 1992), pp. 105–47.

[2] Helgerson, *Forms of Nationhood*, p. 112.

1. Frontispiece to Christopher Saxton's *Atlas of England and Wales* (1579).

of the map, a later addition to fill in the gaps, something marginal that comes only second to the depiction of the territory itself.

If we compare this with William Camden's *Britannia*, a cartographic project printed only seven years after Saxton's, a fundamental change immediately becomes obvious, not to the map of Somerset, which looks very similar to Saxton's, but to the royal arms (Illustration 3). They have vanished and are replaced by a neutral cartouche reading 'Somersettensis' – if the royal arms appear marginal in Saxton's map, Camden obviously believes them to be dispensable altogether. The royal claim has been omitted, and the frontispiece (Illustration 4) underlines this: Elizabeth has simply disappeared as the owner of England. The focus is no longer on the monarch but on the land itself; where there was the Queen there now is the territory of Britain. The logic inherent to the medium of the map shifts the attention away from the ruler to the territory, from the sovereign to the land itself, from 'Elizabeth' to 'Britannia'.

If we, still following Helgerson's line of argument, further consider a third project, Michael Drayton's *Poly-Olbion* of 1612, we see that this shift in perspective away from the ruler towards the territory continues. Drayton's map (Illustration 5) shows no arms or emblems at all but erases all visible claims of ownership. Instead, the land is strangely animated by nymphs and shepherds – it seems to have a life of its own. As Helgerson remarks, it is significant in this regard that *Poly-Olbion* was not merely a collection of maps, as was Saxton's work, but also a chorography. The chorography, however, causes a narrative voice to travel through England, pointing out the particularities of each region and making the land itself speak. If we compare Drayton's frontispiece (Illustration 6) with Saxton's, we see that the land has replaced the Queen: the place of the Queen is taken by an allegorical figure called 'Great Britain' draped in a cloth that shows a map. The territory of Britain is no longer merely property owned by the monarch but becomes the source of power itself, taking the insignia of sovereignty into its own hands. If Saxton's work says 'The Queen is England', Drayton's says 'England is the Queen'. In short: within thirty years, we witness a fundamental shift from perceiving England in terms of its monarchs towards seeing the territory as a power in itself, as Helgerson argues. This shift is not only made visible but is also brought about by cartography: by focusing on the territory of England, maps introduce a source of authority other than the monarchic one. Establishing a territorial, national concept of identification, they question the dynastic one – small wonder that sovereigns did not feel inclined to further sponsor these enterprises.

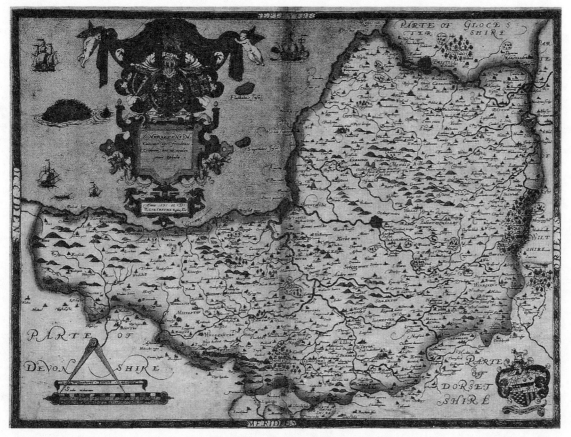

2. Christopher Saxton's map of Somerset (1579).

Of course, this shift is a long and complicated process, and there remains much to be said about this cartographic turn, as I would like to call it. I hope, though, that this brief glance will suffice for my purpose here, which is not to analyse the changes in the cartographic depiction of England as such, for, apart from Richard Helgerson, Bernhard Klein has recently done so in detail.[3] Rather, I want to argue that this shift from focusing on the monarch to focusing on the territory, this revolution in the perception of England described by Helgerson and Klein, shows not only in maps but also on the stage. Analysing the first part of Shakespeare's *Henry IV*, I will follow the traces of the new medium of the map in the equally new medium

of the history play, highlighting the impact of the emerging cartographic perspective on the theatre. What happens when the map is brought to the stage?

★★★

King Lear aside, *Henry IV Part 1* is the only play by Shakespeare that features a map as a stage prop. In the later tragedy, the role of the map is clearly negative: it functions as a decisive tool in Lear's disastrous division of the realm. With its help, he divides the country into three parts to be distributed among his daughters, which sets in motion

---

[3] Bernhard Klein, *Maps and the Writing of Space in Early Modern England and Ireland* (Houndmills, 2001).

3. William Camden's map of Somerset (1607).

the catastrophic action of the play and is the aged king's unmaking. There is an unsettling correlation between the disintegration of the territory of England and that of the body and mind of its former ruler.[4] In fact, Lear's own concept of territory is obviously informed by a belief in an indissoluble link between country and ruler. When he asks Cornwall and Albany to 'digest' (1.1.128) Cordelia's third after she fails to flatter him, this echoes an archaic model that regards the country as not only belonging to but also being incorporated in and embodied by its ruler.[5] The interrelatedness of land and ruler is further suggested by the scarcity of indications of geographically identifiable locations in the stage directions and the characters' speeches – often, we do not know for sure where exactly the action is set. Yet, the play is

peopled with characters whose names link them to particular regions and who are referred to only by their titles. As Cornwall comes to Albany, Cornwall and Albany to Gloucester, Gloucester and

---

[4] For studies on the use of the map in *King Lear* see F. T. Flahiff, 'Lear's Map', *Cahiers Elisabethains*, 30 (1986), 17–30; Terence Hawkes's chapter 'Lear's Maps' in his study *Meaning by Shakespeare* (London and New York, 1992), pp. 121–40; John Gillies, 'The Scene of Cartography in *King Lear*', in *Literature, Mapping, and the Politics of Space in Early Modern Britain*, ed. Andrew Gordon and Bernhard Klein (Cambridge, 2001), pp. 109–37; and Peter Holland, 'Mapping Shakespeare's Britain', in *Shakespeare's Histories and Counter-Histories*, ed. Dermot Cavanagh, Stuart Hampton-Reeves and Stephen Longstaffe (Manchester, 2006), pp. 198–218.

[5] Shakespeare's plays are quoted from the Oxford edition of the *Complete Works*, ed. Stanley Wells and Gary Taylor (Oxford, 1986).

4. Frontispiece to William Camden's *Britannia* (1607).

inhospitable, and much of the dramatic impact of the play derives from the tension between the hostility of an England that finds its most appropriate expression in the barrenness of a heath in a thunderstorm and the aged king's desperate search for a home.

If *King Lear* discredits the map as a tool of disintegration in a rather obvious way, the impact of cartography on *Henry IV Part 1* is more complex. Shakespeare's earlier history play not only prefigures the disintegrative danger of maps we find in *King Lear*, it simultaneously follows a cartographic logic itself, as I shall demonstrate. If in *King Lear* it is paradoxically the king, the supposed source of national unity, who is the agent of national disintegration, in *Henry IV Part 1* Shakespeare puts the map, this potentially separatist tool, appropriately into the hands of rebels – and it is indeed Shakespeare who places the map in the hands of the conspirators who are to revolt against King Henry, for none of his sources on Henry IV mentions a map. Given the scarcity of stage props in the history plays, and the scarcity of maps as props on the early modern stage in general, this underlines how important it must have been to Shakespeare.[7] Yet, why was it so important? This becomes clearer when we look at the relevant scene. A map is introduced when the rebels around Hotspur meet to discuss the imminent revolt against King Henry:

Hotspur. Lord Mortimer and cousin Glyndŵr,
  Will you sit down? And uncle Worcester?
[Mortimer, Glyndŵr, and Worcester sit]
  A plague upon it, I have forgot the map!
Glyndŵr. No, here it is. Sit, cousin Percy, sit . . .
  Come, here's the map. Shall we divide our right,
  According to our threefold order ta'en?
Mortimer. The Archdeacon hath divided it
  Into three limits very equally.
  England from Trent and Severn hitherto
  By south and east is to my part assigned;
  All westward – Wales beyond the Severn shore

Kent to Dover, we witness, as F. T. Flahiff observes, 'the replacing of spatial by human relationships'.[6] Territory hardly appears to exist independently of its representatives; it seems personal in a way that recalls Saxton's depiction of England as indissolubly linked to its queen. In Lear's view, it appears, the territory of England is no authority in itself but a possession to be passed on in an almost corporeal way. Perhaps what makes Lear such a tragic figure is, not least, the fact that he himself eventually suffers from the effects of this reduction of the realm to the possession of its ruler and the concomitant neglect of its inhabitants. As soon as he has handed over his possession and ceded authority, there seems to be no place left for him within the territory of England. The land appears to turn

---

6 Flahiff, 'Lear's Map', p. 19.
7 For the rarity of maps in early modern theatre see Holland, 'Mapping Shakespeare's Britain', p. 200.

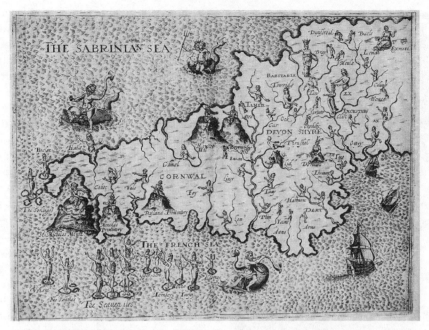

5. Michael Drayton's map of Cornwall and Devon from *Poly-Olbion* (1612).

And all the fertile land within that bound –
To Owain Glyndŵr; *(to Hotspur)* and, dear coz, to you
The remnant northward lying off from Trent.
And our indentures tripartite are drawn . . .
Hotspur. Methinks my moiety north from Burton here
  In quantity equals not one of yours.
  See how this river comes me cranking in,
  And cuts me from the best of all my land
  A huge half-moon, a monstrous cantle, out.
  I'll have the current in this place dammed up,
  And here the smug and silver Trent shall run
  In a new channel fair and evenly.
  It shall not wind with such a deep indent,
  To rob me of so rich a bottom here.
Glyndŵr. Not wind? It shall, it must; you see it doth.
                    (*1 Henry IV*, 3.1.3–103)

We may only speculate but – the obvious anachronism of a sixteenth-century map in the hands of a fifteenth-century rebel aside – the map Shakespeare puts into Hotspur's hands might well have looked similar to those drawn by Saxton or Camden. In a way, these maps mirror precisely the disintegration of England at which the rebels aim. What marks them as signs of the beginning of a

new cartographic era is, not least, their love of detail (Illustration 7); they show almost every village and every river in the country. As a result, one does not, however, get a clearer picture of England; on the contrary, one easily gets lost in a maze of villages, trees and names – one does not see the wood for the trees, or rather, England for its villages. These maps are in themselves already tools of disintegration, separating England into a variety of counties, each on a sheet of its own; they are devices that force attention away from England as a whole towards its individual parts. Encouraging a dissecting gaze, they would be highly appropriate symbols for the rebels' ambitions.[8]

---

8 Indeed, Saxton's map did become a tool of rebellion in the hands of Oliver Cromwell, who directed his revolutionary forces against the king with its help, as the legend in one of the British Library copies suggests. It reads: 'This map was reduced from the county maps of Mr. Saxton by order of Oliver Cromwell for the use of his armies.' Although the truth was perhaps 'less dramatic' and the map was ordered merely by 'a London printseller of parliamentary leaning', as Helgerson (p. 108) suggests, Saxton's maps partook in a

6. Frontispiece to Michael Drayton's *Poly-Olbion* (1612).

7. Detail from Christopher Saxton's wall-map of England (1583).

This dissecting gaze, though, informs not only the rebels' plans; the entire play also seems to imitate their separatist ambition. It is as though there was a disintegrative power at work, and this power already makes itself felt in the spatial setting. If we compare *Henry IV Part 1* with an earlier history play, *Richard III*, we immediately see the change in the handling of space. Clearly, *Richard III* is almost excessively centred on London: in total, 19 out of the 26 scenes are set there and, apart from a short interlude in the third act, it is not until the fifth act, when Richard moves to confront the rebels, that the setting extends beyond it. If we compare this with the spatial setting of *Henry IV Part 1* we immediately realize that here, in the later play, the centre has exploded. The scenes are dispersed all over England, from Warkworth Castle on the Scottish border to the Eastcheap tavern in London, from Bangor in northern Wales to Rochester in the very east, from York to Windsor, from Gadshill near the mouth of the Thames to Shrewsbury. This geographical fragmentation in itself suggests that the court is no longer the centre of gravity – just as Henry IV, the usurper on the throne, is no longer the centre of authority. The claim to sovereignty of Henry, who eliminated the rightful king Richard II, is constantly contested, and if the centre of his realm no longer holds, this shows in the spatial setting of the play that bears his name.

The spatial setting also discloses a cartographic logic. Oscillating wildly between the very north and very south, the very east and very west of the kingdom, measuring its length and width within a few scenes, the setting creates the impression

change of perspective that eventually 'brought the king's enemies to the field'.

of extreme spatial incoherence. While *Richard III* shows hardly any movement in space, the first part of *Henry IV* is the history play as road movie, as it were. Here, we see the protagonists constantly on the move, and the very first scene opens with Henry preparing to leave for a crusade to the Holy Land, only to be stopped in his tracks by the messenger Blunt 'new lighted from his horse, / Stained with the variation of each soil / Betwixt that Holmedon and this seat of ours' (1.1.63–5), bearing news from a battle at the Scottish border. We encounter Hal and his tavern companions moving along the road to Gadshill where they intend to rob pilgrims travelling to Canterbury; we see Falstaff and his soldiers marching along a road near Coventry, towards the decisive battle at Shrewsbury; and we see Hal leaving for North-bridge, where he is to meet the troops of his father. Hotspur alone travels from the Scottish border to Windsor and back, from there to Bangor in north-east Wales, and from Bangor to Shrewsbury, covering a distance of more than a thousand miles in the course of the play. At times he seems to travel with almost superhuman speed, covering the round trip from his home near the Scottish border to Windsor within two weeks, for his wife complains that she has been 'a banished woman from my Harry's bed' for a 'fortnight' (2.4.38–9). Yet, he must leave her again 'within these two hours' (2.4.35–6).

If the protagonists are not transported by magic force, many of their journeys are highly improbable, if not impossible. In other words, the spatial structure of the play hardly accords to human scale; instead, I would argue, it accords to the logic of cartography. Of course, other plays present us with quick successions of locations, too, and certainly, the swiftness with which the spatial setting changes in Shakespearian theatre generally owes as much to an oscillation between *locus* and *platea*, between the symbolic location situated within the world of the play and the non-illusionistic space of the physical stage, as to the fact that locations were indicated verbally rather than through scenery, so that they could shift almost from one word to the next.[9] Yet, in the context of a play that so prominently introduces a map as stage prop, the seemingly effortless

change of location also betrays a cartographic logic. The spatial setting changes with the swiftness of a finger moving on a map: from Eastcheap to Bangor, from Westminster to Shrewsbury, the locations alternate with complete disregard for the possibilities of human travel. With its rapid changes of location and action taking place simultaneously in places scattered all over England, the play stretches geographical coherence to its limits, and within the compass of a two-hour performance, the spectators are transported through more or less the entire kingdom. Hence, they experience the play almost as they would experience a map: *Henry IV Part 1* enacts the simultaneity of the cartographic perspective that places the whole country at one's fingertips.

The centrifugal force is not restricted to the spatial setting, though. It is also shown in the cast – and not only in the radiant figure of Falstaff whose very shape is centrifugal. Whereas the cast of earlier history plays such as *Richard III* is composed almost exclusively of members of the nobility and the clergy, that of *Henry IV Part 1* is extremely diverse. If the spatial setting explodes, so does the social setting: from the robber to the royal, from the pickpocket to the prince, they are all present in this theatrical panorama of Elizabethan society. Thus, the play not only measures the territory of England from north to south and east to west, it also charts its society from top to bottom. The protagonists are not only spatially mobile but also socially, crossing borders of rank – the prime example, of course, being Hal, the Prince of Wales, who miraculously rises from a good-for-nothing into a national hero.

Interestingly, he not only oscillates between two opposing social spheres but also between diverse linguistic realms, between the verse of courtly

---

[9] For the concept of *locus* and *platea* and its impact on the Shakespearian stage see Robert Weimann's *Shakespeare and the Popular Tradition in the Theater: Studies in the Social Dimension of Dramatic Form and Function*, ed. Robert Schwartz (Baltimore, 1978), pp. 73–85 and 208–15, and his chapter 'Space (In)dividable: *locus* and *platea* Revisited' in *Author's Pen and Actor's Voice: Playing and Writing in Shakespeare's Theatre*, ed. Helen Higbee and William West (Cambridge, 2000), pp. 180–215.

speech and the prose of the tavern. He is aware of this himself: 'I am so good a proficient in one quarter of an hour that I can drink with any tinker in his own language during my life' (2.5.17–19). In fact, the entire play swiftly alternates the elaborate rhetoric of the court with the bawdy brawls of the tavern, the 'power of English . . . / Whose arms were moulded in their mothers' womb / To chase these pagans in those holy fields' (1.1.22–4) with ''sblood' (2.2.35) and 'zounds' (2.2.63) and 'I'll be hanged' (2.1.1–2). From high rhetoric to the vernacular, from pathos to bathos, the play captures the whole diversity of the English language.

Thus, it maps out England in its geographical, social and linguistic dimensions. The effect of this survey is fundamentally decentralizing, since the play favours diversity over coherence. Indeed, it is not even clear who is the true protagonist of the play – T. J. King counted that Falstaff, Hotspur, Hal and King Henry are all assigned roughly the same number of speaking lines.[10] The play is deliberately ambiguous in its focus, paralleling the panoramic perspective of the map with its lack of a vanishing point and its denial of clear hierarchies, of foreground and background. Not so much a close-up of one of its characters, it is a broad survey of Elizabethan society that, with its multiple viewpoints, would give headaches to those looking for a clear focus. In fact, *Henry IV* has always been regarded by some as too centrifugal, and productions from early on have merged the two *Henry IV* plays, focusing more strongly on the character of Hal, Hotspur, or Falstaff – Orson Welles's adaptation *Chimes at Midnight*, also known as *Falstaff*, is a notable example. The play almost immediately became Falstaff's play, while later productions have refocused on Hal, narrowing down its heterogeneity to a teleological, *Bildungsroman*-like narrative of a young prince.[11] *Ex negativo*, these interpretations underscore my point: this play has an unsettling power, a disconcerting drive towards disintegration that some find hard to accept.

★★★

From where does this play derive its disconcerting power? Clearly, it must in one way or other engage the spectators, who must feel that what happens on the stage concerns them, too. Yet, how does the play turn the England on the stage into *their* England? First of all, by *not* staging space or, to be more precise, by underdetermining it. It is a small but significant detail that most spectators will not be able actually to see what is on Hotspur's map, it being simply too small to be read from any position not adjacent to the stage. The restricted access might have reminded the audience that maps were luxury goods, a cultural capital to which only few had access. This privilege, however, is clearly abused by the rebels who not only threaten the integrity of the country but also at no moment ask themselves whether they are entitled to divide up its inhabitants. They perceive of England as a vast mass of land to be divided according to mathematical computation and, in arrogantly appropriating political power with the help of their map, they are likely to provoke immediate antipathy in the audience. In fact, the entire scene is likely to prompt an angry rejection of the rebels' selfish plans to dismember the country, and might hence encourage a sense of national unity.

Not only does the audience not see what is on the map, it also does not even know for sure whether the piece of paper in Hotspur's hand is a map at all. It is merely generated verbally: only the fact that the rebels refer to it as such turns it into a map. Indeed, words compensate for the lack of vision in this scene when in Mortimer's explanation of the map and in the ensuing dispute about the boundaries of the separation the geography of England is recreated through language. Hence, the spectators must create a map in their minds and trace the course of the newly drawn borders in their thoughts. Thus, they are encouraged to become cartographers themselves and, by redrawing the lines they, too, temporarily become rebels, splitting up the country in their thoughts. This, however, might make them feel the enormity of

10 T. J. King, *Casting Shakespeare's Plays: London Actors and Their Roles, 1590–1642* (Cambridge, 1992), p. 186.

11 For the stage history of the play see David Scott Kastan's introduction to his Arden edition of *King Henry IV Part 1* (London, 2002), pp. 76–106.

the rebels' plans in a more personal way and might prompt a more emotional rejection.[12]

As in this scene, words in Shakespeare's play frequently define space that otherwise remains unspecified. On the bare stage of *Henry IV*, it is mainly through deictic formulations such as 'this seat of ours' (1.1.65), 'strands afar remote' (1.1.4), or 'this house' (3.3.98) that the spatial setting is specified. In addition, the play abounds with references to off-stage spaces: within the compass of the first scene, for instance, Henry dreams of military glory in the 'holy fields' (1.1.24) of Jerusalem, is confronted with a rebellion in Wales as well as a battle at the Scottish border, and makes plans for a meeting at Windsor Castle. Furthermore, as Matthew Greenfield has noted, 'the characters speculate incessantly about what is happening in the play's other sites': 'the thoughts of Hotspur (1.2, 4.1) and the king (1.1) turn to Hal and his drinking companions; Falstaff and Hal in the tavern discuss Hotspur, Glendower, Douglas, and the king (2.4); and the rebels imagine the king thinking of them (3.1).'[13] Thus, the characters extend the spatial setting beyond the visible space to the invisible space beyond the stage. This contributes to the centrifugal drive of the play, creating the impression that England extends almost boundlessly beyond what we see on the stage. In other words, it evokes England as a vast territory beyond the control of the individual, beyond the control even of the king – there is always something going on somewhere else, and we are not there.

Another strategy for putting the territory of England onto the stage is encoded in the names of some protagonists. Northumberland, Worcester, Gadshill and Westmorland – these are not only the names of characters but refer, of course, also to the geography of England. Needless to say, alluding to the nobility by means of their regionally connoted titles is no Shakespearian invention but was general practice in his time. Yet, it is a revealing one, for it highlights the strong link between land and owner, indicating a territorial concept that is still largely conceived of in terms of property, as we have seen with regard to *King Lear*. Henry Percy, Earl of Northumberland, simply *is* Northumberland – in

a similar way that Elizabeth *is* England in Saxton's frontispiece. Interestingly, though, this mode of referring to persons is less prominent in *Henry IV Part 1* compared not only to *King Lear* but also to earlier history plays such as *Richard III*. Due to the social diversity of the cast, more characters without land or title are shown to play a vital role in the history of England. In other words, the onomastic shift away from equating land and owner through the name of the latter parallels the cartographic shift away from perceiving England in terms of property available only to the few.

If we take a closer look at those names that do bear geographical connotations, we see the centrifugal drive at work once more. Gadshill refers to the hill in Kent where the robbery of the pilgrims takes place. It is a marginal location close to the shore, a place where the land meets the sea and the kingdom its boundary. In *Henry IV Part 1* it is also a marginal place in terms of morals. It is here that Hal assists in the robbery of the pilgrims, it is here that he sinks lowest, turning into a robber who plays tricks on his own friends. Thus, not only is Gadshill spatially on the edge but, in the action taking place, there is also a move towards – and beyond – the margins of accepted behaviour. Westmorland and Northumberland, too, refer to marginal places, situated at the far end of the kingdom, close to the Scottish border – and, in the eyes of some Elizabethans, close to the frontier of civilization. Significantly, the geographical marginality of the region Northumberland borrows his name from mirrors the decentred position he occupies in the plot. Northumberland is the northernmost outpost of England, marking the periphery of the kingdom and the place where English influence begins to fade, a place that is connoted with the constant threat of Scottish invasion. Like the region

[12] For the practical difficulties of employing a map as a stage prop, and various solutions to these difficulties in later productions of *King Lear*, see Holland, 'Mapping Shakespeare's Britain', pp. 210–12.

[13] Matthew Greenfield, '*1 Henry IV*: Metatheatrical Britain', in *British Identities and English Renaissance Literature*, ed. David J. Baker and William Maley (Cambridge, 2002), pp. 71–80; p. 73.

he represents, Northumberland indicates the symbolic point where monarchic power fails, and poses a constant threat. Not only does he support Bolingbroke in his rebellion against Richard II, after Bolingbroke's coronation he again poses a threat to the newly crowned Henry IV, who is dangerously indebted to him, a threat that culminates in his participation in Hotspur's rebellion. Thus, the spatial marginality is equated with a lack of loyalty, and the geography of England is imbued with moral connotations.

Tellingly, the rebels discuss their plan in Wales, a place that is also on the periphery of Henry's kingdom. Yet, not only the place is peripheral; the Welsh of Glyndŵr's daughter would have been foreign to many of the English spectators, too, and when she speaks to her husband Mortimer he, like presumably much of the audience, does not understand a word. This hints at the incompatibility of Wales and England and suggests that the Welsh remain outsiders in the English nation-building process – their voices may be heard but are simply not understood. Glyndŵr's daughter's speaking and singing in Welsh immediately after the rebels seal the tripartition might have reminded the audience that the kingdom was no homogeneous unity, that it was a fragile multi-ethnic compound constantly in danger of disintegration.

Thus, words create territories and speech turns into space. This transfer of the visible into the imaginary fosters engagement, and the centrifugal drive of the play serves to reinforce this involvement, compelling the audience to negotiate the geographical as well as the social diversity of their kingdom. Synthesizing Bangor and Windsor, Northumberland and Gadshill into one coherent mental geography, as well as the king and the tinker into one encompassing social network, calls for a power of abstraction in the audience. The spectators are required to combine the extremely divergent data into one coherent picture – all this is England. This power of abstraction called forth by the play, I would argue, also fosters the concept of the nation as an abstract entity that allows for geographical, social and linguistic differences. In other words, the play not only shows the structural logic

of the map, it also has a similar effect to a map, supporting a conceptual shift away from England as the land and property of the king towards England as a vast, highly varied geography claimed by a socially diverse nation. In short, it takes part in the emergence of national self-awareness.

Shakespeare, of course, must have been conscious of how crucial engaging the audience was for the success of his plays. In the tavern scene immediately preceding the rebels' meeting, Hal and Falstaff play extempore king and prince, swapping roles halfway through their performance. This play within the play is a metadramatic reflection of how *Henry IV Part 1*, and arguably Shakespeare's theatre more generally, functions. Hal and Falstaff turn simple props into signifiers of power: 'This chair shall be my state, this dagger my sceptre, and this cushion my crown' (2.5.380–1), Falstaff declares. Thus, they act out what the audience does without much reflection: imbuing props with significance, creating a kingdom from words and imagination. Asking the audience in the prologue to the ensuing play, *Henry V*, to 'piece out our imperfections with your thoughts' (Prologue, 23), Shakespeare readily admits that he depends on the 'imaginary forces' (Prologue, 18) of his audience to turn 'this unworthy scaffold' (Prologue, 10) into the realm of England. In other words, Shakespeare relies on, and encourages, the spectators' creating their own England, substituting 'a kingdom for a stage' (Prologue, 3). The modesty of Shakespeare the playwright implies an empowerment of the audience that is not merely confronted with a dramatic depiction of England but with the possibility, and the need, to imagine its own kingdom. In terms of reader-response theory: England remains underdetermined and has to be actualized by the individual spectator. Evoking England while deliberately leaving it underdetermined demands the creative appropriation of its spatial, social and linguistic dimensions by the audience, an empathic cartography of sorts.

★★★

How, then, does the England on the stage relate to the England off the stage? How does the *mise-en-scène* of England contribute to a new perspective on its geography and its nation? Among other things, the theatre is a place where imaginary spaces are projected onto the limited space of the stage, where imaginary territories such as that of England are actualized. In a way, it is also a visual tool of sorts, a tool for shaping the optics of an audience, and a device for making visible what so far has been invisible. As such, it contributes towards a more general change of perspectives, a process in which other media, such as maps, also play a role. Helgerson has persuasively demonstrated how the proliferation of maps fundamentally changed the Elizabethans' perspective on the world, and this paper began by following his argument, tracing the change from a monarchic perspective towards a territorial point of view in a sequence of maps and frontispieces. Probably the most immediately striking effect of maps is that of empowerment, and it is this empowerment that fosters the shift from a monarchic towards a national perspective: the kingdom becomes accessible to anyone in possession of a map. Maps render the world at one's fingertips, making the English territory 'appear to be within the reach and grasp of the human subject'.[14]

There is, of course, also a danger inherent to this empowerment. Maps reduce territories to objects, ready for exploitation or separation. More than just one dimension is lost when the three-dimensional world is projected onto the two-dimensional space of the map: all peculiarities of the landscape and of the inhabitants of a specific area are erased. As Klein puts it, the map stands for 'the transfer of organic into functional space', of experienced into abstract space.[15] Like the Renaissance invention of the watch, which marks the transfer of organic and experienced into functional and abstract time, the map contributes to a computation of the world that turns it into gridlines and numbers, making it more rational and calculable but possibly less humane.

Indeed, Shakespeare points to the dangerous side of maps, and the tripartition of England is an obvious instance of abusing them. At no point do the rebels consider their countrymen; for them, England is not an inhabited space that has historically evolved but merely the functional space of a territory to be divided up. If Lear, on the verge of insanity, demands that the 'thick rotundity o' th'world' should be struck 'flat' (3.2.7) as if in a map, this transformation of real into abstract cartographic space has already taken place in the mind of Hotspur, who ignores the real world behind its two-dimensional representation. Tellingly, he would rather alter the course of a river than redraw the lines on the map. He is oblivious to the representational gap between territory and map, between actual space and its mere depiction – he does not see reality for its abstraction. Indeed, he seems to forget England altogether in his plans, as his comical entry suggests: 'A plague upon it, I have forgot the map!' How is he to be trusted with leading England's destinies if he is not even capable of taking care of its miniature representation? Hotspur, whose vocabulary betrays his cartographically informed thinking to his very last breath ('And time, that *takes survey of all the world*, / Must have a stop', 5.4.81–2, my italics), and who is perceived by others in terms of space and territorial ambition (Hal says, 'When that this body did contain a spirit, / A kingdom for it was too small a bound, / But now two paces of the vilest earth / Is room enough', 5.4.88–91), becomes representative of the way of thinking brought about by the map, in particular of its revolutionary and dangerous potential.

It is not until Shakespeare's next play, the more openly pro-monarchic *Henry V*, that the threat of the cartographic revolution is contained again. Here, the monarch is once more clearly the focus of attention. Certainly, the play eschews simple messages, offering various versions of historical truth by juxtaposing the chorus's heroic narration with the often rather shabby reality of war. However, it at least raises the question of whether a monarch such as Henry V might not effectively counter the disintegrative tendencies we have observed in *Henry IV Part 1* and function once more as centre

---

[14] Philip Armstrong, 'Spheres of Influence: Cartography and the Gaze in Shakespearean Tragedy and History', in *Shakespeare Studies*, 23 (1995), 39–70; p. 54.

[15] Klein, *Maps and the Writing of Space in Early Modern England and Ireland*, p. 5.

of national unity. Admittedly, Henry's army falls into factions of quarrelling Scots, Welshmen, Irish and Englishmen, and immediately after the decisive battle, the famously invoked 'band of brothers' (4.3.60) dissolves into, on the one hand, a strictly hierarchical group of nobles, whose deaths are mourned, and, on the other, an indistinct mass of common soldiers whom Henry simply refers to as 'none else of name' (4.8.105). Yet, such is the ambiguity of the play that it is also possible to read it as a eulogy to the king as a national hero who at least temporarily manages to fuse this disparate crew into a band of brothers-in-arms. Thus, if we understand the shift from *Richard III* to *Henry IV Part 1* as one in focus, from centring on the monarch to foregrounding the territory itself, *Henry V* here cautions us against seeing a grand narrative in operation. If early modern cartography suggests the replacement of monarchical by territorial authority, as Helgerson argues, it is worth keeping in mind that Shakespeare's plays oscillate between these alternative forms of authority rather than follow a clear teleological pattern – as *Henry V* shows, the focus can be shifted back towards the monarch as symbol of the nation once more.

The first part of *Henry IV*, however, captures the moment at which the unifying power of Henry V still lies in the future, and nothing less than the integrity of England is under serious threat. The play conveys a palpable impression of this threat through its centrifugal force and the unsettling effect that results. Arguably, this must have been felt even more keenly by Shakespeare's contemporary spectators, for the fear of national disintegration was familiar to the audience of the late 1590s, i.e. at a time when the highly problematic succession of the ageing, childless Elizabeth became a pressing issue. The rebels' tripartition of England mirrors, not least, anxieties about the disintegration of the realm in general, and the relation of England, Scotland and Wales in particular; and the rebellion on stage potentially would have reminded the contemporary audience of their own fears concerning the possibility of civil war.

Yet, although Shakespeare puts the map into the hands of ill-fated rebels, the play is no straightforward denunciation of cartography. If the play shares in the centrifugal power of the map, it also shares in a cohesive force inherent in many of the early modern cartographic projects. Indeed, the far-roaming itineraries of cartographers like Saxton, Camden, Norden or Speed also demonstrate the interconnectedness of the various regions, not just their separateness, and implicitly suggest that regional boundaries may be overcome. Crucially, the inherent logic of their works argues this also. A map of England introduces a similarly national perspective: as the reader's finger, or his gaze, wanders from place to place on a map of England, he imaginatively imitates the cartographer's travels; like the latter, he crosses regional boundaries with ease. Presenting the onlooker with the shape of the entire territory of England all at once, the map allows him to see beyond what he knows from personal experience; it allows him to see England in its entirety and to adopt a national perspective. Yet, it is not only the reader's gaze tracing the contours of England on the national map but also the sequence of the individual county maps within the atlas that follows the route of the traveller journeying through England. Many of these projects pursue itineraries: Camden's *Britannia*, for instance, roughly traces a south-to-north path, and Speed's *Theatre of the Empire of Great Britain* starts off in the south-eastern corner of the kingdom with a map of Kent, then moves on along the southern coast to Cornwall, up to Somerset and back across to Norfolk. These movements do not follow an abstract, alphabetical logic but that of space travelled in. As we move from page to page, from county to county, our imaginative journey mirrors the physical journey of the traveller who crosses boundaries and experiences the various counties of England as one spatial continuum.

Potentially, drama can produce a comparably unifying effect, I would hold. For drama, like the structure inherent in atlases or the movement of the narrative voice of the chorography, is a form of progress, too: as the dramatic focus shifts from location to location, drama can similarly map out England, as *Henry IV Part 1* demonstrates so powerfully. Yoking together in its dramatic structure locations dispersed all over England, it might also suggest that all these locations form part of a greater, national whole, just as the variously set scenes form part of one play. If the variety of regions is still alive in the multitude of figures that stand for, and are named after, them, the fact that they all share the same stage space indicates that, after all, in their representatives the regions do come together. Although these figures are often far from forming a single community, the stage itself provides a frame that makes them, like the regions they stand for and the dialects they speak, part of one greater picture – there is a structural analogy between the atlas that unites depictions of the various English regions and the history play that unites their representatives.

Like a map, *Henry IV Part 1* shows England in its geographical dimension, reducing its vastness to the more manageable scale of the stage. Measuring England's spatial and social dimensions, this play also shares the empowering effect of the map. The audience is put into a position of being able not only to measure for itself the size of the kingdom but also to judge the social balance in England as well as the legitimacy of its rulers. It seems that in a 'circulation of social energies' – to use Stephen Greenblatt's famous phrase – the new cartographic perspective, and with it the questioning of royal authority, permeates from the medium of the map to the theatre.[16] Indeed, there appears to be a close interaction between map and theatre in late sixteenth-century England. At a time when

not only a major theatre is named 'The Globe' but maps are also called theatres – Speed's popular *Theatre of Great Britain* and the first atlas of the world, Abraham Ortelius's *Theatrum Orbis Terrarum*, are prominent examples – cartography and theatre strongly interact. Not only are maps presented as theatres, displaying curtains on their frontispieces and tiny decorations telling narratives of their own, but the theatre also presents itself as a world in a nutshell, a 'wooden O' (*Henry V*, Prologue, 13) that holds the fields of France and the cliffs of England.[17] Indeed, cartography and the history play are not so different: they both make visible and materialize political changes, thus opening them up to reflection, discussion, appropriation or rejection. Whether cartographers are mapping the globe or a playwright such as Shakespeare is mapping 'The Globe', they are all making the world accessible to their audiences. Thus, they contribute to the making of an England that ultimately emancipates itself from its monarchs as it becomes aware of its emerging national identity, and that will eventually even be able to smile at their quirks and oddities; in short, to the making of the England of today.

---

[16] See Stephen Greenblatt, *Shakespearean Negotiations: The Circulation of Social Energy in Renaissance England* (Berkeley, 1988).

[17] For the affinity between theatre and cartography in early modern England see John Gillies, *Shakespeare and the Geography of Difference* (Cambridge, 1994), pp. 70–98.

FALSTAFF'S BELLY: PATHOS, PROSTHETICS AND PERFORMANCE

ROBERT SHAUGHNESSY

BODY PARTS I & II

In March 2008, a number of London newspapers carried press advertisements for the Royal Shakespeare Company's production of the *Henry IV* plays, which ended its run at the Courtyard Theatre in Stratford-upon-Avon towards the end of the month, and transferred to the Roundhouse at the beginning of April. Touted as the centrepiece of a marathon cycle of eight history plays, the two parts of *Henry IV* encapsulate the appeal of an event that drew heavily upon a sense of the RSC's own institutional history, its traditions and its mythologies, which, in the advance publicity, are figured in the persona of the productions' Falstaff, David Warner (Illustration 8). Garlanded with quotes from four-star reviews ('Warner's return to the RSC after more than forty years away proves a triumph,' declared the *Evening Standard*; 'The RSC is making a triumphant return to its roots,' announced the *Sunday Times*), the advertisement remembers the glory days of the early years of the RSC under Peter Hall, with Warner's resurrection in Stratford and London after a gap of four decades summoning memories not only of his own Richard II and Henry VI of 1963–4, but also his gauche, iconic Hamlet of 1965. The narrative is that of a prodigy returned, of a movie actor long exiled from his home in the theatre finally rediscovering his stage vocation. Warner's twice-iterated 'return' is that of the RSC also, which has learned to recall the story of its own youth with him; caught in a carefree pose that seems to catch him toasting his own 'triumph', Warner's Falstaff can barely con- tain his glee over his and his company's success. The compositional centre of this publicity image is Falstaff's belly, here an expanse of red-framed white space that invites us to project upon it a theatrical and institutional history. The viewer's eye is irre- sistibly drawn by the blood-red 'V' (of *Henry IV*), which points arrow-like towards the straining midriff, as if half-consciously tracing 'roots' to the place of the umbilicus, to Falstaff's navel. Having seemingly ingested both whole, this is a Falstaff who stands for both Shakespeare's Histories and the RSC itself. All this, and at the *Round*house too.[1]

The enlistment of the fat knight as poster boy for the *Henry IV* plays is quite routine; and yet there is something that does not quite ring true about this celebratory, would-be carnivalesque config- uration of Warner as a Falstaff. Quite simply, as many reviewers observed when the productions opened at the Courtyard, Warner was 'a thin man in a fat suit', variously described as 'physically and vocally lean . . . equipped with a badly-padded false belly', 'tall, thin and . . . morosely teetotal', and 'a little understuffed', he made at least one critic 'all too conscious of Cyril Connolly's dic- tum that inside every fat man is "a thin one wildly

---

My thanks to Jim Bulman, Andrew Hartley, Barbara Hodg- don, Peter Holland, Cary Mazer and Patrice Pavis for com- menting on earlier versions of this essay.

[1] Unfortunately, copyright complexities rendered it impossible to reproduce the publicity materials for which Illustration 8 was the basis. My thanks to the RSC's David Howells for retrieving this image.

8. David Warner as Falstaff, Royal Shakespeare Company, 2007.

signalling to be let out"'.[2] The actor himself conceded to interviewers prior to opening that his casting seemed wilfully, even perversely, counterintuitive ('I thought that Michael Boyd . . . was mad when he offered it to me'), and he joked about the extent of his physical and mental preparation: 'I did some research in Hamleys at Christmas – Ho, ho, ho.'[3] Approached like this, Falstaff is all contrivance, a stock figure of padding and whiskers outsourced from the traditional haunt of the 'resting' actor, the toystore Santa's Grotto; the task, as Warner recognizes, is to negotiate the gap between caricature and character and thus to bring Falstaff into line with the broadly Stanislavskian demands and priorities that inform most modern Shakespearian acting. The majority of Falstaffs on the modern stage (though not in the more emphatically realist medium of film[4]) confirm that the 'thin man in a fat suit' is the rule, not the exception; the role is, almost invariably, played by ectomorphic rather than endomorphic actors. This is the assumption made by Oliver Ford Davies, for example, when he writes that since it 'seems important' that 'Falstaff is fat', the actor 'might want to wear padding from the start of rehearsals' and that this involves the cooperation of the wardrobe department, since 'they can't make a start on the costume without knowing the shape of . . . the belly'. Ford Davies defines this approach as a form of 'behaviourism': once actors 'have found the "look" – the costume, the hair, the shoes, the

[2] Charles Spencer, *Daily Telegraph*, 18 August 2007; Paul Taylor, *Independent*, 23 August 2007; Ian Shuttleworth, *Financial Times*, 20 August 2007; Robert Gore-Langton, *Mail on Sunday*, 26 August 2007; Michael Billington, *The Guardian*, 18 April 2008.

[3] Tim Walker, 'An Artist Formerly Known as the Prince', *Daily Telegraph*, 11 July 2007; Heather Neill, 'Having it Large', *The Times*, 1 July 2007.

[4] See for example, Orson Welles in *Chimes of Midnight* (1965) and Robbie Coltrane in the flashback sequences of Kenneth Branagh's *Henry V* (1989).

walk – they feel they are some way to discovering the character'.[5] From the outset, Falstaff is a figure constituted and defined by prosthetics, exteriority, supplementation, layers and surfaces. Even Desmond Barrit, an actor not shy of describing himself as larger than average, found that when he played Falstaff for the RSC in 2001 he was compelled to physically expand to fit the production's gargantuan conception of the role: 'Most of my own weight is around the middle, so I needed some padding around the shoulders, and plenty of layers, to fill the costumes out.'[6]

The prevailing assumption that a fat Falstaff is a prosthetic fabrication, and the implication that herein lies at least part of his serio-comic appeal, is implicated within contemporary attitudes towards the oversized and overweight body, attitudes that are shaped not only by immediate considerations of gender, class and race but also by the concerns and pressures of a culture in which prosthesis, both as practice and preoccupation, looms large, and where, as Celia Lurie summarizes, 'the classifications of genre – of gender, class, race, sexuality and age or other natural and social categories – no longer inhere in the individual as they did in plural or synthetic culture; instead, they are seen as the effects of (mechanical and perceptual) prosthesis.'[7] I shall return to the broader cultural implications of the prosthetic Falstaff in the final section of this article. Its theatrical provenance I will examine in two stages: first, by means of a brief history of the character on the postwar English stage and, second, via a close inspection of the last major Falstaff to be seen in London prior to Warner's, Michael Gambon's, for the National Theatre in 2005.[8] Although the casting of David Warner appears to represent an extreme instance of physical, and perhaps temperamental, disparity between actor and role, in actuality it merely confirms a long-term trend; as Peter Thomson observes, the modern Falstaff is almost invariably a 'character' part, 'played for laughs by a "serious" actor'.[9] The tradition extends as far back as the 1930s, to the music-hall comic George Robey's Falstaff at Her Majesty's Theatre in 1935 (whose performance J. C. Trewin later praised as 'seldom externalized'[10]); ten years

later at the Old Vic, Ralph Richardson created a Falstaff 'whose principal attribute', according to Kenneth Tynan, 'was not his fatness but his knighthood'; this was 'not a *comic* performance'.[11]

This change was accelerated as a result of the shift of equilibrium whereby the *Henry IV* plays became, during the postwar period and until very recently, Hal- rather than Falstaff-centred.[12] The beginnings of this shift can be traced to 1951, and to the Festival of Britain production of the Histories directed by Anthony Quayle at Stratford-upon-Avon. Quayle played his Sir John as markedly less benign than those of his predecessors, but his physical conception of the part, and his style of delivery, ran on traditional lines that contrasted sharply with the low-key, intense, semi-naturalistic approach taken by Richard Burton's Hal. As his biographer Melvyn Bragg documents, Burton arrived on the first day of rehearsals 'word-perfect and with the part already sewn onto him like a skin', and from the outset was 'always watching, always using the lines to cut out a space for himself', whilst using this space to conduct a kind

---

5 Oliver Ford Davies, *Performing Shakespeare* (London, 2007), pp. 70–1.

6 Desmond Barrit, 'Falstaff', in Robert Smallwood, ed., *Players of Shakespeare 6* (Cambridge, 2004), 128–44; p. 130.

7 Celia Lurie, *Prosthetic Culture: Photography, Memory and Identity* (London and New York, 1998), p. 17.

8 The major professional productions during the period are: Old Vic, 1945 (Falstaff: Ralph Richardson); Shakespeare Memorial Theatre, 1951 (Antony Quayle; who also played the role in the BBC/Time Life Television Shakespeare version of 1979); Royal Shakespeare Company, 1964 (Hugh Griffith); RSC, 1975 (Brewster Mason); RSC, 1981 (Joss Ackland); English Shakespeare Company, 1986 (John Woodvine); RSC, 1991 (Robert Stephens); RSC, 2000 (Desmond Barrit); National Theatre, 2005 (Michael Gambon); RSC, 2007 (David Warner).

9 Peter Thomson, 'The Comic Actor and Shakespeare', in Stanley Wells and Sarah Stanton, eds., *The Cambridge Companion to Shakespeare on Stage* (Cambridge, 2002), p. 150.

10 J. C. Trewin, *Shakespeare on the English Stage, 1900–1964* (London, 1964), p. 151.

11 Kenneth Tynan, *He That Plays the King* (London, 1950), pp. 48–9.

12 See Scott McMillin, *Shakespeare in Performance: Henry IV, Part One* (Manchester, 1991).

9. Antony Quayle as Falstaff, Shakespeare Memorial Theatre, 1951.

of covert class warfare through his relationship with his superior: 'Falstaff's laughs, his command, were undercut by Burton's proud Prince. The established actor whose plays they ought to have been was out-manoeuvred.'[13] Bragg's epidermal simile evokes a Method-influenced suturing of text, character, actor's persona and performing body to produce Hal as authentic and real; Quayle's fat knight, meanwhile, was visibly and conspicuously a product of theatrical artifice, a second skin worn brazenly on top of his natural body rather than integral to it. The contrast between the performers' personal styles is evident in Angus McBean's posed production photographs included in the volume published to commemorate the season: Burton (already looking more the movie star than the stage actor) as Hal, then Henry, broods, cryptic and expressionless, immersed in both character

and historical role amidst his Leichner-caked colleagues. Most prominent among these is Quayle, a not-yet-forty-year-old unconvincingly accoutred with face paint, whiskers and padding, whose pointed extravagance of gesture and facial expression in every plate insistently mark his performance with the signs of theatricality; not only is he faking it, but he shows himself enjoying himself faking it (Illustration 9). This was in some ways a Falstaff cut from the traditional cloth of manifest artifice, with 'padded belly, the swollen legs and the slightly too clownish pink and white paint on his face', but, according to the critic of the *Manchester Guardian*, Quayle's was also one who appeared to carry within him the seeds of an approach to the character, and

[13] Melvyn Bragg, *Rich: The Life of Richard Burton* (London, 1988), pp. 71–2.

to this mode of characterization, that would expose them for the frauds that they are: beneath the paint and the padding, he suggests, 'modernity is gnawing at a pathological Fat Knight'.[14]

By 1964, modernity was no longer content merely to gnaw at Shakespeare; thanks to Peter Hall's attempts at reform, it had more or less swallowed it wholesale. Presented as part of the extended *Wars of the Roses* cycle, Hall's *Henry IV* contained at its centre a Falstaff, in the diminutively spectacular shape of Hugh Griffith, whose showy individualism, barnstorming mannerisms and vocal relish were not only out of step with the cool, intellectualized detachment of the rest of the cast, but also served to embody his character's resistant role in the scheme of the play. Reviewing the production in *Shakespeare Quarterly*, Robert Speaight highlighted the work that Griffith did with his eyes: 'how they roved! How they rolled! How they flashed – beacons of anarchy in an England which was trying to reduce itself to order.'[15] The Eastcheap tavern over which Falstaff presided was, the *New Statesman* recorded, one of the few remaining 'corners of the old peasant England' to linger on in an encroaching 'iron age of war and despotism'. Between them, Speaight and Bryden unwittingly allegorized Griffith's role in the production. Brought in (like Warner in 2007) solely to play Falstaff rather than participating as a member of the ensemble, Griffith was a man out of time (he had played John of Gaunt, Owen Glendower and the Archbishop of Canterbury for Quayle in 1951), a living demonstration of the kind of broadly declamatory Shakespearian style that Hall was determined to extirpate from the Stratford stage, yet which nonetheless survived as a vital alternative to the rational, intelligent and efficient technologies of acting that he hoped to put in its place. Griffith's Falstaff was celebrated by Bryden as 'a stage-conception as formal and artificial as Punch or Dame Twankey, impossible to imagine outside a theatre', but in the contexts of Hall's Kott–via–Tillyard reading of the plays, and of a company performance style increasingly inflected by realism of an allegedly Brechtian kind, 'the anarchy he represented', Speaight mused, 'was more than

the kingdom could afford', and 'because he is so much larger than life . . . in the end life will have no room for him'.[16] Reflecting the anorexic imperatives of a 1960s Shakespeare that was determined to cut out the excessive and the superfluous, the process of taming, regulating, toning down (and toning up) Falstaff was under way; and a decade on, with a considerably leaner RSC now under the direction of Trevor Nunn and Terry Hands, Brewster Mason, as Falstaff in Hands's 1975 productions of *Henry IV* and *Merry Wives of Windsor*, was singled out for praise by Speaight, in 'a company where the tendency is to overact', for his 'refreshing . . . under-emphasis'; as Stephen Gilbert put it, he was 'no fraud', and his was 'not a gigantic performance, rather a precise character creation'.[17] Joss Ackland in Nunn's production, which inaugurated the RSC's occupancy of the Barbican Theatre in 1981, cultivated interiority even more assiduously, presenting, to Benedict Nightingale, 'not the usual stately sot but a man with a mind and even a philosophy'.[18] To affirm the dominance of mind over theatrical body, Ackland was 'not made up and stuffed into a caricature' but given merely tokenistic padding, his belly appearing 'no more grotesque than that of many City aldermen', thus creating the impression of 'a largish, distinguished-looking citizen who does not seem to be over-indulging in either food or drink'.[19] This shrinkage seemed consistent with a characterization of Falstaff as 'a hard, brutal, earthbound realist',[20] but as Milton Shulman complained, in a comment which seems to express nostalgia for the tradition represented by Quayle and Griffiths, the disavowal of both

---

[14] *Manchester Guardian*, 4 April 1951.

[15] Robert Speaight, 'Shakespeare in Britain', *Shakespeare Quarterly*, 15 (1964), 377–89; p. 383.

[16] Ronald Bryden, *New Statesman*, 24 April 1964; Speaight, 'Shakespeare in Britain', p. 383.

[17] Robert Speaight, 'Shakespeare in Britain', *Shakespeare Quarterly*, 26 (1975), 15–23; p. 18; Stephen Gilbert, *Plays and Players*, July 1975.

[18] Benedict Nightingale, *New Statesman*, 18 October 1982.

[19] John Barber, *Daily Telegraph*, 1982; Milton Shulman, *Evening Standard*, 10 June 1982.

[20] Michael Billington, *The Guardian*, 11 June 1982.

bodily and theatrical excess drained Falstaff of comic appeal: 'If Falstaff is not a caricature, he is a dull dog, indeed.' The culminating instance of downbeat downsizing was in 1991, in Robert Stephens's performance for the RSC in Adrian Noble's production. Likened by Billington to 'a bloated porpoise with the strange daintiness of the truly fat',[21] Stephens possessed a bulk that carried an authenticity transcending theatricality; that of the 'truly' fat; distinct, it seems, from the lying fatness of stage prosthetics or of mimicry. Giving a 'towering performance', and projecting the 'weighty charm' of 'a big man who makes the theatre a small room',[22] Stephens radiated a somatic authority that operated on a tragically vertical rather than comically lateral axis. It was the monumental grounding for an unsentimental portrait of a ruined and bitter man, 'veering melancholically between bouts of hedonistic indulgence and darkly scathing fits of insecurity', that was epitomized by Stephens's delivery of the 'honour' monologue, which he 'snarled out like an indictment, a piece of self-directed misanthropy that would not disgrace Hamlet'.[23] Referencing Hamlet rather than Hamley's, Stephens's Falstaff rendered traditional theatrical prosthesis superfluous.

MORE LAYERS

As with Warner in 2007 to 2008, though with notably greater success, Stephens's reading of Falstaff through Hamlet allies opposites which might have seemed irreconcilable: between the comic and tragic, between external display and enacted interiority, and, not least, between drama's archetypal thin and fat men. But if the almost unanimous, overwhelmingly positive critical response to Stephens's portrayal, seen by many for at least a decade as definitive, confirmed the ascendancy of a certain kind of meticulously plotted, consistent and credible realism, this was for many defined in opposition to a tradition of caricature that is assumed still to be operative: thus Malcolm Rutherford saw him as 'not gross', Carole Woddis praised a Stephens who was 'not the usual roly-poly', for refusing 'to adhere to the usual fat, jolly jester-

like stereotype'; and Kate Kellaway, who found him 'totally uningratiating', concluded that what was 'so delightful about Robert Stephens's performance is that he does not play Falstaff as a buffoon. He is funny, but never ridiculous.'[24] In terms of theatre history, the comments are at least a decade out of date; more importantly, the implication is that Shakespearian realism is, in this instance and perhaps in others, in part an effect of theatrical negation. To seem real, authentic and true, Stephens's performance was defined in relation to its histrionic antitheses: striving to see Stephens's Falstaff for what he was, reviewers could not avoid seeing what he was not. No actor can ultimately constrain the intertexts that a role, especially one as familiar as Falstaff or Hamlet, is liable to generate; but the consistent story of the reviews is that Stephens's Falstaff, producing character by squeezing out any hint of caricature, was an accomplished exercise in containment: described as controlled, introspective, inward-looking, this was a performance in which even the disquisition on honour, treated as Hamletesque soliloquy, was delivered by Stephens as 'a Socratic dialogue, cleverly conducted with himself'.[25] That this was work conducted to a quite significant extent contrary to the representational conventions of Shakespeare's text and theatre, and of the liminal space which Falstaff in particular inhabits, hardly needs stressing here; as a number of recent studies have shown, acting procedures derived from a broadly Stanislavskian twentieth-century training tradition have a habit of producing characters, or character-effects, that are often quite alien to the scripts they claim to serve.[26]

---

[21] Michael Billington, *The Guardian*, 18 April 1991.

[22] John Peter, *Sunday Times*, 21 April 1991; Kate Kellaway, *The Observer*, 2 June 1991.

[23] Michael Coveney, *The Observer*, 21 April 1991; Paul Taylor, *The Independent*, 18 April 1991.

[24] Carole Woddis, *What's On*, 5 June 1991; Kate Kellaway, *The Observer*, 2 June 1991.

[25] Benedict Nightingale, *The Times*, 18 April 1991.

[26] See for example Bridget Escolme, *Talking to the Audience: Shakespeare, Performance, Self* (London, 2005). For a strong counter-argument on behalf on realism, see Roberta Barker, 'Inner Monologues: Realist Acting and/as Shakespearian

If Stephens's Falstaff achieved the coherence and credibility of a 'rounded' character, it did so by suppressing those facets of the role that complicate or disrupt realist coherence and unity (such as Falstaff's inveterate play-acting).

Stephens's Falstaff can be contrasted with the equally acclaimed attempt on the role by Michael Gambon, in Nicholas Hytner's production for the National Theatre in 2005, which, as I hope to demonstrate, can be viewed as a virtuosic example of an actor simultaneously constructing and dismantling Falstaff as character, by turns adhering to and flouting the protocols of embodied enactment, and both affirming and subverting distinctions between the organic and the prosthetic. Performance analysis is well served by this production: not only is it well documented by the National itself, and by an illuminating eye-witness account of the rehearsal process by Bella Merlin; it was also the occasion of a television documentary which offers a fly-on-the-wall record of Gambon and cast in rehearsal.[27] For the purposes of this essay, these records are of particular interest for what they reveal of process, and hence of the labour that produces Shakespearian characters as 'real'.

The two-hour documentary follows one day's rehearsals, during which director and cast work on two tavern scenes, *Part 1*, 2.4, and *Part 2*, 2.4. Given that Gambon is the undoubted focus, these are well chosen, in that they allow him to showcase his full range as a performer (including a brilliant inset play sequence, which amongst other things, sees him mischievously spoofing the production's Henry Bolingbroke, David Bradley); but they are also particularly suited to the production's, and the television documentary's, realist idiom. With their demotic bias and high prose content, the scenes lend themselves particularly well to a vernacular acting style that is tacitly Stanislavskian and whose terms of reference are effortlessly contemporary; what is seen to happen on the rehearsal floor appears to be the combination of immediate, and apparently unmediated, encounter with the text and strategic accessing of character back stories constantly in development.

Consider, for example, the exploration of the account that Falstaff gives to Matthew Macfadyen's Hal of his encounter with the mysteriously proliferating men in buckram (2.4.175–228):

Gambon [as Falstaff]: 'Seven, by these hilts, or I am a villain else.' Hytner [stepping forward]: The last time we were doing this I think that one was, was more, um, disingenuous: in buckram, in buckram; are you sure? Are you sure? Gambon: [affecting bafflement] 'In buckram?' Hytner: Yeah, yeah, yeah; it's as if — Gambon: [indignant]: 'In buckram!' [looks at Hytner, finds confirmation] 'Seven, by these hilts, or I am a villain else.' Hytner [nodding]: Yeah, great, yeah. Macfadyen: And 'buckram' means 'white lycra'. Hytner [laughs]: For our purposes, yes. Gambon: 'So [*sic*] these four came all afront and mainly thrust at me. I made no more ado, but took all their seven points in my target, thus.' Macfadyen: 'Seven? There were but four even —' Hytner [interrupting]: I think you should save the Ninja Turtles stuff for the end [general laughter] . . . it's very good, but, uh, save it up.

This last interjection is prompted by the moves that Gambon executes to re-enact the dispatch of imagined assailants. Michael Cordner's account of this moment cannot be bettered: 'he adroitly spears several with his sword, then spins on his foot and immobilizes another with a back-kick, spins again and repeats the trick in a different direction, then kills a few more with his sword before blithely continuing with his narrative.'[28] Cordner suggests that he 'has obviously been studying films like *Hero, House of Flying Daggers*,

---

Performance Text', *Shakespeare Survey 62* (Cambridge, 2009), 249–60.

[27] The National Theatre's archival records include not only the Theatre's own fixed-camera video recording but also a multi-camera, broadcast-quality recording made for the archive at the V&A Theatre Museum; and the rehearsal period is documented in Bella Merlin, *With the Rogue's Company: Henry IV at the National Theatre* (London, 2005). The *South Bank Show* edition on the production was broadcast on ITV1 on 5 May 2005.

[28] Quoted in Barbara Hodgdon, 'Shakespearean Stars: Stagings of Desire', in Robert Shaughnessy, ed., *The Cambridge Companion to Shakespeare and Popular Culture* (Cambridge, 2007), pp. 46–66; p. 46.

and indeed *Kill Bill'* (and thus, Barbara Hodg-don remarks, 'writing Jet Li, Lucu Liu, or Uma Thurman over "Shakespeare"'[29]); in the context of a setting that is suspended somewhere between the fifteenth century and the twenty-first, kung fu manoeuvres are no more or less anachronistic, or seemly, than anything else in Gambon's wide-ranging gestural repertoire. At one level, Gambon is simply – and wittily – accomplishing what most would recognize as the actor's basic task: to ren-der the text as meaningful bodily action, which in the rehearsal situation involves moving ele-gantly between demonstration, exposition, quo-tation, and paraphrase of the verbal and physi-cal performance text, habitually practising physi-cal and also intellectual analogies that animate the archaic by referencing the local, the immediate and the contemporary. If the physical and vocal work exemplify the ways in which, as W. B. Worthen puts it, '"Shakespeare" appears to enable the body to recapture itself',[30] their contextual frame and explanatory key is contemporary culture: Shake-speare animates and is animated by the 'bodies' of everyday knowledge and popular understanding. It is in this vein that '"buckram" means "white lycra"' (the peasant garb of Falstaff's assailants translated as the street uniform of English working-class youth), and that the Gadshill robbery, 'the biggest heist they've ever done' is dubbed '*Falstaff's Eleven*'.[31]

This is the kind of imaginative, analogical work, essential to the cultivation of a sense of self-identity, that Shakespearian actors undertake the whole time; often it is the harnessing of wil-fully tendentious or unserious reference points that enables the performer to render action, motivation and behaviour plausible, concrete and specific.[32] Recalling Ford Davies's account of the 'behaviourist' aspects of character-building, the distinction that suggests itself here is between the internalized and the externalized, and the organic and the prosthetic; and the performer's skill lies in her capacity to adjudicate fluently between their competing demands and possibilities, to balance the imperatives of the shoes, the hat, the beard or the belly, which demand and facilitate certain kinds of bodily discipline, with those of movement

and gesture, emotion memory and psychological truth, which may dictate others quite different. In practice, of course, the distinction soon blurs; whether it is Gambon's speculation about how Fal-staff and Hal first met ('Probably hanging about in pubs'),[33] or his Ninja moves (which as semi-parodic, demonstrably *quoted* actions, are spectac-ularly *in*authentic indices of 'character'), the tech-niques are no less 'prosthetic', in the sense that they are no less extrinsic to the character's hypoth-esized interiority than the 'mixture of wadding, foam and polystyrene balls' that made up Falstaff's body suit.[34] What is distinctively engaging about the Gambon method, as evidenced in the docu-mentary rehearsal footage, is that he seems fully aware throughout of the wayward, arbitrary and blatantly concocted nature of the persona (or per-sonas) that the work produces: capable of both playfulness and pathos, his Falstaff is characterized by an improvisational unpredictability that, accord-ing to the testimony of his colleagues, was not confined to the rehearsal room floor.[35]

Even in the most sombre and introspective moments, Gambon, who has described stage act-ing as 'shouting in the night', and compared it to tightrope-walking, and who dreams of dancing rather than speaking his art ('If I had been born again, I'd want to be in a different shape. I'd be a ballet dancer'),[36] treads a fine line between invest-ment and detachment. In the final moments of the *South Bank Show* documentary, Hytner outlines his take on the mood of *Part 2*. 'How difficult it is to

---

[29] Hodgdon, 'Shakespearean Stars', p. 46.

[30] W. B. Worthen, *Shakespeare and the Authority of Performance* (Cambridge, 1997), p. 99.

[31] Merlin, *With the Rogue's Company*, p. 39.

[32] See numerous essays in the *Players of Shakespeare* series (Cambridge, 1985–2006) for examples.

[33] Merlin, *With the Rogue's Company*, p. 31.

[34] Merlin, *With the Rogue's Company*, p. 75.

[35] See Emma Brockes, 'Fail Again, Fail Better', *The Guardian*, 28 June 2006. For an account of Gambon's Falstaff in perfor-mance, see Robert Shaughnessy, '"I do, I will": Hal, Falstaff, and the Performative', in Diana E. Henderson, ed., *Alterna-tive Shakespeares 3* (Abingdon, 2008), pp. 14–33.

[36] Mel Gussow, *Gambon: A Life in Acting* (London, 2004), pp. 126, 154.

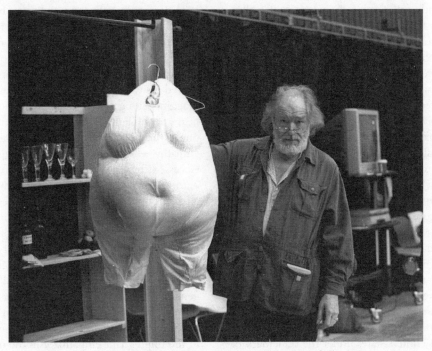

10. Michael Gambon in rehearsal, *Henry IV, Parts 1 & 2*, National Theatre, 2005.

grow old is one of the great themes of the play,' he says, as Gambon, sunk in thought, silently nods; 'And', Hytner turns to Macfadyen, 'the way you deal with Falstaff's vulnerability there is to withdraw from it, and to keep going.' There is a pause, and Gambon ruminatively growls, 'Well. Another layer.' The phrasing is, presumably, entirely innocent, but the double entendre that it contains pulls the ongoing work of character-building simultaneously in different directions: Falstaff's 'layers' are both matters of interiority, depth, subtextual strata to be unearthed through psychological excavation, and exteriorized mimetic and prosthetic accretions; affectively present (if not most 'real') only when self-evidently manufactured. The complex dualities of Gambon's approach to Falstaff are eloquently epitomized by an image included in Merlin's rehearsal log (Illustration 10), which, in the sole moment that the actor plays to camera, catches him in rehearsal holding his fatsuit aloft, and wearing an expression that is tantalizingly unreadable. In the text that accompanies the picture, the produc-

tion's costume supervisor, Emma Marshall, comments on the difficulty of manufacturing the item 'so that it looked real, but wouldn't be too heavy'; packed with lightweight materials, it was designed to 'move about with the actor so that it looks natural'.[37] The point that the effect of 'naturalness' is the product of sophisticated technical contrivance does not needs stressing; what is of more interest is the iconography of disjunction between the bounded self and the role, between the natural body and the manufactured body part, and between Gambon and a kind of amputated synecdoche of his Falstaff, that the image displays. What does Gambon's pose 'say' here? Look at this; look at me; look at us? Isn't it impressive; isn't it ridiculous? It is hard to determine; but the image additionally prompts visual associations beyond the literal. Some of these derive from other Gambon personas: meeting the viewer's eye with his headmasterly

---

37 Merlin, *With the Rogue's Company*, p. 75.

gaze over, rather than through, his spectacles (thus simultaneously accepting and overruling the prosthesis of corrective eyewear), he is the Albus Dumbledore of the *Harry Potter* films (2004 to date); brandishing what looks like a butchered meat carcass, he is also the monstrously funny Albert Spica in Peter Greenaway's *The Cook, The Thief, His Wife and Her Lover* (1989); wisdom and evil simultaneously incarnate.[38] If there is a Shakespearian spirit of carnival also in play here, Gambon, enfolding his play-aristocratic body within a boiler suit that recalls the plebeian styling of the janitor's outfit that he wore to be photographed by Lord Snowdon, is its ideal custodian.[39]

There is more. It is, I suggest, not merely an amusing visual coincidence that the piece of actor's kit sported by Gambon carries a striking family resemblance to a piece of apparatus that, designed for use by pre-pregnant women and their supporters and partners, and manufactured by the Birthways Childbirth Resource Center, Inc., is marketed in the United States under the trademark of the 'Empathy Belly'.[40] A strap-on device weighing thirty pounds (and, at the end of 2009, retailing at 'only' $599), equipped with Barbarella-style conical breasts and a distended abdomen, and containing motorized units to simulate the effect of foetal kicking, the device is for use by those interested in the vicarious experience of the symptoms of pregnancy ('Shallow breathing and shortness of breath / Increased blood pressure, pulse and body temperature / Bladder pressure and frequency of urination / Low backaches; shift in center of gravity; waddling / Fatigue, irritability, and much, much more!'), variously in order to prepare them for its onset, to encourage imaginative identification with it if they are biologically or otherwise excluded from its possibility, or to scare them off altogether (the company's website proudly promotes its success as a tool for 'Teen Pregnancy Prevention'). In form, obviously, the Empathy Belly is closely analogous to the Falstaffian body suit; but it is equally so in function, in that it stages an imaginative extraction of flesh from *within* the fat/pregnant corpus in order to render it as an *external* integument acting upon the wearer's body, and

in so doing not only compels him or her to reconfigure physical actions, posture and gestures, but also encourages (or impels) a degree of emotional resculpting (compare Merlin's report on how, once he starting wearing the fatsuit in rehearsal, Gambon altered his walk, so that 'his feet were now slightly dragging along the floor as if his body was too heavy for his legs').[41] In this light, the harnessing of one of the key terms in the Stanislavskian lexicon – empathy – is bizarrely but revealingly apposite. Accessed through technologies of simulation that enforce their users to a bodily regime characterized as punitive and restrictive, fatness and pregnancy alike are encountered as extrinsic, supplementary, and burdensome; 'empathy', the mechanism through which the self of actor inhabits the space of the other of character, is figured as produced through the subjection, even abjection, that generates Gambon's 'habitual rubbing of the stomach and scratching of the groin'[42] in one sphere, and the breathlessness, backache and incontinence of the unpregnant empathizer in the other.

This apparent identification between obesity and pregnancy, as examples of doubling, inflation, monstrous transformation or grotesque supplementation is grounded in a politics of the body that the Empathy Belly, not unsurprisingly, does not care to interrogate; the question of how the technologies of Falstaffian prosthesis are positioned in relation to these cultural iconographies is the subject of the final part of this article. To conclude this section, however, I want to briefly note that the connection we see here, between the labour that makes a Falstaff and the prosthetic rehearsal of maternity, is no mere contemporary projection but one that, as Valerie Traub has demonstrated, is structurally and thematically central to the *Henry IV* plays. Arguing that Falstaff symbolically

---

[38] Greenaway's *oeuvre*, incidentally, also includes *The Belly of an Architect* (1987).

[39] See Hodgdon, 'Shakespearean Stars', p. 63.

[40] See www.empathybelly.org/home.html. Accessed 29 October 2009.

[41] Merlin, *With the Rogue's Company*, p. 39.

[42] Merlin, *With the Rogue's Company*, p. 39.

occupies the place of the absent mother that Hal mentions (obliquely) but once ('send him back again to my mother,' he says of the nobleman sent to seek him out by his father [*Part 1*, 2.5.294]), Traub reads the physicality of Falstaff as a figuration of 'the female reproductive body' upon which the Henriad's narrative of 'the development of a "prototypical" male subject' depends; his 'somatic iconography', she proposes, 'metonymically positions him as the fantasized pre-oedipal maternal', and his 'corpulence is referred to repeatedly, invoking, in the emphasis on a swollen and distended belly, associations of pregnancy'.[43] Shakespeare's plays, she concludes, represent Falstaff as a monstrous mother in order to secure the project of masculinity that is the shared project of early modern patriarchy and classic psychoanalysis, but is in the end unable to fully contain its transgressive (and here, transgendered) power; because it 'stages its own necessary exclusions', the text ultimately exposes 'phallocentric culture' as 'neither monolithic nor impregnable'.[44] This is not to suggest that the image of a pregnant Falstaff was in any sense intended or even recognized either by Gambon or by the National's production team; but it does indicate performance's potential to articulate the text's unconscious in ways of which its own participants may be unaware.

SUPERSIZE ME

Falstaff's belly is about theatre (perhaps it *is* theatre), but it cannot be ignored that it bears at least some relation to the topic of fatness as well, and that its meanings are also tied up with those attributed to real corporeal shapes and sizes. As the subject of 'personal, medical and cultural deliberation' in 'a world obsessed with abdomens, where the "belly", "tummy", or "gut" are objects of vigilance and, quite frequently, sources of anxiety', the belly, whether addressed in terms of 'size, shape, tone, or internal processes', is, according to Ana Carden-Coyle and Christopher E. Forth, 'an integral aspect of our sense of self as well as a favored site of self-fashioning'.[45] At one level, the relations between the theatrical and social history of Falstaff's

belly can be mapped quite straightforwardly, in that the metamorphoses of the figure during the period with which we have been concerned have been partly shaped by changing attitudes to diet and obesity (and to alcohol consumption). The Festival of Britain audiences who travelled to Stratford to witness Quayle square up to Burton's lean and hungry Hal were themselves subject to the Lenten strictures of the postwar rationing system that remained in place until 1954; this was the end of a period where the strict regulation (and more egalitarian provision) of the nation's diet had created a generally better-fed and physically healthier population than at any other point during the twentieth century, and not until the next decade did the diet industry and medical profession begin to systematically target fat both as public health issue and as lifestyle choice.[46] Nonetheless, the 1950s in Britain marked the beginning of technological and social changes, and of the changing patterns of food production and consumption, working and leisure activities, that would bring about a steady rise in obesity culminating, according to recent Department of Health statistics, in nearly a quarter of the UK adult population being classed as overweight.[47] The stomach that, like

---

[43] Valerie Traub, 'Prince Hal's Falstaff: Positioning Psychoanalysis and the Female Reproductive Body', *Shakespeare Quarterly*, 40 (1989) 456–74; pp. 456, 459, 461–2.

[44] Traub, 'Prince Hal's Falstaff', p. 474.

[45] Ana Carden-Coyne and Christopher E. Forth, 'The Belly and Beyond: Body, Self, and Culture in Ancient and Modern Times', in Christopher E. Forth and Ana Carden-Coyne, eds., *Cultures of the Abdomen: Diet, Digestion, and Fat in the Modern World* (New York, 2005), pp. 1–11; pp. 1–2. Taking as a point of departure in particular Michel Foucault's *The Uses of Pleasure*, translated by Robert Hurley (New York, 1985), related work in this vein includes Jana Evans Braziel and Kathleen LeBesco, eds., *Bodies Out of Bounds: Fatness and Transgression* (Berkeley, 2001); Peter N. Stearns, *Fat History: Bodies and Beauty in the Modern West* (New York, 2002); and Sander L. Gilman, *Fat Boys: A Slim Book* (Lincoln, NE, 2004).

[46] See John Burnett, *Plenty and Want: A Social History of Food in England from 1815 to the Present Day*, 3rd edn (London, 1989), pp. 300–31.

[47] The NHS Information Centre, Lifestyle Statistics, *Statistics on Obesity, Physical Activity and Diet: England, February 2009*

John Bull's, was once mythologically nurtured on the roast beef of Old England was marked with the signs of power, privilege and affluence and of robust patriotism; in a world in which rotundity is more generally perceived as an index of ill-health, self-abuse and low self-esteem, it is more associated with poverty, under-achievement and failure.[48] For the performer aiming to realize Falstaff as an essentially aristocratic and potentially tragic figure (as, to differing degrees, did Mason, Ackland, Stephens and Warner), the belly is not only theatrically bogus but also socially miscast, the property of the low comedian rather than of the actor wishing to be taken seriously.

The patterns of correlation between social and theatrical patterns of bodily expansion and contraction, and of affection and disavowal, are inflected by the contradictions and ambivalences, as well as the often radical variances, that inhere within changing cultural perceptions of weight and the body (itself marked by gender, class and race) in self and others. The ectomorphic body is promoted as normative, yet remains for many aspiration rather than lived actuality; over the past thirty years, while 'modern Western nations are getting fatter, ideal body shapes are getting thinner'.[49] The disjunction between the realities of demography and the fantasy world of corporeal representation can be addressed at the levels of ideology and individual self-perception; here it could be regarded as one of the contexts through which the Falstaffian thin-man-in-fat-suit dyad moves, as a walking embodiment of cultural as well as theatrical contradiction. In terms of the Foucault-influenced paradigm that has informed much recent theorizing about the body and subjectivity, it is clear enough that the fat person, whether male or female, inhabits the wrong side of the cultural binary that opposes the well-regulated, flat-stomached, white male ideal to his disordered and undisciplined, appetite-driven others: 'insofar as they can imply sedentariness, luxury, and the abdication of self-control,' Carden-Coyle and Forth write, 'fat male bodies have continually raised doubts about the "masculine" capacity to conquer appetites, brave hardships, and remain "active" in physical, sexual, and moral terms.'[50] Without for

one moment losing sight of the fact that obesity is not, as some fat activists would have us believe, a tactic of resistance against the hegemony of the svelte but a health hazard whose deadly impact is experienced most acutely (at least in Europe and the United States) by the most socially and culturally deprived members of society, it will readily be recognized that 'fat male bodies' operate within a culture of stigma, one in which they are targeted as objects of mockery and abuse; viewed in this light, the prosthetic fabrication of fat on stage or screen is, at its worse, a mimetic convention as offensive as blackface.[51]

But the example of Falstaff suggests that, at least in the theatre, the belly's propensity to confuse and conflate categories of identity and gender, to transgress boundaries, and to flout the regimes that discipline the bodies of actors and spectators into thinness, hard work and seriousness, mark it also as an object of pleasure and desire, a zone of irresponsibility, indulgence and superfluity whose appeal lies in its limitless capacity to ingest the excessive, the irrelevant and the fantastic. The bulk of this

---

(London, 2009). According to the figures presented in this report, 24% of adults in England in 2007 were officially classed as obese, an increase of 15% since 1993; and 37% had a 'raised waist circumference', compared to 23% in 1993 (p. 7).

48 See Michael Dobson, 'Falstaff after John Bull: Shakespearean History, Britishness, and the Former United Kingdom', *Shakespeare Jahrbuch*, 136 (2000), 40–55.

49 David Bell and Gill Valentine, *Consuming Geographies: We Are Where We Eat* (London and New York, 1997), p. 26.

50 Carden-Coyle and Forth, 'The Belly and Beyond', p. 8.

51 Recent examples of this in popular culture include a number of film comedies which have deliberately engaged in gross violations of cinematic bodily realism, yielding such figures as Robin Williams's cross-dressed *Mrs Doubtfire* (1993), Mike Myers's Fat Bastard in the *Austin Powers* series (1997–2002), Eddie Murphy's turns in *The Nutty Professor* (1996) and *Norbit* (2007), Gwyneth Paltrow in *Shallow Hal* (2001), and John Travolta as Edna Turnblad (a role originally occupied by the performance artist Divine) in the remake of *Hairspray* (2007). Playing Falstaff in an adaptation of *Henry IV* at the Lincoln Center, New York, in 2003, Kevin Kline pandered to this taste for extreme prosthesis by appearing 'nude' in a fatsuit (the pose quotes the infamous image of the pregnant Demi Moore on the front cover of *Vanity Fair* in 1991) in the pages of the *New Yorker*.

article has been concerned with a variety of ways in which Falstaff has been represented, within a broadly realist tradition, as fat but not fat, not 'really fat', not 'really' fat and not really 'fat', a history of prosthetic iteration and equivocation that aptly reflects the fluctuating fortunes of the 'true Jack Falstaff' who is yet his world's most accomplished liar and fantasist and consummate performer, and who is at once king and clown, father and mother, villain and victim – and character and caricature.

The suspicion that the enduring theatrical appeal of Falstaff stems in part from his manifest preposterousness can be confirmed by a comparison of the downsized Falstaff of the *Henry IV* plays on the postwar English stage with the more frequently seen figure of his slapstick, second-order surrogate and even more substantial namesake in *The Merry Wives of Windsor*. Once routinely played by actors who also gave Sir John in *Merry Wives* (among them James Quin between 1720 and 1751, Sir Herbert Beerbohm Tree from 1889 to 1912 and Anthony Quayle in 1955), the Falstaff of the Histories has not, in the modern theatre, generally repeated himself in farce; even more rarely have the plays been presented together.[52] Of course, this partly reflects the consensus that the plays' flatulent knights inhabit parallel but incompatible universes. However, one of the consequences of the clear separation between the Falstaffs of Eastcheap and Windsor has been a sharp tonal and stylistic divergence not only in the plays' respective performance histories (which, generically and event-wise, is to be expected) but also in the representational tactics applied to them. Whereas the styling of Falstaff in productions of *Henry IV* has, as we have seen, tended towards restraint, the Falstaff of *Merry Wives*, as if in compensation, has travelled in exactly the opposite direction, growing larger and more flagrantly bogus by the decade. The culmination of this was seen in the RSC's musical adaptation of 2006, *The Merry Wives – The Musical*, a Christmas show which incorporated song-and-dance numbers and interpolations from the *Henry IV* plays, and which spectacularly featured Simon Callow, burlesquing his own back catalogue (he had played the part in a stage version of Welles's *Chimes at Mid-*

night at the Chichester Festival Theatre in 1998, and written an actor's guide to the play),[53] and sporting the immense fatsuit that had first been worn by the greatest of contemporary operatic Falstaffs, Bryn Terfel, at the Royal Opera House in 1999 (Illustration 11). Beyond parody, Callow's Falstaff caused some critics' imaginations to run riot (polymorphously, he 'wiggles his blubber into his dressing gown like a jelly squeezing through a keyhole');[54] while others remained firmly unconvinced: 'all surface. Marvellous diction, lots of belly, but no inwardness.'[55]

It might be objected, in Callow's defence (not that he needs it), that 'inwardness' – however much one might wish it of the Falstaff of *Henry IV* – was perhaps the last thing to look for in a production conceived and delivered as pantomime; and that, as the antithesis of Falstaffian seriousness, Callow's fully exteriorized Falstaff (he described the role as 'beyond type, certainly beyond morality and even beyond psychology')[56] defined the character's outer limits. I want to suggest that the evidence of the stage history that this article has addressed points to a contrary conclusion: that as a composted composite of speech, belly and surface, Callow's was not the modern Falstaff's antithesis but its apotheosis, a promiscuously versatile, shape-shifting, virtuoso impersonation of a man with nothing beneath his layers but more layers. Perhaps this sounds like the all-too-familiar Foucauldian, decentred, evacuated, post-essentialist subject beloved of post-structuralism and cultural materialism (a dead horse

[52] Productions of *Merry Wives* during the last half-century include the Old Vic, 1960 (Falstaff: Joss Ackland); RSC, 1964 (Clive Swift); 1968 and 1975 (Brewster Mason); 1979 (John Woodvine, who, like Ackland and Mason, subsequently graduated to Falstaff in *Henry IV*, in this instance for the English Shakespeare Company in 1985); 1985 (Peter Jeffrey), 1992 (Benjamin Whitrow), 1996 (Leslie Phillips), and 2002 (Richard Cordery); National Theatre, 1995 (Denis Quilley); Shakespeare's Globe, 2008 (Christopher Benjamin).

[53] Simon Callow, *Actors on Shakespeare: Henry IV, Part 1* (London, 2002).

[54] Susannah Clapp, *The Observer*, 21 December 2006.

[55] Alastair Macauley, *Financial Times*, 13 December 2006.

[56] Simon Callow, 'The Fat Man in History', *Independent*, 11 August 1998.

11. Simon Callow in rehearsal, *Merry Wives – The Musical*, Royal Shakespeare Company, 2006.

that I have no particular desire to flog); but perhaps it also leads us somewhere else, to a place with a little more room for manoeuvre, and even with some scope for fun. Confronted with a pantomime Falstaff, my gut instinct is to recall Ronald Bryden's identification of Hugh Griffith with the archetypal pantomime dame Widow Twankey over forty years earlier. No doubt for Bryden the equation between Falstaff and Aladdin's laundry-basket-wielding mother refers merely to Griffith's staginess and artificiality, but, as the foregoing has suggested, the incidental citation of a fictive icon of the popular stage whose entire comic appeal lies in the fact that 'she' is blatantly a man in drag also – quite unconsciously – penetrates to the heart of Falstaff's mystery.[57] In part, it is a matter of the gender indeterminacy that this essay has sought to map, and that finds its richest articulation in *Merry Wives*: as Patricia Parker has brilliantly demonstrated, the fact that the Falstaff of this play fleetingly appears, in his

penultimate humiliation, in the transvestite guise of the Old Woman of Brainford is an 'explicit embodiment' of the 'effeminate associations throughout the other plays in which he figures', which confirms him as the 'obvious Shakespearean "fat lady"' who is 'ostensibly no lady at all'.[58] But it is also to do with the intercalated effect of the faking of fatness, prosthetically homologous to drag itself. If, as

[57] I cannot resist recording here that the part of Widow Twankey was taken by Ian McKellen at the Old Vic in its Christmas production of *Aladdin* in 2005, in what was a consciously tongue-in-cheek cultivation of a comic alter ego to his (male, tragic) Shakespearian self. As Stephen Purcell notes, McKellen at one point turned to the audience and 'confessed to being "a very foolish, fond old woman"', a line that was 'met with a surprisingly robust laugh': *Popular Shakespeare: Simulation and Subversion on the Modern Stage* (Basingstoke, 2009), p. 99.

[58] Patricia Parker, *Literary Fat Ladies: Gender, Rhetoric, Property* (London, 1987), pp. 200–1.

Judith Butler argues, the pleasurable radicalism of drag lies in its potential to reveal gender identity itself as performative, in that 'all gender is like drag', in that '"imitation" is at the heart of the *heterosexual* project and its gender binarisms, that drag is not a secondary imitation that presupposes a prior and original gender, but that hegemonic heterosexuality is itself a constant and repeated effort to imitate its own idealizations', then the pleasure afforded by the prosthetic theatrical body likewise lies in its potential to travesty the 'normal' body's claims on 'naturalness and originality'.[59] In prosthetic performance, as in prosthetic culture, self-fashioning is achieved through the (counter) 'claiming of the effects of actions that are the outcome of the *extension* of self by means of others, an extension that may involve both humans and non-humans, subjects and objects, things and ideas'.[60] Like the drag queen or panto dame's ensemble of tits, heels and wig, Falstaff's belly subjectifies as well as objectifies: it is an empathy machine that caters to our appetite to suspend or transcend the social and gender roles to which we have been assigned, to divide and to multiply, and to be more than our bodied, bounded selves. If, as Hamlet's pantomime uncle, the riddle posed by Falstaff on the modern stage has been whether he is really fat, or merely pretending to be, then, to paraphrase Hazlitt and Coleridge on the thin prince,[61] it is *we* who are Falstaff – and I have a smack of Falstaff myself, if I may say so.

---

59 Judith Butler, *Bodies That Matter: On the Discursive Limits of 'Sex'* (New York and London, 1993), p. 125.

60 Lurie, *Prosthetic Culture*, p. 218.

61 William Hazlitt, *Lectures on the Literature of the Age of Elizabeth and Characters of Shakespear's Plays* (London, 1900), p. 74; Samuel Taylor Coleridge, 'Table Talk', in Terence Hawkes, ed., *Coleridge on Shakespeare* (Harmondsworth, 1959), p. 159.

'AND IS OLD DOUBLE DEAD?': NATION AND NOSTALGIA IN *HENRY IV PART 2*

NAOMI CONN LIEBLER

The marking and remarking of history – personal or national – is arguably one of the most consistent topoi in the Western canon, let alone in Shakespeare; personal anxieties of ageing persist and prevail in vocal counterpoint to memorial reconstructions of 'historical' or political events. The two justices of *2 Henry IV*, Shallow and Silence, are what Hamlet probably never intended in his reference to the players as 'abstract and brief chronicles' (2.2.524).[1] And yet they are, in another sense, precisely 'abstract' if perhaps not quite '*brief*' almanacs of both personal and political recollections that articulate the relation of war and remembrance to memory and nostalgia. So are several other representations of 'geezerdom' seen and heard throughout the second tetralogy: Gaunt, York and of course Falstaff. In this article I want to trace out the justices' personal frames for measuring and remembering 'history' as localized and alternative versions of their play's (and the tetralogy's) larger concerns with time, succession, memory, obsolescence and war – all inevitable and simultaneously dangerous to incumbent order.

As one-fourth of the second tetralogy, *2 Henry IV* inescapably focuses on time and remembrance, and on the national crisis sprung, two plays and a represented generation earlier, by Richard II's deposition, the consequent breach in succession, and on Henry IV's role in that breach. These of course are the play's large issues; in their midst Shakespeare pauses to reflect on time's passage and remembrance in terms more minutely focused. Shallow and Silence, two ageing country justices, colleagues and cousins-in-law who represent the

judiciary in the lives of ordinary folk, meet and exchange family news for a brief moment before turning to reminiscence and nostalgia:

Shallow. I was once of Clement's Inn, where I think they will talk of mad Shallow yet.
Silence. You were call'd lusty Shallow then, cousin.
Shallow. By the mass, I was call'd any thing, and I would have done any thing indeed too, and roundly too. There was I, and little John Doit of Staffordshire, and black George Barnes, and Francis Pickbone, and Will Squele, a Cotsole man. You had not four such swinge-bucklers in all the Inns a' Court again; and I may say to you, we knew where the bona robas were and had the best of them all at commandement. Then was Jack Falstaff, now Sir John, a boy, and page to Thomas Mowbray, Duke of Norfolk.
Silence. This Sir John, cousin, that comes hither anon about soldiers?
Shallow. The same Sir John, the very same. I see him break Scoggin's head at the court-gate, when 'a was a crack not thus high; and the very same day did I fight with one Samson Stockfish, a fruiterer, behind Gray's Inn. Jesu, Jesu, the mad days that I have spent! And to see how many of my old acquaintance are dead!

This essay began as a short paper in the seminar, 'Shakespeare, War, and Remembrance', led by Clara Calvo at the Shakespeare Institute's biennial conference, Stratford-upon-Avon, 2008; I am grateful to her, to Ton Hoenselaars, and to John Drakakis for encouraging its development. Thanks also go to my colleague Jonathan Greenberg at Montclair State University for generously reading and commenting upon a mediate draft.
[1] Unless otherwise noted, quotations from Shakespeare's plays throughout refer to the *Riverside Shakespeare*, ed. G. B. Evans *et al.* (Boston, 1974).

Silence. We shall all follow, cousin.

Shallow. Certain, 'tis certain, very sure, very sure. Death, as the Psalmist saith, is certain to all, all shall die. How a good yoke of bullocks at Stamford fair?

Silence. By my troth, I was not there.

Shallow. Death is certain. Is old Double of your town living yet?

Silence. Dead, sir.

Shallow. Jesu, Jesu, dead! 'A drew a good bow, and dead! 'A shot a fine shoot. John a' Gaunt lov'd him well, and betted much money on his head. Dead! 'a would have clapp'd i' th' clout at twelvescore, and carried you a forehand shaft a fourteen and fourteen and a half, that it would have done a man's heart good to see. How a score of ewes now?

Silence. Thereafter as they be, a score of good ewes may be worth ten pounds.

Shallow. And is old Double dead?   (3.2.14–52)

This exchange doubles back over Falstaff's career to the time of Gaunt and Mowbray and (for the audience) to the opening scenes of *Richard II* and the launch of the second tetralogy. But it does so by personalizing its reminders of historical figures dramatized in *Richard II*. John of Gaunt is not remembered here as King Henry's father or as the fourth of Edward III's seven sons, but as a courtier who liked to bet on archery contests; Thomas Mowbray's fame is not his implication in Wat Tyler's rebellion or in the murder of Woodstock (*Richard II*, 1.1.95–103), but as Falstaff's early employer. A levelling occurs here, too, in the equal mnemonic attention given to those yet-to-become luminaries and the Staffordshire and Cotswold natives who 'fought' (though in quite a different arena) alongside George Barnes and Francis Pickbone. Later, these or similar sturdy sons perhaps will be recalled by their king only as 'none else of name' (*Henry V*, 4.8.105). In the recollections of their former schoolmates, at least, their names are recorded.

In the interruption of the exchange by reminders of the justices' interests in the market prices of 'bullocks at Stamford fair' (35) and 'a score of ewes now' (46), a *realpolitik* emerges whose irony, in contrast with the roll-call of skinny draftees a few lines later, could not have escaped Shakespeare's audience. As Falstaff observes of Shallow at the end of the scene, 'now has he land and beefs' (327–8). The 'King's justices of the peace' (3.2.58) are thriving,[2] while the injustices of the war eat up the likes of Bullcalf, Mouldy, Feeble and Shadow.

In this central exchange in 3.2, Shallow cannot quite hold on to the fact that Old Double is dead. The name recurs in the dialogue as if remembrance could bring him back, as if the fact of a man's death could be altered by invoking his name (much as Hamlet invokes Yorick, or the hobby horse, or his own father), as if time could be rewound, as if Falstaff could be a boy again and page to Mowbray, as if King Richard's deposition could be undone so that 'today, O Lord' (*Henry V*, 4.1.292–4, noted earlier) his father's sin could be forgotten. Falstaff too remembers the old days, but his 'chronicle' revises Shallow's:

And now is this Vice's dagger become a squire, and talks as familiarly of John a' Gaunt as if he had been sworn brother to him; and I'll be sworn 'a ne'er saw him but once in the Tilt-yard, and then he burst his head for crowding among the marshal's men. I saw it . . .

(3.2.319–24)

Then again, as Falstaff knows better than anyone, old men are given to lying (3.2.303–4).

The exchange between Falstaff and the justices is punctuated by reminiscence (backward) and projection (forward – at least until dinner):

Shallow. O Sir John, do you remember since we lay all night in the Windmill in Saint George's Field?

---

[2] Falstaff's line signals his resentment, but not evidence of some kind of nefarious profit-skimming on the part of Shallow and his fellows. As David Thomas notes, 'local magistrates meeting in quarter or petty sessions still wielded considerable power and the freedom to act with wide discretion. They were the leading figures of their localities, owning much of the land, employing many of the people who might come before them, paying a large portion of local rates and taxes, sitting as of right on the poor law boards.' See 'The Welfare of the Elderly in the Past: A Family or Community Responsibility?', in *Life, Death, and the Elderly: Historical Perspectives*, ed. Margaret Pelling and Richard M. Smith (London, 1991), p. 199. If Shallow and Silence are robber-barons, they are no more so than Falstaff would be if his petty thieving were successful.

Falstaff. No more of that, Master Shallow, no more of that.

Shallow. Ha, 'twas a merry night. And is Jane Nightwork alive?

Falstaff. She lives, Master Shallow.

Shallow. She never could away with me.

Falstaff. Never, never, she would always say she could not abide Master Shallow.

Shallow. By the mass, I could anger her to th' heart. She was then a bona roba. Doth she hold her own well?

Falstaff. Old, old, Master Shallow.

Shallow. Nay, she must be old, she cannot choose but be old, certain she's old, and had Robin Nightwork by old Nightwork before I came to Clement's Inn.

Silence. That's fifty-five year ago.

Shallow. Ha, cousin Silence, that thou hadst seen that that this knight and I have seen! Ha, Sir John, said I well?

Falstaff. We have heard the chimes at midnight, Master Shallow.

Shallow. That we have, that we have, that we have, in faith, Sir John, we have. Our watch-word was 'Hem, boys!' Come let's to dinner, come let's to dinner. Jesus, the days that we have seen! come, come.

(3.2.194–219)

Reminiscence by old men such as these has lately been given constructive attention by sociologists and philosophers of culture. When he was 87 years old, just about Shallow's age (and King Lear's), the Italian political philosopher Norberto Bobbio, who died in 2004 at the age of 94, commented on the significance for old people of acts of memory:

The world of old people, all old people, is to a greater or lesser extent the world of memory. People say that ultimately you are what you have done, thought and loved. I would also say that you are what you can remember . . . Remembering is a mental activity that you often fail to engage in because it is either arduous or embarrassing. But it is a healthy activity. By remembering you rediscover yourself and your identity, in spite of the many years that have passed and the thousands of events you have experienced.[3]

For Bobbio, remembering is not only a kind of action but is the penultimate kind (just before dying), and therefore an important kind. It is just as important as any other kind of action; it is in fact *the* important action of old age: 'The past is the dimension in which the old live.'[4]

Bobbio gives an old man's memories a poetic, even an encouraging, cast; remembering is the business of the old, no less important than the more physically active engagements of youth. Shakespeare seems to take a chillier, less sentimental view. No one pays much attention to old men's memories anywhere in Shakespeare's work – nor, probably, in the world it reflected, except perhaps when kings require the confirmation of precedent. As a measure of human significance, memory alone can be cold comfort. And yet, for a discourse so consistently dismissed, Shakespeare represents old men's reminiscence with surprising frequency. Shallow is particularly given to nostalgia, but in general Shakespeare must have been keenly interested in this phenomenon of elderly yearning for past glory. In *The Merry Wives of Windsor*, sometimes known as 'The Falstaff Play', Shallow is resurrected from the Henriad along with the fat knight and remnants of his entourage and holds the stage as long as Falstaff does. 'I have seen the time', he recalls, 'with my long sword I would have made you four tall fellows skip like rats' (2.1.227–9). It is intriguing that these lines are replicated nearly verbatim three years later in *King Lear*'s 'I have seen the day, with my good biting falchion / I would have made them skip' (5.3.277–9).[5]

---

[3] Norberto Bobbio, *Old Age and Other Essays*, trans. and ed. Allan Cameron (Cambridge, 2001), pp. 12–13.

[4] Bobbio, *Old Age*, p. 12.

[5] Dates for both plays are held uncertain; the abbreviated and problematic Q of *Merry Wives* was published in 1602; *King Lear* is generally set at 1605–6. See R.A. Foakes's Arden 3 *King Lear*, and Giorgio Melchiori's Arden 3 *Merry Wives of Windsor*, respectively, for discussions of chronology. How these reciprocal echoes affect our reception of both the doddering justice and the ruined king is a question for another essay; like Lear, Shallow identifies himself as a man who has 'lived four score years and upward' (*Merry Wives*, 3.1.56; *King Lear*, 4.7.60). Falstaff's resentment of the Justice's bourgeois comfort, first heard in *2 Henry IV* in the snipe about land and beeves (quoted earlier) is heard again when he spites Shallow by admitting publicly, in the opening scene of *Merry Wives*, that he has indeed poached Shallow's deer, broken into his lodge and beaten his servants (111–16).

The personal reflections of Shallow and Silence ring ironically against the play's larger concerns with right rule and its violations, with rebellion at home and war abroad, and other sweeping political concerns. Their choric obituary recitations occupy the central space of the play (3.2) and thus can – and should – be heard as central to Shakespeare's interests in this work. As the king's Justices of the Peace, these old men are not placebos of 'comic relief' but localized and reduced versions of loftier concerns such as succession, redemption and the relegation of those matters to an irrecoverable past, to the nostalgia of the *ubi sunt* tradition. Like tribunes in some of the Roman plays, their job is to mediate the burdens of royal prerogatives on ordinary people and the *im*mediate concerns of those ordinary people never heard at all by royals.

When old men such as these are perceived as 'captivatingly senile',[6] their sense of the past, their *witness*, is immediately invalidated. Why would Shakespeare take time out from his play of war, nation-building and kingship to eavesdrop, as it were, on these reminiscences of schooldays and old rivalries? Why not give us instead another scene with a prologue, another lashing from the tongues of Rumour? What are these old men doing here, in this play, in the *centre* of this play? James Bulman writes that the Gloucestershire scenes involving the justices 'depict a world unlike any other in Shakespeare', an 'idyllic world' to which 'Falstaff brings the predatory ethos of an "old pike" . . . The rural domain of Silence and Shallow is therefore not an idealized garden, but a fallen world.'[7] Bulman is less sympathetically inclined than I towards Shallow and Silence; he finds them 'vain and self-deluding', given to bribery and self-interest, set 'in marked contrast to the integrity' of the Lord Chief Justice's judicial incorruptibility: 'No matter how poignant these Gloucestershire scenes are, they depict an unweeded garden.'[8] He is correct, of course, but distinctions among the three different representations of old men (four, counting the exhausted, insomniac, regretful, ill King Henry) allow us to see that all is not weeds in this garden, and not all the old men are weeds or predatory pikes. As his title denotes, the Lord Chief Justice

stands above the venery of ordinary people, above ordinary local judicial surrogates (indeed the point of their portrayal is that they are absolutely ordinary), even, when necessary, as the king's surrogate above the prince (5.2.70–140), and certainly above manipulative opportunists such as Falstaff. Unlike nearly everyone else in the play, including the king, the Lord Chief Justice has no personal name; he is singular and symbolic of the office he inhabits. He is not a person but a system, represented as patient, incorruptible, kindly even towards the likes of Falstaff and certainly towards his monarch. He is The Law, the opposite of Falstaff who threatens it and him: 'the laws of England are at my commandement . . . and woe to my Lord Chief Justice' (5.3.136–8).[9] Not merely arrogant or ludicrous, Falstaff's words sound dangerous, subversive; not simply imaginary, they can be traced to a historical record.[10]

Yet these distinctions – of personalized/ humanized vs. abstract embodiments of judicial rule – are not so stark and absolute as might at first appear. Granted that Shallow and Silence are Muppet-like[11] in their quaintly repetitive dialogue (Illustration 12), and that right rule prevails when the Lord Chief Justice sentences Falstaff and his companions to the Fleet Prison (5.5.91). Granted too that 'Policy inevitably wins out over humanity',[12] which begs the question of why so

6 A. R. Humphreys, ed., *2 Henry IV*, Arden Second Series (London, 1981), p. 1.

7 James C. Bulman, 'Henry IV, Parts 1 and 2', in *The Cambridge Companion to Shakespeare's History Plays*, ed. Michael Hattaway (Cambridge, 2002), pp. 172–3.

8 Bulman, 'Henry IV, Parts 1 and 2', p. 173.

9 Bulman astutely observes a binary formed by Falstaff and the Lord Chief Justice: 'In a sense, these two old men offer competing centres of authority for England and for Prince Hal' (p. 169). The two country justices then occupy a median space between the absolutes represented by the 'bigger' pair.

10 Humphreys's note to this line in the Arden edition quotes Harold Brooks's observation that attribution of a similar statement to Richard II, 'among those reported by Holinshed', had contributed importantly to his deposition.

11 Statler and Waldorf, the two elderly-gentleman Muppet characters, come to mind.

12 Bulman, 'Henry IV, Parts 1 and 2', p. 174.

12. Statler and Waldorf reminisce (from *The Muppet Show*, Season 1, Pilot 2: 'Sex and Violence').

much and such varied 'humanity' is so appealingly represented. Are we to understand that such 'humanity' will always be crushed by the rule of law? Or that the ruler is not ultimately the rule-bearing Lord Chief Justice but a king whose 'humanity' has been and will continue to be, for better and for worse, disclosed throughout three of the four plays of this tetralogy? As Hal-turned-Henry V will theorize in the next play, the king is

but a man, as I am. The violet smells to him as it doth to me; the element shows to him as it doth to me; all his senses have but human conditions. His ceremonies laid by, in his nakedness he appears but a man; and though his affections are higher mounted than ours, yet when they stoop, they stoop with the like wing.

(*Henry V*, 4.1.101–7)

If the 'project' of Shakespeare's history plays is to understand England's 'history' up to his own time[13] – in Bulman's words a narrative 'less about chronicle history than about the more encompassing "state" of Elizabethan England'[14] – then the

'captivatingly senile' charm of the Gloucestershire justices serves a purpose beyond amusing younger audiences. It slices 'the law' from yet another angle besides those of the Lord Chief Justice, the king and the outlaw knight. *This* law is old, nostalgic, witness to a past it will not efface but keeps alive through reminiscence, even if it has to invent that past. Such a law operates only as long as human memory; it lacks the permanence of statute law but retains some of the flexibility of case law. The two old country justices represent *this* law; their job is, for better or worse, to maintain order among 'the whores, drunks, false captains, country gentlemen, yeomen, and women's tailors who populate the

---

[13] See, among others, Richard Helgerson, *Forms of Nationhood: The Elizabethan Writing of England* (Chicago, 1992). Ton Hoenselaars's discussion locating the Shakespearian 'history play' hermeneutically with others of the period is especially good on this connection. See 'Shakespeare and the Early Modern History Play', in Hattaway, *Shakespeare's History Plays*, pp. 25–40.

[14] Bulman, '*Henry IV, Parts 1* and *2*', p. 174.

world *outside* the court and whose histories have never been recorded'.[15]

The documents of historiography likewise constitute and are constituted by memory, and as most 'new' historicists from Stephen Greenblatt forward have recognized, *everything* depends upon whose memory or record 'counts' as valid, on who, *pace* Foucault,[16] is listening. The sixteenth century 'witnessed an explosion of documentation'[17] and 'a move towards a history based on evidence, whether of documents or existing monuments, and so a stripping away of accretions of legend, and towards a separation of history and myth'.[18] On what did people of prior centuries, particularly the fourteenth and fifteenth (the Hundred Years' War) in which the plays of the second tetralogy are set, rely for their sense of the past? 'One layer of evidence', Alan Macfarlane argues, 'will come from community studies. Without this dimension, the infinite complexity of evidence from a demarcated area, we are left with an impoverished picture of man.'[19]

Reminiscence is a principal component of the 'examined life' and of the Socratic precept *nosce te ipsum*, widely embraced in the sixteenth and seventeenth centuries. On this view, 'ontological issues about the nature of being and human existence, as well as ethical issues, had to be raised from sources deep in subjective experience'.[20] Thus, personal experience counts as a signal validation for knowledge and reminiscence has an important truth-bearing function.[21] Edmund Sherman assigns important salutary functions to such reminiscence, especially among the elderly, chief among which is what he calls 'life review'. 'Even when it occurs spontaneously and without conscious intent or purpose, as it so often does, upon later reflection there is little difficulty in seeing that it has . . . served some purpose . . . in the context of [a] current life situation' such as 'enabling the older person to cope with some problem in the present or anticipated future.'[22] The 'life review' heard in the exchanges of Shallow and Silence marks their nostalgia as a microversion of the play's larger concerns with history. It is not the same story, of course, but a story *about* the story; 'history', Burns observes, 'has a history too.'[23] Shallow's and Silence's reminiscence,

however silly, is one instance of the 'examined life'. Hearing it in relation to Richard II's, Henry IV's and later Henry V's more sombre recollections of prior acts reminds us that a similarly 'examined' and remembered *national* life is presented across the four panels of the tetralogy. 'Many of the historical events invoked in the plays were (just about) in living memory', and the audiences to these plays were people 'for whom a network of memories and information existed'.[24]

Shakespeare's regard for the power of *un*documented data such as reminiscence is nowhere more obvious in *2 Henry IV* than in the presence of the Inductor, Rumour. As Meredith Evans noted recently, Rumour 'initiates a new and demotic form of authority in *2 Henry IV* . . . The multitude, the demi-monde of Eastcheap, the monarchy, the judiciary: each is animated by the force of rumor, which eludes appropriation by eluding ontological stability.'[25] Rumour's opposite in this play, Evans argues, is the rule and order embodied in the Lord Chief Justice; rumour, disruption, 'the unauthorized speech of nobody in particular',

---

[15] Bulman, '*Henry IV, Parts 1* and *2*', p. 174.

[16] 'What is an Author?' *Language, Counter-Memory, Practice: Selected Essays and Interviews*, ed. Donald F. Bouchard (Ithaca, 1977), p. 138.

[17] Alan Macfarlane, Sarah Harrison and Charles Jardine, *Reconstructing Historical Communities* (Cambridge, 1977), p. 31.

[18] Edward Burns, 'Shakespeare's Histories in Cycles', *Shakespeare's History Plays: Performance, Translation, and Adaptation in Britain and Abroad*, ed. Ton Hoenselaars (Cambridge, 2004), p. 151.

[19] Macfarlane, *Reconstructing Historical Communities*, p. 33.

[20] Edmund Sherman, *Reminiscence and the Self in Old Age* (New York, 1991), p. 5.

[21] Sherman, p. 4. He observes further that reminiscence is 'not unique to the elderly' and is indeed just as common among adolescents as among the aged; both periods in life are particularly marked by attention to the self and to one's own experiences, feelings and recollections, to a known past and an uncertain future (p. 6). Both phases, importantly, share a special emphasis on transitions or passages.

[22] Sherman, *Reminiscence and the Self*, p. 28.

[23] Burns, 'Shakespeare's Histories in Cycles', p. 152.

[24] Burns, 'Shakespeare's Histories in Cycles', p. 156.

[25] Meredith Evans, 'Rumor, the Breath of Kings, and the Body of Law in *2 Henry IV*', *Shakespeare Quarterly*, 60 (2009), 4.

subverts authority, 'the ontological stability of bodies and institutions'.[26]

There is, however, another forceful demotic abstraction, another opposition to authority, as persuasive and pervasive as rumour and arguably more so than a nearly abstract, straight-arrow embodiment like the Lord Chief Justice, one equally destabilizing to whatever passes ultimately for political truth, rule of law or any other principle of governance. This one may be, in a sense, more insidious than Rumour precisely because it does not announce itself by means of an actor wearing a symbolic costume; it inheres, in fact, in the seemingly impotent (if not innocent) representation of old men. Rumour's alternative mask is Nostalgia,[27] equally unstable and forceful as a shaper of perceived truths and thus equally capable of moving action, as King Henry V will hear persistently and persuasively in the next play, in arguments from the Archbishop of Canterbury, the Bishop of Ely, the Duke of Exeter and the Earl of Northumberland (*Henry V*, 1.2.102–35). All of them appeal to the new king's sense of family history, both distant and recent. The influence of each depends on who is listening and on the credibility of the speaker. More often than not, however, *because* Nostalgia usually speaks through old men (Shallow, Silence and sometimes Falstaff here, John of Gaunt in *Richard II*), it tends to lack credibility with other characters on stage. But its voice does register on that stage, and on the audience, regardless. Rumour commands: 'Open your ears; for which of you will stop / The vent of hearing when loud Rumour speaks?' (Ind. 1–2), and is confident of its power: 'The posts come tiring on, / And not a man of them brings other news / Than they have learnt of me. From Rumour's tongues / They bring smooth comforts false, worse than true wrongs' (Ind. 37–40).[28] Nostalgia speaks more tentatively, in private conversations among former schoolmates; it asks and repeats questions and seeks confirmation: 'And is old Double dead?' 'Do you remember?' 'Said I well?' (3.2.52, 194, 212–13). Like Rumour's voice, however, once heard, it cannot be unheard.

Representing that quality of nostalgia is perhaps the principal reason Shallow and Silence were invented. For Catherine Belsey, they reflect upon a 'world of plenitude [that] was always already lost [and] has no place outside the memory of an old man'.[29] More likely, that world never existed; it was invoked – or invented – within Shakespeare's work by figures such as John of Gaunt, who dreamed 'This other Eden, demi-paradise' (*Richard II*, 2.1.42) as a counterpoint to Richard's ambivalent relation to tradition and his 'leas[ing] out' (59) of England.[30] Gaunt's nostalgia is nationalistic, of course, and often reinvented as '*this* England' when the plays are performed,[31] though as Edward Burns rightly asks, '*what* England?'[32] 'All nostalgia',

---

[26] Evans, 'Rumor, the Breath of Kings', p. 5.

[27] The *OED* offers the etymology of 'nostalgia' as a combination of the Greek *nostos*, or return home, and *algos*, pain. Thus, *nostalgia* is literally homesickness; its earliest known use is in the *Dissertatio medica de nostalgia* by Johannes Hofer in 1688. *OED* definition 2a authorizes 'the pain of the past' or 'of memory', but that seems to have emerged only in the twentieth century.

[28] Both Humphreys and Evans comment at length on the tradition of reading Rumour as feminine because the tongue-painted costume recalls Virgil's Fama. Shakespeare's text, however, is silent on the matter of Rumour's gender and offers no pronouns to help us.

[29] 'Making Histories', in Holderness, *Shakespeare's History Plays*, p. 118.

[30] I discuss *Richard II*'s (both the play's and the character's) ambivalent relation to tradition in *Shakespeare's Festive Tragedy: The Ritual Foundations of Genre* (London, 1995), pp. 57–85.

[31] For recent discussions of the imaginary/nostalgic in the history redacted in these plays, see especially Burns's essay, 'Shakespeare's Histories in Cycles'.

[32] Burns, 'Shakespeare's Histories in Cycles', p. 151. Emphasis added. Burns's commentary seems to me particularly apt in its general assessment of the political sweep of the plays: 'scepticism seems to me to be a constituent of all the histories, and to be overridden in the "heroic epic of England" reading of them . . . [Soon] after the late Elizabethan popularity of the histories, audiences became alienated from them, largely because an open-mindedly questioning attitude toward historical "truth", and a sense that both nationhood and the sense of history as a linear progression were open to question, became, not so much untenable, as unrecognizable, in the shaping of a contrary idea of history, and in the redefinition of nationhood in the union with Scotland, the creation of "Britain". So the texts are relocated, into – for all their local horrors – an essentially nostalgic myth' (p. 164).

Marjorie Garber writes, 'is really a nostalgia for something that never was' and a 'fantasy of originary cultural wholeness',[33] or what Benedict Anderson calls 'imagined communities'.[34] Shallow's and Silence's nostalgia is personal, local (and to most ears insignificant, unless we hear in it a *memento mori* of lives lost, the 'none else of name' always swept aside by nationalist interests), but occasionally, as is the case here, remembered as also part of the human landscape and thus of national identity.

The figures of old men in this part of the tetralogy, and particularly in *Part 2*, are necessary constructions, conjoined with the functions of memory and the embodiment of Rumour. If these sagas of monarchs and their temporary grasp on the sceptre of power are the thematic subjects of these plays, if *history* is understood as the passage from one generation to another and of one set of values to another (not always different, but always 'passed'), then representations of old age in both its dignified and grotesque faces must be part of the dramatized 'picture' worth the proverbial thousand words. Falstaff certainly, as Graham Holderness argues, 'performs the functions . . . of carnival . . . His attitude to authority is always parodic and satirical; he mocks authority, flouts power, responds to the pressures of social duty and civic obligation by retreating into Bacchanalian revelry.'[35] Falstaff is the iconic representation of old age as misrule, the *pantalone*, the monstrous, horny, inebriated, breathless image of superfluity. But power and authority are also represented as elderly – sometimes anxious and guilt-ridden (King Henry IV), at other times open and honour-bound (the Lord Chief Justice; especially 5.2.35–41, 73–140), and sometimes just comfortably bourgeois, tipsy and generally oblivious to everything but their own personal concerns (Shallow and Silence, especially 5.3).

As one section of this four-part portrait of ageing authority, Shallow and Silence are intermediary figures between Falstaff's ludic lawlessness, the old king's exhaustion and then his death, and the rectitude of the Lord Chief Justice, who becomes the new king's 'father' (5.2.140) in matters of policy.[36] They are part of what Holderness identifies as

the Henry IV plays' 'separate and incompatible visions of history . . . celebrat[ing] the dialectical conflict of these contradictory cultural energies.'[37] Their concerns are other than the fate of the nation or the outcome of the war against France. Their quaint (in 3.2) and drunken (in 5.3) dialogue offers a context for the conversation in the next play between King Henry V and his soldiers Williams and Bates (*Henry V*, 4.1.84–215). Shallow and Silence converse quite easily with Bardolph, Falstaff and the servant Davy in 5.3; in contrast, the new King Henry (who, as Hal, once boasted that he could 'drink with any tinker in his own language', *1 Henry IV*, 2.4.19), masquerading briefly as 'Harry le Roy' (*Henry V*, 4.1.49), cannot in fact understand his soldiers' real concerns, as his comments show when he is again alone at the end of that scene (4.1.230–84). The scene of two old country justices drinking and singing throughout 5.3, actually complicates reception of the play's more serious concerns. John Dover Wilson noted that 'on the death of a king a J.P.'s office terminated';[38] in that case, our jolly country justices, though they do not yet know it, are out of office even while in their cups, and are about to be arrested along with the disgraced Falstaff in the play's last lines. The new world order ushered in with Henry V is already under way, and the transition, served by these scenes with Shallow and Silence, is complete.

---

[33] 'Shakespeare as Fetish', in *Profiling Shakespeare* (New York, 2008), pp. 110–11.

[34] See *Imagined Communities: Reflections on the Origin and Spread of Nationalism* (London, 1983).

[35] '*Henry IV*: Carnival and History', in Holderness, *Shakespeare's History Plays*, p. 154.

[36] Evans proposes that, 'in a sense', it is Rumour who 'fathers' the new king (p. 19).

[37] Holderness, *Shakespeare's History Plays*, p. 163. Humphreys, leaning heavily on Tillyard's *Shakespeare's History Plays* (1944), reads the two justices simply as representatives of 'country life', inserted into this play for the sake of panoramic inclusion – this too is England: see notes to the openings of 3.2 and 5.3, both set in Gloucestershire.

[38] *2 Henry IV*, New Shakespeare, quoted in Humphreys' note to 5.3.112.

Once he is crowned, Henry's personal memory is necessarily bound in with political time, as befits an incumbent whose persona(l) is inevitably shaped by his political role. Moments after dismissing his soldiers' spoken fears for their immortal souls and their mortal families as 'the breath / Of every fool whose sense can no more feel / But his own wringing' (*Henry V*, 4.1.234–6), Henry remembers (and urgently begs God *not* to remember) 'the fault / My father made in compassing the crown' (*Henry V*, 4.1.293–4). For the king's military agenda, forgetting serves better than remembering;[39] his role – like God's – in the larger state requires it, though at a micro-level he will remember Williams later in the matter of the glove (*Henry V*, 4.8.25–56).

The infamous iteration of Henry's body-count later in the same scene – the long list of French slain, the much shorter list of four noteworthy English, 'None else of name; and of all other men / But five and twenty' (4.8.103–6) – stands in significant contrast to the justices' roll-call of the dead and of absent school friends in *2 Henry IV*. Perhaps because the consequences of local remembrance and nostalgia have smaller than national scope, their scene is often heard as comedic, to the extent that *2 Henry IV* is 'often' performed at all. But the giggles sometimes invited by the justices' scenes betray a nervousness confronting, even at the remove of theatrical representation, the inevitable, un-heroic, un-Crispian obituary that no one in the audience can avoid. It echoes later, in *Henry V*, when Pistol, demobilized and demoralized, knows his only pension will be what he can steal:

> News have I that my Doll is dead i' the spittle
> Of a malady of France,
> And there my rendezvous is quite cut off.
> Old do I wax, and from my weary limbs
> Honour is cudgell'd. Well, bawd I'll turn,
> And something lean to cutpurse of quick hand.
> To England will I steal, and there I'll steal;
> And patches will I get unto these cudgell'd scars,
> And swear I got them in the Gallia wars.
>
> (5.1.81–9)

This little speech is packed with ironies, coming as it does just dramatic moments after Harry's 'band of brothers' speech in 4.3:

> He that shall see this day, and live old age,
> Will yearly on the vigil feast his neighbours,
> And say, 'To-morrow is Saint Crispian.'
> Then will he strip his sleeve and show his scars,
> And say 'These wounds I had on Crispin's day.'
>   . . . Be he ne'er so vile,
> This day shall gentle his condition . . .
>
> (4.3.44–8, 62–3)

As in the scene with Williams and Bates, Harry's idea of the spoils of war does not quite mesh with the experience of his soldiers; Pistol's condition will not be 'gentled', though he will show his scars, and he will never 'feast his neighbours'. France has victory over him, whoever wins the war – his Nell is dead of syphilis, the 'malady of France' – and now he waxes old.

Pistol's monologue and Henry's casualty notices would have been heard on the stage as a sharp counterpoint for an audience who had recently attended the justices' moments in *2 Henry IV*.[40] Shallow's and Silence's – and Falstaff's – meta-commentaries are focused on their personal histories and nostalgia for their long-lost glory days and the 'bona robas' of their youth. For them in ways quite different from Henry's, the personal *is* political and politics *are* local. They do not concern themselves with the consequences of depositions, usurpations, displacements, who's in, who's out (as King Lear puts it: 5.3.15); those are matters for monarchs. As Henry IV pivots between memories of the king he displaced and apprehension of the son who, in 4.5, performs his displacement, the 'history in all men's lives' alternates with the 'hatch and brood of time' (3.1.80, 86). Shallow's chronicle of days and nights at Clement's Inn is remembered

---

39 On *Henry V*'s 'brutal campaigns of forgetting', see Jonathan Baldo, 'Wars of Memory in *Henry V*', *Shakespeare Quarterly*, 47 (1996), pp. 132–59, and Dermot Cavanagh, 'History, Mourning and Memory in *Henry V*', *Shakespeare's Histories and Counter-Histories*, ed. Dermot Cavanagh, Stuart Hampton-Reeves and Stephen Longstaffe (Manchester, 2006), pp. 32–48.

40 Humphreys accepts 1597–8 for *2 Henry IV*'s first performances and 1599 for *Henry V*, citing also the reference to Justice Silence in Jonson's *Every Man Out* (1599). See his Arden Introduction, p. xiv.

only there, 'where I think they talk of mad Shallow yet' (3.2.11–13), if at all, and is of no public consequence. Macro- and micro-cosms tumble around and over each other in *2 Henry IV*, whose playing with the past performs in recollected images what resists discursive articulation.

In the middle of this play, 3.1 (right before the justices' first scene), King Henry complains of insomnia and blames his responsibilities: 'Uneasy lies the head that wears a crown' (31). But the crown is not what keeps him from sleeping; as the rest of the scene makes clear, it's remembering the way he got it and its blood-price in rebellion and civil war that keeps him up this night. 'O God, that one might read the book of fate, / And see the revolution of the times' (45–6). The king is a bit disingenuous here; fate and the inexorable march of time had nothing – even under the 'providential' banner of the Tudor Myth[41] – to do with the national predicament in which he finds himself. These lines are just his warm-up; he gets to the heart of the matter in relatively short order after this, and then, in the lines I italicize, he lies outright:

> 'Tis not ten years gone
> Since Richard and Northumberland, two great friends,
> Did feast together, and in two years after
> Were they at wars. It is but eight years since
> This Percy was the man nearest my soul,
> Who like a brother toil'd in my affairs,
> And laid his love and life under my foot,
> Yea, for my sake, even to the eyes of Richard
> Gave him defiance. But which of you was by –
> [*To Warwick*] You, cousin Nevil, as I may remember –
> When Richard, with his eye brimful of tears,
> Then check'd and rated by Northumberland,
> Did speak these words, now prov'd a prophecy?
> 'Northumberland, thou ladder by the which
> My cousin Bullingbrook ascends my throne'
> (*Though then, God knows, I had no such intent,*
> *But that necessity so bow'd the state*
> *That I and greatness were compell'd to kiss*)
> 'The time shall come,' thus did he follow it,
> 'The time come, that foul sin, gathering head,
> Shall break into corruption' . . .   (57–77; italics added)

Henry needs an ally, or an alibi, for this 'corruption'; rhetorically and loyally, Warwick nominated

time itself as the 'necessary cause', the root of inevitability in Richard's deposition. Henry wants to hear again about the 'history in all men's lives, / Figuring the natures of the times deceas'd, / . . . Such things become the hatch and brood of time' (80–6). The king is eager for this, like a child begging for a favourite bedtime story. As greedy for affirmation as Shallow in 3.2, the king jumps on Warwick's seeming reassurance: 'Are these things then necessities? / Then let us meet them like necessities' (92–3). Henry, of course, had learned the political utility of 'necessity' (and of equivocation) from his father Gaunt – 'There is no virtue like necessity' (*Richard II*, 1.3.278) – on the occasion of his banishment. Recalling that earlier training, he now leans on recollection for supportive 'precedent'.

Their common reliance on reminiscence links the king and his local justices, whose long exchange in 3.2 is more than comedic interlude; it is the foil to Henry's opportunism, and casts a shadow over the reliability of memory and nostalgia as justification for his present aggressions. The justices' reminiscence, narrowing the play of history to selective frames of personal memory, is a dark metonymy for the audience's nostalgia, for Old Gaunt's nostalgia in *Richard II*, for (perhaps) the author's politically cautionary/cautious nostalgia.[42] Maybe, to paraphrase Lear on seeing Poor Tom, man really *is* 'no more than' (*King Lear*, 3.4.103) these, generalized from self-referential old geezers lost in dubious recollections of a personal past. And yet, their recollections are not to be dismissed; in so far as narrative is the way human experience is made meaningful,[43] episodic reminiscence is a microversion of larger forms of narrative structure such as myth, legend, epic and various forms of historical record, all of which, it needs be said, likewise

---

41 See Phyllis Rackin, *Stages of History: Shakespeare's English Chronicles* (Ithaca, 1990), p. 38.

42 Bulman notes that the popularity of the two parts of *Henry IV* on the Elizabethan stage 'no doubt resulted in part from their use of the past to comment on the present' (p. 158).

43 Sherman, *Reminiscence and the Self*, p. 39.

present their 'truths' episodically, their 'narratives' giving 'form and meaning to the discrete and discontinuous contents of reminiscence'.[44] In *2 Henry IV* the separation of private and public collapses in ways that readers may forget but audiences to performed plays cannot. What really matters in this play of remembrance, and to whom does it matter? Chronicles or no, the history encompassed by Hall, Holinshed[45] and other recorders of the matter condensed in Shakespeare's second tetralogy (which, as Henry reminds us in the speech at 3.1.57 quoted earlier, is only the matter of a decade) is not only too big for the stage, as *Henry V*'s first Prologue 'admits' (11–32); it is also, in a sense, irrelevant. The large sweep of time, its 'hatch and brood', is interesting to historians and historiographers, and to kings; as Shakespeare is very careful to draw them for us, however, ordinary folks – soldiers, draftees, old country justices – measure time differently and take its passing personally. Does it really matter who occupies the throne when all around you are dying or dead? Perhaps, at the end of the day, the lofty crises of 'history' do in fact devolve to personal reminiscence and the price of sheep.

---

[44] Sherman, *Reminiscence and the Self*, p. 41.

[45] Annabel Patterson notes that the Chronicles attributed to Holinshed were too big even for Holinshed; she emphasizes repeatedly throughout *Reading Holinshed's Chronicles* (Chicago, 1994) that the work was a collaboration of many voices, many pens and many kinds of records.

PERFORMING THE CONFLATED TEXT OF *HENRY IV*: THE FORTUNES OF *PART TWO*

JAMES C. BULMAN

In 1995, BBC television broadcast what it called Shakespeare's *Henry IV* in a radical abridgement and conflation of *Part One* and *Part Two*. Directed by RSC associate John Caird, this was the BBC's most lavish and ambitious Shakespeare production since the conclusion of its marathon filming of all the plays ten years earlier (1978–85), and for a new generation of television viewers it set a standard for performing Shakespeare's history plays.[1] Caird focused his production on what he imagined to be prince Henry's long-standing relationship with Hotspur: the two are glimpsed together as children witnessing the deposition of Richard II, and their growing rivalry climaxes at the Battle of Shrewsbury, when the prince defeats his former friend, winning his 'proud titles' from him and with them, the king's paternal approval.

Caird thus uses *Part One* to provide a structure for the whole, and most of the material in *Part Two* is jettisoned, both the historical (the flight of Northumberland to Scotland, the thwarting of the Archbishop's rebellion at Gaultree) and the non-historical (most of the scenes at Justice Shallow's farm, and much of Falstaff's comic banter with his tavern cronies). Instead, Caird ingeniously grafts speeches and snippets of scenes from *Part Two* onto *Part One* to reinforce themes or to create ironic counterpoints. For example, Hotspur's farewell to Lady Percy is preceded by Falstaff's farewell to Doll Tearsheet (an exchange that now occurs prior to Falstaff's march to Shrewsbury), the king's chastising his son in *Part One* is intercut with the Lord Chief Justice's interrogation of Falstaff in *Part Two*,

and the king's soliloquy on the unease of king-ship from *Part Two* is spoken immediately prior to the Gadshill robbery, as a kind of meditation on political theft, while other lines spoken by the king later in that scene ('O God, that one might read the book of fate, / And see the revolution of the times')[2] are interpolated as ominous glosses on the play-extempore in which Hal and Falstaff each assume the role of king. Following the rebels' defeat at Shrewsbury, Caird swiftly concludes the royal history with the death of the king, the accession of Henry V and the rejection of Falstaff – the only sequence from *Part Two* preserved without radical alteration.

For audiences who had never seen the two parts of *Henry IV* in the theatre, Caird's montage of disparate but thematically related moments offered a politically coherent interpretation of Henry's reign.[3] Those familiar with the complete texts of

---

[1] With an unusually large budget of one million pounds, the production featured a stellar cast including Rufus Sewell as Hotspur, Jonathan Firth as the prince, Ronald Pickup as the king and John Calder as Falstaff. To shape his history, Caird, working from a script adapted by Michael Hastings, liberally interpolated material from *Richard II*, *Henry V*, *Henry VI Part 3* and *Merry Wives*, as, for example, when he concludes with Falstaff's death – a borrowing from *Henry V* also used by Orson Welles in *Chimes at Midnight*. For brief accounts of this *Henry IV*, see *BFI Screenonline: Henry IV* (1995), and René Weis, ed., *Henry IV, Part 2* (Oxford, 1998), pp. 76–7.

[2] See *Part Two*, 3.1.44–5. All references are to Weis's edition.

[3] In *Shakespeare in Space: Recent Shakespeare Productions on Screen* (New York, 2002), pp. 45–52, H. R. Coursen objects to Caird's use of montage to underscore verbal echoes as

the two plays, however, would have been aware of what had been lost; for while the linear narrative of *Part One* was kept intact, *Part Two* was only mined for 'bits', its more discursive structure and unhistorical characters sacrificed to the need for clarity and compression. As the reviewer in the *Daily Mail* objected, 'Director John Caird brutally re-ordered *Henry IV*, changing the order of scenes to sharpen up the story line, and more or less abandoned Shakespeare's wider historical perspective to concentrate on the father–son relationship' (30 October 1995).[4] The sacrifice of the 'wider historical perspective' offered in *Part Two* has a performance history of its own.

I. PART TWO ALONE

Henry IV Part Two has seldom been a popular play. Since its first performances (*c.*1597–8), it has lived in the shadow of its more famous older brother. As centuries of theatre history attest, *Part One* can be staged very successfully on its own as a study of the prodigal prince's growth to maturity, culminating in his defeat of Hostpur at the Battle of Shrewsbury. Political events in *Part Two*, however, depend in part on one's knowledge of what has occurred in *Part One*; and scholars have long speculated that the two plays may originally have been planned together, even as one ten-act play.[5] Yet there is no evidence that *Part Two* was ever performed with *Part One* during Shakespeare's lifetime;[6] and indeed, prior to the mid-twentieth century, it was most often performed independently. Billed as a Falstaff play, it provided a star vehicle for great actors to exploit the humorous potentials of the fat knight, with its scenes of chronicle history truncated in order to foreground scenes of comedy until Falstaff – unjustly, in the view of most audiences – was banished by the newly crowned king.[7]

Thomas Betterton's adaptation of *Part Two*, which held the stage for forty years, is a case in point. Betterton had played Hotspur and then Falstaff in *Part One* to great acclaim during the Restoration, and his decision to revive *Part Two* in 1704 was no doubt opportunistic – a way to capitalize on the popularity of Falstaff. His

The Sequel of Henry the Fourth altered the play in various ways, most notably by featuring Falstaff as

---

'much more heavy handed' than television can accommodate. Coursen's detailed analysis of various sequences in the production is valuable, even if one discounts his argument that Caird's 'reordered, chopped-up version' ultimately confuses the historical chronology and thematic patterns of the plays.

4 As was true for many directors before him, Caird's overriding concern in the *Henry IV* plays was 'the way in which they talk about inheritance and father/son relationships': see Lisa Vanoli's interview with Caird, 'Fascinating Time Spent with Henry', in *The Stage* (5 October 1995), p. 34; also Anthony Davies, 'Falstaff's Shadow', in Sarah Hatchuel and Nathalie Vienne-Guerrin, eds., *Shakespeare on Screen: The Henriad* (Rouen, 2008), pp. 99–117.

5 For evidence that Shakespeare planned the two parts together from the outset, see John Dover Wilson, 'The Origins and Development of Shakespeare's *Henry IV*', *The Library*, 4th Series, 24 (1945), 2–16. This view was modified by Harold Jenkins who, in *The Structural Problem in Shakespeare's Henry IV* (London, 1956), argues that the two parts were originally conceived, and perhaps written, as one five-act play which was divided only when Shakespeare realized he had too much material to dramatize in one. Alternatively, Matthias A. Shaaber, 'The Unity of *Henry IV*', in James G. McManaway et al., eds., *Joseph Quincy Adams Memorial Studies* (Washington, DC, 1948), pp. 217–27, offers evidence that *Part Two* was an unpremeditated sequel which Shakespeare wrote only when *Part One*, and especially Falstaff, had proved popular with audiences.

6 Mary Thomas Crane makes this point in 'The Shakespearean Tetralogy', *Shakespeare Quarterly*, 36 (1985), 291–5, as does Paul Yachnin in 'History, Theatricality, and the "Structural Problem" in the *Henry IV* Plays', *Philological Quarterly*, 70 (1991), 163–79. The two plays were performed at Whitehall during the festive season of 1612/13, the first part titled *The Hotspur* and the second, *Sir John Falstaffe*; but they were not staged as one continuous play, and even the titles given them suggest dramatic foci at odds with a unitary focus on the royal narrative.

7 The earliest responses to the play reveal how sympathetically Falstaff was received. Nicholas Rowe, for example, observed in 1709 that many lamented seeing Falstaff so abused by his old friend: see Brian Vickers, ed., *Shakespeare, The Critical Heritage*, vol. 2 (London, 1974), p. 195. Corbyn Morris in 1744 viewed Falstaff as 'entirely an amiable character ... superior to all other Men', whose 'Imprisonment and Death' were warranted not by anything he had done to deserve such punishment, but to comply 'with the *Austerity* of the Times, and in order to avoid the Imputation of encouraging *Idleness* and mirthful *Riot* by too amiable and happy an example': see Vickers, vol. 3 (1975), pp. 122–9. And even the

the only character of any consequence in the first three of its five acts.[8] All references to Hotspur and to the Northern rebellion so central to *Part One* were expunged: the Induction and the opening scene in which Northumberland receives word of his son's death were cut entirely, as was the scene in which Northumberland is urged by his wife and daughter-in-law to flee to Scotland.[9] With these scenes removed, all connections between *Part Two* and the climactic Battle of Shrewsbury in *Part One* were severed. The political action of Betterton's first three acts involved only an abbreviated scene to introduce the Archbishop's rebellion in Act 1, and a conflation of the Gaultree scenes to conclude it in Act 3. Furthermore, the scene that introduces the king (3.1) was omitted – as it had been in the first issue of the quarto in 1600 – and instead the insomniac king's soliloquy concluding 'Uneasy lies the head that wears a crown' was transposed to the scene of his death. The result of such alterations was to create a three-act prose comedy in which Falstaff holds the stage for all but a minor and quickly quelled political uprising; and notably, his great tavern scene (2.4) and his long recruiting scene at Justice Shallow's farm (3.2) were juxtaposed, as they were in the first issue of the quarto, yielding 658 lines of Falstaffian comedy uninterrupted by any chronicle history.

Betterton's compression of the climactic scenes at court – the king's illness and death and the new king's confrontation of the Lord Chief Justice – into one act (Act 4) may have been prompted by the same neoclassical impulse to avoid unnecessary changes of locale that caused Dryden to reduce the number of scenes in his adaptation of *Troilus and Cressida*. Arguably, though, Betterton was more concerned with the decorum of genre and intended to segregate the 'tragick part' from the rest of the play as a discrete dramatic unit, tonally distinct from the prose comedy that had preceded it.[10] And while Betterton was unique in borrowing material from the opening of *Henry V* to flesh out his fifth act following the rejection of Falstaff, the practice of segregating the historical plot from the comic scenes continued into the nineteenth century, as John Bell's acting edition of

1773 and J. P. Kemble's of 1804 attest. Indeed, even the most celebrated 'royal' production of the play – mounted in 1821 to commemorate the accession of George IV – which embellished Hal's coronation with four added scenes of ceremonial spectacle at the end, drew on a text that rearranged the play in the same vein as Betterton, allowing Falstaff to dominate the stage until the scene of the king's death.[11] At the same time, those productions that adhered more closely to the structure of Shakespeare's play typically shortened the scenes of chronicle history in order to emphasize the fortunes of Falstaff; and up to the middle of the twentieth century, *Part Two* continued to be produced on its own as an autonomous play, independent of *Part One*.[12]

---

moralist Samuel Johnson, in a note on 5.5.92 in his 1765 edition, objected to Falstaff's being carried to the Fleet, since 'he had committed no new fault, and therefore incurred no punishment': see Vickers, vol. 5 (1979), p. 123.

[8] Thomas Betterton, *The Sequel of Henry the Fourth: With the Humours of Sir John Falstaffe, and Justice Shallow* (London, 1721). Betterton had died in 1710, so his edition was printed posthumously, and possibly, despite the date of imprint, as early as 1719.

[9] Lois Potter speculates that Northumberland's speeches were cut because they had been recently appropriated by Colley Cibber for use in his production of *Richard III* in 1700: see 'The Second Tetralogy: Performance as Interpretation', in Richard Dutton and Jean Howard, eds., *The Blackwell Companion to Shakespeare: The Histories* (Oxford, 2003), p. 287.

[10] Samuel Johnson identifies King Henry's death and its aftermath as the 'tragick part' of *Henry IV* in his 1765 edition: see Vickers, vol. 5, p. 124.

[11] See *Henry IV, Part 2: Coronation Production 1821* (London, 1971). For this production, William Macready used J. P. Kemble's 1804 acting text, published by Mrs Inchbald in 1808, which reorganized Act 5 so that the rejection of Falstaff *preceded* the new king's reconciliation with the Lord Chief Justice. The spectacular coronation scenes were Macready's addition.

[12] The performance archives of the Royal Shakespeare Company, for example, reveal that between 1894 and 1932, *Part Two* was staged at the Memorial Theatre in twelve different seasons, but only twice – 1905 and 1932 – in the same season as *Part One*, which was staged less often than *Part Two* and not at all between 1909 and 1923. After 1932, *Part Two* was absent from the repertory for twenty years, until 1951, when it was revived in a production discussed below.

JAMES C. BULMAN

II. THE RISE OF THE TWO-PART PLAY

The decision by Anthony Quayle and Michael Redgrave to stage the two *Henry IV* plays together as part of a grand history cycle at Stratford-upon-Avon in 1951 to celebrate the Festival of Britain significantly altered the fortunes of *Part Two*. Inspired both by John Dover Wilson's argument that the two parts of *Henry IV* dramatize one of history's great conversion stories in which 'the technical centre of the play is not the fat knight but the lean prince'[13] and by E. M. W. Tillyard's hypothesis that Shakespeare had a 'grand design' for the history plays to be seen together as a providential epic of England,[14] this cyclical conception placed the royal *Bildungsroman* front and centre. Hal's coming of age became emblematic for England's emergence from the Second World War and the restoration of order; his accession to the throne an affirmation of English nationhood and the legitimacy of tradition. *Part Two* served as the linchpin for this ideologically conservative interpretation, because in its final two acts rebellion is finally put down; King Henry IV dies; the prince, vowing to pin his legitimacy on linear succession, is crowned Henry V; and at his coronation he banishes the vicious misleader of his youth. From this perspective, Falstaff represents a crucial obstacle to the prince's moral reformation, and thus his rejection should be viewed as necessary and played dispassionately, not sentimentally, as it had been for more than two centuries. *Part Two*, therefore, began to be performed regularly with *Part One* as a *history* play – an essential part of the royal narrative – whose comic digressions and potential for subversion served to justify the political imperatives of what had come to be known as the second tetralogy. Since 1951, it has almost never been performed without *Part One*.

Ironically, however, as the twentieth century drew to a close, *Part Two* – now seen by audiences largely as Shakespeare had written it – came to be regarded by scholars as a distinctly different sort of history play, as much the obverse as the sequel of *Part One*,[15] its darker and more cynical tone, particularly in Prince John's Machiavellian double-crossing of the rebels at Gaultree, appealing to audiences whose view of politics and 'official history' had grown sceptical in the wake of the Vietnam war, Watergate and its aftermath, or in the face of Thatcherism with its opportunistic view of the social contract and its promotion of predatory forms of privatization. In such political contexts, *Part Two* seemed to reflect the *realpolitik* of government more accurately than *Part One*, its opposition to the earlier play's chivalric affirmations more in line with audiences' recent experience – a study, as Stephen Greenblatt would have it, in how those in power allow anarchic forces (such as those embodied by Falstaff) to operate only to be able to contain them.[16]

In performance, however, the two plays were not kept as tonally distinct as scholarly arguments were suggesting they should be. Increasingly, *Part One* took on some of *Part Two*'s darker coloration and was played as if to anticipate the end in the beginning. Hal's soliloquy in 1.2, for example, invariably became a revelation of his capacity for political calculation (not unlike his father's), and his 'I do, I will' at the end of the play extempore, an ominous threat to banish Falstaff (2.4.468), the comic 'I do' chillingly anticipating the more tragic 'I will'.[17] In many productions Falstaff shed some weight and acquired a dangerous dignity, and his merriment in the tavern scenes in *Part One* was tempered by more sober concerns about mortality borrowed from *Part Two*. At the extreme, as in a production of the history cycle by the English Shakespeare Company which toured internationally (1986–9), *Part One* was made to dramatize an ethos as duplicitous as

---

[13] *The Fortunes of Falstaff* (Cambridge, 1943), p. 17.

[14] See *Shakespeare's History Plays* (London, 1944). On p. 264, Tillyard argues that it is imperative to 'treat the two parts [of *Henry IV*] as a single play' in order to realize this design.

[15] This is Peter Davison's formulation in his New Penguin edition of the play (London, 1977), pp. 9–10.

[16] See 'Invisible Bullets: Renaissance Authority and its Subversion, *Henry IV* and *Henry V*', in Jonathan Dollimore and Alan Sinfield, eds., *Political Shakespeare: New Essays in Cultural Materialism* (Manchester, 1985), pp. 18–47.

[17] All references to *Part One* are from David Kastan, ed., *King Henry IV Part 1* (London, 2002).

that of the court in *Part Two*. At the climax of this production, Hal's defeat of Hotspur at Shrewsbury represented a dirty repudiation of the military code of honour he had sworn to uphold. Hotspur, the better fighter of the two, had 'knocked the sword and shield out of Hal's hands and forced him to his knees'; but then 'chivalry intervened as a piece of stupidity'. Unwilling to kill an unarmed man, Hotspur slid Hal's sword back to him, and Hal, seizing the opportunity, drove his sword into Hotspur from behind.[18] This revisionist staging of Hal's killing of Hotspur was ethically of a piece with Prince John's betrayal of the rebels at Gaultree, where 'commandos marched them off to execution' to the mocking strains of Handel's 'The King shall rejoice!',[19] and it anticipated the new king's abuse of power at the end of *Part Two* when, in a scene often omitted in performance, officers brutally beat Doll Tearsheet as they hauled her and Mistress Quickly off to prison – evidence of the ruthlessness with which state power would be exercised under Henry V.

In such productions, furthermore, the discursive structure of *Part Two*, which offers a welter of alternative histories to rival the official one – those of the women, menials, peasants, unemployed and hangers-on who populate Falstaff's world – was seen to promote a Marxist understanding of history from the bottom up, as a study of economic relations, class struggle and hegemonic oppression, rather than from the top down.[20] Those characters who offer so much of the play's amusement – Mistress Quickly in her absurd quest for social respectability, Ancient Pistol in his ludicrous recitation of an outmoded heroic rhetoric, Justice Shallow in his desire to have a friend at court (and his willingness to pay for it) – now appeared not simply as comic diversions, but as parodic reflections of the self-interest and political hypocrisy of those in power: in the words of Barbara Hodgdon, 'Falstaff's comic world . . . was revealed not as history's amusingly playful carnival alternative, but as its dangerous double' (132). Paradoxically, then, the cycle mentality that gave rise to a new popularity for *Part Two* as a crucial cog in the royal narrative led to its discovery as a cynical gloss on the very history that the cycle was intended to validate.

III. DERING'S *HENRY IV*

The impulse to regard the two parts of *Henry IV* as a coherent coming-of-age story goes back much further than Tillyard. An abridgement prepared by Sir Edward Dering for a private performance in 1622 or shortly thereafter – but never finished – suggests that readers and performers have wanted to combine the two parts as one since shortly after Shakespeare's death.[21] The Dering manuscript foregrounds the royal history and the conflict between father and son at the expense of those marginalized characters whose 'unofficial' histories no doubt were seen as digressions from the narrative of the prince's reformation. Dering's skilful conflation of the two parts – which together total 6148 lines – to a playable 3401 lines reflects a popular bias in favour of *Part One*. Of the 2968 lines in the fifth Quarto of *Part One*, which was his source, Dering kept 2621, or 88 per cent; he omitted only two scenes in their entirety – one involving the carriers in Rochester, the other introducing the Archbishop's rebellion, a plot he eliminated entirely from *Part Two* – and cut portions of other scenes, the longest of which was the exchange in which Lady Percy and Lady Mortimer are asked to

---

[18] See Scott McMillin, *Henry IV, Part One*, Shakespeare in Performance Series (Manchester, 1991), p. 120.

[19] See Barbara Hodgdon, *Henry IV, Part Two*, Shakespeare in Performance Series (Manchester, 1993), p. 136.

[20] For particularly astute cultural materialist analyses of the two *Henry IV* plays, see Jean Howard and Phyllis Rackin, *Engendering a Nation: A Feminist Account of Shakespeare's English Histories* (London, 1997), pp. 160–85, and Phyllis Rackin, *Stages of History: Shakespeare's English Chronicles* (Ithaca, 1990), *passim*.

[21] See the Folger Library facsimile edition of *The History of King Henry the Fourth, as revised by Sir Edward Dering, Bart.*, prepared by George Walton Williams and Gwynne Blakemore Evans (Charlottesville, 1974), p. viii. The back of a scrap of paper containing eight lines of text to be inserted in the king's speech following 1.1.20 includes an apparent cast list, drawn from among Dering's friends and relatives, for a private performance of Fletcher's *The Spanish Curate* at Dering's Surrenden estate. *The Spanish Curate* was licensed to be played in 1622, and Francis Manouch, whose name heads the cast list, moved away from the region in 1624, thus providing the dates within which Dering's performance of *Henry IV* must have been intended to occur.

sing (3.1.192–271).[22] From *Part Two*, in contrast, Dering kept little more than those scenes involving the prince or the king, a total of 806 lines, or 25 per cent, of the 3180 lines in the second issue of the quarto. Scenes drawn from *Part Two* begin late in Dering's Act 4 with a truncated version of Northumberland's hearing news of Hotspur's death at Shrewsbury – a direct connection to the scenes from *Part One* that precede it – and continue with Lady Percy's persuasion of Northumberland to fly to Scotland. With the elimination of the Archbishop's plot, Dering used these scenes to put a period to the rebellion that opened the play: news of Northumberland's capture brought to the dying king ensures that rebellion will be given no chance to divert attention from the conclusion of the royal history.

Sandwiched between the two Northumberland scenes is a brief comic squabble over debts between Falstaff and the Hostess extracted from *Part Two* (2.1); otherwise, Falstaff appears only in the rejection scene, in which he is granted a scant four and a half lines. Gone are Falstaff's scenes with the Lord Chief Justice, with Doll Tearsheet, and with the Ancient Pistol; gone, the wonderful scenes of Falstaff's recruiting soldiers, drinking and reminiscing with Justices Shallow and Silence. Dering allows nothing to impede the conclusion of the main plot: the illness and death of the king (a clever splicing together of 3.1 and 4.3); Prince Henry's accession and reassurance of his brothers (a reduction of 5.2); and, immediately following as part of the same scene, his rejection of Falstaff in a speech that concludes with five rather clumsy interpolated lines wherein the new king vows to 'change our thoughtes for honour and renowne' and set his sights on 'the royalty and crowne of Fraunce' (5.10.77–8).[23]

Dering's conflation thus uses portions of *Part Two* – most of them from Acts 4 and 5 – to provide a swift resolution of the royal narrative dramatized in *Part One*, culminating in the reformation of the Prince of Wales, who has already proved himself in battle at Shrewsbury, as a responsible king. For this reformation, it was unnecessary that the Falstaff scenes from *Part Two* be included, for they add

nothing to the relationship Prince Henry has had with him: they dramatize a Falstaff who, capitalizing on his 'honours' falsely won at Shrewsbury, presides over a comic world that no longer includes the prince. Indeed, the prince in *Part Two* has little to do before his exchange with his father in Act 4: having apparently lapsed after his defeat of Hotspur, he is full of self-recrimination, and his scene with Poins and Bardolph is more bitter than comic. Dering's abridgement of the two texts thus offers a coherent dramatic action that some scholars speculate may have been Shakespeare's original design for *Henry IV*, before he realized that he had too much chronicle material to include in one play, or before the character of Falstaff grew out of all compass, prompting him to end his play at Shrewsbury and, as a result, leaving little history to be dramatized in the sequel. Given his emphasis on the royal narrative, it is not surprising that less than a quarter of Dering's play is drawn from *Part Two*.

IV. WELLES'S *CHIMES AT MIDNIGHT*

In recent decades there have been several attempts to perform *Henry IV* as a conflation of the two parts. As with Dering's abridgement, such attempts have tended to foreground the narrative of Hal's coming of age as a triumph of the state over forces of anarchy, and consequently to suppress those aspects of *Part Two* that would call such ideological certainty into question. The earliest and best known of these conflations is Orson Welles's 1965 film *Chimes at Midnight*. Based on two short-lived stage adaptations which Welles had attempted, in the US in 1938 and Ireland in 1960,[24] it offers

---

22 I am indebted to Williams and Evans, pp. viii–ix, for their comprehensive review of Dering's use of *Part One*.

23 In *The End Crowns All* (Princeton, 1991), pp. 168–9, Barbara Hodgdon assesses Dering's conservative abbreviation of the play's final scenes and the function of the prince's last lines as an anticipation of the 'Chronicle deeds' to be dramatized in *Henry V*.

24 For discussion of these stage versions, see Robert Hapgood, '*Chimes at Midnight* from Stage to Screen: The Art of Adaptation', *Shakespeare Survey 39* (Cambridge, 1987) 39–52. The

a complex portrait of Falstaff, its emphasis falling heavily on both the comic resourcefulness and the inevitable tragedy of a great but mistreated hero, and its ingenious cutting and splicing of the two *Henry IV* plays including more of the social panorama from *Part Two* than Dering allowed. In carefully arranged segments of the tavern scenes, Mistress Quickly, Doll Tearsheet and the Ancient Pistol are all allowed to revel with Falstaff, and Falstaff visits Justice Shallow's farm twice, once to recruit soldiers, and again to bilk Shallow of a thousand pounds. The title itself comes from Falstaff's wry acknowledgement to Justice Shallow, in a moment that opens the film, that their youth has passed: 'We have heard the chimes at midnight, Master Shallow' (3.2.206–7). Age, remembrance and a sense of loss pervade the film and heighten the sympathy one feels for Falstaff.

Nevertheless, although Welles foregrounds his own performance as Falstaff, the overall dramatic arc of his film is determined primarily by the royal coming-of-age story. All references to the Northumberlands and to the Archbishop's rebellion are expunged following the royal victory at Shrewsbury, and the portion of the film drawn from *Part Two* soon narrows to Hal's emergence as a 'true prince'. Rather than political history, Welles explores the psychology of the father–son triangulation, with Hal craving the affection of a surrogate father, Falstaff, who stands between him and the approval he seeks from the emotionally remote king, and eventually emerging unscathed by 'the two fathers who threaten to submerge his own unique identity, either through guilty rule or gilded license'.[25]

Welles is careful to avoid the backsliding in Hal's relationship with the king in *Part Two* that often puzzles those who expect narrative consistency with *Part One*, as if Hal had never redeemed himself on Percy's head and won the confidence of his father. Rather, he shapes their encounters in *Part One* to suggest that the king is unpersuaded by evidence of his son's sincerity: distant and cold at their meeting in 3.3, the king scarcely credits Hal's offer to engage Hotspur in single combat, and his expression of pleasure in his son's heroic resolve,

'A hundred thousand rebels die in this!' (3.2.160), is cut. Even more tellingly, Welles omits Hal's rescue of his father from Douglas at Shrewsbury, a rescue that in *Part One* redeems the prince's 'lost opinion' (5.4.47) and provides prime evidence of his loyalty to the king. Most significantly, in a tactical revision of *Part One* that allows the alienation between the prince and king to continue into *Part Two*, Falstaff claims to have killed Hotspur *while the king is present to hear him*. Believing that his son has falsely taken credit for defeating Hotspur, the king turns his back in disgust, obviating any possibility for protest from Hal.[26] The purpose of such textual manipulation is to postpone the reconciliation of father and son to the king's deathbed scene in *Part Two*; but it also allows Hal to prolong his decision to relinquish Falstaff as a surrogate father.

Hal signals his growing displeasure with Falstaff 'four times during the movie', according to Welles, each instance adding cumulative force to the final rejection.[27] The first time, Hal delivers his 'I know you all' soliloquy so that Falstaff can hear him, thus changing the dynamic between the two men (as the camera reveals in Falstaff's reaction to Hal's words) and anticipating the more explicit threat of banishment in the 'I do, I will' concluding the play extempore. The third time – notable because it was invented by Welles – occurs at Shrewsbury when, after the king has left in disgust, Falstaff attempts to placate Hal with the false bonhomie of his paean to sherris sack (transposed from 4.3). The prince, no longer amused by the corrupt knight who has severely discredited his rightful claim to

---

film was released in the United States as *Falstaff*. Welles's script, edited by Bridget Gellert Lyons, has been published as *Chimes at Midnight: Orson Welles, Director* (Rutgers, 1988).

25 Samuel Crowl, 'The Long Goodbye: Welles and Falstaff', *Shakespeare Quarterly*, 31 (1980), 372.

26 The device of having the king credit Falstaff, not his son, for Hotspur's defeat was borrowed by Michael Bogdanov for his English Shakespeare Company history cycle, denying *Part One* its customary resolution and signalling that a sequel in which the king and prince would reconcile was still to come.

27 See Hapgood, '*Chimes at Midnight*', p. 50; also Juan Cobos and Miguel Rubio, 'Welles and Falstaff', *Sight and Sound*, 35 (1966), 159.

chivalric rehabilitation in the eyes of his father, turns his back on Falstaff and walks away, casting aside the proffered cup as he goes. Thus, however one is encouraged to regard Welles's film as Falstaff's tragedy, with his stark final banishment and long, solitary exit followed by a poignant account of his death borrowed from *Henry V*,[28] ultimately Falstaff's fate is subsumed in Hal's coming-of-age story, just as it had been in Dering's abridgement, to clarify the play's focus on royal succession and what has to be sacrificed to maintain the order of state.

V. BARTON'S *WHEN THOU ART KING*

John Barton's adaptation of the two *Henry IV* plays, performed by the Royal Shakespeare Company as a Theatregoround production in 1969 and revived in 1970, was tellingly titled *When Thou Art King*.[29] Although it may have been inspired by Welles's film, released only four years earlier, it is in spirit much closer to Dering's abridgement. Barton divided *Henry IV* so that each part was given an act, though *Part One*'s act was significantly longer than that for *Part Two*.[30] Barton's rehearsal notes printed in the programme reveal how deeply indebted he was to the views of John Dover Wilson about the play as allegorical history:

Henry IV reflects the Morality school: enter at one door the young Prince Hal; at the other, the Reverend Vice Falstaff – the tempted and the tempter. It is a Catholic conflict: to achieve salvation you have to experience and overcome sin . . . Falstaff embodies every aspect and degree of Vanity. A self-indulgent whoremaster, a thief, a liar, a cutpurse, a cheat, a braggadocio, in love with himself and his own company, immensely and seductively attractive. If Hal can survive such a mountainous attack on the senses, then it is certain that Vanity will one day be outfaced.

Clearly, Barton's emphasis would fall on Hal's growth to moral maturity, signalled most potently by his rejection of Falstaff. As in the RSC history cycles wherein *Part One* was made to antici-

pate *Part Two*, such as the one Barton himself co-directed with Peter Hall in 1964, Barton insists that '[t]he rejection of Falstaff' in *When Thou Art King* is 'clearly provided for throughout'. Indeed, he argues, the rejection itself 'is not so surprising as the moderation of the sentence'; and to underscore the new king's moral maturity, he omits the lines in which the Lord Chief Justice commits Falstaff to the Fleet. 'Justice is done', Barton comments, 'but this time with humanity.'

To narrow the focus of his play to the royal *Bildungsroman*, Barton significantly curtails the scenes of rebellion in *Part One*, preserving only those portions involving Hotspur and Northumberland, whose father–son tensions parallel those between the king and the prince. He eliminates Worcester, Glendower, the scene in the Welsh camp and the scene with the Archbishop. He splices together portions of the rebels' scenes at Shrewsbury; eliminates all of the scene in which Worcester confronts the king and the prince except Falstaff's speech on honour, which is appended to an earlier scene (4.2); and merges the scenes remaining in Act 5 into one seamless denouement, with the deepest cuts coming in the rebels' dialogue. In fact,

---

28 Welles's 'overriding visual and structural emphasis . . . to signal farewell' to Falstaff has achieved iconic status. For the most articulate analysis of that cinematic emphasis, see Crowl, 'The Long Goodbye', pp. 369–80.

29 The programme for *When Thou Art King* when it was performed at the Roundhouse in London in 1970 explains the rationale for the RSC's Theatregoround productions. Based 'on the principle of the Elizabethan touring company which often used small casts and condensed texts', such productions were bare-bones, with minimalist sets and a heavy use of doubling. Thus they were economically viable to tour to regional theatres and other venues, schools and colleges as well as playing seasons as 'main house repertoire' in Stratford and London.

30 Each part was given a title: *Part One* was The Battle of Shrewsbury; *Part Two*, The Rejection of Falstaff. Eventually Barton added an act for *Henry V* as well, titled The Battle of Agincourt; but in any given performance only two acts were presented, and most often they were the two parts of *Henry IV*, the abridgement of *Henry V* having been drubbed by critics as no more than 'a brief précis . . . with all the best bits in' (B. A. Young, *Financial Times*, 17 July 1969).

Barton does not introduce the rebels until the play is well underway. Where, in Shakespeare's text, Northumberland, Worcester and Hotspur confront the king in Act 1, Barton postpones that confrontation until scene 6, nearly a third of the way into his abridgement of *Part One*. Prior to it, he signals his focus on the conflict between the king and the prince by having the play open with the king asking a question adapted from *Richard II*, 'Can no one tell me of my wayward son?',[31] which leads to an exchange where he contrasts his own prodigal Hal with the heroic Hotspur (adapted from *Part One*, 1.1.77–89). In this exchange, however, Barton substitutes for Westmoreland the Lord Chief Justice, who reports that the Sheriff has sent Hal and his companions to prison.

Barton then provides evidence of Hal's madcap youth never dramatized by Shakespeare. As he had done brilliantly in his adaptation of the *Henry VI* plays in 1963–4 titled *The Wars of the Roses*, for which he drew on various sources to insert pseudo-Shakespearian scenes of his own devising, Barton includes a legendary episode that was dramatized in a source play, *The Famous Victories of Henry the Fifth* (*c*.1588), but to which Shakespeare alludes only fleetingly in *Part Two*. When the Lord Chief Justice has arraigned Bardolph for a crime, Hal enters the chamber, demands Bardolph's release and, when the Lord Chief Justice refuses, strikes him 'on the cheek' (Shakespeare reports it as a 'box of th' ear', 1.2.188), for which he is committed to the Fleet. Following this, in a scene clearly inspired by Hal's play extempore with Falstaff, Francis the drawer and the newly freed Bardolph re-enact the arraignment in sport, with Francis taking the role of Bardolph and Bardolph the role of the Lord Chief Justice. This scene establishes a tone of comic anarchy in anticipation of the scene in which Falstaff asks Hal (now released from prison) what will happen 'when thou art king' (*Part One*, 1.2.22). In answer to that question, Hal's 'I know you all' soliloquy promises the reformation that, as Barton argues, is prepared for throughout the play.

If, in Barton's abridgement of *Part One*, the Northern rebellion is narrowed to a personal rivalry between Hal and Hotspur, rebellion is all but absent from his abridgement of *Part Two*. The scene of Northumberland's receiving news of Hotspur's death is drastically reduced, as is his scene with Lady Percy; and, as in Dering's *Henry IV*, the Prelate's rebellion is cut entirely: there is no aggrieved Archbishop, no royal double-cross at Gaultree. The effect of this abridgement is to tighten the dramatic focus on the contest between the king and Falstaff for Hal's soul – the son torn between two fathers, rather like an Everyman who is tugged by the forces of good and evil: the one father cold but politically astute, the other warm but morally corrupt.

Barton keeps enough material from the early scenes of *Part Two* to foreground Falstaff as the abstract of all sins: he cleverly splices together portions of the scenes in which Falstaff tries to borrow money from the Hostess and then from the Lord Chief Justice (whose role continues from the first act), and he leaves intact most of the long tavern scene in which Falstaff consorts with Doll Tearsheet and the Ancient Pistol. But the scenes at Justice Shallow's farm in Gloucestershire are eliminated, and with them, a more genially rounded portrait of Falstaff. Instead, Barton turns his gaze on the king's illness and his final reconciliation with the prince. In a conflation that harks back to Betterton's, Barton merges 3.1 – the king's soliloquy on sleep and subsequent musings on the state of the kingdom – with 4.3, in which the king asks, 'Where is the Prince, my son?' (an adaptation of 'Where is the Prince your brother?' at 4.3.13). The question is asked of the Lord Chief Justice, for Barton, intent on keeping his cast to a minimum, has eliminated the king's other sons, Clarence and Gloucester, and chosen to move quickly to the king's falling into a swoon, the entry of the prince and his exit with the crown. Some of the longer

---

[31] Quotations are from the promptbook for *When Thou Art King*, Shakespeare Centre Library, Stratford-upon-Avon. The king's actual line is 'Can no man tell me of my unthrifty son?' (5.3.1): Charles R. Forker, ed., *King Richard II* (London, 2002).

speeches in the tense confrontation of father and son are pared down, but the scene itself provides an emotional climax for the play. It marks Hal's ultimate choice to accept his father's mantle and to abjure his former life.

Barton compresses the final scenes to build up the significance of Hal's last encounter with Falstaff. Much of the ancillary material in Act 5 of *Part Two* is eliminated. Falstaff, presumably on his way north following the Battle of Shrewsbury, says to Bardolph 'we must a dozen miles tonight' (adapted from 3.2.278–9), then delivers a composite soliloquy that begins by paraphrasing the speech in which, in Shakespeare's original, he mocks the pretensions of Justice Shallow, but whose object of ridicule now is Bardolph, from whom he vows to 'devise matter to keep the Prince in continual laughter' (from 5.1.70–1). This speech segues into his unfavourable comparison of Prince John with Prince Hal (from 4.2.84–120), at which point Pistol enters with news of the king's death, and Falstaff proceeds to brag that 'the laws of England are at [his] commandment . . . and woe to my lord Chief Justice' (an adaptation of 5.3.82–135 which now excludes Shallow). In an ironic juxtaposition, Barton moves directly to a compression of two scenes: the first, in which the new king rewards the Lord Chief Justice for honourable service to his father; the second, in which he banishes Falstaff, the decisive event towards which the whole play, according to Barton, has tended.

While critics generally praised the 'coherence and drive' that Barton's adaptation gave to the saga of 'Hal's relationship with Falstaff and his education in the art of kingship' (Michael Billington, *The Times*, 4 November 1970), they also regretted the price that had to be paid to achieve such coherence. 'We need to see the circumstances, the concerns of society from which the Prince appears to escape,' complained Nicholas de Jongh (*The Guardian*, 4 November 1970): in particular, he lamented the simplification of political history and cultural contexts – 'the internal dissensions, the complex of dynastic disputes and the spectrum of life' – from which Hal would emerge as a popular but astute leader. This loss was most keenly felt in the abridge-

ment of *Part Two*, which, more than *Part One*, offers a 'panoramic vision of English society: thus we lose both the mellow comedy of Shallow and Silence and, at the other end of the scale, a crucial incident such as Prince John's betrayal of his pardon to the northern rebels. The latter is particularly significant since, without it, we never see in action the kind of treacherous political pragmatism that is no part of Hal's concept of kingship' (de Jongh). What Barton sacrifices in conceiving *When Thou Art King* as Hal's Morality play, therefore, is the subtle balance Shakespeare provides between humane governance and political expedience, between chronicle history and cultural memory.

VI. MATTHEWS'S *HENRY IV*

This tradition of sacrificing the peculiar merits of *Part Two* as social history to the interests of a coherent coming-of-age story was followed by Dakin Matthews in his popular adaptation of the two *Henry IV* plays. Matthews's 'compilation', as he calls it, was first workshopped at Julliard in 1972, just two years following the run of Barton's *When Thou Art King*. It was performed at the Goodman Theatre in Chicago in 1974; revised and performed again by the California Actors Theatre in 1980; further revised for performance by the Denver Center Theatre Company in 1990; re-adapted and lengthened for the 1995 season at the Old Globe in San Diego, where it was directed by Jack O'Brien; and reworked into its final form for the successful Lincoln Center production in 2003, directed by O'Brien and starring Kevin Kline as Falstaff. Since its 100 sold-out performances at Lincoln Center, Matthews's adaptation has achieved a popularity unprecedented among recent adaptations of Shakespeare – in part, I suspect, because the conflated text purports to *be* Shakespeare's *Henry IV*, its interpolations and manipulations largely unrecognized by critics; and in part because it allows audiences to get the whole royal history in one sitting, without theatre companies running the risk of staging the less popular *Part Two* at considerable financial loss, as was the case when the Shakespeare Theatre Company in Washington, DC, mounted both parts in 2004.[32] The economics of staging both parts as one play have proved especially attractive to regional theatres, among them the Pittsburgh Irish and Classical Theatre Company, which staged *Henry IV* in 2005, and the Seattle Shakespeare Company in 2008.

Like the Dering manuscript and subsequent conflations of the *Henry IV* plays, Matthews's adaptation draws more heavily from *Part One*. He divided the play into three acts – the first two compressing (though not drastically) material from *Part One*; the third and shortest telescoping events from the final two acts of *Part Two*. With a direct debt to Welles, whose prince signals displeasure with Falstaff at four key moments in the film, Matthews structured his adaptation to foreground the increasingly strained relationship between Prince Henry and Falstaff, pointing the way to Henry's rejection of Falstaff at the end of *Part Two* and thus, inevitably, focusing on the royal *Bildungsroman*. I quote Matthews (pp. 7–8):[33]

The three-act structure is mounted on the triple rejection of Falstaff, each rejection more serious and more painful for the Prince. The first occurs in jest – at the end of the extempore play in the first major tavern scene; it is the climactic moment of my Act One. The second, an intensely personal leave-taking, occurs on the battlefield of Shrewsbury, when the Prince discovers the body of Falstaff lying next to Hotspur's corpse; this farewell to an (apparently) dead comrade is the climax of my Act Two. The third rejection occurs right after the coronation, and is public, painful, and final. This is the climactic moment of my Act Three.

The first and third of these rejections, of course, are in the Shakespearian text. Matthews is disingenuous about the second, however. When he alludes to the prince's 'farewell' to an apparently dead Falstaff, he doesn't use the word 'rejection': the reason, I think, is that he wants to avoid drawing attention to lines he himself wrote for this scene in which Hal actually *does* reject Falstaff. In Shakespeare's text, when Falstaff comes back to life carrying with him the corpse of Hotspur, Hal's generous sanctioning of his behaviour is the last he speaks to Falstaff in *Part One*: 'Come, bring your luggage nobly on

your back. / For my part, if a lie may do thee grace / I'll gild it with the happiest terms I have' (5.4.156–8). Matthews keeps these lines, but then adds an exchange in which the prince, in exasperation, turns his back on Falstaff, as he does in *Chimes at Midnight* (p. 76):

Falstaff. Well, Hal – and shall we to the west together, to baste the devil Welshman with his own leeks?
Prince Henry. No. No, 'twere best to part; go then with my brother John; for heaven's witness, I have no care to fight with thee. Farewell.

These pseudo-Shakespearian lines explain Falstaff's appearance at Gaultree with Prince John's army in the final act and thus serve a function required by the conflation. But in them, Matthews also chooses to fabricate a repudiation of Falstaff totally unwarranted by the text of *Part One*, in which Hal's final words *grace* Falstaff's lies. Matthews thus works against the Shakespearian text to achieve the structural balance and thematic coherence he desires.

Like previous adapters, then, Matthews acknowledges that his primary intention is to 'tell of the transition of power from father to son', in which 'Hal is the real focus of the narrative' and for which *Part Two* is important largely because 'it ties up all the loose ends left dangling from the first play' (p. 5). Yet Matthews also admits that in abridging the plays he was loath to relinquish 'that handful of magnificent scenes from *Part Two*' (p. 7) – scenes not essential to the political plot – in which, for example, Lady Percy eulogizes Hotspur, Falstaff confronts the Lord Chief Justice and extols the virtues of alcohol, and Falstaff recruits soldiers in Gloucestershire. For most audiences,

---

[32] The productions were directed by former RSC associate Bill Alexander. In a Shakespearian irony, the role of the king was played by Keith Baxter, who forty years earlier had played the prince to John Gielgud's king in *Chimes at Midnight*. Despite being less popular than the better-known comedies and tragedies, Shakespeare's histories are now performed more frequently in regional theatres in North America than in the UK, probably because American companies can still afford the larger casts demanded by these plays.

[33] *William Shakespeare's Henry IV*, adapted for Lincoln Center Theater by Dakin Matthews (North Hollywood, 2003).

Matthews observes, 'all these would pass unseen and unheard into oblivion' (p. 7) – and so he chose to keep them, though in abbreviated form. However laudable his preservationist impulse may be, he does not preserve the scenes as Shakespeare wrote them. Instead, he picks and chooses parts of scenes – though less artfully than Welles had done – so that the resulting text plays like a 'greatest moments from *Henry IV*', fattening Falstaff's role but reducing the characters who surround him to mere caricatures. Mistress Quickly, Doll Tearsheet, Bardolph, Ancient Pistol and Justices Shallow and Silence, who in the full text of *Part Two* create a rich alternative world to that of the court, are robbed of life – and most of their lines – in Matthews's adaptation.

Let me illustrate how Matthews grafts some of the best material from the first three acts of *Part Two* onto scenes in *Part One*. To the lively tavern scene early in Matthews's second act (taken from *Part One*, 3.3) – on the eve of the march to Shrewsbury – he transfers a lot of material from the long tavern scene in *Part Two* (2.4). Falstaff's banter with Pistol and Bardolph, his being overheard and called to account by Hal and Poins disguised as drawers, and his affectionate farewell to his favourite whore Doll are all interpolations from the later play. Mistress Quickly's comic complaint about Falstaff's promise to marry her is interpolated from an earlier scene in *Part Two* (2.1). By grafting this material onto the tavern scene from *Part One*, Matthews argues that he saves colourful characters and unmatchable dialogue that otherwise would have been sacrificed. Yet the effect is not, as it is in the full text of *Part Two*, to dramatize the stories of marginalized people who had no voice in the writing of 'official' history. Instead, the interpolations succeed only in beefing up the role of Falstaff as a great comic adversary for Hal, much as Orson Welles foregrounded Falstaff by diminishing the roles of everyone around him.

The same thing happens two scenes later when Matthews, like Welles, preserves another scene from *Part Two* in which Falstaff arrives at the Gloucestershire farm of Justice Shallow to recruit soldiers. To a degree, his decision to relocate this scene from *Part Two* as a prelude to the Battle of Shrewsbury makes sense, for by doing so he is quite possibly returning it to its original place in the narrative structure of *Part One*. The scene's placement in *Part Two* is problematic because, since Falstaff has been sent north from London to Yorkshire with Prince John's army, it isn't logical for him to recruit soldiers in Gloucestershire, which lies considerably to the *west* of London. It would be perfectly reasonable, though, for him to pass through Gloucestershire on his way to Shrewsbury. One could reasonably speculate that Shakespeare wrote the scene to occur before the Battle of Shrewsbury but, when the original *Henry IV* play grew unwieldy, decided to replace it with a soliloquy in which Falstaff simply confesses that he has 'misused the King's press damnably' (*Part One*, 4.2.12–13); and that he resurrected the scene when he was looking for new comic material to flesh out the sequel but, in an oversight, forgot to change its location.[34]

Matthews thus may have had some justification for preserving and transposing the recruitment scene, yet he ransacked it in much the same way he ransacked the tavern scene in *Part Two* – for good bits to flesh out Falstaff's role. He radically reduces the conversation between Justices Shallow and Silence about country life and Shallow's years at the Inns of Court, and the ragtag recruits from whom Falstaff must choose – each brilliantly individualized by Shakespeare – are seen but not heard. In sum, the scene is shorn of the details of quotidian life which help to imprint the Gloucestershire idyll so indelibly in the memory. Instead, Matthews moves quickly to Falstaff's acceptance of bribes from the two recruits who can afford to buy out their service (bribes dramatized in the full text,

---

[34] In *Part Two*, Gloucestershire is not identified as the site of Shallow's farm until 4.2.79, possibly owing to Shakespeare's having placed Shallow there in *Merry Wives*, whose writing, some scholars argue, interrupted his work on *Part Two*. Thus it is conceivable that the recruiting scene in 3.2 was written for a location closer to Lincolnshire. But apart from the reference to Stamford Fair, most of the places mentioned by Shallow are in or near the Cotswolds, not Lincolnshire, making Gloucestershire the more likely site of Shallow's farm from the outset.

but here, as in *Chimes at Midnight*, only reported by Bardolph) and to his settling for the least likely recruits instead ('food for powder'). Moreover, as a coda to this action, when Shallow and the others have exited, Falstaff delivers a portion of the soliloquy from *Part One* in which he confesses that he has misused the king's press, something Matthews has just *dramatized*: first he shows, then he tells. Although there is little logic in this redundancy, Matthews clearly wants the play to be about Falstaff, and that he succeeded in making it so is amply evident in the enthusiastic critical response to Kevin Kline's performance at Lincoln Center. Yet like a new historicist, he also wants to contain Falstaff's anarchic energies within the bounds of the narrative of Hal's reformation. In a sense, then, the fattening of Falstaff's role at the expense of everyone else's makes him a more formidable influence on Hal, and this heightens the significance of Hal's repeated rejection of him — the structural premise of the whole adaptation.

Matthews's conflation of the two parts of *Henry IV*, then, is consistent with the conception of these plays as part of a grand history cycle that emerged more than a half century ago. It is a text bent on foregrounding the royal narrative and suppressing those other narratives — those of the tavern low-lifes, the country justices and recruits — that have the potential to subvert the 'official' version of events: a potential which, in the last thirty years, has made *Part Two* speak as very much a play for our time. My concern is that the popularity of Matthews's conflated text, and its attractiveness to North American theatre companies reluctant to take the financial risk of staging the two parts of *Henry IV* in their entirety, have diminished the number of productions of *Part Two* that companies have been willing to undertake, substituting for it a royalist and ideologically conservative version of *Henry IV* just at a time when audiences have themselves been in conservative retreat. Today, when staging *Part Two* as an anti-masque to *Part One* — as a study of political opportunism and how history is constructed by those in power — could have a cautionary influence on audiences who have grown cynical about government, Matthews's conflated text may have the effect (as Hal has on those former companions who, by his order, wind up in the Fleet) of silencing the voices of opposition in *Part Two*.

MEDLEY HISTORY: *THE FAMOUS VICTORIES OF HENRY THE FIFTH TO HENRY V*

JANET CLARE

More than any other playwright of the period, Shakespeare dramatized English history and in so doing experimented with different ways of representing the past. Within as well as between the tetralogies of pre-Tudor history, spanning at least a decade of composition, there are quite evident differences in style and form. The Henry VI plays, largely dependent on the chronicle of Hall and those compiled by Holinshed, have been appositely labelled 'heroical histories':[1] an epithet which is equally applicable to the Agincourt scenes of *Henry V* and the 'patriotic triumphalism' of the play's Chorus.[2] *Richard II*, with its Marlovian tragic influence, and specifically that of *Edward II*, is written almost entirely in verse, and the only popular voices in the play are the royal gardeners, who comment on, but do not influence, the action of the play. In contrast, *1 and 2 Henry IV* mark a radical departure in the composition of the history play. The advertisements on the title-pages of the quartos remind readers of what they would have seen on the stage, namely the dramatic interplay of the heroic, the dynastic and the comic encapsulated in allusions to the Battle of Shrewsbury, the coronation of Henry V and the 'humorous conceits' or 'humours' of Falstaff. Similarly, the title-page of the 1600 quarto of *Henry V* advertises the Battle of Agincourt and the conceits of Ancient Pistol. In the co-existence of the comic and the serious there is a recuperation of pre-Marlovian drama or that of Marlowe himself before the publisher Richard Jones had expunged the indecorous comedy which he had deemed unfit for the weighty tragedy of the two parts of *Tamburlaine*.[3] It is the purpose of this article to consider the stimuli for the composition of such 'medley history' and to recover something of the reception of Shakespeare's last Elizabethan history plays in the light of the popular *Famous Victories of Henry the Fifth*, to which they are clearly indebted.

The conventional defence of the history play, that it served collective memory in representing the nation's heroic past, was famously articulated by Thomas Nashe:

First, for the subject of them (for the most part) it is borrowed out of our English Chronicles, wherein our forefathers valiant acts (that have lain long buried in rusty brass and worm-eaten books) are revived, and they themselves raised from the Grave of Oblivion, and brought to plead their aged Honours in open presence . . . How would it have joyed brave Talbot (the terror of the French) to think that after he had lain two hundred years in his tomb, he should triumph again on the stage, and have his bones new embalmed with the tears of ten thousand spectators at least (at several times), who, in the Tragedian that represents his person, imagine they behold him fresh bleeding.[4]

---

[1] See David Riggs, *Shakespeare's Heroical Histories: Henry VI and its Literary Tradition* (Cambridge, MA, 1971).

[2] *King Henry V*, ed. Andrew Gurr, updated edition (Cambridge, 2005), p. 2.

[3] 'To the Gentlemen Readers: and Others that Take Pleasure in Reading Histories', *Tamburlaine the Great* (1590). See Kirk Melnikoff, 'Jones's Pen and Marlowe's Socks: Richard Jones, Print Culture, and the Beginnings of English Dramatic Literature', *Studies in Philology*, 101 (2005), 184–209; pp. 205–9.

[4] *The Works of Thomas Nashe*, ed. R. B. McKerrow, 5 vols. (Oxford, 1958; revised edition, 1966), vol. I, p. 212.

Theatre revives history's valiant acts. The open presence of Talbot, so feared by the French, and the number of spectators witnessing his death simulated in *1 Henry VI* give to the play greater significance than the chronicle in fashioning memory. Over a decade later Thomas Heywood produced a similar argument.[5] Such an interpretation, however, is hardly apposite to plays where clowning and tavern scenes occupy more theatrical time than heroic action. In *1* and *2 Henry IV* it is the dominant presence of an Elizabethan underclass, which refuses to be marginalized, that creates a rupture of theatre and chronicle. Whereas in *Richard II* the gardeners are conservative and loyal as they elaborate on the topos of commonwealth and garden, the underclass of *1* and *2 Henry IV* and *Henry V* appear in scenes that barely mask a pragmatic self-interest, that is, before they are pushed aside in the interests of royal authority.

In their diminishing reliance on chronicle material and in their generic hybridity *1* and *2 Henry IV* and *Henry V* are experimental in terms of both dramaturgy and historiography. Yet the plays are backward looking in so far as their generic inclusivity harks back to the influence of the Queen's Men and what the authors of a study of their plays aptly term a 'medley' style of theatre.[6] Why should such an apparently outmoded formula for the history play be adopted or at least reinvented at this stage in Shakespeare's career? We can speculate on the pressures that may have dictated a new redaction of history or more precisely a return to the very beginnings of the English history play. It is entirely feasible to suggest that the problems encountered through the censorship of *Richard II*[7] determined the production of a history that laid claim to be as much a fictive comedy as a political play. In *Richard II* Shakespeare had confronted the highly contentious subject of rebellion against a weak and unjust ruler, leading to his deposition. The play was censored, an experience that can hardly have failed to affect the composition of subsequent history plays. One evident way of diverting the attentions of a stage or press licenser was by diluting the political content of a history with the 'humours' of an invented character.

If some such consideration lay behind the diminution of history in *1* and *2 Henry IV*, equally significant is the stimulation of theatrical pre-text, that of *The Famous Victories of Henry V*, a play usually considered to be the first extant chronicle history.[8] The play is of uncertain authorship[9] and is known to have been performed by the Queen's Men at the Bull in Bishopsgate before 1588, the year of the death of the popular comic actor Richard Tarlton.[10] In a collection of anecdotes affectionately commemorating Tarlton, the compiler recalls a performance of a scene in *The Famous Victories* when Tarlton, obliged to double as clown and as the justice, was given a blow on the ear by the prince. According to the report, Tarlton, in the part of the clown, extemporized in the course of a dialogue in which he detached himself from his part and alluded to his cheeks as still burning from the prince's blow, and this was much enjoyed by the crowd. The story in Tarlton's *Jests*, not published until 1611, is indicative of how *The Famous Victories* was not only a vehicle for the talents of Tarlton in the role of the clown

---

5 Thomas Heywood, *An Apology for Actors* (1612), B4r.

6 Scott McMillin and Sally-Beth MacLean, *The Queen's Men and Their Plays* (Cambridge, 1998), pp. 124–7.

7 Andrew Gurr, writing of the patriotic appeal in 1599 of the battles and victories of Henry V, observes that Shakespeare was on much safer ground than he had been with the preceding plays, see *Henry V*, p. 16. *1* and *2 Henry IV* were not, however, immune from censorship: lines relating to the rebellions against Henry IV appear to have been cut, see Janet Clare, '*Art made tongue-tied by authority*': *Elizabethan and Jacobean Censorship* (Manchester, 1990), pp. 68–70.

8 McMillin and MacLean state: 'Among the commercial companies, it is possible to think that the Queen's Men invented the English history play. No example from the professional theatre can be dated earlier than *The Famous Victories of Henry V* on the basis of factual evidence': *The Queen's Men and their Plays*, p. 167.

9 Philip Brockbank has suggested that the play was written by Robert Greene, which would help to account for Greene's jibe against Shakespeare: Shakespeare's Henry VI plays had rivalled *The Famous Victories*. See 'Shakespeare: His Histories, English and Roman', in *English Drama to 1700*, ed. Christopher Ricks (London, 1971), pp. 166–99; p. 168.

10 For a discussion of Tarlton's acting and stage persona, see David Wiles, *Shakespeare's Clown: Actor and Text in the Elizabethan Playhouse* (Cambridge, 1987), pp. 11–23.

Derrick but an indication of how he had helped to perpetuate the play in theatrical memory. 'To this day', adds the compiler of the *Jests*, 'I have heard it commended for rare, but no marvele for he had many of these.'[11] Clearly the play continued to exert appeal: it was reprinted in 1617 and, if the attribution on the title-page is to be credited it had become the property of the King's Men.[12]

As the dramatic pre-text to three of Shakespeare's histories, *1* and *2 Henry IV* and *Henry V*, memories of the performance and publication of *The Famous Victories* initiated a dialogue about ways of recreating and representing the past quite distinctive from earlier heroical history. The argument, as with the chronology of the composition of Shakespeare's English histories, might seem a little back to front. By the time Shakespeare was working on the *Henry IV* plays, *The Famous Victories*, the property of an obsolete theatre company, would surely have appeared old-fashioned, a hymn to a kind of actors' theatre that had been overtaken by the work of more literary professional playwrights. Yet, this appears not to have been the case in the mid 1590s. As has been said, the part played by Tarlton enlivened memories of *The Famous Victories*, much as Falstaff's presence did for *1* and *2 Henry IV*. The use of *The Famous Victories* as pre-text for plays of the second tetralogy can be traced to the vagaries of publication history when in May 1594 Thomas Creede, who was to publish Shakespeare's *Henry V*, entered *The Famous Victories* into the Stationers' Register. As amongst the first plays from the adult professional companies to reach print, there must have been considerable interest in the plays of the Queen's Men from theatre personnel as an experiment in the transition from stage to print.[13] Although the play had reached the publishing industry by 1594, the earliest known edition is that of 1598, the same year as the publication of *1 Henry IV*. That Shakespeare was not relying entirely on theatrical memory, either personal or collective, but on some closer acquaintance with the text of *The Famous Victories* is suggested by verbal resonance, heard in the scene of the death of Henry IV, and the repetition of formal structures in *1* and *2 Henry IV*. The 1594 Stationers' Register

entry indicates that a manuscript of *The Famous Victories* good enough to serve as a copy text of the play was in circulation, and we can assume that, through the connection with Creede, Shakespeare had access to it. Giorgio Melchiori has suggested that it was Shakespeare and the Chamberlain's Men who were the stimulus for the publication of *The Famous Victories*. He speculates that there was no decent text available in 1594 and so the company were induced to hand in a 'wretched summary reconstruction only in 1598, to cash in on the current success of the Shakespearean Henry plays that the Chamberlain's Men had started staging at the time'.[14] But we do not need such an elaborate hypothesis. Creede entered *The Scottish History of James IV* on the same day as *The Famous Victories* and that too was only published in 1598. The quality of the text of *The Famous Victories* is poor, in the main because prose is printed as verse, but, in general, its alleged defects are characteristic of the published plays of the Queen's Men and early ventures such as this one in the translation of a stage text to a literary one.

The Famous Victories trades on anecdotes and folkloric material about the early life of Henry V and in this sense the play's title is misleading. The opening scene boldly defies any audience expectations of a play about the nation's heroic past as embodied in one of its most martial kings. For,

---

[11] *Tarleton's Jests and New out of Purgatory: with notes and some account of the life of Tarleton* by James Orchard Halliwell (London, 1844), pp. 24–5.

[12] There is some scholarly disagreement here. See Andrew Gurr, *The Shakespeare Company* (Cambridge, 2004), p. 125, and Roslyn Lander Knutson, *The Repertory of Shakespeare's Company 1594–1613* (Fayetteville, 1991), p. 212.

[13] The text is unusually printed in black letter, used for the Bible, chronicles, jest books, ballads and news pamphlets. Chiaki Hanabusa observes that Creede's choice of black letter acknowledged the popular character of *The Famous Victories*. See *The Famous Victories of Henry the Fifth 1598*, The Malone Society Reprints, prepared by Chiaki Hanabusa (2007), p. xv.

[14] *The Second Part of King Henry IV*, updated version, ed. Giorgio Melchiori (Oxford, 2007), p. 8. See also *The First Part of King Henry IV*, ed. A. R. Humphreys (London 1961), p. xxxvi, and *The First Part of King Henry IV*, ed. Herbert and Judith Weil (Cambridge, 1997), p. 25.

although referred to as Henry V in the speech prefixes throughout the text, Henry is only king for about half of it: in the early scenes he occupies still the role of a dissolute prince in waiting. His lines in the opening scene, as he addresses his companions, Ned and Tom, announce him a thief: 'Tell me, sirs, think you not that it was a villainous part of me to rob my Father's receivers?' and with Ned, Tom and Sir John Oldcastle (referred to as Jockey) he proposes celebrating his ill-gotten gains in the old tavern at Eastcheap. As is well known, when composing the *Henry IV* plays Shakespeare took over the name Oldcastle from *The Famous Victories* and loosely modelled Hal's drinking companion and surrogate father on the character in *The Famous Victories*.[15] Oldcastle's nickname Jockey is a diminutive or familiar form of John, but it also carries associations of craft and fraudulence, characteristics attributed to a horse dealer, which are played upon in the Oldcastle of *The Famous Victories* and, although without the name prompt, carried over to Falstaff. Such an ignoble stage representation of a Lollard martyr celebrated by John Foxe was apparently judged slanderous by Oldcastle's descendants and at some stage in the play's performance history, though apparently after stage licensing, the character was renamed Falstaff.[16] It is interesting that no such pressures were brought to bear on *The Famous Victories* where the name of Oldcastle remains in the text. This may simply be because Oldcastle is usually referred to as 'Jockey' and so the revered family name does not resonate much on stage or in the text. Neither is Oldcastle so prominent a character as Falstaff. When he rejects his former companions, it is Tom and not Oldcastle whom Henry addresses specifically. But as with most cases of early modern censorship, the censorship of *1 Henry IV* is very much tied to the moment of production: William Brooke, Lord Cobham, Oldcastle's descendant, was Lord Chamberlain for eight months from August 1596, while the play was enjoying great success. *The Famous Victories*, on the other hand, would have been licensed and performed a decade earlier and once licensed for performance did not, in this period, need to be re-licensed for publication.

A refrain in the scenes between the prince and his companions alludes to their common expectations in lawless pleasure at the accession of Henry V. In a parodic version of social levelling, the prince promises his companions that they would all be kings if the old king were dead. The prince does not hide his longing for power and 'When my father is dead' is repeatedly held out as a prospective ushering in of a new anarchic commonwealth. Even as he leaves for the court to attend his dying father, the prince anticipates eagerly his new authority: 'for the breath shall be no sooner out of his mouth, but I will clap the crown on my head' (v. 34–5). An intent which is half realized in the prince's taking of the crown before the breath is out of his father's body. There is little of a prince in the Henry of *The Famous Victories*. Robert Weimann's comment on one of the scenes in *The Famous Victories* that 'princely prerogative is played out from a complementary and thoroughly plebeian point of view', would seem to be apt for all of the first half of *The Famous Victories*.[17] Henry is not a prince playing a commoner; he is a commoner playing the prince, which accords with the idea of the Queen's Men as an actors' theatre. Just as Tarleton was identified with Derrick, John Knell was known as the actor who played the prince.

With only passing reference to the reprobate behaviour of the king's son in the chronicles, *The Famous Victories* clearly offered a model for the Hal of *1 and 2 Henry IV*. The subversive, bold opening of *The Famous Victories*, with the heir to the throne exulting in robbery, makes its mark on the second scene of *1 Henry IV* located in the tavern.

---

[15] See *The Oldcastle Controversy: Sir John Oldcastle, Part I and The Famous Victories of Henry V*, ed. Peter Corbin and Douglas Sedge (Manchester, 1991), pp. 9–12. All quotations are from this edition.

[16] See Clare, '*Art made tongue-tied by authority*', pp. 76–9; *The Oldcastle Controversy*, pp. 9–12; David McKeen, *A Memory of Honour: The Life of William Brooke, Lord Cobham*, 2 vols. (Salzburg, 1986); and Gary Taylor, 'The Fortunes of Oldcastle', *Shakespeare Survey 38* (Cambridge, 1985), 85–100.

[17] Robert Weimann, *Shakespeare and the Popular Tradition in the Theater: Studies in the Social Dimension of Dramatic Form and Function* (Baltimore and London, 1978), p. 188.

The verbal recall of *The Famous Victories* is clear in Falstaff's wheedling dialogue with Hal: 'Marry, then, sweet wag, when thou art king, let not us that are squires of the night's body be called thieves of the day's beauty' (1.2.23–5). There is a crucial difference, of course, in that it is only Falstaff who projects into the reign of Henry V such inversions of order. The shift from the refrain of 'when I am king' of *The Famous Victories* to the 'when thou art king' of *1 Henry IV* is decisive and telling. Similarly, when there is talk of robbery on Gadshill, this is projected and not, as in *The Famous Victories*, accomplished, nor will Hal be complicit: 'Who, I rob? I a thief? Not I, by my faith' (1.2.136). This departure of text and pre-text does not signify a less lawless prince in *1 Henry IV* but a more complex or devious one. As Hal and Poins devise the plan of setting on Falstaff and Bardolph and taking the booty they have stolen from the defenceless pilgrims, Hal takes a vicarious enjoyment in the robbery. Thievery is turned to jest: 'The thieves have bound the true men; now could thou and I rob the thieves, and go merrily to London. It would be argument for a week, laughter for a month, and a good jest for ever' (2.3.1–4). The prince's involvement in criminal activity is one stage removed, not as in *The Famous Victories*, and so he cannot be indicted in the manner of his counterpart in the pre-text. The difference is that Hal in *1 Henry IV* is willing to take pleasure in the subordination of order and yet cunning enough to avoid directly inculpating himself.

The carnivalesque element of *The Famous Victories* is exemplified in the prince's challenge to the authority of the Lord Chief Justice. The prince is no sooner released from the Counter following the drunken brawl in Eastcheap than he is again threatening authority. One of his servants is in custody for the robbing of the clown Derrick on Gad's Hill. The prince, incensed, demands his servant's release and when the justice refuses thus to contravene the law the prince gives him a blow on the ear. This famous episode was recounted by Thomas Elyot in *The Book named the Governor*[18] and re-narrated at the beginning of the account of the reign in Stow's *Annals* with significant changes. In Elyot's

relation of the story, it is given an exemplary reading; when faced with the determination of the Chief Justice to correct him, the prince recognizes the error of his ways and, according to Elyot, by allowing reason to overcome anger, illustrates the virtue of 'placability'. Stow's marginalia indicate that he took the incident from Elyot, yet he modifies the detail.[19] In this version there is no boxing of the Lord Chief Justice's ears, although Stow reports that the prince's threats were such that onlookers thought the prince would slay the judge. Again, the Chief Justice's steadfastness moves the Prince, who feels compelled to lay aside his weapons and goes 'to the king's bench as he was commanded'. Stow, like Elyot, extracts a moral from the encounter which demonstrates a judge not fearing to execute justice, a prince who reconsiders his corrupt example and a father who rejoices at the conduct of the judge and repentance of the son. As if in confrontation with such pious interpretations, *The Famous Victories* represents the scene without any such moral resolution. The prince is unrepentant in a vociferous exchange with the Chief Justice, during which Ned intervenes demanding to cut off the justice's head. While such extravagant threats provide comic theatre, the subsequent action of the king in ordering his son's release exposes the subordination of the law. The message is unequivocal: there is one law for the powerful, another for the powerless: the king is a law unto himself.

Curiously Shakespeare makes little use of this particular confrontation of judge and prince, although he evidently relied on his audience's familiarity with the earlier play. The crucial encounter of prince and Chief Justice comes at the end of *2 Henry IV* and the meeting is manipulated as part of Hal's public transformation. In *1* and *2 Henry IV* it is Falstaff, and not the prince, who is the Lord Chief Justice's adversary, again indicating Hal's more marginal involvement with

[18] See Sir Thomas Elyot, *The Governor*, ed. S. E. Lehmberg (London, 1962), p. 114.
[19] J. Stow, *The Annales of England, faithfully collected out of the most autenticall Authors, Records, and other Monuments of Antiquitie* (1592), pp. 547–8.

the lawless activities of his companions. Following the announcement of the king's death, the Chief Justice receives the condolences of Warwick and the younger sons of Henry IV. Against his better judgement, Clarence advises the judge that he must now be friends with Falstaff if he is to prosper at all under the incoming regime. When the new king enters he reminds the Lord Chief Justice of the hitherto unheard of 'indignities' he has suffered at his orders: 'What – rate, rebuke, and roughly send to prison / Th'immediate heir of England?' (5.2.69–70). As in Elyot and Stow, the Chief Justice defends his action; whereupon Henry V, without indicating whether he is swayed by the judge's persuasive words or by political necessity, confirms him in his office. In doing so, he prepares the way, through his use of filial imagery, for the banishment of Falstaff, that other father-substitute. This neat patterning is Shakespeare's and as such characteristic.

In both plays the suddenness – at least in public – of the prince's transformation puts his credibility at stake. In *The Famous Victories*, the prince's dramatic credibility might also be at stake for there has been no hint of an imminent reformation. As Henry V, he must convince his father, his subjects, foreign foes and the audience that his reformation is real, allowing a new and convincing character to emerge. There are two roles and two characters in one, the prince and the king, and little room to elaborate movement psychologically from one to the other. Yet the play effectively communicates that Henry has changed. This is done simply by a series of statements. He tells his dying father 'And no doubt but this day, even this day, I am born new again' (vi. 37–8) and his father prophesies that he will be 'as valiant and victorious a King as ever reigned in England' (viii. 4–5). Henry admonishes his former associates, who accuse him of feigning grief at his father's death, 'Thou say'st I am changed; so I am indeed, and so must thou be, and that quickly, or else I must cause thee to be changed' (ix. 39–41). There is no acknowledgement that he has strung these men along. One moment Oldcastle comments on Hal's god-like identity at his coronation, the next the king tells

him and his companions that he has abandoned them and abolished their company forever. Without pause for thought, Henry begins to fulfil his dying father's prophecy. Within the same speech he banishes Jockey and Tom and turning to the Archbishop of Canterbury, announces that he has 'other matters to talk on' and then consults about the legality of the French war. Henry V's promotion of the Lord Chief Justice to the role of Protector, ordering him to govern during his absence in France, is illustrative of the change in style accorded to him on his accession: 'Tut. my lord! you are not unworthy, Because I think you worthy; for you, that would not spare me, I think will not spare another' (ix. 149–50). Here, every word that the king utters impresses on the audience that he is not the feckless prince of old. The prince's sudden change in *The Famous Victories*, with its popular impulse, may be seen simply as the effect of moving from relative impotence to a position of immense power, and this would accord with the play's popular emphasis and perspective on power from below.

The prince's conversion is intimately bound up with his emergence as a patriotic, martial ruler. Seen thus, to speculate that *The Famous Victories* was originally a two-part play[20] does not make dramaturgic sense in the way it does for *The Troublesome Reign of King John*. It is the broad historic sweep of *The Famous Victories*, rather than any sense of interior revelation, that gives theatrical integrity to the play and coherence to Henry. His career as reprobate prince and victorious monarch is represented in bold and continuous outline and within the same frame; the conversion from one to the other mediated, clearly and simply, by the death of his father.

The shifts in emphases and transcodifications of *1* and *2 Henry IV* are illustrative of different dramaturgic practices and the plays strive for different theatrical effect. Shakespeare appropriates the up-front criminality of the prince and his tavern

---

[20] First suggested by John Dover Wilson, 'The Origin and Development of Shakespeare's *Henry IV*', *The Library*, 4th series, 24 (1945), 2–6. See also Melchiori, *The Second Part of Henry IV*, pp. 8–9.

associates of *The Famous Victories* and infuses into it the ruthlessness and manipulations of *realpolitik*. From the very beginning of *1 Henry IV* and the soliloquy of Act 1 ('I know you all...' 1.2.192), we know what Hal's strategy is and how, in manipulating his image, he is using Falstaff as much as Falstaff hopes to use him. Hal is confidential about his duplicity; he will use these commoners and Falstaff until such a moment as he will discard them, the more to impress the world by his reformation. We are always aware with Hal, as with his later incarnation as Henry V, of the public persona and of another that lies behind the mask. Hal understands the exigencies that attend or will attend the exercise of power and manipulates the rituals and exploits accordingly the masks of public life. In this sense, the power-hungry prince of *The Famous Victories* offers a stimulus for Shakespeare's more expressly calculating Hal in both *Henry IV* and in *Henry V*, even though his roles as king in waiting and king are so different.

There is, however, another way of looking at the changed perspective other than in demonstrating Hal's evident political guile. An audience with expectations based on the legacy of *The Famous Victories* would be prepared for Hal's reformation; but, once such a pivotal scene had been integrated into the dynamics of one play, *The Famous Victories*, it could hardly be replicated with the same effectiveness in another. Henry's apparently unpremeditated reformation in the presence of his dying father and, after the king's death, the dismissal of his old companions have a more immediate impact in *The Famous Victories* than in *2 Henry IV*, startling both on- and off-stage audiences. Audiences watching the latter play, through recall of *The Famous Victories* or of Hal's soliloquy in *1 Henry IV*, anticipate the transformation in Hal. In *2 Henry IV* dramatic interest lies in how the promised reformation will be effected and in the ironic discrepancy between Falstaff's expectations of reward, fully articulated in the Gloucestershire scenes, and Hal's planned rejection of Falstaff signalled in the confirmation of the Lord Chief Justice in his office.

It has been said of the plays of the Queen's Men that what is missing entirely is 'poetry capable of expressing the pressures of realistic psychological experience'.[21] This is well demonstrated when scenes of *The Famous Victories* are compared with the involved and psychologically complex dialogue of *2 Henry IV*. What *The Famous Victories* might lack in verbal sophistication is strongly compensated for by moments of visual effectiveness. Representing an account in Stow's *Annals*, the prince goes to the court wearing a cloak 'full of needles' and carrying a dagger. Face to face with his son, the king tearfully rebukes him, alluding to his costume as typifying the prince's feelings towards him:

Aye so, so, my son, thou fearest not to approach the presence of thy sick father in that disguised sort. I tell thee my son, that there is never a needle in thy cloak but it is a prick to my heart, and never an eyelet hole but it is a hole to my soul; and wherefore thou bringest the dagger in thy hand I know not, but by conjecture.

[*He weeps*] (vi. 5–10)

Apart from the striking visual effect, why the prince appears thus before his father is not entirely clear. Before he goes to court, he offers Tom some specious reasoning: 'Why, man, 'tis a sign that I stand upon thorns, till the crown be on my head' (v. 40–1). This is consonant with all that the prince has held out for the future once he becomes king, although it does undermine the credibility of his reformation. The *Henry IV* plays refuse to go along with this conception of two roles in one character; despite the apparent change from prince to king, the playing out in public of his reformation, Hal's character is entirely consistent. Throughout the trilogy he is self-aware and self-questioning. It is evident that Hal is consciously acting out the role he chooses for himself while, later, he performs the role chosen for him. This contrasts with the Henry V of the pre-text who never reveals his plans to the audience; the audience accepts the two images of dissolute prince and martial king with little mediation. Dramaturgically, though, the scene in *The Famous Victories* between repentant son and dying father makes complete sense. In

---

[21] McMillin and MacLean, *The Queen's Men and Their Plays*, p. 145.

the surrender of his dagger to the king and in the removal of the coat of needles, the scene produces effective symbolic theatre. The prince's acts signify absolute reformation. No stage directions are necessary, as in the prince's lines visual and verbal imagery coalesce: 'this ruffianly cloak I here tear from my back, and sacrifice it to the devil, which is master of all mischief' (vi. 24–5). This arresting stage imagery is effectively translated into verbal imagery in *2 Henry IV*. In the meeting of king and heir, the visual imagery of weaponry is completely abandoned as the king accuses his son of hiding a thousand daggers in his thoughts and whetting them on his stony heart. The visual image has been internalized and reproduced in the shape of an elaborate metaphor. Emblematic morality drama has been displaced by a fraught humanized exchange.

The resonances of pre-text and text in the scene of the king's death are remarkable, demonstrating how affective theatrical moments are transmitted from one play and playgoing experience to another. Power is symbolically transferred from father to son as the old king accepts his son's reformation. In *2 Henry IV* the solemnity and intimacy of the scene of *The Famous Victories* are recreated in the same mould of confessional impulse and affirmation of kinship. But, as we have seen, in *The Famous Victories* the reformation of the prince is sudden and apparently unpremeditated, and the attendant reconciliation with his father is brought about with less of the anguish, distrust and final uncertainty that accompany the scene in *2 Henry IV*. Both plays make effective spectacle from the anecdote, briefly reported in Holinshed, recounting the prince's stealing of the crown from his father's pillow. It is this act in *The Famous Victories* which undermines the dying king's confidence in his son established by the prince's previous act of surrendering cloak and dagger. There is the same structure in *2 Henry IV* as Hal convinces his father that he has changed and then, after removing the crown from his father's pillow and arousing afresh his father's suspicions, has to restore his father's belief in his reformation. The deathbed scene in *The Famous Victories* lacks the involved and com-

plex emotions conveyed in the dialogue of the scene's counterpart in *2 Henry IV*, and yet expressively the scenes are the same. There is a simple directness in the king's accusation in *The Famous Victories*:

Why how now, my son? I had thought the last time I had you in schooling I had given you a lesson for all; and do you now begin again? Why, tell me, my son, dost thou think the time so long that thou wouldest have it before the breath be out of my mouth?   (viii. 35–8)

The idea here of a pattern of reformation and lapse is one which is considerably enlarged and interred in the structure of *1 and 2 Henry IV*. This produces dramaturgical problems as the prince, after convincing his father of loyalty after Shrewsbury, has to convince him anew in the second play that he is fit to govern.[22] In words which are appropriated in *2 Henry IV*, the king alludes to his acquisition of the crown: 'For God knows my son, how hardly I came by it, and how hardly I have maintained it' (viii. 56–7), prompting the prince to profess loyalty to father and crown in words that, again, resonate in *2 Henry IV*. Henry IV's maintenance of the crown, so pervasive a theme in *1 and 2 Henry IV*, is of marginal significance in *The Famous Victories*. The 'hardly' maintained crown in the above lines can be seen as a prompt for the king's weary comment on the crown 'how troublesome it sat upon my head' (*2 Henry IV*, 4.5.186). In this instance the crown is a synecdoche for the king's disturbed reign which has been much of the focus of the preceding drama. In *The Famous Victories* the king is alluding to a state of affairs we have not seen. Nevertheless, these brief, passing references to a troubled reign and a troubled conscience

---

[22] Much has been written about the duplication of structure in *2 Henry IV*. See, for example, Harold Jenkins, *The Structural Problem in Shakespeare's Henry the Fourth* (London, 1956); G. K. Hunter, 'Henry IV and the Elizabethan Two Part Play', *Review of English Studies*, n.s., 5 (1954), 236–48. Edgar T. Schell argues that the reformation scene in *Part One* is in fact a reformation, but the corresponding scene in *Part Two* turns on misunderstanding and clarification, 'Prince Hal's Second "Reformation"', *Shakespeare Quarterly*, 21 (1970), 11–16, p. 13.

in the final encounter between the prince and his father in *The Famous Victories* can be seen as the stimulus for the king's anguished conscience suggested throughout the *Henry IV* plays and starkly exposed in his dying moments.

The 'medley' style of history play – alternation and the interaction of the comedic and the serious – is exemplified in *The Famous Victories* by the various character groupings representative of different classes and commensurate power. John Cobler, an officer of the watch, and the clown Derrick act as a kind of chorus as they comment on reports of the reprobate prince and in so doing they offer a critique of the social hierarchy. John Cobler comments to Lawrence Costermonger that the prince is a 'toward young Prince' whom he would not care to meet by the highway, but his subordination makes him circumspect; he names the prince's thievery by not naming it: 'I dare not call him thief, but sure he is one of those taking fellows' (ii. 10–12). Later Derrick and Cobler discuss the prince's slapping of the Lord Chief Justice, and Cobler confides 'there had been no way but one with us – we should have been hanged' (iv. 93–4). Here, again, *The Famous Victories*, representative of a more genuinely popular theatre than that of Shakespeare, unequivocally demonstrates, in a way that *1* and *2 Henry IV* eschews, that there is one law for the powerful and another for the commonalty. *The Famous Victories* in the early scenes presents a prince who seems to aspire to be one of the people. When his companions announce that they will follow him to the tavern, he rejects such formality and promises again a world of fair shares when his father is dead: 'Gogs wounds, wait. We will go all together; we are all fellows. I tell you, sirs, and the King, my father, were dead we would be all kings. Therefore, come away' (i. 78–80). Simultaneously, he denies and asserts rank ('I tell you, sirs'). Later, in the prince's assumption that his regal position entitles him to special treatment at the hands of the law, the play treats such levelling instincts ironically. As a result of the sojourn in the tavern the prince is involved in a drunken brawl and sent to the Counter. His father intervenes and reprimands the mayor and sheriff for punishing him in

this way, unbecoming to a prince: 'What although he be a rude youth and likely to give occasion, yet you might have considered that he is a prince, and my son, and not to be hauled to prison by every subject' (iii. 7–10). The sentiment is echoed mockingly by the prince in dialogue with Oldcastle after he has been released for abusing the Lord Chief Justice:

Prince. How now Sir John Oldcastle! What news with you?
Oldcastle. I am glad to see your grace at liberty. I was come, ay, to visit you in prison.
Prince. To visit me? Didst thou not know that I am a prince's son? Why 'tis enough for me to look into a prison, though I come not in myself. But here's such ado nowadays, here's prisoning, here's hanging, whipping, and the devil and all. But I tell you, sirs, when I am king, we will have no such things. But, my lads, if the old King, my father, were dead, we would be all kings. (v. 5–13)

The prince is not asserting royal prerogative now (there is no need), but he is exulting in the advantages that come his way even while ridiculing his father. Feckless, irresponsible and opportunistic, the prince advocates an anarchic commonwealth which privileges his friends.

The ambivalence towards authority in *The Famous Victories* is expressed through its comic subversion. One of the play's dramatic strategies is the parodic repetition of serious action in the play. Clowns advertently or inadvertently mimic their social superiors, thus flattening out social difference. The prince colludes in robbery, and his servant is simultaneously apprehended for a different thieving episode. When the clown Derrick – the role played by Tarlton – and John Cobler hear of the prince's detention, they are so taken with the occasion of the prince's affront to the Lord Chief Justice that they decide to enact out the confrontation (scene iv). Although they have not witnessed the scene between prince and justice, their words echo those of the prince and the justice. The comic exchange culminates in Derrick administering the blow, but the two are incapable of sustaining their roles and find in role-playing a threat to their identities.

Cobler's threat to Derrick as prince, 'Why, then, to teach you what prerogatives mean I commit you to the Fleet' (iv. 120–1), mimics the line spoken in earnest by the Lord Chief Justice in the preceding scene and the comic effect of the refrain would much depend on intonation and delivery. As indicated earlier, Robert Weimann discusses this scene as anticipating a Shakespearian synthesis where clowning is skilfully related to the larger meaning of the play.[23] In their play-acting these clowns are exposing the pretensions of their social superiors. When Cobler asks 'who am I?' and Derrick incredulously replies 'Dost not know thy self?' 'Thou art John the Cobler', there is more to this than amateur actors being unable to sustain their roles. Cobler echoes the rhetorical questions of the Lord Chief Justice and the prince who, full of their own eminence, ask of the other 'Who am I?' In the voice of the clown this rhetorical trick becomes bathos and an opportunity to deflate the self-regard of hierarchy.

The play-acting scene would seem to be a prompt for the similar assumption of parts between prince and clown in *1 Henry IV*. When Hal hears that he has been summoned to court to meet his father, Falstaff's reaction is to turn the anticipated rebuke and reprimand into the mirth of role playing, as do Derrick and Cobler. With Falstaff and Hal, however, the script has to be improvised. 'If thou love me, practise an answer' (2.5.377–8) says Falstaff, whereas Derrick gives Cobler his lines. Again, in contrast to Derrick and Cobler, the prince and Falstaff, as one would expect from characters skilful in duplicity, sustain their parts to perfection, each pursuing their own agenda and refusing to adopt the role and response the other would prescribe. The relative scenes are quite differently nuanced. In *1 Henry IV* the play acting anticipates rather than mimics a serious encounter to which it bears little resemblance, suggesting a discontinuity of comic and political worlds that are reinforced in *The Famous Victories*. For an Elizabethan audience the comedy of the mock court scene in *1 Henry IV* springs from its intertextuality. There is incongruity in Falstaff's aping of the precious style of courtly theatre associated with Lyly

and the discrepancy between this idiom and that of the king, so that at the end of the playlet Hal questions quizzically 'Dost thou speak like a king?' (2.5.436). Falstaff's comic exploitation of euphuistic speech cannot entirely conceal his shameless exploitation of the role to advance his cause. As prince he defends himself, warning the real prince that if he does banish him he will 'banish all the world'. Abandoning the role of his father, but still playing in Falstaff's eyes the role of his father, Hal anticipates the moment when he will break with Falstaff: 'I do: I will' (2.5.485–6). It is a tantalizing, half-realized theatrical moment which for all its subtleties of characterization and exposure of Machiavellian politics brings the play back to the actors' theatre of the Queen's Men. As with the scripts of the Queen's Men we have no way of knowing precisely how this comic interlude would have been played: comic charade or a baiting game.

The juxtaposition of knock-about comedy and matters of national and international import continues in those scenes in which Henry has emerged as heroic king. In the play's episodic structure, scenes represent the impact of the war on the commoners and how they turn it to their advantage. John Cobler has been recruited against his will for the French campaign. The clown Derrick is also destined for France and enters the recruitment scene carrying the pot lid of Cobler's wife as a shield, which elicits a beating from the quarrelsome wife. The scene shifts to France, where Cobler takes a French prisoner who promises him a ransom but easily gives him the slip. Following the peace treaty, Cobler and Derrick meet up, each carrying the spoils of war, Derrick with a girdle full of shoes and Cobler with a pack of apparel which he plans to take home to his wife. It can be seen how these homely episodes are re-presented in *Henry V* in scenes between Bardolph, Nim, the braggart Pistol and Mistress Quickly, now Pistol's wife, with greater vibrancy, but also with a notable harshness. Falstaff is dead and the conviviality of the Eastcheap tavern of *1 Henry IV* has gone. Bardolph,

---

[23] Weimann, *Shakespeare and the Popular Tradition in the Theater*, p. 187.

Nim and Pistol embark for war, driven entirely by self-interest, encapsulated in Pistol's rally: 'Let us to France, like horseleeches, my boys, / To suck, to suck, the very blood to suck!' (2.3.51–2). As minor players in international affairs, both Derrick and Cobler, like Pistol, Nim and Bardolph, aim to profit from the war, but whereas the former return to England with their modest booty, Cobler's to please his shrewish wife, there is a grimness in the fates of Bardolph and Nim, executed, on the orders of the king, for looting. Pistol, now a widower, is dismissed by Fluellen, the king's Welsh compatriot, as 'a scurvy, lousy knave'. Cobler and Derrick, the latter identified with Tarlton, are there to entertain, and the audience are on their side. Even their manner of returning to England shows their comic ingenuity: they will accompany the Duke of York's funeral procession and as one of them engages the sexton in conversation, the other will eat and drink as much as he can and they will then swap roles. In *Henry V* little if anything of this kind of clowning is transmitted; instead, there is a brutishness in the legacy of the comic world of *1 Henry IV* conveyed through self-revelation and through Shakespeare's brilliant invention of the boy, who accompanies Pistol, Bardolph and Nim from London and later becomes a guardian of baggage. With forthright scepticism, in his first monologue, the boy exposes the gross dishonesty of his fellows: 'they will steal anything and call it "purchase"' (3.2.22–3). He finds their conduct so repellent that he determines to leave them and seek other employment. The boy's second monologue sees Pistol's bombast for what it is:

I did never know so full a voice issue from what so empty a heart. But the saying is true: 'The empty vessel makes the greatest sound.' Bardolph and Nim had ten times more valour than this roaring devil i'th'old play, that everyone may pare his nails with a wooden dagger, and they are both hanged, and so would this be, if he durst steal anything adventurously.   (4.4. 63–9)

Pistol's bombast masks his pusillanimity and to an extent reverberates with the king's rhetoric, of the Crispin Day speech, for example, which masks his uncertainty about the war and glosses over resid-

ual guilt at the murder of Richard II. Whereas the comic scenes of *The Famous Victories* stand up on their own, in the more textually layered *Henry V* the words and acts of the Eastcheap veterans contribute to the moral dubiousness of a campaign undertaken to busy 'giddy minds'. The boy's choric commentary has the reverse intention to that of the Chorus, whose rhetoric orientates the audience towards the heroic and gives 'ambiguous support' to Henry's glorification.[24] Both are Shakespearian additions, working against each other to contribute to the play's ambiguous heroics largely absent in the play's pre-text.

The 'victories' of *The Famous Victories* get scant attention. The Siege of Harfleur is reported, not depicted, and, despite the publicity of the title-page, Agincourt is a fairly cursory battle scene. It is notable, however, that the quarto text of *Henry V*, published in 1600, is in many ways closer to *The Famous Victories* than the version of the play we are familiar with from the Folio.[25] As has been convincingly argued, the 1600 text is probably an authoritative player's text and, in its two hours' stage traffic, reflective of the play that Shakespeare's company first put on the stage at the Globe in 1599.[26] In cutting the Chorus and most of the Siege of Harfleur, more emphasis falls on the comic interpolations while the heroic idiom becomes less pronounced. With the cuts to the Harfleur scenes Henry's chivalric image is less tarnished. The military centre of the quarto version, as with the latter part of *The Famous Victories*, becomes Agincourt, where we hear the articulation of a military rhetoric quite different from that of Harfleur.

---

24 See Gurr, *King Henry V*, p. 13, and Sharon Taylor, '"Minding True Things": The Chorus, the Audience and *Henry V*', in *The Theatrical Space*, Themes in Drama, 9, ed. James Redmond (1987), pp. 69–80.

25 I am not suggesting verbal echoes, although it has been conjectured that the printers of Q1 either added recollections of or referred to a printed text of *The Famous Victories*, notably in the final act of the play. See Robert A. H. Smith, 'Thomas Creede, *Henry V* Q1, and *The Famous Victories of Henrie the Fifth*', *Review of English Studies*, n.s., 49 (1998), 60–4.

26 See Andrew Gurr, *The First Quarto of Henry V* (Cambridge, 2000), p. 9.

Audiences watching Shakespeare's *Henry V* in 1600 may not have considered its representation of the war a very different play from that of *The Famous Victories*. Indeed, one might speculate that Shakespeare's play was adapted so that it more resembled its immensely popular precursor.

In his last Elizabethan histories Shakespeare reworks a great deal from *The Famous Victories*. The three plays *1* and *2 Henry IV* and *Henry V* follow exactly the contour of *The Famous Victories*, beginning with images of a prince restlessly in waiting for the crown and misspending his time, continuing with the waging of a morally dubious war in France and concluding with a marriage alliance and treaty, giving little more than was on offer before the war. There is, however, more of a rupture in the popular tradition than continuity. Shakespeare's trilogy emulates the stagecraft of *The Famous Victories* while subverting the popular ethos of the Queen's Men's play and extending and at the same time complicating its heroics.

The mingling of clowns and kings gives the two plays only a superficial generic resemblance: *1* and *2 Henry IV* reject the popular, anti-authoritarian history play as exemplified in *The Famous Victories* and its fantasies of insubordination. We can locate the different perspectives in the Henry/Hal role. Hal is always the prince, even when he is playing the commoner and mixing with his so-called social inferiors. There is a distance, an hauteur, throughout, which is most in evidence when he is ragging Falstaff. The intimacy with Falstaff allows Falstaff's foibles and faults to be named unsparingly, whether as a token of trust and affection or by way of cool, clear-eyed appraisal that motivates and justifies a withdrawal. This ambivalence of mood complicates their relationship and drives the plays. Compared with *The Famous Victories*, there is in *1* and *2 Henry IV* a tangle of psychological and dramatic problems of which the former is largely unaware. In place of the narrative which links Henry's conversion directly with his succession, Shakespeare depicts Henry as consciously acting out roles: royal

with a common touch, the warrior king, the conqueror, the man amongst men, the bluff soldierly wooer. As prince and king, Henry is supremely aware of his situation and the role he has to play. In this, his conception is, of course, radically different from that of his predecessor: this difference may be interpreted as an imaginative alternative to the conversion line of *The Famous Victories*, something set against it, prompted and provoked by it.

An analysis of dialogue between the plays demonstrates how Shakespeare turned a levelling play performed by the Queen's Men at the Bull into more hierarchical plays performed by the Chamberlain's Men. *The Famous Victories* cannot simply be dismissed as inferior source material, as it frequently has been, particularly in studies of Shakespeare's histories.[27] An intertextual approach enlarges *The Famous Victories* and illuminates its plebeian emphasis, articulating the viewpoint of the lower echelons, ironically through the mouth of the prince. This in turn reinforces our understanding of the hierarchical nature of the *Henry IV* plays. In both plays kings and clowns are mingled; in one the distinction is questioned, and in the other the distinction remains intact. The difficulty for *The Famous Victories* is that *1* and *2 Henry IV* and *Henry V* have become the norms against which *The Famous Victories* appears a corrupted version.[28] Yet in its own terms it strongly and persuasively initiates a dramatic tradition.

---

[27] See, for example, Irving Ribner, *The English History Play in the Age of Shakespeare* (Princeton, 1957), pp. 56, 68–71; Robert Ornstein, *A Kingdom for a Stage: The Achievement of Shakespeare's History Plays* (Cambridge, MA, 1972), pp. 6, 86; M. M. Reese, *The Cease of Majesty: A Study of Shakespeare's History Plays* (London, 1961), p. 293. Robert Weimann redressed the balance.

[28] This is perhaps suggested in the precedence – inadvertently – given to Shakespeare's play by Hanabusa in the introduction to the Malone Society Reprint of *Famous Victories*: 'The play appears to fall into two sections – one corresponding roughly to Shakespeare's *1* and *2 Henry IV* and the other to his *Henry V*' (p. xix).

GEORGIC SOVEREIGNTY IN *HENRY V*

DERMOT CAVANAGH

Over twenty years ago, James C. Bulman made the striking claim that Virgil's *Georgics* provided one of the 'deep sources' for Shakespeare's understanding of historical life in his first and second tetralogies.[1] Scholarship had long recognized a sporadic pattern of allusion to the *Georgics* throughout these plays, especially in *Henry V*. Indeed, in the latter work, Shakespeare returned to the original text of Virgil's poem rather than its first complete English translation made by Abraham Fleming in 1589 or the versions of its topoi found in vernacular writings such as Thomas Elyot's *The boke named the governour* (1531) and John Lyly's *Euphues and his England* (1580).[2] However, Bulman's argument extended beyond conventional studies of sources and influences. His suggestion was that the political sensibility expressed in these plays was essentially Virgilian, more specifically georgic in character. This can be detected in both their imagery, where conflict is portrayed recurrently in terms of its drastic effect on husbandry, and in their ambivalent mode of political reflection. In both Virgil and Shakespeare, the laborious struggle to restore prosperity to the blighted land is presented as heroic, yet this endeavour is shadowed throughout by an awareness that political stability is desperately hard to maintain.

This article makes a new claim about the significance of the *Georgics* that helps both to reappraise the neglected relationship between Virgil and Shakespeare and to shed new light on the political significance of one of these history plays, *Henry V*.[3] My argument is that a more detailed examination of georgic idioms in the play reveals how it contributes to the urgent contemporary debate on political sovereignty. This aspect of *Henry V* is also shaped, in turn, by two contrasting viewpoints that affect profoundly its reception of Virgil's poem: the divergent accounts of sovereignty offered, firstly, by the period's foremost theorist of the subject, Jean Bodin, and, second, by its foremost sceptic, Michel de Montaigne. Understanding the significance of these conflicting views reveals both what is at stake in Shakespeare's political curiosity about the *Georgics* and how this informs the dramatic process of the play. *Henry*

---

[1] James C. Bulman, 'Shakespeare's Georgic Histories', *Shakespeare Survey 38* (Cambridge, 1985), 37–49. See also Katherine Maynard, 'Shakespeare's Georgic Nationalism', *History of European Ideas*, 16 (1993), 981–7.

[2] See T. W. Baldwin, *William Shakspere's Small Latine and Lesse Greeke*, 2 vols. (Urbana, IL, 1944), vol. 2, pp. 472–9; John H. Betts, 'Classical Allusions in Shakespeare's *Henry V* with Special Reference to Virgil', *Greece and Rome*, 15 (1968), 147–63; John H. Betts, 'Shakespeare's *Henry V* and Virgil's *Georgics*', *Notes and Queries*, 25 (1978), 134–6.

[3] Robert S. Miola notes the 'slight and desultory' critical recognition of 'the complex and pervasive influence of Vergil on Shakespeare' in 'Vergil in Shakespeare: From Allusion to Imitation', in *Vergil at 2000: Commemorative Essays on the Poet and His Influence*, ed. John D. Bernard (New York, 1986), pp. 241–58. This view is disparaged by Charles Martindale in the only essay on 'Shakespeare and Virgil' included in *Shakespeare and the Classics*, eds. Charles Martindale and A. B. Taylor (Cambridge, 2004), pp. 89–106. For further analysis, see A. D. Nuttall, 'Virgil and Shakespeare', in *Virgil and his Influence*, ed. Charles Martindale (Bristol, 1984), pp. 71–93; Heather James, *Shakespeare's Troy: Drama, Politics and the Translation of Empire* (Cambridge 1997); Margaret Tudeau-Clayton, *Jonson, Shakespeare, and Early Modern Virgil* (Cambridge, 1998).

V's account of sovereignty is not advanced as a set of static propositions but unfolds gradually as a sequence of insights concerning its nature, insights that are challenged as much as affirmed.

I

The role of the *Georgics* in *Henry V* seems surprising despite Shakespeare's habit of 'analogical thinking' across otherwise disparate texts.[4] Virgil's poem is technically detailed and it deals with the planting of grain and the cultivation of vines, livestock and bees. The *Georgics* evoke seasonal change and describe the qualities of the land, offering instructive precepts on the process of cultivation and reflections on what constitutes the good life.[5] There would seem little in this combination of elements to inspire Shakespeare in the composition of *Henry V*. However, Virgil's concern with husbandry in the *Georgics* has long been recognized as possessing a political dimension. It embodies, especially, his reflections on the triumph of Octavian, later Augustus Caesar, after a prolonged period of crisis and civil war. The *Georgics*' broader concern with national and imperial renewal interested Shakespeare; the poem is full of political reflection inspired by the cultivation of the natural world.[6] One lesson it proposes is that the growth and vitality of the state requires the determination to bring diverse and sometimes recalcitrant elements into a fruitful harmony. Such an understanding of the task of sovereignty finds a powerful echo in *Henry V*'s portrayal of imperial kingship.

This becomes clear in the play's first major exposition of a georgic theme drawn from the fourth book of Virgil's poem: the Archbishop of Canterbury's panegyric to the bees during his persuasion of the king to invade France. This speech is of crucial significance for this essay even if, at first hearing, it appears simply to reiterate the unremarkable lesson found by Thomas Elyot in this part of 'the Georgikes of Virgil': that 'undoubtedly the best and most sure governance is by one kynge or prince'.[7] Yet its implications can be grasped more fully by taking a step back to consider the rhetorical context in which Canterbury

ventures this elaborate Virgilian analogy. A little earlier, as part of his vindication of Henry's claim to the French crown, the Archbishop exposes French Salic law to hostile scrutiny. This reveals how the true extent of Henry's sovereign power dispels this poorly founded customary tradition. In his vindication of the English claim to the French crown, Canterbury makes fulsome acknowledgement of the king's stature as his 'gracious sovereign', the incumbent of 'this imperial throne' (1.2.33, 35). In contrast, the French have misconceived culpably the basis upon which succession to the crown rests; the fundamental law of their realm derives from a custom which has no proper basis. Canterbury reveals that the French prohibition on succession through the female line, which would prevent Henry's claim, originated with an edict of Charlemagne's based on his distaste for the habits of German women; it has no relevance for France and has only been adhered to sporadically. This leads to an astonishing claim: that the English sovereign possesses a superior sense of the origin and limits of French customary law.[8]

Even earlier, the Archbishop had stated his elevated conception of the king's sovereign mastery as deriving from a divine seizure of his will. In his view, Henry's eloquence and decisiveness are not the result of a gradual acquisition of

---

[4] Robert S. Miola, *Shakespeare's Reading* (Oxford, 2000), p. 6.

[5] For a concise overview of the mode and its reception, see Alastair Fowler, 'The Beginnings of English Georgic', in *Renaissance Genres: Essays on Theory, History, and Interpretation*, ed. Barbara Kiefer Lewalski (Cambridge, MA, 1986), pp. 105–25.

[6] For an illuminating study of how Virgil's conception of husbandry could be elaborated for imperial purposes in the Renaissance, see William A. Sessions, 'Spenser's Georgics', *English Literary Renaissance*, 10 (1980), 202–38.

[7] Thomas Elyot, *The boke named the governour* (1531), fol. 8r; fol. 7r.

[8] For the contemporary pertinence of Salic law and succession for *Henry V*, see David Womersley, 'France in Shakespeare's *Henry V*', *Renaissance Studies*, 9 (1995), 442–59, esp. pp. 454–8, and Richard Dutton, '"Methinks the truth should live from age to age": The Dating and Contexts of *Henry V*', *Huntington Library Quarterly*, 68 (2005), 173–204, esp. pp. 185–9.

aptitudes. Instead, they result from a sudden irresistible influx of God's grace that transforms the
delinquent prince into a paragon of monarchic
accomplishment. Canterbury's attack on Salic law
and advancement of the king's claim to the French
crown follows from this emphasis on the ordained
quality of Henry's self-command and command
over others. Establishing Henry's authority over
France demands, of course, a resort to force: 'O
let their bodies follow, my dear liege, / With blood
and sword and fire, to win your right' (1.2.130–
1). It is in this context of exalting the scope of
Henry's powers over custom that the Archbishop
draws upon Virgil in his portrayal of the bees and
he succeeds in eliciting this commitment from the
king:

> France being ours we'll bend it to our awe,
> Or break it all to pieces. Or there we'll sit,
> Ruling in large and ample empery
> O'er France and all her almost kingly dukedoms.
>
> (1.2.224–7)

In his disquisition on the bees, Canterbury is
deploying Virgil as part of an insistent argument:
that Henry needs to realize the full scope of his
sovereign powers by subordinating claims which
derive from custom. The terms of this case converge with those proposed by Jean Bodin, in his
influential *Six Livres de la République* (Paris, 1576),
a work translated in 1606 but widely read, disseminated and discussed before then.[9] In this work
Bodin had frequent resort to Octavian and the subsequent *Pax Augusta* as a source of inspiration for
his contention that sovereign power should be concentrated in the person and will of 'a sole Monar-
que, and soveraigne Prince'.[10] Crucially, Bodin also
insisted that customary practices be subordinated
by the sovereign who had the power to make the
law:

custome hath no force but by sufferance, and so long
as it pleaseth the soveraigne prince, who may make
thereof a law, by putting thereunto his owne confirmation: whereby it is to be seene, that all the force of
lawes and customes lieth in the power of him that hath
the soveraigntie in a Commonweale.[11]

For example, the achievements of Octavian's
rule derived from his realization: 'That the prince
is acquitted from the power of the laws: and this
word the Law, in the Latine importeth the com-
maundment of him which hath the soveraigntie'.[12]
For Bodin, the essential attribute of sovereignty is
the power to declare or suspend legal rules and this
is marked by the supersession of 'custom as the
chief source of law'.[13]

---

[9] The extent of Bodin's reception in Elizabethan England is captured by Gabriel Harvey's remark that 'You can not stepp into a schollars studye but (ten to on) you shall litely finde open ether Bodin de Republica or Le Royes Exposition uppon Aristotles Politiques or sum other like Frenche or Italian Politique Discourses', in *Letter-Book of Gabriel Harvey, A.D. 1573–1580*, ed. Edward John Long Scott, Camden Society, n.s., vol. 33 (London, 1884), p. 79. On the circulation of Bodinian and absolutist ideas in English culture, see Johann P. Sommerville, 'English and European Political Ideas in the Early Seventeenth Century: Revisionism and the Case of Absolutism', *Journal of British Studies*, 35 (1996), 168–94.

[10] Jean Bodin, *The Six Bookes of a Commonweale*, trans. Richard Knolles (1606), ed. Kenneth Douglas McRae (Cambridge, MA, 1962), p. 419. For further instances of Bodin's admiration for Octavian, see, for example, p. 91 and pp. 196–7.

[11] Bodin, *The Six Bookes of a Commonweale*, p. 161. Bodin defended Salic law but not in terms of its customary origins. It provided both a bulwark against the female sovereignty he opposed (see pp. 752–4) and, more importantly, constituted a fundamental law that established and ensured the succession of the crown. In this respect, it helped preserve 'the greatnesse and majestie of a true soveraigne prince' and upheld the principle: 'that which it pleaseth the king to like or dislike of . . . is holden for law', p. 95.

[12] Bodin, *The Six Bookes of a Commonweale*, p. 91. James VI's writings helped disseminate Bodin's ideas: see, in particular, his claim in *The Trew Law of Free Monarchies* (1598): 'that the kings were the authors and makers of the Lawes, and not the Lawes of the kings'. In *King James VI and I: Selected Writings*, ed. Neil Rhodes, Jennifer Richards and Joseph Marshall (Aldershot, 2003), pp. 259–79, p. 269. The first edition of this work was published anonymously. Its significance lies, in part, in reiterating James's insistence, as Rebecca Bushnell puts it, that the monarch was 'able to break free from precedent and custom'; see 'George Buchanan, James VI and Neo-classicism', in *Scots and Britons: Scottish Political Thought and the Union of 1603*, ed. Roger A. Mason (Cambridge, 1994), pp. 91–111, p. 111.

[13] J. U. Lewis, 'Jean Bodin's "Logic of Sovereignty"', *Political Studies*, 16 (1968), 206–22, p. 208.

It is in this spirit that Canterbury interprets the Fourth Georgic. As a 'Bodinian' reader of the poem, he finds in both apian life and in the transcendence of custom, material with which to inspire Henry's ambitions. As he recounts the habits of bees, the Archbishop aims to convince the king that a multitude of activities and aims can have a unifying purpose. Henry should not be wary, therefore, of dividing his forces between those committed to defending the border with Scotland and the army that will accompany him overseas. To persuade the king towards this goal, the Archbishop indulges in a broader evaluation of those crucial qualities of obedience and hierarchy that should underpin a well-functioning community, however heterogeneous its roles and functions. The lives and labours of the bees are an example of this and 'by a rule in nature teach / The act of order to a peopled kingdom' (1.2.188–9). They live under a king and 'officers', especially those who 'like magistrates correct at home' (190–1). This stratified community includes merchants, masons, citizens, porters and adventurous 'soldiers', who:

> armèd in their stings,
> Make boot upon the summer's velvet buds
> Which pillage they with merry march bring home
> To the tent royal of their emperor,
> Who busied in his majesty surveys
> The singing masons building roofs of gold.   (193–8)

In the bees' commonwealth, political supremacy lies with the 'emperor' who exercises legislative authority over this interdependent social world. Consequently, the 'lazy yawning drone' (204) is condemned to execution through the vigilance of his magistrates. Furthermore, both the majesty of the sovereign and the productivity of the community are only made possible through the audacity of its 'soldiers' who replenish it by rifling the booty of nature. Canterbury's inference from this excursion into natural history is clear. The bees are an inspiring example of how complex and customary patterns of life are harmonized productively in accordance with monarchical will. As long as 'many things' possess 'full reference / To one consent' they may conclude triumphantly 'in one purpose' (205–6, 212). This famous vision of a hierarchy unified by a common goal testifies to the resonances of Virgil's *Georgics* for Shakespeare as a work which exalts imperial command.[14]

II

Canterbury's disquisition on the bees is a perfectly coherent appropriation of this sequence from Virgil's work and, more broadly, of its political engagement with nature. As Michael Putnam has argued, we need to 'eradicate from our minds any lingering notion that the poem is utilitarian' in its concerns; indeed,[15] it has little practical value as a guide to husbandry. Instead, the historical context of the work has been seen as crucial for uncovering its deeper motivations and concerns. Virgil is reputed to have read the poem to Octavian upon his triumphant return from the East after crushing Antony at Actium in 31 BCE and, at the outset of its third book, he describes the entire poem in allegorical terms as a temple dedicated to him as its deity.[16] Consequently, the *Georgics* have been

---

[14] Such analogies were common; see, for example, Charles Butler's commendation of bees in *The feminine monarchie or a treatise concerning bees* (1609) as 'an expresse patterne of a perfect monarchie, the most natural & absolute form of government', sig. A3r. See also Thomas Floyd, *The Picture of a perfit Common wealth* (1600), esp. p. 29.

[15] Michael C. J. Putnam, *Virgil's Poem of the Earth: Studies in the 'Georgics'* (Princeton, 1979), p. 7. R. O. A. M. Lyne observes that 'Virgil gives selective and often unhelpful advice to a type of farmer who was increasingly an irrelevance in contemporary Italy.' See 'Introduction to C. Day Lewis's Translation of Vergil's *Eclogues* and *Georgics*' (1983), in *Collected Papers on Latin Poetry* (Oxford, 2007), pp. 101–14, p. 109. For a contrary view, see M. S. Spurr, 'Agriculture and the *Georgics*', *Greece & Rome*, 33 (1986), 164–87.

[16] References are to the Loeb edition of *Virgil: Eclogues, Georgics, Aeneid, 1–6*, trans. H. R. Fairclough; revised G. P. Goold (Cambridge, MA, 1916; rev. edn 1999), 3.1–39. The seriousness of this passage has been questioned: see Louis L. Martz, '*Paradise Regained*: Georgic Form, Georgic Style', *Milton Studies*, 42 (2003), 7–25, pp. 17–18. For an overview of the poem's context, see Gary B. Miles and Archibald W. Allen, 'Vergil and the Augustan Experience', in *Vergil at 2000*, pp. 13–41, pp. 21–9; see also Christopher Nappa, *Reading After Actium: Vergil's 'Georgics', Octavian and Rome* (Ann Arbor, 2005).

defined as one of Virgil's literary 'affirmations of faith in Octavian and in the values and achievements of imperial Rome', a testimony to the poet's belief in a 'redeemed future'.[17] On this view, the poem envisions a new age of prosperity secured by Octavian's providential overcoming of the unnatural forces of anarchy and civil destruction. As Bulman summarizes this interpretation, by 'their glorification of the social stability and moral regeneration inherent in . . . husbandry, the *Georgics* anticipate the *Pax Augusta*'.[18] This sense of the equivalence between poetic and imperial achievement in the poem has been enduring. In his influential reappraisal in 1697, Joseph Addison reminded his readers not to be deceived by its seemingly humble subject-matter and commended Virgil's presence in this work as possessing a 'rustic majesty like that of a Roman dictator at the plowtail'.[19]

In the Fourth Georgic, the bees are indeed presented as epitomizing the collective energy required for a community to flourish. In Virgil's account, this involves the many working together at a task that is never truly finished; this is the mode best 'suited to the establishment of civilization and the founding of nations'.[20] The bees are conceived as a 'wondrous pageant of a tiny world' which reveals its 'chiefs great-hearted' as well as 'a whole nation's characters and tastes and tribes and battles' (4.3–5). The similitude between the bees and human society offers an example of how the latter might achieve discipline and order, with all the plenitude of its habits and customs dedicated to a single unifying goal. It is this aspect of bees that Shakespeare's Archbishop admires and his expansive use of a georgic analogy stresses the capacity of Virgil's poem to 'naturalize' an imperial mode of sovereignty. The appearance of such a topos at this stage within *Henry V* adds lustre to the king's pursuit of the French crown: this too is a form of heroic labour that will unify and enrich his kingdom.

Yet the context in which this georgic modulation appears is not straightforward. The Archbishop is a speaker with strong motivations and these affect his exposition of the *Georgics*. Caution should be exercised, therefore, before crediting T. W. Baldwin's claim that in this passage Virgil's poem was reshaped 'in accordance with his [i.e. Shakespeare's] own fundamental concept of the English commonwealth'.[21] As is well known, at the outset of the play Canterbury and the Bishop of Ely share their concerns over a 'bill / Urged by the Commons' that proposes to expand the king's temporal powers at the expense of the church (1.1.71–2). Bequests of land are to be appropriated for 'the King's honour', increasing Henry's retinue, establishing new charitable foundations under the control of the crown and enriching the 'coffers of the King' (7–19). Henry 'seems indifferent' (73) to this proposal, even sympathetic to the church's concern; both clerical figures agree that he must use his power to mitigate or countermand the aims of this bill. Consequently, the ecclesiastical hierarchy is determined to augment Henry's sovereignty in another way: by endorsing his imperial endeavour to seize the French crown.[22]

It is not so much, therefore, that the play adopts a georgic ethos to exalt Henry's power but that Canterbury does so. Furthermore, his account of the bees does not simply distil the essence of Virgil's lengthier portrayal but presents an emphatic, even a one-sided, act of interpretation. This succeeds in spiriting away some discomfiting details. Virgil's poem hints that the lives of bees could endorse

---

[17] Christine G. Perkell, *The Poet's Truth: A Study of the Poet in Virgil's 'Georgics'* (Berkeley, 1989), p. 3. This is not Perkell's own view.

[18] Bulman, 'Shakespeare's Georgic Histories', p. 40.

[19] Joseph Addison, 'An Essay on Virgil's *Georgics*' (1697), in *Eighteenth-Century Critical Essays*, ed. Scott Elledge, 2 vols. (Ithaca, NY, 1961), vol. 1, pp. 1–8, p. 6.

[20] Anthony Low, *The Georgic Revolution* (Princeton, 1985), p. 12.

[21] Baldwin, *William Shakespere's Small Latine*, vol. 2, p. 477. Baldwin demonstrates how the ordering and categories of Canterbury's speech indicate that Shakespeare was familiar with an edition of Virgil with a commentary by, most probably, Willichius.

[22] A motivation captured in Holinshed's terse comment on the determination of the clergy 'to assaie all waies to put by and overthrow this bill: wherein they thought best to trie if they might moove the kings mood with some sharpe invention'; see Raphael Holinshed, *The Third Volume of Chronicles* (1587), p. 545.

equally well alternative models of action and governance.[23] For example, as Baldwin acknowledged, their portrayal in the *Georgics* begins not with their king or emperor but by noting 'that the bees "pass their life under majesty of law"'.[24] Virgil's bees are intensely communitarian: they hold children and property in common and return goods to the 'common store' (4.153–7) not to Canterbury's 'tent royal of their emperor'. Their interdependence is indeed stressed and, in Virgil, the sentries welcome and 'take the load of incomers'; drones are excluded from the hive rather than handed over to execution by magistrates (165–8). In many respects, Virgil's bees function like a self-regulating urban community, rather than the Archbishop's image of a royalist polity. They are self-sacrificing and resourceful in ensuring their own continuity but they also establish the conditions of their own governance: 'of themselves provide a new monarch and tiny burghers' (201–2). Canterbury's citation of Virgil is highly selective and it emphasizes some members of the community – merchants, soldiers and magistrates – at the expense of others.

To be sure, Virgil also depicts the bees as an intensely monarchical society showing how subjects are concealed within citizens. In this respect, however, their behaviour is presented in an equivocal manner that demonstrates Virgil's capacity to explore contradictions within the *Georgics*. This is part of the poem's reflection on the efficacy of using the natural to make foundational statements about matters of sovereignty and governance. The admirably communitarian nature of the bees is stressed in the Fourth Georgic, but there is a strong insinuation that this also makes them incapable of individual and reflective action. Similarly, their obedience to their king has an uncritical, even slavish, dimension leading to their suggestive comparison to effeminate and 'oriental' subjects – 'neither Egypt nor mighty Lydia . . . show such homage to their king' – and exposing their impulse to self-destruction when he dies (210–14). The accumulation of detail concerning the king-worship of the bees has an unsettling effect as it documents their fanatical degree of subservience, especially in mili-

tary conflict: 'to him [i.e. their king] they do reverence; all stand round him in clamorous crowd, and attend him in throngs. Often they lift him on their shoulders, for him expose their bodies to battle, and seek amid wounds a glorious death' (215–18). The soldier-like belligerence of the bees means, as Christine Perkell observes, that they 'prepare with excitement for wars without substance, sacrificing their lives with alacrity in battles that have no urgency'.[25] From another viewpoint, these struggles are futile and insignificant: 'These storms of passion, these savage conflicts, by the tossing of a little dust will be quelled and laid to rest' (86–7).[26] Even the bees' eager harvesting of nature's bounty has an unappealing aspect, making them acquisitive: they 'freely yield their lives under their load – so deep is their love of flowers' (204–5) and are driven by 'an inborn love of gain' (177).

Emphasizing Canterbury's divergences from and elisions of the *Georgics* demonstrates how enlisting Virgil's poem in the interests of a monarch-dominated society requires the artful constraint of its implications. Traces of the strain this involves remain even in Canterbury's sanitized account. 'Pillage' is an odd word to choose for the bounty the soldier-bees deliver to their emperor. Similarly, the acknowledgement that this diverse range of activities 'may work contrariously' is curious. As Andrew Gurr notes, it hints at that 'series of private motives which work contrariously through the play', indeed at the self-interest we might suspect is animating the Archbishop's own discourse: 'As Mandeville put it much later, all bees are out for

---

[23] In John Lyly's *Euphues and his England* (1580), for example, Fidus describes how the king-worshipping bees are also constitutional monarchists with an elective monarchy and rights of deposition: 'albeit they lyve under a Prince, they have their Priveledge, and as great lyberties, as streight lawes'. See pp. 20–2, p. 21.

[24] Baldwin, *William Shakespere's Small Latine*, vol. 2, p. 474 (translating 'magnisque agitant sub legibus aevum', 4: 154).

[25] Perkell, *The Poet's Truth*, p. 128.

[26] This passage was cited by Montaigne to deflate martial pretensions. See 'An Apology for Raymond Sebond', *The Complete Essays*, trans. M. A. Screech (London, 1991), 2: 12, p. 530. All subsequent references to Montaigne are to this edition.

themselves.'[27] Furthermore, it suggests that even their heroic and martial aspect draws them into pointless conflicts that foster submissiveness.

The absence of these ironies or contradictions in Canterbury's account is suggestive because its implications filter back into the play. The Archbishop may be a 'Bodinian' reader of the *Georgics*, but this requires a creative pruning of the poem's implications; the play does not consistently follow his lead in this matter. For example, Shakespeare's soldiers have variegated attitudes and motivations and they do not share the uniformity of purpose the Archbishop imputes to them. They range in temperament from the self-seeking Pistol, to the unswerving loyalty of Fluellen, to the disputatious Michael Williams who engages with the disguised king very much as a citizen questioning the legitimacy and costs of the war. Commentators on its ambivalence have long noted that *Henry V* contains, as John Arden puts it, 'a secret play inside the official play', at least in the longer version printed in the First Folio.[28] As many of these readings have shown, the play contains a range of perspectives, including those that express doubts about the legitimacy, conduct and outcome of the war or that expose the king's bad faith or self-deception.[29] The key issue for this argument is how the *Georgics*, including Virgil's critical reflection on imperial power, provide a medium in which the king's mode of sovereignty is both illuminated and questioned.[30]

III

One key issue that helps foreground the selectivity of Canterbury's response to the *Georgics*, in contrast to the fullness of the play's, is the interest both works share in cultivation. This is one of the richest areas of correspondence between the two works and it is a constitutive element of the political interests of Virgil's poem. The *Georgics* begin with a panegyric to Octavian as a divine sovereign whose 'care for our lands' will restore their fertility and they end by celebrating the imperial expansion of Roman power as it imposes 'victor's laws on willing nations' (1.23–8; 4.561–2). One of Virgil's preoc-

cupations is that the account of agricultural labour in the poem should also convey the difficulty of the task Octavian faces and this demands 'something of the heroic warrior's resourcefulness, determination, and aggressiveness'.[31] Like the farmer, the statesman will 'discipline the ground, and give his orders to the fields' and this results in an acute form of political husbandry: 'sharpening men's wits by care, nor letting his kingdom slumber in heavy lethargy' (1.98–9; 123–4). The work suggests that the peace and prosperity of the state can only be secured by a georgic form of sovereignty dedicated to the same skilled and demanding activity of cultivation that the farmer brings to the land. This possibility has been established by Octavian, who has achieved an unquestioned supremacy over all those forces that threaten to divide the land or to debilitate its fecundity.

The conception in the *Georgics* of sovereignty as an inspiring, if arduous, task of cultivation caught Shakespeare's interest in *Henry V* as did its celebration of the struggle against seemingly insurmountable difficulties. This is apparent in the analogy drawn by the Bishop of Ely between Henry's maturation and that of the strawberry which ripens best in the shadows. Ely admires the new king's patience and craft when he observes how astutely Henry has chosen the most propitious soil from which to absorb strength:

> The strawberry grows underneath the nettle,
> And wholesome berries thrive and ripen best

[27] Andrew Gurr, '*Henry V* and the Bees' Commonwealth', *Shakespeare Survey 30* (Cambridge, 1977), pp. 61–72; 70, 72.

[28] Quoted in *The First Quarto of King Henry V*, ed. Andrew Gurr (Cambridge, 2000), p. 10.

[29] See Steven Marx, 'Holy War in *Henry V*', *Shakespeare Survey 48* (Cambridge, 1995), 85–97 and Stephen Greenblatt's influential essay, 'Invisible Bullets', in *Shakespearean Negotiations* (Oxford, 1988), pp. 21–65, esp. 47–65.

[30] Annabel Patterson has analysed the political resonances of the georgic mode as it explores a 'culture's relationship to agriculture' throughout the Renaissance: see, 'Pastoral versus Georgic: The Politics of Virgilian Quotation', in *Renaissance Genres*, pp. 241–67, p. 242.

[31] Gary B. Miles, *Virgil's 'Georgics': A New Interpretation* (Berkeley, Los Angeles, London, 1980), p. 77. See also, A. Betensky, 'The Farmer's Battles', *Ramus*, 8 (1979), 108–19.

Neighboured by fruit of baser quality;
And so the Prince obscured his contemplation
Under the veil of wildness – which, no doubt,
Grew like the summer grass, fastest by night,
Unseen, yet crescive in his faculty.   (1.1.61–7)

This is echoed later in the play by the Constable, who reminds the French court not to be deceived by Henry's reputation for vanity. This simply concealed 'discretion with a coat of folly, / As gardeners do with ordure hide those roots / That shall first spring and be most delicate' (2.4.38–40). These are not simply testimonies to the king's powers of self-cultivation, skills which Virgil also commends in Octavian as one of those 'men whose watchful care nothing escapes' as they learn how to nurture the soil (2.265). The play is also alert to the potential of English land from which the king draws strength. The Dauphin is baffled by how the degraded issue of the Norman Conquest have returned to assert themselves on unfamiliar terrain:

> Shall a few sprays of us,
> The emptying of our fathers' luxury,
> Our scions, put in wild and savage stock,
> Spirt up so suddenly into the clouds,
> And over-look their grafters?   (3.5.5–9)

This disdain is shared by the Constable in his scorn for the deleterious English climate, where 'the sun looks pale, / Killing their fruit with frowns' and the 'sodden water' and 'barley-broth' that feed horses and men has constituted such surprising 'mettle' (15–20). '[I]f they march along', Bourbon adds, 'Unfought withal, but I will sell my dukedom / To buy a slobb'ry and a dirty farm / In that nook-shotten isle of Albion' (11–14). In this respect, the French are poor interpreters of georgic qualities and cannot comprehend how such a seemingly dispiriting island could be transformed into 'the world's best garden' (Epilogue, 7).

It is to this realization of heroic potential that Henry is dedicated, inspiring himself and others to exceed their own expectations. This endeavour may also require political ruthlessness and this necessity too was acknowledged by Virgil, '[i]f a leader is determined to reform and cultivate a peo-ple, and eventually to bring them to full ripeness'.[32] It is in relation to these moments that some of the most controversial ambivalences in both works emerge. In each of the four parts of the *Georgics*, the effect of political achievements, but also of political turmoil, is assessed in terms of its impact upon the natural world and especially upon farming and customary life. In this respect, there are many elements of Virgil's poem that are difficult to square with the beneficent effects of sovereign power that we find in Canterbury's exposition of a georgic motif.

For example, it is true that the *Georgics* begin by evoking Octavian's divine sovereignty and his 'care for our lands'. However, the poem continues to wonder what form Octavian will take: 'whatever you are to be' might also involve the 'monstrous lust of empire' (1.36–7). Similarly, the cultivation of the earth and Octavian's political activities do not always equate with each other smoothly. The values of the husbandman sometimes point in a contrary direction to the imperatives that drive political aspirations. In the second book of the poem, the simplicity of the countryman's life, 'far from the clash of arms' is portrayed: 'they have sleep free from anxiety, a life that is innocent of guile and rich with untold treasures' (2.458–74; 459; 467–8). In stark contrast, political life is associated with violence and treachery. It involves struggle, invasion and conspiracy and the excesses of those who 'steep themselves in their brothers' blood and glory in it' (510). As Gary B. Miles notes, in this sequence of the poem Octavian's compulsion to tame and cultivate the land shapes his toughness and ambition but it can also involve 'a ruthless violation of the landscape'.[33] Traditional stewardship of the land remains 'untroubled by Rome's policies spelling doom to kingdoms' (498). Cultivation involves an effortful learning from nature and it requires accommodation to its demands; control cannot simply be imposed upon it. Learning those customary practices which work most successfully to harvest the natural world requires

---

[32] Low, *Georgic Revolution*, p. 47.
[33] Miles, *Virgil's 'Georgics'*, p. 131.

endurance and sustained patterns of usage; it also involves understanding one's own vulnerabilities and dependencies. These resonances of the georgic tradition have significance for the play as well and they offer another and competing view of imperial sovereignty.

We can glimpse this in passages of the play that suggest another and more forbidding potential within Henry's kingship: the unflinching rapidity with which he advances his imperial enterprise. The play records, for example, the alacrity with which the king's cultivation of his realm involves the forceful excision of unwholesome elements of the commonwealth, exactly as the Archbishop's disquisition on the bees had recommended. In 2.2, for example, Henry moves with overwhelming force against the traitors in a scene redolent with the language of sovereign presence. The king repeatedly uses the formulation 'our person' and 'our royal person' (41, 163) and on the traitors' part there is an equally fulsome recognition of the inescapable extent of sovereign power. This is acknowledged insincerely before their apprehension ('your majesty', 'your grace', 'sovereign', 'your highness', 'my royal sovereign') and abjectly thereafter: 'Beseeching God and you to pardon me', 'pardon, sovereign' (26, 38, 45, 48, 62, 156, 161). This scene presents a startling exercise of prerogative power. The king provides the evidence to implement his own instantaneous condemnation to death of 'these English monsters', including Lord Scroop whose revolt is like another 'fall of man' (82, 139). This is dealt with curiously. Henry acts so as to protect the safety of the kingdom, 'to her laws / We do deliver you', but this is followed immediately by the abrupt injunction: 'Get you therefore hence, / Poor miserable wretches, to your death' (173–5). There are similar discordances in the presentation of further regal acts of exclusion or execution. These include, most movingly, the death of Falstaff, but also the condemnation of his old companion Bardolph who is executed for robbing a church in France: 'We would have all such offenders so cut off... For when lenity and cruelty play for a kingdom, the gentler gamester is the soonest winner' (3.6.108, 112–14).

Of course, a powerful appeal can be and is made from necessity in all these cases to defend the king's actions. In this respect, the play could be seen as endorsing what Andrew McRae terms 'georgic economics', another crucial strain of Virgilian discourse in the period. On this view, Henry's antipathy towards delinquent subjects is cognizant with a broader impatience in late Elizabethan society towards those on the social margins who were deemed to be unproductive. In McRae's account, this moral vision pervaded late Elizabethan writing. It advanced a new kind of social order based on the initiative of those who pursued national improvement, including those were willing to take up the sword.[34]

Yet *Henry V* questions the assumptions and consequences of this moralized discourse, most signally by the manner in which the georgic ethos of the play also appears in disconcerting and disruptive ways. For example, there is the king's terrifying and anti-georgic invocation of 'impious war / Arrayed in flames' at the gates of Harfleur; a spectre 'like to the prince of fiends... / Enlinked to waste and desolation' (3.3.98–101). The consequences of this are imagined starkly: the 'fleshed soldier'... 'mowing like grass / Your fresh fair virgins and your flow'ring infants' (94–7). However, in terms of the play's reflection on the nature of sovereignty, there are two highly charged moments where georgic allusions and idioms emerge in their most provocative guise. The first is Henry's soliloquy on the night before Agincourt where the disguised king has been shaken by his encounter with the soldiers, especially by Michael Williams's hostility to the war. This leads Henry to reflect on the responsibilities of his great office and his consequent vulnerability to being 'subject to the breath / Of every fool, whose sense no more can feel / But his own wringing' (4.1.231–3). The soliloquy concludes with an outpouring on the insensate life of 'the wretched slave' (265). In this extensive passage, the king turns upon the cycle of cultivation canonized by georgic tradition to

---

[34] Andrew McRae, *God Speed the Plough: The Representation of Agrarian England, 1500–1660* (Cambridge, 1996), ch. 7.

expose its vacuous contentment: the 'slave', 'like a lackey, from the rise to set / Sweats in the eye of Phoebus, and all night / Sleeps in Elysium' (269–71). Henry seems to have rapidly forgotten his earlier pride in the 'good yeomen / Whose limbs were made in England' and his appeal that they demonstrate the 'mettle of your pasture' at Harfleur (3.1.25–7). It is equally surprising that Henry's scorn for those subjects who remain oblivious of his efforts to preserve the peace is made most stridently on the night before Agincourt.

This passage is undoubtedly a disturbing one and calls into question the authenticity of the king's association with georgic tradition. However, it is succeeded by a far more testing evocation of the mode: Burgundy's lament for France in the final scene of the play.[35] This speech is the second of *Henry V*'s most substantial evocations of georgic discourse. If it is less celebrated than Canterbury's disquisition on the bees, it is an eloquent counter-reflection on the nature of Henry's sovereignty. It achieves this by returning in a disturbing way to one of the core qualities of georgic tradition: the value of custom.

Burgundy's entreaty to the French king is to accept peace on English terms, but the support he offers Henry is not ratified so easily by his piteous account of the desolation that has followed Agincourt. Burgundy portrays the ruination of 'this best garden of the world, / Our fertile France' and its customary life (5.2.36–7). As Donald R. Kelley reminds us, at the basis of the idea of custom and providing 'its most concrete expression' lies 'the long-enduring institution of the cultivated field' imagined as '"the characteristic creation of the West . . . the nature and spirit of its civilisation"'.[36] In Burgundy's account, this foundation has been destroyed. Nature, once harvested and harmonized for human benefit, now runs wild and the distinctive presence of French custom has been erased from the land: 'Even so our houses and ourselves and children / Have lost, or do not learn for want of time, / The sciences that should become our country' (56–8). In his view, the English king's ascendancy over customary life results in its despoliation; husbandry has stagnated and the uncultivated land

has returned to wilderness. The first casualty of sovereignty imposed by violence is the destruction of its steadily accumulated traditions of cultivation. Under military dominion, French life can only be captured in anti-georgic idioms:

> And all her husbandry doth lie on heaps,
> Corrupting in it own fertility.
> Her vine, the merry cheerer of the heart,
> Unprunèd dies; her hedges even-plashed
> Like prisoners wildly overgrown with hair
> Put forth disordered twigs; her fallow leas
> The darnel, hemlock, and rank fumitory
> Doth root upon, while that the coulter rusts
> That should deracinate such savagery.   (39–48)

The inhabitants of France are similarly degraded into 'savages' who act 'as soldiers will / That nothing do but meditate on blood' (59–60). It is a crucial part of the awkwardness of this scene that the figure responsible for this devastation is also expected to redeem it. This too is an ambivalence that resonates with the *Georgics* as one of the poem's most unsettling effects lies in portraying the tragic consequences of political struggle.[37]

Burgundy's speech also proposes an alternative evaluation of the relationship between sovereignty and custom to that commended by the Archbishop of Canterbury's 'Bodinian' reading of Virgil. This stresses the importance of customary patterns of life that develop slowly and by accretion in contrast to the immediacy of sovereign power, a distinction

---

[35] On this speech's recapitulation of Virgil's poem, see Betts, 'Shakespeare's *Henry V*', p. 135, and on its topical resonances see Womersley, 'France in Shakespeare's *Henry V*', pp. 445–8.

[36] Donald R. Kelley, '"Second nature": The Idea of Custom in European Law, Society, and Culture', in *The Transmission of Culture in Early Modern Europe*, ed. Anthony Grafton and Ann Blair (Philadelphia, 1990), pp. 131–72, p. 135. The quotation is from Gaston Roupnel. See also J. G. A. Pocock's classic account of custom in *The Ancient Constitution and the Feudal Law* (Cambridge, 1957), esp. pp. 30–55, and, more recently, Adam Fox, *Oral and Literate Culture in England 1500–1700* (Oxford, 2000), pp. 259–98.

[37] Book 1 of the *Georgics* comments memorably on the futility of human endeavour in the face of recalcitrant circumstances: 'by law of fate all things speed towards the worse and slipping away fall back' (199–203).

crucial for Bodin: 'custome by little and little take force; and in many yeres by the common consent of all or most part; but the law commeth forth in a moment and taketh strength of him which hath power to commaund all'.[38] My argument is that the reflections on customary life expressed by Burgundy coincide with those of Bodin's contemporary, Michel de Montaigne, whose influence upon Shakespeare is more usually associated with the speculative *Hamlet* than the strident *Henry V* although both plays were composed proximately. Yet an association between Burgundy's speech and Montaigne is also surprising because the latter, like Bodin, was not an admirer of custom and had indeed equated its force with that of a tyrant who promotes the unquestioned acceptance of traditions and habit.[39] However, Montaigne could also perceive the value of custom, as I'll now suggest, in contexts that are of great significance both for Burgundy's lament and for the unfolding inquiry of Shakespeare's play into political sovereignty.

In his great essay on custom Montaigne engages, as we might expect, in a rhetorically complex 'trying' or trial of the subject. On the one hand, the essay presents a shattering demonstration of the infinite variety of ways in which human beings impose order upon their experience of the world. In this respect, Montaigne shares with Bodin an understanding of the plurality of customary traditions. In a dazzling catalogue of examples from different periods and cultures, Montaigne shows that nothing that is now (customarily) conceived of as taboo or unnatural has not been made habitual within human societies. Political structures, codes of property and possession, sexual hierarchies, emotions, religious beliefs, forms of pleasure, all take on a bewildering diversity of entirely customary forms across the range of human societies. More radically, Montaigne suggests that assumptions regarding human nature or natural law are groundless: 'there is nothing that custom may not do and cannot do'.[40]

Yet as Victoria Kahn reminds us, it was Montaigne's habit 'in the course of any one essay [to] contradict whatever statement he seemed to

support'.[41] This commitment to sceptical inquiry is powerfully at work in the essay on custom. In an intriguing shift of emphasis, Montaigne recuperates its value because it is, in the end, the principal way in which human beings sustain themselves in communities. Furthermore, as Biancamaria Fontana suggests of Montaigne's view of custom: 'the sudden tearing of this connective tissue by a divisive intervention . . . could bring unforeseen disruption and suffering'.[42] In this sense, custom was of great value and, Montaigne observes, 'it is greatly to be doubted whether any obvious good can come from changing any traditional law'.[43] These traditions constitute an intricate and distinctive set of practices whose value demands respect. This is not quite as quiescent or conservative a position as it appears. Montaigne was well aware that 'the idea of custom [was] situated at the very storm center of modern political and constitutional debates'.[44] In this respect, his essay takes a further surprising turn when it acknowledges the great value of custom in the specific context of political domination. He confesses his pride that it was 'a Gascon gentleman from my part of the country whom Fortune led to be the first to object when Charlemagne wished to impose Imperial Roman Law on us'.[45] Custom takes on a new power, Montaigne argues, when traditional communities are threatened with

---

[38] Bodin, *The Six Bookes of a Commonweale*, p. 160.

[39] See Michel de Montaigne, 'On habit: and on never easily changing a traditional law', 1: 23, p. 122. Montaigne was a passionate, although not uncritical, admirer of the *Georgics*. He acclaimed the work as 'the most perfect achievement in poetry', 2: 10, p. 461, yet criticized passages that appeared to indulge in emperor-worship, deriding Virgil's recounting in Book 1 of the 'mad official belief' that a solar eclipse accompanied the assassination of Julius Caesar: see 2: 13, p. 686. For Montaigne's equivocal attitude towards Bodin, see 2: 32, esp. pp. 818–19.

[40] Montaigne, 'On habit', p. 129.

[41] Victoria Kahn, *Rhetoric, Prudence, and Scepticism in the Renaissance* (Ithaca and London, 1985), p. 146.

[42] Biancamaria Fontana, *Montaigne's Politics: Authority and Governance in the 'Essais'* (Princeton, 2008), p. 40.

[43] Montaigne, 'On habit', p. 134.

[44] Kelley, '"Second nature": The Idea of Custom', p. 136.

[45] Montaigne, 'On habit', p. 132.

suppression and it exposes the motives of those who endeavour to do so. In this way, custom can foster an actively critical response to domination (rather than serving simply to reconcile subjects to their condition). In these circumstances, it helps foster resistance to those who would obliterate an enduring sense of rights:

If you are resisting the growth of an innovation which has recently been introduced by violence, it is a dangerous and unfair obligation to be restrained by rules everywhere and all the time in your struggle against those who run loose, for whom anything is licit which advances their cause, and for whom law and order means seeking their own advantage.[46]

It is in this respect that Burgundy's lament carries a political charge because it recollects custom in the moment of its violation, a force that is preserved in memory and one that is not of the king's making, even if the latter has the power, if not the right, to vanquish it.

'[N]ice customs curtsy to great kings,' Henry declares to the French princess at the end of the play, when she insists on observing '*la coutume de France*' (5.2.267; 257). Henry glosses 'custom' as 'fashion', an ephemeral matter. The future royal couple 'cannot be confined within the weak list of a country's fashion. We are the makers of manners, Kate, and the liberty that follows our places stops the mouth of all find-faults, as I will do yours' (268–71). This silencing and dismissal of custom is another equivocal moment in a scene which refers to the contrasting importance of written treaties and articles of agreement. Yet from the georgic perspective that discloses the devastation of French agricultural life, imperial endeavour is caught in a disquieting relationship to custom as it attempts to diminish or correct the insufficiency of its claims.[47] In this way too, the play explores one of its defining questions: whether an expansionist war of conquest contributes to or detracts from the common good.[48] Furthermore, unlike Virgil's poem, which addresses Octavian as a supreme sovereign in the making, Shakespeare's play recounts a history that has vanished along with the king's legacy for his son: 'Whose state so many had the managing /

That they lost France and made his England bleed' (Epilogue, 11–12).

In an illuminating account of the legal discourses that inform *1* and *2 Henry IV*, Lorna Hutson has argued that the representation of monarchy in these plays is also suffused with a form of 'civic consciousness', a concern with the common weal as distinct from its embodiment in the king.[49] In *2 Henry IV*, Hutson suggests, there is a growing emphasis on Hal's intention to ensure that justice serves the public good. This perception is crystallized at the play's conclusion when the newly crowned Henry V acknowledges the law, in the person of the Lord Chief Justice, as a constitutional restraint upon his royal authority. Consequently, the play reveals 'a general good intended by justice which will curb Hal's magisterial power'.[50] In this article, I've argued that the evolving nature and extent of Henry V's sovereignty is re-examined by Shakespeare in a new context of imperial enterprise. The action of conquest also involves an expansion in the scope of sovereign powers. It is part of *Henry V*'s appeal that the decisive agency of the monarch is given inspirational rhetorical and dramatic force and the georgic mode of Virgil's writing undoubtedly contributes to this. However, the play also draws on the georgic legacy to sanction alternative reflections upon sovereignty; these provide significant testimony to the customary life

---

[46] Montaigne, 'On habit', p. 138. For an alternative analysis of Montaigne's view of custom see Ullrich Langer, 'Montaigne's Customs', *Montaigne Studies*, 4 (1992), 81–96.

[47] Bradin Cormack considers the tense relationship between territorial claims based on antiquity of occupation and usage in contrast to the rights of conquest primarily with reference to Spenser's *The Faerie Queene* (1590/96): see *A Power to Do Justice: Jurisdiction, English Literature, and the Rise of Common Law, 1509–1625* (Chicago, 2007), ch. 3.

[48] See Rita Banerjee, 'The Common Good and the Necessity of War: Emergent Republican Ideals in Shakespeare's *Henry V* and *Coriolanus*', *Comparative Drama*, 40 (2006), 29–49, esp. pp. 31–9.

[49] Lorna Hutson, 'Not the King's Two Bodies: Reading the "Body Politic" in Shakespeare's *Henry IV*, Parts 1 and 2', in *Rhetoric and Law in Early Modern Europe* (New Haven, 2001), pp. 166–98.

[50] Hutson, 'Not the King's Two Bodies', p. 188.

of the common weal in contrast to the immediacy of sovereign actions. On the one hand, Virgil's poem provided a way of conceiving Henry's kingship in a Bodinian manner: as an example of the heroic dedication required to cultivate and extend a political patrimony. On the other, the ambivalent representation of imperial sovereignty in the

Georgics also allowed Shakespeare to explore Montaigne's understanding of how domination alters understanding of both monarchical authority and the common good. *Henry V* presents a debate, not a thesis, concerning the king's sovereign powers and understanding of the terms and implications of this are deepened when its georgic aspect is perceived.

THE TROUBLESOME REIGN, RICHARD II, AND THE DATE OF KING JOHN: A STUDY IN INTERTEXTUALITY

CHARLES R. FORKER

I

Scholars continue to be increasingly aware of the extent to which Shakespeare habitually drew upon earlier drama for the verbal details, staging effects, dramatic situations, thematic ideas and even plot elements of his own plays. The playwright's use of prior dramas seems to have been especially pervasive among the chronicle histories.[1] Much of this assimilation was undoubtedly unconscious, at least in the case of verbal echoes, since Shakespeare seems to have known many of the plays from practical experience in the theatre, although he probably consulted playbooks and even published dramas as well. It is well known, for example, that *The Famous Victories of Henry the Fifth* (*c.*1586) lies behind *1* and *2 Henry IV* and *Henry V*, and many scholars believe that *The True Tragedy of Richard III* (1590–1) was a source for Shakespeare's play on the same subject.[2] Despite MacDonald Jackson's strong argument that *Woodstock* (1592–3?) post-dates *Richard II* (1595), many scholars still contend that Shakespeare echoed the anonymous play for his dramatization of Richard's fall; Marlowe's *Edward II* (1591–2) is also an undoubted source for numerous passages in the same play.[3] And as I have recently argued, *The True Chronicle History of King Leir* (1589–93?) served the dramatist not only as a source for his most cataclysmic tragedy but also for the verbal texture of both *Richard III* and *Richard II*.[4] Shakespeare seems to have imitated Kyd's *Spanish Tragedy* for at least one phrase referring to Richard II ('that sweet lovely rose') in *1 Henry IV* (1.3.175).[5]

Although the two-part history, *The Troublesome Reign of King John* (1589–91), has been much

---

[1] Of course the tragedies and comedies of Shakespeare were hardly exempt from the influence of earlier drama. We have Nashe's famous reference to 'whole Hamlets' in Greene's *Menaphon* (1589), pointing to Kyd as the probable author of the so-called *Ur-Hamlet*, besides which there are the numerous parallels between Shakespeare's *Hamlet* and *The Spanish Tragedy* (1587–90); see Geoffrey Bullough, *Narrative and Dramatic Sources of Shakespeare*, vol. 7 (London, 1978), pp. 15–19. Arthur Freeman establishes Shakespeare's use of Kyd's *Solyman and Perseda* in *Romeo and Juliet* in addition to having alluded to one of its characters in *King John*; see 'Shakespeare and "Solyman and Perseda"', *Modern Language Review*, 58 (1963), 481–7. G. K. Hunter notes the 'definite traces of a study and imitation' of Lyly's dramas in such comedies as *A Midsummer Night's Dream* and *Love's Labour's Lost*: see *John Lyly: The Humanist as Courtier* (London, 1962), p. 300. Antony Hammond points out Shakespeare's debt to Lyly's *Campaspe* (*c.*1584) in *Richard III*: see Hammond, ed., *Richard III* (London, 1981), pp. 95–6.

[2] See for instance J. Dover Wilson, 'Shakespeare's *Richard III* and *The True Tragedy of Richard the Third*, 1594', *Shakespeare Quarterly*, 3 (1952), 299–306; also G. B. Churchill, *Richard the Third up to Shakespeare*, *Palaestra X* (Berlin, 1900), pp. 497 ff.; Wilson, ed., *Richard III* (Cambridge, 1954), pp. xxviii–xxxiii; Bullough, *Narrative and Dramatic Sources*, vol. 3, pp. 222, 238–9, 241, 248; Kenneth Muir, *The Sources of Shakespeare's Plays* (London, 1977), p. 35.

[3] See Jackson, 'Shakespeare's *Richard II* and the Anonymous *Thomas of Woodstock*', *Medieval and Renaissance Drama in England*, 14 (2001), 17–65. For the majority view, see Charles R. Forker, ed., *Richard II*, Arden Shakespeare (London, 2002), pp. 144–52; and for Marlowe, pp. 159–65. The impact of *Woodstock* and *Edward II* upon Shakespeare's play went well beyond mere verbal imitation.

[4] Forker, 'From Political Revolution to Apocalypse: *Richard II* as a Precursor of *King Lear*', in '*Richard II*' *de William*

---

discussed in connection with the ongoing debate about its problematic relationship to Shakespeare's *King John*, its impact on other plays of the period has received scant attention. My contention in this essay is that *The Troublesome Reign*, which Sir Brian Vickers, assembling an impressive body of evidence, has recently ascribed to George Peele,[6] was well enough known by Shakespeare for him to have echoed it repeatedly in works other than *King John* – notably *Richard II*. Scholars agree that the date of *Richard II* is almost certainly 1595[7] and, further, that the numerous stylistic, prosodic and intellectual links between it and *King John* are too remarkable to be coincidental. There is warrant indeed for considering *Richard II* a companion piece to *King John* on the theme of royal legitimacy. If, therefore, it can be established that *The Troublesome Reign* served Shakespeare as a minor source for *Richard II* and other plays composed later than 1591 (when Peele's play was published), such evidence should materially strengthen the orthodox, but as yet not universally accepted, belief in the priority of *The Troublesome Reign* to *King John*. It would also reaffirm the basis for dating *King John* 1595–6 and for regarding *The Troublesome Reign* as its principal source.[8]

II

J. Dover Wilson long ago noted a few parallels between *The Troublesome Reign* and *Richard II*, implying that Shakespeare clearly knew the earlier play.[9] Scholars, however, have tended to ignore this evidence, and certainly no one has yet suggested that Peele's drama was prominent enough in the poet's memory or experience to serve him as a possible source for particular phrases, stage effects, imagery and other stylistic elements that would find their way into *Richard II*. That this should be so is scarcely surprising. We know that *The Troublesome Reign* was a Queen's Men's play, as were *The Famous Victories* and *King Leir* – both of them well-known sources for Shakespeare, who may perhaps have begun his career in the theatre as a member of the Queen's Players.[10] Shakespeare could have acted in Peele's play. I note some seventy verbal, thematic, thought-related, staging and situational links (some involving collocation of ideas)

Shakespeare: Une oeuvre en contexte, ed. Isabelle Schwartz-Gastine (Caen, 2005), pp. 13–14, n. 5.

5 Cf. Philip Edwards, ed., *The Spanish Tragedy* (London, 1959), p. 43 n. on 2.5.46. The Chadwyck-Healey database, *English Drama*, shows no other instances of the phrase.

6 Vickers, '*The Troublesome Raigne*, George Peele, and the Date of *King John*', in *Words that Count: Essays on Early Modern Authorship in Honor of MacDonald P. Jackson*, ed. Brian Boyd (Newark, 2004), pp. 78–116. Vickers, building on an early essay by H. Dugdale Sykes, '*The Troublesome Reign of King John*', in *Sidelights on Shakespeare* (Stratford-upon-Avon, 1919), pp. 99–125, documents numerous respects in which *TR* conforms to Peele's stylistic habits including self-repetition, the use of the same favourite words (e.g., *remunerate, gratify, pheere* [= spouse]), distinctive use of the vocative, self-naming, similar patterns of complex alliteration, the use of Latin tags (with *translatio*), feminine endings, pause patterns and the like. Sykes thinks that the stylistic uniformity of *TR* 'preclude[s] any supposition of mixed authorship' (101); Vickers, who applies a number of different stylistic and metrical tests and who demonstrates the general homogeneity and evenness of the Peele characteristics, arrives at the same conclusion.

7 See Forker, ed., *Richard II*, pp. 111–16.

8 The debate as to whether *The Troublesome Reign* is the source of *King John* or a derivative of it has been continuous since Peter Alexander in 1939 and E. A. J. Honigmann in 1954 proposed that Shakespeare's play preceded and was the source of the two-part drama; see Alexander, *Shakespeare's Life and Art* (London, 1939), pp. 85–6, and Honigmann, ed., *King John*, Arden Shakespeare (London, 1954), pp. xliii–lviii. As A. R. Braunmuller points out, however, a third possibility exists, namely that both *TR* and *KJ* derive from an earlier 'unknown text' – either a complete play or a mere scenario or 'plot' – and that 'the two surviving plays were written by authors aware of this hypothetical text' (*The Life and Death of King John* [Oxford, 1989], p. 10). E. M. W. Tillyard, for instance, suggested that *TR* might be a 'bad quarto . . . not of *King John* as we have it but of an early play by Shakespeare on the same theme. This play would then be the original both of the *Troublesome Reign* and of *King John*': see *Shakespeare's History Plays* (New York, 1946), p. 217. Suzanne Tumblin Gary went on to argue that *TR* is a 'plot-based adaptation' of *King John*, i.e. that it derives from an outline of the action of a play by Shakespeare, 'possibly based on shorthand notes taken during performance' in which the 'anonymous author' expanded his imperfectly absorbed original, substituted his own language for Shakespeare's, and emphasized the 'anti-Catholic potential of the material': see Gary, 'The Relationship between *The Troublesome Reign . . . and Shakespeare's King John*' (unpublished Ph.D. dissertation, University of Arizona, 1971),

that, taken in the aggregate, suggest a considerable impact of *The Troublesome Reign* upon *Richard II*.[11] It would be absurd to claim that each of these correspondences represents deliberate imitation by Shakespeare. Some of the details are conventional, proverbial, or commonplace; others involve parallel stage directions or dramaturgical decisions that may be coincidental, similarities of plot partly explainable by source material, or links that could be byproducts of like situations or even of the same dramatic genre. Nevertheless the number of specific phrasal connections between the two plays, not infrequently in analogous contexts, points unmistakably to direct influence (see Table I, pp. 130–1).

As several of my footnotes indicate, it would be rash to assume that even these correspondences are unique in every case to *The Troublesome Reign* and *Richard II*. A search of the Chadwyck-Healey database, *English Drama*, however, discloses no other examples for items 3, 5, 8, 12, 15, 18 and 19 in plays anterior to 1596. In a few additional cases (items 6, 16, 17) it is the similar contexts rather than mere verbal likeness that make borrowing probable.

The two plays share a number of common phrases and related locutions not listed in Table I: '**But who commes** posting **heere**?' (*TR*, 2:51) and '**But who comes here**?' (*RII*, 2.3.20, 2.3.67, 3.2.90, 3.3.19, 5.3.22); '**Well hath** my Lord . . . tolde his tale' (*TR*, 2:420) and '**Well have** you argued' (*RII*, 4.1.151); 'a **King annoynted**' (*TR*, 2:463) and 'an **anointed king**' (*RII*, 3.2.55); '**Till time** be minister of more amends' (*TR*, 2:511) and '**Till time** lend friends' (*RII*, 3.3.132); '**speake** them **faire**' (*TR*, 2:620) and '**speak** so **fair**' (*RII*, 3.3.128);[12] '**ill becomes**' (*TR*, 2:653) and '**ill become**' (*RII*, 3.3.97); '**The divell take** the Pope' (*TR*, 2:706) and '**The devil take** Henry of Lancaster' (*RII*, 5.5.102); 'your **nurse**' as a figure for England (*TR*, 2:759) and 'This **nurse**' referring also to England (*RII*, 2.1.51); 'stand not **wayling** on our present harmes . . . but seeke our harmes redresse' (*TR*, 2:780–1)[13] and 'wise men ne'er sit and **wail** their woes, / But presently prevent the ways to **wail**' (*RII*, 3.2.178–9); '**be**

our **owne carvers**' (*TR*, 2:986) and '**Be** his own **carver**' (*RII*, 2.3.144);[14] '**It bootes not** me . . . **To** . . .' (*TR*, 2:1167–9, 2:1173) and '**It boots** thee **not to** . . .' (*RII*, 1.3.174, 3.4.18); 'From out these loynes shall **spring** a Kingly **braunch**' (*TR*, 2:1084) and 'seven fair **branches** [i.e., the sons of Edward III] **springing** from one root' (*RII*, 1.2.13).[15] Vocabulary choices are also worth noticing. Both plays invoke the myth of Phaëton (*TR*, 1:338; *RII*, 3.3.178),[16] both use the word *lineal* in the special sense of 'conferred by

---

p. vi. Since there is no reliable evidence for the existence of this 'hypothetical' play in any form, it seems safest to discount it as a factor in an argument about priority and dating.

9 See Wilson, ed., *Richard II* (Cambridge, 1939), pp. x n., xliv n., lvii–lviii, 142, 151, 193; also Vickers, '*Troublesome Raigne*', p. 115 n. 57. Wilson speculates that 'The striking parallels between *Richard II* and *The Troublesome Reign* may be explained as due either to proximity of the dates of *Richard II* and *King John* or to *The Troublesome Reign* and the play used by Shakespeare for his *Richard II* being written by the same author' (p. x n.). Wilson's theory that a lost play on Richard's reign stood in relation to *Richard II* in a manner analogous to that of *The Troublesome Reign* and *King John* (pp. lxiv–lxxvi) has, however, failed to gain general acceptance.

10 See Scott McMillin and Sally-Beth MacLean, *The Queen's Men and Their Plays* (Cambridge, 1998), pp. 160–6.

11 For *The Troublesome Reign* I cite the edition by Geoffrey Bullough in vol. 4 of *Narrative and Dramatic Sources of Shakespeare* (London, 1962); for *Richard II* I quote from my own edition for the Arden Shakespeare (London, 2002).

12 Cf. also 'speak him fair' (*2 Henry VI*, 4.1.120; *The Comedy of Errors*, 4.2.16); 'speak us fair' (*The Comedy of Errors*, 4.4.152); 'speak me fair' (*The Merchant of Venice*, 4.1.275).

13 Peele's source was probably Arthur Brooke's *Romeus and Juliet* (1562): 'A wise man in the midst of troubles and distress, / Still standes not wayling present harme, but seeks his harmes redres' (ll. 1359–60); see Bullough, *Narrative and Dramatic Sources*, 1 (1957), 321. Since *Romeo and Juliet* was written the same year as *Richard II*, Brooke may also have been Shakespeare's source. Cf. also *3 Henry VI*: 'wise men ne'er sit and wail their loss, / But cheerly seek how to redress their harms' (5.4.1–2).

14 Cf. *Hamlet* (1.3.20). The phrase has proverbial overtones: see R. W. Dent, *Shakespeare's Proverbial Language: An Index* (Berkeley, 1981), C110.

15 Cf. *3 Henry VI*: 'That from his loins no hopeful branch may spring' (3.2.126).

16 Cf. *3 Henry VI*: 'Now Phaëton hath tumbled from his car' (1.4.33).

Table I

The Troublesome Reign	Richard II
1	**'Why (foolish boy)'** (1:206)	**'Why, foolish boy'** (2.3.97)[17]
2	'we will **away to France'** (1:305)	'you must **away to France'** (5.1.54)
3	'Ile **ceaze** . . . **lands / Into my hands** to pay my men of warre' (1:309–10)	'we **seize into our hands** / His . . . **lands** [to fund war in Ireland]' (2.1.209–10).[18]
4	**'Why lookst thou pale?** The colour **flyes thy face'** (1:898) Cf. 'your cullor gins to change' (2:1024)	**'Why looks your grace so pale?** . . . / But now the blood of twenty thousand men / Did triumph in **my face**, and they are **fled**.' (3.2.75–7) 'Have I not reason to **look pale** . . . ?' (3.2.79). 'Yea, **look'st thou pale?**' (5.2.57)[19]
5	'his **knee** . . . shall cleave / Unto . . . **the earth, / Till** *Fraunce* and *England* graunt this glorious boone' (1:919–21)	'may my **knees** grow to **the earth** . . . Unless a pardon ere I rise or speak' (5.3.29–31) 'Our **knees** still kneel **till** to the **ground** they grow' (5.3.105)
6	**'dreadfull drums'** (1:1039)	**'drums,** / With . . . trumpets' **dreadful** bray' (1.3.134–5)
7	'Why **how now** sirs, **what** may this outrage **meane?**' (1:1337). Arthur cries out when the executioners enter his cell.	**'How, now! What means Death** in this rude assault?' (5.5.105). Richard cries out when the murderers enter his cell.
8	**'staine the beautie of** our garden plot' (1:1544)	**'stained the beauty of** a fair queen's cheeks' (3.1.14)
9	'the **withered flower** [i.e., Prince Arthur dead]' (2:33)	'a . . . **withered flower** [i.e., Gaunt dying]' (2.1.134)[20]

(cont.)

hereditary authority' (*TR*, 1:353; *RII*, 3.3.113),[21] and both refer to Englishmen 'slaughtered' in warfare (*TR*, 1:694; *RII*, 3.3.44). Accoutrements of 'palmers' are mentioned in both dramas (*TR*, 2:98; *RII*, 3.3.151) and both use the verb *convey* for removing corpses or carrying dying men off-stage (*TR*, 2:102, 109; *RII*, 2.1.137). Both employ the rare verb *unsay* (*TR*, 2.130; *RII*, 4.1.9),[22] and both use *undo* in the context of royal displacement or deposition (*TR*, 2:224; *RII*, 4.1.203). *Usurp*, including its variants, appears twice in one play (*TR*, 1:511, 2:669), three times in the other (*RII*, 3.3.81, 4.1.257, 5.1.65). Simple chance might account for some of these parallels, but their density suggests a more than coincidental relationship.

Examples of related imagery may also owe something to conscious imitation. A queen or England itself as the 'womb' of 'kings' relates *The Troublesome Reign* (1:6–7) to *Richard II* (2.1.51), as does the

association of political ambition with the soaring of birds (*TR*, 1:261–2, 528–9; *RII*, 1.1.109, 1.3.129–

[17] Cf. Lyly, *Sapho and Phao*: 'foolish boy' (2.1.11); *Complete Works of John Lyly*, ed. R. Warwick Bond (Oxford, 1902), II, p. 380.

[18] Holinshed does not connect Richard's seizure of Gaunt's property with his need to finance the Irish war; see Forker, ed., *Richard II*, pp. 238n., 259n., 262n.

[19] Cf. also *2 Henry VI* (3.2.27). Unless otherwise noted, citations of Shakespeare are taken from *The Riverside Shakespeare*, ed. G. Blakemore Evans and J. J. M. Tobin (Boston, 1997) to which the standard Harvard Concordance is keyed.

[20] Cf. also *The Rape of Lucrece*: 'the withered flow'r' (line 1254). Peele repeated the phrase in the revised text of his poem, *The Tale of Troy* (1604), line 477; see *The Life and Works of George Peele*, gen. ed. Charles Tyler Prouty (New Haven, 1952–70), vol. I, p. 202.

[21] Cf. *1 Henry VI*: 'by lineal descent' (3.1.165).

[22] This use is one of only four instances in Shakespeare; the others are *A Midsummer Night's Dream* (1.1.181), *1 Henry IV* (1.3.76) and *Henry VIII* (5.1.175).

Table I (*cont.*)

The Troublesome Reign	Richard II
10 'Remove the **Sunne** from our Meridian, / Unto . . . **thantipodes**' (2:124–5)[23]	Richard likens himself to the sun, 'the searching eye of heaven . . . wand'ring with the **Antipodes**' (3.2.37–49)
11 '**cursed fall**' (2:149)	'**fall** of **cursed** man' (3.4.76)
12 '**a traitor with the rest**' (2:216)	'**a traitor with the rest**' (4.1.248)
13 '**gives away** the **Crowne**' (2:271) '**give my Crowne**' (2:322) '**give my Crowne with** this right **hand**' 2:325)	'**With** mine own **hands I give away my crown**' (4.1.208)
14 '**Why am I sent for to** thy cursed selfe?' (2:287).	'**why am I sent for to** a king . . . ?' (4.1.163).
15 'curst **without redemption**' (2:299)	'damned **without redemption**' (3.2.129)
16 King John takes up arms against the French: '**Come** lets **away**' (2:347)	Bolingbroke takes up arms against the Welsh: '**Come**, lords, **away**' (3.1.42)
17 Philip the Bastard tries to cheer King John when he is threatened by Lewis the Dauphin and his alliance: '**Comfort my** Lord' (2:710)	Aumerle tries to cheer up King Richard when Bolingbroke's military power seems overwhelming: '**Comfort, my** liege' (twice; 3.2.75, 3.2.82)[24]
18 '**I know not, nor I care not**' (2:988).	'**I know not, nor I** greatly **care not**' (5.2.48)
19 King John reflects upon his evil rule: 'Me thinks I see a cattalogue of **sinne**, / **Wrote** . . . in Marble characters' (2:1046–7)	King Richard has a similar moment of reflection, looking into his mirror: 'I do see the very book indeed / Where all my **sins** are **writ**' (4.1.274–5)

30). Both playwrights are attracted to the contrast of 'shadow' with 'substance' for expressing fantasy-versus-reality issues (*TR*, 1:513–14; *RII*, 2.2.14, 4.1.294–9), and both apply the imagery of pruning 'branches' (*TR*, 1:1481–2; *RII*, 3.4.63–4) and of 'rooting' out 'weeds' (*TR*, 1:1543–5; *RII*, 3.4.37–8) to the suppression of political enemies. Both name mountain ranges – 'the frozen Alps' (*TR*, 2:1033–4) and 'the frosty Caucasus' (*RII*, 1.3.294–5) – to vivify antitheses of heat and cold. Both mention 'meteors', 'moons' and 'prophets' in connection with the future toppling of kings (*TR*, 1:1593, 1602; *RII*, 2.4.9–15) although Shakespeare also probably consulted Daniel's *Civil Wars* for the omens.[25] Familiar sentiments, though they can scarcely be called uncommon, may carry over from the earlier to the later play. Both dramas present characters who inveigh against the shame of ceding French possessions won by heroic predecessors such as Richard Coeur de Lion, Edward III or the Black Prince (*TR*, 1:832–4; *RII*, 2.1.178–81); both draw upon the proverbial notion that dying men

(Meloun, Gaunt) can be relied upon to speak the truth (*TR*, 2:724–5; *RII*, 2.1.5–6);[26] both express the conviction that internal dissension is a greater danger to England than threats from abroad (*TR*, 2:1187–8; *RII*, 2.1.65–6),[27] and both voice the

---

23   Cf. Marlowe, *2 Tamburlaine* (1.2.51–2): 'Phoebus leaping from his hemisphere / Descendeth downward to th'Antipodes'; also 5.3.148–9: 'the sun, declining from our sight, / Begins the day with our Antipodes.' Peele could be imitating Marlowe. Of course Shakespeare's source could be either Marlowe or Peele. The edition cited is J. S. Cunningham, ed., *Tamburlaine the Great* (Manchester, 1981).

24   Cf. *3 Henry VI* (4.8.28).

25   See Forker, ed., *Richard II*, p. 307n.

26   Forker, ed., *Richard II*, p. 242n.

27   Cf. *The True Tragedy of Richard Duke of York*: 'Let England be true within it selfe, / We need not France nor any alliance with them' (*The Complete Works of William Shakespeare*, ed. Herbert Farjeon [London, 1953], vol. II, p. 869). This reading from the so-called bad quarto of *3 Henry VI* could be Peele's source, but the uncertainty of date and the possibility that actors were recalling a line heard earlier in the theatre makes it impossible to know in which direction the indebtedness runs. The Folio reading of *3 Henry VI*: 'England is safe, if true

doctrine that subjects must passively obey divine-right monarchs, even when they are guilty of murder (*TR*, 2:463–7; *RII*, 1.2.37–41). On the last point, Virgil Whitaker has suggested that, when composing *Richard II*, 'Shakespeare probably owed a great deal' to the Bastard's defence of John as 'a King annoynted by the Lord' (*TR*, 2:463).[28]

The number of staging and situational parallels is also striking. Both plays make use of the upper stage to represent castle battlements for a confrontation between opposed political forces above and below (*TR*, 1:613; *RII*, 3.3.61.2); both introduce symmetrical heralds to represent their hostile masters ceremonially in combat (*TR*, 1:671–8; *RII*, 1.3.104–16); and both feature an aborted chivalric contest between a pair of dukes (*TR*, 1:924–59; *RII*, 1.3.118–53). The ritualistic laying down of hands beside each other or upon the hilt of a sword accompanies oath-swearing in both dramas (*TR*, 2:494, 619; *RII*, 1.3.179–80), and the use of trumpets to announce a 'parley' between competing kings or claimants to the same throne contributes to a similar pageantry in both (*TR*, 2:1142.1; *RII*, 3.3.61.1). In each a sick or dying character (King John, Gaunt) is borne on and off-stage in a chair (*TR*, 2:785.1, 868; *RII*, 2.1.0.1, 138), and both plays conclude solemnly with funeral processions (*TR*, 2:1192–4; *RII*, 5.6.51–2). Constance despairs of Arthur's prospects for rule ('**I see the fall** of all thy hopes' [*TR*, 1:784]) in an episode that Salisbury may recall when he predicts Richard's defeat: '**I see** thy glory like a shooting star / **Fall** to the base earth' (*RII*, 2.4.19–20). Both plays contain scenes in which one claimant to the throne confronts his rival (*TR*, 1:1097–8; *RII*, 4.1.175–6, 220), and both utilize the device of having successive messengers arrive with bad news to create crescendos of disaster (*TR*, 2:953–5, 962, 969–70; *RII*, 3.2.119–20, 200–3). *The Troublesome Reign* presents two coronations on stage, the second an obvious echo of the first (1:1537.1, 2:1184.1). Although Henry IV's crowning takes place off-stage in the later tragedy, Shakespeare gives it unusual prominence ('On Wednesday next we solemnly set down / Our coronation. Lords, prepare yourselves' [*RII*, 4.1.319–20]), adumbrating it powerfully through

Richard's invented ceremony of self-divestiture – a coronation in reverse: 'I give this heavy weight from off my head, / And this unwieldy sceptre from my hand…'; 'With mine own hands I give away my crown' (*RII*, 4.1.204–5, 208).

A few details of plot and characterization in *The Troublesome Reign* could have influenced *Richard II*. Especially notable are the similar ways in which King John and Henry IV hint at their desire to have their royal kinsmen murdered (*TR*, 1:1121–3; *RII*, 5.4.2), then cynically repudiate their agents when they suppose that the crime has been accomplished (*TR*, 1:1722; *RII*, 5.6.39–44). Significantly, Holinshed's treatment of Richard's reign provides no warrant for either action. Both John and Richard appoint regents (Essex, York) to govern England while they lead armies abroad (*TR*, 1:307; *RII*, 2.1.219–20); and the two plays also refer to the custom of 'taking the assay' (i.e., testing the royal food to make sure it is not poisoned) in connection with the assassinations of the two kings (*TR*, 2:1012–13; *RII*, 5.5.99). Although Shakespeare relied mainly on Holinshed for these last two elements,[29] their presence in *The Troublesome Reign* could have reinforced Shakespeare's decision to include them. The character of King John in Peele's play may have suggested to Shakespeare a few touches for his portrait of Richard II. John anticipates deposition and death before he learns that Lewis has been proclaimed king just as Richard does in similar circumstances (*TR*, 2:178–81; *RII*, 3.2.95–103). John rails against his subjects who defect to the enemy, proclaiming them traitors, in the same way that Richard, misunderstanding their actions, damns Bushy, Green and

---

within itself' (4.1.40) appears further removed from the language of *TR*. Dover Wilson believed that Peele might have contributed to *3 Henry VI* and indeed that Shakespeare in the Henry VI trilogy was revising plays originally composed by others; see Wilson, ed., *2 Henry VI* (Cambridge, 1952), p. xxviii. If Wilson is correct, the close similarity between the line on England's being true to itself in *TR* and its counterpart in *True Tragedy* might conceivably be explained as Peele repeating himself.

28 Whitaker, *Shakespeare's Use of Learning* (San Marino, CA, 1964), p. 139.

29 For Richard's appointment of York as regent, see Forker, ed., *Richard II*, 264n.; for Richard's taster, see p. 472n.

the Earl of Wiltshire (*TR*, 2:201–10; *RII*, 3.2.129–32). John agonizes about submitting to the Pope before finally yielding, as does Richard when reluctantly acceding to Bolingbroke's demands (*TR*, 2:300–5; *RII*, 4.1.200–2); and both kings in similarly plangent tones lament being forced to give up their thrones: '**I must loose** my realme' (*TR*, 2:321); '**Must** [I] **lose** / The name of King?' (*RII*, 3.3.145–6).

Clearly the two plays are related conceptually, both being centrally concerned with dynastic conflict and with questions of lineal inheritance, *de facto* versus *de jure* rule, primogeniture and usurpation. In the earlier play, a dispute about true heredity involving the half-brothers, Robert and Philip Falconbridge, parallels the debate as to whether Prince Arthur or John is the rightful king of England. The issue of possession versus theoretical entitlement informs both conflicts and seems to carry over into Shakespeare's drama where we can see the issue of dual claimants to the throne within the same royal family (a nephew versus an uncle) reprised in the antagonism between Richard and Bolingbroke (royal cousins). Both plays make much of taking off and putting on crowns, actions shown visually as well as articulated politically. A few of the same names even appear in both plays – Fitzwater, Percy, Ross and Mowbray. These are merely mentioned in Peele and do not attach to characters who appear on stage as in Shakespeare.[30] Moreover, they come in both cases from Holinshed, not from dramatic sources. But even though the naming links are accidental, they nevertheless illustrate the interest in similar subject matter that both dramatists shared and might prompt a playwright who was working from an array of source materials to recall an earlier use of the same families or titles.

A certain stylistic carry-over may also be noted, particularly in the comic rhyming that Shakespeare introduces into the scene where Aumerle and his parents beg Henry IV at cross purposes:

> *King Henry.* Our scene is altered from a serious thing,
> And now changed to 'The Beggar and the King'. –
> My dangerous cousin, let your mother in.
> I know she's come to pray for your foul sin.

> [*Aumerle opens the door.*]
> *Enter* Duchess [of York].
> *York* [*to King Henry*]. If thou do pardon whosoever pray,
> More sins for this forgiveness prosper may.
> This festered joint cut off, the rest rest sound;
> This let alone will all the rest confound.
>
> (*Richard II*, 5.3.78–85)

As Wilson notes, 'This farcical upshot is quite in the manner of *The Troublesome Reign*'.[31] The passage to which Wilson refers is that in which Philip the Bastard reacts facetiously to the revelation that he is the natural son of Richard Coeur de Lion:

> Then *Robin Fauconbridge* I wish thee joy,
> My Sire a King, and I a landles Boy.
> Gods Ladie Mother, the word is in my debt,
> There's something owing to *Plantaginet*.
> I marrie Sir, let me alone for game,
> Ile act some wonders now I know my name.
>
> (*Troublesome Reign*, 1:412–17)

Introducing a note of jocosity into an otherwise serious situation is indeed the kind of rapid shift in tone that Shakespeare could have picked up from a cruder drama on a similar subject. Another stylistic similarity is the use of anaphora in both plays, particularly as exemplified by rhetorical questions in series. The villainous monk who poisons John is given to such patterned speech:

> Is this the King that never lovd a Frier?
> Is this the man that doth contemne the Pope?
> Is this the man that robd the holy Church
> And yet will flye unto a Friory?
> Is this the King that aymes at Abbeys lands?
> Is this the man whome all the world abhorres,
> And yet will flye unto a Friorie?
>
> (*Troublesome Reign*, 2:869–75)

Richard's address to the mirror is rhetorically similar:

> Was this face the face
> That every day under his household roof

---

[30] *The Troublesome Reign*, 2:354, 359. It hardly needs mentioning that 'L. *Fitz Water*,' 'L. *Percy*,' 'L. *Rosse*' and 'Lord *Mowbrey*' are different historical personages from characters with the same titles in *Richard II*.

[31] Wilson, ed., *Richard II*, p. 226.

Did keep ten thousand men? Was this the face
That like the sun did make beholders wink?
Is this the face which faced so many follies,
That was at last outfaced by Bolingbroke?
(*Richard II*, 4.1.281–6)[32]

Shakespeare would seem, then, to have had Peele's play at the back of his consciousness as he composed *Richard II*, recalling particular situations or ideas presented on stage or summoning up incidental phrases or bits of dialogue, perhaps subliminally, from having read or heard or acted them in the theatre. The validity of this assumption can be supported by instancing echoes from the same play in other dramas by Shakespeare.

III

Various scholars have noted parallels in *The Troublesome Reign* to a large range of Elizabethan plays, a circumstance that has led to the assumption that the author was 'a shameless borrower' or, as E. A. J. Honigmann puts it, a 'writer with a memory-box filled with scraps from other men's plays'.[33] Peter Alexander, who believed in earlier dates for many of Shakespeare's plays than traditionalists such as E. K. Chambers, referred to the drama as 'a tissue of borrowed and only half-assimilated phrases from *Henry VI*, *Richard III*, as well as *King John* itself'.[34] There can be no doubt that *The Troublesome Reign* is indeed replete with many parallels to contemporary plays although, unfortunately, it is sometimes difficult to establish their precedence. An excellent example of this problem is the anonymous *Arden of Faversham* (tentatively dated by M. L. Wine 1588–91), which contains several striking parallels to *The Troublesome Reign*, the priority of which it is impossible at the present time to determine.[35] A goodly number of the verbal similarities are to plays by Peele himself, which (if we accept Vickers's attribution) are best explained as mere repetitions by a playwright who was in the habit of reusing favorite locutions, vocabulary and rhetorical mannerisms in different contexts.[36] Among the most indubitable parallels are a substantial group from *3 Henry VI* and *Richard III*, the most con-

vincing of which Professor Honigmann has conveniently assembled for us.[37] Although these may look, as Honigmann argues, like desultory echoes of Shakespeare in *The Troublesome Reign*, to accept each of them as such requires us to date *Richard III* as early as 1590 whereas the preponderance of other kinds of evidence, most thoroughly summarized by Wells and Taylor, points to 1592–3 as the date of composition.[38] Indeed the Wells–Taylor chronology of Shakespeare, on which the present discussion is founded and which takes into account extensive studies of rhyming, metrics, vocabulary, linguistics and other kinds of evidence, makes 1591 the earliest possible date for any of Shakespeare's histories. Honigmann, following A. S. Cairncross, says that in the case of one of the several *Troublesome*

---

[32] Although such rhetoric could have been prompted by the passage in *TR*, the more likely source (probably recognizable to many in the audience) was the famous passage in Marlowe's *Doctor Faustus*: 'Was this the face that launched a thousand ships?' (A-text, 5.1.91–2); see my note in *Richard II* (408). Peele indeed may well have picked up the technique from Marlowe if (as some think) *Doctor Faustus* preceded *TR*.

[33] J. C. Maxwell, ed., *Titus Andronicus*, 3rd edn (London, 1961), p. xxii; Honigmann, *Shakespeare's Impact on His Contemporaries* (Totowa, NJ, 1982), p. 79.

[34] Alexander, *Shakespeare's Life and Art* (London, 1939), p. 85.

[35] See Wine, ed., *The Tragedy of Master Arden of Faversham* (London, 1973), pp. xliii–xlv. Among the closer parallels are the following: '**Ile** not **infringe my vow**' (*TR*,1:375; 'if **I infringe my vow**' *Arden*, 4.70); 'The world **can witnes**' (*TR*, 1:443; 'The heavens **can witness**' *Arden*, 1.194); 'I **venter life**' (*TR*, 2:3; 'You'll **venture life**' *Arden* 1.271); '**Disturbed thoughts**' (*TR*, 2:110; '**Disturbèd thoughts**' *Arden*, 8.1); '**life** . . . **is leveld at**' (*TR*, 2:266; '**life is levelled at**' *Arden*, 3.196). The passages in which 'Disturbed thoughts' occurs are both gloomy soliloquies in which King John and Mosby, respectively, ruminate; the database, *English Drama*, suggests that the phrase is unique to these two plays.

[36] See Sykes, especially pp. 108–24; also Honigmann, *Shakespeare's Impact*, p. 79.

[37] Honigmann, *Shakespeare's Impact*, p. 80.

[38] See *William Shakespeare: A Textual Companion*, ed. Stanley Wells and Gary Taylor (Oxford, 1987), pp. 115–16. Matthew McDiarmid points out that *Richard III* must postdate Marlowe's *Edward II* (1591–2), since two minor characters, Tressel and Berkeley (*Richard III*, 1.2.225), derive from the Marlowe play in which Trussel and Berkeley are 'authorized by chronicle'; see 'Concerning *The Troublesome Reign of King John*', *Notes and Queries*, n.s. 4 (1957), 435.

Reign–Richard III parallels in which the echoed phrase happens to be 'devine instinct' (*TR*, 2:518; cf. 'divine instinct' [*RIII*, 2.3.42]), Shakespeare cannot be the debtor because he is rewriting Holinshed's 'secret instinct of nature' whereas the source material for the King John play contains no comparable phrase.[39] But as the Chadwyck-Healey database, *Early English Books Online* (*EEBO*), reveals, 'divine instinct' was in fairly common use (we find at least eight instances before 1590 in the works of Lodge, Spenser and others), so that Shakespeare's use of it in *Richard III* as a paraphrase of Holinshed could have been prompted by Peele's play, or by Lodge or Spenser, or indeed have occurred to him spontaneously as a locution in popular circulation. There is no Stationers' Register entry for *The Troublesome Reign* (printed 1591), but it could hardly have been performed for the first time any later than 1590–91, and its composition probably dates from earlier still.[40] The likelihood of Shakespeare's having drawn upon Peele's play both for the Henry VI plays and for *Richard III* is therefore strong.

Two additional parallels to *Titus Andronicus* and *The Comedy of Errors* present the same kind of chronological issue. There is an obvious connection between 'Even now I curse the **day** . . . Wherein I did not **some notorious ill**' (*Titus*, 5.1.125–7) and 'a **day** / That tended not to **some notorious ill**' (*TR*, 2:1060–1); and also between '**Hopeless and helpless** doth Egeon wend' (*Errors*, 1.1.157) and 'Poore helples boy, **hopeles and helples** too' (*TR*, 1:894). The Chadwyck-Healey database, *English Drama*, shows that these parallels are unique in plays written before 1642. To assume with Honigmann, however, that *The Troublesome Reign* was invariably the borrower forces us to date both *Titus* and *Errors* no later than 1590 – an obstacle for chronological traditionalists who tend on the basis of evidence of other kinds to date the revenge tragedy in 1592 and the Plautine comedy as late as 1594.[41] That *The Troublesome Reign* contains imitations of earlier plays is probable (*Arden of Faversham* may be an example), but that these include known dramas by Shakespeare seems most unlikely if we accept the chronologies of E. K. Chambers and Wells–Taylor. On the contrary, there is every reason to think that Shakespeare and other dramatists drew upon Peele's play for striking or even serviceable phrasing. I have argued elsewhere that Shakespeare and Marlowe borrowed from and strongly influenced each other in a way that amounted almost to symbiosis, as is especially apparent in the close verbal and conceptual ties between *Edward II* and the first historical tetralogy and then again between *Edward II* and *Richard II*.[42] The professional relationship between Peele and Shakespeare appears to have been more of a one-way street in the latter's direction, but we know now, as Brian Vickers has demonstrated, that the two collaborated on *Titus Andronicus*.[43] We should note, by the way, that Shakespeare's echo of *The Troublesome Reign* in *Titus* occurs in a part of the latter play (5.1) *not* composed by Peele, although the collaboration might partly account for Shakespeare's attraction to the echo of 'some notorious ill', remembered from an earlier play by his working partner.

If we could be certain, as most recent scholars contend, that *1 Henry VI* was composed in 1592, basing their conclusions on Henslowe's entries for 'Harey the vj' that year and on Nashe's famous reference in *Pierce Penniless* (1592) to a recent play

---

39 Honigmann, *Shakespeare's Impact*, pp. 82–3.

40 Honigmann, who posits 1590–1 as the date when *TR* was written, ascribes the brief interval between the play's performance and its publication to 'financial difficulties of the Queen's Men' at the time (*Shakespeare's Impact*, pp. 86–7). My inclination is to date *TR* about 1589–90, earlier than Shakespeare's first tetralogy according to Wells and Taylor's chronology.

41 1592 and 1594 are the dates assigned by Wells and Taylor in their *Textual Companion*, pp. 113–15, 116–17. E. K. Chambers dated *Titus* 1593–4 and *Errors* 1592–3; see *William Shakespeare: A Study of Facts and Problems* (Oxford, 1930), vol. I, p. 270.

42 See Forker, ed., *Marlowe's Edward II* (Manchester, 1994), pp. 17–41; also Forker, ed., *Richard II*, pp. 159–64.

43 See Vickers, *Shakespeare, Co-Author: A Historical Study of Five Collaborative Plays* (Oxford, 2002), pp. 148–243. Shakespeare may have drawn upon Peele's *Battle of Alcazar* (1588–9) as well as Marlowe's *2 Tamburlaine* for Pistol's rant in *2 Henry IV*, 2.4; see A. R. Humphrey, ed., *2 Henry IV* (London, 1966), pp. 73–4 nn.

on 'brave *Talbot*',[44] we might add another echo of Peele's King John drama to our list of Shakespearian imitations. In *The Troublesome Reign* the French lord Meloun expires from wounds after having warned his English allies that if they continue to support Lewis as claimant to the English throne, he will reward their loyalty with death. Salisbury then orders Meloun's corpse to be removed from the stage: '**Beare hence** the **bodie**...' (2:778). Shakespeare (or perhaps Nashe himself if he was responsible for the corresponding scene)[45] gave the same line to Talbot, who orders the removal of another slain hero (coincidentally named Salisbury) from the battle: '**Bear hence** his **body**, I will...bury it' (*1 Henry VI*, 1.4.87). If this is a legitimate Shakespearian echo (we find no other instances in the Chadwyck-Healey database apart from *Romeo and Juliet* [1595], 3.1.196), it illustrates the point that verbal borrowings were often virtually subliminal – useful phrases from a probably unsorted store of theatrical utterances that had become commonplace in the minds of their users.

Lest it should be thought too hazardous to rely for dating purposes exclusively on plays by Shakespeare composed so near in time to the publication date of *The Troublesome Reign*, we may point to two additional Shakespearian parallels where priority is not in question. In the 'anonymous' King John play, Cardinal Pandulph acclaims the Dauphin Lewis as the 'victorious Conqueror' (*TR*, 2:655) whose military powers have brought most of England under French control, only to be told that on the threshold of his success he must withdraw his forces because John has at last submitted to Rome and acknowledged the Pope as his liege lord. When Lewis is advised 'quietly [to] returne to *Fraunce* againe: / For all is done the Pope would wish thee doo,' he responds defiantly, '**But al's not done** that *Lewes* came to doo' (*TR*, 2:663–5). Shakespeare seems to have recalled this moment in *Henry V* (1598–9) when another royal conqueror comments during the Battle of Agincourt, 'Well have we done, thrice-valiant countrymen, / **But all's not done** – yet keep the French the field' (4.6.1–2). Shakespeare's reminiscence here seems the more likely since both contexts involve mili-

tary conflicts between French and English armies. Moreover, the database, *English Drama*, reveals no other examples of the phrase in plays of the Tudor period. The second probable echo from *The Troublesome Reign* seems to have been prompted by a speech by Philip the Bastard in reaction to King John's impending death: '**O piercing sight**, he fumbleth in the mouth, / His speech doth faile' (*TR*, 2:1103–4). Shakespeare in *King Lear* (1605–6) may have recalled this expression when Edgar, encountering his crazed sovereign on the heath, exclaims, 'O thou side-**piercing sight**!' (4.6.85). In both instances the exclamations, glancing as they do at the Gospel account of Christ's pierced body on the cross (John 19:34), come from loyal subjects appalled by the stricken condition of their royal masters.[46]

The case of verbal parallels to Marlowe and Kyd in *The Troublesome Reign* is more complex because the chronologies of these playwrights are notoriously difficult to fix with certainty and have yet to be studied with the same ingenious intensity that has characterized investigations of Shakespeare. Nevertheless, there is general scholarly consensus that *1* and *2 Tamburlaine* (1587–8) preceded *Edward II* (1591–2) and *The Massacre at Paris* (1592–3); and also that *The Spanish Tragedy* (1587–90) preceded *Solyman and Perseda* (1590–2).[47] *The*

---

44 See Edward Burns, ed., *Henry VI, Part I*, Arden Shakespeare (London, 2000), pp. 1–9.

45 Burns, ed., *Henry VI, Part I*, pp. 73–6. Debate as to the possibly collaborative genesis of *1 Henry VI* is ongoing.

46 *English Drama*, the Chadwyck-Healey database, lists the phrase 'piercing sight' as appearing also in Beaumont and Fletcher's *The Woman-Hater* (1607) and Middleton's pageant, *Triumphs of Truth* (1613), but in contexts where acuteness of vision, not penetrating grief, is the point. In any case these instances are later than *King Lear*.

47 The two parts of *Tamburlaine* were published together in 1590 (Stationers' Register entry, 14 August 1590) and, as J. S. Cunningham explains in his Revels edition, 'Some two or three years separate the first performance' of the two plays 'from the 1590 printing' (22). *Edward II* cannot have been composed earlier than 1591 (see Forker, ed., pp. 14–17) whereas *The Massacre at Paris*, a reported text, contains reminiscences of *Edward II* (as well as of *2* and *3 Henry VI*) and is probably to be dated 1592 or 1593 shortly before Marlowe's death. The upward limit for the date of *The Spanish Tragedy*

Troublesome Reign contains convincing parallels to all these plays some of which are almost certainly earlier compositions (pre-1591) and others of which are probably later (post-1591).[48] The precise details of Peele's relationship to Marlowe and Kyd, taking into account uncertainties of dating as well as the mixed evidence of verbal indebtedness provided by the Chadwyck-Healey database, must await further research. But in the meantime it is reasonable to assume that the three dramatists knew and drew upon each other. Honigmann bases his claim that the borrowing in *The Troublesome Reign* must all be on one side mostly upon his preconception of an anonymous theatrical hack (he wrote before Vickers had confirmed Peele's authorship) whose 'literary talent' was 'essentially derivative, or parasitic'. He describes a playwright who cobbled up a 'strangely uncelebrated' play in a hodgepodge of styles including 'attempted blank verse, rhymed pentameters, fourteeners, Skeltonics and other forms of doggerel, as well as prose'. Clinging to the belief that such an unusually pedestrian drama derives from Shakespeare's *King John* as opposed to its being that play's principal source, he characterizes the writer as 'an imitator of popular styles, as well as phrases, and this makes it all the more likely that he also imitated another man's plot'.[49] What such a view fails to recognize is that verbal imitation was a stock-in-trade of the commercial theatre, and that popular dramatists such as Peele, Marlowe, Kyd and Shakespeare all practised it to varying degrees.

Scholars who have studied the controversial but obviously close relationship between *The Troublesome Reign* and Shakespeare's *King John* have understandably concentrated on similarities and differences in characterization, plot, political or religious bias and general style. The point usually stressed is the seeming paradox that one of the two plays should follow the other so closely in respect of its outline and sequence of scenes, yet depart from it so strikingly in the use, or rather non-use, of its language. Although verbal parallels between the two dramas are indeed more numerous than has sometimes been realized, these tend to consist of utilitarian or unremarkable phrases and almost never

involve the arresting images or turns of phrase that we might expect an eager dramatist to remember or appropriate. The closeness in wording of several stage directions in the two plays is also worth remarking. The following table (see pp. 138–9) shows the kinds of imitation employed.

The five closely related stage directions that obviously link the two plays in some fashion have been discussed by Alice Walker (items 1, 6, 23 and 24) and by Sidney Thomas (item 3). Walker points out that the close similarities in wording and in the order of characters named betoken a 'documentary link' between the two plays since the precise formulation of stage directions could not have been so imitated if the transmission had been merely auditory or memorial. One of the two dramatists, she implies, must have had a paper text before him as he composed, and since *The Troublesome Reign* was the only one of the two dramas in print during the period when *King John* could have been written, Shakespeare very probably was the borrower. If Peele had been the copier of these stage directions, he would presumably have had to work in 1589–90

---

is its entry in the Stationers' Register (6 October 1592) while its dependence on a sonnet by Thomas Watson (1582) establishes the anterior limit. Most scholars have favoured 1587 as the date of composition although Philip Edwards on stylistic and other grounds suggests 1590 as more probable; see Edwards, ed., pp. xxi–xxvii. Frederick S. Boas places *Solyman and Perseda* in 1588, later than *The Spanish Tragedy* (*The Works of Thomas Kyd*, rev. edn [Oxford, 1955], p. lvii); E. K. Chambers suggests 1589–92 (*The Elizabethan Stage* [Oxford, 1923], vol. IV, p. 46). But Arthur Freeman presents strong reasons for dating it after 1591, just before its publication in 1592; see 'Shakespeare and "Solyman and Perseda"', *Modern Language Review*, 58 (1963), 483–7.

48 *TR*, 1.1154 ('stop **the organ of** her **voyce**'), echoes *1 Tamburlaine*, 2.7.8 ('arrests **the organ of** my **voice**'); *TR*, 1:1158–9 ('**tongue is tunde** ... **to tell** a pleasing **tale**'), echoes *The Spanish Tragedy*, 4.4.85 ('**tongue is tun'd to tell** his latest **tale**'). For echoing of other plays in *TR*, see Rupert Taylor, 'A Tentative Chronology of Marlowe's and Some Other Elizabethan Plays', *PMLA*, 51 (1936), 643–88; H. B. Charlton and R. D. Waller, eds., *Edward II*, rev. F. N. Lees (London, 1955), pp. 8–10; Forker, ed., *Edward II*, pp. 14–17, 152, 235, 267. See also Kenneth Muir, 'The Chronology of Marlowe's Plays', *Proceedings of the Leeds Philosophical and Literary Society*, 5 (1938–43), 345–56.

49 Honigmann, *Shakespeare's Impact*, p. 81.

Table II

The Troublesome Reign	King John
1	S.D. '*Enter K. John, Queene Elinor* . . . , *William Marshal Earle of* **Pembrooke**, *the Earles of* **Essex** *and of* **Salisbury**' (1:0.1–2)	S.D. '*Enter King Iohn, Queene Elinor, Pembroke, Essex, and Salisbury*' [Folio] (1.1.0.1)
2	'the Lordship of *Ireland, / Poit[i]ers, Anjow, Torain, Main*' (1:33–4)	'To **Ireland, Poitiers, Anjou, Touraine, Maine**' (1.1.11)
3	S.D. '*Enter the Shrive, & whispers the Earle of Sals.* **in the eare**' (1:65.1)	S.D. '*Enter a Sheriffe*' [Folio] (1.1.43.1); '**whispers in** your **ear**' (1.1.42)
4	'Next **them a Bastard of the Kings deceast**' (1:490)	'With **them a bastard of the King's deceased**' (2.1.65)
5	'*Q. Elinor*: . . . **I can** inferre **a Will**, / **That barres the** way he urgeth by discent. / *Constance:* **A Will** indeede, **a** crabbed **Womans will**' (1:519–21)	'*Queen Eleanor*: . . . **I can** produce / **A will that bars the** title of thy son. / *Constance:* . . . **A will** – a wicked will, / **A woman's will**, a cankered grandam's will!' (2.1.191–4)
6	S.D. '*They summon the Towne, the* **Citizens** *appeare* **upon the walls**.' (1:612.1)	S.D. '*Trumpet sounds. Enter a* **Citizen vpon the walles**' [Folio] (2.1.200.1–2)
7	'**You men of** *Angiers*, **and** as I take it **my** loyall **Subjects**' (1:613–14)	'**You men of Angers, and my** loving **subjects**' (2.1.203)
8	'The beauteous **daughter of** the King **of** *Spaine*, / Neece to K. *John*' (1:752–3)	'That **daughter** there **of Spain**, . . . / Is near to England' (2.1.424–5)
9	'[**King**] *Philip*: **Brother of England**, what dowrie wilt thou give?' (1:820)	'*King Philip*: . . . **Brother of England**, how may we content / This widow lady?' (2.1.548–9)
10	'**Then I** demand *Volquesson, Torain, Main,* / *Poiters* **and** *Anjou*,**these five Provinces**' (1:827–8)	'**Then** do **I** give **Volquessen, Touraine, Maine, / Poitiers, and Anjou, these five provinces**' (2.1.528–9)
11	'And **thirtie thousand markes of** stipend **coyne**' (1:841)	'Full **thirty thousand marks of** English **coin**' (2.1.531)
12	'**Lets in** and there prepare **the mariage rytes**, / Which in **S.** *Maries* **Chappell presently** / **Shalbe** performed' (1:856–8)	'**Let in** that amity which you have made, / For at **Saint Mary's Chapel presently** / **The rites of marriage shall be** solemnized' (2.1.538–40)
13	'**Tell** thy Maister . . . and say, *John* **of** *England* said it, **that** never an **Italian Priest** of them all, **shall** either have **tythe, tole, or** poling penie out of *England*, **but** as I am King, so wil I **raigne** next **under God, supreame head** both over spirituall and tem[p]rall' (1:979–84)	'**Tell** him this tale, and from the mouth **of England** . . . : **that** no **Italian priest** / **Shall tithe or toll** in our dominions. / But as we, **under God, are supreme head**, / So, under Him, that great supremacy / Where we do **reign**, we will alone uphold' (3.1.152–7)
14	'*John: Philip*, **though thou and all the** Princes **of Christendome** suffer themselves to be abusde by a Prelates slaverie' (1:987–8)	'*King John:* **Though you and all the** kings **of Christendom** / Are led so grossly by this meddling priest' (3.1.162–3)
15	'*John:* Brother of *Fraunce*, **what say you to the Cardinall?**' (1:1010)	'*King John:* Philip, **what sayst thou to the Cardinal?**' (3.1.202)
16	'*Philip*: . . . Nobles, **to armes** . . . . *Blanche:* And will your Grace upon your **wedding day** / Forsake your Bride . . . ?' (1:1033–9)	'*Louis the Dauphin:* Father, **to arms!** *Blanche:* Upon thy **wedding-day**?' (3.1.300)

(cont.)

Table II (*cont.*)

The Troublesome Reign	King John
17	'[King] *Philip*: . . . come *Constance*, **goe with me**' (1:1168)	'*King Philip*: . . . I prithee, lady, **go** away **with me**' (3.4.20)
18	'The Pope **sayes I** [= ay], and so is *Albion* thine' (1:1175)	'If you **say ay**, the King will not say no' (3.4.183)
19	'*Arthur*: . . . **O** helpe me **Hubert**, gentle keeper helpe' (1:1338)	'*Arthur:* **O** save me, **Hubert**, save me!' (4.1.72)
20	'**ere Ascension day** / Have brought the Sunne unto his usuall height, /Of **Crowne**, Estate, and Royall dignitie, / Thou shalt be cleane dispoyld and dispossest' (1:1637–40)	'**ere** the next **Ascension Day** at noon, / Your highness should deliver up your **crown**' (4.2.151–2)
21	'*John*: . . . *Enter Hubert*. How now, **what newes with** thee' (1:1660)	'*Enter Hubert. King John* . . . Hubert, **what news with you**?' (4.2.66.1–68)
22	'*Hubert*: Why **heres** my Lord your Highnes **hand & seale**, / Charging on lives regard to doo the deede' (1:1715–16)	'*Hubert*: **Here is your hand and seal** for what I did' (4.2.215)
23	S.D. '*Enter yong Arthur on the walls*' (2:0.1)	S.D. '*Enter Arthur on the walles*' [Folio] (4.3.0.1)
24	S.D. '*Enter Pembrooke, Salsburie, Essex*' (2:26.1).	S.D. '*Enter Pembroke, Salisbury, & Bigot*' [Folio] (4.3.10.2)
25	'and not a foote **holds out** / **But** *Dover* **Castle**' (2:645–6)	'nothing there **holds out** / **But Dover Castle**' (5.1.30–1)
26	'*Mel*[oun]: . . . **if** *Lewes* **win the day** . . . ' (2:738)	'*Melun*: . . . **If** Louis by your assistance **win the day**' (5.4.39)
27	'*Mel*[oun]: . . . **For that my Grandsire was an Englishman**' (2:748)	'*Melun*: . . . **For that my grandsire was an Englishman**' (5.4.42)

from a playhouse copy or independent manuscript of *King John*, access to which (even if we can imagine the Shakespeare text having been written so early) would be difficult to explain. It is striking, for example, that the designations '*upon the walls*' (item 6) and '*on the walls*' (item 23) each appear at corresponding places in the action of both Peele's play and Shakespeare's. We should recall in addition that '*on the walls*' occurs also at a significant point in *Richard II* (3.3.61.2) and could conceivably have been repeated from *The Troublesome Reign* although Shakespeare uses the formula with both '*on*' and '*upon*' in *3 Henry VI* (4.7.16.1 and 5.1.1.0). Honigmann responded to Walker's argument by calling attention to the fact that both dramatists consulted the 1587 edition of Holinshed independently, and that the chronicle narrative of John's reign might account for the same sequence of names in both

plays. Alternatively, suggests Honigmann, an editor of the 1623 Folio in which *King John* was first printed could have consulted *The Troublesome Reign* (an inferior quarto version of the same play as he would have considered it) to supply stage directions omitted in the manuscript he was preparing for the press.

Thomas observed that the stage direction, '*Enter a Sheriffe*' (*KJ*, 1.1.43.1), introduces a 'ghost' or mute character for whom no reason or function is evident in the rest of the play, and that Shakespeare may have taken over this unneeded entrance from *The Troublesome Reign* where the Sheriff actually does speak and take part in stage action involving the quarrelling brothers Falconbridge. Thomas thinks that Shakespeare originally intended to develop the scene along the same lines as Peele but then decided to 'simplify and condense the action' by deleting the Sheriff and in haste left the 'vestigial' evidence of his first thought in his copy. Honigmann attributes the unnecessary stage direction to a hypothetical (but mistaken) interpolation on the part of a First Folio editor who supposedly consulted *The Troublesome Reign* in his preparation of copy for *King John*.[50] As Paul Werstine has noticed, to accept Honigmann's hypothesis forces us to believe in an editorial interventionist who was by turns both extraordinarily precise and careless.[51] In the absence of proof, Walker and Thomas seem to me to present the simplest and most likely account of the obviously related stage directions in the two plays. And the additional verbal links noted above would appear to strengthen the assumption that Shakespeare was drawing upon Peele from knowledge of the play on stage, perhaps having acted in it himself as a member of the Queen's Men, from the quarto text, or even from both. A few scholars seem to have assumed that the similar stage directions might conceivably be explained by a hypothetical 'plot' or theatrical outline upon which both Peele and Shakespeare could have drawn independently.[52] This seems to me to be grasping at straws. There is no external evidence for such a document, and the hypothesis forces us to imagine a scenario in which different playwrights at different times copied directions for stage action with extraordinary exactitude in the use of prepositions and the sequence of names. We may doubt indeed whether such 'plots' would ordinarily contain such precise or detailed wording. Suzanne Gary, for example, imagined a plot 'based on shorthand notes taken during performance' (vi).

Stage directions apart, what of the twenty-two other phrasal echoes in the two dramas – those that appear in the dialogue? What we immediately notice about these is that nearly all of them contain factual information necessary for purposes of clarification or unremarkable, even routine, language unlikely to stick in a poet's memory or to stimulate his creative imagination. In most cases they could have been taken over, almost semi-consciously, from a text that the dramatist was using chiefly as a plot outline or narrative layout for a succession of scenes. In a few places the revising

dramatist would need to pay fairly close attention to details – for lists of names, for instance (items 2 and 10), for blood and marital relationships (items 4, 8 and 27), for a specific amount of money (item 11), for a crucial religious or military location (items 12 and 25), or for the calendrical terms of a prophecy (item 20). But quite ordinary utterances such as those in items 7, 9, 14, 15, 16, 17, 21, 22 and 26 a professional dramatist might easily appropriate from his source almost without noticing.

A few additional features of the borrowing are worthy of remark. Two of the parallels (items 13 and 14) are cases in which one of the playwrights transforms a prose passage into verse, or vice versa. Anyone familiar with Shakespeare's way with sources (Plutarch and Holinshed are obvious examples) will find no difficulty in adducing instances of his turning prose, some of it merely functional and pedestrian, into iambic pentameter. Certainly the reverse process would be possible, but examples come less readily to mind, and indeed the movement from prose to verse seems to have been a natural pattern of composition for Shakespeare, especially during his so-called lyrical period when he was writing plays such as *Richard II* in which prose is totally excluded.[53] If we assume that *The Troublesome Reign* derives from *King John*, it would mean that Peele converted verse lines into prose – a

[50] The controversy about the linked stage directions in *TR* and *KJ* begins with a review of Honigmann's edition of the latter play by Alice Walker in the *Review of English Studies*, 7 (1956), 421–3. Honigmann responded to Walker in his *Shakespeare's Impact*, pp. 60–2. Sidney Thomas drew attention to the 'ghost' character in *KJ* in '"Enter a Sheriff"': Shakespeare's *King John* and *The Troublesome Raigne*', *Shakespeare Quarterly*, 37 (1986), 98–100. Thomas's note then provoked further commentary by Honigmann, Paul Werstine and Thomas himself in an 'Exchange', *Shakespeare Quarterly*, 38 (1987), 124–30. Werstine in this discussion suggests that the 'ghost' character could have been created by a 'theatrical annotator' of *KJ* who deleted a speech or speeches by the Sheriff but forgot to remove the introductory stage direction.

[51] Werstine, 'Exchange', p. 127.

[52] See note 8 above.

[53] Jonson told Drummond of Hawthornden 'that he wrote all his [verses] first in prose, for so his master Cambden had Learned him' (*Ben Jonson*, ed. C. H. Herford and Percy and Evelyn Simpson [Oxford, 1925–52], I, p. 143).

process for which I have found no parallel in Peele's handling of source material. Peele does occasionally write scenes or parts of scenes in prose, but for none of these, unless *The Troublesome Reign* is an exception, can we trace an original in verse.

Peele frequently writes without the concision that often marks Shakespeare's dramatic style, especially in the mid-1590s and later. Notice, for example, items 20 and 22 in which two passages in *King John* are notably briefer and rhetorically sparer than their counterparts in *The Troublesome Reign*. In the first instance one of the two poets either reduces four lines to two, or expands two lines to four. Again, in the second example, one of the writers either shrinks Hubert's excuse for his action regarding Arthur from two lines to one, or inflates a single line into two. No doubt Peele would be capable of the latter procedure, but it seems likelier that Shakespeare's rhetorical tightening and dramatic economy are in evidence here. Not that Shakespeare invariably avoids lengthening when there is good reason for it. Item 5 provides an example in which adding an element to an already established rhetorical pattern (technically defined as epistrophe) heightens one of Constance's speeches and thereby intensifies her excoriation of Queen Eleanor. When the queen mentions a will that would bar Arthur's claim to the throne, Peele's Constance puns, 'A Will indeede, a crabbed Womans will'; Shakespeare's version of the same retort is 'A will – a wicked will, / A woman's will, a cankered grandam's will!' which, because of the quadruple repetition of 'will,' is even fiercer. Is it likelier that Shakespeare enhanced Peele's effect by adding iteration, or that Peele weakened Shakespeare's speech by shortening it?

As Vickers has shown, Peele displays a fondness for the rhetorical figure known as ploce (in which the writer repeats a word with other words intervening) and also for its cousin epanalepsis (in which the same word or phrase occurs at both the beginning and end of a clause).[54] Item 19 offers an example of the latter technique: Peele has Arthur cry out, 'O helpe me *Hubert*, gentle keeper helpe'; Shakespeare preserves the repetitive pattern but, using up only three feet of his pentameter line,

gives us a terser and psychologically more realistic version, 'O save me, Hubert, save me!' Who borrowed from whom at this point? That Shakespeare's speech is dramatically superior does not of course demonstrate that he was improving upon Peele. But to suppose that Peele relaxed a line of Shakespeare merely in order to fill out his decasyllabic line seems much less probable. Although dwarfed by Shakespeare as a writer for the theatre, Peele was no amateur dramatist nor poetic dunderhead. It is hard to conceive of him as consistently worsening even minor Shakespearian effects, let alone shunning almost everything of genuine beauty in the poetic texture of *King John*, which would be the case if he were deriving *The Troublesome Reign* from Shakespeare's play. It is surely more reasonable to imagine Shakespeare using Peele's drama for its artful reorganization of materials derived from Holinshed while going on to write a fresh play with greater nuance in the characterization, less stridency in the political and religious components of the narrative, a greater emphasis on the complexity of human motive and behaviour, a tighter linkage of cause and effect, and a firmer control of imagery, metre and sonority than he had met in the drama of a professional colleague and competitor.

We must also enquire whether the clustering of parallels in the two plays throws any light on the issue of priority. Unfortunately the two sets of related stage directions, concentrated as they are within three corresponding scenes from each play (*1TR*, 1, 2, and *2TR*, 1; *KJ*, 1.1, 2.1, 4.3), tell us nothing about precedence, since they merely reflect similarities of action in two plots that diverge from each other in only minor ways. Of the twenty-two parallels in the dialogue, it is interesting that nineteen are distributed fairly evenly throughout Part I of *The Troublesome Reign* (there is a gap between lines 34 and 490), whereas only three show up in Part II, all clustering within about a hundred lines in the midst of a run of 1197 lines (645–748). These correspond to passages

---

[54] Vickers, '*Troublesome Raigne*', pp. 85–6.

from *King John* in 1.1 (one), 2.1 (eight), 3.1 (four), 3.4 (two), 4.1 (one), 4.2 (three), 5.1 (one) and 5.4 (two). If Shakespeare was the borrower, as I believe, he leaned more heavily on the language of Peele's text for Act 2 and the first scene of Act 3 of *King John* than for the rest of the drama. This is a central section of the play, running a little over nine hundred lines, that dramatizes the complicated political confrontation between England and France before Angers with its cynical upshot, the marriage of Blanche to the Dauphin, followed by Constance's lamentation, Pandulph's intervention, and King Philip's fracturing of the compact of peace with John. We can imagine Shakespeare attending a bit more closely to his source at this point in the story on account of the intricacies and ironic shifts involved. On the other hand, if Peele were indebted to *King John*, he would have lifted more than half the borrowed phrases from the two scenes of Shakespeare's play just described, a concentration not especially characteristic of his widespread echoes from other plays.

IV

The close relationship between *King John* and *Richard II* was a subject about which there was virtually no disagreement until Alexander and Honigmann attempted to alter the traditional landscape of Shakespearian chronology by arguing that the former play is the source of *The Troublesome Reign* rather than its offspring. But, as Vickers correctly avers, 'whoever wishes to dislodge *King John* from its position in 1595–96 is going to have to do the same with *Richard II*' (105). For the latter play we know that Shakespeare drew upon the first instalment of Daniel's *Civil Wars*, published early in 1595, and, as Dover Wilson pointed out in his edition of *King John*, '*Richard II* . . . seems to be closer to it [in time] than any other of his plays.'[55] If *King John* were the precursor of *The Troublesome Reign*, as Honigmann and his scholarly allies contend, it could have been written no later than 1590–1, which would mean separating it from *Richard II* by four years or more. Leaving aside the question of whether *King John* preceded or followed Peele's

play, we may note that nearly all the scholarly evidence of other kinds – stylistic, metrical, prosodic, vocabulary-related and the like – points to a close chronological link between it and *Richard II*.

As Stanley Wells and Gary Taylor report, *King John* is more closely related to *Richard II* in terms of rare vocabulary than any other play in the canon with *Richard III* and *1 Henry IV* as followers up, although the same genre may partly account for this correspondence.[56] *King John* and *Richard II* represent two of the four Shakespearian plays (the others are *1* and *3 Henry VI*) that are wholly in verse. We find couplets and quatrains in both although rhyme is somewhat more prominent in *Richard II* than in *King John*. Vickers has summarized much of the 'empirical and quantitative' evidence (105) to establish the close chronological relation between the two histories, laying particular stress on Ants Oras's meticulous study of pause patterns in Shakespeare and MacDonald Jackson's analysis correlating each Shakespearian play to every other play in the canon using Oras's data.[57] As these correlations show, 'Strong links exist' (108) among seven of Shakespeare's dramatic works written, according to Wells and Taylor's chronology, between 1594–5 and 1597–8. The earliest of these is *Love's Labour's Lost* while the latest is *2 Henry IV*. *Richard II* and *King John* are both included among the seven interrelated plays and, although the pause patterns of *King John* correlate with four other plays (*A Midsummer Night's Dream*, *Romeo and Juliet*, *Love's Labour's Lost* and *The Comedy of Errors*) a little more closely than with *Richard II*, the numerical differences are negligible.[58] In addition to epitomizing

---

[55] Wilson, ed. *King John* (Cambridge, 1936), p. viii.

[56] Wells and Taylor, *Textual Companion*, pp. 100, 119.

[57] Vickers, '*Troublesome Raigne*,' pp. 104–11, drawing upon Oras, *Pause Patterns in Elizabethan and Jacobean Drama; An Experiment in Prosody*, University of Florida Monographs, Humanities, 3 (Gainesville, 1960), and MacD. Jackson, 'Pause Patterns in Shakespeare's Verse: Canon and Chronology', *Literary and Linguistic Computing*, 17 (2002), pp. 37–46.

[58] Vickers, '*Troublesome Raigne*,' pp. 108–9. Jackson's figures for plays with the five highest correlations of pause patterns to *King John* (as reported by Vickers) are A *Midsummer Night's Dream* (9957), *Romeo and Juliet* (9872), *Love's Labour's Lost*

the more technical investigations of Shakespearian chronology relating to the date of *King John*, Vickers sketches a vivid portrait of Peele as a versatile playwright and 'university wit', who by the time he came to write *The Troublesome Reign* 'had shown his competence in three different theatrical contexts' (109) – university drama, court theatre and civic pageantry – and hence had much to teach Shakespeare, his less experienced contemporary. The gravamen of Vickers's objection to Honigmann's 'early start' theory is that the author of *King John* was still learning his trade in 1590–1, was about to collaborate with Peele on *Titus Andronicus* (c.1593), and would hardly have composed a play on the same subject as Peele's at this point in his career – especially a play with such close ties to *Richard II* about the composition of which in 1595 we can be virtually certain.

For purposes of strengthening the assumption that *King John* and *Richard II* were written in close proximity to each other, it may be helpful to detail some of the ways in which the two histories are related in terms of shared imagery, themes, dramaturgy and political outlook. But we may begin with a list of verbal details that obviously link the two plays. As we know from his echoes of other plays, Shakespeare had a long memory. Nevertheless, it seems likely that plays exhibiting so many linguistic parallels as those listed below – parallels quite evenly distributed throughout both plays – were composed close to each other in the playwright's career (see Table III, pp. 144–5).

Patterns of imagery also link *Richard II* with *King John*. The word *blood* (with its relatives) appears fifty-three times in the first play, sixty-seven in the second. In both, Shakespeare associates it doubly with inheritance, kinship and legitimacy on the one hand and with warfare and violence on the other. The colour contrast between red and green in *Richard II* – 'earth... soiled / With... blood' (1.3.125–6), a 'crimson tempest... bedrench[ing] / The... green lap' of England (3.3.46–7), the 'bedew[ing]' of 'grass with... blood' (3.3.99–100) – has its counterpart in *King John* where the French king and his army 'tread / In warlike march' upon 'these greens before' Angers

(2.1.241–2) or where fallen soldiers stain 'the bleeding ground' and embrace 'the discoloured earth' (2.1.304–6). The term *usurp* and its derivatives appear regularly in both plays (five times in *Richard II*, nine times in *King John*). Both dramas go in for lion and eagle imagery,[59] hardly surprising in plays about kingship concerned with contests for royal possession and with pride, supremacy and aggression. The imagery of blots and stains suffuses both dramas as does that of tears and sorrow.[60] The focus on grief links up in both with further water images concerned with flooding and with the idea of Britain as an island fortress. Both invoke rivers overflowing their banks (*RII*, 3.2.107; *KJ*, 3.1.23), both allude to Neptune (*RII*, 2.1.63; *KJ*, 5.2.34), and both conceive of England as a 'water-wallèd bulwark' (*KJ*, 2.1.27) encircled by an ocean 'Which serves it in the office of a wall / Or as a moat defensive' (*RII*, 2.1.47–8). Each play makes use of the biblical story of Cain (*RII*, 1.1.104, 5.6.43; *KJ*, 3.4.79), each mentions Fortune repeatedly in both its personified and unpersonified forms (twelve times in *Richard II*, sixteen times in *King John*), and each contains characters who experience time as rushing too fast (*RII*, 2.1.223, 2.2.121, 3.2.69, 5.5.49, 5.5.58–9; *KJ*, 5.1.48, 5.2.161, 5.6.26–7) or creeping too slowly (*RII*, 1.3.213, 2.1.77, 5.5.58; *KJ*, 3.3.31, 4.1.47).

The two histories both show an interest in altered complexion: Richard associates the ruddiness of his face with the 'twenty thousand men' who once were loyal to him and have now made him pale by their defection to Bolingbroke

---

(9870), *The Comedy of Errors* (9840) and *Richard II* (9814). The spread between the highest and fifth highest correlation is only 143.

59 For lion imagery, cf. *Richard II*, 1.1.174, 2.1.173, 5.1.29, 5.1.34; *King John*, 1.1.266–8, 2.1.3, 2.1.138, 2.1.142, 2.1.291–4, 2.1.453, 2.1.460, 3.1.259, 5.1.57, 5.2.75. For eagle images, cf. *Richard II*, 1.3.129, 3.3.69; *King John*, 5.2.149.

60 For blots and stains in *Richard II*, see Forker, ed., *Richard II*, p. 78; cf. *King John*, 2.1.45, 2.1.114, 2.1.132–3, 2.1.357, 3.1.45, 4.2.6. For weeping and sorrow, see Forker, ed., *Richard* II, p. 79; cf. *King John*, 2.1.303, 3.1.29–30, 3.1.68, 3.1.70–3, 3.4.43, 3.4.105, 4.1.36, 4.1.62, 4.2.102, 4.3.50, 4.3.105, 5.2.29, 5.2.47–9, 5.7.44, 5.7.109.

Table III

Richard II	King John
1 'I **do defy** him' (1.1.60)	'I **do defy** thee' (2.1.155)[61]
2 'His **deputy anointed**' (1.2.38) 'The **deputy** elected by the Lord' (3.2.57)	'**anointed deputies** of God' (3.1.136)
3 '**trumpets**' dreadful **bray**' (1.3.135)	'**braying trumpets**' (3.1.303)[62]
4 '**wade** even **in** our kindred's **blood**' (1.3.138)	'**Wade** . . . **in** Frenchmen's **blood**' (2.1.42)
5 '**eye of heaven**' (1.3.275, 3.2.37)	'**eye of heaven**' (4.2.15)[63]
6 '**ear** . . . **stopped with** . . . flatt'ring sounds' (2.1.16–17)	'**ear** / Is **stopped with** dust' (4.2.119–20)
7 '**silver** sea' (2.1.46) '**silver** rivers' (3.2.107) '**silver** fountain' (5.3.60)	'**silver** water' (2.1.339) '**silver** currents' (2.1.442)
8 '**How fares** our . . . uncle Lancaster?' (2.1.71) '**how fares** your uncle?' (2.3.23)	'**How fares** your majesty?' (5.3.2, 5.7.34)
9 '**ague's** privilege' (2.1.116)	'**ague's** fit' (3.4.85)[64]
10 'Make pale our **cheek, chasing** the . . . blood . . . from his **native** residence' (2.1.118–19)	'**chase** the **native** beauty from his **cheek**' (3.4.83)[65]
11 'The pale-faced moon looks **bloody**' (2.4.10)	'The sun's o'ercast with **blood**' (3.1.326)
12 'I **like** it **well**' (3.2.4)	'It **likes** us **well**' (2.1.534)
13 '**Arm, arm**, my name!' (3.2.86)	'**Arm, arm**, you heavens . . . !' (3.1.107)
14 '**Too well, too well**' (3.2.121)	'**Too well, too well**' (3.4.59)
15 '**this flesh** which **walls** about our life' (3.2.167)	'**this wall** of **flesh**' (3.3.20)
16 '**a sacred king**' (3.3.9)	'**a sacred king**' (3.1.148)[66]
17 '*King Richard*: We are **amazed**' (3.3.72)	'*King John*: . . . I was **amazed**' (4.2.137)

(cont.)

(*RII*, 3.2.76–9); Salisbury notices that John's 'colour . . . doth come and go / Between his purpose and his conscience' when he is about to order the blinding of Arthur (*KJ*, 4.2.76–7). Other instances of the same motif are noticed above, and it should be added that both plays make paleness of cheek a reaction to the news of military danger.[67] Both histories explore the idea of shadows elaborately as aspects of self-identity – Richard responding in a wittily conceived manner to Bolingbroke's comment after the cracking of the mirror that his 'sorrow' is mere 'shadow' (*RII*, 4.1.292–8), the Dauphin applying the same image to Lady Blanche's reflective eye as a means of expressing his dual relationship to her and his father (*KJ*, 2.1.497–501). Both plays also associate shadows with flattery. Note, too, that the interest

in paleness of face and the symbolic properties of shadows may have been prompted by *The Troublesome Reign*.[68] Richard and Constance, the two principal grievers of these complementary dramas,

---

[61] Cf. also *Romeo and Juliet* (5.3.68); *1 Henry VI* (3.1.27); *1 Henry IV* (4.1.6).

[62] Cf. also *Venus and Adonis*, 'churlish drum' (line 107), and 'churlish drums' in the same line of *KJ* (3.1.303). See also Table I, item 6.

[63] A fairly common phrase but used by Shakespeare only here and in *The Rape of Lucrece* (line 356). See also, however, *The Comedy of Errors* (2.1.16), and *Sonnets* (18.5).

[64] Shakespeare's only two uses of *ague* in the possessive.

[65] Cf. Table I, item 4.

[66] Shakespeare's only two uses of this phrase.

[67] Cf. also 'Where is that blood / That I have seen inhabit in those cheeks?' (*KJ*, 4.2.106–7).

[68] See note 72 below; also *TR*, 1:513–14.

Table III (*cont.*)

	Richard II	King John
18	'thy **lawful king**' (3.3.74)	'his **lawfull king**' (2.1.95)
		'your **lawful King**' (2.1.222)[69]
19	'my large **kingdom** for a **little grave**' (3.3.153)	'His **little kingdom** of a forcèd **grave**' (4.2.98)
20	'**make** foul **weather**' (3.3.161)	'**make** fair **weather**' (5.1.21)[70]
21	'I must **not say no**' (3.3.209).	'the King will **not say no**' (3.4.183).
22	'**harsh rude** tongue' (3.4.74)	'**rude harsh**-sounding rhymes' (4.2.150)
23	'In thy heart-**blood** . . . **stain** . . . my . . . **sword**' (4.1.29–30)	'**stain** your **swords** with **blood**' (2.1.45)
24	'**let it not be so**' (4.1.149)	'**let it not be so**' (3.1.249)
25	'**well** / That owes two **buckets**' (4.1.184–5)	'like **buckets** in concealèd **wells**' (5.2.139)
26	'the **face** which **faced** so many follies, / That was at last **outfaced**' (4.1.285–6)	'a half-**face** like my father! / With half that **face** . . . A half-**faced** groat' (1.1.92–4)
		'**Outfacèd** infant state' (2.1.97)[71]
27	'In . . . **tedious** nights . . . let them tell thee **tales**' (5.1.40–1)	'**tedious** as a twice-told **tale**' (3.4.108)
28	'**look's't thou pale**?' (5.2.57)	'**Look'st thou pale** . . . ?' (3.1.195)[72]
29	'the **flinty ribs**' (5.5.20)	'**The flinty ribs**' (2.1.384)[73]
30	'thoughts are **minutes** . . . they jar / Their **watches** . . . tells what **hour** it is' (5.5.51–5)	'**watchful minutes** to the **hour**' (4.1.46)
31	'**Hail**, royal **Prince**!' (5.5.67)	'**Hail**, noble **Prince**' (5.2.68)
32	'bear a **burden** like an **ass**' (5.5.93)	'upon an **ass**. / But, **ass**, I'll take that **burden** from your back' (2.1.144–5)
33	'**wish him dead**' (5.6.39)	'**wish him dead**' (4.2.206)

both use the *memento mori* emblem of the smiling death's head at points of despair: Richard conceives of Death as an 'antic . . . grinning at his pomp' (*RII*, 3.2.162–3), while Constance invites Death to 'grin on [her]' as a lover: 'I will think thou smil'st / And buss thee as thy wife' (*KJ*, 3.4.34–5). Finally, Richard and Arthur, as rightful, God-appointed monarchs, both die voicing their sense of possessing two bodies, physical and mystical: Richard's soul 'mount[s] . . . up on high' while his 'gross flesh sinks downward' (*RII*, 5.5.111–12); Arthur invites 'Heaven' to 'take [his] soul' and 'England' to 'keep [his] bones' (*KJ*, 4.3.10).

Rhetorical similarities also relate *Richard II* to *King John*. One noticeable feature of the style is the wordplay on *face*, an example of polyptoton in which a speaker repeats words deriving from the same root (see Table III, item 26). Another is the use of privatives as, for example, *uncurse*,

undeaf, *undeck*, *undo*, *unhappied*, *unkinged*, *unkiss* and *unsay* in *Richard II*, and *uncleanly*, *unfenced*, *unhacked*, *unowed*, *unswear*, *unthread*, *untread*, *unurged*, *unvexed* and *unwashed* in *King John*. A particular form of epanalepsis (repetition of the same word at the beginning and end of a phrase or clause) characterizes both texts and is related to a dramatic style grounded, like the dramaturgy itself, in antithesis; compare, for example, 'this house against this house' (*RII*, 4.1.146) and 'the word . . . against the

---

[69] A phrase much used in Shakespeare's histories: *1 Henry VI* (5.4.140); *2 Henry VI* (5.1.4); *3 Henry VI* (1.1.137, 1.1.150, 2.2.86, 3.3.29, 5.1.88).

[70] Cf. 'make fair weather' (*2 Henry VI*, 5.1.30).

[71] Cf. also *Love's Labour's Lost* (5.2.622–3) and *1 Henry IV* (2.4.256).

[72] Perhaps prompted by *TR*, 1:898; 2:1024.

[73] According to the Chadwyck-Healey database, *English Drama*, a unique phrase in Shakespeare.

word' (*RII*, 5.3.121, 5.5.13–14) with 'Thy tongue against thy tongue' (*KJ*, 3.1.265). A related use of epanalepsis occurs in the latter play when Hubert observes: 'Blood hath bought blood, and blows have answered blows; / Strength matched with strength, and power confronted power' (*KJ*, 2.1.329–30). In the mid-1590s Shakespeare was attracted to a form of declarative sentence in which the relative clause is separated from the subject it modifies. *Richard II* offers an example of this syntax, enriched by polyptoton: 'A beggar begs that never begged before' (5.3.77). We find other examples in *King John* ('He talks to me that never had a son' [3.4.91]) and *Romeo and Juliet* ('He jests at scars that never felt a wound' [2.2.1]). All three of these plays, judged by other criteria, are usually placed close to each other chronologically, and no wonder. Another point that might be thought to relate *Richard II* to *King John* is the use in both of the same proverb, 'Dying men speak true' (Dent, M514). Gaunt's speech, 'they say the tongues of dying men / Enforce attention like deep harmony' (*RII*, 2.1.5–6) finds its counterpart in the final words of Melun: 'Why should I then be false, since it is true / That I must die here and live hence by truth?' (*KJ*, 5.4.28–9). Although no dramatist needs a source for a proverbial idea, Shakespeare, as the context shows, seems to have followed Peele for *King John* and may have done so even for *Richard II* (cf. *TR*, 2:724–5).

Like-minded decisions about staging are notable in both *Richard II* and *King John*. Much of course may derive from *The Troublesome Reign*, but it is interesting none the less to observe the several points at which the dramaturgy of *Richard II* coincides with that of *King John*. The throne (or 'state') dominates much of each play and is symbolically central in five scenes (1.1, 1.3, 4.1, 5.3, 5.6) of *Richard II* and in three (1.1, 4.2, 5.1) of *King John*. We see John ascending his throne and Bolingbroke, although prevented by Carlisle, attempting to do likewise. In both plays also, Shakespeare places characters antithetically to enhance the effect of balance or symmetry. Mowbray and Bolingbroke, Bagot and Aumerle, and Bolingbroke and Richard confront each other on either side of the stage, as do

the disputatious sons of Falconbridge and, later, the quarrelling kings, John and Philip. The two depressive figures, Richard and Constance, both make a point of sitting on the ground to emblematize their mortality and grief. The kneeling competition between the parents of Aumerle in which they attempt to wring opposing verdicts from Henry IV is replicated in another key by Blanche and Constance as they beg the Dauphin to keep and break his alliance with King John. Richard gives his crown away on-stage in an act of ceremonial humiliation while John, also forced to surrender his crown, receives it back again from Cardinal Pandulph in full view of the audience. Appearances on the upper stage representing a castle wall are heralded by trumpet fanfares in both dramas, and both also feature prison scenes in which the victims, Richard and Arthur, are suddenly rushed upon by their enemies. Gaunt and John are both carried in a chair when too ill to walk, and both plays end with the corpse of the dead king being ritually carried off-stage. The rushing into a prison, the carrying in a chair, and the funeral cortège appear also in *The Troublesome Reign*.

As an ancillary observation, it is worth mentioning that for the blinding scene in *King John*, Shakespeare went well beyond the details that would have been available to him had he relied exclusively on Holinshed and *The Troublesome Reign*. Neither the chronicler nor Peele, for instance, mentions the 'red-hot' iron (*KJ*, 4.1.61) that Shakespeare makes so threatening a property throughout his episode, and it seems probable that for this scene he recalled the murder of Edward II in Marlowe's tragedy, which we know he drew upon as both a model and a minor source for *Richard II*.[74] In *The Troublesome Reign*, the signal for the executioners to '*issue forth*' (*TR*, 1.336.1) to assault Arthur is Hubert's phrase, '*God save the King*' (*TR*, 1.1322, 1336). In Shakespeare, Hubert says only 'Come forth!' (*KJ*, 4.1.71), although he must also stamp his foot because he has earlier specified to the executioners that he will 'strike [his] foot / Upon...the

---

[74] See Forker, ed., *Richard II*, pp. 159–64.

ground' (4.1.2–3). In *Edward II* Lightborn gives explicit instructions to Gurney and Matrevis about the instrument of execution: 'See that in the next room I have a fire, / And get me a spit, and let it be red hot' (*Ed.II*, 5.5.29–30). When he is ready for his assistants to rush on stage, his words are, 'Matrevis, come!' (5.5.106). He also instructs his assistants to 'stamp' on the table under which the victim is pinioned (5.5.111). The prominence of the hot iron, the stamping, and the verbal signal 'Come' in both *King John* and *Edward II* make it likely that Marlowe's play was in Shakespeare's mind at the time he wrote both *Richard II* and *King John*.

Even minor elements of plot and touches of characterization, in most cases untraceable to independent sources, link the two plays and would seem to reflect a particular cast of mind at a given point in Shakespeare's career. A concern with naming and proper rank, for instance, characterizes *Richard II* and *King John*: Bolingbroke insists on being addressed as Duke of Lancaster (*RII*, 2.3.70–3), York rebukes Northumberland for neglecting to give Richard his royal title (*RII*, 3.3.7–8), and Philip the Bastard reproves his mother for failing to acknowledge his new knighthood (*KJ*, 1.1.244–5). Bad news prompts arias of despairing lamentation in both Richard (*RII*, 3.2.144–77) and Constance (*KJ*, 3.4.23–105), and both characters rebuff attempts to cheer them up. Popular rebellion becomes the occasion in both plays for vivid descriptions of civil disorder (*RII*, 3.2.106–20; *KJ*, 4.2.185–202). False rumour feeds the political chaos in both plays: Richard's Welsh supporters disband, believing he is dead (*RII*, 2.4.7), and the assumption that John has murdered Arthur fuels the French invasion (*KJ*, 4.2.161–6, 199–202). The fall of a king together with social upheaval is accompanied in both dramas by unnatural prophecies and astral disturbances (*RII*, 2.4.8–17: *KJ*, 4.2.143–52, 182–6). Tidings of a lady's death – the Duchess of Gloucester in *Richard II* (2.2.97), Queen Eleanor in *King John* (4.2.119–21) – add to the acceleration of impending doom in both plays, and in each instance the receiver is thrown into psychic confusion. York dithers indecisively where 'everything is left at six and seven' (*RII*, 2.2.122) while John

is 'made . . . giddy' (*KJ*, 4.2.131) by the bad news. Both dramas depict a similar means of financing foreign wars, Richard seizing his uncle's estates and John ransacking abbeys. Here the source, at least for *King John*, was probably Peele (*TR*, 1:308–10). In addition, both Richard's and John's murders involve mentioning the tasting of the monarch's food or drink before it could pass the royal lips (*RII*, 5.5.99; *KJ*, 5.6.28). Although in the case of Richard's death Shakespeare undoubtedly took the detail from Holinshed,[75] its use by Peele in *The Troublesome Reign* (2:1012–13) may have reinforced the suggestion.

Perhaps the most telling plot similarity between *Richard II* and *King John* is the manner in which the order to commit violence on a royal prisoner is delivered. This parallel was noted years ago by C. H. Herford, who pointed out that Henry IV's reported hint, 'Have I no friend will rid me of this living fear?', together with his knowing look 'As who should say, "I would thou wert the man / That would divorce this terror from my heart"' (*RII*, 5.4.2–9), prompts Exton to murder Richard with a concern for deniability like King John's circuitous directive to Hubert for the blinding of Prince Arthur (*KJ*, 3.3.19–69).[76] Interestingly, the parallel continues in the way both kings denounce their human instruments after the order has supposedly been carried out, a detail, in John's case, obviously derived from *The Troublesome Reign* (*TR*, 1:1722). Bolingbroke cynically exiles Exton with a curse and the statement that 'They love not poison that do poison need' (*RII*, 5.6.38–44), while John, also regretting his crime, laments that

> It is the curse of kings to be attended
> By slaves that take their humours for a warrant
> To break within the bloody house of life,
> And on the winking of authority
> To understand a law, to know the meaning
> Of dangerous majesty, when perchance it frowns
> More upon humour than advised respect.
>
> (*King John*, 4.2.208–14)

---

75 Forker, ed., *Richard II*, p. 472 n.
76 Herford, ed., *Richard II*, Warwick Shakespeare (London, 1893), p. 204.

Then, in an extended speech of guilty self-exculpation, John tries to blame his interlocutor for Arthur's death before Hubert can allay his qualms with the news that Arthur is in fact still alive. Since the episodes involving Exton and Hubert seem to have been partly prompted by *The Troublesome Reign* (Peele's John also hints to Hubert of his lethal intentions; cf. 1:1121), it is tempting to suppose that both would have occurred to practising dramatists in close proximity to each other.

V

As I have tried to illustrate, close similarities in phrasing, word choice, imagery, rhetoric, staging and plot detail make the ties between *Richard II* and *King John* undeniable. Indeed, all our evidence points to the strong probability that both plays were written within a year or so of each other. If this proximity be granted, it cannot possibly be squared with a theory that would make *King John* the source of *The Troublesome Reign* and push the date of Shakespeare's play back to 1590–1 or earlier. It is true of course that any attempt to establish chronology on the basis of verbal and other parallels is risky – especially when some of those adduced come from plays whose own dates cannot be fixed with certainty or from plays whose texts may be so-called bad quartos or compilations based on reports by actors. Such uncertainties, however, are relative, not absolute, and forceful probabilities should be preferred to militant nescience or impatience with an educated and reasoned weighing of alternatives. *The Troublesome Reign* has sometimes been thought an unreliable text. Honigmann includes it, for instance, in a list of dramas 'widely thought to belong to the . . . category' of 'bad quartos or . . . derivative plays closely modelled on Shakespearian originals'.[77] But, apart from the attempt by publishers long after Peele's death to pass off an anonymous play as Shakespeare's for commercial advantage in 1611 and 1622,[78] there is no reason to suspect that *The Troublesome Reign* is other than it purports to be, an original

chronicle play on the reign of King John, '*sundry times . . . acted*' by the Queen's Men in 1591 or earlier. Like many Elizabethan quartos, *The Troublesome Reign* is not without its textual difficulties, but these are hardly sufficient to relegate the play to a special or unusually problematic class. We could only judge this text to be 'corrupt' or memorially redacted if we had some superior version with which to compare it. J. W. Sider, the most authoritative editor, makes no such claim, although he seems to be impressed by Gary's suggestion that the anonymous author may have been working from the mere scenario of an earlier version of Shakespeare's play rather than from a playhouse copy.[79] But the notion of a lost play by Shakespeare in any form from which both Peele's work and the published version of *King John* derive has nothing to support it but fantasy. It is hard, indeed, to disagree with T. M. Parrott, who observed half a century ago that Peele's play 'lacks all the "stigmata" of a bad quarto' and who invokes the 'firmly drawn character' of Philip the Bastard as an indication that *King John* cannot belong 'to Shakespeare's apprentice period'.[80]

The intertextual relationships between *The Troublesome Reign* and *Richard II*, and between it and *King John*, remain revealing and instructive. If Shakespeare drew upon *The Troublesome Reign* (1589–90) for *Richard II* (1595) as I have tried to show, and if *Richard II* and *King John* are as closely related chronologically as I have also argued, the conclusion that *King John* (1595–6) derives from *The Troublesome Reign* rather than vice versa would seem to be inescapable.

---

77 Honigmann, *Shakespeare's Impact*, p. 45.
78 In Q$_2$ and Q$_3$ of *The Troublesome Reign* authorship is claimed, respectively, for 'W. Sh.' and 'W. Shakespeare'.
79 Sider, ed., *The Troublesome Raigne of John, King of England* (New York, 1979), p. xxv.
80 Parrott, Review of Peter Alexander's *A Shakespeare Primer*, *Shakespeare Quarterly*, 3 (1952), 368. Although Honigmann distinguishes between 'bad quartos' and 'derivative plays', he thinks that in the latter category 'some "bad quarto characteristics" may be found' (*Shakespeare's Impact*, p. 57).

THE TRIALS OF QUEEN KATHERINE IN *HENRY VIII*

JANETTE DILLON

Henry VIII is remarkable for its unusually full stage directions: the fullest of any play in the Shakespeare canon. It is well known that many of these stage directions follow Holinshed's *Chronicles* virtually word for word, but those who have noted this point have not gone on to remark on what it suggests about the interest of early modern historians in issues of space: namely that they devote almost as much attention to spatial layout and the way space is occupied as a dramatist might.[1] In this respect not only do Holinshed and his revisers follow the practice of earlier sixteenth-century historians, whom they are often incorporating word for word, but all these historians taken together place tremendous importance on outlining spatial practice in often minute detail. This tells us something about early modern priorities. When Mary Queen of Scots was tried for treason in 1586, for example, one of the greatest problems exercising Lord Burghley in the weeks leading up to the trial was how to lay out the hall for the trial of an anointed monarch. So concerned was he that he sketched out a possible layout in his own hand, placing Mary centrally but below the judges.[2] And so important were the messages conveyed by the organization of the space that the positioning of Mary's chair had changed by the time of the trial itself. Robert Beale's official drawing of the trial shows her chair further up but left of centre, a more demeaning position than Burghley's sketch first proposes.[3] Central at the top of the hall in both drawings was the empty chair of estate representing the absent presence of Elizabeth I; and Mary's first remark upon entering the hall for the first day of the trial was, according to one

record: 'I am a Queen by right of birth, and my place should be there, under this canopy.'[4]

---

[1] Holinshed's *Chronicles*, and particularly the revised edition of 1587, completed after his death, was a collaborative work. Holinshed worked with Reyner Wolfe, his printer, on the first edition of 1577, and a team of writers, led by Abraham Fleming and including John Stow, worked on the second edition (see further Elizabeth Story Donno, 'Abraham Fleming: A Learned Corrector in 1586–87', *Studies in Bibliography*, 42 (1989), 200–11; Annabel Patterson, *Reading Holinshed's Chronicles* (Chicago, 1994); and Patterson's study of the collaborative Holinshed in relation to *Henry VIII*: '"All is True": Negotiating the Past in *Henry VIII*', in *Elizabethan Theatre: Essays in Honor of S. Schoenbaum*, ed. R. B. Parker and S. P. Zitner (Newark, NJ, 1996), pp. 147–68. Though I will continue to use the name 'Holinshed' as a form of reference here in distinguishing this chronicle from others, this should be understood as shorthand in relation to the multi-authored 1587 edition.

[2] BL MS Cotton Caligula C IX, f.635r. The drawing is reproduced in Charles Dack, *The Trial, Execution and Death of Mary Queen of Scots* (London, 1889). The planning of space for Mary's trial and its implications are further discussed in my *The Language of Space in Court Performance, 1400–1626* (Cambridge, 2010).

[3] Beale's drawing (BL Add. MS 48027, f.569*, the asterisk indicating that this folio is separately catalogued from the rest of the manuscript) is confirmed by 'a note of the procedyngs at Fotherynghay' on fol. 570r: 'At the vpper end of the Chambre vnto [SIC: for 'under'?] the Clothe of estate on that syde next vnto the L. of Burgaveny was a Chaire sett vppon a Carpett w[i]th a Cusshion on w[hi]ch the Q. of Scottes satt, and hir feete vppon the Cusshion, w[i]th hir face towarde the Earles & somewhat enclynynge to the people'. Beale, who was principal Clerk to the Privy Council, was probably commissioned by the Council to produce the drawing.

[4] 'Je suis reine par droit de naissance . . . ma place devrait être là, sous ce daïs' (R. de Chantelauze, citing the journal of Mary's

The point here is that space mattered almost as much in early modern history as it did in early modern plays. The organization of the space was understood to encode key messages about the relative importance of, and relationships between, the individuals who occupied it. In this article I will look closely at the scene of the Black-friars trial, Act 2, scene 4 (usually attributed to Shakespeare), paying particular attention to issues of space arising in Shakespeare, Holinshed and other sources and exploring how seemingly minor changes to spatial protocol affect the spectators' understanding of the scene and how such changes line up alongside or against other decisions about the content and sequence of the scene. I will be comparing the play primarily with the sources and the fuller historical record but also briefly with an earlier play that I will argue has some bearing on our assessment of what is at stake in representing Katherine's position: the anonymous *Godly Queen Hester*, probably written and performed in the immediate aftermath of the Blackfriars hearing in 1529, but not printed until 1561.[5]

Though this article will refer to the hearing in Blackfriars as a trial, it should be made clear that this was not the trial of an individual, but a general commission convened on the Pope's instruction by two legates, Cardinal Campeggio (or Campeius) and Cardinal Wolsey, with the object of testing a cause, not a person.[6] The cause, of course, was the legitimacy of the king's marriage, and the king himself had set the process in place with the aim of achieving a divorce, but he would no more have welcomed this public hearing than Katherine. He had undoubtedly hoped to obtain the Pope's consent to the annulment of his first marriage without undergoing a formal investigation of this kind. In convening this commission the Pope was subjecting Henry and Katherine equally to his jurisdiction, summoning them both to appear before the court to give evidence. Their positions in relation to this court were thus technically almost parallel. (They could never be fully parallel in any situation because the king was the reigning monarch and the queen merely his consort.)

George Cavendish, Wolsey's gentleman usher, whose *Life of Wolsey* was not printed in Shakespeare's lifetime, gave utterance to the sense of shock that such a procedure sent through the nation:

the kyng & the Quene ware dewly Cited and Sommoned to appere/ W^che was the strayngest & newest sight & devyse that euer was rede or hard in any history or Cronycle in any Region/ That a kyng and a quene/ to be convented and constrayned by processe compellatory to appere in any Court (as comen persons) w^t in ther owen Realme or domynyon to abyde the Iugeme^t & decrees of ther owen subiectes.[7]

physician, *Marie Stuart, son procès et son exécution d'après le journal inédit de Bourgoing, son médecin, la correspondance d'Amyas Paulet, son geôlier, et autres documents nouveaux* (Paris, 1876), p. 193.

[5] For a more detailed analysis of the case that *Godly Queen Hester* reflects on Katherine of Aragon's position, see Janette Dillon, 'Powerful Obedience: *Godly Queen Hester* and Katherine of Aragon', in *Interludes and Early Modern Society: Studies in Gender, Power and Theatricality*, ed. Peter Happé and Wim Hüsken (Amsterdam and New York, 2007), pp. 117–39. David Bevington argued some years ago that it may have been written for performance by the Queen's Chapel (*Tudor Drama and Politics: A Critical Approach to Topical Meaning* [Cambridge, MA, 1968], p. 94).

[6] Wolsey had hoped for a decretal commission, which it would have been easier to manipulate towards the intended judgement. On the differences between the two, see Peter Gwyn, *The King's Cardinal: The Rise and Fall of Thomas Wolsey* (London, 1990), pp. 522–4.

[7] *The Life and Death of Cardinal Wolsey*, ed. Richard S. Sylvester, EETS 243 (Oxford, 1959), p. 78. All subsequent references to Cavendish are to this edition. Cardinal Campeggio, as an Italian, was not literally a subject of the King of England, but his status was more generally that of a subject, inferior to any monarch. Cavendish's *Life* (completed in 1558) was not printed until 1641, but Holinshed's account of the Blackfriars trial was mainly derived from John Stow's *Chronicles of England* (1580), which in turn reproduced much of Cavendish's *Life* very closely. (Stow was also one of the group of writers responsible for the 1587 edition of the *Chronicles* known as 'Holinshed's'.) This passage, however, does not appear in either Holinshed or Stow's *Chronicles*, though it appears in Stow's *Annals* of 1592. Judith Anderson has shown that Shakespeare probably had access to Stow's fuller rendition of Cavendish in his 1592 *Annals* (*Biographical Truth: The Representation of Historical Persons in Tudor–Stuart Writing* [New Haven, CT, 1984], pp. 136–42), and Matthew C. Hansen has further argued that Shakespeare was familiar with, indeed

Cavendish does not comment here on the physical layout of the court, but it is certain that its spatial protocols would have encoded this outrageous subjection of a king and queen to the judgement and decrees of their own subjects very clearly. That disposition of the space would have been the first thing visible to those present at the trial; and it would also have been the first thing an audience of 1613 would have seen at the opening of this scene on stage. By a peculiar irony of fate, furthermore, the venues of both trial and performance were probably one and the same. The Dominican settlement known as the Blackfriars, established in the thirteenth century, had been the location for the occasional church council, heresy trial or meeting of Parliament before 1529, and was chosen on the occasion of this tribunal, says Cavendish, for its convenience to the king and queen, who were to reside at Bridewell Palace next door (connected to Blackfriars by a passageway) for the duration of the trial (p. 78). After the dissolution of the monasteries a mere decade later, Blackfriars was taken over for a variety of secular purposes, including lodgings for Sir Thomas Cawarden, Master of the Revels, a fencing school and the Society of the Masters of Defence.[8] In 1575 the First Blackfriars Playhouse was established in the Old Buttery; and in 1596 the Second Blackfriars Playhouse was built in the adjoining Upper Frater, the room known as the Parliament Chamber, which, as the biggest room in the complex, measuring approximately 100 feet by 46 feet, was almost certainly the one Edward Hall and Holinshed refer to as the 'great hall' where the legatine court sat.[9] Though the only recorded performance of *Henry VIII* was at the Globe, the King's Men were regularly using the Blackfriars at this time, and it is likely that the play would have been performed in both playhouses.

Shakespeare's stage directions, as so often in this play, script the layout of the space and entry into it in great detail, and his directions are in turn very closely based on Holinshed; but what is interesting here is the marked difference between the way Holinshed and Shakespeare describe the organization of the space for the trial and the way Hall relates it. Here are Hall, Holinshed (the revised

edition of 1587) and Shakespeare in chronological order:

In the beginning of this yere, in a great Hal within the black Friers of London, was ordeined a solempne place for the two legates to set in, wyth two cheyers covered with cloth of gold, and cushyons of the same, and a Dormant table railed before, lyke a solempne courte, al covered with Carpettes and Tapissery: on the right hand of the court was hanged a clothe of estate, with a chayer and cushyons of ryche Tyssue, for the kyng, and on the left hand of the courte was set a ryche chayer for the quene . . . At the daye assigned, the Legates came to the forenamed place, with Crosses Pillers, Axes, and al the Ceremonyes belonginge to their degrees, and after that thei wer set (the Cardinal of Yorke sitting on the right hand) their Commission was redde.

The place where the cardinals should sit to heare the cause of matrimonie betwixt the king and the queene, was ordeined to be at the Blacke friers in London, where in the great hall was preparation made of seats, tables, and other furniture, according to such a solemne session and royall apparance. The court was platted in tables and benches in manner of a consistorie,[10] one seat raised higher for the judges to sit in. Then as it were in the midst of the said judges aloft above them three degrees high, was a cloth of estate hanged, with a chaire royall under the same, wherein sat the king; and besides him,

---

inspired to return to the writing of a history play, by the 1605 edition of Stow ('"And a Queen of England, Too": The "Englishing" of Catherine of Aragon in Sixteenth-Century English Literary and Chronicle History', in *'High and Mighty Queens' of Early Modern England: Realities and Representations*, ed. Carole Levin, Jo Eldridge Carney and Debra Barrett-Graves (New York, 2003), pp. 79–99; p. 90.

[8] See Ian Borden, 'The Blackfriars Gladiators: Masters of Fence, Playing a Prize, and the Elizabethan and Stuart Theater', in *Inside Shakespeare: Essays on the Blackfriars Stage*, ed. Paul Menzer (Selinsgrove, 2006), p. 134.

[9] For more detail and sketches of the Blackfriars complex see Richard Hosley's chapter on 'The Second Blackfriars Playhouse', in *The Revels History of Drama in English*, vol. 3, ed. J. Leeds Barroll, Alexander Leggatt, Richard Hosley and Alvin Kernan (London, 1975).

[10] 'In manner of a consistorie' means 'like a council chamber', that is, with tables and benches laid out along the direction of the longer side of the hall, facing inwards, like choir stalls. A photograph of the Consistory Court Room at Chester Cathedral is reproduced in Lena Cowen Orlin's *Locating Privacy in Tudor London* (Oxford, 2007), p. 195.

some distance from him sat the queene, and under the judges feet sat the scribes and other officers.

Trumpets, sennet and cornetts. Enter two Vergers, with short silver wands; next them two Scribes in the habit of doctors; after them, the Archbishop of Canterbury alone; after him, the Bishops of Lincoln, Ely, Rochester, and St Asaph: next them, with some small distance, follows a Gentleman, bearing the purse with the great seal and a cardinal's hat; then two priests, bearing each a silver cross: then a Gentleman Usher, bare-headed, accompanied with a Sergeant-at-arms, bearing a silver mace; then two Gentlemen bearing two great silver pillars: after them, side by side, the two Cardinals; two Noblemen with the sword and mace. The King takes place under the cloth of state. The two Cardinals sit under him as judges. Queen Katherine[, attended by Griffith,] takes place some distance from the King. The Bishops place themselves on each side the court in manner of a consistory; below them the Scribes [and a Crier]. The Lords sit next the Bishops. The rest of the attendants stand in convenient order about the stage.[11]

Shakespeare, then, was following Holinshed (1587) rather than Hall, though he had access to both. Holinshed (1587) was following Stow's *Chronicles* of 1580 (and in so doing deviating from the 1577 edition of Holinshed);[12] and Stow was bringing together two extracts from Cavendish's *Life of Wolsey* (pp. 78–9), which he possessed in manuscript.[13]

Stow, however, was not following Cavendish absolutely precisely, because Cavendish nowhere mentions the location of the throne. The relevant text from Cavendish reads as follows:

ffirst there was a Court placed w[t] tabylles, benches, & barres, lyke a consistory a place Iudicyall for the Iuges to sytt on/there was also a clothe of estate vnder the w[che] sate the kyng/ & and the Quene sat some distaunce benethe the kyng.   (p. 79)

Richard Sylvester, Judith Anderson and Annabel Patterson note Stow's practice of editing what he took from Cavendish, but the emphasis of their analysis falls solely on his omissions.[14] They do not discuss his interpolations. Although Stow's primary source for this material was Cavendish, he himself does also suggest that his account is indebted to oral testimony ('as I have bin enformed by persons of good credite'), so it is possible that some of

his alterations or additions to detail derive from another unidentified source or sources.[15]

Holinshed follows Stow's deviation from Cavendish's wording by adding the important detail that the king's seat was 'in the midst of the said judges aloft above them three degrees high'. Shakespeare, though he does not specify where the chair of estate should be, by implication follows Holinshed/Stow in placing it centrally above the judges. This would be the natural and expected position for the royal chair of state under normal conditions,

---

[11] Hall is quoted from Janette Dillon, *Performance and Spectacle in Hall's Chronicle* (London, 2002), p. 123; Holinshed is quoted from Geoffrey Bullough, *Narrative and Dramatic Sources of Shakespeare*, 8 vols. (London and New York, 1957–75), vol. IV, pp. 466–7; and all quotations from the play are taken from Gordon McMullan's Arden edition (London, 2000). References to Hall and Holinshed below are to these editions except where otherwise noted. Bullough notes (p. 466) that Shakespeare supplemented his stage direction from Holinshed's description, several pages below, of Wolsey's normal manner of proceeding, with the crosses, pillars and mace borne before him, but Shakespeare could have found these details in direct relation to the Blackfriars trial in Hall's Chronicle.

[12] The 1577 edition of Holinshed is much briefer than 1587 on the subject of the Blackfriars trial, and has no detail on the placing of the king's chair of estate. Its only description of the space states that 'in the greate Hall was preparation made of seates, tables, & other furniture, accordyng to suche a solemne Session and apparance': *The firste volume of the chronicles of England, Scotland, and Irelande . . .* , 3 vols. (London, 1577), vol. III, p. 1552.

[13] See John Stow, *The Chronicles of England from Brute vnto this present yeare of Christ*, 2nd edn. (London, 1580), pp. 959–63. Stow's ownership of the manuscript now known as Lambeth 179 is known from an inscription inside it (see Sylvester, ed., *Life and Death*, p. 285). The first edition of Holinshed's *Chronicles* lists the names of sources after the Preface to the Reader, singling out Stow alone for more extended acknowledgement: 'by whose diligent collected summarie, I haue ben not only ayded, but also by diuers rare monuments, ancient writers, and necessarie register Bookes of his, which he hath lente me out of his owne Librarie'.

[14] Sylvester, ed., *Life and Death*, p. 271; Anderson, *Biographical Truth*, pp. 136–7; Patterson, '"All is True"', pp. 152–3. Paul L. Wiley's article, 'Renaissance Exploitation of Cavendish's "Life of Wolsey"', *Studies in Philology*, 43 (1946), 121–46, also focuses only on Stow's deletions, though it does discuss Holinshed's additions to Stow (pp. 127–32).

[15] Stow is here quoted from Patterson, '"All is True"', p. 152.

and if William Montgomery is right that the throne is scripted to remain on stage throughout the performance, this would be its likely position.[16] In a stage direction of this precision, if Shakespeare were placing it anywhere other than its usual position, he would have had to spell that out.

Such a position, however, as we have seen, goes against the authority of the two contemporary sources and potential eyewitnesses, Hall and Cavendish. Hall's description strongly implies a position below the 'solempne place' erected for the judges, and Cavendish's recording of the widespread feeling that subjecting a king and queen to the judgement of mere subjects was against the natural order of things also conveys the strong sense that such a subjugation would have had to be scripted into the physical layout of the hall in order for the proceedings to go ahead and the legates to sit in judgement over Henry and Katherine. Hall was, furthermore, a lawyer, and likely to have paid close attention to the layout of legal proceedings in such a special case. Special as it was, however, it was not the only case Shakespeare would have heard of in which a monarch was put on trial. As noted at the start of this article, Mary Queen of Scots had been tried for treason at Fotheringhay Castle under English law in 1586; and the degree to which the layout of the space for that preoccupied contemporaries is indicative of how clearly all concerned understood the degree to which spatial signifiers affected both the course of events and the public reception of them. Though the moving of her chair shows concern and uncertainty about how much respect to accord an anointed monarch who was also accused of treason, there is never any suggestion that she can occupy a position above the judges who are to pronounce judgement on her. It is worth noting here too that the trial and execution of Mary Queen of Scots may have held personal significance for Fletcher, whose father, as Dean of Peterborough Cathedral, preached at both her trial and her execution, and hence had firsthand experience of occupying these spaces as laid out for each occasion. He died in 1596, but may well have talked to his son about these momentous events before he died.

From Shakespeare's point of view, in this scene, we can say that he had two different written versions available to him (and perhaps also Fletcher's hearsay) of how the space was configured for the Blackfriars trial and he chose the one that gave the king more rather than less authority. This will be important in terms of the development, and particularly the close, of the scene; for as soon as the scene opens the king is taking control of the proceedings away from the cardinals:

Wolsey. Whil'st our Commission from Rome is read
 Let silence be commanded.
King.   What's the need?
 It hath already publicly been read,
 And on all sides th'authority allowed;
 You may then spare that time.
Wolsey.   Be't so. Proceed.

(2.4.1–5)

This breaks with Holinshed, who reports a procedurally correct opening of the trial: 'The judges commanded silence whilest their commission was read, both to the court and to the people assembled' (p. 467).

The criers call the king and queen, who are already seated in their places, and the stage direction for the queen's response follows Holinshed very closely:

The Queen makes no answer, but rises out of her chair, goes about the court, comes to the King, and kneels at his feet. Then she speaks.   (line 10)

Holinshed follows Cavendish/Stow in noting the marked distance between the king and queen as the reason why Katherine has to '[go] about by the court' in order to kneel before him (p. 467);[17] and Shakespeare follows both in turning this into a direct and personal confrontation between Katherine and Henry which highlights the isolation Katherine now feels, as 'a most poor woman' of foreign birth seeking 'right and justice' and

---

[16] See his interpolated stage direction at 1.1: '[*A cloth of estate on stage throughout*]': *The Complete Works*, ed. Stanley Wells and Gary Taylor, 2nd edn (Oxford, 2005).

[17] As Annabel Patterson notes, Abraham Fleming inserted this and Katherine's following speech into the much briefer account in Holinshed's 1577 edition ('"All is True"', p. 161).

Henry's pity (lines 11–16). Her speech in Shakespeare is based very closely on Holinshed (who, following Stow's *Chronicles*, closely reproduces the first part of Cavendish's report of Katherine's speech, but truncates the latter part); but none of this corresponds with Hall, whose Katherine is constructed with more emphasis on dignity and formality than on the personal relationships between her and Henry or Wolsey. Holinshed describes only the full court of 21 June, to which both the king and queen were summoned; but Hall makes clear the distinction between two separate occasions. The first, on 18 June, was a hearing to which the king sent a proctor rather than appearing in person. It was not expected that Katherine would appear in person either, but she did appear, very fully escorted, in order to appeal formally and in person against the validity of this court's jurisdiction. Hall's text focuses on Katherine's appearance on the first occasion:

the Quene was called, which wythin short space, beyng accompaignied wyth the foure Bishoppes and other of her counsaill, and a greate compaignie of Ladies and gentle women folowing her, came personally before the Legates, and after her obeysaunce, sadly and wyth greate gravitie done, she appeled from them, as Judges not competent for that cause, to the court of Rome, and after that done she departed againe. (pp. 132–3)[18]

His description of 21 June reports only the king's speech, adding this single sentence:

When the kyng had sayd, the Quene departed withoute any thing saiyng, then she was called, to know whether she would bide by her appeale, or answer there before the Legates, her Procter answered, that she would byde by her appeale. (p. 133)

He thus shows the queen surrounded by those who support her; directs her appeal to the legates as judges; and focuses on procedural rather than personal matters. There is no extended solitary progress around the court, no prolonged kneeling and no personal appeal to Henry.

Shakespeare, though he takes Katherine's direct appeal to Henry from Holinshed, scripts Wolsey to answer her. (In Holinshed she receives no answer,

and simply leaves, according to the text at this point [p. 468]; but we shall see below that Holinshed's account of how much is said before Katherine departs is curiously unclear.) Wolsey, in Shakespeare's version, insists on the proper constitution of the court, and Campeius supports him, urging that the proceedings continue without further delay. Katherine then turns to address Wolsey on a personal level, moving from sorrow to anger:

> Sir,
> I am about to weep; but, thinking that
> We are a queen, or long have dreamed so, certain
> The daughter of a king, my drops of tears
> I'll turn to sparks of fire. (lines 8–71)

Holinshed seems to incorporate two versions of Katherine's departure. Following Cavendish/Stow, he first reports a dramatic exit immediately after her plea to Henry: 'With that she arose up, making a lowe curtesie to the king, and departed from thence' (p. 468). But considerably later, after a lengthy description of speeches by Henry and Wolsey to which we will return, and after reaching the point in his narrative at which the court has been adjourned, he adds this:

Heere is to be noted, that the queene in presence of the whole court most greevouslie accused the cardinall of untruth, deceit, wickednesse, & malice, which had sowne dissention betwixt hir and the king hir husband; and therefore openlie protested, that she did utterlie abhorre, refuse, and forsake such a judge, as was not onelie a most malicious enimie to hir, but also a manifest adversarie to all right and justice, and there with did she appeale unto the pope, committing hir whole cause to be judged of him. (pp. 469–70)

Neither Stow nor Cavendish nor Hall includes any such statement, or any exchange between Katherine and Wolsey at the trial itself, though the 1577 edition of Holinshed contains these words almost verbatim (p. 1533), whilst omitting any mention of her departure from the court. Holinshed here seems to be drawing either on material that is

---

18 Hall's dates are unreliable. He writes 28 May for 18 June and leaves a blank space for the number to be filled in later in referring to the June date.

attributed by Hall to Katherine's interview with the legates at Bridewell prior to the trial or on Polydore Vergil's account of the trial.[19] Vergil is the only earlier source I have found that shows Katherine accusing Wolsey publicly at the trial:

Then the queen made her appearance, and publicly denounced Wolsey for his perfidy, trickery, iniquity, and improbity for creating dissent between herself and her husband, and she made this public declaration, 'I accuse, abhor, and shun such a judge, being a most hostile enemy of right and justice, and I appeal to the Pope alone, and commit my cause to him alone for judgment.' As she tearfully said these words, you could see Wolsey receiving hard looks from nearly everybody. And so the hearing was suspended.[20]

Shakespeare develops the passage from Holinshed into a bruising and highly personal confrontation between Katherine and Wolsey, drawing on Holinshed's wording:

You shall not be my judge. For it is you
Have blown this coal betwixt my lord and me,
Which God's dew quench. Therefore I say again,
I utterly abhor, yea, from my soul
Refuse you for my judge, whom yet once more
I hold my most malicious foe, and think not
At all a friend to truth.   (lines 76–82)

Wolsey denies having any 'spleen' against Katherine or having stirred the king to move against her but Katherine condemns his cunning and hypocrisy alongside his 'arrogancy, spleen and pride', submits her formal appeal to the Pope, '*curtsies to the King and offers to depart*' (lines 87, 108, 119). The details of Henry's command to the crier to call her back, her gentleman usher's intervention, her refusal to respond to the command to return and her determination never again to appear in any court, correspond closely with Holinshed. So too does the content of the king's speech in praise of her wifely virtues and noble bearing, but Shakespeare adds the humanizing touch of his first words: 'Go thy ways, Kate' (line 130). Not only does the direct address to the absent Katherine rather than the assembled court change the nature of the speech, but so too does the choice of the affectionate and very personal 'Kate', a name, as

Gordon McMullan points out, with resonances of Shakespeare's other Kates (in *1 Henry IV*, *Henry V*, *Love's Labour's Lost* and *The Taming of the Shrew*, as well as Fletcher's *The Woman's Prize*). Shakespeare chose the name Kate for Hotspur's wife in *1 Henry IV*, even though her historical name was Elizabeth, and humanized and anglicized Henry V's French future wife by having him address her as Kate. It was a name Shakespeare used with affection and usually of women who show spirit; and this is the only moment in *Henry VIII* where Queen Katherine becomes, briefly, Kate.[21]

Wolsey's request that Henry justify his own behaviour and correct Katherine's accusation that he was first to 'broach this business to your highness', and Henry's endorsement of Wolsey's position, follow Holinshed; and it is in Holinshed's reporting of those speeches that Shakespeare and Fletcher may first have been struck by the potential resonance and ironies to be developed around the word 'conscience'. Henry's speech is full of it:

The speciall cause that mooved me unto this matter was a certeine scrupulositie that pricked my *conscience*, upon certeine words spoken at a time when it was, by the bishop of Baion the French ambassador, who had been hither sent, upon the debating of a marriage to

---

[19] See Hall, *The Union of the Two Noble and Illustre Famelies of Lancastre [and] Yorke* (London, 1550), 'The triumphaunt reigne of Kyng Henry the VIII', fol. clxxxiir (a version of events confirmed by the Spanish Ambassador's letter to the Emperor in *Calendar of State Papers, Spanish*, ed. G. A. Bergenroth, Pascual de Gayangos and Martin A. S. Hume (London, 1862–1954), vol. III, part. ii, #586, p. 841). The 1587 edition of Holinshed's *Chronicle* acknowledges sources in the margin, but the only sources acknowledged for this section of text are Hall and Abraham Fleming (drawing on Stow): 'Abr. Fl. ex I. S. pag. 959' (*The First and Second Volumes of Chronicles* [London, 1587], vol. III, p. 907).

[20] Polydore Vergil's text is here cited in translation from the online critical edition by Dana F. Sutton, which includes both Latin and English texts (www.philological.bham.ac.uk/polverg/).

[21] Though Hansen does not cite it, it would also contribute to his argument that the play seeks to 'English' Katherine ('"And a Queen of England, Too"'). Patterson notes Stow's omission of the detail in Cavendish's *Life* that Katherine spoke 'in broken Englysshe' as demonstrating this wish to anglicize her ('"All is True"', p. 162).

be concluded betweene our daughter the ladie Marie, and the duke of Orleance, second son to the king of France . . .

Which words once conceived within the secret bottome of my *conscience*, ingendered such a scrupulous doubt, that my *conscience* was incontinentlie accombred, vexed, and disquieted . . .

Thus my *conscience* being tossed in the waves of a scrupulous mind . . .

the weightie burthen of my weake *conscience* . . .

[judges] to whose *conscience* & learning I have committed the charge and judgement . . .

after that I perceived my *conscience* so doubtfull.

(pp. 468–9; my italics)

Shakespeare follows the first part of Holinshed's reported speech here very closely, other than to change the verb 'pricked' to accommodate the noun 'prick':

My conscience first received a tenderness,
Scruple and prick, on certain speeches uttered
By th' Bishop of Bayonne, then French ambassador,
Who had been hither sent on the debating
A marriage 'twixt the Duke of Orléans and
Our daughter Mary. (lines 167–72)

This minor change highlights a set of nuances that Shakespeare and Fletcher have been building up since the king's first meeting with Anne Boleyn. The sexual undertow is obvious in this early exchange between the Lord Chamberlain and the Duke of Suffolk:

Chamberlain. It seems the marriage with his brother's
  wife
  Has crept too near his conscience.
Suffolk.   No, his conscience
  Has crept too near another lady. (2.2.16–18)

Henry himself then picks it up in his own agonizing over whether to leave his wife:

Would it not grieve an able man to leave
So sweet a bedfellow? But conscience, conscience –
O, 'tis a tender place, and I must leave her.
(2.2.142–4)

The Old Lady uses it to taunt Anne Boleyn for her hollow claim that she would not wish to be a queen:

You, that have so fair parts of woman on you,
Have, too, a woman's heart which ever yet
Affected eminence, wealth, sovereignty;
Which, to say sooth, are blessings; and which gifts –
Saving your mincing, the capacity
Of your soft cheverel conscience would receive,
If you might please to stretch it. (2.3.27–33)

And when Anne is finally crowned, an anonymous gentlemen is scripted to hint very strongly that the king's reasons for discarding his queen are not primarily moral scruples:

Our King has all the Indies in his arms,
And more, and richer, when he strains that lady.
I cannot blame his conscience. (4.1.45–7)

The excessive use of the term dominates Henry's self-defence in this scene, as it does in Holinshed, and the scene becomes as much a trial of Henry and Wolsey as of Katherine.

Shakespeare's representation of Henry, then, hovers between exploiting the full defensive potential of Holinshed and showing the seamy underside. In showing Henry turn to the Bishop of Lincoln and the Archbishop of Canterbury for endorsement of how he first sought their advice about this course of action and how they urged him to pursue it he seems to transfer responsibility to them for any injury to Katherine; and his ringing oath that, should the court prove his marriage lawful, he will keep his queen 'before the primest creature/ That's paragoned o' th' world' (lines 226–7) sounds suitably high-minded. If Shakespeare knew Stow's *Annals*, however, as Anderson argues, he knew that Holinshed had omitted the opposition of John Fisher, Bishop of Rochester, Katherine's confessor, and acting for her defence in this court. After the Archbishop of Canterbury's agreement that he set his hand and seal to the king's proposed course of action, Fisher in fact interrupted to contradict the king's line of argument that he had the agreement of the clergy behind him:

No my lord (quoth the bishop of Rochester,) indeed you were in hand with me to haue both my hand and seale, as other of my lords haue done, but then I said againe to you, that I would neuer consent to any such act, for it was much against my conscience, and therefore my hand and seale should neuer be set to any such instrument, God willing, with much more matter touching the same communication betweene vs.[22]

Shakespeare does not include this testimony but finds another way of undercutting Henry's self-justification. He has Campeius adjourn the court 'till further day' and Henry slip in an aside that shows his real mind, before wresting control from the judges again to disperse the court:

> I may perceive
> These cardinals trifle with me. I abhor
> This dilatory sloth and tricks of Rome.
> My learned and well-beloved servant, Cranmer,
> Prithee return. With thy approach I know
> My comfort comes along. – Break up the court
> I say, set on.
> *Exeunt in manner as they entered.*　　　(2.4.232–8)

Although Shakespeare's scripting of Henry's frustration implies that the adjournment was a significant and lengthy one, designed to halt Henry in his tracks, this stage did not come until much later. What happened in fact on this day, when Katherine refused to return after three calls to do so, was that she was pronounced contumacious and the court continued to examine the cause in her absence, with Fisher leading her defence. Not until 23 (or possibly 31) July did Campeggio adjourn the court for the summer vacation; and by the time it would have been due to resume again in October, the Pope had already sent letters of inhibition putting an end to it.[23] Henry's closing aside is probably developed from Holinshed's remark following the July adjournment of the trial: 'This protracting of the conclusion of the matter, king Henrie tooke verie displeasantlie' (p. 471); and that displeasure, it has been more recently argued, was more performed than felt.[24]

There was, as noted at the start, another play dealing with this moment in English history written very close to the events themselves: *Godly*

Queen Hester. As the titles of both plays reveal, this is a play, unlike *Henry VIII*, which focuses primarily on the queen rather than the king, and its content shows how very differently the same subject matter could be dramatized at these two distinct cultural moments. Probably written within a few months of the Blackfriars trial, and around the time of Wolsey's fall, *Godly Queen Hester* presents a startlingly radical portrait of a queen whose integrity and determination eventually allow her to show her husband the way to just rule.[25] This radical stance is veiled to a degree by being filtered through the allegorical lens of the biblical Queen Esther, and Hester's boldness is further masked by being framed in a verbal and bodily language of deference and submissiveness; but the implications are nevertheless clear. King Assuerus is blind to the threat posed by Aman (Wolsey), persecutor of the Jews (the religious orders in England). Hester, like Katherine, is a foreigner in a strange land (a point

---

[22] *The Annales of England* (London, 1592), p. 913. Stow is here following Cavendish.

[23] J. J. Scarisbrick, *Henry VIII*, 2nd edn (New Haven and London, 1997), p. 227. On the question of the date of the adjournment see further Gwyn, *The King's Cardinal*, pp. 527–8 and n. 4.

[24] See Gwyn, *The King's Cardinal*, pp. 527–30. As Gwyn points out, Cavendish reports that the Duke of Suffolk's famous declaration (pp. 159–60 below) was not spontaneous, but made by order of the king (Cavendish, p. 90).

[25] David Bevington has suggested that the play may have been performed under the auspices of Katherine's own chapel, to encourage and console her in time of peril and dates the play to a time 'perhaps very shortly before' the fall of Wolsey in the autumn of 1529 (*Tudor Drama and Politics*, p. 92). Greg Walker, focusing more on the play's agenda with regard to the monasteries than on the queen, and noting the parallels between the Lords' Articles of December 1529 and the charges laid against Aman (a figure for Wolsey) in the play, argues for a probable date of Christmas 1529, just after Wolsey's fall (*Plays of Persuasion: Drama and Politics at the Court of Henry VIII* (Cambridge, 1991; ch. 4). Others have dated the play to 1541, following the fall of Thomas Cromwell: Ian Lancashire, *Dramatic Texts and Records of Britain: A Chronological Topography to 1558* (Cambridge, 1984), p. 22 and Alistair Fox, *Politics and Literature in the Reigns of Henry VII and Henry VIII* (Oxford, 1989), pp. 240–5, but the evidence for the connection with Wolsey's fall is overwhelming.

emphasized by Katherine herself at the Blackfriars trial and also taken up by Shakespeare), but it falls to her to protect her people (and by implication the whole country) from the dangers of Aman's wickedness. Though her requests to the king are all framed with careful courtesy and meekness, and she explicitly acknowledges the dangers of speaking openly before a king ('To speake before a king, it is no childes playe,/ Therfore, I aske pardon of that I shall saye' (lines 269–70)), the play gives her extraordinary power to direct the king towards the decision and outcome she believes to be right.[26]

Her reminder of the subjection of a queen consort to the authority of her husband:

> No quene there is, but by marriage of a prince,
> And under covert, according to the lawe.
> So that the jurisdiction of the whole province,
> To the kynge perteineth, this is the trewe sawe;

quickly turns in a different direction with the next line:

> Albeit, sometyme more for love than for awe,
> The king is content to bee counselled by the queene,
> In many sundrye causes, as ofte hath been seene;
>
> (lines 277–9)

and ends up putting a king and a queen on fairly level footing, arguing that the queen must be as virtuous as the king so that the realm is safeguarded against any 'treason unjust' that may 'falsely convince' (lines 289–90).

In a very few lines, then, Hester has moved from a typically submissive and obedient female figure to one who speaks out boldly in favour of a role for queens equal to that of kings; and Assuerus, furthermore, is given lines endorsing that bold claim to equal partnership:

> Then, I doute not, but the wysdome of vs two,
> Knytte both to gether in parfytte charyte,
> All thynges in thys realme shall cumpas so,
> By truth and Justice, law and equitye,
> That we shall quenche all vice and deformitie.
>
> (lines 296–300)

This is a remarkable agenda to present for approval in 1529; and one that it would certainly have been easier to perform within the queen's household than anywhere outside it. Whether performed before or after Wolsey's fall, it has about it a strong element of wish-fulfilment, in that the play shows Aman brought low by the queen's careful and strategic pursuit of opposition and her ability to manage the king. By the time the play drew to a close, the audience might have been hard pressed to remember that the lesson of the play, according to the prologue, was to instruct wives how to behave with proper duty and humility:

> Come nere vertuous matrons and women kind
> Here may ye learne of Hesters duty;
> In all comlines of vertue you shal finde
> How to behave your selues in humilitie.

The prologue, however, may have been written later for the printed play when it appeared in 1561. Whether it was performed then, or later, and whether Shakespeare could have seen it, there is no record, though he might have read it.

His treatment of the material is so different from this, in any case, and so dependent on Holinshed, that there is no question of influence here. The comparison is revealing only in terms of showing what another dramatist might do with the same material in another time and place, and thus concentrating the focus on how Shakespeare's play fits within its own cultural moment. Here is where the play's alternative title, *All Is True*, becomes importantly suggestive of the available perspectives of 1613. In the context of the whole play, the Blackfriars trial takes its place amongst a sequence of other more or less formal trials. There is first the Duke of Buckingham's trial: a formal state trial for treason, but reported rather than staged (2.1). Its outcome, within the context of the play, is clearly to be understood as false rather than true, because the evidence, set up by Wolsey, is demonstrably unreliable. The duke is thus, in the context of the play, executed for treason without just cause. The Blackfriars trial follows close on its heels (2.4), and its representation of Katherine as true

---

[26] Quotations are taken from *The Enterlude of Godly Queen Hester* in *Medieval Drama*, ed. Greg Walker (Oxford, 2000).

finds confirmation via her subsequent vision of being crowned by angels, while at the same time it leaves room for more than one version of the truth about Henry. Wolsey's own trial, an informal testing of his integrity by the king once he has discovered evidence of Wolsey's corruption (3.2), produces a kind of truth, partly in allowing the truth about Wolsey's double-dealing to emerge, and also in the emergence of Wolsey's realization that:

> Had I but served my God with half the zeal
> I served my King, he would not in mine age
> Have left me naked to mine enemies.   (456–8)

Lastly, Cranmer's trial (5.1), a private trial before the King's Council rather than a public state trial, forces Cranmer's innocence into the open, despite the best efforts of several members of the council to bring him down falsely.

There is thus, as Anderson and Patterson have already suggested, no position of clear and evident truth in the play, but rather a sequence of versions of truth and a parallel dramaturgy of testing truth which requires the spectator to set scenes in dialogue with one another. The chronicle sources already explicitly suggest this struggle for truth even before Shakespeare and Fletcher dramatize it as such. Holinshed, writing about the later sessions of the court following the adjournment of the first day, writes, in relation to the question of whether Katherine's first marriage was consummated:

This matter was verie vehementlie touched on that side, and to prooue it, they alleaged manie reasons and similitudes of truth: and being answered negatiuelie againe on the other side, it seemed that all their former allegations were doubtfull to be tried, and that no man knew the truth.[27]

Holinshed, as usual in this section of the *Chronicles*, is following Stow's 1580 *Chronicles*; but Stow's *Annals* (1592), which Shakespeare and Fletcher could have known, continues as follows:

Yes (quoth the bishop of Rochester) I know the truth: how know you (quoth my L. cardinall) the truth more than any other person? Yes forsooth my lord (quoth he) *Quia ego sum professor veritatis*, therefore I know the

truth: I know that God is truth it selfe, & he neuer saith but truth, and God said: *Quos Deus coniunxit, homo non separet.*[28]

The emphasis on truth in Holinshed, and more especially in Stow, though less intense than the repetition of 'conscience' discussed above, is quite sufficient to have suggested the play's alternative title.

Godly Queen Hester, by contrast with *Henry VIII*, is a partisan piece of writing produced at a time when Katherine of Aragon's fate really did hang in the balance, depending on what the court upheld as true and right. As such, it not surprisingly presents a clear through-line of where the truth lies. The use of the scriptural Book of Esther in particular endorses the idea that right will emerge as triumphant over wrong in a divinely ordained world. There is only one possible godly outcome, as the title indicates from the start: the triumph of Hester's truth over the wicked Aman and the easily led Assuerus. But Shakespeare and Fletcher in 1613 found themselves at a point where truth seemed less monologic, and a point where, as Gordon McMullan has shown, truth had very particular connotations linking the play closely to 'the politics of Protestantism' for a contemporary audience.[29] The Reformation had created a struggle between Catholic and Protestant for the moral high ground of 'truth', producing literature and performances that sought to appropriate the iconography of truth for either side. Further, audiences in 1613 could not have been unaware that the adjournment of the Blackfriars trial represented a turning point in relations between England and the papacy. As the Duke of Suffolk famously said at the point of adjournment: 'It was neuer

---

27. *The First and Second Volumes of Chronicles*, vol. III, p. 908. Bullough omits this passage from his selection of relevant material, presumably because the play does not literally cover this section of the trial, but the wording here is very suggestive for the title and perspective of the play.

28. Stow, *Annals*, pp. 915–16. Patterson cites the 1580 *Chronicles*, but rejects Anderson's proposal that Shakespeare also knew the 1592 edition ('"All is True"', p. 165, n. 15).

29. McMullan, *King Henry VIII*, p. 70; and see further his discussion pp. 63–73.

mery in England...while we had any cardinals among vs.'[30] But there was no consensus
in Jacobean England about either Protestantism
or Henry VIII. Even Protestants had reservations
about the king who had set England on the path
towards Protestantism with such very mixed and
questionable motives.

The names Henry and Elizabeth may have suggested the same kind of figuring of living beings
through historical ones that is so central to *Godly
Queen Hester*. They were after all the names of two
of the present king's children, the first a hero of
militant Protestantism who had died just months
before and the second a princess literally espousing
the Protestant cause by marrying the Elector Pala-
tine. Indeed her wedding, it has been suggested,
may have been the occasion for the writing and
first performance of *Henry VIII (All Is True)*.[31] But
the figuring of the prince and princess through the
historical King Henry VIII and his daughter, Elizabeth I, could have had no such clarity as the figuring of Queen Katherine through Esther. Where the
earlier play seeks to align its audience on the side
of Queen Hester/Katherine, the later one has no
such clear position. The title *All Is True* is at best
open-ended and dialogic, at worst cynical. Even
the Blackfriars location, which is not a figure but a
literal reoccupation of the earlier space of Katherine's trial, does not speak clearly to the audience. It
may fill them with curiosity, nostalgia and concern
for the earlier events that so memorably took place
in it; or it may leave them with that slightly disappointed sense of irony and reductiveness that Sir
Henry Wotton so famously voiced in response to
the Globe performance, finding the play 'set forth
with so many extraordinary circumstances of Pomp
and Majesty . . . sufficient in truth within a while
to make greatness very familiar, if not ridiculous'.[32]
Reflection on the fact that real moments of truth
on trial in history had, first, produced no clear
position from which to judge them almost a century later and, second, become scenes in a play
staged for mass popular entertainment, could have
produced a more widespread awareness of how far
greatness had indeed been made ridiculous by that
transition.

The positioning of the throne in the trial scene,
and indeed throughout the play, is thus not a trivial point, but a crucial metaphor for the major
questions the play raises about what is or was true
and what truth might be understood to mean.
Put simply, in a pre-Reformation world the king's
authority was subject to that of the Pope, whilst
in a post-Reformation world the English church
was subject to the king's authority. The Blackfriars trial, of course, took place at a date prior to
the break with Rome, but may have seemed, ret-
rospectively at least, to represent the determining
moment in reaching the point of that break. In
moving the king's chair of estate from a position
below and to the right of the judges to a position
amongst but above them Holinshed was following
Stow; but, as indicated above (p. 152), I have not
found any historical authority for Stow's introduction of this change. Perhaps what accounts for the
change, however, is not an alternative source, but
a change in sensibility. In describing the scene this
way, Stow and Holinshed are perhaps importing
a post-Reformation sensibility, a feeling that the
monarch *belongs* in a position above rather than
below his judges. Fleming, who oversaw the 1587
edition of Holinshed, was strongly Protestant in
religious affiliation, whilst Stow's position was one
of more moderate conformism with the Church of
England. The contents of his library led to accusations of sympathy with Roman Catholicism, but
his behaviour provides no evidence of this and
suggests a more detached and tolerant position.[33]
Certainly his placing of the throne suggests a felt
need to conform with the Elizabethan sense of
the monarch as the head of church and state and

---

[30] Stow, *Annals*, p. 918. This passage is not in Holinshed or
Stow's *Chronicles* of 1580, but was taken into the *Annals* of
1592 from Cavendish (p. 90).

[31] See R. A. Foakes, *Henry VIII*, 3rd edn (London, 1964),
pp. xxxi–xxxii.

[32] The quotation is given in full in McMullan, ed., *Henry VIII*,
pp. 59–60.

[33] See further Barrett L. Beer's biography in the *Oxford Dictionary of National Biography*, online at www.oxforddnb.com/
public/index.html?url=%2Findex.jsp, accessed 2 December
2008.

subject to no higher authority except God himself. And by 1613, when Shakespeare and Fletcher were writing, a positioning of the monarch below ecclesiastical judges, even if the two dramatists were aware of that position as correct in its own time, would have been virtually impossible to stage in a public playhouse, far less in the presence of the reigning monarch, so thoroughly embedded was the ideology of the king's position at the apex of the state and so insistent was James I's own rhetoric on this point.

It is likely, then, that the play's alternative title arises directly out of an awareness, and the wish to signal such awareness, that historical sources are as easily manipulated as trials themselves and as theatre audiences. All versions of the Blackfriars trial, the rise of English Protestantism, or indeed any aspect of history, may be equally 'true' in as far as most readers and audiences are not in a position to dispute the version they see in front of them or may be unable to resist it openly even when they know it is not true. And nothing could have acted more strongly or ironically as a reminder of the degree to which 'truth' is determined by the limits of what can or cannot be said at any given time than the continuous and commanding presence of the throne, whether empty or filled, dominating the stage from the same central and most authoritative position throughout the performance. As Mary Queen of Scots knew at her trial in 1587, the location of the English monarch's throne, whether or not it was physically occupied, determined in advance what would be pronounced as 'true' when the court gave its verdict.

'WATCH OUT FOR TWO-HANDED SWORDS': DOUBLE-EDGED POETICS IN HOWARD BARKER'S *HENRY V IN TWO PARTS* (1971)

VANASAY KHAMPHOMMALA

Among the many contemporary pretenders to the throne of Shakespeare, Howard Barker (born in 1946) has often been regarded either as one of the most convincing contestants or as 'a charlatan, a poseur and a prig'.[1] Although the latter view has found ample support in reviews of his plays, Barker has gained increasing credit from both academics, actors and directors, and a powerful champion in Sarah Kane, who claimed in an article published shortly before her death that, misunderstood though he was in his own time, 'in two hundred years' time Howard Barker [would] be thought of a bit like Shakespeare',[2] an opinion that has been widely circulated since then. Aside from a debatable similarity of style and compositional practices, there is ground for such a claim. Barker has devoted most of his writing, both dramatic and theoretical, to a generic refashioning of tragedy into what he has called the Theatre of Catastrophe, a transformation that has necessarily taken into account Shakespeare's contribution to our understanding of tragedy. Moreover, his attempt to re-create a poetic and lyrical language for the stage has often been termed, notably by actors, Shakespearian. Two of Barker's best known plays, *Seven Lears* (1989) and *Gertrude – the Cry* (2002), use Shakespeare's tragedies as their main source and testify, along with his rewriting of Middleton's *Women Beware Women* (1986), to his interest in Renaissance drama, an interest which he has also manifested in choosing to locate several of his plays in this period, most notably *Brutopia* (1993) and *The Seduction of Almighty God* (1997), set during the dissolution of the English monasteries in the 1530s.

Barker's challenge to Shakespeare, however, far from being a late development in his work, reaches back to his earliest efforts and to his lesser-known plays. His unpublished *Henry V in Two Parts*, broadcast by the BBC in 1971, shows the then young playwright trying to assert his own identity by confronting not only an iconic character, but an iconic character as defined by the most iconic figure of English literature: William Shakespeare. It is certainly unfair for an author as prolific as Barker, who has now been writing for almost forty years, to be judged according to his early plays, and for critics to try and identify distinctive traits in his work according to what still very much resembles the blueprints of the plays to come. In fact, much has changed since Barker was a promising young playwright, both in his work and in his political stance. Whereas he then freely self-identified as a young socialist author, Barker now recoils from political affiliation and in fact spends a lot of time and energy in rejecting the values of liberal humanism, which he now considers empty if not downright dictatorial. There is therefore necessarily something of a retrospective illusion in trying to extract some of Barker's current artistic features from the plays of his very first period, a period he now disowns. But

---

[1] Fiachra Gibbons, 'Honour Without Profit: Actors Love Him, So Why Don't Audiences?', *The Guardian*, 6 May 1998, p. A14.

[2] Gibbons, 'Honour Without Profit'.

it is worth taking a look at this play, as it contains an ambivalent attitude towards Shakespeare which, even if in a different context, will then flow directly into Barker's mature work.

Barker's play reads as a literal parody (*para odē*), a parallel narrative to Shakespeare's play with which it intersects in the key episode of the Battle of Agincourt. However, instead of focusing on the heroic king, it takes as its anti-hero a popular nobody bearing the unfortunate name of Dick Oldham. The play opens on a scene in Harfleur, in 1415, where Oldham, a merchant from Yorkshire, is staying for business of a professional as well as private nature. When his affairs come to a sudden end, he decides to go back to his wife in England, but is conscripted against his will in Henry's army. Having no disposition at all for the military trade nor any desire of glory, he attempts, but to no avail, to escape his fate, until he finally reaches Agincourt, on the eve of Saint Crispian. There, King Henry's powerful rhetoric and his promise that 'he today that sheds his blood with [him] / Shall be [his] brother; be he never so vile' (p. 14)[3] manage to overturn Oldham, who goes to combat, dreaming of the eternal glory that will await him on his return home. These dreams, however, are dashed as soon as the war ends when Dick meets with indifference and even contempt on his way back to Yorkshire. And on his arrival in his hometown, instead of the expected triumph, nobody seems to be impressed by his feats of war nor by his new-found kinship with King Henry. He then decides to complain directly to the king, 'his brother', and goes to London, where he is coldly received by an arrogant civil servant, until by chance he manages to have an audience with Henry. The king then shatters Dick's illusions by revealing the metaphorical nature of his speech, thereby denying his supposed relation to Oldham, and by further revealing to him a secret: he did not even fight in Agincourt, but was replaced on the battlefield by his counterpart, Henry V Part Two, a brutish and barely articulate warrior with whom he trades places whenever the dirty work needs to be done. The *coup de grâce* comes when the king lets it slip before leaving that the outcome of the battle in Agincourt had been decided in advance.

Appalled and disgusted by these revelations, Oldham understands that power only depends on the gullibility of others. When the civil servant who had received him mocks him on his way out, he therefore decides to impress him by pretending that he will soon be knighted by his friend the king, and gets the civil servant to pay for his journey back to Yorkshire.

OVERT SUBVERSION, COVERT FASCINATION

Although humour has always been one of Barker's fortes, the extent of its use in *Henry V in Two Parts* will be surprising to most readers familiar with his later work, which is mainly interested in the development of a new tragic form. In fact, Barker's talent for satire and his 'gift of the gab' (p. 38), which earned him his reputation in the 1970s, are features of his writing which he was later to reject, especially in the 1980s when he came to redefine his approach to theatre. In his 'Forty-nine asides for a tragic theatre', he thus claims: 'The time for satire is ended. Nothing can be satirized in the authoritarian state',[4] while in his recent *Death, the One and the Art of Theatre*, he goes as far as to write: 'It is healthy to laugh says the satirist – on the contrary we are poisoned by it.'[5] *Henry V in Two Parts* is therefore of special interest in Barker's canon, as a witness to a time in which Barker still indulged in comedy and defined himself, with characteristic irony, as 'Britain's leading socialist playwright'.[6] The play may use Shakespeare as a source, but in many respects it is written under the influence of Brecht (whom Barker later repudiated, along with

---

[3] *Henry V in Two Parts*, p. 14. All references to Barker's *Henry V in Two Parts* are taken from the original, unpublished script used by the BBC when the play was broadcast in 1971, and kindly provided to me by Howard Gooding. I also thank Howard Barker for giving me permission to quote from his play.

[4] Howard Barker, *Arguments for a Theatre*, 3rd edn (Manchester, 1998), p. 17.

[5] Howard Barker, *Death, the One and the Art of Theatre* (London, 2005), p. 80.

[6] Gibbons, 'Honour Without Profit'.

Shaw) as 'the Great Illuminator'.[7] Barker's rewriting of *Henry V* is indeed mainly social and political, and serves the demonstration of a thesis, admittedly very consensual in the early 1970s: that of antimilitarism and the absurdity of war on the one hand, and that of the exploitation of the masses by the ruling classes on the other. *Henry V in Two Parts* is the work of a 25-year-old baby-boomer, born in the aftermath of the Second World War to a family that had first-hand experience of the disillusionment brought about by war, even when fought victoriously. Postwar scenery was, however, to become a recurrent feature in Barker's plays: *Claw* begins when World War II ends, *Victory* takes place in the early stages of the Restoration, *The Europeans* in a Vienna destroyed by the Turks and *The Bite of the Night* in the ruins of a university which simultaneously represent the fallen Troy. These post-traumatic settings will later offer the playwright a context to explore and speculate on human drives and actions when the structures of society that dictate ordinary behaviour have collapsed, and thus to expose the mendacity of civility and the frailty of idealism in conflict with self-interest.

In *Henry V in Two Parts*, however, Barker has not yet come to that point, nor have social structures been completely destroyed: characterization, on the contrary, mainly rests on social distinctions and on a strict opposition between the higher classes embodied by the king, and the plebs championed by Oldham. In that opposition, Barker seems to side with the common man, whose banality is underlined by the choice of the commonest possible name for the hero, Dick, a choice that is commented on within the play when the civil servant remarks to Oldham that 'the Tower of London is not a free house for any Tom, Dick or Harry to doss down in' (p. 24). Language, as could be expected in a play written for the radio, is also used to signify the social gap between the characters, in the contrast between the 'raucous voice' (p. 30) of Oldham and the 'smooth accent, effeminate at times' (p. 24) of characters at court, but also in the contrast between the king's exquisite English, directly borrowed from Shakespeare, and Oldham's 'misuse of the English tongue' (p. 30), further stigmatized

by Barker's choice to partially reproduce his accent in the spelling of the script.

This strong demarcation between social classes serves the demonstration of the play's overt thesis, articulated by Oldham when he leaves the king:

[*Oldham.*] A've been led up garden path! Not just me! Everyone! Oh, it's so easy to mislead people! It's so bloody simple, they're eating out your hand before you know it, lapping it up, grinning all over their stupid faces! . . . Human nature stinks. It's just one lie after another, one deception after another. It's all a matter of gullibility. If you can tell a big enough lie, someone'll believe you! And the bigger the lie the more people'll believe you. (p. 38)

In a satirical tone, *Henry V in Two Parts* denounces the cynical exploitation of lower classes by the elite, much in the same manner as Barker's first known play, *One Afternoon on the 63rd Level of the North Face of the Pyramid of Cheops the Great*.[8] In this play, broadcast by the BBC in 1970, in which the motif of disguise already makes an appearance, Cheops passes himself off as a slave in order to spur his fellow workers to build the pyramids at an even faster pace than the one that is exacted from them, in an act of paradoxical defiance against the terrible oppression they suffer. Both plays, beside their obvious political partisanship, also endeavour, as Brecht advocated in such poems as 'Fragen eines lesenden Arbeiters' in his *Svendborger Gedichte* (1939), to look at history from the perspective of those who have been not remembered but forgotten.

But even if the political message of the play seems clear enough – all the more so if one takes into account Barker's professed leftist tendencies when the play was written – one cannot but notice that, for all the apparently clear-cut depiction of

---

7 Barker, *Arguments*, p. 183. On Barker's relationship with Brecht, see Heiner Zimmermann, 'Howard Barker's Brecht or Brecht as Whipping Boy', *CDE Studies*, 8 (2001), pp. 221–5.

8 Information about this play, also unpublished, can be found in David Ian Rabey, *Howard Barker: Politics and Desire, An Expository Study of His Drama and Poetry, 1969–87*, 2nd edn (Basingstoke and New York, 2009), pp. 10–12.

the mechanisms of society, some ambiguities linger. Henry may be a deceitful leader, but he wields a language whose beauty is irresistible, even for the audience. As for Oldham, as an amusing comic type and a victim of Henry's schemes, he may elicit the audience's sympathy, but mostly as an object of mockery whose morality often seems far from being beyond reproach. This ambiguity mainly derives from Barker's complex attitude towards his source. There is certainly, in his iconoclastic gesture towards Henry V and Shakespeare's eponymous play, something that pertains to a form of populist provocation. But the provocation in turn derives its strength from Barker's ambiguous relationship to the idol he is about to destroy. That is precisely the question he addresses in his article 'Murders and Conversations: The Classic Text and a Contemporary Writer':

The highest pleasures of delinquency come from an affront to an authority that cannot be moved. To deface a monument, to smear a public property, is an act of reverence more profound, because of the investment of will, than any common genuflection of the uncritical believer. It is the continuity and immobility of things that supplies the authentic shock behind all acts of desecration.[9]

It is this paradox that lies at the heart of Oldham's ambiguous and amazed reaction to Henry's revelation: 'You were a bluddy myth with us . . . an idol . . . and now . . . my God!' (p. 31). Beyond Henry, the idol whose twilight Barker slowly prepares is of course Shakespeare himself.

BARKER'S SHAKESPEARE

Barker's treatment of Shakespeare's *Henry V* is not only parodic in structure, it is also parodic in tone and thematic contents: *Henry V in Two Parts* is essentially a short comical play that attempts to deflate the myth that Henry V has become, for which Shakespeare is to a large extent responsible, and thereby to debunk the Shakespearian myth itself. It does so by referring to its model in an invariably offhand manner that necessarily simplifies and caricatures the original play. Barker's selective reading does away with the complexities of

Shakespeare: the interpretation is deliberately simplistic so as to conform to the received idea of the play and to allow parody and confrontation. From *Henry V*, Barker only keeps (if one excepts Katherine's short appearance in the end) Henry V, and from Henry V, only the character's most famous passages. The other characters who contribute to defining the ambiguities of the main character have disappeared, as have the passages in the text in which his frailties could be (and have been) seen. By a series of simplifications, Shakespeare's play is thus reduced to its eponymous hero, and its eponymous hero to his warlike speeches, with a deliberate ambiguity between the historical and the fictitious character. Shakespeare's play thus becomes equated with the myth it has created, in contempt of the subtleties of the text, while three different instances of Henry V are conflated into one: the historical king, the fictitious character and the play itself. This confusion, as well as Barker's tongue-in-cheek attitude towards Shakespeare's play, are all confirmed by the amusingly deceptive title chosen by the playwright for his work. *Henry V in Two Parts* leads the reader or audience to expect a long epic in two parts, such as Marlowe's *Tamburlaine* or, for that matter, Shakespeare's *Henry IV*, only to deceive them into a short play that has very little to do with epic, and in which it is the protagonist, and not the play at all, that is split into two.

Barker's approach to Shakespeare's text is therefore neither deferential nor erudite, it does not aim at refining our perception of the play or at unveiling unsuspected aspects of it, nor does it strive to do justice to the play's complexity. It aims at dramatic efficiency and, in order to do so, caricatures the play to fit exactly what popular culture has turned it into. *Henry V* is a particularly felicitous choice to approach Shakespeare from that angle. Even if there has been a shift in postwar criticism and if recent research[10] and productions have attempted, as Barker has, to erode a monolithic perception of

---

9 Barker, *Arguments*, p. 153.
10 See for instance John Sutherland and Cedric Watts, *Henry V War Criminal? and Other Shakespeare Puzzles* (Oxford, 2000).

the play, it remains in popular culture the patriotic monument erected by Sir Laurence Olivier during the Second World War, first in his 1942 radio broadcast, and then two years later in his film. Barker's decision to quote only from the two speeches broadcast by Olivier, coincidental though it may be, reveals his interest in the play as a cultural phenomenon rather than as a text, an interest which commands most of his forays into intertextuality, or what he calls his 'conversations with dead authors',[11] invariably chosen for the iconic cultural status of their plays. It is that cultural perspective that partly accounts for Barker's choice, when it comes to his other 'conversations' with Shakespeare, to deal only with his tragedies, and more precisely with two of his most famous creations, Hamlet and Lear, taken as symbols of Western culture at least as much as Shakespeare's literary inventions. As Barker himself notes:

[T]he conversations I describe with regard to Shakespeare, Chekhov or Lessing, are partly inspired by authorship, partly by the use to which these authors have been put by contemporary ideologues, and partly by my own resistance to the forces and inertias that govern the contemporary theatre.[12]

In other words, Barker's approach to intertextuality rests less on the texts themselves than on the cultural emblems they and their authors have come to represent.

However, Barker's choice of reducing Shakespeare's play to its most basic traits so as to fit its popular perception does not mean that some of its more complex features do not infiltrate the play in other, less clearly identifiable ways. The very theme, as well as dramatic motif, of *Henry V in Two Parts*, that of usurpation and pretending, is of course central to Shakespeare's *Henry V*, and notably to the episode of the night watch before the Battle of Agincourt, when Henry passes himself off as Harry Le Roy in order to assess his army's opinion of him. Moreover, although Barker decides to counterbalance Shakespeare's choice of the king as a main character by focusing on a popular character, the popular (and often comic) perspective is also present in Shakespeare's history thanks to such

characters as Pistol, Nim and Bardolph. In fact, by depicting Dick Oldham as a variation on the stock type of the *miles gloriosus*, Barker resorts to many of the comic features that Shakespeare used for comic relief in his own play. Similarly, Shakespeare's dramatic use of different accents as well as different languages for both characterization and comic effect finds its way into Barker's contrastive use of Oldham's Yorkshire accent and the king's 'Etonian accent and/or Sandhurst' (p. 13). And if, in Barker's play, Katherine has already been wooed and won, the playwright offers his own, derisory version of the bilingual wooing scene at the beginning of his play, in which Dick and his lover Chérie, though long past wooing, still stumble on the language barrier:

Chérie. My pretty little cochon...
Oldham. Pretty little what?
Chérie. Mmmmmm... my darling cochon...
Oldham. (*playing too*) Oh, A'm a chochon [*sic*], am
    A... Oh... aye... A am that...   (p. 2)

Chérie's use of the word 'cochon', once she finds out about Oldham's marriage, becomes much less endearing and all too clear to Oldham:

Chérie. Get out, you stupid pig!
Oldham. All right, all right, no need to use bad language!
Chérie. Get out!   (p. 4)

It is of course difficult to demonstrate the hand that Shakespeare may or may not have had in scenes that do not explicitly quote him: such is the pervasiveness of influence, and even more so of Shakespearian influence, that its identification and gauging have become theoretical issues far beyond the scope of this article. In both *Seven Lears* and *Gertrude – the Cry*, this influence is mainly a matter of speculation: the nature of intertextuality is questioned by blurring the relation to the source texts to the point where they become disfigured and even unidentifiable. But in *Henry V in Two Parts* the link with Shakespeare's history play is clearly established by a number of explicit quotes, which

---

[11] Barker, *Arguments*, p. 154.
[12] Barker, *Arguments*, pp. 155–6.

are moreover chosen from the purple patches of the play, precisely the two speeches broadcast by Olivier: Henry's address to his soldiers on the eve of Saint Crispian (4.3.35–67, quoted extensively by Barker pp. 13–15), and the opening speech of Act 3, 'Once more unto the breach' (3.1.1–34, quoted in fragments pp. 33 and 38).

It is revealing that, among all the possibilities to refer or allude to another text, Barker should have chosen the most explicit to quote from and that he should have selected passages that have long taken on a life of their own, severed from their dramatic context, to become readily quotable. These passages are indeed meant to be recognized as borrowings, when recognition is precisely what the audience will be deprived of in Barker's later Shakespearian rewritings, in favour of speculation. As a matter of fact, Barker insists on the specific status of these quotes even within his own text. This comes in part from the versification, which Barker faithfully reproduces and which marks their difference from the rest of the text written in prose. But more importantly, unlike the rest of the play (and in contradistinction to their use in the original), these quotes do not pretend to be a spontaneous oral outburst from the characters, rather they present themselves, in their artificiality and even their artfulness, as the repetition of something which has already been written and rehearsed. Barker thus uses them as a deliberate narrative and stylistic disruption, as the irruption of a different form of theatricality in the flow of his narrative: a self-conscious and here literally Shakespearian theatricality. The oddity and incongruousness of Henry's Saint Crispian speech is underlined by the very context in which it is uttered: it is not at all integrated into the rest of the scene. Henry enters, delivers his speech from 'He that has no stomach' (p. 13) to 'while any speaks / That fought with us upon Saint Crispin's Day!' (p. 15) without any alteration and leaves. Even if the other characters react to his speech, he himself has no interaction with them at all, thus underlining the aloofness and unchangeable quality of an address that seems to be set in stone. This impression is later confirmed when Henry, during his interview with Oldham, is able to repeat his speech

on demand, and proves that its rhetorical power has nothing to do with the specific context in which it was first uttered (p. 28). By mere repetition, Barker reveals the intrinsic inauthenticity of the theatrical language, repeatable with equal efficiency on a number of occasions. A similar eroding of the efficiency of speech through repetition is given to such passages as 'For Harry, England and Saint George' (originally 3.1.34), which Henry himself identifies as 'stock phrases' (p. 33) of the kind even a man 'not over-endowed with intelligence' (p. 34) such as his *doppelgänger* can master, and which he himself keeps repeating (p. 33 and 38). Similarly, 'Once more unto the breach' (originally 3.1.1) is here applied to an altogether different context and transformed into 'Once more into the breech' (p. 38) when Henry leaves Oldham to go back to Katherine (although the pun, on radio, would of course be lost to listeners). Borrowings from Shakespeare are thus constantly underlined and introduced as such: powerful, theatrical quotes that are, however, devoid of intrinsic meaning and repeatable at leisure. Their foremost function is no longer dramatic, lyrical or even poetic but pragmatic. In Barker's *Henry V in Two Parts*, Shakespeare's language is turned into an empty sign of social status that is the privilege of the powerful, and whose beauty is all the more dangerous when it is explicitly histrionic and disconnected from the characters' actual thoughts. Henry himself owns up to that much to Oldham:

Oldham. You didn't mean what you said! It was just . . .
Henry V. Well, really, I think you are taking an extreme view. I honestly don't think an enlightened government can rule without a little friendly deception – deception in the public interest, of course, good deception. In fact, I don't think I'd call it deception at all . . . it's sort of white lying . . .   (p. 35)

One quotation escapes this rule, and it is significantly one that is attributed not to Henry but to Oldham, and is woven into his speech rather than cut out as a disposable, ready-to-use piece of oratory: the intertextual mode chosen here is allusion rather than quotation. Before leaving his wife to call on the king in London, Oldham tells her: 'No,

A'm a wounded man, Mable. Wounded where it hurts most, in ma soul... These last few weeks have been the worst in all my life, even worse than the slings and arrows of the Frogs' (p. 24). It is of course a far cry between Hamlet of Denmark and Oldham of Battersby, and it is precisely that difference that is underlined in Oldham's literalization of Hamlet's metaphor and in his substitution of the bathetic 'Frogs' for Hamlet's abstract 'Fortune'. Here again, the different use of quotations by the characters serves to enhance a social distinction in mastery of language. While Henry makes a conscious and even cynical use of Shakespeare's text to achieve his goals, Oldham speaks it incorrectly, lowering sublime metaphors to the level of plain description.

WIELDING LANGUAGE

However, even if in a different manner, these references to Shakespeare's original text all serve one and the same purpose: a deflating, comic denunciation of the power of rhetoric as dangerous, empty words. Barker thus pays his model a paradoxical compliment by insisting on the beauty and efficiency of his speeches while suggesting the dangers that come from misusing their power. Throughout the text, attention is called to the almost magical persuasiveness of Henry's speech, with so much insistence, and coming from such unpolished characters, that the compliment ends up appearing somewhat strained:

Regimental Sergeant Major. Pure poetry!
Cockney 1. He can't half speak, can't he? That was bloody marvellous!
R.S.M. It was beautiful...
Oldham. Aye, it were grand. His brother, he said. His brother! (p. 15)

Henry's speech is so powerful indeed that the king himself gets carried away by its poetry when he repeats it to Oldham:

Henry V. That was a good speech, yes, a very good speech...
Oldham. It were marvellous!
Henry V. Do you want the rest?

Oldham. Oh aye, if it's no trouble.
Henry V. (recalling himself) No, no, no! Look, the crux! It's time we got to the crux! (p. 28)

This paradoxical homage, flaunted with so much ostentation that it becomes suspect, repeats within the text the double movement from tribute to burlesque that characterizes the play as a whole, already suggested in the grandiloquent but deceptive and derisive title. Barker, as a playwright with a hammer, conjures up the myth the better to smash it to pieces, whether this myth be Henry V or Shakespeare. In fact, the play hinges on a clear identification of both in the figure of the writer. This confusion between author and character, frequent when it comes to dramatic literature, is playfully underlined by the characters themselves when Oldham, in doubt about the king's identity, eventually asks him if he truly is the author of his speech:

Oldham. What you're saying is, it wasn't you who made the speech at all? It was sumone else?
Henry V. Someone else? Of course I made it! Me, Henry the Fifth, I made it! Tell me who else could have produced a minor masterpiece like that? Go on, tell me. You can't. Of course not, there is only one person who could have written that speech and that's me. After all, speech-making is my forte. (pp. 31–2)

The ambivalent attitude of Oldham towards Henry, his mistrust and admiration of him, could be seen to replicate Barker's own position towards Shakespeare, as defined by his ambiguous comments about him in his theoretical writings. Barker's radical deformation of *Henry V* may thus well derive from the need to stabilize a text which he defines as 'pliable':

Shakespeare has always been a source for transfusions of patriotic inspiration when a national crisis necessitated it. It seems possible to argue that it is this pliability of the text that, in the end, lends it its classic status, for all forms of society, and all modes of opposition, require the endorsement of smothered genius. Are we immune? Obviously not. Shakespeare will always be our contemporary for this reason: his texts are perpetually plundered by the existing dispensation whatever its current preoccupations.[13]

But Barker's assessment of Shakespeare also appears as profoundly pliable, especially when it comes to his own assessment of his moral stance. Even if he acknowledged Shakespeare as perhaps the only conscious influence in his writing, his position towards Shakespeare as an embodiment of moral consensus seems more ambiguous. On the one hand, he claims that 'Shakespeare was the last English writer who was not a moralist',[14] and praises the excessive situations in which he unleashes his characters. On the other, he finds fault with Shakespeare for surrendering to moral diktats at the end of such a play as *King Lear* ('When Shakespeare made Lear rage, did he not love him more than when, humiliated and broken by events, he brings him to the brink of an apology?'),[15] or for refusing to explore the darker aspects of desire at which *Hamlet*, according to him, only hints ('Gertrude's sketchily described character [in Shakespeare's *Hamlet*] is saddened with shame and regret').[16] 'The form of [Shakespeare's] tragedy,' according to Barker, 'is that, having put the character into a position of excess, he would withdraw it again, in order to produce an aura of relaxation on his public.'[17] When he discusses Shakespeare, Barker thus seems torn between the disruptive potential he acknowledges in his work and the embodiment of accepted morals he has come to represent.

Barker's ambivalence towards Shakespeare is literalized in his decision to split Henry into two characters: an excessively refined and Machiavellian rhetorician and a brutish warrior barely capable of thought. The motif of splitting, of division, and the questioning of the integrity of the body and the mind are announced early in the play, even before their spectacular materialization in Henry's division. The war context in which the play takes place offers many opportunities for Barker to introduce them, and body mutilation and dismemberment are thus conjured up, literally, in scenes of military preparation. While training Oldham, the sergeant major threatens to 'cut one of [his] ears

off' if he does not learn how to lop an arm off (p. 10), a treatment which almost backfires on Oldham himself at the end of the play ('Thank your lucky stars I haven't lopped your arm off for insolence', p. 30). Even its most explicit form, Henry's division, is foreshadowed at the beginning of the play when a fellow soldier warns Oldham about the dangers of two-handed swords: 'Watch out for two-handed swords. One blow from them and you're in two halves – flip, flap, half of you on either side of where you stood. It's quite pretty, really' (p. 9). Through rhetorical legerdemain and thanks to the emphasis laid on the motif of doubleness and duplicity, whose key is struck in the very title, this literal evocation of body splitting is made to refer metaphorically not only to Barker's treatment of Henry V but also, retroactively, to Shakespeare's impression on us. The two-handed sword seems also double-edged and swings both ways.

As a matter of fact, Barker's questioning of Shakespeare in *Henry V in Two Parts* does not only read as a one-way indictment of duplicity and of the treachery of Shakespeare's rhetoric, but also as a mirror held up to Barker's own use of language and to the intrinsic duplicity of theatre. If Henry is insistently described as a figure of the writer, and therefore as a direct representative of Shakespeare within the play, especially in the final scene in which he discloses his secret, so is paradoxically Oldham himself. Throughout the play, Barker sprinkles scenes in which Oldham is heard writing letters (p. 4, 8, 11, 16), signalled by the sound of 'a scratchy pen on parchment' (p. 4). In these, the audience is given direct access to his thoughts in an interesting, radiogenic twist on the tradition of the soliloquy, also present in the play (pp. 18, 38). But these scenes do not simply counterbalance Henry's

---

[13] Barker, *Arguments*, p. 155.

[14] Interview with Nick Hobbes in the programme notes for *Scenes from an Execution*, Dundee Rep, April 2004.

[15] Barker, *Arguments*, p. 157.

[16] Programme notes for Barker's production of *Gertrude – the Cry* with his company, The Wrestling School, 2002.

[17] *Transfuge*, 19 January 2009, p. 61. The interview was published in French; I thank Donatien Grau for the original passage.

deceitful use of writing with Oldham's honest use of it: on the contrary. In spite of all that separates them, their difference of accent, language, education and social status, what Henry and his opposite Oldham do share is a cunning and dishonest use of language, and especially of writing. Just as Henry's speech at Agincourt is disconnected from any real feeling that his words, however, are able to fake successfully, so is Oldham able to write almost the same letter twice, once *'in an indifferent tone of voice'* (p. 4) and once *'with real feeling'* (p. 8). Moreover, Henry is not the only one to comment, metapoetically and self-consciously, on his own writing ('That was a good speech, yes, a very good speech' [p. 28], 'Tell me who else could have produced a minor masterpiece like that... There is only one person who could have written that speech and that's me' [p. 32]). These comments are also to be found, albeit in a slightly less elegant way, in Oldham's own commentary on his verbal skills: 'How A long to be beside you again, with baby, rocking him beside the fire and listening to your voice... Aye, I like that bit, that's nice, is that. I remain your luvving husband, Dick' (p. 4). Writing is thus introduced in the first pages of the play as a morally ambiguous motif, liable to manipulation and deceit, which Henry will only take to another level.

The joint emphasis on writing and deceiving, writing as deceiving, calls attention to what is perhaps the major theme of the play, that of imposture. It is again in a biased way that Barker introduces this theme into the fabric of his drama, when Oldham is refused access to a packet which he wanted to board to go back to England, and fulminates against the seaman in tones that might also echo *Coriolanus*:

[Oldham.] Of course A could have showed my scars, rolled up my sleeve and said – look here, here's my ticket! Oh, that would have been different, that would have put him in his place. A expect there's plenty of rogues who've pretended they were there on Crispin's Day. A shall have to watch out for imposters, A can see. When A get to England A shall make a point of sorting out imposters. A expect the country's full of them by now... (p. 18)

Little does he know that King Henry himself is one of these rogues and 'imposters' he will have to sort out. But here again, Barker prevents the audience from too easy an opposition between the duplicitous king and the honest countryman, by closing the play on a final development in which Oldham, introducing himself as the future 'Sir Richard Oldham of Battersby' (p. 39), is seen to yield to the temptation of imposture:

[Oldham.] Oh, it's a gift, this governing business. A rare gift. A've always said leaders were born... Understand human nature and you're half way there. Oh, it's a gift alright, people aren't in high positions for nuthing... (*Pause*)
A must say, A think *this is the style A should be accustomed to*... this is the way a man like me should travel... *in style*, like... (pp. 39–40, my emphasis)

From a metapoetic point of view, Oldham is of course not the only one to pretend to be someone else, to use, if not borrowed robes, at least a borrowed style: so also is Barker, by integrating into his play quotes that are originally Shakespeare's. Barker will later use a similar technique in his *(Uncle) Vanya* (1996), and even more explicitly in his alternative rewriting of *Women Beware Women*, labelled as being written 'in collaboration with Thomas Middleton', and whose first part is an almost verbatim reproduction of Middleton's first four acts, transposed into prose. Barker's *tour de force*, in identifying Henry V with Shakespeare himself and suggesting that both are impostors, consists in undermining the very authority of the playwright from whom he borrows, in dissolving the author into his character, so as to legitimate his own appropriation of his words. Though *Henry V in Two Parts*, at first sight, may read as a minor and derisive parody of Shakespeare's great war play, it thus reveals the (losing) battle fought by Barker in his attempt to come to terms with his literary legacy. This re-appropriation hinges on their paradoxical identification as authorial figures, through the characters of Oldham and Henry. As dramatic authors, and in spite of their differences, they share indeed the same status: that of people who stand in for others, and sometimes for one another, when they claim for themselves someone else's language – literally, the status of impostors.

Barker's *Henry V in Two Parts* appears as an interesting symptom in the history of the play's reception: the playwright's choice to split the main character into two separate entities can be seen as a dramatization of the two critical attitudes that have come to prevail and that Gary Taylor sums up in the opening paragraph of his introduction to the play:

[C]ritics almost all divide into two camps: partisans of Henry and partisans of pacifism. Partisans of Henry generally like the play, interpreting it as a blunt straightforward Englishman's paean to English glory . . . Partisans of pacifism either dislike the play intensely, or believe that Shakespeare (Subtle rather than Blunt, and never straightforward) himself intensely disliked Henry, and tried hard to communicate this moral distate to the more discerning members of the audience.[18]

But as one of Barker's earliest plays, it also testifies to the author's long-standing interest in Shakespeare as well as in the questions of intertextuality and the related problem of the nature of authorship. Although its mostly comic tone and socio-political agenda are now features that Barker has forsaken, or that have transformed beyond recognition, its ambiguous relation to its model, halfway between celebration and desecration, paves the way for Barker's later encounters with Shakespearian tragedy. Even if Henry is mostly a comic character, his superb rhetoric and fascinating intelligence announce the monarchs that will populate, in a drastic change from satire to tragedy, later plays such as *Seven Lears* and *Gertrude – the Cry*. Their egoism, though no more likeable than Henry's, will then be justified on the ground of their quest for the sublime, a quest for which Barker will no longer borrow his words from others, but invent his own tragic language.

---

[18] William Shakespeare, *Henry V*, ed. Gary Taylor (Oxford, 1982), p. 1.

DAUNTED AT A WOMAN'S SIGHT?: THE USE AND ABUSE OF FEMALE PRESENCE IN PERFORMANCES OF THE HISTORIES AS CYCLES

ANNA KAMARALLI

Shakespeare's history plays show a man's world more unequivocally, more inescapably, more impenetrably than his comedies or Romances, perhaps even more than most of his tragedies. Yet when women appear in these plays they are rarely presented as mere victims of the system, or of individual men, but as having agency. Sometimes that agency even extends to become power. These instances open up a space to examine what power a woman can have in a man's world, and how we identify and reflect on such power. The process of staging the text will establish the position from the artists on what quantity but also what different qualities of power a woman can enact within a framework that is unabashedly patriarchal. Performance offers an excellent canvas on which to draw images of the potential varieties of female power and, whether deliberately or not, the performance practitioners who create those images also give indications of approval or censure. At first glance the history plays tend to offer less to the female performer than those of other genres, but the exceptions are exciting ones. Queen Margaret is an acknowledged *tour de force* of a role, stretching over four plays. The relative obscurity of *1 Henry VI* means that many people remain unaware that Shakespeare wrote of Joan of Arc (or Jeanne la Pucelle here), but what he created was a virtuoso role startlingly modern in its conception. *Richard III* is often thought of as a vehicle for a single, male star, but not only includes four strongly differentiated female characters but shows them conversing together. In performances that can struggle to distinguish the many Lords from one another,

the women trumpet their distinctiveness and individuality.

Since the second half of the twentieth century it has become increasingly common for some or all of Shakespeare's eight core English history plays to be performed as a cycle, often compressed and amalgamated into a more compact version.[1] This is now such a standard approach to the *Henry VI* plays (most often by editing down the three parts into two) that it has become unusual for them to be performed any other way. Edward Hall's Propeller theatre company gave such a three-in-two production in 2001, dubbed *Rose Rage*, as did Australia's Bell Shakespeare Company in 2005, and Northern Broadsides in 2006, both called *Wars of the Roses* for the purposes of the exercise. An exception is Michael Boyd's 2000 production for the Royal Shakespeare Company, which gave all three *Henry VI* plays in full, with *Richard III* added in 2001, and which was revived for the 'Complete Works' festival in 2006, then expanded into the full cycle of eight plays in 2007. Benedict Andrews for the Sydney Theatre Company in 2009 went furthest in the other direction, editing down all eight English history plays into two nights, running at just under eight hours in total. All of these were shaped by a larger conception than would be apparent in a single play. Audiences were being offered theatre on an epic scale, requiring a commitment of more than one night, and investment in a grand narrative arc, including an intricate plot and a large set

---

[1] I omit *King John* and *Henry VIII* as not having a history of being incorporated into cycles as part of a unified production.

of characters, and calling for a challenging goal of unity in design and character development. These directors had a great deal to think about in getting works of such scale onto the stage, and one place their consciousness of the need to communicate a strong message played itself out was in the persons of the female characters, as most latched gratefully onto opportunities to generate images accessible to a modern audience.

Female presence in these productions was shaped by an intriguing variety of strategies that included the doubling of Jeanne and Margaret (Boyd), complete excision of Jeanne and the Duchess of Gloucester (Hall and Andrews), costuming that resisted the temptation to mark the women with anything more than their nationality (Rutter), or that bombarded them with pop culture signifiers (Bell), men playing women (Hall and Andrews) and women playing men (Andrews). So we have female bodies representing male presences and male bodies representing female presences, as well as female bodies creating female characters who embody a range of traditionally masculine and feminine behaviours. Modern staging (from around the mid-twentieth century) is the first style to allow such flexibility in representation. Audiences generally accept a variety of techniques within the one performance, including some naturalistic and some more presentational moments, and with actors embodying characters who might or might not resemble themselves in any of numerous ways. Today's conventions instruct us to accept casting with fewer rules for race and gender than in any previous era (though perhaps more for appropriateness of age). Five productions at different ends of the world, including different combinations of plays with different degrees of textual editing, and with different artistic goals, and yet each of these recent examples gives the impression of a shared directorial worry that these plays are likely to be difficult for a modern audience to follow, or to be perceived as dense, complicated or boring. Each employed discernible strategies aimed at enhancing clarity, pace and audience engagement. What quickly becomes clear is how easily a position that presents itself as unconcerned with the rep-

resentation of gender can default to a misogynist one.

Performing a series of plays as a cycle makes particular demands on a production. The director will be looking for unifying features, and a way to strengthen the narrative spine. Streamlining the plot by reducing the exposition, the number of events and the list of characters is inevitable. Editing will influence the impression given to an audience of any character, but the pressures of truncation will always affect the presentation of women disproportionately, because of there being fewer female characters than male. Reducing the number of male characters will not significantly reduce the male presence, whereas the female presence can be almost extinguished. On the other hand, although it is commonplace to see several Lords combined into one person in performance, this will rarely happen to female characters, a fact which makes apparent how highly individuated they are. Female characters may be more affected by a directorial desire to enhance clarity by offering the audience a shorthand guide to the personalities they are observing. If characters are marked as types, there are fewer female archetypes than male from which to select, although at the same time the semiotic indicators for making that type easy to identify are stronger. Our society provides a plethora of visual markers designed to allow the observer to read the female body, dress being the most obvious, but demeanour being just as important to a performer. Put simply, our culture is not short on over-simplified images of women, and a director who exploits this as a storytelling convenience runs the risk of denying the female actors, and the audience, the nuanced character development afforded by the text, and comparable with the major male roles.

Edward Hall's *Rose Rage* offers the most obvious example of the effect of compression and simplification on the female characters. As Hall employs only male actors in his company it might be expected that any Propeller production would generate interesting material for the study of how women are represented on stage, since nothing can be taken for granted in the creation of female presence in their performances. Female characters have to be entirely created, without an actual female body taking care of much of the work. Although there is no reason why the fact that men are playing the female roles should mean that they are treated in a more perfunctory or broad-brush manner, that is, unfortunately, what seems to have happened here. Queen Margaret, Lady Elizabeth Grey and Lady Bona (who has only one scene) were the only female characters kept. Although a token gesture was made at including portions of Part One, the central character of Jeanne la Pucelle was completely eliminated. Hall also removed the Duchess of Gloucester and her plot of witchcraft. The 'cycle' approach has a particularly significant impact on Margaret, who has very different relationships to the characters around her in her second play from those in her third. For example, if the three *Henry VI* plays are reshaped into two then Margaret's adultery with Suffolk and grief at his death can occur in the same play as her defence of her husband's title and their son's birthright, and the vindictiveness of her treatment of York in the third part may appear an echo of that which she has shown to Gloucester, instead of being fuelled by a very different imperative. In this case such subtleties were obliterated by the decision of Robert Hands to play a female impersonator rather than a woman. Reviewers observed that 'He injects a great deal of camp humour, looking as if he has minced straight from *La Cage aux folles*'[2] and 'Forever fiddling with lipstick, hand on hip, Robert Hands gave the impression that he'd seen *Some Like It Hot* a lot more often than he'd ever talked to girls.'[3] Hall's interest in working exclusively with male actors, and probably a sense that these plays are mostly about men and male things, appears to have resulted in a lack of concern with developing the female roles, and the choice to use the most prominent of these as a vehicle for easy laughs. The dominance of masculinity in these plays need not render what female presence there is an inconvenience or an irrelevance, but here the caricaturing of Margaret and the elimination of Jeanne gave the English the ultimate victory in their battle to silence these troublesome Frenchwomen.

If Hall has as his excuse the abbreviated form of his production and his minimalist use of resources, Michael Boyd could be expected to offer something greatly contrasting in his full-length RSC productions. Boyd made what is an unusual choice in the modern age when he staged all three parts of *Henry VI* in full in the Swan theatre in 2000. He added *Richard III*, using the same cast, in 2001, and then adapted and remounted them in the new Courtyard theatre in 2006. Finally, the production was expanded to the full eight plays in 2007. Doubling of roles was an important thematic strategy for Boyd, as were strong visuals, and what might be considered a simplification of the characters into 'good' and 'bad' categories, to aid clarity of storytelling. Both Jeanne and Margaret, doubled by Fiona Bell in the original, were played very much from the assumption that Shakespeare, as an Englishman, would portray these women as clear-cut villains. However, historicizing seems to have been Boyd's excuse rather than his guide. Hardin in his detailed study found 'no specifically English legend hostile to Joan'[4] and an ambivalence among the English historians who do begin to chronicle her story in the sixteenth century. Margaret is treated mostly negatively by Edward Hall in his *Chronicle*, but her inclusion in Thomas Heywood's list of 'nine female worthies' shows that it was considered reasonable at the time to admire her as a historic personage. Historically speaking, both women had both positive and negative characteristics attributed to them. Obviously Shakespeare's version of these famous figures shows no intention to depict them as idealized or virtuous, but neither does he present them as bad or wrong in every scene. In the presentation of character, Shakespeare's writing may at times be confusing, dense or contradictory, but it is not simplistic, and

[2] Philip Fisher, www.britishtheatreguide.info/reviews/roserage1-rev.htm, 2002.

[3] Michael Dobson, 'Shakespeare Performances in England', *Shakespeare Survey 56* (Cambridge, 2003), p. 279.

[4] Richard F. Hardin, 'Chronicles and Mythmaking in Shakespeare's Joan of Arc', *Shakespeare Survey 42* (Cambridge, 1989), 25–35; p. 26.

the Jeanne and Margaret of his text are as often appealing, admirable or sympathetic figures as they are villainous. Boyd drew on selective moments of the text to confirm a negative perspective on the characters, instead of engaging with this textual complexity.

From the beginning of Boyd's production it was made clear through his staging that Jeanne's power came from a combination of witchcraft and sexual bribery, expanding on any opportunities in the narrative to show her performing magic or behaving promiscuously, and minimizing or trivializing points where she demonstrates physical skill or verbal mastery. Boyd took the finely constructed elusiveness of the Joan of the text and bludgeoned her into vulgar certainty. Margaret was visually identified with Joan's 'fiends' through her red gown and also clearly marked as a demonic presence. Fiona Bell articulates the director's position thus: 'I think it was Michael's intention that Margaret was, to an extent, a conduit for evil. Joan was alive and had crossed the Channel and until we encounter Richard III no-one can match her for badness.'[5]

Bell's analysis of playing these dual roles reveals much about the attitude to female power that fuelled the rehearsal process. She mentions both as having a 'manipulative sexuality', locking herself into the stereotype that bad women are sexual and sexual women are bad. She reflects the common tendency to consider a woman responsible for a man's sexual response to her, in her take on Joan's encounter with the Dauphin. Examining the text shows that it is the Dauphin who introduces a sexual element to their interaction, and it also suggests that her response is to deflect this kind of speech.

Charles. Stay, stay thy hands! Thou art an Amazon
  And fightest with the sword of Deborah.
Joan. Christ's Mother helps me, else I were too weak.
Charles. Whoe'er helps thee, 'tis thou that must help
  me:
  Impatiently I burn with thy desire:
  My heart and hands thou hast at once subdued.
  Excellent Pucelle if thy name be so,
  Let me thy servant, and not sovereign be.
  'Tis the French dauphin sueth to thee thus.

Pucelle. I must not yield to any rites of love,
  For my profession's sacred from above.
  When I have chasèd all thy foes from hence,
  Then will I think upon a recompense.   (1.3.83–95)

The way Bell saw this meeting was that Joan is exploiting her sexual power over the Dauphin. If this were the case, there would surely be more direct ways to go about it than to challenge him to single combat. When Joan makes her first entrance to the French court the text implies that there are numerous characters on stage. The Dauphin tries to disguise himself among his courtiers and Joan calls for him to come 'from behind', showing that she can pick him out in a crowd. In this production (which did not skimp on extras as a rule) only the speaking characters, numbering three lords in addition to the Dauphin, were on stage for this scene; 'from behind' was taken to mean merely that he should come from upstage to down. When Joan and the Dauphin 'talk aside' the others exited the stage completely, which meant that Joan's defeat of the Dauphin in single combat did not take place in the public domain. This results in an uncalled-for diminishment of Joan's power, especially given that she is supposed to be impressing the French army enough for them to follow her into battle. The combat concluded with the two of them lying on their backs in the middle of the stage, laughing and panting in a very post-coital fashion. Joan's indication that later on she will 'think upon a recompense' was quite openly seductive.

Joan's single combat with the Dauphin and later with Talbot both included sequences where ringing sounds and the circular motion of Joan's sword had a hypnotic effect on her antagonist. Boyd obviously wanted to emphasize the mystical element of Joan's military power, but what he did was take a scene where a woman demonstrates exceptional physical skill and ensure that it can only be interpreted as witchcraft. Joan even drew one of her mysterious circles on the floor with the point of her sword before her speech persuading Burgundy

---

5 Fiona Bell, 'Joan of Arc and Margaret of Anjou', in *Players of Shakespeare 6*, ed. Robert Smallwood (Cambridge, 2004), 163–84; p. 172.

to change sides. Even her rhetorical power here was not permitted to be seen as 'real' power, but trickery.

Boyd found ways to make sure the audience would side with the male characters who disbelieve Joan's professed role as a holy virgin. Until her claim of pregnancy preceding her execution the only hints in the text that she might not be the chaste woman she claims are name-calling by her enemies and the fact that she enters at the same point as the Dauphin in 2.1 when the French have been attacked at night. It must be stressed that *all* she does with the Dauphin in this scene is enter at the same time; there is no more explicit indication of a relationship. There are plenty of points in the text where Joan is referred to with terms designed to label a woman sexually promiscuous, but we should be careful about where we locate the judgement delivered upon characters in situations like this. It is not Shakespeare who calls Joan a 'strumpet' or 'trull', but Talbot and Burgundy.[6] When there is no authorial commentary, but only the words of characters who are inevitably shaped by their place within the dramatic narrative there is no reason to credit the insults with more than the eternal tradition of men accusing non-conforming women of being whores. Boyd, however, used this as his inspiration to go 'one step further than Shakespeare and intimated that she was in fact sleeping with several members of the French court'.[7] This taking of abuse from other characters as stage directions firmly allies the director with the enemies of the woman in question, and forces her to present herself from their point of view. Shakespeare's very subtle ambiguous moments were used to authorize a version of Joan that removed any need to question the moral superiority of the English.

From a textual point of view, the only thing that unambiguously marks Joan as not what she claims to be is the fact that her soliloquy is addressed to 'fiends'. Here, both actor and director took the appearance of the fiends as a revelation of what has been happening all along, a statement that the Virgin Mary has never appeared to Joan and that she has been lying from the beginning, which required Bell to read Joan's displays of admirable

qualities as worthless: 'she is putting on a pious act, feigning the sort of bold timidity of one who is driven by, and herself given over to, a higher power. Behind this façade she is undoubtedly self-possessed.'[8] Boyd introduced the fiends to earlier scenes with Joan, and Bell sees this as simply making clear what an Elizabethan audience would have assumed: 'By objectifying her magic in the shape of the "fiends", Michael relieved me of the burden of having to give a modern audience hints as to her true nature.'[9] The fiends were represented by three women, and sometimes also a man (the 'keeper', a recurring figure in Boyd's production), dressed in long, red robes. It was implied that these were supernatural forces working with and for Joan. Bell's quotations from Boyd suggest the director's two-dimensional understanding of character was particular to Joan, and went unquestioned by the actress. When she is bad she is her 'true' self, when she is noble she is 'lying'.

Bell's analysis of her performance after her transformation into Margaret, as in her discussion of Joan, does not question her director's impression that the play is divided into good and bad characters, and that the women are bad. In Parts Two and Three her sympathy is all with York and she does not seek her own character's point of view. For example, she refers several times to Margaret's 'torturing' of York, but does not use similar language for the scenes of Joan's capture (which was unremittingly brutal in this version) or the scene where Margaret's son is killed before her eyes. This is not a theoretical stance based on a position that a fully developed character would be an anachronism – she still looks for motivation and personality traits, and describes 'plotting Joan's emotional and mental journey'.[10] Rather it is an example of the common pattern of male actors being encouraged to find their own position, the women to

---

[6] It would be a similar choice to look to Tamora to decide how Titus Andronicus should be played.

[7] Bell, 'Joan of Arc', p. 167.

[8] Bell, 'Joan of Arc', p. 164.

[9] Bell, 'Joan of Arc', p. 167.

[10] Bell, 'Joan of Arc', p. 167.

understand the position of the men. Bell herself does not describe the production as limiting in its presentation of the characters she played. In fact, she praises Boyd for having 'shaped both the text and my performance in such a way as to remind me always that first and foremost these women are only human',[11] despite offering no example of anything resembling this perspective in the details she gives about the production or her reports of Boyd's directives. Is she perhaps protesting too much?

This approach to the characters was carried over to the 2006 revival, when Katy Stephens took over the two roles. Alastair Macaulay's review demonstrates how much misogynist baggage Stephens was asked to carry: 'Margaret becomes, as Joan became, a perilous woman who cancels her own femininity and dons armour to fight in battle . . . She is a *femme fatale* many times over.'[12] Woman can be dangerous because of her femaleness, or her shedding of it; evil because she fights openly, or persuades subtly; somehow able to be all these contradictory bad things at once, yet not the contradictory good and bad things that Shakespeare included in his text.

Hall showed how the representation of female power can be curtailed by simple elimination of roles and introduction of parody, Boyd by diverting the source of that power away from the characters' possession of genuine skills, and reshaping it as the kind of power our society finds easy to imagine in women: sex and witchcraft. John Bell's production demonstrates that these are not the only measurable effects on female presence arising from the pressure to produce a slick and accessible story. For a company producing Shakespeare's history plays in Australia, the concern is not that the audience will associate the Wars of the Roses with schoolbook history but that the story is completely unknown: British history is not taught in schools. This can result in an even greater than usual emphasis on simplifying complex twists of plot and character, and finding a strong narrative thrust and moments that will be recognizable to a modern audience. The advantage for Australian productions of Shakespeare can be the absence of a weight of preconception or performance history, when assumptions about characters that are frequently seen in British

productions are not made, simply because there has been no local precedent. However, there is a corresponding disadvantage in the pressure to avoid presenting anything in a way that might be obscure or hard to follow. The Bell Shakespeare Company, named after its founder and Artistic Director, veteran actor John Bell, places great emphasis on touring (to both larger cities and regional centres) over the whole country, and takes its educational arm very seriously. It runs workshops for students, and always includes designated schools' performances for its shows. Casting itself in the role of reaching out to non-established audiences, it sees itself as 'founded on the ideals of uninhibited access to the great classics for as many Australians as possible'.[13] In 2005 Bell's company staged an amalgamation of the three parts of *Henry VI* which illustrated a paradox that emerges from this philosophy. The company's mission statement is socially progressive, in that it advocates theatre for all, Shakespeare for all, and the unequivocal belief that the plays in performance can communicate something of value to people regardless of their geographical or educational background. However, to validate this belief the imperative becomes to prove that the performances can be popular with everyone, which usually results in drawing on popular culture for images and references, with all its attendant conventionality. Making the production accessible meant making it socially conservative, in that it did not aim to challenge our society's dominant assumptions about powerful women.

Joan was presented as a martial arts movie 'girlpower action heroine who can fly through the air and kickbox in slow-mo'.[14] The style was something like a Manga cartoon, with combat trousers, a plastic breastplate bearing a sacred heart design, and rollerball knee and elbow pads. The other French characters performed with comically exaggerated, Monty-Pythonesque French accents, but

---

[11] Bell, 'Joan of Arc', p. 184.

[12] Alastair Macaulay, *Financial Times*, 11 August 2006.

[13] See under headings Company/Introduction at www. bellshakespeare.com.au/ (accessed 31 July 2009).

[14] John McCallum, *The Australian*, 15 March 2005.

Joan was exempted from this. Her scene speaking to fiends was cut altogether, as not fitting in with the modern caste of the piece, or perhaps the director simply didn't know what to do with such an unusual moment. This removed a speech that is usually an opportunity for a virtuoso performance by a woman in a play dominated by men, and also eliminated any questions about whether or not Joan is genuine. Instead, the production made reference to the Abu Ghraib torture scandals that had recently erupted by covering her head with a bag and wheeling her around in a shopping trolley, while the English soldiers took photographs and jeered. Some of the less sophisticated reviewers were impressed with the up-to-the-minute politics, others felt it was a cheap and easy grab at 'relevance' that was not supported by the context. Local blogger Alison Croggon was one who thought through the dramaturgical implications of the staging decision:

This snatch at contemporary events is gratuitously shallow: are we now supposed to equate France with occupied Iraq? And if so, why are we caricaturing the enemy? Or is the whole issue of torture merely the occasion (as I fear) for a jokey aside?... Aside from a scene showing Joan's dealings with demons and witchcraft (absent from this version), Shakespeare is fairly even-handed in his portrayals of the French and the English, with both armies demonising each other. Dehumanising the enemy is one of the time-honoured (or dishonoured) staples of warfare, and Shakespeare clearly demonstrates its mechanisms. By eliciting easy laughs at the expense of the French, Bell neatly fillets out this moral equivalence, and with it a great deal of tragic power.[15]

In this climate it was inevitable that Margaret would be reduced to that other female cartoon staple, what one reviewer called a 'blood-lusting rock 'n' roller: big hair, boobs and leather',[16] and another a 'leather-clad dominatrix'.[17] Croggon summarized her simply as a 'manipulative sex bomb', and noted that this was 'an interpretation that, like her outrageous accent, obscures her warrior ruthlessness'.[18] Like Fiona Bell, Blazey Best played Henry's warrior queen as 'outrightly sexual and manipulative',[19] but with even less subtlety this approach was signalled in costume by her 'tottering

about in stilletos and wearing a vinyl/leather raincoat of amazing tartishness'[20] in the early scenes, and then changing into more bondage-style leather once she began to lead Henry's army. Best used an unabashedly fake French accent, and enthusiastically reduced herself to a stereotype on the grounds of making it easier for the audience to understand the play.

Best illustrates the tangle of issues at work for an actor trying to see her character's point of view in the way she chooses to defend her character in interview. Her main interest is in arguing for Margaret's ultimate femininity: 'Generally, the way Western society views women in power is that they have to be de-feminised. Think of Margaret Thatcher or Condoleezza Rice – people think of them as ball-breakers', but Best believes 'There's a very feminine quality to the power Margaret wants' in that 'she doesn't want it for herself, she wants it firstly for her husband so he can rule the kingdom, and secondly for her son (Edward), so he can become king. At first she's quite sexually manipulative, but in the second half she's like a lioness protecting her cub. Once the rule of her family is threatened all hell breaks loose.'[21] The only choices Best sees open to her are portraying Margaret as a woman without sexual or feminine qualities or a woman who uses these qualities manipulatively.

The greatly reduced role of the female characters in this production was born of a very specific set of priorities. Bell does not seem to have been antagonistic towards women, but his anxiety about whether his audience would follow and respond to the story led him to disregard the hard questions about what message is communicated by the use of

[15] Alison Croggon, http://theatrenotes.blogspot.com, 28 May 2005.
[16] Colin Rose, *Sun Herald*, 13 March 2005.
[17] Martin Portus, *Sydney Star Observer*, 17 March 2005.
[18] Croggon, http://theatrenotes.blogspot.com, 28 May 2005.
[19] Keith Gallasch, www.realtimearts.net, 17 May 2005.
[20] Neil Whitfield, http://ninglun.wordpress.com/my-canon-whats-yours/the-bard-a-rabbit-and-ninglun/, 8 March 2005.
[21] Blazey Best interviewed by Luke Benedictus, *The Age*, 15 May 2005.

stereotyping. These two characters were far from being the only ones who were reduced in scope or caricatured in this production, and it would be unfair to imply that male characters were not treated similarly, but the similarity extends only to their being stereotyped. They were not similarly sexualized. The direction taken by this production says a great deal about the social context within which Bell was working. When the goal was to find images of powerful women that would be comprehensible to his audience, what the director (in conjunction with the designer and presumably with input from the actors) came up with were comic-book types. This is what the company felt it had available to draw upon in looking for a visual language with which to communicate with its audience. The production did not treat it as a component of its brief to critique these perceptions of gender roles, they were merely regarded as useful.

In the discussion surrounding both the Boyd and Bell productions, it is hard to miss that the phrase 'sexually manipulative' and its variants crops up repeatedly, in the former relating to both Joan and Margaret, the latter only in relation to Margaret. Can such a description of these characters claim to be textually based? Joan has only one line in which critics have argued for the presence of sexual innuendo: 'When I have chasèd all thy foes from hence, / Then will I think upon a recompense' (1.3.94–5). Tenuous at best, especially given its placement immediately after a flat rejection of the Dauphin's quite explicit advances. Margaret is definitely shown as a sexual being, but does she use that sexuality to achieve her ends? In her relations with her husband Margaret's approach is based around complaint and command, rather than seduction and the conditional promise of sexual favours. She does tell him, in Part Three:

> . . . I here divorce myself
> Both from thy table, Henry, and thy bed,
> Until that act of parliament be repeal'd
> Whereby my son is disinherited.   (1.1.248–51)

But a public divorce is surely the precise opposite of manipulative. That is, it does not use sex to facilitate the achievement of a disguised end; it is an open declaration of exactly what she wants and intends. And she hardly needs to manipulate Suffolk, who shares her agenda already. In fact, in the concluding lines of Part One he declares his plan to use his seductiveness to control her: 'Margaret shall be Queen and rule the King; / But I will rule both her, the King and realm' (5.6.107–8). I have yet to find an account of the play or a performance of it that describes Suffolk as 'sexually manipulative'.

At this point it is beginning to seem as if evidence is needed that it is possible to stage these plays without resorting to crude stereotypes in the female characterization. Barrie Rutter's 2006 Northern Broadsides production at the West Yorkshire Playhouse may be the place to look. There are both underlying similarities to and striking differences from Bell's production in this version, given the same title: *Wars of the Roses*. Both companies frame their work around the idea of a core ensemble of actors who work repeatedly with the company, local accents, regional touring and a philosophy of creating a 'people's Shakespeare'.

Rutter was most interested in these plays as a reflection and investigation of a Britain divided against itself, and consequently was perhaps least interested in the sequences involving Joan. Her appearances were heavily cut, as were her longer speeches. This de-prioritizing of her story did, however, result in a presentation that did not seek to make judgements on her character: the audience was simply shown two groups of warriors in opposition, without implications that either side was wrong or right, evil or virtuous. Her costume was a simple blue tunic and loose trousers (the French wore blue to distinguish them from the English in Lancastrian red and Yorkist white) and she carried a broadsword (the production used weaponry from all periods). There was no attempt to sexualize her character or make her seductive. In fact, two reviewers commented (disparagingly) that she looked most like Peter Pan.[22] Though

---

[22] *The Stage Inc*, 27 April 2006; J. D. Atkinson, *British Theatre Guide*, 5 April 2006.

her Act 5 soliloquy was severely truncated, it was also ambiguously situated. There were no textual changes to re-address the speech to the Virgin Mary (as in the Bogdanov production of 1986) or similar, but the 'fiends' were two singing women who were angelic rather than demonic: dressed in long robes and carrying a cross and a palm frond.

The text was trimmed to the point where entire scenes would sometimes be represented by a single speech. So it was that Joan's first appearance was only to recite, in isolation, an amalgamation of several of her speeches in 1.2, amounting to twenty lines. Her recognition of the Dauphin, her challenge to him and their fight, indeed, all her interaction with the people she is to lead, disappeared. The scene of Joan's persuasion of Burgundy was cut entirely. The battle scenes were all performed in various symbolic and ritualistic ways, generally involving clog dances or the beating of drums, rather than as actual swordfights. All the scenes set in France were greatly reduced, group battle scenes were not played out and individual confrontations between Joan and Talbot were what remained. Talbot was wheeled on in a kind of simple cart, beating a large drum 'while Joan clog-danced around him brandishing her sword'.[23] The drastic nature of the cutting was not unique to Joan, other characters with prominent roles in Part One were similarly affected (Talbot's role was shortened, the Dauphin did not appear until the section derived from 2 Henry VI, which began halfway through the first play in Rutter's two-part amalgamation, and Burgundy was cut altogether), but for anyone familiar with Part One the difference made to the presentation of Joan was staggering. There was really no remaining representation of the range or extraordinary nature of her powers.

The ensemble nature of the company's approach meant that all twenty-one actors appeared in all three parts of the cycle (which consisted of the three Henry VI plays compressed into two, with the split occurring after the reporting of the death of Suffolk, followed by Richard III in its standard form), and the programme listed the actors in alphabetical order with the three plays listed across the page from them, and the names of the

characters each played under each one, in a kind of grid. This makes it instantly apparent that Helen Sheals as Queen Margaret is the only actor playing just one role, and the only one playing the same character in all three plays. For an audience watching the whole cycle, this makes her the only figure that can be followed from the beginning of the story to the end. Again, there seems to have been no attempt to imbue her with an obvious sexuality. Rather, reviews refer to her in terms such as 'diminutive but indomitable',[24] 'brash, almost vulgar toughness'[25] and 'diminutive spitfire'.[26] The heavy textual editing did not affect Margaret in quite the same way as Joan. She did not lose any full scenes, plot points or representations of the scope and variety of her powers. However, the consistent thinning out of her many speeches removed some of the most articulate and emotive writing in these plays. Passages that, in full, are passionately poetic (such as her separation from Suffolk or the death of Edward) were narrowed to be tightly functional in moving the plot along.

Reviews of the production, hampered by the need to reflect on seven hours of theatre in a few hundred words, make small mention of the female roles, even Margaret, and many do not speak of them at all. Susannah Clapp, of The Observer, found that the production's goal of dynamic, action-driven storytelling came with the price of reduced subtlety and inflection, and that this was particularly apparent in the changes to the roles of Joan and Margaret: 'The women's parts have been reduced: Maeve Larkin's piping Joan of Arc has little more than a twirl of a fight, and mostly sounds petulant; Queen Margaret's lament for her dead son is severely stripped down so that a layer of feeling in the plays is diminished.'[27]

Though it is a shame to see roles of such extraordinary sinew and distinctiveness curtailed, at least

---

[23] Kate Wilkinson, *Shakespeare Bulletin*, 24.3 (2006), 113–20, p. 116.

[24] Dominic Cavendish, *Daily Telegraph*, 5 April 2006.

[25] Peter Whittle, *Sunday Times*, 9 April 2006.

[26] J. D. Atkinson, *British Theatre Guide*, 5 April 2006.

[27] Susannah Clapp, *The Observer*, 9 April 2006.

Rutter did not come to the plays with an interest in channelling our society's hostility to women who display skills and achievements that fall outside traditional gender roles. There was a willingness to engage with the women exhibiting a variety of forms of power: spiritual, political and physical, if less of the rhetorical than they show in uncut versions.[28] There was no attempt to limit them to sexual power alone, or to identify sexual power as 'bad' power.

Certainly the most complex and varied uses of female presence in any of these examples were in Benedict Andrews's Sydney Theatre Company production in early 2009, a compression of all eight Wars of the Roses plays into two nights' performance. That description is already a little misleading: as Andrews's interest was very obviously with the two Richards, so much more was cut out of the intervening Henrys. The first night gave *Richard II* before the interval and *Henry IV* and *V* after; the second night gave all parts of *Henry VI* in the first half, *Richard III* in the second, with the obvious results in the balance of editing. In many ways this version was the most interesting for drawing in all the elements involved in the use and representation of women into one place. Andrews had two extraordinary female actors he wanted to display in showpiece roles, and so Cate Blanchett took on Richard II and Pamela Rabe Richard III, using female bodies to comment on masculinity by constructing it through nothing more than the acting (all the women playing men wore gender-neutral modern clothes and kept their feminine haircuts). Conversely, his sense that the *Henry IV* and *V* plays operate with a purely masculine energy meant all the female roles in that portion were cut except Princess Katherine, who was played by a man (Luke Mullins), which explored the possibilities of symbolic representation of female presence (and shared nothing stylistically with Hall's use of male actors in female roles). In the section devoted to the *Henry VI* series cross-casting was still used but less featured (Rutland was played by a woman, but as a boy, while Warwick was played by a woman as a woman), but the pressure to compress the enormous and complex narrative into less than two

hours resulted in some moments of stereotyping and trivializing the female characters in a way similar to that encountered in Bell and Boyd. The motivation for the cross-casting used by Andrews seemed thematic in the case of *Henry V*, but in the two Richards may well have emanated from nothing more than a desire to see his best actors given the chance to dominate the stage in a way that is not afforded to women playing female roles.

The sole use of a man playing the woman's part began when Luke Mullins was revealed in the final minutes of the second segment as a bloodied corpse lying on a bare stage. Ewan Leslie, who had been playing Henry V bare-chested and covered in blood, and Mullins were ritually washed in enamel basins by the other actors, who then dressed the latter in a white lace dress, without any attempt to disguise his masculine identity. Mullins's demeanour during the courtship was passive, his face immobile. Apart from a completely anachronistic kiss that concluded the scene, the two actors did not interact with each other, standing at the extreme edges of the large, empty stage. It was a clever representation of the symbolic way a woman was used in such historic circumstances. The Princess is currency being exchanged to forge a treaty, much more than she is a person, and so she was presented as a body put into a dress, going through a prescribed ritual of words and gesture.

Governed by the need to get the three *Henry VI* plays into half an evening, Joan and the Duchess of Gloucester were predictable excisions. Marta Dusseldorp's Margaret made the most of the moments of power permitted her, when expressing triumph or grief, but her natty cream dress and gold high heels worked with the heavily trimmed text to make it almost impossible to pick up the fact that she was commanding Henry's army. More concerning was the depiction of her relationship with Suffolk. Her speech comparing her husband to

---

[28] For some interesting observations on comparative cuts to the role of Margaret, see Randall Martin, 'Queen Margaret Thatcherized in Recent Productions of *3 Henry VI*', in *Shakespeare and His Contemporaries in Performance*, ed. Edward Esche (Aldershot, 2000), pp. 321–38.

Suffolk was kept, but performed as a disengaged monologue while pulling up her skirt and writhing in a parody of lust. Suffolk watched from upstage, then grabbed her from behind and held a hand over her mouth as she struggled. There were no more lines, or further indication of why their romance should be depicted as a rape, just a minute or two of the actors standing centre-stage waggling their tongues at each other. Whatever else the Margaret of the text may be, she is unquestionably articulate, but denying her voice in preference for a visually signalled caricature of femininity (drag queen, scarlet woman, dominatrix, porn siren) is by now looking like a habitual feature of staging her.

The problem was repeated at the introduction of Elizabeth, Lady Grey. Surtitles were used throughout this segment of the production, summarizing the incident being played out underneath, and in this case 'The Seduction of Elizabeth' was put up, while Elizabeth and Edward removed each other's clothes and retired upstage, in passionate embrace, without a word being spoken. This is virtually a reversal of the scene it replaced, which is an attempt at seduction through persuasion that fails to work on a woman who demands that the king treat her honourably. Once again, a woman's eloquence was replaced with an image of her as a sexual plaything.

This *Richard III* gave a female performer an unusual opportunity to be a dominant physical presence on the stage. Pamela Rabe, whose dark pageboy haircut was a neat reference to Olivier's incarnation of the role, employed no deformity in representing Richard, except occasionally to stoop and twist her arm up in mocking exaggeration of the cliché of the hunchback. In a production that often held to rigid restraint in its interactions between actors, Andrews gave Rabe free rein to use her remarkable physicality. Richard bore down on Cate Blanchett's Anne, whose fragile, haunted demeanour was an effective contrast to Rabe's vitality, and wrestled just as enthusiastically with Clifford, Richmond or his brothers' offspring.

A most inventive use of an additional female presence was the expansion of the role of George's daughter, Margaret (Holly Fraser), whose one scene is almost always cut in production. Fraser

was on-stage for almost the entire performance, becoming an ally and a chorus figure supporting Rabe's Richard, with remarkable focus. The set consisted of a bleak children's playground, with swings, slippery slide, roundabout and jungle gym, and Fraser, sometimes with the boys playing the princes, used all these, generating a continuous sense both of motion and of watchfulness. It was she who concluded the production, the last figure on an empty stage, holding the crown that had been passed from one king to another all the way back to Richard II.

In the opening segment of this two-night production, this filigree crown had topped off the fastidious white trousers and crisp shirt that instantly made Cate Blanchett stand out from the other actors, who were all costumed in rehearsal-type clothing. This *Richard II* was unashamedly a vehicle for Blanchett's luminous presence. Andrews placed her physically front and centre, the only actor seated on a setless stage, the others standing in the weaker positions in the space. Shimmering gold foil confetti fell in a constant rain over them all, until Richard's confrontation with the returned Bullingbrook. There was virtually no motion up to this point, with lines generally directed out to the audience, and the scenes run on without entrances and exits. This left clarity of diction and expressiveness of delivery in the lines as the actors' only means of communicating with the audience, which is precisely where Blanchett excels. Richard's many long speeches were executed with virtuosic style; precise, lucid and fresh. Once the confetti had settled on the ground Richard's capriciousness had a physical outlet in the gathered piles, as he retreated upstage to sulk, lay on his back wriggling bare toes up the wall and played with the fallen gold. His ostentatious self-assurance devolved into defiant, over-compensatory showing-off, kissing Bullingbrook's feet with insulting obsequiousness, feigning casualness at the handing over of the crown, with comic pretence at its heaviness. Richard's imprisonment was represented by a black stocking mask with a hole cut for the mouth, leaving Blanchett no resources besides her mellifluous voice to make this famous speech work. Reduced, as it was, to a single act, this was nothing like watching a complete *Richard II* but, still, there have been few opportunities to hear Richard's words given such life. The chief female presence in this segment may have been representing a man, but it still offers a lesson to many other productions, including the remainder of this one. Give a good actor the lines and the space to interpret them and an audience will listen. When a director has some faith in the audience members' ability to involve themselves, stereotyping characters to aid comprehension is revealed as counterproductive.

The surprising thing about this *Richard II* was how rarely an instinct to simplify a complex narrative results in a staging that is actually simple, as this was. Instead of stripping away the peripherals to allow the text to do the work, most directors have layered on semiotic signifiers, and removed text. This has a palpable effect on the presentation of the female characters, as they are shown less as articulate, verbal people, and more as representatives of visually identified types. In Andrews's STC, Rutter's Northern Broadsides and Hall's Propeller productions there was heavy cutting or removal of Jeanne's and Margaret's speeches that are the most dazzling pieces of rhetoric and the most extraordinary opportunities for female performers. In Boyd's RSC production the concern about complexity mainly manifested itself in the over-simplification of the female characters into out-and-out villains, preoccupied with their sexuality, and in Bell's production it was both. Andrews's production both expanded and contracted the female presence through his use of cross-casting, but some of the same sticking points did manifest themselves, such as in portions of the presentation of Margaret, and also of Elizabeth, Lady Grey.

In a series of plays that seem to be exploring the possibility of female martial, spiritual, administrative, rhetorical and political power, seeking to reduce these many things to sexual power alone makes a strong statement about the interpreter's attitude to women and power. The reductive drawing of Margaret, and in some instances Jeanne or Elizabeth as the fear/fantasy of a woman whose mastery over men resides in her sexuality displays a need to render them simple and conventional. It is notable that, despite being comparatively uninterested in dwelling on the female characters, Northern Broadsides gave (perhaps as a result?) the least narrow or judgemental presentation of them. It is easy to question whether Boyd's selective historicization was an excuse, allowing him to stage a fear of female power. Bell's reliance on the populist to sell the plays to a potentially resistant audience shows that the most common images of female power currently in circulation for him to draw upon are cartoon staples, including hypersexualized images that have no male equivalent. Andrews had the imagination to use female performers in a wide variety of ways, but failed to find a vision of heterosexual passion that did not draw on the most hackneyed images of male predators and female victims and vamps. It is astonishing how some of the world's most celebrated, most intelligent, most experienced directors seem to flounder when asked to represent a woman who falls outside a few common ranges of behaviour.

When Shakespeare's histories are performed today they are almost always subject to heavy editing of all the characters; narrative streamlining is *de rigueur*, and commercial imperatives prompting a fear of the over-complicated can understandably lead to the temptation to over-simplify. Still, what a shock it would be to find that a four-hundred-year-old text offers us a greater capacity to represent complex and sophisticated images of women exhibiting many different kinds of power than we, with all our advances in critical discourse and theatre practice, can imagine how to use.

THE RSC'S 'GLORIOUS MOMENT' AND THE MAKING OF SHAKESPEARIAN HISTORY

ALICE DAILEY

Whose forgetting? Whose memory? Whose history?
Joseph Roach, *Cities of the Dead*

Before I left Philadelphia on a madcap voyage to Stratford to see Shakespeare's two history tetralogies[1] performed over a four-day weekend, a colleague who thought me rather deranged for undertaking this adventure during the teaching term remarked sardonically that 'Jack Cade's Rebellion, the most trite episode in all of Shakespeare', would surely make my trip worthwhile.[2] Admittedly, Michael Boyd's 'Glorious Moment' – the title of this 'once in a lifetime' theatrical event – was a form of Extreme Shakespeare not for the faint of heart (or hind). But its rendition of Cade's Rebellion provides an improbably elegant entry point for theorizing the intersection between event-based theatrical phenomena and the construction of Shakespearian history. In this production of *2 Henry VI*, Dick the Butcher, one of Cade's followers, wore a bloody apron and punctuated his speech with the emphatic wave of a bloody meat cleaver. Stripped to the waist, he had scrawled on his chest (in more blood) the obstinate declaration, 'WE'RE 'ISTRY'.

Who are 'we', and what history is being claimed here? On its surface, the statement asserts the rebels' right to control and construct events according to popular rather than aristocratic prerogative; they'll 'set London Bridge afire, and, if [they] can, burn down the Tower too', erasing others' history to clear ground for their own (*2 Henry VI*, 4.6.14–15).[3] Colloquially, the phrase is an acknowledgement of mortality, even imminent death, and this

meaning also had significant resonance in Boyd's productions. Jack Cade's entourage was composed of the animated corpses of characters who had been killed off earlier in this and previous plays, including Lord Talbot and his son John, Margery Jourdain and John Hume, the murdered Duke of Gloucester, and a headless Suffolk, led haltingly around by the elbow. As an ironic analogue to Henry's court, Jack Cade's followers suggested that the world of the living – was equally 'history', equally doomed. Through the device of the zombie rebels, the production literalized the claim, 'WE'RE 'ISTRY', by making the 'we' not only deceased but bloodied, headless, and wounded. This freezing in time dramatized the paradoxical nature of history as both living and dead, recuperative and impotent, animated and static. Populating Cade's ranks with wounded zombies exposed the fact that what we were seeing was not so much history as it was theatre, the only space where the figures of the past can have three-dimensional

---

I want to thank Donnacadh O'Briain, Dan Usztan, and Roger Watkins at the RSC, as well as Regina Buccola, Lowell Gallagher, Matthew Kozusko, Zachary Lesser, Kristen Poole, Katherine Rowe, Lauren Shohet, Jonathan Walker and Josh Dailey.

[1] I use the terms 'first' and 'second' tetralogy throughout this article as they are conventionally used in Shakespeare studies, not to describe the order in which the tetralogies were performed, which was the opposite.

[2] I quote my irrepressible and incomparable colleague in the Villanova Theatre Department, Professor Shawn Kairschner.

[3] All quotations of Shakespeare's plays are from *The Complete Works*, ed. John Jowett, William Montgomery, Gary Taylor and Stanley Wells, 2nd edn (Oxford, 2005).

animation. Boyd's interpolation of Cade's Rebellion thus deconstructed the boundary between
living and dead and interrogated the distinction
between the explicitly theatrical (headless zombies
on stage) and the ostensibly historical (the events
of Henry's rule).

I want to suggest that the phrase, 'WE'RE 'ISTRY',
ultimately functions as a frame for reading the Glorious Moment – that it works as a self-reflective,
metatheatrical, and metahistorical statement about
what happened as these plays were staged and
received during this exceptional event. This was
the first time in the history of the Royal Shakespeare Company that a single ensemble produced
all eight plays, and this was the only weekend
in their two-year residence in Stratford that they
were staged in this way.[4] On the previous weekend (6–9 March 2008) all eight plays were performed over four days in compositional order. The
term, 'The Glorious Moment', however, does not
include these performances; it was used by the
RSC specifically to denote the weekend of 13–
16 March 2008,[5] when the plays were performed
in episodic order. The event commemorated the
end of the Histories' residence in Stratford before
they moved to London's Roundhouse.

The word 'event' is essential to considering what
occurred in Stratford during the weekend of the
Glorious Moment. By assigning a name to this
and only this block of performances, the RSC
explicitly marked it out as an event, a singular
instance of *something happening* – something different from what had happened during the preceding,
no-title, non-event, eight-play weekend of performances or what would happen a month later at the
Roundhouse.[6] The RSC sold a Glorious Moment
Package consisting of tickets to all eight plays,
programmes, interval cocktails, a Sunday brunch
before *Richard III* and admission to a final wrap-
up gala.[7] Those of us not fortunate enough to
afford the Package (£400–500, depending on seats)
were nonetheless invited into the event's conscious
and cooperative construction of something special, something singular. This singularity is now
reinforced by the RSC website, which showcases
reaction interviews with the actors and pre- and

post-event interviews with audience members, all
of whom articulate the extraordinary nature of the
experience.[8]

---

4 Jami Rogers provides a concise summary of Michael Boyd's
progressive engagement with the *Henry VI* plays and the
octology, beginning with the *This England* project in 2000:
'"Staging History": The RSC's *Histories* for the New Mil-
lenium', *Cahiers Élisabéthains*, 73 (2008), 57–73; p. 57. For a
history of the RSC's stagings of the two tetralogies, see Stuart
Hampton-Reeves, 'Theatrical Afterlives', in *Cambridge Companion to Shakespeare's History Plays*, ed. Michael Hattaway
(Cambridge, 2002), pp. 229–43. While the RSC advertised
Boyd's 'The Histories' project as the first staging of all eight
plays by a single ensemble, Peter Hall and John Barton produced the plays at the RSC with one company in 1963–4,
although Barton had compressed the three parts of *Henry VI*
into two plays. The English Shakespeare Company also produced a seven-play cycle titled *The Wars of the Roses* in 1986–9,
detailed in Michael Bogdanov and Michael Pennington's *The
English Shakespeare Company: The Story of 'The Wars of the
Roses' 1986–1989* (London, 1990).
5 Incidentally, this was the same weekend as the 2008 Shakespeare Association of America conference in Dallas, Texas.
This coincidence meant that American Shakespeare scholars
were absent from the Glorious Moment, which in turn made
me persistently aware that an alternative marathon Shakespeare event was unfolding simultaneously across the Atlantic.
6 V. V. Montreaux observes that 'The title, however derived,
must submit to its own logic of uniqueness: when the cycle
is repeated at London's Roundhouse theatre in April with
an identically intense long weekend, there is no "Glorious Moment" denomination or package. History is now
and Stratford': '32 Short Thoughts about "The Glorious
Moment"', *Shakespeare Bulletin*, 26.4 (Winter 2008), 65–75;
p. 67.
7 The RSC's web advertisement for the Glorious Moment
Package is at www.rsc.org.uk/content/5102.aspx. Montreaux
offers a detailed price breakdown of what was included ('32
Short Thoughts', p. 67). According to RSC sales records, 601
Glorious Moment Packages were sold. The Courtyard's seating capacity of 1000 people would equal the largest possible
number who witnessed the entire event.
8 These videos can be viewed at www.rsc.org.uk/content/
6838.aspx. Performances of Wagner's complete *Ring Cycle*
represent an analogously monumental theatrical enterprise,
one that generates audience response similarly befitting the
magnitude of the undertaking. Beyond the significant differences in content (mythic vs. historic) and genre (operatic vs.
dramatic), however, there are notable distinctions between
the two phenomena. A typical *Ring Cycle* lasts about fifteen
hours, its final, longest evening (*Götterdämmerung*) running at
most five hours. The Glorious Moment was a twenty-four-
hour event (not including a twenty-minute intermission per

The specific language demarcating the weekend as a 'Glorious Moment' is itself worth considering. While merely giving these performances a title constructs their exceptionality, the word 'moment' highlights their ephemerality, a quality that no doubt contributes to their character as exceptional. It also constructs the content of the experience in specific ways. The title announces in advance of the event that what we're about to see will be glorious, predetermining the audience's reception of what is seen. Certainly we expected to see Shakespeare's rendering of a significant period of English history. What the title of the event draws our attention to, however, is the theatrical ·moment – the gloriousness of this moment in the history of Shakespearian performance and, more specifically, of the RSC. In other words, the title, 'The Glorious Moment', calls attention not to the plays themselves or the 'glorious moments' of English history they may represent but to the staging of them at this place, at this time, in this way, by this company. The history represented in the plays is thereby subtly supplanted by the historic theatrical event of their staging.

This shift in focus is consistent, I want to argue, with the productions' broader meditation on the relationship between historicity and theatricality. Like Dick the Butcher's claim, 'WE'RE 'ISTRY', the paradoxical title of 'The Glorious Moment' calls attention to the relationship between the ephemeral and the memorable, a relationship imminent to the domains of both history and theatre. And in the same way that 'The Glorious Moment' focuses attention on the productions themselves, 'WE'RE 'ISTRY' works as a self-referential commentary on both the remarkable and fleeting character of what's happening on stage. Both phrases tell us that the event happening now is important and will persist. And both phrases tell us that as soon as these actions and utterances are performed, they will disappear. Even the space in which the plays were performed iterates this paradox. Built on the car park of the Other Place, the Courtyard Theatre is a temporary structure slated to be torn down when the new RST auditorium is complete. Not only are the plays now gone but

the theatre itself will soon be dismantled and presumably reconverted back into a car park – or, rather, a palimpsest of the car park, the Other Place, the Courtyard and the layers of histories and 'moments' that have unfolded on that plot of ground.

The connective tissue between what disappears and what persists is the continuously reconstitutive power of memory – or, in the case of photographic and videographic recording, of memory technologies.[9] In *The Haunted Theatre*, Marvin Carlson describes theatre as 'a memory machine', a unique physical, imaginative and cultural space where human beings rehearse stories they already know, watch actors they've seen before, sit in spaces – maybe even seats – they've sat in on previous occasions and observe the work of a director who is preceded by reputation or is familiar from past playgoing experience.[10] How the play signifies in performance – what it means – is therefore contingent to a large degree on the information supplied by the audience's memory. Carlson writes,

the retelling of stories already told, the re-enactment of events already enacted, the re-experience of emotions already experienced, these are and have always been central concerns of the theatre in all times and places, but closely allied to these concerns are the particular production dynamics of theatre: the stories it chooses to tell, the bodies and other physical materials it utilizes to tell them,

---

play). Two of the four days (Friday, March 14, and Saturday, March 15) were trilogy days of nine hours of theatre per day, beginning at 10:30 a.m. and ending at around 11:00 p.m. Further, one of the distinguishing characteristics of Wagner's *Ring* is its status – for several of the opera companies that perform it – as a repeated event, one that occurs nearly every year (Bayreuth) or every few years (such as Seattle) in the same space. This defines many complete performances of *The Ring* in the context of repetition and of performance history, in contrast to the RSC's construction of the Glorious Moment's as a first and 'once in a lifetime' event.

9 I borrow the concept of memory technologies from Katherine Rowe's '"Remember Me": Technologies of Memory in Michael Almereyda's *Hamlet*', in *Shakespeare the Movie II*, ed. Richard Burt and Lynda E. Boose (New York, 2003), pp. 37–55.

10 Marvin Carlson, *The Haunted Stage: The Theatre as Memory Machine* (Ann Arbor, 2001), p. 142.

and the places in which they are told. Each of these production elements are also, to a striking degree, composed of material 'that we have seen before', and the memory of that recycled material as it moves through new and different productions contributes in no small measure to the richness and density of the operations of theatre in general as a site of memory, both personal and cultural.[11]

The phenomena Carlson describes – 'the operations of theatre . . . as a site of memory' – are particularly central to a theatrical experience like the Glorious Moment in which the director, actors and production team have the opportunity to carefully construct a set of experiences that then form a reliable source of recent, shared information from which subsequent plays can draw to make meaning. The layered meanings of the Glorious Moment – 'the stories it chooses to tell' – are constructed from the audience's memory of 'bodies and other physical materials' used in these productions and of 'the places in which [those stories] are told'.

What I want to explore in the remainder of this article is the Glorious Moment's use of bodies, materials, and physical space to iterate multiple historical modes, all of which are connected, like theatre itself, to the operations of memory. This unique event made meaning by creating its own internal history, a history that accrued gradually as we saw the same actors, costumes, visual tropes and stage space reused and transformed, play after play and day after day. Embedded in the Glorious Moment was a driving tension between the emphatic singularity of the event and the inherent necessity of its continuous recycling. The modes of history-telling it successively and simultaneously performed – traumatic, archetypal, parodic, didactic, providential, progressive – exploited this tension by dramatizing the complex, layered interplay between past and present, between what we had seen and what we were now seeing. By simultaneously performing and deconstructing the historical narratives by which we organize things seen, the Glorious Moment staged both the inadequacy and inescapability of those narratives.

The first play, *Richard II*, opened with a traditional Elizabethan dance but without music. The company moved in quiet, sombre unison, transforming the elegance of a pavane into an eerie index of what was to come. The uncanny centre of the play was made disquietingly clear when one of the dancers fell to the ground, bleeding and unremarked, while the others continued to move around him. As the dispute between Thomas Mowbray and Henry Bolingbroke unfolded in the play's first scene, the subject of their animosity – the murder of the Duke of Gloucester – became poignant and inexorable through the victim's awful presence on stage.

Like the ghost of Hamlet's father, killed before the action begins, Gloucester (Chuk Iwuji) haunted the play as a silent, persistent 'remember me' (*Hamlet*, 1.5.91). This moment both introduced and summarized Boyd's principal interpretive and dramaturgic approach to staging Shakespeare's histories, one that depended on ghosts, various modes of haunting, and acts of remembering. Boyd's strategic doubling of actors within and across plays – 34 actors played a total of 264 parts – meant that the dead were always reappearing in the guise of the living, rendering the living as sites of stratified meaning. Carlson describes this kind of theatrical layering as 'ghosting', the process by which an audience's experience in the theatre is informed by the lingering presence of information that precedes the present. This information may include familiarity with the story being dramatized; knowledge of an actor's previous roles or the details of his or her private life; associations, either individual or cultural, with costumes or sets used in the production; familiarity with the theatrical space as it has been employed on past occasions; or all of these.[12] Whatever the particular content of the audience's recollections, Carlson writes, 'The

---

[11] Carlson, *Haunted Stage*, pp. 3–4.

[12] Peter Holland's edited collection, *Shakespeare, Memory and Performance* (Cambridge, 2006), includes two essays that address and complicate these phenomena in relation to costume and props, respectively: Barbara Hodgdon, 'Shopping in the Archives: Material Memories', pp. 135–67; and Carol Chillington Rutter, '"Her first remembrance from the Moor": Actors and the Materials of Memory', pp. 168–206.

present experience is always ghosted by previous experiences and associations while these ghosts are simultaneously shifted and modified by the processes of recycling and recollection.'[13]

What Carlson's study does not address are the particularly concentrated effects of ghosting in a single theatrical production that uses actors in multiple roles and recycles the same space and props to represent disparate moments. To Carlson's 'ghosting', then, we might add the term 'doubling', which usefully connects the layering effects of the event to Elizabethan stage practice. While 'ghosting' speaks to the ways in which the ghost of the murdered Gloucester 'bleed[s] through'[14] the actor's subsequent roles in the octology, 'doubling' articulates the multiple meanings that the actor's body accrues – even within a single play – through the operations of the audience's memory.[15] 'Ghosting' addresses the spectral lingering of the past; 'doubling' addresses the multiplicity of the present.

In addition to ghosting or doubling, the plays made elaborate use of material residue to express the past's survival. One of the most remarkable scenes of the eight-play sequence was that of Richard's formal deposing in Act 4, scene 1 of *Richard II*. Richard (Jonathan Slinger) – formerly distinguished by an extravagant wardrobe of ruffled-and-ribboned finery in tones of pink and ivory, a wig of red curls and Elizabethan whiteface – was poignantly dismantled before our eyes, a collapse punctuated by his tearing off the wig to reveal a bald scalp infected with syphilitic sores. As he wiped off the makeup – 'Now mark me how I will undo myself' – his guise of snarling superiority gave way to naked anguish and vulnerability (*Richard II*, 4.1.193). A spotlit stream of fine white sand fell softly on his head and shoulders, pooling in the space around him to create an image of heavenly light and of impending burial in the hourglass of time. Heartbreaking and luminously beautiful, the moment at once marked Richard's transition into death and announced the complications created by this act of usurpation. The pile of sand now dusting the centre of the stage raised several deceptively pragmatic questions: what would happen to it? How would they clean it up without

an intermission? Wasn't it going to make a mess of everything?

Yes, it was – and that turned out to be exactly the point. It wasn't cleaned up; it didn't go away. It got tracked around the stage as the remainder of the play unfolded. And as the action moved towards the inexorable murder of Richard, the stage floor was gradually transformed into an abstract painting in blood and sand. The final scene at Bolingbroke's newly constituted court necessarily took place amidst the residue of Richard's overthrow and murder. The sand of Richard's deposing and the blood of his death became both the physical foundation on which Henry IV's throne rested and the inescapable past that would pollute his reign. When Henry (Clive Wood) ascended his staircase-throne in the final tableau of the play – with bloody sand crunching underfoot – he had to step over Richard's coffin, now resting centre-stage, and over bleeding bags of decapitated heads that lay at the base of the stairs. It was an ominous ending – and beginning.

The visual vocabularies of haunting and residue established so persuasively in this first play were then invoked, revisited and revised as the cycles unfolded. In this way, the Glorious Moment parlayed the concept of a cycle into a meditation on theatrical and historical *recycling*. *2 Henry IV* opened where *1 Henry IV* had ended, the nooses tied for Henry IV's new enemies swinging gently over the stage, linking precedent with imminent threat. The figure of Rumour then dragged a coffin onto the stage, opened it and released the ghost of Richard II, who lingered around the play. Turning to exit at the end of 3.1, Henry IV was confronted with the source of his insomnia in the form of

---

[13] Carlson, *Haunted Stage*, p. 2.

[14] Carlson, *Haunted Stage*, p. 133.

[15] Carol Chillington Rutter suggests that for audience members who had seen earlier iterations of Boyd's first tetralogy in which Iwuji played Henry VI, Iwuji-as-Gloucester's-ghost was himself complexly ghosted. Lying dead on the stage at the opening of *Richard II*, he was 'in roughly the same position, dead, as Henry VI, murdered by the actor now playing Richard II': 'Shakespeare Performances in England, 2008', *Shakespeare Survey* 62 (Cambridge, 2009), 349–85; p 351.

Richard's ghost, who descended down the throne-stairs to briefly obstruct Henry's exit from the stage. The two stood facing each other, frozen in a surreal moment of tension, as sand was again released momentarily from above, this time on the head of Henry. Henry's subsequent deathbed confession of having stolen his crown from Richard resonated for an audience made to recognize – through the recycling of sand – that for all his killings and rebellion he was becoming a mirror image of Richard, 'a mockery king of snow' (*Richard II*, 4.1.250).

These scenes illustrate another way that the plays were haunted, not merely by recycled bodies, images and space but by actual ghosts. The only ghosts who appear in Shakespeare's eight play-texts are the victims of Richard III, who visit Richard and Richmond in their prophetic dreams. But Boyd's productions included countless extra-textual walking dead, such as Cade's rebels and the ghost of Richard II. This dramatic interpolation expands the notion of 'ghosting' not only to describe theatrical productions that are 'haunted' by what came before but to function as the visual representation of trauma, not coincidentally described by Cathy Caruth as a past that 'returns to *haunt* the survivor later on' (italics mine).[16] Unlike the insomniac Macbeth, who knows that he 'hath murder'd sleep' and actually sees the ghost of Banquo (*Macbeth*, 2.2.40), Henry IV does not know what troubles him. Rather, his soliloquy on sleep is a series of questions: 'O sleep, O gentle sleep, / Nature's soft nurse, how have I frighted thee[?]' (*2 Henry IV*, 3.1.5–6). With no answers to explain his insomnia, he concludes – famously but vaguely – 'Uneasy lies the head that wears a crown' (*2 Henry IV*, 3.1.31).

The source of uneasiness that Henry cannot articulate was supplied visually in this production in the form of Richard II's ghost. The audience saw Richard, but we had no evidence that Henry did; their moment of face-to-face confrontation was dreamy and surreal. When the sand began to fall on Henry's head – just as it had in the fateful scene of Richard's deposing – we were watching what Caruth describes as 'the experience of trauma [which] repeats itself, exactly and unremit-

tingly, through the unknowing acts of the survivor and against his very will'.[17] As Henry is on his own deathbed, he at last locates the source of his uneasiness in the usurpation – 'God knows, my son, / By what bypaths and indirect crook'd ways / I met this crown; and I myself know well / How troublesome it sat upon my head' – and devises a plan by which Hal can escape the shared burden of their past by 'busy[ing] giddy minds / With foreign quarrels' (*2 Henry IV*, 4.3.312–15, 342–3). But as Heather Hirschfeld reminds us in her discussion of *Hamlet*, 'it is the sinful bequest – the chronologically older experience – rather than the salvific offering of the later one that ends up holding hermeneutic and psychic priority'.[18] The wars that occupy the next three plays inevitably function as what she calls 'a means of revisiting a traumatic scene, not one for resolving it'.[19] In Boyd's productions, the haunting of history by the ghosts of wronged dead thus operated as a device for constructing that history as traumatic – as what Caruth describes as the repetitious, 'unwitting re-enactment of an event that one cannot simply leave behind'.[20]

The inability to leave the past behind – the paradox of both remembering and not remembering – was a central preoccupation of the Glorious Moment. The realization of this traumatic history depended simultaneously on the audience's memory – our recognition that '*we are seeing what we saw before*'[21] – and the characters' failure to recognize. *Henry V* introduced its own vocabulary of haunting and residue when, as in the preceding plays, the stage was gradually polluted with evocative remains and what initially appeared as ephemeral

---

[16] Cathy Caruth, *Unclaimed Experience: Trauma, Narrative, and History* (Baltimore, 1996), p. 4.

[17] Caruth, *Unclaimed Experience*, p. 2.

[18] Heather Hirschfeld, 'Hamlet's "first corse": Repetition, Trauma, and the Displacement of Redemptive Typology', *Shakespeare Quarterly*, 54.4 (2004), 424–48; p. 434.

[19] Hirschfeld, 'Hamlet's "first corse"', p. 438.

[20] Caruth, *Unclaimed Experience*, p. 2.

[21] Carlson, *Haunted Stage*, p. 1: '[O]ne of the universals of performance, both East and West, is its ghostliness, its sense of return, the uncanny but inescapable impression imposed upon its spectators that "*we are seeing what we saw before*".'

again persisted. The Dauphin's 'present' in Act 1 to the young Henry V (Geoffrey Streatfeild) was suspended overhead in the form of a French-blue trunk – coffin-sized and -shaped – that dropped some hundred tennis balls onto the stage when struck by Henry's sword. When the Chorus figure came on at the change of scene, he used an enormous push broom to sweep many of the tennis balls off-stage. But the upstage area remained littered with tennis balls until they were cleared away at intermission, the remaining balls working in tacit dialogue with Henry's preparations for war and early victories in France. The persistent 'Paris balls' articulated the relationship between bloody war and Henry's need to convert a problematic adolescence into heroic kingship. Further, they made visual Henry's strategic translation of the Dauphin's mock into an excuse for war, fulfilling the promise that 'this mock of his / Hath turn'd his balls to gun-stones' (*Henry V*, 1.2.281–2).

The broom and tennis ball props thus functioned in another of the cycle's constructions of history. Drawing on the repository of cultural memory for the symbolic action of sweeping something away, the moment with the brooms acted as a visual metaphor for Hal's already much metaphorized 'reformation in a flood / With such a heady currance, scouring faults', or the process of radical conversion by which he is 'perfected' (*Henry V*, 1.1.34–5, 69). The resistance of the tennis balls to sweeping suggested the intrusion of a traumatic rendering of history – the stubborn, unperceived persistence of the past – on the more transformative, redemptive model offered by the brooms. In the final scenes, this privileging of a traumatic over a redemptive view of the events of the play was fully realized. As the company sang the *Te Deum* on the field of Agincourt, they gradually covered the central playing space with more – and more – pine coffins. They then brought out platforms to place on top to form a new stage floor that rested on the bodies of the dead, literalizing the dark subtext of conquest and colonization that underlies the political and romantic negotiations of Act 5. It was upon this foundation that Henry wooed and won his Kate and that the future of England

would be built. This would be his son's traumatic inheritance, one not unlike his own.

In its invocation of culturally resonant tropes, the Glorious Moment offered a meditation on our narratives of history as archetypal – as a set of recurrent actions (like redemptive transformation) that are summarized in symbolic acts (like sweeping). The casting of Jonathan Slinger as both Richard II and Richard III demonstrated the cycle's consistent interest in an archetypal visual vocabulary by constructing a complex dialogue between the first play's victim and the final play's villain. The introspective poetry of Richard II's final soliloquy gathered particular pathos in Slinger's delivery, its tone of delicate fragility so unlike the haughty sneer that marked his earlier scenes in the play. His white nightshirt ragged with wear, his pink nail polish bloodied from clawing at stones, Richard was humanized in his suffering and solitude. This Richard – the Richard who commanded our pity – persisted through *2 Henry IV* as a rarefied ghost in angelic white, all the more sympathetic for the contrast he provided to the guilt-ridden, power-hungry, black-clad Henry. As the violence escalated, claiming more and more victims with each successive play, Henry's usurpation took on the character of a primal scene. For all its waste and folly, the kingdom of Richard II ironically began to look like John of Gaunt's 'other Eden', and the ghost of Gloucester, that 'vial full of Edward's sacred blood . . . cracked' before our plays began, receded from memory (*Richard II*, 2.1.42, 1.2.17–19).

Boyd didn't allow this amnesia to persist. Rather, the productions complicated any impulse towards martyr-making by casting Slinger as the archvillain Richard III and doubling a number of significant tropes from the earlier play. Richard II's dramatic removal of his wig during the scene of his defrocking was the first move towards his humanization. The young Richard of Gloucester also wore a red wig, this one cut in a youthful, if vaguely sinister, pageboy. But his removal of it as he lividly recounted his physical defects – his 'disproportion . . . in every part' – signalled something radically different (*3 Henry VI*, 3.2.160). In contrast to the vulnerability conveyed by Richard II's exposed scalp, Richard III's naked head signalled naked rage – an id free of its superego, Hyde without the encumbrance of that pesky, repressive Jekyll. The wounded scalp beneath also signified differently. Whereas Richard II's sores made him pathetic and frail, the blood-coloured birthmark revealed on Richard III's scalp was the physical marker of internal 'disproportion' – of still bloodier thoughts. What was born into the world in this moment of revelation wasn't a chastised, 'gentle Richard' but the 'hell-hound that doth hunt us all to death' (*Richard II*, 5.2.28; *Richard III*, 4.4.48).

Inverting the wig-removal trope complicated the symbolics of ornamentation and nakedness that were set up in the earlier play. In this production, Richard II's sartorial extravagance was a principal marker of his negligence as a leader, in particular his squandering of England's resources after his own fancy. While working with a similar vocabulary of signifiers, Boyd shifted the semiotic code for Richard III, for whom bodily ornament functioned as an oppressive constraint. In the scene of Richard III's dream in Act 5, the character appeared on stage in nothing but a t-shirt and briefs, celebrating a fantasized freedom from physical blight. In contrast to the pathos generated by Richard II's 'undeck[ing]' (*Richard II*, 4.1.240), this moment of Richard III's nakedness provoked disgust, its rawness situating us as uncomfortable voyeurs to deep moral deformity. The more naked he was, the more grotesque he appeared, even when momentarily free of his physical defects. He could be made reasonably presentable by 'fashions' and a wig, but without them he was monstrous (*Richard III*, 1.2.244).

The cycle's double symbolism of removing a wig expressed the paradoxical relationship between appearance and human identity – the way our outer trappings function to shelter the frail, naked thing that lies beneath from the ruthless eyes of the world and, conversely, to protect the frail, naked eyes of the world from the ruthless thing that lies beneath. By doubling the Richards and inverting the visual vocabularies of bodily concealment and disclosure, these productions bookended the octology with

a meditation on the age-old paradox of physical masking – the paradox of those legendary fig leaves. In this way, the Glorious Moment represented history as a set of timeless conflicts, inherited, narrativized and dramatized by successive generations. Not incidentally, this particular conflict is one of Shakespeare's central preoccupations. It is difficult to articulate the effect of Richard II's unmaking without reference to Lear's tragic 'unbutton[ing]' or to describe the rise and fall of Slinger's Richard III without allusion to Macbeth, the failed equivocator who grows progressively unable to 'look like the innocent flower, / But be the serpent under't' (*Lear* F, 3.4.103; *Macbeth*, 1.5.64–5). The vision of history articulated in these multiple doublings – of actor, prop and action – was both archetypal and Shakespearian.

The doubling of the Dauphin with Jack Cade, both played by John Mackay, relied on the operations of memory and ghosting to perform quite a different historical mode: the parodic. In our first introduction to the Dauphin, he and his courtiers were perched on swings suspended over the stage. Boyd used the trapeze to situate the French court of *Henry V* on an alternative plane, creating an ephemeral, insubstantial world floating above the ground. Mackay's Dauphin was the flightiest of the flighty, a lithe and limber, pink-cheeked effete with perfect blonde ringlets who never merely sat nor stood but sashayed from one pretentious pose to another. Jack Cade also descended from the flies on a trapeze, holding court among his followers while hovering mid-air. Like the Dauphin, he was explicitly theatrical – vigorously invested in playing what he imagined to be the persona of royalty while simultaneously exposing the superficiality and artificiality of the role. Boyd's doubling of the Dauphin and Cade accentuated their symmetry, drawing, for an audience privileged with the remembered history of the trapeze and the actor's body, a parodic equation between the ludicrous pretences of Cade and the impotent French court – an equation further heightened by Cade's grotesque zombie comrades. This parody both depended on and rewarded the audience's superior knowledge: through ghosting and doubling, we recognized the Dauphin and Cade as the same. History had taught us, and parody both performed and repaid our memory of its lessons.

Carlson's discussion of the relationship between parody and ghosting emphasizes the centrality of the audience's shared knowledge and the community such knowledge creates. He writes, 'In order to enjoy a theatrical parody the audience must be essentially composed of a community that shares a common theatrical history of attending the work being parodied.'[22] This 'common theatrical history' was particularly assured and immediate in an event like the Glorious Moment, which parodied its own internal constructions. When combined with the parodic elements embedded in *2 Henry VI*, the doubling of Mackay brought several characters from the octology into meaningful conversation with one another. The parallels between authentic aristocratic power and the pretensions of an upstart beggar are central to the argument of *2 Henry VI*, which insistently interrogates and dismantles the distinction. Ghosting Cade with the Dauphin extended this political commentary beyond the limits of this single play to illustrate the elements of fantasy and theatricality necessary to performances of legitimate authority. The make-up and exaggerated effeminacy of Cade and the Dauphin also linked them to Slinger's Richard II, another figure in Boyd's cycle who was more attracted to the 'pomp and majesty' of kingship than to the substance of government (*Richard II*, 4.1.201). And not far from these explicit examinations of kingship's inherent theatricality lies Shakespeare's more nuanced meditations on their interdependence. Walking cloaked through his camp, unrecognized by his troops because he comes 'not like [him]self' and looks 'as a common man', Harry le Roi learns what Jack Cade knows: that little more than 'thrice-gorgeous ceremony' marks the difference between king and commoner (*Henry V*, 4.8.51–2; 4.1.263). The doubling of Cade and the Dauphin thus constellated a number of relationships that unfolded diachronically across the event, demonstrating the symmetry between the 'dread sovereign' and the bricklayer's son and illustrating

the role of theatre in constructing an illusion of difference (*Henry V*, 1.2.97). At the centre of that constellation was the audience, whose constitutive mental labour in the 'working-house of thought' peopled the stage (*Henry V*, 5.0.23).

The casting of Katy Stephens as Joan la Pucelle and Queen Margaret created an ongoing dialogue between the two characters that challenged both archetypal and didactic constructions of historical meaning. In place of a stable, legible narrative of the past, this doubling created an emotional and epistemological paradox as we were repeatedly called upon to respond in ways that were radically at odds with the internal history the cycle itself had generated. Boyd's script reorganized Act 5 of *1 Henry VI* so that Margaret did not appear until after Joan's death. Margaret stepped forth from the discovery space almost immediately after Joan was swallowed into the burning hell mouth of one of the stage's trapdoors. Unlike the cycle's other significant doublings, this one was not separated by multiple plays nor even multiple scenes. The effect of Stephens's almost instantaneous transformation from Joan to Margaret was to suggest that Joan had been reincarnated as Margaret – that they were the same woman. The 'ugly witch', 'fell banning hag, [and] enchantress' may have been burned to death, but in her instant resurrection as the 'She-wolf of France', Joan was always ghosting Margaret (*1 Henry VI*, 5.4.4, 13; *3 Henry VI*, 1.4.112).

This ghosting – reinforced by visual echoes between Margaret and Joan's fiends – methodically constructed a symmetry between Joan and Margaret and between the feminine and the demonic, a symmetry that encouraged the audience to read Margaret typologically and unsympathetically. The fact that these expectations were generally fulfilled by Shakespeare's, Boyd's and Stephens's representations of Margaret ratified our sense that we knew who this figure was. But this knowledge left us unprepared for the devastating moments of pathos to come. In the scene of farewell between Margaret and Suffolk in *2 Henry VI*, we were confronted with

---

[22] Carlson, *Haunted Stage*, p. 39.

one of the few examples of true romantic attachment in the eight-play cycle, one whose depth, articulated with beauty and conviction, forced us to reconsider the assumption that the relationship was merely physical or political. Her banished lover gently touching her cheek, Stephens's Margaret wept as a widow in mourning whose vow of love is 'printed' and 'seal[ed]' with a sacramental kiss (*2 Henry VI*, 3.2.347–8). It was an expression of true marriage unmatched by anything we had observed between Margaret and Henry. For those audience members who knew the play, her self-sacrificial promise to Suffolk, 'I will repeal thee, or, be well assured, / Adventure to be banishèd myself; / And banishèd I am, if but from thee', was all the more tragic for the fact that she would never see him alive again (*2 Henry VI*, 3.2.353–5). The scene produced a collision of contradictory knowledge and emotion: Margaret was inextricably bound up with the figure of Joan, but here she was decidedly sympathetic, especially in light of what we knew of the future. The most powerful certainty the scene produced was the certainty of not knowing – not knowing who this character was, what was authentic or what was mere manipulation.

While the violent, mocking role she takes in York's murder returned us to the Margaret we knew how to read, our expectations were again confounded in the scene in *Richard III* in which old Queen Margaret, supplanted and ruined, curses the faction of York. In the most compelling scene of Katy Stephens's steadily magnificent performance, the disenfranchised crone, like a folktale hag who's skulked out of the woods to terrorize polite society, unfolded her filthy pack to disclose the bones of her murdered son. As she cursed first King Edward, then Queen Elizabeth, Dorset and Rivers, Lord Hastings and finally Richard, she methodically laid out the bones of her son in the shape of a human body, kissing and weeping over them as she howled. Amidst the bickering and backstabbing Yorkists, Margaret again emerged as the only character with true familial attachment in a scene that elicited deep sympathy. In this moment of emotional resonance, however, Margaret was unmistakably ghosted by Joan, who similarly knelt over a pile of bones while mumbling her demonic incantation. The effect was to destabilize our readings of both characters and both moments as well as to challenge the very categories of villain and victim by which so many of our historical narratives are organized. The advantages of categorical, retrospective construction were shattered by our own sympathy, and we were no closer to understanding Margaret than we were when the plays began. History did not teach us how to read this scene, nor did the scene teach us how to read history.

As the Glorious Moment moved towards its climax in *Richard III*, it unfolded a broad meditation on the historical mode with which the final play, the tetralogy and the octology concluded: history as a document of God's divine providence.[23] The interrogation of providential history was conducted principally through the recycling of the theatre space itself. With no other significant scenery, the plays relied on the central copper cylinder – sparse, industrial, monolithic – for a wide range of practical and symbolic functions.[24] As the symbolics of the cylinder accrued over the eight plays, the politics of verticality became increasingly complex. The structure worked beautifully, for example, to convey the hierarchical implications of Richard II's 'Down, down I come', as he moved from the second level to meet Bolingbroke on the stage floor (*Richard II*, 3.3.177). When it functioned later as the Tower of London, as a vantage point for the many ghosts who haunted the plays and as a lookout for the ominous gatekeeper to the world of the dead, the cylinder's seeming simplicity betrayed the complex and contradictory character of ascent.

The instability of the cylinder signifier was only one aspect of the shifting symbolics of playing space that the cycle invoked to develop and destabilize

---

23 That is, when the eight plays are seen in this order. Rogers compares the experiences of seeing Boyd's two tetralogies in compositional versus episodic order, especially as regards ghosting, doubling and the development of characterological through-lines ('Staging History', pp. 61–4).

24 For a full description of the histories' set, see Rutter, 'Performances 2008', pp. 350–61.

meaning – in particular, to interrogate the possibility of divine justice or organization. *1 Henry IV* made extensive use of the space beneath the stage floor, where a number of elaborately decorated traps were used to suggest Hal's Eastcheap tavern world. Here the up-down symbolism held as Hal's lowbrow excursions originated from a space that was physically beneath the more elevated world of the court. In *Henry V*, the subterranean maintained its association with Hal. In contrast to the garish French, who occupied the plane above the stage, the dingy English conducted their assault on France from the underground up, erecting ladders through the open traps to climb their way to Harfleur. Ironically, Hal had left the Eastcheap underground to tunnel through foreign land; when he finally transcended the terrestrial, he held court atop the coffins of the dead. In the opening scene of *1 Henry VI*, he descended the throne-stairs back to the subterranean world, this time into a foggy, blue-lit grave.

When the trapdoors opened again at the end of *1 Henry VI* to consume the burning Joan la Pucelle, the space beneath the stage began to take on a different character – no longer the quiet grave of the heroic Henry V but an underworld of punishment and pain. This had important implications for the productions' representation of divine justice, suggesting that Henry was in hell – with Joan, no less, the demonic agent of France. The proximity – visual, spatial and symbolic – of Joan's smoky pit to Henry's foggy tomb functioned to interrogate both Henry's heroics and the concept of an afterlife that neatly, justly organizes good from evil. When the traps opened up again early in *2 Henry VI* to reveal the valiant Talbots, arguably the moral centre of Boyd's cycle, the space had reverted fully to its traditional theatrical function as a hell mouth.[25] The Talbots' apparent relegation to hell raised the same troubling implications that had been introduced by the Henry-Joan mirroring.

Further complicating matters were the use of the above-stage space and the materials that drifted through that space. While most of the dead in the first tetralogy were escorted off-stage by the extra-textual figure of the Keeper, Cardinal Beaufort's body ascended from the stage into what would conventionally signify the heavens. Beaufort's ascension was incoherent with the figurative meanings of both the motion and the implied destination, meanings that the audience provided through powerful cultural associations with ascent and descent and with subterranean and supernal space. This information ghosted our experience of moments like Beaufort's ascent to contradict the notion of a just eternity. Additionally, the productions made extensive use of red and white feathers, dropped from above at varying moments throughout the cycle to punctuate a conflicting range of states and events: battle, murder, martyrdom, prophecy, coronation, justice, innocence, guilt. The message dropped from the heavens was ultimately an inscrutable series of contradictions, 'like ambiguously compassionate or mocking commentaries from a distant and otherwise aloof God'.[26] Boyd's productions frustrated any attempt to refer the actions of the cycle to a providential design that organizes human events or to a just dispensation of eternal punishment and reward. Those structures were insistently challenged by the cycle's spatial and material symbolism, leaving human ambition and its promise of violence as the plays' only transcendent forces.

By setting *Richard III* as the only one of the eight plays in explicitly modern time, designer Tom Piper undermined any possibility that the present would be substantively different from this brutal past. Analogizing the nightmare world of *Richard III* and our own, Boyd's cycle confounded the fantasy of evolution that informs progressive constructions of history. The argument made through the translation of *Richard III* from the fifteenth century to the twenty-first was one that both took us by

---

[25] For an extended discussion of Boyd's treatment of the Talbots and the doubling of actors Keith Bartlett and Lex Shrapnel in multiple father–son pairs across the octology, see Rogers, 'Staging History', pp. 73–4.

[26] Michael Dobson, 'Shakespeare Performances in England, 2001', *Shakespeare Survey 55* (Cambridge, 2001), 285–321: p. 287. Dobson's remark is made in reference to the use of feathers in Boyd's first staging of the *Henry VI* plays, but the trope was carried over to the later Histories productions.

surprise and for which we had been carefully prepared. Although the costumes for the first seven plays were neither consistently medieval nor Elizabethan, they were suggestive enough of Ye Olde Times that *Richard III* caught us off guard. Moreover, the use of swords through the first seven plays decidedly, if non-specifically, grounded them in pre-modern time and space. However, the constant presence of ghosts – characters representing the walking dead as well as actors and dramatic elements layered with previous meaning – created a temporal flexibility that destabilized place and time to create an audience receptive to the suggestion that, all along, these plays had been showing us ourselves.

The updating of *Richard III* summarizes what was perhaps the most persuasive historical mode dramatized by the Glorious Moment. By drawing an analogy between the world of *Richard III* and our own, these productions argued chillingly that the narrative of history is not one of progress but of repetition. Their world is our world; their crimes are our crimes. The Glorious Moment resonated powerfully beyond the tumultuous period of the Wars of the Roses, exposing the ways that our own conflicts and tenuous amities are haunted by atrocity, by murderous ambition and by the enduring imperatives of a violent past. We too walk among the dead, carrying on their legacies, resisting in vain their dictates, labouring by turns to appease and ignore their ghosts. In this way, a theatrical event constructed out of recycled material concluded by making an argument about that very recycling. The claim for the inescapably repetitive nature of history, especially in this final move to telescope pre- and post-modernity, represented one of the most essential ways in which the Glorious Moment did metatheatrical and metahistorical work. Our participation in the event thus constituted multiple forms of *seeing what we saw before*. Essential to these layered acts of spectatorship and participation was individual and collective memory, where *before* resides to be performed, recognized and forgotten again.

One of the principal achievements of the Glorious Moment was its intelligent framing of these multiple historical modes, simultaneously with their equally intelligent deconstruction. The essential content of the event, however, did not reside merely in these critically sophisticated, metatheatrical moves. There was yet something else staged by the Glorious Moment that articulated its own singular experiential properties. The extraordinary scene of old Queen Margaret's cursing the royal family offers a concise example. In *Richard III*, the Marquis of Dorset was played by the same actor (Wela Frasier) who played the young Prince Edward in the Second and Third Parts of *Henry VI*. This produced a peculiar kind of doubling as the figure of Prince Edward resided at once in two on-stage bodies, the living Dorset and the decaying, skeletal corpse. Not only did this render Margaret's cursing of Dorset ironic but the production used this glitch in the time-space continuum to startling effect. When Margaret addressed Dorset, she was momentarily arrested by silent, subtle recognition of her son, a look of pained longing crossing her face. She then seemed to shake off the spectral image and resume the business of rage. But the emotive force of that moment of recognition – one that the audience shared as we recognized with Margaret – transcended history. It disrupted the meaning of the lines and the logic of the scene, creating an alternative signifying plane that reminded us that what appeared to be happening was the mere shadow of a complex, layered and inarticulable past. The moment's phenomenological content resided outside the temporal altogether, insisting that there was *something happening* that neither the playtext nor the production script could represent. That ineffable something was theatre, another historical mode that asserted itself across the experience of the Glorious Moment with its own vocabulary for making meaning of the past.

The surplus content of moments like this – their phenomenological excess – interacted uncomfortably with the RSC's reductive packaging of the event. No written or oral account of the productions can accommodate the force of those four days in Stratford. No DVD series of the plays, even one supplemented with extensive commentary from

13. The 'Glorious Moment' curtain call: a photo taken from the stage by ensemble member Roger Watkins.

the audience and production team, will approximate the individual and communal experience that unfolded at that time, in that place. In short, no memorial form can reproduce the content of Margaret's silent recognition. And yet the event, deeply committed to staging the inadequacy of historical constructs, was defined in advance by a name that sought – indeed, still seeks – to rigidly fix the terms of its signification and reception. Even Cade's zombies enjoyed existential ambiguity; but the title, 'The Glorious Moment', names a desire to embalm – to counteract ambiguity and ephemerality by anxiously ensuring that *moment* doesn't slip into *momentary* but instead becomes *momentous*. The experiential expansiveness of the event was contracted by a framework that declared it as an already-past object of nostalgic and conservative longing.

This construction of itself became the only mode of history-telling about which the Glorious Moment was uncritical. By foreclosing interrogation of its own claims as a historic event, the Glorious Moment scripted audience response into uniform, homogeneous approval. In the final scenes of the drama, the entire company and Michael Boyd took the stage for an extended curtain call and a standing ovation that lasted several minutes. The house lights came up, and Boyd stepped forward to acknowledge those involved in the project, including us. As if by prior unspoken understanding, hundreds of audience members threw thousands of flowers onto the stage. It was, after all, a glorious moment. But in order to participate in that moment – to be ready with the requisite carnations – one must have purchased flowers in advance of the final play. One must have agreed with the RSC that the moment would be glorious even before it had entirely unfolded.

Time and again we had watched the playing space polluted with feathers, rose petals, blood and gore. Like Richard II's sand, these remains functioned symbolically as the lasting evidence of violence. Now, to a theatrical experience preoccupied with recurrence and a playing space crowded with ghosts and remains, we had added a residue of our own: flowers in red and white, tossed from above to be crushed beneath an actor's shoes, yet another mess for the stage crew to sweep away. Yes, history had repeated once again, but this repetition was even more eerie than *Richard III's* – meticulously scripted and yet unbounded by the constructs of theatrical fiction. Some of the company threw flowers back to the audience appreciatively, and many held cameras and video recorders aimed not at each other but at us (Illustration 13). While we imagined that we'd come to watch the dramatizing of history, in the end we ourselves became the event – the spectacular object recorded by the technologies of memory to be reseen, relived, remembered, misremembered. We had joined the ranks of Cade's Rebellion, leaving our own mark on Shakespeare's great work and standing alongside bloody Dick the Butcher to unwittingly declare, 'WE'RE 'ISTRY'.

SHAKESPEARE AS WAR MEMORIAL: REMEMBRANCE AND COMMEMORATION IN THE GREAT WAR

CLARA CALVO

War memorials have long been regarded as the most visible form of Great War commemoration practices.[1] Whether through public memorial or private grave, the First World War has been fixed in collective memory for its numerous dead. The word 'remembrance' is inextricably associated, at least in the collective imagination of many European and Commonwealth countries and the US, with the poppy and 11 November. Commemorating the First World War is often equated with remembering the dead. As public sites of mourning, Sir Edward Lutyens's Monument to the Missing of the Somme at Thiepval and his Cenotaph in Whitehall contrast with the private space of the soldier's regular slab, on which very little room is left for a personalized inscription.[2] The private space of commemoration is reduced to a line or two – while the public rite of enforcing the same gravestone for all soldiers enacts a communal practice of remembrance.[3] War memorials, as Jay Winter has argued, can be read as sites of both memory and mourning, places where collective grief and individualized remembrance are materially located.[4] Whether public, as the Somme memorial at Thiepval, or private, as soldiers' graves, war memorials and war cemeteries together give form to a material culture of Great War commemoration which is literally linked to a fixed, permanent, singular location.

It has not been sufficiently stressed that the materiality of Great War commemoration and its remembrance rites stretches beyond sculpture, architecture, gardens of remembrance and the iconological programmes of communal or private

funereal art and that war memorials for the dead of the Great War began to appear in the form

Research for this article has been financed by MICINN Research Project EDU2008–00453. I am also grateful to the library staff at the Imperial War Museum and the Shakespeare Centre Library and Archive (especially Helen Hargest and Mairi MacDonald) for their help.

[1] The seminal study on First World War memorials is Jay Winter, *Sites of Memory, Sites of Mourning: The Great War in European Cultural History* (Cambridge, 1995). For a very useful survey of the interest aroused by war memorials in both Fine Art and History Studies and its continuing growth in the last thirty years, see Catherine Moriarty, 'The Material Culture of Great War Remembrance', *Journal of Contemporary History*, 34 (1999), 653–62, and John Stephens, 'Memory, Commemoration and the Meaning of a Suburban War Memorial', *Journal of Material Culture*, 12 (2007), 241–61. See also John R. Gillis, ed., *Commemorations: The Politics of National Identity* (Princeton, NJ, 1994); William Kidd and Brian Murdoch, eds., *Memory and Memorials: The Commemorative Century* (London, 2004); William Logan and Keir Reeves, eds., *Places of Pain and Shame: Dealing with 'Difficult Heritage'* (London, 2009); Daniel J. Walkowitz and Lisa Maya Knauer, eds., *Memory and the Impact of Political Transformation in Public Space* (Durham and London, 2004); and Joachim Wolschke-Bulmahn, *Places of Commemoration: Search for Identity and Landscape Design* (Washington, DC, 2001).

[2] Tim Skelton and Gerald Gliddon, *Lutyens and War Memorials* (London, 2008) includes useful images of the Somme memorial at Thiepval (p. 137), the Whitehall Cenotaph (p. 44), the Cross of Sacrifice in its central position at Villers-Bretonneux (p. 155) and the standard headstone for Imperial soldiers (p. 110).

[3] The Imperial War Graves Commission (today the Commonweath War Graves Commission) regulated that all officers and soldiers should have the same gravestone to prevent display of differences in wealth or religion in war cemeteries. This official stone allowed some space for the expression of private grief and personal remembrance and it could include a

of printed matter long before the end of the war itself.[5] Unlike architecture, sculpture or gardens, books are movable objects, not anchored to a fixed, permanent 'site' or unique *locus*. In spite of this, books, like crosses, needles and cenotaphs, can become sites of grief and mourning, portable war memorials that mix memory and commemoration into one single material practice, namely the commemorative volume, whose function is primarily but not exclusively to keep collective remembrance alive. In 1916, the celebrations for the 300th anniversary of Shakespeare's death provided ample opportunity for transforming books into war memorials and, as I hope to show, Shakespeare the patriot, Shakespeare the soldier, who did his bit for the war effort by helping to collect funds for the Red Cross and the soldiers' huts run by the YMCA, also fuelled the material culture of First World War acts of remembrance. Any attempt at tracing the 'cultural biography' of Shakespeare's works cannot neglect the material practices of commemoration and remembrance triggered by the 1916 Tercentenary and the First World War.[6]

I. SHAKESPEARE AND THE MATERIAL CULTURE OF GREAT WAR COMMEMORATION

During the Tercentenary year, commemoration of Shakespeare's life and works was often linked to the war effort. Charity and commemoration became inextricable in matinées which were meant both to commemorate the playwright and collect funds for the Red Cross, the YMCA or the YWCA.[7] The celebrations also gave occasion to several volumes of Shakespearian interest. The official commemorative volume, *A Book of Homage to Shakespeare*, edited by Israel Gollancz, the Honorary Secretary of the Shakespeare Tercentenary Committee, is presented in its preface as a replacement memorial, 'a worthy Record of the widespread reverence for Shakespeare as shared with the English-speaking world by our Allies and Neutral States'.[8] For Gollancz, this book would have to do in lieu of a true, real memorial, since the war put an end to plans for building the truly 'fitting memorial' for Shakespeare, the projected National Shakespeare Memorial Theatre in London, which Shaw, Barrie, Jones, Pinero and many other playwrights had actively campaigned for.[9] The proceedings from the sale of the book, Gollancz advanced as he closed the preface, would be devoted to an annual volume of

---

chosen religious symbol such as a cross. Relatives had to accept that the bodies of soldiers, even after death, belonged to the Army and personal grief could not be displayed through an individual's personalized monument. Any attempt to individualize the dead had to be confined within the standard rectangular slab with rounded top that fills war cemeteries with regular, identical rows of gravestones. See, for instance, Hooge Crater Cemetery in Skelton and Gliddon, *Lutyens*, p. 109.

[4] Winter, *Sites of Memory*; Jay Winter, *Remembering War: The Great War Between Memory and History in the Twentieth Century* (New Haven and London, 2006).

[5] Samuel Hynes, in his seminal study on the First World War and English culture, *A War Imagined: The First World War and English Culture* (London, 1992, first published 1990), is aware of the existence of a trend of 'monument-making in the publishing world' (p. 277) but is slightly dismissive about its importance or significance. He mostly examines 'monumental' works of history, memoirs by politicians and army leaders but ignores the kind of war memorials discussed here. In 'Personal Narratives and Commemoration' (in *War and Remembrance in the Twentieth Century*, ed. Jay Winter and Emmanuel Sivan (Cambridge, 1999), pp. 205–20), he doubts if diaries, journals and letters are also war memorials and concludes that they contribute to the construction of myth rather than history.

[6] For the notion of the 'cultural biography' of objects, see Igor Kopytoff, 'The Cultural Biography of Things: Commoditization as Process', in *The Social Life of Things: Commodities in Cultural Perspective*, ed. Arjun Appadurai (Cambridge, 1986), pp. 64–91.

[7] Sir James Barrie was actively involved in two of these charity galas which capitalized on the Tercentenary celebrations. On 14 April 1916, a skit by Barrie, *Shakespeare's Legacy*, was performed at Drury Lane Theatre as part of a 'war matinée' organized by Olga Nethersole for the YWCA. The proceedings were to provide hostels, canteens and restrooms for 'girl shell makers' (*The Daily Mirror*, 14 April 1916, p. 6). A month earlier, on 7 March, Barrie had also contributed to a special matinée in aid of the YMCA held at the Coliseum, in which his *Macbeth* film parody, *The Real Thing at Last*, was premiered.

[8] Israel Gollancz, ed., *A Book of Homage to Shakespeare* (London, 1916), p. viii.

[9] See Geoffrey Whitworth, *The Making of a National Theatre* (London, 1951).

Shakespeare studies, thus perpetuating the culture of commemoration and remembrance triggered by the Tercentenary.

The Tercentenary also became an occasion for books of Shakespearian interest that use their preface to remember those at war. Charlotte Carmichael Stopes felt the urge to produce a book that would appear on what she herself calls 'the commemoration year' and, failing to produce the book, she collected several papers, 'new and old,' into a volume entitled *Shakespeare's Industry*.[10] In the Preface, Stopes spares a thought for remembrance, turning her commemorative volume into a site of memory in which First World War soldiers are remembered:

> if this prove my last effort in the *field*, I do it full of the desire to help to keep Shakespeare's *flag flying* during the commemoration year, while so many of my fellow-students are torn away from their studies, to defend 'This blessed spot, this earth, this realm, this England'. In their names and my own I dedicate my work to Shakespeare.[11]

If Gollancz offers his book of homage as a surrogate memorial for the fitting memorial the war has precluded from being erected, Stopes makes use of the Shakespeare Tercentenary to create a site of remembrance for the scholar turned soldier and – although she conspicuously elides the subject – the glorious dead. The tone of her dedication acquires here military and war-like resonances – 'my last effort in the *field*' 'to keep Shakespeare's *flag flying*' – more redolent of medieval jousting and *Henry V* than evocative of the trenches and the muddy fields of Flanders. Like other war memorials, Stopes's Preface does what Samuel Hynes says that monuments do, i.e. 'to affirm the value and significance of the war's sacrifices'.[12] Stopes's metaphor – 'to keep Shakespeare's flag flying' – evokes both the patriotic gesture of a bystander – waving Shakespeare's flag to see her fellow-students off to the front – and the gallop of the warrior scholar that carries Shakespeare's ensign on the critical battlefield. Shakespearian scholarship joins here the war effort and makes room for propaganda as Stopes helps to glorify the war and contributes to the number of war memorials that appeared at the

home front before 1918.[13] Both Gollancz's volume of homage to Shakespeare and Stopes's collection of essays nod gently towards the war in their prefaces, and become what Jay Winter would call 'an act of citizenship' and a form of 'collective affirmation in wartime', but their central aim is to commemorate the Bard rather than to remember and mourn the dead.[14]

There were, however, other Shakespearian books published during or after the war which openly presented themselves as war memorials. Three books of Shakespearian interest that can be read as sites of memory and mourning will be discussed here and in the process I hope to show how Shakespeare was recruited to help in the erection of a war memorial. These books are an edition of the Complete Works, a critical monograph and a collection of letters from the Western Front by a Shakespearian actor. Taken together, these three books – and First World War memorials – show three different ways of conducting a close encounter with Shakespeare, even though they constitute cultural practices far removed from the close reading of the words on the page.

II. SHAKESPEARE AND BOOKS AS SITES OF MEMORY

In 1916, four days after the Battle of Jutland, the death of the Secretary of State for War Lord Kitchener when HMS *Hampshire* struck a mine and sank off the Orkney Islands on 5 June left Britain in a state of shock. The unexpectedness of the news was soon followed by an intense drive to mourn his death. Kitchener's revolutionary scheme of voluntary recruitment – Kitchener's 'New Army' as it was called – was enormously

---

[10] Charlotte Carmichael Stopes, *Shakespeare's Industry* (London, 1916). Stopes's book was widely reviewed and won the Rose Mary Crawshay award (*The Athenaeum*, May 1916, p. 220).

[11] *Shakespeare's Industry*, p. viii. My italics.

[12] Hynes, *A War Imagined*, p. 275.

[13] For memorials and commemoration before the end of the war see Winter, *Sites of Memory*, pp. 80–2.

[14] Winter, *Sites of Memory*, p. 80.

successful. His personal involvement in the scheme is clear from the famous poster bearing his portrait and a finger pointing at the viewer with the slogan 'BRITONS [Kitchener] WANTS YOU. JOIN YOUR COUNTRY'S ARMY! GOD SAVE THE KING.'[15] Although often despised by the regular, professional army men, it was Kitchener's 'Falstaff's Army' that manned the trenches of the Western Front and filled the lists of casualties. Kitchener's death was not only lamented but immediately commemorated – one of the earliest acts of remembrance and public mourning for Lord Kitchener was in fact a book. Kitchener's body was never found, so there could be no official site of mourning for the national hero but, as Moriarty points out, memorials can function as substitute graves.[16] Only a week after the shipwreck of HMS *Hampshire*, the *Illustrated London News* produced a special memorial number dedicated to Lord Kitchener (13 June 1916).[17] The Lord Kitchener National Memorial Fund, founded by the Lord Mayor of London a month after his death, was unable to provide a ceremonial burial, but soon produced the *Lord Kitchener Memorial Book*, a life tribute profusely illustrated with photographs, adorned with personal memories of those who knew him well and displaying after the frontispiece a seating plan for the cabinet with the signatures of all the members of the British goverment.[18]

The *Lord Kitchener Memorial Book* was not the only book memorial in honour of this controversial war hero. In January 1917, Sir Sidney Lee, as Chairman of the Kitchener Souvenir Committee of the League of the British Empire, presented Princess Louise, Duchess of Argyll, with copies of Shakespeare's Complete Works. The princess, in turn, presented the same copies to men who had been blinded at the front – luckily, for the soldiers, the act of presentation included two Shakespeare recitations by Sir Johnston Forbes-Robertson (*The Times*, 25 January 1917). The presentation took place at St Dunstan's Hostel on 24 January and the event had been previously announced by *The Times* on 22 January. This was not the only occasion on which copies of Shakespeare's works were distributed to disabled veterans, as *The Times* records

a similar event taking place at the Royal Star and Garter Home on 26 January (*The Times*, 27 January 1917). Once again, Forbes-Robertson recited to the men and Sidney Lee gave a speech. The book was clearly conceived as a joint memorial to Shakespeare and Lord Kitchener. The copy at the Imperial War Museum has pasted into its inside cover a letter from Buckingham Palace conveying the approval of His Majesty the King for the gift, for the idea of celebrating the memory of Lord Kitchener and for 'the form which it is to take'.[19] The volume opens with a biographical introduction, unsigned, but possibly an abridged version of Sidney Lee's biography of Shakespeare. The introduction is followed not with a critical introduction to the plays, but with an essay on Shakespeare and Bacon by Sir Henry Irving. The plays appear next, followed by the poems. The volume is rounded off with an Index to Characters in Shakespeare's Dramatic Works and a glossary.

Blinded soldiers were not occasional casualties. The use of gas in the Western Front rendered the blind soldier a common war casualty. Sir John Singer Sargent's *Gassed* (1919) shows blinded soldiers in a line staggering to a dressing station while many more lie on the ground with their eyes hidden behind bandages.[20] Sargent's monumental oil painting and Wilfred Owen's 1917 poem, 'Dulce

---

[15] The poster is Catalogue no. IWM PST 2734 in the Imperial War Museum Art collection. It can be accessed at www.iwmcollections.org.uk/qryArt.php. It can also be viewed at http://vads.ahds.ac.uk.

[16] Moriarty, 'Material Culture', p. 653.

[17] See www.iln.org.uk/iln_years/year/robinhunt/huntspecialsp72.htm.

[18] Sir Hedley Le Bas, *The Lord Kitchener Memorial Book* (London, New York and Toronto, 1916).

[19] *The Complete Works of William Shakespeare with Biographical Introduction* (London, 1916). IWM Catalogue no. 86/784. As the date on the king's letter is 27 October 1916, it is quite possible that this edition of Shakespeare's Works was amongst the first Kitchener memorials conceived and produced.

[20] This large oil painting was one of several paintings commissioned by the Imperial War Museum and it is now part of its permanent art collection. See Catalogue no: IWM ART 1460 at www.iwmcollections.org.uk/qryArt.php or at http://vads.ahds.ac.uk/. See also Eric Henri Kennington, *Gassed and Wounded* (1918), Catalogue no. IWM ART 4744.

14. Crested china models of Sir Edwyn Lutyens's Cenotaph in Whitehall bearing the arms of the City of London.

et decorum est' ('All lame, all blind') underline the magnitude of the effects of mustard gas. The numbers of gassed men who suffered impaired vision at the front must have been so considerable that charity organizations multiplied not only in Europe but in America – a Franco-American organisation, 'The Committee for Men Blinded in Battle', collected funds through charity peformances in the US and kept a home in Paris, known as 'Le Phare de France', for the instruction of blinded soldiers.[21]

Beyond its surreal, Kafkaesque implications, the gift of Shakespeare's Complete Works to blinded soldiers offers an example of how the plays acquired a new 'social life' in the context of war commemoration.[22] Divested of its use as text, as drama, as literature, the Complete Works could be equated with the 'crested' china souvenirs manufactured in Staffordshire, meant no doubt to rest

on the mantelpieces of British homes. If originally these pieces of porcelain bric-à-brac bearing the coat of arms of the town in which they were bought mainly consisted of miniature pots, jugs, mugs, vases, plates, teapots, cats and cottages, the war put them to use as commemorative objects. Minute models of Lutyens's Whitehall Cenotaph (Illustration 14) were soon produced and bought in large quantities.[23] Like a crested model of the

21 For the activities of the Committee and its home in Paris see the History collection at University of Wisconsin Digital Collections: http://digital.library.wisc.edu/1711.dl/History.

22 Appadurai, *Social Life of Things*.

23 Lutyens's Cenotaph was a favourite subject for crested china manufacturers. The fashion for crested china during the First World War has been surveyed by Barbara Jones and Bill Howell in their study of popular art, trench art and

Cenotaph bearing the London coat of arms or a crested bust of Kitchener with the arms of Belgium and the Triple Entente, the function of the Kitchener Souvenir Shakespeare is that of an object to be displayed – possibly also on the mantelpiece – rather than a book to be read. As such, Shakespeare's works are divested of their primary, original function and become Baudrillard's 'l'objet pur', an object which has been deprived of its use and *raison d'être* and has become an item in a collection.[24] In *Le Système des objets*, Baudrillard defines 'l'objet pur' in contradistinction to 'l'objet practique', which has its social function intact. Instead, 'l'objet pur, dénué de fonction, ou abstrait de son usage, prend un status strictement subjectif'.[25] The pure object is deprived of its social function and 'devenu relatif au sujet' and it acquires a new function, the function 'd'être possédé'.[26] Like Baudrillard's *objet pur*, the Kitchener Souvenir Shakespeare becomes, in the hands of blinded veterans, an object whose function is that of being possessed.

It is tempting to enquire into the motivations of the League of the British Empire and its Kitchener Souvenir Committee – why Shakespeare? Why not Chaucer or Milton? Why not the Bible? The topicality of the Tercentenary was doubtless behind the choice, but very conveniently so, as other options might have proved unsuitable. The Bible would not have been a wise choice. As the tense struggle between Sir Edward Lutyens and others such as Sir Reginald Blomfield indicates, there was a conflict between those who, like Lutyens, wanted to erase Christian symbols from memorials and acts of war commemoration and those who, like Blomfield, staunchly advocated the presence of the cross.[27] At the Thiepval Memorial to the Missing of the Somme, Blomfield's standard Cross of Sacrifice (which can still be found today in many British towns and villages, as well as in many small, rural church graveyards) stands in stark contrast to the absence of religious iconography in Lutyens's War Stone or Great Stone of Remembrance, a rectangular stone 3.5 m long and 1.5 m high, surrounded by three steps.[28] There is no religious symbolism either in the pure, sober geometry of Lutyens's Whitehall Cenotaph. Shake-

speare's works provided a non-religious symbol of national glory, a useful equivalent of Lutyens's abstract and secular replacement of Christian symbols with unadorned Portland stone and entasis. At the same time, what Shakespeare's Complete Works could provide in 1916 was the soothing, healing effect of 'the turn back to the familiar'.[29] For Jay Winter, mourning practices of the First World War often resorted to classical, Romantic and Christian sources because 'in these traditions contemporaries found the language in which they could mourn'.[30] Unlike 'modern memory', Shakespeare still enjoyed a capacity to heal. The Complete Works offered a convenient, non-religious but traditional site of mourning for the multi-creed disabled soldiers of an imperial army.

If the Kitchener Souvenir Complete Works enacts a public ritual of collective mourning and remembrance, Shakespeare could also be the vehicle for the expression of private grief. In 1916, the Shakespeare Head Press published in Stratford a volume of Shakespearian criticism by Lacy Collison-Morley entitled *Shakespeare in Italy*, which attracted enough attention to be

---

souvenirs, *Popular Arts of the First World War* (London, 1972). Many of these souvenirs, which included shells and soldiers' caps, are still auctioned today, indicating their abiding popularity.

[24] Jean Baudrillard, *Le Système des objets* (Paris, 1968), p. 121.

[25] Baudrillard, *Le Système*, p. 121.

[26] Baudrillard, *Le Système*, p. 121.

[27] For the clash between the diverging ideological programmes of Lutyens and Blomfield and the role played in this by the Imperial War Graves Commission, see Gavin Stamp's study *The Memorial to the Missing of the Somme* (London, 2006). The controversy became so much a matter of public interest that in 1920 there was a parliamentary debate at the House of Commons on the Commission's ban of religious symbols.

[28] See the chapter dedicated to 'The War Stone' in Skelton and Gliddon, *Lutyens*, pp. 23–35.

[29] Jay Winter and Antoine Prost, 'Agents of Memory: How Did People Live between Remembrance and Forgetting?', in *The Great War in History: Debates and Controversies, 1914 to the Present*, ed. Jay Winter and Antoine Prost (Cambridge, 2005), p. 182.

[30] Winter and Prost, 'Agents of Memory', p. 182. See also Winter, *Sites of Memory*, pp. 2–5 and pp. 223–9.

prominently reviewed in *The Athenaeum*.[31] This study of Shakespeare's afterlife in Italy since before Voltaire to the end of the nineteenth century was turned by the author into a private war memorial that commemorates the death of his brother in the Western Front at the battle of Loos. The dedication is self-explanatory:

> *To the memory of my brother*
>
> LIEUT.-COLONEL
>
> *HAROLD DUKE COLLISON-MORLEY,*
>
> soldier and artist,
>
> *The Buffs, commanding the 19th London Regt., T. F. (St. Pancras Battalion), who was killed at the head of his men, after being twice wounded, just before reaching the German trenches in the attack on Loos on the 25th September, 1915, aged 37.*
>
> *Men must endure*
> *Their going hence, even as their coming hither.*
> *Ripeness is all.*
>
> *An enthusiastic Shakespeare lover, he had maintained ever since the South African war that Henry V was the ideal 'soldier's play'. A copy of it, which he had carried with him throughout the present campaign, was found upon him after his death. Only five days before he was killed he wrote: 'There is no hardship or terror or doubt that happens out here that Shakespeare does not touch on or give advice for.'*

With this dedication in a book published in the tercentenary year, 1916, Lacy Collison-Morley turns a volume of Shakespearian criticism into a personal, private memorial. A brother's sorrow (and pride) for his brave sibling is transmogrified, by virtue of being appended to a piece of criticism on Shakespeare, into a permanent site of both memory and mourning. At the same time, by virtue of the materiality of printed matter, private grief is released from the domain of intimacy and becomes public. Shakespeare – or rather his afterlife in Italy – becomes part of a commemoration practice that translates transient feeling into war memorial. A few yards away from Holy Trinity Church and Shakespeare's grave, the Second

World War Memorial in Stratford-upon-Avon's garden of remembrance (see Illustration 15) displays an inscription from what Collison-Morley's brother called the ideal 'soldier's play': 'From this day to the ending of the world, but we in it shall be remembered, we few, we happy few, we band of brothers' (taken from *Henry V*, 4.3.58–61). Collison-Morley also resorts to a Shakespearian quotation, 'Men must endure . . . Ripeness is all' (*King Lear*, 5.2. 9–11), to mourn and cope with grief.[32]

Lieutenant-Colonel Harold Duke Collison-Morley is buried at the Dud Corner Cemetery in Loos. Unlike Lutyens's Cenotaph, the memorial at Loos sports a Christian Cross – Blomfield's Cross of Sacrifice – but the memorial also extends all round the walls of the cemetery where the names of the 20,000 soldiers who were missing in action during the Battle of Loos are inscribed and remembered.[33] Here the memorial closely recalls the pages of a book, as the names of the soldiers are carved on huge rectangular stone slabs placed on the inside walls of the cemetery.[34] These slabs, covered in written characters from top to bottom, create an uncanny sight, as if pages from a book had been carefully torn out from a spine and pasted on the walls. The Loos memorial shares with books the materiality of the written word. A visitor so inclined could read the names of the missing moving from slab to slab as one moves from page to page when reading a book. The materiality of Great War commemoration, by virtue of its oscillation between the public and the private, the collective

---

[31] Lacy Collison-Morley, *Shakespeare in Italy* (Stratford-upon-Avon, 1916). See review in *The Athenaeum*, November 1916, p. 409. I must record here my gratitude to Ton Hoenselaars for drawing my attention to the existence of this monograph-cum-war memorial.

[32] Quotations from Shakespeare have been taken from the New Cambridge Shakespeare editions of the plays.

[33] For a view of the Cross of Sacrifice at Dud Corner Cemetery, see for instance www.cwgc.org/CWGCImgs/dud%20corner2006.JPG.

[34] For the inner walls of Dud Corner Cemetery and the Loos Memorial see http://yourarchives.nationalarchives.gov.uk/index.php?title=Dud_Corner_and_the_Loos_Memorial.

15. The Second World War Memorial in Stratford-upon-Avon's garden of remembrance with quotation from *Henry V*, 4.3.

and the individual, favours these transformations of books into portable war memorials and of war memorials into stone books.

In 1926, eight years after the Armistice, Vera Leslie, wife of Shakespearian actor Henry Doughty, also known as 'Gunga Din' – presumably for his dexterity at entertaining the troops with recitations of Kipling's famous poem about an Indian water-bearer – presented the Imperial War Museum with a copy of a book which strangely inhabits a realm astride the public and the private: *An Actor-Soldier. Extracts from his Letters, 1914–1919. Henry Doughty ('Gunga Din').*[35] Doughty enlisted in 1914, at the outbreak of war, long before conscription was enforced, and was allocated to Horse Transport in an artillery company. In his earliest letters he writes: 'Work is the word. We start at 6 tomor-row. I think our "Falstaff's army" will really do quite well with discipline. They are much bet-ter as soon as they get into uniform' (p. 18). A female pony allocated to his unit seems deranged

and when he notices that the soldiers have plaited hay in her mane, he christens her 'Ophelia' – a name the soldiers do not relate to and replace with 'Amelia' or 'Camelia' (pp. 34–6). Doughty begins to give recitations early in the war and continues to take part in concerts arranged by the YMCA (p. 44). Together with Kipling's 'Gunga Din' and other poems, his repertory includes 'Seven Ages', 'St Crispin' and scenes from *Othello*. He continues to perform throughout the Tercentenary Year, even though he is training to become an officer: 'The tests are pretty stiff – foot-drill, riding, driving and supply. We did the "Othello" scene last Sunday and it made quite a sensation' (p. 52). On Boxing Day 1916, Doughty recited from *Othello* again during a YMCA concert, this time, he says, 'in costume'.

---

[35] Henry Doughty, *An Actor-Soldier: Extracts from his Letters, 1914–1919. Henry Doughty, 'Gunga Din'* (London, *c.*1926?). IWM Catalogue No.: 11789.

The Allied Advance in 1918 finds him in the thick of the action, at the Ypres Salient, and he writes:

I have been up to my new location in search of a site. The country is awful, indescribable. I had to go through one of the worst, I should think really the worst devastated of all. The whole countryside is pock-marked with shell holes and there are dozen of smashed–up tanks and aeroplanes. Scorched stumps of trees show what once were woods. If I were an artist, I could paint a weird picture of 'The Blasted Heath' for *Macbeth*. The approach is awful. My wagons will be up to their axles in mud. (p. 80)

The published volume of Doughty's letters ends with the following colophon, a printed memorial which bears a noticeable resemblance to the text of an epitaph:

In Memory of

Henry Doughty

Actor and Soldier (1914–1919)

Lieut. Horse Transport, R.A.S.C.

Forgotten 1919–1922

Passed away 27th November, 1922

≪THE REST IS SILENCE≫

Hamlet's famous and final words are quoted knowingly by Vera Leslie, a wife who presents herself, in the copy of the book donated to the Imperial War Museum, as 'the Writer's wife and Comrade in Art (Drama)'. The war could not silence the Shakespearian actor, but the return to civil life did. On a typescript note pasted onto the back cover of the Imperial War Museum copy, Doughty is described as an actor who before the war had 'an excellent position' and was 'connected with most of the London theatres'. He had been actor-manager of the 'Doughty Leslie' touring company. As a Shakespearian actor, he had performed at the Lyceum under Sir Henry Irving and also played secondary roles in the Shakespearian repertory company of Robert Taber and Julia Marlowe who toured in the US. The war allowed him to continue to perform but, the note tells us,

'From the time of his demobilisation to the date of his death, he could get no dramatic work.'

Doughty was one of many veterans who found it difficult to find employment after demobilization. The multiplicity of posters encouraging employers to take in veterans as employees testifies to this considerable social problem.[36] Unrest and riots occasioned by the masses of unemployed ex-service men were a feature of the postwar period.[37] Doughty found occasional work as a cinema actor, but in the six months prior to his death the only job he found was that of Father Christmas at Selfridges. After exposure to a heavy storm of rain and a brief illness, he died – possibly of Spanish fever. 'A slaughter by itself is too commonplace for notice' – writes Paul Fussell in *The Great War and Modern Memory* – 'When it makes an ironic point it becomes memorable.'[38] An actor voluntarily enlists, trains and becomes an officer, is willing to fight not only for 'King and country' but also for his national Bard, and survives the war after getting close enough to the Ypres Salient to describe it in detail as a set fit for *Macbeth*, but he fails to survive a London winter. The life and death of Henry Doughty, minor Shakespearian actor, becomes memorable through the irony of his death.

Henry Doughty's letters, which originally belonged to the realm of the individual, transgress that confinement when his wife publishes them, turning private correspondence into a war memorial. A book that has its origin in a personal, intimate exchange between man and wife, actor and

---

[36] For First World War posters that encouraged employers to employ veterans see IWM PST 13800, 13801, 13802 and 13803 at www.iwmcollections.org.uk/qryArt.php.

[37] On 19 July 1919, the very day London was celebrating Peace Day with marching troops parading in front of Lutyens's original Cenotaph, a riot in Luton ended with unemployed veterans setting fire to the Town Hall (Hynes, *A War Imagined*, p. 281) and the army had to be brought in to end the disturbances, resulting in Luton being occupied by military troops for several days (Neil Hanson, *The Unknown Soldier* (London, 2007, first published 2005), pp. 416–17). Commemoration and social unrest often took place in unison.

[38] Paul Fussell, *The Great War and Modern Memory* (Oxford, 1975), p. 31.

actress, becomes, by virtue of the materiality of its publication and presentation to the Imperial War Museum, a public site of memory and mourning. As the colophon suggests, the drive behind this war memorial is the desire to preclude oblivion: 'Forgotten 1919–1922'. The letters of Henry Doughty are not particularly literary – they simply encapsulate a syncopated narrative of the war years – but the act of publication places them in a public space that memorializes individual experience. If, as Baudrillard argues, 'Forgetting extermination is a part of extermination, because it is also the extermination of memory, of history, of the social',[39] Vera Leslie's printed memorial for her husband turns her into an 'agent of memory',[40] a 'social agent of remembrance',[41] and a solo 'memory activist',[42] who actively contributes to the shaping of cultural memory. The function of memorials is precisely to preclude oblivion, a feeling which tainted the report of an eye-witness at the Peace Conference in 1919. William Orpen, who had been, like Paul Nash and Wyndham Lewis, Official War Painter at the Front, was allowed to see the signing of the Treaty of Versailles in the Hall of Mirrors and his comment on such a crucial occasion was: 'The Army was forgotten. Some dead and forgotten, others maimed and forgotten, others alive and well – but equally forgotten.'[43]

'Forgotten 1919–1922' expresses the wish that the period of oblivion may be finite, of limited duration, but it also shapes Vera Leslie's memorial for her husband and fellow actor into what Samuel Hynes has called an 'anti-monument'. For Hynes, anti-monuments are 'monuments of loss' (loss of values, of a sense of order, of beliefs) and they testify to 'a sense of impoverishment' expressed in 'the language of disillusionment and rejection'.[44] Doughty's life is a story of hope abridged and disillusionment, not with the war as in the case of Robert Graves, Siegfried Sassoon and many others, but with the aftermath of a war supposedly fought to preserve civilization and the status quo.[45] Like Virginia Woolf's Septimus in *Mrs Dalloway*, he survives the war to be killed by the postwar, which makes it impossible to resume civilian life in the same terms as before the war. Leonard V. Smith

has shown how First World War narratives often construe the soldier as victim and 'tragic hero'.[46] Doughty's epitaph rewrites the usual First World War tragic narrative and replaces it with a 'veteran as victim' narrative that links the end of the actor-soldier to Hamlet's death.

III. SHAKESPEARE AS *L'OBJET PUR* – THE CULTURAL BIOGRAPHY OF THE PLAYS

Reading these three books as war memorials shows how Shakespeare may crucially contribute 'to approach[ing] the history of collective remembrance from the angle of small-scale, locally rooted social action',[47] expanding thus our knowledge of the material practices of commemoration and the cultural history of the First World War. I hope to have shown (a) that war memorials in the shape of books appeared long before the end of the war itself; (b) that a study of the cultures of commemoration and remembrance which sprouted during and after the 1914–1918 war should take into account the function of books as portable war memorials and sites of mourning; and (c) that Shakespeare and his works played a substantial role in the material culture of Great War commemoration, partly because Shakespeare's

---

[39] Jean Baudrillard, *Simulacra and Simulation*, trans. Shelia Faria Glaser (Ann Arbor, 1994, first published 1981), p. 49.

[40] Winter and Prost, *The Great War*, p. 173.

[41] Winter, *Remembering War*, p. 136.

[42] Carol Gluck quoted in Winter, *Remembering War*, p. 136.

[43] Quoted in Hynes, *A War Imagined*, p. 294.

[44] Hynes, *A War Imagined*, p. 307.

[45] For the contested role of 'disillusionment' in representations of the First World War and its texts (diaries and letters), see 'The Soldier's Story: Publishing and the Postwar Years', in Janet S. K. Watson's study of war as lived experienced versus war as memory, *Fighting Different Wars: Experience, Memory, and the First World War in Britain* (Cambridge, 2004), pp. 185–218.

[46] Leonard V. Smith, 'Narrative and Identity at the Front: "Theory and the Poor Bloody Infantry"', in *The Great War and the Twentieth Century*, ed. Jay Winter, Geoffrey Parker and Mary R. Habeck (New Haven and London, 2000), pp. 132–65; p. 135.

[47] Winter, *Remembering War*, p. 150.

16. Stratford-upon-Avon's First World War Memorial in its original location at the top of Bridge Street.

status as national poet was fuelled and enlarged by the celebrations of the 1916 Tercentenary of his death during the second year of the first world-wide conflict.

Shakespeare should naturally be part of the study of cultural memory and the dynamics of cultural transmission. If, as Assmann suggests, 'Cultural memory is at the furthest remove from individual memory',[48] by turning the works of Shakespeare into a memorial for a lost leader, a text read by a soldier in the trenches, or a play performed at the front, these encounters with Shakespeare transcend individual memory and enter the land of cultural memory. Assmann also distinguishes cultural memory from communicative or oral memory and from Halbwachs's collective, bonding memory. Unlike communicative memory, cultural memory 'encompasses the age-old, out-of-the-way, and discarded' and by contrast with collective memory, it 'includes the noninstrumentalizable, heretical, subversive, and disowned'.[49] Cultural memory is the closest we may ever be to Benjamin's ideal of history which is only available to a 'redeemed mankind' on Judgement Day: 'nothing that has ever happened should

be regarded as lost for history'.[50] Messy, unruly, unstructured as it is, cultural memory ignores the discontinuities that challenge a unitary conception of human history and overcomes the fear that feeds Benjamin's vision of the angel of history.[51] Age-old, out-of-the-way, discarded and disowned by scholarship as these three Shakespearian war memorials might be, they have an important role to play in the cultural memory of the First World War.

---

[48] Jan Assmann, *Religion and Cultural Memory*, trans. Rodney Livingstone (Stanford, 2006), p. 27.

[49] Assmann, *Religion and Cultural Memory*, p. 27.

[50] Walter Benjamin, 'Theses on the Philosophy of History', in *Illuminations*, ed. Hannah Arendt, trans. Harry Zorn (London, 1999), p. 246. First published as *Schriften* (1955).

[51] Benjamin's angel of history, inspired by Paul Klee's painting 'Angelus Novus', is willing to face the past but caught in the stormy wind of history is inevitably pushed backwards into the future. The stormy wind blows from Paradise and is what we call 'progress' (Benjamin, 'Theses', p. 249). Our postcolonial, postmodern view of history partly stems, according to Modris Eksteins, from the cultural legacy of the First World War, which has taught us to replace hope and confidence with humility and respect (Modris Eksteins, 'The Cultural Legacy of the Great War', in *The Great War*, ed. Winter, Parker and Habeck, pp. 331–49; p. 344).

Although the role played by Shakespeare in commemoration and memory rites around 1916 must necessarily be of interest to British First World War historians and cultural historians, what benefit a study such as this entails for Shakespearian scholarship may appear to be a moot point. There are, however, some directions – provisional no doubt – in which a cultural history of war may illuminate our knowledge of Shakespeare the icon and Shakespeare the body of texts. It seems that beyond their function as texts, the works of Shakespeare enjoyed a new social life during the First World War. Shakespeare – his works, their afterlives in a foreign country, the performance of his plays at the Front – provided an occasion for the erection of sites of public memory and private mourning, a chance for the ritualized practice of commemoration and remembrance to expand into book gifts and dedications. Two of the three Shakespearian war memorials discussed here – Lacy Collison-Morley's dedication and Vera Leslie's epitaph – make use of Shakespearian quotations to cope with grief and bereavement; the third one is a gift edition of the Complete Works for those who have suffered pain and hardship. Shakespeare is thus called upon to provide comfort. A few days before the Battle of Loos, Lieutenant-Colonel Harold Duke Collison-Morley, according to his brother, wrote: 'There is no hardship or terror or doubt that happens out here that Shakespeare does not touch on or give advice for.' He has become the universal, ultimate advice-giver and his plays, now as a surrogate religion, provide moral guidance.

The Kitchener Souvenir Complete Works, intended as a joint memorial for both Lord Kitchener of Khartoum and William Shakespeare of Stratford, may provide a useful site, a foundation stone for a cultural biography of the plays. As Kopytoff suggests, when aiming to trace the cultural biography of a thing, 'one would ask questions similar to . . . How does the thing's use change with its age, and what happens to it when it reaches the end of its usefulness?'[52] For a disabled soldier, and particularly for a blinded one, the meaning of the works of Shakespeare may not be enshrined in their value as literature but rather in a symbolic

17. Stratford-upon-Avon's First World War Memorial after having been hit by a lorry in 1927.

value as gift and memorial, rendering the plays' use, meaning and value close to that of a Staffordshire crested souvenir. To imagine the works of Shakespeare on the mantelpiece of a British home, between a crested bust of Kitchener and a miniature replica of the Cenotaph is to begin to see how Shakespeare's plays have acquired a social life as object, and even *objet pur*, independent of their life in academia or on the stage, whose symbolic meaning stems from the very act of being possessed.

The commodification of Shakespeare's plays through the Kitchener Souvenir – Shakespeare as war memorial – took place precisely at a time in which the cultural life of the plays on the London stage was declining. The demise of the system of the actor-manager, to which Doughty's life and

---

[52] Kopytoff, 'The Cultural Biography of Things', pp. 66–7.

18. Stratford-upon-Avon's First World War Memorial in its present location, with Holy Trinity Church emerging through the trees in the background.

death testify, also account for the decline of 'live Shakespeare' in the metropolis – and his highlights from Shakespeare at the Front, delivered as part of a YMCA 'concert', suggest that a sizeable section of Edwardian Shakespeare was 'music-hall' or 'revue' Shakespeare. As the – real or imaginary – presence of a copy of *Henry V* upon the dead body of a British officer after the attack on German positions at Loos in 1915 suggests, individual plays may also generate cultural biographies of their own. The presence of Shakespeare and his plays in the practices of First World War commemoration indicates that a cultural biography of the Works would not prove a simple, uncomplicated pursuit – and that there are many and varied ways of engaging in close encounters with Shakespeare other than the close reading of the plays.

Shakespeare himself was of course well aware of the value and usefulness of memorials and shrines. In Sonnet 55 ('Not marble nor the gilded monuments') he contended that poetry and the written word make better, more reliable sites of remem-

brance than funereal monuments. The Shakespeare war memorials discussed here have in fact lasted longer than some WWI war shrines that have been 'besmear'd with sluttish time'. The Maltese Cross erected in Hyde Park in August 1918 to commemorate the fourth anniversary of the start of the war remained in place only for fifteen months, as it was damaged and had to be removed in October 1919.[53] Lutyens's original Cenotaph, made of wood and plaster, was initially raised only to commemorate the fallen during Victory Parade in July 1919 and was, as an afterthought, left in place until the Armistice commemoration on 11 November 1919. At the end of this year, the Cenotaph was 'badly dilapidated' and was dismantled in January 1920,[54] so the very same structure that Foch and marching Allied soldiers saluted on Peace Day, having been exposed to London's weather, only lasted six months. Even war memorials made of

---

[53] Hanson, *The Unknown Soldier*, p. 420.
[54] Hanson, *The Unknown Soldier*, p. 421.

stone, such as Stratford-upon-Avon's Cross of Sacrifice, which stood at the top of Bridge Street (Illustration 16), did not last long in their original locations. Erected in 1922 and hit by a lorry in 1927 (Illustration 17), this memorial has seen two earlier sites, before finding its actual prominent place in Stratford's garden of remembrance for the glorious dead of several wars, situated just outside Holy Trinity Church, within a stone's throw of Shakespeare's own grave and shrine (Illustration 18). In contrast to the stone crosses of the First World War, the Shakespearian war memorials memorialized in these pages remain for the eyes of all posterity movable, portable memorials while equally serving as lasting sites and a living record of memory and mourning.

SHAKESPEARIAN BIOGRAPHY, BIBLICAL ALLUSION AND EARLY MODERN PRACTICES OF READING SCRIPTURE

RANDALL MARTIN

Modern narratives of Shakespeare's life have tended to expand our sense of the playwright's representativeness of his own culture in perhaps every area but one:[1] his use of the Bible. The boundaries of this subject have long been shaped by two biographical assumptions about Shakespeare's encounters with scriptural texts: that they occurred mainly when he was a boy in school and later when he attended church services. Both assumptions have sedimented into part of our cultural memory of Shakespeare that no recent biographer, as far as I am aware, has questioned.[2] They constitute what one might call, following Pierre Bourdieu,[3] the historical field that determines the social value and scholarly production of Shakespeare's discursive relationship with the Bible. The critical result, evident in any modern edition, has been a reduction of Shakespeare's biblical references to the level of proverbial wisdom or unproblematic doctrine. These scholarly tendencies have been reinforced by wider cultural attitudes, such as long-standing admiration for the plays' absence of religious dogma, as well as wariness of provoking outdated polemics or fanciful speculations about Shakespeare's personal beliefs.

The current consensus has had the less desirable effect, however, of inhibiting historicized investigations of Shakespeare's biblical intertexts and early modern English culture, including potentially diverse responses by original spectators and readers to scriptural allusions in the plays. While modern scholars have catalogued scores of references to the Bible in Shakespeare, most of these remain untouched by recent theoretical discourses and cross-disciplinary methodologies which have transformed Shakespearian historicism in other areas, including early modern contexts of religious politics and the theatre.[4] Contacts with modern

---

[1] Douglas Bruster, *Shakespeare and the Question of Culture: Early Modern Literature and the Cultural Turn* (London, 2003), p. 4.

[2] Park Honan, *Shakespeare: A Life* (Oxford, 1998); Anthony Holden, *William Shakespeare: His Life and Work* (London, 1999); Katherine Duncan-Jones, *Ungentle Shakespeare* (London, 2001); Stanley Wells, *Shakespeare for All Time* (Oxford, 2003); Michael Wood, *Shakespeare* (London, 2003), the book published to accompany Wood's BBC television series, *In Search of Shakespeare*; Stephen Greenblatt, *Will in the World: How Shakespeare Became Shakespeare* (New York, 2004); James Shapiro, *A Year in the Life of William Shakespeare: 1599* (London, 2005). Like his other recent criticism, Greenblatt's biography does have much to say about the cultural contexts of religion, especially Catholicism (as does Michael Wood), but little about Shakespeare's specific reading of scripture other than a remark that Bottom's mixed-up quotation from 1 Corinthians (*A Midsummer Night's Dream*, 4.1.208–11) was familiar 'from endless repetitions in church', but that its alleged original source was the Bishops' Bible, the version 'Shakespeare knew and used most often' (35).

[3] Pierre Bourdieu, *Distinction: A Social Critique of the Judgement of Taste*, trans. Richard Nice (Cambridge, MA, 1984); *The Field of Cultural Production*, ed. Randal Johnson (New York, 1993). See n. 5 below.

[4] For example: Huston Diehl, *Staging Reform, Reforming the Stage* (Ithaca, 1997); Jeffrey Knapp, *Shakespeare's Tribe: Church, Nation and Theater in Renaissance England* (Chicago, 2002); Patricia Parker, 'The Bible and the Marketplace: *The Comedy of Errors*', *Shakespeare from the Margins* (Chicago, 1996), ch. 2, pp. 56–82; Debora Shuger, *Political Theologies in Shakespeare's England* (New York, 2001); Paul W. White, *Theatre and Reformation: Protestantism, Patronage, and Playing in Tudor England* (Cambridge, 1993). Overall, the recent 'turn to religion' has focused more on the plays' thematic relationships to wider

biblical scholarship are rare, even though many of the methodological breakthroughs of Renaissance humanists anticipate the revisionist studies of modern New Testament hermeneutics and feminist theologians.

In this article I'd like to begin redrawing the biographically oriented field of Shakespeare's scriptural intertexts by outlining several early modern categories of knowledge that prepared him and other English readers to interpret biblical associations independently and creatively.[5] I'll begin by surveying the construction of the prevailing scholarly narrative about Shakespeare's biblical allusions. Focusing attention on Paul's New Testament letters, my second and third sections will outline two biographically implicated but culturally integrated reading practices: (1) the significance of Shakespeare's grammar-school education for stimulating professional interest in Paul's writings as rhetorical and inherently theatrical dialogues; (2) early modern habits of letter-writing and the vernacular diffusion of humanist biblical criticism, both of which taught readers to see Paul's epistles as locally targeted interventions into historically situated debates over religious authority, not as timeless theological statements. By way of illustrating the critical possibilities of these two perspectives, my final section will turn to *Pericles*, where I explore Marina's scenes in the brothel in relation to certain allusions to political and gender controversies in Paul's letters.

CHILDISH THINGS AND BIBLICAL WISDOM

The biographical turn in studies of Shakespeare's biblical knowledge is a product of late nineteenth- and twentieth-century secular scholarship. It represents a reaction against the overweening piety of Victorian divines such as T. R. Eaton, author of *Shakespeare and the Bible: showing how much the great dramatist was indebted to Holy Writ for his profound knowledge of human nature* (1860). Charles Wordsworth's *Shakespeare's Knowledge and Use of the Bible* (1864 (twice), 1880, and 1892) aimed

to refute Thomas Bowdler's iconoclastic view that Shakespeare had profaned religion merely by referring to the Bible in his plays, references which Bowdler expunged with other alleged indecencies in his notorious 'Family Shakespeare' (1807, 1818). Wordsworth's method was to argue from copious lists of parallel passages that Shakespeare was 'a diligent and devout reader of the Word of God'.[6] His study decisively influenced the opinions of widely read nineteenth-century biographers and critics such as Hermann Ulrici, first president of the *Deutsche Shakespeare-Gesellschaft*, founded in 1864, and the Irish academic Edward Dowden, who opined that Shakespeare, while not a 'religious fanatic', possessed the 'habits of thought and feeling . . . belong[ing] more especially to the Protestant ideal of manhood'.[7] One exception among

---

intellectual and cultural contexts than on the heuristic and methodological connections between Renaissance humanist and modern theological scholarship, or the diffusion of humanism's new epistemologies among early modern English Bible readers.

[5] Bourdieu tends to be sceptical about the ability to alter historical fields. On the one hand he argues that it is virtually impossible for critics working within a literary or scholarly field to position themselves outside the network of received opinion or to replace that network with something entirely new, since the field operates quasi-autonomously as an objectified body of historically constituted knowledge (*Distinction*, p. 496). On the other hand the field is not immune from temporal contingency nor does its status preclude attempts to identify new relationships with fields outside the discipline (*The Field of Cultural Production*, p. 184). Historical and interdisciplinary bridges between early modern and present-day New Testament scholarship represent a way of potentially defamiliarizing and reconfiguring the current Shakespearian field.

[6] *Shakespeare's Knowledge and Use of the Bible* (1864; London, 4th edn, 1892).

[7] Hermann Ulrici, *Shakespeare's dramatische Kunst*, 2 vols. (Leipzig, 1839), translated as *Shakespeare's Dramatic Art* by L. Dora Schmitz (London, 1846, 1976, 1880), citing Wordsworth in I. 259; Edward Dowden, *Shakespere: A Critical Study of His Mind and Art* (1875; London, 16th edn, 1900), p. 39. Ironically, Dowden dismisses J. W. Birch's *An Inquiry into the Philosophy and Religion of Shakespeare* (London, 1848), which makes use of the atomized parallel-passage methodology to prove that Shakespeare, *pace* Wordsworth, was a militant atheist (*Shakespere: A Critical Study of His Mind and Art*, p. 38). My information about German Shakespeare

these commentators was German literary biographer Karl Elze, who argued that Shakespeare was indeed 'a diligent reader of the Bible', but that his use of scriptural references was (echoing a term of Goethe's) 'dramatico-objective', that is, a pragmatic and aesthetic response to the dramatic goals of mimetic naturalism. Such artistic negotiations, Elze maintained, reveal nothing about Shakespeare's personal beliefs.[8]

The strategic response to Wordsworth and like-minded critics dates from Sir Sidney Lee's influential *Life of William Shakespeare* (1898, 1905), which expanded on his ground-breaking *Dictionary of National Biography* entry (1897). Lee described the playwright's biblical references as those

which a clever boy would be certain to acquire either in the schoolroom or in church on Sundays. Shakespeare quotes or adapts biblical phrases with far greater frequency than he makes allusion to episodes in biblical history . . . [This suggests] youthful reminiscence and the assimilative tendency of the mind in a stage of early development rather than close and continuous study of the Bible in adult life.[9]

Lee's became the standard *Life* during the first quarter of the twentieth century.[10] His speculation that Shakespeare's biblical knowledge was acquired in and limited to juvenile and publicly authorized contexts was energetically affirmed by T. W. Baldwin's massive study, *William Shakspere's Small Latine & Lesse Greeke* (1944). Basing his conclusions on an exhaustive survey of Tudor grammar-school curricula, Baldwin argued that

Shakspere's knowledge of the Old Testament [was] predominantly the result of grammar school practice . . . [T]here is no evidence that he was later an assiduous reader of these sections. His knowledge is too well confined to grammar school limits to permit much individual and aggressive endeavor at any time on his part. He was no John Milton.[11]

From Lee's theory, backed by Baldwin's erudition, it was a short step to critical fossilization. Summarizing the state of scholarship on Shakespeare's reading at mid-century, F. P. Wilson mentioned the Bible among books the playwright

typically 'chewed and digested'. But unlike his discussions of Ovid, Plutarch, Holinshed or Montaigne, Wilson had nothing new to report about it.[12] In a similar survey of biography, C. J. Sisson, author of a famous British Academy lecture rubbishing the nineteenth-century state-of-mind school ('The Mythical Sorrows of Shakespeare'

---

biographers derives partly from a paper presented by Wolfgang Weiss at the 2008 International Shakespeare Conference, 'The Argument about Shakespeare's *Weltanschauung* (World View) and Religion in Ninteenth-Century Germany'.

8 *William Shakespeare* (Halle, 1876), pp. 42, 439, 443–4. Moreover, Elze argues, the only certain claim which can be made about Shakespeare's Christian subjectivity was that he, like everyone else in the period, was culturally interpellated within its common system of symbolic signs and values: 'Shakespeare . . . not only recognized Christianity to be a factor in the human world he wished to represent, but it was to himself personally an element of culture from which he could as little free himself entirely as anyone else, even though he had wished to do so [sic] . . . The poet . . . moves within the mental atmosphere of Christian conceptions, ideas, and figures of speech, and it is impossible in every single case to point out with certainty how far the poet is actually imbued with its substance, or how far the thoughts, hopes, feelings, and convictions expressed in his works are identical with his own' (pp. 444–5, 453). Later, Elze again echoes Goethe in venturing to interpret Shakespeare's avoidance of confessional didacticism as an indication that his outlook was liberal humanist, and that Shakespeare believed the overriding point of religion was 'our conscience, the fulfilment of our duty, not dogma; in every case he insists upon an active life in the service of morality and the active exercise of charity' (p. 449).

9 In his revised edition (1905) Lee downplayed earlier speculations about school and church. He argued that because 'Elizabethan English was saturated with scriptural expressions', and biblical texts recur frequently in Holinshed and other secular sources, these were the main source of Shakespeare's biblical references. 'Yet', Lee added, 'there is a savour of early study about his normal use of scripture phraseology, as of scriptural history . . . [which] bear trace [sic] of the assimilative or receptive tendency of an alert youthful mind' (p. 23). Lee maintains that Shakespeare grew out of this unconscious susceptibility.

10 S. Schoenbaum, *Shakespeare's Lives* (Oxford, 1991), pp. 378, 380.

11 (Urbana, 1944), I. 685.

12 'Shakespeare's Reading', *Shakespeare Survey 3* (Cambridge, 1950), p. 18.

(1934)), simply omitted the Bible in his section on Shakespeare's education and 'library'.[13] Among later twentieth-century biographers, Samuel Schoenbaum approved Baldwin's basic arguments, albeit with characteristically greater restraint, in *William Shakespeare: A Documentary Life* (1975). Schoenbaum's became the standard biography for the remainder of the century, and arguably remains so today.[14]

The narrative dating from Lee's biographical turn restricts consideration of Shakespeare's scriptural references to paths of reception that were officially under interpretive control. Whether derived from school or church, they are conceived largely as reminiscences. The medium of transmission is predominantly aural. This profile perhaps explains the long-standing fashion to speak of Shakespeare's biblical *allusions*;[15] that is, covert, implied or indirect references (*OED* 4) rather than culturally dynamic ones. Above all, these assumptions situate Shakespeare's scriptural education within the non-metropolitan bourns of Stratford-upon-Avon. The traditional and still current story of Shakespeare's encounter with biblical texts therefore portrays him as an immature, critically passive and uninquisitive reader, as well as a conforming member of the Church of England.[16] While the latter view is probably historically accurate, its implications continue to underwrite eighteenth- and nineteenth-century constructions of him as the national poet whose quintessential Englishness was defined by implicit approval of establishment institutions.

In an under-noticed article written twenty years ago, Naseeb Shaheen challenged this narrative by demonstrating that most of Shakespeare's Bible references must have derived from dedicated personal reading as an adult, not from school or church services.[17] The implications of his arguments have yet to be followed up, in particular his revisionist insight that Shakespeare read scripture with purposeful intelligence, just as other literate early modern men and women did. Yet the Shakespearian field, and even Shaheen's main work,[18] has continued to under-historicize the relationship between

the plays' biblical associations and the diversity of early modern interpretation. One explanation for this is Shaheen's and others' persistent view that Shakespeare favoured Old Testament texts. Baldwin regarded Shakespeare's greater familiarity with the Old Testament as a sign of his grammar-school training.[19] His opinion expanded upon that of Richmond Noble, whose secular-minded study *Shakespeare's Biblical Knowledge* (1935) argued that

---

[13] 'Studies in the Life and Environment of Shakespeare Since 1900', *Shakespeare Survey 3* (Cambridge, 1950), pp. 5–6.

[14] *William Shakespeare: A Documentary Life* (Oxford, 1975), pp. 47–57. Schoenbaum also noted a characteristic wobble in Baldwin's argument (which the latter was aware of but downplayed (I. 687)) about the priority of the Old Testament: in Baldwin's section assessing Shakespeare's possible knowledge of Greek, Elizabethan pedagogues all recommended working from the New Testament Acts of the Apostles with an accompanying English translation (*William Shakspere's Small Latine*, II. 632, 645; *Shakespeare's Lives*, p. 531). Writing with an overt Catholic agenda, Peter Milward expressed doubts about Baldwin's grammar-school deductions but nonetheless argued that Shakespeare's familiarity with the Bible in church, along with the Book of Common Prayer and government-commissioned Homilies, was 'more than could have been derived from hearsay, or even from a literary study of the books in question' (*Shakespeare's Religious Background* (Bloomington, IN, 1973), p. 37).

[15] For instance, Steven Marx, *Shakespeare and the Bible* (Oxford, 2000), p. 13.

[16] Of his adult church-going in London, we know virtually nothing. The intermittent records of his failure to pay taxes, Easter payments, and parish dues between 1597 and 1600 at two London churches (Schoenbaum, *William Shakespeare*, pp. 162–3) may suggest irregular attendance, or some avoidance of church to evade prosecution for debt, just as his father had apparently done when William was a boy (Wells, *Shakespeare for All Time*, pp. 23–5). Katherine Duncan-Jones speculates that Shakespeare's non-payment of parish dues and lapses in church attendance may indicate he was either 'indifferent or resistant to public devotion' in London or that he was simply busy and peripatetic (*Ungentle Shakespeare*, p. 195).

[17] 'Shakespeare's Knowledge of the Bible – How Acquired', *Shakespeare Studies*, 4 (1988), 201–14.

[18] *Biblical References in Shakespeare's Tragedies* (Newark, NJ, 1987); *Biblical References in Shakespeare's History Plays* (Newark, NJ, 1989); *Biblical References in Shakespeare's Comedies* (Newark, NJ, 1993).

[19] I. 684–5. See quotation p. 4.

Shakespeare read scripture 'in the spirit of recreation' as well as for poetic inspiration and dramatic insight:

My own impression is that the wisdom of *Ecclesiasticus* appealed to Shakespeare. Probably its keen observation of human society provided him with a parallel to his own, and a man of his temperament would enjoy its reprehension of immoderation, whether it concerned grief, food, wine, or the pursuit of revenge. So I think now and again he refreshed himself with a perusal of its pages.[20]

Shaheen likewise steered readers' attention towards Shakespeare's Old Testament references. He drew implications about what Shakespeare would and would not have heard in church from the institutional practice of alternating 'ordinary' and 'proper' (i.e. occasional) first lessons appointed for Sundays and holy days. In both cases these were Old Testament lessons. Their most frequent passages were taken from 'the books of Isaiah, Ecclesiasticus, and Genesis in that order'.[21] There were fewer 'proper' alternatives for second-lesson New Testament readings. Shaheen inferred that because first lessons changed more often, they would have been noticed more. But this depends on a professional awareness of the possibility of alternative lessons in the church lexicon and a subjective view of deviations from the 'ordinary' readings as 'interference', both of which seem questionable suppositions for ordinary parishioners. Moreover, while Shaheen argues against Baldwin and earlier commentators about Shakespeare encountering the Bible mainly in church, he treats the psalms as an exception. On this point his views are traditionally biographical: Shakespeare knew the psalms from Sunday services, and he learnt them by heart at school.[22]

Distinct critical implications flow from an emphasis on Shakespeare's alleged preference for the Old Testament. Philologically and semantically, it was less controversial in the early modern period than the rediscovered Greek New Testament and its vernacular translations. The latter, and Paul's letters in particular, became foundational texts for Christian humanists and Protestant reformers and were saturated with political controversy. In this regard it may be telling that Peter Milward endorses Baldwin's and Noble's emphasis on the Old Testament since it serves his purposes of distancing a 'Catholic' Shakespeare from the 'Protestant' New Testament.[23]

Thus, an interrelated process of biographical fashioning, historical attenuation and scholarly preference has tended to under-represent the New Testament in studies of Shakespeare's biblical references and to de-historicize its relationship to contested early modern interpretive contexts. An Old Testament focus has also underwritten still popular notions that Shakespeare's plays transmit unchanging values. Ever since Romantic scholars constructed the image of Shakespeare as the supreme secular poet of nature,[24] commentators have argued that the meanings and effect of his scriptural knowledge are universalizing. Steven Marx's recent study *Shakespeare and the Bible* (2000), admirable in many respects, tends to reproduce these assumptions, assessing Shakespeare's relationship to scripture mainly in terms of formal dramatic features, moral themes and problems of characterization. And while Marx discusses allusions to both parts of the Bible, he too places greater emphasis on Old Testament texts, the Gospels and Revelation. His consideration of Pauline texts is limited to small parts of Acts and Romans.

THE THEATRICALITY OF PAULINE RHETORIC

The main drawback of studies such as Baldwin's is that they focus rather mechanically on Shakespeare's early formation as a writer rather than as

---

[20] *Shakespeare's Biblical Knowledge and Use of the Book of Common Prayer* (London, 1935), p. 43.

[21] 'Shakespeare's Knowledge of the Bible', pp. 210–11.

[22] *Biblical References in Shakespeare's Tragedies*, p. 36; *Biblical References in Shakespeare's History Plays*, pp. 23–4; *Biblical References in Shakespeare's Comedies*, pp. 25–6. See also Milward, *Shakespeare's Religious Background*, p. 86.

[23] *Shakespeare's Religious Background*, p. 102, citing Noble, p. 43, and Baldwin, I. 687.

[24] Jonathan Bate, *The Genius of Shakespeare* (London, 1997), pp. 173–80.

an adult creative reader. Tudor grammar schools such as the one Shakespeare attended in Stratford-upon-Avon educated boys chiefly in the arts of rhetoric. The standard curriculum was designed by sixteenth-century humanists John Colet and Desiderius Erasmus to train morally upright and well-spoken candidates for civil administration and the professions. Pupils were taught to learn persuasive arguments and moving styles of eloquence (*ratio* and *oratio*) from classical authorities such as Cicero, then to identify examples in Greek, Latin and biblical texts, and finally to compose and perform original debates and orations.[25] By the time he left school, Shakespeare shared this rhetorical knowledge not only with his European contemporaries but also his ancient Roman counterparts – including the educated Roman citizen and Jew, Paul. Twentieth-century scholars have amply documented the impact of grammar-school rhetoric on the linguistic fluency and critical imagination of playwrights such as Christopher Marlowe and Ben Jonson. In Shakespeare's case, however, connections between this cultural competence and his plays' biblical allusions have been surprisingly neglected owing to the delimiting and/or secularizing assumptions outlined in the previous section. Here Marlowe provides a corrective, if characteristically flamboyant, analogy for Shakespeare and his educated contemporaries as imaginative readers of scripture. According to Richard Baines and Thomas Kyd, Marlowe described Paul as a 'juggler' (i.e. someone who used rhetoric duplicitously) and thought the apostles to be 'neither of wit nor worth . . . only Paul had wit' (i.e. persuasive eloquence).[26] Setting aside his intention to shock, Marlowe is showing off his grammar-school training: he judges the apostles' writings according to their verbal dexterity and purity of Greek usage and finds Paul's (ambiguously) superior. Implicitly Marlowe recognized that Paul's social identity shifted in response to local auditors and that his protean gifts were theatrical. Such traits, I suggest, also explain Shakespeare's career-long interest in Pauline rhetoric and ideas: e.g. the Ephesian setting and marital dilemma of 'one flesh' in the face of extramarital sex in *The Comedy of Errors* (of

which more below);[27] the St Paul-avowing and ironically shape-shifting Richard of Gloucester; Erasmian arguments deriving partly from Paul supporting the moral and economic benefits of peace over war that appear throughout the English history plays; Hamlet's scepticism about the value of Western introspective conscience associated with Paul through Augustine and Luther; Isabella's moving appeals to Pauline principles of equitable justice in *Measure for Measure*; or Paulina, who opposes tyrannical misogyny in *The Winter's Tale* by transforming Paul's traditional negativity towards women's public speech into righteous female eloquence.

The Marlowe anecdote further indicates the potential for independent critical responses to dramatic appropriations of scripture by educated early modern audiences. Colet, Erasmus, Sir Thomas More and other humanists in fact reached conclusions about Paul similar to Marlowe's, albeit deferentially. They admired and emulated his witty 'language of accommodation' and 'often and soden chaunge of persones' (or 'change of masks', as a modern English translation puts it); i.e. shifting verbal registers and strategic impersonations designed to mollify or refute the positions of opponents.[28] The huge output of humanist

---

[25] Baldwin, *William Shakspere's Small Latine & Lesse Greeke*, vol. 1; Brian Vickers, *Classical Rhetoric in English Poetry* (London, 1970).

[26] Millar Maclure, *Marlowe: The Critical Inheritance* (London, 1979), pp. 35, 37.

[27] Shakespeare returned to the marital concept of one-flesh repeatedly. To cite just a few instances: *Hamlet* 4.3.52; *All's Well That Ends Well* 1.3.47–8; *Pericles* 5.3.46.

[28] John Colet, *An Exposition of St. Paul's Epistle to the Romans*, trans. J. H. Lupton (London, 1873), p. 55; *An Exposition of St. Paul's First Epistle to the Corinthians*, trans. J. H. Lupton (London, 1874), pp. 8–9; Desiderius Erasmus, *Paraphrase on the Acts of the Apostles* in *Collected Works of Erasmus*, vol. 50, ed. John J. Bateman, trans. Robert D. Sider (Toronto, 1995), pp. 108 (alluding to 1 Corinthians 9.19–22), 114; 'Argument to Romans' and 'Argument to Ephesians', in *The seconde tome or volume of the Paraphrase of Erasmus vpon the newe testamente* (1549), sigs. a4v, AA1r; *Paraphrases on Romans and Galatians*, in *Collected Works of Erasmus*, vol. 42, ed. Robert D. Sider, trans. John B. Payne, Albert Rabil Jr and Warren S. Smith Jr (Toronto, 1984), p. 13.

sermons, commentaries, treatises and public correspondence popularized this image of 'cunnyng
craftesman[ship]' and role-playing.[29] Like some
readers, however, both lay and clerical, Shakespeare
recognized the ambiguities of Paul's protean identity in ironic portrayals such as 'honest Iago', who
deploys the Pauline strategy of improvised retrospective argument to 'prove' alleged but unwit-
nessed events.[30]

LETTER–WRITING AND
LETTER–READING

Another major focus of the Tudor curriculum
which shaped Shakespeare's and other readers'
understanding of the New Testament was letter-
writing. Epistolary pedagogy was a high priority on
the edifying agenda of Renaissance humanists, and
Paul's letters exemplified their favoured meeting-
place of classical rhetoric and Christian ethics.[31]
Lynne Magnusson has shown how Shakespeare's
formal education in letter-writing, systematically
exemplified by Erasmus's *De Conscribendis Episto-
lis* (1522), introduced the playwright to constructions of dynamic social identity which shaped the
dialogic character of his dramatic language.[32] The
same training allowed Shakespeare and his contemporaries to read Paul's epistles as situationally interactive transactions among writers, scribes, messengers and listeners/readers.[33] Erasmus had differentiated these social functions in a series of prefaces
to Paul's epistles in his *Paraphrases on the New Testament* (1547), copies of which were required by successive Tudor governments to be placed in every
English parish church, and which circumstantial
evidence indicates were widely read.[34] Erasmus not
only drew attention to problems of provenance,
authenticity, transmission and reception, but also
outlined the epistles' historical contexts of political and religious controversy, thereby destabilizing literal and traditional readings.[35] By popularizing the results of his philological and historical
research, Erasmus's *Paraphrases* gave common readers new mental categories for interpreting Paul's
words independently.[36]

Shakespeare's understanding of Paul's letters as
rhetorically crafted responses to social and religious controversies is evident in the rival arguments of Luciana and Adriana over patriarchal

29 'Argument to Romans', in *The seconde tome or volume of the
Paraphrase of Erasmus vpon the newe testamente*, sig. a2v. Citing
Origen in the same passage, Erasmus says that the overall
effect of Paul's role-playing is that he seems like a trickster
who leads readers into a labyrinth where they 'neither seeth,
where [Paul] came in, nor yet well knoweth, which way to
go out'. See also *Annotations on Romans* in *Collected Works
of Erasmus*, vol. 56, ed. Robert D. Sider and John B. Payne
(Toronto, 1994), p. 37.

30 In a different perspective on Paul's idea of becoming all things
to all men, Knapp argues that Shakespeare's fellow actors
appropriated the language of homiletic accommodation and
ecclesiastical communion to deflect anti-theatrical criticism
and develop an inclusive image of dramatic good fellowship
(*Shakespeare's Tribe*, ch. 1, pp. 23–57, especially pp. 32–9).

31 Baldwin, *William Shakspere's Small Latine & Lesse Greeke*,
vol. 2; Judith Henderson, 'Erasmus on the Art of Letter-
Writing', *Renaissance Eloquence*, ed. J. Murphy (Berkeley,
1983), pp. 331–55.

32 Lynne Magnusson, *Shakespeare and Social Dialogue* (Cambridge, 1999).

33 For an illuminating modern discussion of these issues, see
E. Randolph Richard, *Paul and First-Century Letter Writing*
(Downers Grove, IL, 2004).

34 Hilmar M. Pabel and Mark Vessey, eds., *Holy Scripture Speaks:
The Production and Reception of Erasmus' Paraphrases on the New
Testament* (Toronto, 2002), pp. 19–21. In the same volume,
John Craig documents copies of the *Paraphrases* in three
parishes associated with Shakespeare's London residences:
St Michael Wood Street (Nathan Field); St Olave's Silver
Street (Mountjoys); and St Saviour's Southwark ('Forming
a Protestant Consciousness? Erasmus' *Paraphrases* in English
Parishes 1547–1666', pp. 350–2).

35 In his Argument to 1 Corinthians, for example, Erasmus
questions whether the order of certain passages is correct (sig.
Aaiir); in the Arguments to 1 and 2 Thessalonians he raises the
more radical possibility of co-authorship (sig. AAAa1r). Such
questions of textual instability sound familiar to modern
Shakespearians. For comparable approaches in New Testament studies see, for example, Richard A. Horsley, ed., *Paul
and Politics: Ekklesia, Israel, Imperium, Interpretation* (Harrisburg, PA, 2000).

36 Erasmus seems to have regarded the opening up of diverse
readings among lay-readers as a desirable opportunity for collective debate. By contrast, the *Paraphrase* prologues or prefaces written by Miles Coverdale and Jonathan Olde admit
no keys to, or questions of, historical or textual criticism.
Their rhetorical mode is uniformly moral and didactic.

authority and gender equality in *The Comedy of Errors*, 2.1. As they wait for the tardy Antipholus of Ephesus to return home for dinner, the sisters debate the question of a husband's personal freedom and authority over his wife. Editors have long noted how their opposing positions allude to passages in Ephesians and other scriptural texts. They have not directed much attention to the original rhetorical context of Paul's letter, however, and, specifically, the patterned alternation of often-quoted commands he gives to wives and husbands at 5.21–33.[37] These form part of the epistle's wider prescription of traditional domestic hierarchies (viz. husbands and wives, parents and children, masters and slaves). Luciana's model of universal degrees in nature mandating female subordination in marriage (2.1.16–25)[38] elaborates Paul's well-known admonition that wives should 'submit to' and 'feare' their husbands (Ephesians 5.22–4, 33).[39] Adriana's complaints about her husband's neglect and mistreatment, here and again 'directly' in her pleas to Antipholus of Syracuse at 2.2.113–49, allude to Paul's rules for husbands based on two metaphorically linked concepts: Christ's headship of the church based on self-sacrificing love, and marriage as a union of one flesh (originating in Genesis 2.24):

Housbands, loue your wiues, euen as Christ loued the Church, & gaue him self for it.

So oght men to loue their wiues, as their owne bodies: he that loueth his wife, loueth him self.

Therefore . . . let euerie one loue his wife, euen as him self. (Ephesians 5.25, 28, 33)[40]

Ephesians juxtaposes the radically new concept of universal equality based on Christian love with the patriarchal social order of Hellenistic Judaism and classical antiquity.[41] While Western Christianity resolved this fundamental contradiction in favour of Jewish and Roman custom,[42] Adriana's position reflects the subversive reading of Ephesians 5 put forward by some early modern English women, after the Reformation encouraged ordinary people to read Paul's letters for themselves. One such reader was Dorothy Leigh, author of a popular

family advice book, *The Mother's Blessing*, reissued nineteen times between 1616 and 1640. Her discussions echo Adriana's argument that the Judaeo-Christian law of one flesh obliges marriages to function socially and spiritually as equal partnerships. In chapters 12 and 13 on a husband's conduct, Leigh advises her son to

marry with none, except you loue her, and be not changeable in your loue; let nothing, after you haue made your choise, remoue your loue from her (sig. C7r)

If shee bee thy wife, she is always to good to be thy seruant, and worthy to be thy fellow. (sig. D1r)

Recalling the alternatives of Ephesians 5, Leigh interprets the Protestant theory of companionate marriage as mutuality and not just complementarity, and she anticipates Mary Wollstonecraft's famous complaint about wives being no better than 'upper-servants', which is essentially Adriana's criticism too.[43] Both Leigh and *The Comedy*

---

[37] Made more conspicuous typographically by the unusual use of paragraph signs (¶) before 'Wiues' (line 22) and 'Husbands' (line 25).

[38] All Shakespeare quotations are taken from *The Complete Works*, ed. Stanley Wells, Gary Taylor, John Jowett and William Montgomery, 2nd edn (Oxford, 2005), except for *Pericles*, ed. Roger Warren (Oxford, 2003).

[39] Similarly, Colossians 3.18–41, 1 Peter 3.1–11.

[40] *The Geneva Bible, a facsimile of the 1560 edition*, intro. Lloyd E. Berry (Madison, 1975). All quotations are taken from this edition.

[41] Elisabeth Schüssler Fiorenza, *In Memory of Her: A Feminist Theological Reconstruction of Christian Origins* (New York, 1983), pp. 269–70. Paul's most famous statement of universal social equality is Galatians 3.28.

[42] This remains the dominant reading. Compare, for instance, the concept of marriage defined by one standard American reference work, *The Guide to American Law: Everyone's Legal Encyclopedia*, 12 vols. (St Paul, MN, 1983–5): 'The traditional legal principle upon which the institution of marriage is founded is that a husband has the obligation to support a wife and a wife has the duty to serve' (VII. 275).

[43] The principle of equality recurs prominently throughout Leigh's *Mother's Blessing*. In chapter 11 on rearing children, for example, unlike traditional advice books to children, Leigh refrains from differentiating between sons or daughters in terms of her advice about appropriate reading material, schooling or choice of vocation.

of Errors demonstrate, moreover, how rhetorically attuned readings of Paul's letters by early modern readers and writers anticipate the reconstructive methodologies and historicist criticism of present-day theologians.[44]

Through both humanist education and publicly accessible models, Shakespeare and his scripturally literate audiences acquired new tools to analyse the meanings and authority of biblical texts. And when he relocated their ideas to the ethical and situational conflicts of his dramatic fictions, Shakespeare tested their human motives and psychology in collaboration with his scripturally discerning audiences. In Marina's founding of an income-generating house of virtuous women in Pericles, to cite a further example, Shakespeare dramatized concepts of female community leadership and openly embodied spirituality, which are discernible in Paul's verbal anticipations of the submerged voices of his opponents in 1 Corinthians.

MARINA, PAULINE RHETORIC AND FEMALE SPIRITUALITY

The biblical aspects of Marina's rhetoric have, as far as I know, not yet been explored, and neither have her subversions of Pauline ideology. Modern critical interest in the scattering and reunion of Pericles's family has tended to keep attention focused on Marina's relationship with her father and mother, rather than on what she represents or achieves in her own right. This is particularly true of the brothel scenes.[45] Marina ultimately survives by using persuasive speech to defend her body from personal violence and a degrading sexual ethos of economic utility.[46] She also changes the moral outlook and material lives of others in Mytilene, beginning with the three gentlemen clients we see leaving the brothel at the beginning of scene 19 (traditionally numbered 4.5), by 'preaching divinity' and 'freezing the god Priapus' (i.e. delegitimizing male sexual desire and local idols). Her piety is rhetorical and charismatic: 'she has me

her quirks, her reasons, her master reasons, her prayers, her knees' (16–17), complains the Bawd. Part of the moment's humour lies in Jacobean spectators' awareness that Marina's skills contradict one of Paul's most (in)famous prohibitions against women teaching or speaking publicly on religious matters.[47]

Marina's powers of conversion are more severely tested by the arrival of Lysimachus, governor of Lesbos. Their confrontation begins with the discrepancy between her real and apparent sexual status before turning to Lysimachus's political authority. At this point the original quarto text becomes confusing because Lysimachus claims he did not come to the brothel with a 'corrupted mind' or 'ill intent', and yet Marina's two short speeches so amaze him that his intentions change. As Philip Edwards observed:

after what is really only a passionate and inarticulate cry [in the quarto text], [Lysimachus] is marvelling at [Marina's] eloquence . . . What we need is amplification of these ejaculations into really persuasive arguments.[48]

---

[44] For example: Elisabeth Schüssler Fiorenza, 'Women in the Pre-Pauline and Pauline Churches', Union Seminary Quarterly Review, 33 (1978), 153–66; In Memory of Her; Lauri Thurén, De-Rhetorizing Paul (Harrisburg, PA, 2002); Antoinette Clark Wire, The Corinthian Women Prophets: A Reconstruction Through Paul's Rhetoric (Minneapolis, MN, 1990); Ben Witherington, Women and the Genesis of Christianity, ed. Ann Witherington (Cambridge, 1990).

[45] Pre-twentieth-century productions were scandalized by their sexual candour. Modern ones tend to caricature them as sexual farce (Roger Warren, ed., Pericles, p. 50).

[46] In Suzanne Gossett's words, the 'end of Pericles is calculated to keep the focus on parental love rather than restored marital happiness' (ed., Pericles (London, 2004), p. 145). The latter, as Roger Warren further notes, is the dramatic point of the final scene, but it tends to be theatrically discounted in performance.

[47] 'Let your women keepe silence in the Churches: for it is not permitted vnto them to speake, but they ought to be subiect, as also the Law saith. / And if they will learne any thing, let them ask their husbands at home: for it is a shame for a woman to speake in the Church' (1 Corinthians 14.34–5).

[48] 'An Approach to the Problem of Pericles', Shakespeare Survey 5 (Cambridge, 1952), p. 44, cited in Warren, ed., Pericles, p. 50.

The quarto fails to substantiate how or why Lysimachus's conversion happens. Wilkins's *Painful Adventures* (1608), which derives partly from the original play, supplies Marina's missing arguments, and on this assumption both the Oxford *Complete Works* and Roger Warren's Oxford Shakespeare edition restore Marina's speeches to the scene. The 'divinity' in her preaching, originally audible to Jacobean spectators, also becomes more visible to us.

Lysimachus initially positions himself as an early modern tyrant by justifying his powers according to personal whims of 'displeasure' or 'pleasure'. Marina challenges him using a version of what Lynne Magnusson calls 'rebuke and repair' rhetoric, in which early modern letter-writers aiming to criticize a higher-status recipient simultaneously softened any impressions of offence or impertinence, and levelled social differences between the speaker and hearer – a mitigating strategy of reprimand and soothing familiarity equally characteristic of Paul's epistles:[49]

> My lord, I entreat you but to hear me.
> If as you say you are the governor,
> Let not authority which teaches you
> To govern others be the means
> To make you misgovern much yourself.
> If you were born to honour show it now;
> If put upon you, make the judgement good
> That thought you worthy of it. (scene 19, 103–10)

Marina tempers her assertiveness with implicit praise of Lysimachus's nobler self-image. She distinguishes carefully between this imagined identity and his potential misdeed – a division already signified theatrically by his arrival in disguise – and then persuades the 'true' Lysimachus to embrace the virtue they both share (111–48). In epistolary pedagogy this kind of 'strategic presumption' was gendered masculine;[50] by deploying it successfully, Marina not only refashions the power imbalance between herself and Lysimachus but also appropriates the masculine apostolic voice associated with the rhetoric's Pauline exemplars.[51]

Her words also point Jacobean spectators in the direction of wider political arguments. Marina calls upon Lysimachus to treat his subjects on the basis of the same principles from which he derives his right to govern. She supposes these powers could derive from either primogeniture or public consent – a contentious choice of alternatives under James, author of *The True Law of Free Monarchies* (1598). Morally, obedience to Lysimachus is contingent on his own just and reasonable behaviour.[52] London playgoers had recently heard arguments similar to Marina's rehearsed by Isabella in *Measure for Measure* (2.2.111–30). They were even more widely known from frequent sermons on its controversial scriptural warrant, Romans 13.1: 'Let euery soule bee subiect vnto the higher powers: for there is no power but of God: and the powers that bee, are ordained of God.' Marina's confrontation with Lysimachus implicitly makes Paul's call to obey public authorities contingent on evaluation of a just relationship between rulers and the governed, rather than on divine fiat. From at least the 1580s onward, Puritans and others had argued that ungodly rulers could be challenged or corrected by the will of the people acting through Parliament. Before then, humanist scholars such as John Colet had revolutionized scriptural hermeneutics by relating the meaning of Paul's words to the 'crisis' of Roman Jewish Christians who were facing punitive taxes and expulsion under the emperor Claudius.[53] In this context, Paul's advice in Romans 13 to lie low and obey civil

---

[49] Magnusson, *Shakespeare and Social Dialogue*, pp. 68–74.

[50] Magnusson, *Shakespeare and Social Dialogue*, p. 72.

[51] See, for instance, the echoes of Galatians 4 in 'Make me your servant, I willingly obey you, / Make me your bondmaid, I'll account it freedom' (scene 19, 138–9).

[52] Wilkins clarifies this point further (Warren, ed., *Pericles*, p. 288).

[53] *An Exposition of St. Paul's Epistle to the Romans*, trans. Lupton, pp. 1–2, 91–103. The Geneva translation avoids historical specificity: 'And that, considering the season, that *it is* now time that we should arise from sleepe: for now is our saluation neerer, then when we believed it' (Romans 13.11); and its marginal note is comparably vague, 'An application taken of the circumstance of the time'.

laws was prudently tactical, not a universal ethic. Neither Shakespeare nor Wilkins probably knew Colet's famous *Exposition of Romans* directly,[54] but they may have encountered its innovative historicism through his friend Erasmus, who incorporated Colet's methodology in his *Paraphrase on Romans* (1547) and other writings.[55]

The effects of Marina's 'reformation[s]'[56] do not end in the brothel but determine the play's future political and marital alliances, beginning with Lysimachus in his capacity as governor. As he rounds on Bolt while leaving the brothel, his outrage recalls Vincentio's spluttering indignation after seeing 'corruption boil and bubble / Till it o'errun the stew' (*Measure for Measure*, 5.1.315–16). But unlike Vienna's Duke, Lysimachus takes practical steps to remedy such problems by paying Marina for her 'holy words'. He substitutes a virtuous circle for the vicious one Bolt continues to defend with surprisingly forceful eloquence.[57] Marina dispels Bolt's topically resonant fears of unemployment and starvation by transferring Lysimachus's gold.[58] Bolt will now tout her new foundation – a kind of ladies' academy and cottage industry rolled into one. Her skills are conventional to early modern English gentlewomen – singing, weaving, sewing and dancing. But rather than being merely decorative, they actively generate an income for her house. Her teaching, moreover, includes 'other virtues which I'll keep from boast'. The dramatic context suggests these are related to the persuasive rhetoric she has used to convert Lysimachus and will now use publicly to 'dumb' 'deep clerks'.[59] Marina's Pauline/Erasmian 'language of accommodation' tailors her roles and messages to meet the knowledge and status of diverse listeners in Mytilene.

But Marina's Pauline associations also become more complex as the immediate threat to her physical safety recedes. As her community of virtuous women thrives, Marina's bounty flows non-judgementally back to the brothel – surprisingly, even to the 'cursèd Bawd'. Her motive seems to be kindness, and perhaps conversion. Audiences may connect this impulse to the *caritas* which moved her father to relieve the famine at Tarsus in scene 4 (2.1), a story she has heard

from her nurse Lychorida before Dionyza turned on them both. Yet Gower's 'story' insists that Marina's ethos is gendered differently from the personally sacrificing love of 1 Corinthians 13 or her father's *noblesse*: 'She sings like one immortal, and she dances / As goddess-like to her admirèd lays' (20.3–4). Freed from the brothel's dangers, Marina's wisdom finds confident expression in the ecstatic female body. Dervish-like in her sensibility, she rejects the body–soul binary of Hellenized Judaism and Western Christianity that imposed a self-shaming discipline on prophetic women and female speech.[60] Marina's divine gifts

---

[54] Though reprinted and widely circulated during the sixteenth century, it remained untranslated from Latin into English until 1873 (ed. Lupton).

[55] *Paraphrases on Romans and Galatians*, ed. Sider, trans. Payne et al., pp. xiv–xix.

[56] As Wilkins calls them in *Painful Adventures*, sig. H4r.

[57] His topical speech at 19.219–21 ('What would you have me do?') is not paralleled in *Painful Adventures*.

[58] Marina never answers Bolt's arguments directly. In *Painful Adventures* the brothel keepers 'first tak[e] away the golde which [Lysimachus's] charitie (and not injury of all who had beene there) had giuen her to releeue her with' (sig. H4r). But Marina has previously kept some in reserve and uses it to pay Bolt (sig. I1r).

[59] Scene 20, line 5. *Painful Adventures* is more explicit, yet also revealing, about Shakespeare's additions and different interpretation of Marina's knowledge. At this point she states, 'I am skilfull in the seauen Liberall Sciences, well exercised in all studies, and dare approve this, that my skill in singing and playing on Instruments exceeds any in the citty' (sig. I1r). Bolt advertises 'her excellencie in speaking, and in singing' (sig. I1v), and later, when the stricken Pericles arrives at the harbour, Lysimachus 'sodainely remembring the wisedom that he had known *Marina* had in persuasion: and hauing heard since of her excellent skill in musicke, singing, and dauncing: he ... caused her to be sent for' (sig. I3v). Marina's teachable and profit-making skills in needlework and weaving are thus Shakespeare's inventions, as is Gower's report that her audiences admire her singing and dancing as 'goddess-like' expressions. For gendered differences from medieval versions of the story, see also Elizabeth Archibald, '"Deep clerks she dumbs": The Learned Heroine in *Apollonius of Tyre* and *Pericles*', *Comparative Drama*, 22 (1988–9), 289–303.

[60] In his *Historical Commentary on Galatians* (London, 1899), William Ramsay suggests that ancient rites of the Anatolian mother-goddess Cybele, ancestor of the Near Eastern Artemis/Diana, lie beneath the ecstatic dance-worship of

and unselfconscious physical integrity recall the religion and iconography of the play's 'presiding deity',[61] the physically revitalizing Diana/Artemis in her Near-Eastern identity as earth-mother goddess – an identity Erasmus distinguished clearly from 'Diana the huntour, vnto whome the Poetes attribute bowe and arrowes' in his Argument to the *Paraphrase on Ephesians*.[62]

As she becomes identified with Diana of Ephesus, Marina's practices mirror those of Paul's opponents in letters such as 1 Corinthians. Her openly embodied spirituality, for example, recalls that of the Corinthian women, who represent a threat to patriarchal headship and liturgical decorum in Paul's letter.[63] The apostle's arguments point to their alternative ideas of human bodies freely exercising re-creative energies of the materially integrated divine. Paul associates house-churches led by local leaders such as Priscilla and Aquila, who were based in Ephesus as well as Corinth, with this kind of spontaneous and under-regulated spiritual practice (1 Corinthians 16.19; Romans 16.5).[64] Priscilla and Aquila originally taught the Alexandrian Jew Apollos (Acts 18.18, 27), who had become Paul's powerful competitor in Corinth at the time he wrote his letter (1 Corinthians 1.12).[65] Paul's strategy consisted partly of challenging Apollos's ascendancy indirectly by advocating a social model based on his preferences for patriarchally ordered, sex-specific rituals.[66] Invoking his authority as an apostle, Paul called ultimately for these Corinthian spiritual women to be domestically segregated and submissive.

Shakespeare, by contrast, directs Marina's influence outward from her house into the community. She and one of her 'companion maid[s]' first stir Marina's father out of his catatonic state with their song. This prepares him to hear the heavenly music following his recognition of Marina as his daughter, and to receive Diana's vision that will lead to his final reunion with Thaisa in the goddess's temple at Ephesus. Traditional criticism tends to link Pericles's revelations to his personal discipline, visually coded by his unshaven head, and/or his psychological doubling of Thaisa through Marina. But Marina also journeys into social power and

higher consciousness through persuasive speech and charismatic fellowship. In the context of the play's wider Pauline associations, she valorizes the local customs of Paul's opponents, in particular the female-centred traditions of pre-Pauline

---

the Mevlevi Dervishes (cited in H. V. Morton, *In the Steps of St Paul* (London, 1936), p. 166). As Maurice Hunt observes in 'Shakespeare's *Pericles* and the Acts of the Apostles', the play's dialogue and action repeatedly 'cross over major historical thresholds', and 'suggest that Shakespeare is not trying to fix the events of *Pericles* in an exact cultural moment or century in the ancient world' (*Christianity and Literature*, 49 (2000), 296, 301).

[61] Warren, ed., *Pericles*, p. 221, n. 225.2; Gossett, ed., *Pericles*, p. 117.

[62] *The seconde tome or volume of the Paraphrase of Erasmus vpon the newe testamente*, sig. AA1r. The Ephesian goddess was 'Diana with many pappes, whome the Grecians call Polymaston, and saye, she is the nource of all manner of beastes'. Shakespeare combines attributes of both Dianas in *Pericles*. For further discussion, see F. Elizabeth Hart, '"Great is Diana" of Shakespeare's Ephesus', *Studies in English Literature 1500–1900*, 43 (2003), 347–74; R. Martin, 'Rediscovering Artemis in *The Comedy of Errors*', in *Shakespeare and the Mediterranean: The Selected Proceedings of the International Shakespeare Association World Congress, Valencia, 2001*, ed. Tom Clayton, Susan Brock and Vicente Forés (Newark, 2004), pp. 363–79.

[63] Wire, *Corinthian Women Prophets*, ch. 6, pp. 116–34. 'Dare any of you, hauing busines against another, bee iudged vnder the vniust, and not vnder the Saints?' / 'The wife hath not the power of her owne body, but the husband; and likewise also the husband hath not the power of his owne body, but the wife.' / 'There is difference also betweene a virgin and a wife: the vnmarried woman careth for the things of the Lord, that she may be holy both in body and spirit: but she that is maried, careth for the things of the world . . .' / 'But euery woman that prayeth or prophecieth bare headed, dishonoureth her head' (1 Corinthians 6.1, 7.4, 7.34, 11.5).

[64] Wire, *Corinthian Women Prophets*, ch. 7, pp. 135–58. Household churches provided essential physical and spiritual sustenance for first-century Christians and were often led and organized by relatively well-off women in the community. In Corinth as elsewhere, their locally authorized customs and independence sometimes clashed with the imported ideas of itinerant preachers such as Paul. See Witherington, *Woman and the Genesis of Christianity*, pp. 180–5; Schüssler Fiorenza, *In Memory of Her*, pp. 175–84.

[65] Schüssler Fiorenza, 'Women in the Pre-Pauline and Pauline Churches', pp. 153–66.

[66] 'For this cause haue I sent vnto you Timotheus . . . which shal put you in remembrance of my wayes in Christ' (1 Corinthians 4.17).

Corinth and pre-Christian Ephesus. Dramatically, her actions prepare Jacobean audiences for Paulina's more audacious opposition and spiritualized re-creations in *The Winter's Tale*. And as I have tried briefly to show here, they illustrate some of critical possibilities that a biographically reoriented and rehistoricized perspective on Shakespeare's scriptural associations might generate.[67]

---

[67] I am grateful to the Social Sciences and Humanities Research Council of Canada for supporting the research undertaken in this article.

FILLING IN THE 'WIFE-SHAPED VOID': THE CONTEMPORARY AFTERLIFE OF ANNE HATHAWAY

KATHERINE SCHEIL

Shakespeare's domestic life has been the subject of much recent scholarly and creative interest. At least three new plays have appeared in the last decade with his wife Anne Hathaway at the centre, and Germaine Greer's biography (*Shakespeare's Wife*, 2007) has similarly generated intense discussion. Anne Hathaway wrote nothing that survives (if she was in fact literate), few material details remain about the realities of her life and no representations exist of what she looked like. Yet, just as Shakespeare has been used for a variety of social, cultural and political causes, so too has his wife been appropriated, perhaps more easily because she lacks a body of creative work with which adapters must grapple and there are few stable points of reference for her. To some degree, anyone writing about Anne Hathaway (whether biographer, scholar, novelist, etc.) must invent material to fill in the gaps of her life story, and some of the most recent examples have constructed her in relation to contemporary life.

Married to one of the most famous men in history and firmly entrenched in the world of domesticity through the preservation (and global proliferation) of her famous cottage, the afterlife of Anne Hathaway is ideal for articulating the relationship between husband and wife, and between domestic responsibility and the workplace, in scholarly and imaginative works alike.[1] Three stage versions of Shakespeare's domestic life: Avril Rowlands's *Mrs Shakespeare . . . The Poet's Wife* (2005), Vern Thiessen's *Shakespeare's Will* (2002) and Amy Freed's *The Beard of Avon* (2001) have used Shakespeare's marriage, and particularly the 'wife-shaped

void' of Anne Hathaway, as a canvas for expressing contemporary women's struggles – over independence, single motherhood, sexual freedom, unfaithful husbands, child care, women's education and the power relations between husband and wife.[2] Likewise, Germaine Greer's 2007 biography

---

[1] Anne Hathaway's cottage is her central symbolic image, perhaps because we lack any illustration of the woman herself. The Hathaway cottage also functions as a portable representation of Shakespearian domesticity in a wide variety of locales around the world, including Anne Hathaway Cottages in Green Lake, Wisconsin; Wessington, South Dakota; Perth, Australia; Victoria, British Columbia; and Anne Hathaway's B&B and Garden Suites in Ashland, Oregon. Nicola J. Watson provides an excellent discussion of Anne Hathaway's cottage in 'Shakespeare on the Tourist Trail', in *The Cambridge Companion to Shakespeare and Popular Culture*, ed. Robert Shaughnessy (Cambridge, 2007), pp. 199–226. See also Marjorie Garber, *Profiling Shakespeare* (New York, 2008) and Barbara Hodgdon, *The Shakespeare Trade: Performances and Appropriations* (Philadelphia, 1998). In 'The Second Best Bed and the Legacy of Anne Hathaway', I offer an overview of how Hathaway's afterlife has been constructed in relation to the infamous bed and its associations of sexuality and domesticity: *Critical Survey*, 21.3 (2009), 59–71.

[2] For summaries of the many fictional works about Shakespeare, see Douglas Lanier, *Shakespeare and Modern Popular Culture* (Oxford, 2002) and 'Shakespeare™: Myth and Biographical Fiction', in *The Cambridge Companion to Shakespeare and Popular Culture*, ed. Robert Shaughnessy (Cambridge, 2007); Maurice J. O'Sullivan, 'Shakespeare's Other Lives', *Shakespeare Quarterly*, 38 (1987), 133–53; and Samuel Schoenbaum's *Shakespeare's Lives* (New York, 1970). Enno Ruge's article '"We Begin to be interested in Mrs. S.": Male Representations of Anne Hathaway in Fictional Biographies of Shakespeare', *Zeitschrift für Anglistik und Amerikanistik*, 50 (2002), 411–22, focuses on James Joyce's *Ulysses* (1922), Anthony Burgess's *Nothing Like the Sun* (1964) and Robert

of Hathaway as well as recent biographies of Shakespeare engage with many of these same issues, and the separation between biography and fiction blurs as writers fill in the 'wife-shaped void' with narratives that fulfil political, social and personal agendas.

In the last decade, several contemporary playwrights (and, to some degree, also biographers) have sought to give meaning to the domestic world of the Shakespeares by taking on concerns of financial security, sexual fulfilment, domestic significance and the balance between home life and the professional world through various constructions of Anne Hathaway. We can perhaps explain some of the 'Anne Hathaways' in these texts by looking at the 'Shakespeares' they produce; this article will explore what these various versions of 'Shakespeare' tell us about the creators and consumers of both fictional works and biographies.[3] If Shakespeare is a 'visual anchor for a body of connotations', to use Douglas Lanier's phrase, which myths and narratives about the Shakespeares' domestic life are disseminated to particular audiences and what's at stake in those representations? Where is the dividing line between biography and imaginative work? And how might we explain the disparity between a recent (2004) best-selling biography of Shakespeare that describes Anne Hathaway as a woman who 'filled [Shakespeare] with revulsion' and 'sour anger', and a play published a year later (2005) that imagines Anne Hathaway as the real author of the Shakespeare plays?[4] I am particularly interested in how forms of 'popular biography' are circulated, both in actual biographies and through biographically based works in other genres, as well as the preoccupation that numerous recent texts have with constructing Shakespeare's domestic life in comparison with biographical works.

VERN THIESSEN'S *SHAKESPEARE'S WILL* (2002)

The circumstances of the Shakespeares' probable long-distance marriage of almost twenty years (from the early 1590s on) have provided a background for exploring and imagining an account of that period. In *Shakespeare's Will* (2002), Canadian playwright Vern Thiessen constructs a lonely and neglected Anne Hathaway, who survived as a single mother for nearly two decades without her husband in permanent residence. Thiessen conveys this solitude by setting up his play as a monologue spoken by Hathaway as the sole character in the play, without a single appearance by Shakespeare (though he exists as a subject of her conversation).[5] Instead of exploring biographical questions about Shakespeare himself, Thiessen focuses on Anne Hathaway, describing his play as 'the journey of a woman who faces adversity, rises above it, and ultimately re-kindles faith in herself'.[6] *Shakespeare's Will* recasts the poet's domestic life into a familiar narrative for a twenty-first-century audience, a sort of inspirational 'Chicken Soup for the Lonely Married Woman' based on the Shakespeare marriage.

In this play, despite her unfulfilling marriage, Anne Hathaway is a self-sufficient and resourceful woman. Thiessen invents a relationship of mutual sexual gratification and companionship between

---

Nye's *Mrs Shakespeare* (1993). The 'wife-shaped void' is Germaine Greer's term from *Shakespeare's Wife* (London, 2007), p. 4.

[3] See, for example, Graham Holderness, *Cultural Shakespeare: Essays in the Shakespeare Myth* (Hertfordshire, 2002), p. 4. Douglas Lanier provides a helpful discussion of the Shakespeare 'franchise' in 'Shakespeare™: Myth and Biographical Fiction', pp. 94–5.

[4] Stephen Greenblatt, *Will in the World: How Shakespeare Became Shakespeare* (New York, 2004), pp. 129, 387. In Avril Rowlands's play *Mrs Shakespeare . . . The Poet's Wife* (2005) Anne Hathaway is the real author of the plays.

[5] As Ann Wilson has put it, Thiessen constructs a 'portrait of the playwright through the imagined memories and musings of his wife'. 'Waves and Wills: Vern Thiessen's *Shakespeare's Will*', *Borrowers and Lenders*, 3 (Fall/Winter 2007). Wilson argues that Thiessen's play 'speaks to contemporary Canada and the shifts in understanding around marriage', and that 'another indication of *Shakespeare's Will*'s Canadianness is Thiessen's refusal to create a portrait of the Bard and so, his refusal to give Shakespeare "center stage"', though I think this is a bit narrow, given the similar concerns of other plays about domestic Shakespeare.

[6] Vern Thiessen, *Shakespeare's Will* (Toronto, 2002), p. 74.

the Shakespeares; they both confess to liking boys, and their secret shared desire bonds them throughout their separate lives:

> We make a vow:
> to wed yes
> but to live
> our own lives.
> To treat each other well
> but allow for our
> separate desires.   (p. 12)

Rather than remaining in Stratford as a passive neglected wife, Anne Hathaway takes advantage of the freedom of a long-distance marriage and engages in an active extra-marital sex life: 'I have only now discovered / being married / it is far more respectable to have many lovers' (p. 35). Thiessen does not cast Hathaway as a lascivious and adulterous wife, as is the case in numerous other texts; he sets her pursuit of sexual fulfilment amid a mutual agenda that both partners attain independently.[7]

One of the topics that Thiessen tackles is the sacrifice made by Hathaway to allow Shakespeare to have his career, adapting the Shakespeares into a familiar modern paradigm of working husband/stay-at-home mother. At one point, William tells her, 'You give me my work. / You give me my words. / You give me my life, Anne' (p. 43). Yet this is also the story of a woman who has failed in her domestic responsibilities, specifically in her duty to care for her children. During a time of plague, she takes the children to the sea, where their son Hamnet drowns when she looks away for a moment to swat a wasp. At the end of the play, Anne Hathaway learns the contents of Shakespeare's will and interprets the infamous 'second best bed' as a punishment for her failings as a mother. She ends the play with a Malvolio-style curse to Shakespeare: 'To hell. / To hell with your words' (p. 72), a resounding condemnation of his disregard for the sacrifices she has made for him, and the tragic denouement of her domestic life in comparison to his eternal fame. 'Shakespeare' in this play is a vengeful husband who sets up a marriage of convenience so that he can pursue his

artistic life, but at a cost which the play dramatizes. *Shakespeare's Will* was commissioned by the Free Will Players and premiered at the Citadel Theatre in Edmonton, Alberta on 3 February 2005; since then, it has been performed widely, notably at the Stratford Festival (Ontario) in 2007. Theatre audiences seem receptive to a play about a stay-at-home mother's inspirational story of struggle and triumph, even though it contains an unflattering rendering of Shakespeare as a self-interested husband who has little appreciation for the sacrifices his wife made to foster his career.

AVRIL ROWLANDS'S *MRS SHAKESPEARE . . . THE POET'S WIFE* (2005)

Avril Rowlands's two-act play *Mrs Shakespeare . . . The Poet's Wife* (2005) takes up contemporary topics of career and motherhood by portraying Anne Hathaway as a work-at-home mother who manages her household and writes the plays of 'Shakespeare' in her spare time, perhaps the ultimate example of a multi-tasking woman. Rowlands explicitly puts Anne at the centre of the play, noting that 'Anne definitely should remain on stage throughout. It is, after all, her production!'[8] In this version, Anne was a writer before she married

---

7 Three examples might suffice for illustrating the numerous promiscuous and sexually voracious Anne Hathaways. John Brophy's novel *Gentleman of Stratford* (New York, 1939) contains an Anne who is 'tireless in the hot response', prompting Shakespeare to complain that he is 'kept like a stallion for stud' and must take desperate measures to escape before he has 'a family to be counted by the dozen' (pp. 55–6). Edward Fisher's *Shakespeare & Son* (New York, 1962) casts Hathaway as a nanny in the Shakespeare household, who keeps an upper hand by bedding John Shakespeare before marrying his son. Anthony Burgess's *Nothing Like the Sun* (1964) involves an Anne Hathaway whom he describes as a 'sexual monster' in order to produce a Shakespeare who was 'very heavily seduced and, eventually, rendered sick . . . of the varied patterns of heterosexual lust'. Anthony Burgess, 'Genesis and Headache', in *Afterwords*, ed. Thomas McCormack (New York, 1969), p. 36.
8 Avril Rowlands, *Mrs Shakespeare . . . The Poet's Wife* (Malvern, 2005), p. 7.

Shakespeare, and 'tends the farm at Shottery, looks after her younger brothers and sisters and scribbles up in her room – a shocking thing for a woman!' (p. 11). Unlike the many works about Anne Hathaway that construct Stratford as a place of domestic tranquillity, Rowlands recasts Stratford as a site of artistic production, where Anne lays claim to some of her husband's most famous lines: 'I always was a writer . . . stories were there in my head . . . in the fields, in the forest, everywhere there were "tongues in trees, books in the running brooks, sermons in stones and good in everything"' (p. 18).

In Rowlands's account of the Shakespeares' domestic life, 'Shakespeare' is merely a player whose nickname is 'Wandering Willy' for such acts as 'star[ing] down at the rows of tightly-laced bosoms below, wondering which of them was softest to the touch and which you would fondle next' (p. 10). Their marriage is more a business partnership than a companionate relationship; when they meet, Anne tells him, 'I think, Will lad, you and I can do business together' (p. 14). She supplies the plays to make his reputation on the London theatre scene and married him only because he could provide an outlet for her creative work. Rowlands's plot is the antithesis of the narrative of Shakespeare miserably trapped into marrying a calculating and controlling older woman who hinders his artistic career.[9]

In keeping with her revisionist agenda, Rowlands does not hesitate to give Anne Hathaway polemical feminist statements about motherhood and the importance of her work (writing), emphasizing her portrait of Hathaway as a modern work-at-home mother who intersperses her work amid her domestic duties: 'It is said that women are too weak to bear the pains of writing. But what is writing save giving birth, and in this alone we have the edge on men. I wrote when I should have been at my tasks . . . feeding the hens . . . mending the linen . . . busy about the stillroom . . . Like a thief I stole away and hid my scribblings – inside this very bed' (pp. 20–1). As well as giving credit for the Shakespeare canon to his wife, Rowlands attributes to Anne several of the biographical stories about

Shakespeare: she was inspired to write after seeing a group of touring players, for example, and she learns Latin and Greek at school. In this play, the material for rounding out a life of Anne Hathaway is appropriated from the biography of her husband, leaving him with a sketchy existence as a mediocre player who has little literary talent and is dependent on his wife for his reputation as a playwright (and, in turn, his immortality).

Rowlands also incorporates issues of domestic responsibility by making Will the caregiver of their three young children while Anne works:

> *Will (Off-stage).* Anne? Anne? (*Enters.*) Anne, I'll not endure it!
> *Anne.* What?
> *Will.* Three babes and a wife who shuts herself in her room for hours on end! What kind of a wife is that?
> *Anne.* An obedient wife, Will, to have given her husband such fine proofs of her love. (pp. 16–17)

Supporting an untalented aspiring playwright-husband, Anne spends her time in Stratford writing plays which her husband passes off as his own, even penning the sonnet 'My Mistress' Eyes are Nothing Like The Sun' to her friend Alice. Anne is able to dominate her husband because she is the source of his oeuvre, and she does not hesitate to remind him of his inferior place: 'the audience flock to see *my* plays, written, if they did but know it, by a woman's hand, created by a woman's brain . . . You are not the writer, Will. Never forget that. You are a player, playing a part of my devising, dancing to my tune!' Tellingly, his response to this tirade is 'You unman me' (p. 50). Shakespeare must also take up his share of domestic duties so that his wife can work, i.e. compose the plays to make his name. When Queen Elizabeth commands a play about Falstaff in love, Shakespeare begs his wife to compose a play so that he can maintain his reputation as a playwright. Again, she does the work while he attends to the household tasks, ordering him to 'send the maids away. And take the children to Alice' so that she can write in peace (p. 44). He keeps her glass of ale

---

[9] This narrative will be familiar to readers of Stephen Greenblatt's biography *Will in the World*, discussed later in this article.

filled and her candle lit while she labours to write, a reversal of the traditional housewife who supplies her husband with necessary domestic comforts so that he can succeed in the workplace.[10]

Rowlands ends her play by overturning some of the persistent myths about Anne Hathaway as a shrewish and illiterate woman; Anne declares, 'I'm the greatest playwright that never was, but I'll be remembered as the shrew from Stratford who drove her genius husband away to fame and fortune. Anne Hathaway's name will never blaze like a comet to the stars. No. Yours will, even though you could never spell your name the same way twice' (p. 58). Rowlands's version of Anne Hathaway certainly extends beyond plausible belief, but her play is an obvious attempt to give meaning and significance to the domestic aspects of the Shakespeares' life by depicting Anne as a work-at-home mother and 'unmanning' Shakespeare. In turn, by making Shakespeare do his share of domestic labour and making Anne the source of their household income, Rowlands also validates gender equality in the household through an updated version of the Shakespeare marriage.

AMY FREED'S *THE BEARD OF AVON* (2001)

A third play about Shakespeare and his wife, and the most successful of the lot, Amy Freed's play *The Beard of Avon* (2001) depicts an independent-minded Anne Hathaway who exacts revenge against a cheating husband (Shakespeare), amid a tale of Oxfordian authorship. Described in the cast list as 'Lively, illiterate, promiscuous', Hathaway follows Shakespeare to London disguised as a prostitute so that she can torment him: 'He knew me not as his wife, but thought me a wicked whore. He took me to his rooms, and we've scarcely been apart for a week. I've been just AWFUL to him. It's been WONDERFUL. Well, he himself hath taught me cruel inconstancy, since faithful kindness prompted him to flee.' In the process, she discovers his seedy sex life, and they engage in 'wild and stormy expanses of uncharted filth' involving whips and bondage.[11] Freed does not

employ the work-at-home or stay-at-home mother paradigms, but instead devotes her play to the story of a woman's victory over her philandering husband.

Freed's Anne Hathaway gets even with Shakespeare by perhaps committing the ultimate act of Shakespearian adultery: copulating with the Earl of Oxford. When they first meet, Oxford describes her as a 'hot bitch' (p. 52); after discovering that she is Shakespeare's wife, Oxford is even more attracted to her: 'I find my appetite revives! Honor then demands I do the job. Why, e'en now my friend doth feel the horns burst forth upon his brow and knows not why – ' (p. 56). Anne returns to Stratford triumphant over her husband and sexually fulfilled from a 'wicked and a sweet night' that 'showed me what life might be, if only I had not been me' (p. 62). The Earl of Oxford procures both Shakespeare's identity and his wife, in the process revealing Shakespeare as incompetent in bed and on paper.

In addition to the revenge that Anne Hathaway attains in this play, Freed also employs the Shakespeare marriage as a site of negotiation between the competing demands of the household and the workplace; William tells Anne, 'You kill all that gives me pleasure . . . You take from me all heart. And do deprive me of my necessary space!' She in turn accuses him, 'You provide nothing and blame me for it!' Will warns her, 'You have killed my soul already! . . . There is a great spirit in me that thou seekest to subdue – it will rebel' (p. 15). In order

---

[10] We might see Rowlands's play in contrast to Tim Kelly's *Second Best Bed* (1970), which validates Hathaway as a stay-at-home mother whose sacrifices enabled the plays of Shakespeare to be written, and who is rewarded at the end of the play. In this brief skit designed for young girls, Hathaway discovers a love letter from Shakespeare after she has dutifully followed his posthumous instructions to cut open the mattress on the second best bed. Inside she finds a pouch of jewels and a letter praising her for being a supportive wife: 'If you had not been so sympathetic all these years, if you had not sent me on to London when you did, I should very likely have ended a poor farmer and a poorer husband.' Tim Kelly, *Second Best Bed: A Romantic Speculation in One Act for Eight Girls* (New York, 1970), p. 15.

[11] Amy Freed, *The Beard of Avon* (New York, 2004), p. 50.

for Shakespeare to attain his career goals, Anne must give him his 'space', stop demanding that he 'provide' for her and become self-sufficient, both financially and sexually. Thus, in this play the creation of the Shakespeare canon is dependent on a wife who agrees to give her husband his freedom while she manages the household and attends to her own needs, whose only recourse is to cuckold her husband. Though this Anne Hathaway obtains autonomy and sexual satisfaction, she must adhere (though not without a fight) to the domestic role of obedient wife whose submission facilitates her husband's achievements.

The Beard of Avon was commissioned by the South Coast Repertory in Costa Mesa, California, where it premiered in 2001. Since then, it has been performed in such venues as the Vortex in Austin, Texas; the Goodman Theatre in Chicago; City Theater Company in Delaware; the Rorschach Theatre in Washington, DC; Portland Center Stage in Oregon; and Off Broadway at the New York Theater Workshop. The play's popularity gives some indication of its appeal to contemporary audiences, perhaps because of its engagement with contemporary gender politics in the household and its clever employment of the authorship question as a way to produce a sexually satisfied Anne Hathaway.

ANNE HATHAWAY IN BIOGRAPHIES: GERMAINE GREER'S *SHAKESPEARE'S WIFE* (2007)

The predominant 'Anne Hathaway' constructed in recent imaginative texts is a modern woman of sexual desire, at times financially independent, with a domestic life that the work endorses and validates, while often critiquing a 'Shakespeare' who pursues his own career without regard to the domestic costs of such an agenda. The three stage versions under consideration can be linked to a larger effort to rehabilitate Anne Hathaway and validate domesticity through the Shakespeare marriage. Germaine Greer's biography of Anne Hathaway, *Shakespeare's Wife* (2007), picks up on many of the threads from

these stage versions of Hathaway, offering a similar but more extended articulation of feminist concerns through Anne Hathaway.

Both Greer's title and her introduction situate her biography within a larger context of women's issues, extending beyond a more narrow reappraisal of an early modern woman from Stratford. Rather than using the more straightforward title *Anne Hathaway*, Greer's choice of *Shakespeare's Wife* underlines the significance of each of those terms – the cultural cachet and authoritative power associated with the name 'Shakespeare' reveals her desire to chip away at the patriarchal authority represented by Shakespeare. Throughout her biography Greer deliberately uses honorific titles for Shakespeare, frequently referring to him as 'the Bard' and 'the Man of the Millennium', so that he represents the male sex in general as a sort of über male against whom she can argue, rather than a historical figure confined to his own time period. The 'Wife' in Greer's title links Hathaway to a long history of silent 'wives', and in the process redefines the possibilities for understanding the status of wives in the early modern period. Hathaway's probable adherence to the role of silent and submissive wife has prevented us from knowing much about her, and has left open numerous possibilities for conscripting her life to serve other narratives. As Greer puts it, 'By doing the right thing, by remaining silent and invisible, Anne Shakespeare left a wife-shaped void in the biography of William Shakespeare, which later bardolaters filled up with their own speculations, most of which do neither them nor their hero any credit' (p. 4). Biographers of Shakespeare and misogynists (sometimes, as she points out, one and the same) have thus filled in this gap with material to suit a Shakespeare-centred narrative which often devalues both Anne Hathaway and domesticity.

To remedy this, though Greer locates her project in the genre of biography rather than fiction, she nevertheless takes up some of the topics we have seen in the imaginative works discussed earlier in this essay. Like Avril Rowlands's construction of Anne Hathaway as a Renaissance work-at-home mother, for example, Greer suggests that

Stratford was a site not only of domestic space, but also of women's work. She contends that Anne may have provided for her family through some sort of employment and that she was financially self-sufficient, the equivalent of a working single mother: 'Anne Shakespeare could have been confident of her ability to support herself and her children, but not if she had also to deal with a layabout husband good for nothing but spinning verses, who had the right to do as he pleased with any money she could earn.' In Greer's narrative, Hathaway is a self-sufficient woman whose financial acumen may have led her to purchase New Place and even instigate the First Folio project.[12] This account gives meaning to domesticity by associating Anne with some type of household work, while making Shakespeare a 'layabout husband' who does not produce anything of value and exploits the fruit of his wife's labour.

While many reviewers of Greer's work have appreciated her willingness to overturn every stone in Anne Hathaway's life, others have taken on an unusually vitriolic tone. Peter Conrad, for example, attacks Greer's wider agenda, calling her biography 'reckless, baseless', 'grim and gloating', a 'war of attrition against the chromosome-deficient male sex' by a 'spinster professor' with a 'wild-eyed, foamy-lipped enthusiasm' who has a 'sacred rage on behalf of her victimized sisters'.[13] For Conrad, Greer's biography is not so much about the individual woman from Stratford as it is a war against men.

Yet stage plays that tell a parallel (and at times a more blatantly revisionist) story have not received the same type of criticism, even though they have a similar goal of exploring possibilities for Shakespeare's domestic life. Are theatre audiences more willing to accept versions of 'Shakespeare' that validate (and even rehabilitate) Shakespeare's wife, while in the process painting him as a cheating husband, a sham playwright and a vengeful selfish spouse? Is a story such as 'the journey of a woman who faces adversity, rises above it, and ultimately re-kindles faith in herself' (to reiterate Vern Thiessen's description of his play *Shakespeare's Will*) only suitable for a stage audience?

Why should a biography provoke such hostility, whilst these plays seem to have passed unscathed? For some answers, we might look to the way Anne Hathaway is constructed in recent biographies of Shakespeare.

ANNE HATHAWAY IN RECENT BIOGRAPHIES OF SHAKESPEARE

Biographers of course are not immune to imaginative work and participate in disseminating various narratives about Shakespeare's life (and about Anne Hathaway) to a wide audience with expectations that come with the genre of biography. Samuel Schoenbaum, for example, remarked that the 'task of the responsible biographer' is to 'clear away the cobwebs and sift, as disinterestedly as he may, the facts that chance and industry have brought to light'.[14] One could argue that biographers have a more urgent responsibility for the narratives they circulate because the genre of biography comes with the assumption that the biographer is not pursuing an imaginative trajectory at will but rather is 'disinterestedly' adhering to

---

[12] Greer, *Shakespeare's Wife*, pp. 162, 221, 345–6.

[13] Peter Conrad, 'Dr Greer on the Warpath', *The Observer*, 2 September 2007. Other reviews have praised Greer's work; René Weis says 'she dares to think the unthinkable and sometimes it works well' and the book 'does a huge favour to its subject as wife and woman': *The Independent*, 7 September 2007. Jonathan Bate commends the book as 'a marvellous imagining of the life of Shakespeare's wife and a devastating exposure of the misogyny of the male biographers who have disparaged her': *Daily Telegraph*, 7 August 2007. Duncan Wu similarly applauds Greer's work as 'a corrective to the fantasies of her predecessors': 'On Mrs Shakespeare's Kitchen Table', *Daily Telegraph*, 1 September 2007. Katie Roiphe criticizes Greer for romanticizing female independence but concludes that 'Greer's speculations are, for the most part, surprisingly responsible': 'Reclaiming the Shrew', *New York Times*, 27 April 2008. Stanley Wells praises Greer's biography for opening up 'new perspectives' and 'offering alternative hypotheses to many of the all-too-easy assumptions about Shakespeare's wife and his relationship to her': 'Mistress Shakespeare', *New York Review of Books*, 55.6 (17 April 2008).

[14] Samuel Schoenbaum, *William Shakespeare: A Compact Documentary Life* (Oxford, 1977), pp. 75–6.

some version of 'truth'. In addition, I would argue that the uses to which biography is put are much wider than stage plays (like the three I discussed earlier); one does not expect an audience member to rely on a work like Vern Thiessen's *Shakespeare's Will* as a source of information about Shakespeare's life. Biographies remain available to a wide reading public in diverse geographical areas, whereas stage productions depend on either proximity to a theatre performing that play, or to a more narrow set of readers who might obtain a text of the play to read. Even so, biographies share some common ground with these other imaginative works – they both engage in constructing an account of Shakespeare's life, guided by fact, but necessarily inventive to some degree where facts are sparse or inconclusive. Thus, given the many recent efforts to rehabilitate Anne Hathaway in imaginative works, one might expect contemporary biographies of Shakespeare to approach the subject of his domestic life in a similar manner.

Stephen Greenblatt's biography *Will in the World: How Shakespeare Became Shakespeare* (2004) has been praised as 'a beautifully assembled mosaic of Shakespeare's life, work, time, and place'; a 'series of beautifully crafted episodes'; and a 'magnificent digest of our knowledge', among other epithets.[15] Yet *Will in the World* includes one of the harshest and most negative portrayals of Anne Hathaway in the last fifty years, with no apparent regard for the revisionist initiatives we have seen elsewhere in recent depictions of Anne Hathaway.

In her biography, Germaine Greer has already taken Greenblatt to task for this representation, so there is no need to repeat her arguments here. Rather, I am interested in how Greenblatt's portrayal of Anne Hathaway fits in with other ways this famous wife has been imagined, what that might reveal about how Anne Hathaway is constructed for a particular audience, and why perhaps the most widely distributed biography of Shakespeare ever written includes one of the most negative portrayals of Anne Hathaway ever written, in stark contrast to other contemporary narratives about her, both fictional and biographical.

Throughout *Will in the World*, Greenblatt constructs an extended narrative of Shakespeare as an artist trapped in a loveless marriage, miserably yoked to a woman who cannot share his art, from whom he must eventually escape to find love, success and sexual satisfaction. Greenblatt headlines his discussion of Shakespeare's marriage with the foreboding chapter title 'Wooing, Wedding, and Repenting'. In this account, although Shakespeare must have been sexually attracted to Anne, his parents objected to the marriage because he 'was not making a great match'; a reluctant and unwilling Shakespeare was thus 'dragged to the altar' and he viewed his wife with 'distaste, and contempt' (pp. 121, 124, 123).[16] Greenblatt extends his anti-Anne Hathaway diatribe by alleging that she may have 'filled [Shakespeare] with revulsion', that Shakespeare experienced the 'misery of the neglected or abandoned spouse' (pp. 129–30), that Shakespeare 'made a disastrous mistake, when he was eighteen' (p. 140), and that his imagination and experience of love 'flourished outside of the marriage bond' (p. 143). He leaves little room in this story for other possible interpretations of the Shakespeare marriage, and the Anne Hathaway sections have surprisingly little of the conditional language that permeates most other biographies.

In contrast to Greer's biography of Hathaway, which suggests that the domestic world of Stratford may have involved a space for women's work, and the more fanciful depiction of Hathaway in Avril Rowlands's play as the real author of the Shakespeare canon, Greenblatt claims it is likely that

---

[15] Laura Shapiro, 'Greer Tames the Shrew', *Slate*, 31 March 2008; Lois Potter, review in *Shakespeare Quarterly*, 56 (2005), 374; Colin MacCabe, 'The Bard as a Chat-Show Celeb', *The Independent*, 5 November 2004. Of course, *Will in the World* has received its fair share of critiques, most notably Alastair Fowler's review in the *Times Literary Supplement*, 20 February 2005.

[16] Germaine Greer challenges this story; she asserts that Anne 'was a spinster and at her own disposal, but only misogyny would assume on the available evidence that she was pushing for the marriage and Will was resisting' (*Shakespeare's Wife*, p. 73).

Shakespeare's wife 'could not read or write' and maintains that 'it is entirely possible that Shakespeare's wife could never read a word he wrote' (p. 125). In Greenblatt's story, Hathaway is severed from any possible connection with Shakespeare's creative work and she remains exiled to the grim domestic world of Stratford as a mistake the young poet would rather forget.

Any biographer of Shakespeare wanting to make an argument for a miserable marriage must account for the fact that Shakespeare returned to Stratford in the last few years of his life. Greenblatt addresses this by claiming that Shakespeare wanted to live near his daughter and her family, but not near his wife, for whom he felt only 'sour anger' (p. 387). Indeed, in this tale, Shakespeare 'could scarcely be expected to find comfort in the enduring bond with his wife' (p. 361), but instead harboured a 'strange, ineradicable distaste for her that he felt deep within him' (p. 145). Greenblatt repudiates any possibility that Shakespeare may have had a joyful reunion with his wife in his last years of life, and even refuses to allow any sort of amiable alliance in their side-by-side burial: 'So much for the dream of love. When Shakespeare lay dying, he tried to forget his wife and then remembered her with the second-best bed. And when he thought of the afterlife, the last thing he wanted was to be mingled with the woman he married' (p. 147).

The intensity with which Greenblatt denigrates Anne Hathaway throughout his biography is striking and the usual linguistic turns common to biography ('may have', 'it is likely that', 'perhaps', etc.) are notably absent: Shakespeare was 'dragged to the altar', Hathaway 'filled him with revulsion' and an 'ineradicable distaste', he knew the 'misery of the neglected or abandoned spouse', his marriage was a 'disastrous mistake', his love 'flourished outside of the marriage bond', and he felt 'sour anger' towards his wife even in his last years of life. Is it sheer fantasy that Shakespeare's relationship with Anne Hathaway could have been anything but revulsion, misery, sour anger, a disastrous mistake? Are more charitable explanations of

Anne Hathaway only found in works of fiction, such as the three stage plays discussed earlier? We might be tempted to explain Greenblatt's 'Anne Hathaway' by proposing a split between academic and popular representations of Hathaway, with academic biographers taking a more negative interpretation, and popular works imagining a more positive (but ultimately illusory) story.[17] Yet this is not the case.

In *Ungentle Shakespeare: Scenes from his Life* (2001), Katherine Duncan-Jones gives readers an Anne Hathaway much closer to the fictional one imagined in recent works. Here she is a 'mature and spirited country girl' who 'exploited her freedom to consort with the local youth'. Duncan-Jones suggests that 'A combination of boredom with the sexual curiosity natural to his years led to Shakespeare's dalliance with her, and to what was probably his first experience of sex.' She finds it feasible that 'the union was a lovematch . . . A young man of extraordinary talent and imagination, stuck in uncongenial employment with no prospects except the possibility of one day managing the family business better than his father was doing, found, as other men of genius have done, an outlet in sex.'[18] To be fair, Duncan-Jones also suggests that Shakespeare 'was very probably sulky and reluctant' about the likelihood that his marriage would inhibit his artistic career, and may have felt 'deep resentment at this premature yoking' (p. 20). Even so, Duncan-Jones allows for a wider range of possible interpretations of the Shakespeare marriage.

Park Honan, in *Shakespeare: A Life* (1999), similarly offers a more balanced interpretation of the marriage. We might note that he titles this chapter 'Love and Marriage' as opposed to Greenblatt's not-so-subtle choice of 'Wooing, Wedding, and Repenting'. In Honan's account, Anne's age is a

---

[17] I am using 'popular' to denote texts not designed primarily for an academic/scholarly audience, but aimed at the general public.

[18] Katherine Duncan-Jones, *Ungentle Shakespeare: Scenes from his Life* (London, 2001), pp. 17–18.

virtue, not a detraction: 'William can hardly have acquired a maturity of outlook that years would have given Anne.' The death of her father and marriage of her brother may have 'led Anne to take a lover', giving both agency and choice to Anne. Honan contends that Shakespeare was 'evidently in love, and his problem in November was to arrange for his future as quickly as he could'.[19] Greenblatt's interpretation was that Shakespeare's family did not support the marriage but Honan argues that the Shakespeare family respected the Hathaways and they 'were likely to find her age and practicality of benefit to their son, a young man lively, eloquent, with a "mint of phrases in his brain" but of small practical experience' (p. 82). Overall, Honan makes an argument for an amiable relationship between the Shakespeares throughout the poet's life: 'his apparently regular visits to Stratford, his investments and care to establish himself there, do not suggest he found Anne immaterial to his welfare', adding that the first biographers of Shakespeare (Rowe and Theobald) 'imply he chose marriage, not that he was trapped' (p. 87). In Honan's narrative, Shakespeare sought a playwriting career not as an escape from his wife, but rather as the best way to support his family: 'The birth of twins virtually assured that Shakespeare's future would be more problematic, that he would be concerned to make up for lost time in a calling, and would undertake nearly anything required of him to get money. He would also know, surely, the pain of separation for long periods from a substantial and consoling family.' This is hardly the tale of escape that Greenblatt proposes; in Honan's account, 'Shakespeare hoped to better himself; he could serve his family best by removing himself from Stratford' (p. 91). This is a significantly different trajectory for Shakespeare than the one Greenblatt asserts – in Honan's interpretation, Shakespeare leaves Stratford for London in order to best support his family and yearns to return at the end of his career. The 'Shakespeare' that Honan thus constructs is both a successful artist and a responsible family man, whose career goals did not necessitate rejecting his domestic life or discarding his wife.

In light of the contrasting portraits of Anne Hathaway in recent biographies and in imaginative portrayals, how might we explain Greenblatt's interpretation? Why would a contemporary biographer go against the prevailing 'climate' of rehabilitative portraits of Anne Hathaway, given that *Will in the World* is not based on any new information about Shakespeare's wife or his domestic life nor does it employ a new methodology? We might ask what are the ideological and political implications involved in constructing a 'Shakespeare' who renounces his domestic life and feels only 'sour anger' towards his wife throughout his life.

Will in the World, a 'blockbuster popular work' designed both for academics and for a popular readership, disseminates a portrait of Anne Hathaway to an unprecedented number of readers, from the book tables at big box retailers, to the legions of students who buy the Norton Shakespeare.[20] According to one analysis, Greenblatt's aim was to use his academic reputation to cross the boundary between high culture Shakespeare and popular culture Shakespeare and 'extend his influence into the general public'.[21] If Greenblatt's intended audience is 'the lay reader and nonacademic Shakespeare fan', in the estimation of *New York Times* reviewer Michiko Kakutani, there seems to be a disturbing correlation between constructing a 'Shakespeare'

---

[19] Park Honan, *Shakespeare: A Life* (Oxford, 1999), pp. 80–1.
[20] M. G. Aune, 'Crossing the Border: Shakespeare Biography, Academic Celebrity, and the Reception of *Will in the World*', *Borrowers and Lenders*, 2.2 (Fall/Winter 2006). Aune's article also provides extensive details of the marketing, sales and critical reception of Greenblatt's book. On a number of occasions, Greenblatt has remarked that he intended to reach the general public as well as an academic audience. See for example his interview with Sara F. Gold in *Publishers Weekly*, 19 July 2004. John Simon points out the correlation between speculation and academic status, particularly 'if a conjecture is developed in great detail and often enough repeated – and if the author is the Cogan University Professor of the Humanities at Harvard, as well as the editor of the *Norton Shakespeare* and the author of a number of books': 'Bardolatry Made Easy', *New Criterion*, April 2005.
[21] M. G. Aune, 'Crossing the Border'.

for a popular audience and offering a pejorative portrayal of Anne Hathaway.[22]

Perhaps the million-dollar advance that Greenblatt reportedly received for the book necessitated 'the greatest [story] of all time', as he promises in his preface, and thus the creation of 'the Shakespeare of a celebrity booker for the Oprah Winfrey show'.[23] Perhaps the narrative of a genius husband trapped in an unhappy marriage (like a tormented Romantic poet), who upon escaping from that stifling world, is then able to write the greatest plays in the history of drama, is a way to increase the sensationalism of the biography in light of the imperative for a publisher to market and sell yet another biography of Shakespeare. Indeed, more than one reviewer has suggested that financial gain may have been a motivating factor in the genesis of this biography; in his review in *The Guardian*, 'Where there's a Will there's a payday', John Sutherland, for example, criticizes Greenblatt for writing 'books which the hucksters in the book trade want rather than the books their discipline needs' and for accepting 'the Mephistophelean invitation to write the great book about the great dramatist for a great sum'.[24] The repercussions of associating financial success with the story of a maligned wife are troubling. We might explore the implications of this point further by asking how future work on Shakespeare, women and domesticity will be influenced by this model of Anne Hathaway as woman who entrapped Shakespeare in a world of domestic misery.[25]

Empowering Anne Hathaway through association with a modern paradigm for women's lives that contemporary audiences can relate to (such as a work-at-home mother or stay-at-home mother) also has the effect of giving value to her domestic life, in line with the many recent revisionist works on the history of domesticity.[26] In contrast, *Will in the World* suggests that a repudiation of domesticity is one answer to 'How Shakespeare Became Shakespeare', the agenda of the book's subtitle. The narrative of Shakespeare's domestic life in Greenblatt's biography is strikingly similar to more regressive accounts of what one historian has termed the

'stifling, oppressive, and old-fashioned domesticity' of the late nineteenth century, where anxieties about domesticity inspired 'all-male fantasy worlds in which domesticity was a state and, often literally, a place from which to escape if full selfhood was to be realized'.[27] Likewise, Greenblatt's Shakespeare must escape his wife and her world of domesticity in order to achieve full artistic and personal satisfaction.

Victorian poet Mathilde Blind described Anne Hathaway as 'She, whose mortal lot / Was linked to an Immortal's unaware', and Anne Hathaway's immortality shows no signs of abating. Let's hope

---

[22] Michiko Kakutani, 'Shakespeare Attracts a New Pursuer', *New York Times*, 1 October 2004.

[23] Gary Taylor remarks that *Will in the World* 'tells a better story than other Shakespeare biographies' and is one of many reviewers who mention the million-dollar advance: *The Guardian*, 9 October 2004. The Oprah Winfrey reference is from Colin MacCabe's review, *The Independent*, 5 November 2004.

[24] John Sutherland, *The Guardian*, 16 February 2005.

[25] Gary Taylor contends that the anti-Anne Hathaway thread is a validation of Greenblatt's own life: 'Greenblatt has mined his own life to supply the emotional raw materials that energise this book. Like Shakespeare, Greenblatt writes convincingly of the "complex states of estrangement" in a bad marriage, "as if the misery of the neglected or abandoned spouse was something he knew personally and all too well". Like the author of the sonnets (and me), Greenblatt knows about the "erotic virtue of mendacity", how "the age difference" between two lovers can be "a paradoxical source of excitement", and why "The woman who most intensely appealed to Shakespeare in his life was 20 years younger than he."' Taylor concludes that 'what purports to be an image of Shakespeare is really an idealized image of the biographer himself': 'Stephen, Will and Gary Too', *The Guardian*, 9 October 2004.

[26] See for example Lena Cowen Orlin, *Private Matters and Public Culture in Post-Reformation England* (Ithaca, 1994); Frances A. Dolan, *Dangerous Familiars: Representations of Domestic Crime in England 1550–1700* (Ithaca, 1994); Viviana Comensoli, *Household Business: Domestic Plays of Early Modern England* (Toronto, 1996); Wendy Wall, *Staging Domesticity: Household Work and English Identity in Early Modern Drama* (Cambridge, 2002); Catherine Richardson, *Domestic Life and Domestic Tragedy in Early Modern England: The Material Life of the Household* (Manchester, 2006).

[27] Judy Giles, *Parlour and Suburb: Domestic Identities, Class, Femininity, and Modernity* (Oxford, 2004), pp. 3, 13.

that future work on women's domestic history, in various imaginative genres, will further illuminate 'the shadowy figure in the corner of the great house in Stratford',[28] rather than perpetuate a regressive fantasy of escaping domesticity.

[28] Mathilde Blind, 'Anne Hathaway', in *The Poetical Works of Mathilde Blind*, ed. Arthur Symons (London, 1900), pp. 439–40. The 'shadowy figure' phrase is from Katie Roiphe, 'Reclaiming the Shrew', *New York Times*, 27 April 2008.

SHAKESPEARE AND MACHIAVELLI: A CAVEAT

N. W. BAWCUTT

Readers of this article may well regard it as old-fashioned and disappointing. It has no subtle and ingenious connections to make between Shakespeare and Machiavelli, indeed the opposite. No indisputable borrowing from Machiavelli has so far been discovered in Shakespeare – certainly nothing remotely resembling the clear and detailed use of Florio's translation of Montaigne in *The Tempest* – and I believe that scholars have been too ready to invoke Machiavelli's influence on seriously inadequate grounds.

I

Until about the middle of the twentieth century Machiavelli was not a particularly important presence in scholarly discussions of Shakespeare. He hardly figures, for example, in the standard accounts of Shakespeare's sources by Kenneth Muir and Geoffrey Bullough. In *Shakespeare's History Plays* (1944), a book once regarded as authoritative, but now mentioned only to be patronizingly dismissed, E. M. W. Tillyard asserted that Machiavelli ignored what for the Elizabethans was a central issue in discussion of politics:

Thoughtful Elizabethans agonised over the terrible gaps between the 'erected wit' and the 'infected will' of man and between the majestic harmony of an ideal state and the habitual chaos of the earthly polity. Machiavelli spared himself such agonisings by cutting out the 'erected wit' altogether, thereby making irrelevant the questions that most disturbed men's minds.[1]

Tillyard was of course aware that Machiavelli was read and quoted in the period, but for him 'the age, while making much use of certain details of his writing, either ignored or refused to face what the man fundamentally stood for'.[2] He ended on a dismissive note:

The conclusion is that in trying to picture how the ordinary educated contemporary of Shakespeare looked on history in the gross we do not need to give much heed to Machiavelli. His day had not yet come.[3]

Few if any modern scholars would want to say this, though it is arguable that Machiavelli did not have a profound and genuine influence on English political thinking until the middle seventeenth century, when the collapse of monarchy made republicanism a potentially viable option, and here the influence came from the *Discourses* rather than *The Prince*.[4]

---

[1] E. M. W. Tillyard, *Shakespeare's History Plays* (London, 1944), p. 21. Tillyard was influenced by the sceptical account of Machiavelli's later influence in J. W. Allen's *A History of Political Thought in the Sixteenth Century* (London, 1928), pp. 488–94. Despite its age Allen's book, written in a crisp and pungent style, is still a useful overview of the period.

[2] Tillyard, *Shakespeare's History Plays*, p. 22

[3] Tillyard, *Shakespeare's History Plays*, p. 23.

[4] According to Felix Raab, the years 1640 to 1660 mark 'the high point of Machiavelli's influence on English political thought. During these years, consciously Machiavellian criteria of political judgement become more prominent in contemporary polemic and analysis than in any period before or since': *The English Face of Machiavelli* (London, 1964), p. 102.

In the second half of the twentieth century the picture altered strikingly. A whole series of articles appeared attempting to link Machiavelli to individual plays, a process which could be said to climax in 2002 when two full-length studies appeared, John Roe's *Shakespeare and Machiavelli* and Hugh Grady's *Shakespeare, Machiavelli, and Montaigne: Power and Subjectivity from 'Richard II' to 'Hamlet'*.[5] One could say, perhaps over-harshly, that Machiavelli became fashionable. Most discussions by literary critics of Elizabethan political attitudes in literature would feel it obligatory to fit in some account of him. There are indeed exceptions: Robert S. Miola, in his *Shakespeare's Reading* (2000), ignores him. Stuart Gillespie, in *Shakespeare's Books, A Dictionary of Shakespeare Sources* (2001), displays what I would regard as an admirable scepticism. Attempts to assert Machiavellian influence on Shakespeare rarely display specific reference, 'commentators usually comparing only generally "Machiavellian" principles of character and action with the content of the plays'.[6] And Machiavelli says so much about 'kings, governance, rebellion, and so on' that 'it is all too easy to isolate parallels in his writings for attributes and behaviour found at one point or another in the many Shakespeare plays which involve similar elements'.[7] His conclusion is decidedly unenthusiastic: 'the quantity of work is disproportionate to the security with which any direct use of Machiavelli can be demonstrated'.[8]

We might reasonably ask why Machiavelli became so popular among scholars. One perfectly respectable answer could be that we are now much more aware than in, say, the nineteenth century that Machiavelli's writings were widely available in sixteenth-century England and Scotland, in the original or in translation, and that there was even a London printing in Italian of some of his most important works. There was thus no need to argue that because a translation of *The Prince* into English was not printed until 1640, and of the *Discourses* until 1636, the Elizabethans could not have known about him and must have relied for their knowledge on the attack on him by Gentillet, though this sometimes led to a mistaken denial of Gentillet's influence, which can be shown to have been quite substantial.[9]

Another factor was a marked swing towards the left in politics among literary scholars during the twentieth century, a trend which has continued despite the collapse of belief in Marxism. The Elizabethan age was no longer seen as a period of great and glorious national achievement. Contemporary assertions of English superiority were said to be obtained by reference to the inferiority of other races such as the Irish, and attempts to acquire overseas territory were stigmatized as imperialism and colonialism. What Tillyard presented as a politically neutral Elizabethan World Picture, with its emphasis on order and hierarchy, was seen as ideological propaganda designed to support a harsh and oppressive ruling class. Of course no one suggested that this all derived from Machiavelli, but this darker vision was accompanied by an increasing stress on the influence of Machiavellianism in Elizabethan political thinking. The tendency affected attitudes to Shakespeare's kings: it was intolerable to see Shakespeare as a naively patriotic admirer of Henry V and, in both of his manifestations as Prince Hal in *Henry IV* and the king in *Henry V*, Henry was seen as a Machiavellian, whose splendid utterances masked brutal calculation. This is not universal: in the introduction to his 1982 edition of *Henry V* Gary Taylor saw no need to refer to Machiavelli and defended some of the king's more questionable actions, and Tom McAlindon

---

5 John Roe, *Shakespeare and Machiavelli* (Cambridge, 2002), and Hugh Grady, *Shakespeare, Machiavelli, and Montaigne: Power and Subjectivity from 'Richard II' to 'Hamlet'* (Oxford, 2002); henceforth referred to as 'Roe' and 'Grady'. The *World Shakespeare Bibliography* contains 97 items referring to Machiavelli since 1961; to list them all would be impracticable, and to select a few might seem invidious, as I obviously disagree with them.

6 Stuart Gillespie, *Shakespeare's Books, A Dictionary of Shakespeare Sources*, Athlone Shakespeare Dictionary Series (London, 2001), p. 313.

7 Gillespie, *Shakespeare's Books*, p. 313.

8 Gillespie, *Shakespeare's Books*, p. 315.

9 See my article, 'The "Myth of Gentillet" Reconsidered: An Aspect of Elizabethan Machiavellianism', *Modern Language Review*, 99 (2004), 863–74.

has portrayed Prince Hal as an honourable man who keeps his promises and should not be seen as a Machiavellian.[10]

Reservations could be expressed about various aspects of the modern vogue for Machiavelli. Too often he is seen in isolation; in some discussions we might get the impression that he is the only sixteenth-century political writer of any importance. Certainly when Ben Jonson's ludicrous Sir Politic Would-be wanted to demonstrate his knowledge of the best authors he mentioned 'Nic Machiavel', but he linked him with 'Monsieur Bodin' (*Volpone*, 4.1.26). A remark of Gabriel Harvey is often quoted:

You can not stepp into a schollars studye but (ten to on) you shall litely [*sic*] finde open ether Bodin de Republica or Le Royes Exposition uppon Aristotles Politiques or sum other like Frenche or Italian Politique Discourses.[11]

Jean Bodin's major works were widely known in sixteenth-century England but, if there has been any attempt to assess Bodinian influence on Shakespeare, I have yet to come across it. Similarly Giovanni Botero's *Della Ragion di Stato* (1589), which originated the phrase 'reason of state', was influential (Ben Jonson quotes the phrase in its Italian form in *Cynthia's Revels*, 1.4.84, and *Volpone*, 4.1.141). But I doubt if Botero is much mentioned in Shakespeare criticism. One explanation for this may be that these treatises are inaccessible and sometimes very substantial, whereas Machiavelli, with typical cunning, compressed his most outrageous assertions into a relatively small treatise which has been repeatedly translated into English, so that it is perfectly easy to compare *The Prince* and a Shakespeare play.

It is not always sufficiently recognized that a great many 'Machiavellian' ideas circulated in the sixteenth century which have nothing to do with Machiavelli. I will confine myself to two illustrations, one ancient and one modern. Fletcher and Massinger's *The False One* (?1620) is set in Egypt shortly after the shattering defeat of Pompey the Great at Pharsalia by Julius Caesar in 48 BC. Pompey is fleeing to Egypt in search of help, and the Egyptians have to decide how to receive him.

The old blind priest Achoreus points out that Ptolemy owes his crown to Pompey, and should remain loyal to him. The evil counsellor Pothinus praises Achoreus, perhaps sarcastically, but says that his advice is mistaken:

> What in a man sequester'd from the world,
> Or in a private person, is preferr'd,
> No policy allows of in a king:
> To be or just, or thankful, makes kings guilty;
> And faith, though praised, is punished, that supports
> Such as good fate forsakes: Join with the gods,
> Observe the man they favour, leave the wretched;
> The stars are not more distant from the earth
> Than profit is from honesty; all the power,
> Prerogative, and greatness of a prince
> Is lost, if he descend once but to steer
> His course, as what's right guides him: Let him leave
> The sceptre, that strives only to be good,
> Since kingdoms are maintained by force and blood.
> (1.1.299–312)

Machiavellian, of course! In fact it is a reasonably close translation from a source for the play, Lucan's *Pharsalia*:

> 'ius et fas multos faciunt, Ptolemaee, nocentes;
> dat poenas laudata fides, cum sustinet,' inquit
> 'quos fortuna premit. fatis accede deisque,
> et cole felices, miseros fuge. sidera terra
> ut distant et flamma mari, sic utile recto.
> sceptrorum uis tota perit, si pendere iusta
> incipit, euertitque arces respectus honesti.
> libertas scelerum est, quae regna inuisa tuetur,
> sublatusque modus gladiis. facere omnia saeue
> non inpune licet, nisi cum facis. exeat aula
> qui volt esse pius. uirtus et summa potestas
> non coeunt; semper metuet, quem saeua pudebunt.'
> (VIII. 484–95)

[He said: 'Ptolemy, keeping the laws of God and man makes many guilty: we praise loyalty, but it pays the price when it supports those whom Fortune crushes. Take the side of destiny and Heaven, and court the prosperous, shun the afflicted. Expediency is as far from the

---

[10] Tom McAlindon, 'Swearing and Forswearing in Shakespeare's Histories: The Playwright as Contra-Machiavel', *Review of English Studies*, n.s., 51 (2000), 208–29.

[11] *The Letter-Book of Gabriel Harvey*, ed. E. J. L. Scott (London, 1884), p. 79.

right as the stars from earth or fire from water. The power of kings is utterly destroyed, once they begin to weigh considerations of justice; and regard for virtue levels the strongholds of tyrants. It is boundless wickedness and unlimited slaughter that protects an unpopular sovereign. If all your deeds are cruel, you will suffer for it the moment you cease from cruelty. If a man would be righteous, let him depart from a court. Virtue is incompatible with absolute power. He who is ashamed to commit cruelty must always be apprehensive.']¹²

My modern example comes from the French king Louis XI, who reigned from 1461 to 1483, and had a reputation in some ways similar to that of the English king Richard III. He is supposed to have originated the saying, 'Qui nescit dissimulare nescit regnare' ('He who knows not how to dissemble knows not how to reign'). It caught on, became proverbial (Tilley, D386), and is found all over the place in Elizabethan and Jacobean literature.

The term 'Machiavellian' deserves closer scrutiny. It could refer to a precise echo of a specific statement in one of Machiavelli's writings. For example, the notion that a prince should take pains to appear religious and devout even if he is not could legitimately be termed 'Machiavellian' since Machiavelli gave this advice in Chapter 18 of *The Prince*. (Of course, mention of this would not necessarily indicate a first-hand knowledge of *The Prince*, since opponents like Gentillet, Book 2, maxim 1, attacked the idea.) But the word can be used, and by some modern critics is used, to indicate practically any kind of behaviour which exhibits trickery, deceit and ruthless self-interest. As used in this way it is a convenient shorthand term, but it may have only a very vague and generalized relationship to Machiavelli himself, or even none at all. It is evasive, as though the critic wants to hint that a text has some sort of relationship to Machiavelli, but doesn't want to be obliged to examine it in detail, to spell out precisely the degree to which the author of the text may be supposed to have studied the actual writings of Machiavelli.

A good instance of what I would regard as the illegitimate use of 'Machiavellian' occurs in Grady's treatment of *Richard II*. Bolingbroke, of course, is a Machiavellian, which is unsurprising and per-

haps has a superficial plausibility, but so, surprisingly, is Richard himself, though he has failed to study his copy of *The Prince* closely enough (p. 73). We have phrases like 'the Machiavellian contest for power between Richard and Bolingbroke' (p. 74), and on pages 78–9 there is a succession of such items: 'a paradoxical Machiavellian vision', 'a deadly Machiavellian game', and 'Bolingbroke's personal triumph of Machiavellian political skill'. In several of these phrases the word 'Machiavellian' could be omitted without destroying the sense. In the end, the constant repetition makes the reader feel that the play is saturated with Machiavellianism, though at no point is a direct connection made between a quotation from the play and a specific idea in Machiavelli's writings. It therefore seems odd that older editors of the play, such as Peter Ure in his Arden edition of 1956, or Stanley Wells, in his New Penguin Shakespeare edition of 1969, did not find it necessary to apply the word to the play in their introductions.¹³ Either they failed to notice something which should have been evident to them, or Grady is forcibly injecting 'Machiavellianism' into the play. It will be obvious which alternative I find more plausible.

What I have termed the evasive use of 'Machiavellian' can sometimes lead to an inadequate presentation of what the reader experiences in making contact with Machiavelli's actual writings. This applies even to full-length studies of the subject: Grady uses the words 'Machiavellian' and 'Machiavellianism' over and over again, but he has very few quotations from Machiavelli, and often seems more concerned to discuss modern schools of theory and to establish the right way of looking at someone like Althusser, than to give anything like an extended account of Machiavelli himself, who

---

¹² Lucan, *Civil War VIII*, edited with a Commentary by R. Mayer (Warminster, 1981), pp. 56–9.

¹³ Ure does refer to 'Machiavels' (p. xxxvi) and 'Machiavellian' (p. xlix), but not in connection with *Richard II*. According to Ure, p. lxvii, 'Power slides from the absent and silent Richard with the speed of an avalanche: this is not a play about how power is gained by *expertise*.' If this is so, there is no 'contest for power', and Bolingbroke has little need to be a Machiavellian.

can be pungent, violent, even outrageous, though you would hardly gather this from reading Grady.[14] Many of the earliest attacks on Machiavelli would probably now be dismissed as naive, prejudiced, based on inadequate evidence, and so on, but in some cases it is perfectly clear that they are responding directly to a Machiavellian text. A good example is found in a Latin treatise published in Rome in 1552 by Lancelotto Politi, who took the religious name of Ambrosius Catherinus. He had obviously read *The Prince*, and was deeply scandalized by it, backing up his case by translating into Latin the unpardonable horrors of Chapter 18.[15]

This leads to another of my general points. Very few modern scholarly discussions of Shakespeare's relation to Machiavelli make any extended effort to look at sixteenth-century responses to Machiavelli, apart perhaps from a brief reference to Gentillet; sometimes they base their work on an extremely sophisticated modern analysis which may be partly derived from material, such as Machiavelli's biography, and his letters and diplomatic reports, which was not available to early readers. Shakespeare was obviously a man of the sixteenth century, and if we are to 'historicize' our approach we should surely take into account how his contemporaries responded to Machiavelli.[16] This is more varied than is sometimes realized. There were, of course, innumerable expressions of disgust and indignation. Some writers were rude about Machiavelli whenever they mentioned his name but elsewhere were happy to steal from him without acknowledgement. In his *Solon His Follie* (1594), a treatise on Elizabethan policy towards Ireland, Richard Beacon made extensive use of Machiavelli's writings but never mentioned his name. A few writers were openly laudatory, such as Thomas Bedingfield in the dedication to Sir Christopher Hatton of his translation of *The History of Florence* (1595). Alberico Gentili, an Italian living in London, claimed that the *Discourses* were 'plane aureas' ('outstandingly valuable') and recommended them for imitation; he asserted that Gentillet misunderstood Machiavelli and frequently slandered him.[17]

It is also the case that sixteenth-century readers sometimes responded very powerfully to ideas in Machiavelli that might not make much impact on modern readers. In *Discourses*, II. 2, Machiavelli argued that Christianity glorified humility, contempt for worldly things and passive endurance of suffering, thereby making Christians weak and easily conquered by evil men, whereas the pagan religion of Rome, with its blood sacrifices, celebrated power and worldly glory. A Portuguese humanist, Jeronimo Osorio, published his five-book treatise *De Nobilitate* in Lisbon in 1542. He obviously knew a range of Machiavelli's writings, but it was the doctrine just summarized which particularly offended him, and he attacked it as an insult to Christianity.[18] In 1576 Gentillet turned it into one of the wicked Machiavellian maxims he aimed to confute (Book 2, maxim 3). When two sixteenth-century Englishmen selected a small number of maxims from Gentillet in order to attack Machiavelli, this was among them; for John Stockwood (1578) it was 'most horrible', and for Thomas Bowes (1594) it was one of Machiavelli's 'horrible blasphemies against pure religion, and so against God the Author thereof'.[19] Not all responses were so extreme; Bacon quoted the doctrine in his essay

---

[14] This criticism does not apply to Roe, who looks at, and quotes from, the more questionable chapters of *The Prince*.

[15] For a detailed but very unsympathetic account see Sydney Anglo, *Machiavelli: The First Century, Studies in Enthusiasm, Hostility, and Irrelevance*, Oxford-Warburg Studies (Oxford, 2005), pp. 167–71. Among the Englishmen who attacked Machiavelli by summarizing the content of Chapter 18 of *The Prince* were John Case, *Sphaera Civitatis* (Oxford, 1588), Aaa3r–v, and John Dove, *A Confutation of Atheism* (1605), pp. 5–6.

[16] I tried to do this in an article published some while ago, 'Machiavelli and Marlowe's *The Jew of Malta*', *Renaissance Drama*, n.s., 3 (1970), 3–49. One important point made there was that Machiavelli's ideas were often assimilated to Aristotle's account, in his *Politics*, Book v, chapter 11, of the devices used by tyrants to preserve their power. Now that we have Anglo's splendid book (see note 15) there is no excuse for ignorance about the early response to Machiavelli.

[17] See Anglo, *Machiavelli: The First Century*, pp. 367–8.

[18] For a full account of Osorio see Anglo, *Machiavelli: The First Century*, chapter 5.

[19] Full details are given in Bawcutt, 'The "Myth of Gentillet" Reconsidered', pp. 865–8.

'Of Goodness, and Goodness of Nature', naming Machiavelli but not in terms of outraged condemnation, and Barnabe Barnes, in *Foure Bookes of Offices* (1606), pp. 172–3, quoted it approvingly, though he referred to its author as 'a wily commonwealths man'.

II

We do know for certain that Shakespeare was aware of the 'Machiavel' figure so common in Elizabethan drama. There are three references to him in the accepted Shakespeare canon. One is near the end of *1 Henry VI*, where Joan, named Puzel or Pucell in F, asserts that she is pregnant by 'Alanson', i.e. Alençon, prompting a reply by Richard Duke of York:

> *Alanson* that notorious Macheuile?
> It dyes, and if it had a thousand liues.
> (5.6.74–5; TLN 2714–15)[20]

She then claims that the child's father is Reignier, Duke of Anjou and King of Naples, but it is clear that her pregnancy is merely a device to escape execution. Another is spoken by the Host of the Garter in *The Merry Wives of Windsor*, where he congratulates himself on his skill as a plotter: 'Am I politicke? Am I subtle? Am I a Machiuell?' (3.1.92–3; TLN 1246). In the 1602 quarto of the play this is given as 'Am I wise? am I politicke? am I Matchauil?' The third instance is spoken by Richard Duke of Gloucester, later Richard III, in *3 Henry VI*, but this deserves separate consideration.

In a long soliloquy half-way through the play he reveals himself fully for the first time (3.2.124–95). He is desperate to become king, but it looks as though this is impossible because there are too many people with a better claim to the throne than he has. He could perhaps console himself with sexual pleasures, but quickly rules this out because his physical deformities make him repulsive to women. He reverts to his wish to 'catch the English crown', and has a sudden burst of self-confidence – he has the political skills and the ruthlessness which will enable him to achieve his goal:

> Why I can smile, and murther whiles I smile,
> And cry, Content, to that which grieues my Heart,
> And wet my Cheekes with artificiall Teares,
> And frame my Face to all occasions.
> Ile drowne more Saylers then the Mermaid shall,
> Ile slay more gazers then the Basiliske,
> Ile play the Orator as well as *Nestor*,
> Deceiue more slyly then *Vlisses* could,
> And like a *Synon*, take another Troy.
> I can adde Colours to the Camelion,
> Change shapes with *Proteus*, for aduantages,
> And set the murtherous *Macheuill* to Schoole.
> Can I doe this, and cannot get a Crowne?
> Tut, were it farther off, Ile plucke it downe.
> (182–95; TLN 1706–19)

In the version of the text known as *The True Tragedie of Richard Duke of Yorke* (Octavo 1595, Quarto 1602), generally accepted as a memorial reconstruction, the speech is abbreviated (lines 3–9 of the above quotation are omitted) and line 12 is given as 'And set the aspiring *Catalin* to schoole'.

The first two of these allusions can be disposed of fairly quickly. Gary Taylor and Brian Vickers have convincingly established that *1 Henry VI* is a collaborative play. Act 1 is by Nashe, Shakespeare wrote a few scenes in Acts 2 and 4 (2.4 and 4.2–4.5) and the rest is by another dramatist.[21] He has recently been identified by Vickers as Thomas Kyd, though Vickers's methods and conclusions have been challenged by MacDonald Jackson.[22] The description of Alençon as a Machiavel is in Act 5 and is therefore not by Shakespeare. The allusion by the Host of the Garter is amusing but not particularly

---

20 In this and the next paragraph I quote old-spelling texts in order to illustrate the various forms 'Machiavel' can take.

21 Gary Taylor, 'Shakespeare and Others: The Authorship of *Henry the Sixth, Part One*', *Medieval and Renaissance Drama in England*, 7 (1995), 145–205, and Brian Vickers, 'Incomplete Shakespeare: Or, Denying Co-authorship in *1 Henry VI*', *Shakespeare Quarterly*, 58 (2007), 30–52.

22 'Thomas Kyd, Secret Sharer', *Times Literary Supplement*, No. 5481, 18 April 2008, 13–15, and MacDonald P. Jackson, 'New Researches on the Dramatic Canon of Thomas Kyd', *Research Opportunities in Medieval and Renaissance Drama*, 47 (2008), 107–27. Vickers now believes that Shakespeare wrote only two scenes in the play, 2.4 and 4.2.

significant. Clearly the allusion in *3 Henry VI* is the one that really matters.

It is possible to take the final section of Richard's speech as a series of highly rhetorical and hyperbolical assertions in which he claims to outgo and surpass a number of stock figures, drawn from mythology and natural history, who are notorious for their power to influence or even destroy an audience. Similarly the chameleon and Proteus symbolize an ability to change appearances which is often used for sinister purposes.[23] But it needs to be emphasized that they are stock figures; we could not possibly tell how and when Shakespeare acquired his knowledge of them, and in the context the Machiavel and Catiline are equally appropriate.[24] The mention of the Machiavel no more proves that Shakespeare was well-read in Machiavelli's writings than references to the basilisk and chameleon indicate that Shakespeare was deeply learned in natural history.

We may wish to give more weight to the allusion to the Machiavel but if so we should be sure to understand what it means. To say that 'Richard announces himself as a Machiavel', or 'Richard adopts the role of the stage "Machiavel"' is to misunderstand the line.[25] If you claim that you can set someone to school you are asserting that you are very much cleverer than he is; the relationship is one of master to pupil. Richard is not a Machiavel, he is greatly superior to the Machiavel. The tone of the phrase 'murtherous *Macheuill*' seems to be jeering and contemptuous, even if we remember that Richard himself emerges at the end of the play as distinctly 'murtherous'; he shares in the stabbing to death of young Prince Edward, is quite willing to murder Edward's mother Queen Margaret, and rushes off to the Tower to assassinate King Henry.

Clearly, then, Shakespeare knew of the stereotypical 'Machiavel' figure but was unimpressed by it. What of Machiavelli himself? Here perhaps we should remind ourselves of what was said at the beginning of this discussion, that no verbal proof exists that Shakespeare read his works. Even writers of full-length studies of the subject concede this: for Roe it is an 'open question' whether or not Shakespeare had read *The Prince* (pp. 93, 206),

and Grady is more outspoken: 'there is no direct evidence that he ever read a page of Machiavelli's works' (p. 20). This might seem decisive, but both scholars do their best to weaken the effect of their concessions. Roe says that Shakespeare 'can hardly have failed to have access to Machiavelli, either directly or at a slight remove' (p. 4). This has some resemblance to an earlier remark by Anne Barton:

I think myself that it would be more surprising if it could be proved that Shakespeare had managed to avoid reading Machiavelli than if concrete evidence were to turn up that he had.[26]

Grady ingeniously frees himself from his earlier scepticism by arguing that 'the ideas embodied in the Machiavellian texts came to circulate independently of those texts, carried by the political and cultural institutions which absorbed, modified, and disseminated them' (p. 29). So Shakespeare could have come into contact with Machiavelli's ideas without having had to read his books. This is not impossible, but if it did take place we should surely expect some direct echo of the ideas in the large canon of his writings, and of this there is not a trace.

But the argument does not stop there. According to Grady, 'in the end, it matters little whether Shakespeare directly read either Machiavelli or Montaigne' (pp. 29–30). Barton, who is discussing the relationship between Shakespeare's *Coriolanus* and Machiavelli's assessment of Coriolanus in the *Discourses*, i. 7, says that there is 'no real need to make an issue of Shakespeare's actual acquaintance with the *Discourses*' (p. 149). It seems to me muddled and contradictory to claim that Shakespeare

---

23 See Jonas Barish, *The Antitheatrical Prejudice* (Berkeley, 1981), pp. 99–107.

24 For an argument to this effect see Bernard Spivack, *Shakespeare and the Allegory of Evil* (New York, 1958), pp. 377–8.

25 Phyllis Rackin, *Stages of History: Shakespeare's English Chronicles* (London, 1991), p. 72, and Michael Hattaway, ed., *The Third Part of King Henry VI*, The New Cambridge Shakespeare (Cambridge, 1993), p. 140 (commentary on 3.2.193).

26 Anne Barton, 'Livy, Machiavelli, and *Coriolanus*', in *Essays, Mainly Shakespearean* (Cambridge, 1994), p. 149. This essay first appeared in *Shakespeare Survey 38* (Cambridge, 1985).

must have come into contact with Machiavelli's ideas in some form or other, and it would be deeply surprising if he hadn't, and then to assert that it doesn't matter whether or not he did. If we simply wish to read Shakespeare in the light of Machiavelli, as we might wish to read him in the light of Marx or Freud or Foucault or any other modern sage, then perhaps it does not matter. But if we believe that Shakespeare's way of thinking was deeply influenced by Machiavelli, then the relationship needs to be established with the precision and accuracy that good scholarship demands.[27]

Let me be clear on an important point. I am not for a moment trying to assert that Shakespeare could not possibly have read Machiavelli. *The Prince* and *Discourses* were available in Italian, French and Latin, and *The Art of War* and *The Florentine History* were translated into English in the sixteenth century. Shakespeare could have read some or all of them, but there is no evidence to prove that he did.[28] Scholars who find it hard to believe that he did not read Machiavelli often make a further assumption, that the reading made a great impression, that he absorbed and digested a large number of Machiavelli's ideas. If the whole question is merely one of theoretical possibilities, is it not conceivable that perhaps Shakespeare did indeed read something of Machiavelli's – most probably *The Prince* – but found it uncongenial or even downright repulsive, that it taught him nothing which he could not otherwise get from Plutarch or Holinshed? Many of his contemporaries were horrified by Machiavelli, and we should not conclude that by being so they merely showed themselves to be fools. Certainly Machiavelli was a patriot who desperately wanted to free Italy from enslavement by foreign occupiers, though ironically the final chapter of *The Prince* seems to have made very little impression on sixteenth-century readers. But it could be said that the world he portrays is one of brutal calculation and opportunism, with a conspicuous lack of human warmth and generosity.

An example of something in Machiavelli which Shakespeare might well have found offensive, if he did come across it, is the notorious Chapter 18 of *The Prince*, 'Quomodo fides a principibus sit ser-

vanda' ('How princes should keep their faith'). I propose to give only a very brief summary of the contents: it begins with a perfunctory nod to keeping one's word as praiseworthy, but rapidly shifts into a kind of eulogy of lying, cunning and deception, of which Pope Alexander VI is held up as a supreme master. A wise prince, however, must take great pains to appear pious, honest and truthful, even if he is forced, in order to preserve his power, to take actions which are contrary to faithfulness, contrary to charity, contrary to humaneness and contrary to religion ('contro alle fede, contro alla carità, contro alla umanità, contro alla religione'). It is not surprising that Gentillet was horrified by this chapter and drew several of his maxims from it. For example, Book 3, maxim 21, 'A wise prince ought not to keepe his Faith, when the observation therof is hurtful to him, and that the occasions for which he gave it be taken away', is a literal translation of a sentence in the Italian. Gentillet then did all he could to demolish the maxim, with a long list of examples from ancient and modern history.

Obviously we cannot know what precisely Shakespeare himself thought on the matter, but it is undeniable that frequently in his plays the question of keeping or breaking oaths and promises is treated as a matter of the utmost seriousness.[29] This particularly applies to the history plays, where the future of the whole kingdom may be involved in the making or breaking of an oath. In *3 Henry VI* King Henry agrees to pass the inheritance of his crown after his death to Richard Duke of York if the latter takes an oath to remain loyal to the

---

[27] I am obviously out of sympathy with the more extreme forms of what is now termed intertextuality.

[28] Roe, p. 143, says that there is 'no knowing' whether he read Bedingfield's translation of the *Florentine History*, and Grady, p. 45, 'suspects' that he did not read the *Discourses*. These opinions are merely subjective and impressionistic, and can hardly count as evidence.

[29] See, for example, Faye Kelly, 'Oaths in Shakespeare's *Henry VI* Plays', *Shakespeare Quarterly*, 24 (1973), 365–71, Frances Shirley, *Swearing and Perjury in Shakespeare's Plays* (London, 1979), William Kerrigan, *Shakespeare's Promises* (Baltimore, 1999), and McAlindon, 'Swearing and Forswearing in Shakespeare's Histories', 208–29.

king during his lifetime. York agrees: 'This oath I willingly take and will perform' (1.1.202). But in the next scene his sons urge him to break it; York says 'I took an oath that he should quietly reign' (1.2.15), but Edward contemptuously replies:

> But for a kingdom any oath may be broken.
> I would break a thousand oaths to reign one year.
>
> (16–17)

This perhaps sounds pseudo-Machiavellian, but the first line seems to be an adaptation of the proverbial 'For a kingdom any oath may be broken' (Tilley K90), which derives eventually from Cicero, De officiis, 3.21. York's son Richard, later King Richard III, says 'God forbid your grace should be forsworn' (18), but this is not from any concern for honourable behaviour, because he then produces a blatantly specious and spurious argument that the oath was not properly executed and is therefore not binding. York is easily persuaded and decides to attack the king.

Something similar occurs in King John. The French King Philip and King John swear to a peace treaty (though their reasons for doing so are mocked by the bastard Falconbridge in his famous speech on 'commodity', 2.1.562ff.). But Philip had promised to support Arthur, the son of Constance, in his claim to the English crown, and she bitterly accuses him of being 'forsworn' and 'perjured' (3.1.27, 37). Cardinal Pandulph enters and (to summarize briefly) excommunicates John for failing to obey him, and orders Philip to make war on John, again with the threat of excommunication if he fails to do so. Philip makes a deeply felt and moving defence of adhering to his promise:

> This royal hand and mine are newly knit,
> And the conjunction of our inward souls
> Married in league, coupled and linked together
> With all religious strength of sacred vows;
> The latest breath that gave the sound of words
> Was deep-sworn faith, peace, amity, true love,
> Between our kingdoms and our royal selves;
> And even before this truce, but new before,
> No longer than we well could wash our hands
> To clap this royal bargain up of peace,

> God knows, they were besmeared and over-stained
> With slaughter's pencil, where Revenge did paint
> The fearful difference of incensed kings;
> And shall these hands, so lately purged of blood,
> So newly joined in love, so strong in both,
> Unyoke this seizure and this kind regreet,
> Play fast and loose with faith, so jest with heaven,
> Make such unconstant children of ourselves,
> As now again to snatch our palm from palm,
> Unswear faith sworn, and on the marriage-bed
> Of smiling peace to march a bloody host,
> And make a riot on the gentle brow
> Of true sincerity? (3.1.152–74)

The treaty of friendship is given a powerful significance: it is compared to a marriage, and the vows made in it are 'religious' and 'sacred'. It has only recently put an end to the vividly portrayed bloodshed of war, and to break it so soon afterwards would be to 'jest with heaven' and once again commit violence on 'smiling peace'. Pandulph manages to coerce Philip into breaking his oath, but in comparison to Philip's speech his arguments seem contrived and casuistical.

Shakespeare's concern with the topic is not confined to the history plays. What plot there is in Love's Labour's Lost derives from a failure to keep promises: the play contains seventeen uses of 'forsworn' and seven of 'perjured', in both cases more than is found in any other Shakespearian play. Four young men swear an oath to study for three years and to avoid any contact with women; as we might expect, at the approach of four attractive young women they immediately fall in love. Berowne's great speech in 4.3, which Shakespeare revised and expanded to get it right, is a wholly specious attempt to justify their behaviour, to offer 'some salve for perjury' (4.3.287). But the women are aware of their promise-breaking, and take it seriously; as the princess puts it, 'Nor God nor I delights in perjured men' (5.2.347), and she does not accept that falling in love is an adequate excuse:

> So much I hate a breaking cause to be
> Of heavenly oaths, vowed with integrity.
>
> (5.2.356–7)

At the end of the play the men are forced to undergo a kind of year-long penance, in order to prove that their protestations of undying love are well founded. It does indeed seem that in both affairs of state and affairs of the heart Shakespeare took very seriously the making and breaking of oaths and promises.

III

It would clearly be impossible to comment in detail on every attempt that has been made to link a Shakespeare play with Machiavelli. In some cases the exaggeration and overstatement seem to me to be blatantly obvious, as when Leon Harold Craig asserts that when *Macbeth* is read in a philosophical spirit, that is to say with minute attention to detail, 'the first conclusion to emerge is that the play is designed to illustrate the political teachings we associate most readily with Machiavelli's *The Prince*'.[30] The play is about the ruthless seizure of power, and inevitably there are aspects of it that can be compared to aspects of *The Prince*, but 'designed to illustrate' seems to suggest, to my mind quite implausibly, that Shakespeare sat down to dramatize Machiavelli, almost that he had a copy of *The Prince* in front of him, and checked it from time to time to make sure he had covered everything. When Craig says casually of one of Machiavelli's pieces of advice that it is 'something every successful polititian knows' (p. 43), it helps to undermine his case: if every successful politician knows it, the idea comes from experience and common sense, not from Machiavelli.

The most extensive collection of parallelisms between Shakespeare and Machiavelli is in Roe's book. Repeatedly we are told that something in Shakespeare 'echoes' or 'resembles' or 'is similar to' something in Machiavelli, but only too often the resemblance is strained and unconvincing. Roe himself occasionally seems to have second thoughts about an assertion, to state it categorically and then somewhat withdraw from it, as when he claims that Cleopatra's rebuke to Antony:

> Good now, play one scene
> Of excellent dissembling, and let it look
> Like perfect honour.
>
> (*Antony and Cleopatra*, 1.3.78–80)

'derives from' Chapter 18 of *The Prince*, but then qualifies it: 'though of course it may not do so directly, given the pervasiveness of Machiavellianism in contemporary drama' (p. 188). This apparently implies that Shakespeare may have got the idea at second-hand from some other contemporary dramatist, but if this is what Roe means surely we should be given chapter and verse, in other words examples of the same idea being used by other dramatists.

Understandably Roe is impressed by some of the more vivid of Machiavelli's remarks. One of these occurs at the end of Chapter 25 of *The Prince*; Machiavelli has been saying that men must know how to vary with fortune, to be impetuous at some times and cautious at others. But he concludes that on the whole it is better to be impetuous, because fortune is a woman and needs to be forced to submit by means of violence. As the recent translation of J.G. Nichols puts it:

One thing I am certain of: it is better to be impetuous than cautious; for Fortune is a woman, and it is essential, in order to keep her under control, to beat her and attack her. And one can see that she allows herself to be overcome more readily by one who does this than by one who approaches her coolly; and so, being a woman, she is always friendly towards young men, because they are less cautious, more fiery, and dominate her with more audacity.[31]

Roe takes it for granted that Shakespeare was deeply impressed by the passage (he does not consider the possibility that Shakespeare might have found it repulsive), and relates it to three locations in Shakespeare. One is Richard's wooing of

---

30 Leon Henry Craig, *Of Philosophers and Kings: Political Philosophy in Shakespeare's Macbeth and King Lear* (Toronto, 2001), p. 40.

31 Machiavelli, *The Prince*, translated by J. G. Nichols (London, 2009), p. 73.

Lady Anne in *Richard III*, 1.2, which bears a 'close resemblance' to the Machiavellian passage (p. 18), the second is Falconbridge's approval of his mother for yielding to what almost seems to be rape by his father Richard Coeur de Lion in *King John*, 1.1.259–76, which 'carries an echo' of the passage (p. 98) and the third is Hamlet's account to Horatio of how he rewrote the commission carried by Rosencrantz and Guildenstern: 'Hamlet here uses expressions which recall those of Machiavelli in his exhortation to use fortune impetuously' (p. 22). The first two items certainly show men behaving in an overbearing way towards women, but it is hard to believe that Shakespeare needed to be inspired by Machiavelli to write them. The *Hamlet* passage seems to me to have no relationship to Machiavelli at all.

Another famous episode repeatedly referred to by Roe occurs in Chapter 7 of *The Prince*. Cesare Borgia won control of the Romagna in Italy but found it full of anarchy and crime because its previous rulers had been greedy and incompetent. So he appointed Remirro de Orco, a man cruel and quick to act ('uomo crudele ed espedito'), as a governor and he soon brought things under control. But Borgia realized that Remirro's severities had brought hatred upon himself, and he wanted to show that any cruelty had been caused by the harsh nature of his deputy. So one morning (in December 1502), Remirro's body was discovered in the square at Cesena, cut into two pieces and with a piece of wood and a bloodstained knife beside it. (Machiavelli does not explain the significance of the piece of wood.) Not surprisingly, the ferocity of the spectacle made the people simultaneously satisfied and stupefied ('satisfatti e stupidi').

Roe brings in references to this notorious incident in a variety of contexts. On p. 72 he suggests fairly casually that Machiavelli would have approved of the rejection of Falstaff at the end of *2 Henry IV* ('think only of the calculated disposal of the wretched Remirro de Orco'). No doubt many critics consider Henry's behaviour to be cold-blooded and heartless but he merely orders Falstaff not to approach within ten miles of him and

provides Falstaff with a pension, which is very different from the bisection of Remirro. Some lines from a speech of Brutus in *Julius Caesar*, 2.1, where the conspirators are debating how to assassinate Caesar, are 'a fairly obvious echo of the notorious Orco anecdote' (p. 165):

> And let our hearts, as subtle masters do,
> Stir up their servants to an act of rage,
> And after seem to chide 'em.   (2.1.175–7)

But there is nothing in Machiavelli's account to suggest that Cesare needed to 'stir up' Remirro, a man cruel by nature, and his punishment was to be brutally executed, not merely 'chided'.

Roe's most extended allusion occurs in his discussion of the banishment of Mowbray at the beginning of *Richard II*. He speaks of the 'Machiavellian treatment' of Mowbray, and considers that Machiavelli's anecdote 'finds special relevance to the event' (p. 37). The 'special relevance' appears to be that in this case there is a fairly close plot-connection between the two events: both are concerned with men who perform violent acts to help their masters, but are then punished instead of rewarded. Roe makes the connection more in terms of Samuel Daniel's version of his banishment (he speaks of Daniel's 'close application of the Remirro model'), though it seems clear that we are expected to see a relationship to the Remirro incident in Shakespeare's version. But the English historians that were easily available to Shakespeare provided him with an ample range of material relevant to the banishment of Mowbray; there is simply no need to invoke Machiavelli (and banishment, though harsh, is very different from a horribly violent execution).

I will conclude with one more attempt to relate the Remirro incident to Shakespeare, which Roe is aware of but does not discuss in detail. In 1959 Norman Holland asserted that the appointment of Angelo as the Duke's deputy in *Measure for Measure* was modelled on Machiavelli's anecdote.[32] He

---

[32] Norman N. Holland, '*Measure for Measure*: The Duke and The Prince', *Comparative Literature*, 11 (1959), 16–20.

did not, however, believe that Shakespeare could read Italian, and argued that the influence came from Gentillet via Simon Patericke's English translation of 1602. Gentillet was obviously horrified by the incident, and referred to it at some length on three separate occasions. I have space for only a few observations on this suggestion. In his discussion in 1.3 of his motives for appointing Angelo the Duke certainly assumes that he will restore order to Vienna, but also stresses that the appointment will test whether Angelo's apparent rectitude is genuine. As the play progresses, the first of these motives fades from sight and the second predominates. Furthermore, at the beginning of the play Angelo is not ordered to be severe; he is given the full powers of the Duke himself and is told to use them entirely at his own discretion:

> Your scope is as mine own,
> So to enforce or qualify the laws
> As to your soul seems good.   (1.1.64–6)

But Angelo is still uncertain about what is expected from him, and he and Escalus agree to meet later and discuss their commissions. In the final scene Angelo is sentenced to death not because of the Duke's ingratitude but because he has (apparently) violated a virgin and wrongfully executed her brother, a sentence he accepts and welcomes. In the end he is not executed but pardoned and married to Mariana.

It is perfectly legitimate to compare incidents in Machiavelli with incidents in Shakespeare. What usually emerges is that Shakespeare is much the more humane of the two and has a richer sense of the complexities of human motivation. But in no case is the parallelism so close and precise and detailed that we are obliged to conclude that Shakespeare could not have written what he did without the stimulus of Machiavelli.

SHAME AND REFLECTION IN MONTAIGNE AND SHAKESPEARE

LARS ENGLE

This article discusses the presentation of reflective retreat in Shakespeare and Montaigne, noting that for both of them reflection frequently follows an experience of shame. Moreover, for both reflection offers no path out of embodiment. That is, neither embraces a hallowed Platonic (and an imminent Cartesian) idea that a focus on mental life extricates one from the difficulties of embodiment.

Being seen in a bad light, gazed at with a critical, superior eye, promotes shame. As Silvan Tomkins comments,

The shame response is an act which reduces facial communication. It stands in the same relation to looking and smiling as silence stands to speech and as disgust, nausea and vomiting stand to hunger and eating. By dropping his eyes, his eyelids, his head and sometimes the whole upper part of his body, the individual calls a halt to looking at another person, particularly the other person's face, and to the other person's looking at him, particularly at his face.[1]

Closing eyes or bowing the head to break eye contact with the shamer, covering the face or the exposed body parts, are, in effect, an attempt to enlarge or barricade the space between the shamed body and the shaming, gazing body of the other. Flushing (more involuntary than the first two, but not much more involuntary) may in some physical or residually animal way be an attempt to accomplish the same thing by changing colour, radiating heat, producing a warning sweat, stoking the metabolism for conflict or flight. These are potential first steps towards reflective isolation, just as shame is an internally isolating affect, as Tomkins

says with his characteristic combination of technical and literary intensity:

In contrast to all other affects, shame is an experience of the self by the self. At that moment when the self feels ashamed, it is felt as a sickness within the self. Shame is the most reflexive of affects in that the phenomenological distinction between the subject and object of shame is lost. Why is shame so close to the experienced self? It is because the self lives in the face, and within the face the self burns brightest in the eyes. Shame turns the attention of the self and others away from other objects to this most visible residence of self, increases its visibility and thereby generates the torment of self-consciousness.

(*Affect*, p. 133)

Shame plants the mind's eye. The shamed person breaks contact, retreats, licks wounds in private and (if at all reflective) has a strong reason to think about what has happened and possibly replay it in an inner theatre. As Shakespeare puts it in a sonnet on reflection I will discuss below, 'in disgrace with fortune and men's eyes, / I all alone beweep my outcast state' (29:1–2).[2]

Shakespeare, as these lines and this article will suggest, has a relatively normal sensitive person's relation to shame. Montaigne, however, at least in

---

[1] Silvan S. Tomkins, *Affect Imagery Consciousness*, Volume II: *The Negative Affects* (New York, 1963), pp. 119–20. Further citations will appear parenthetically. Both of the passages I have quoted also appear in Adam Frank and Eve Kosofsky Sedgwick, eds., *Shame and Its Sisters: A Silvan Tomkins Reader* (Durham, 1995).

[2] *Shakespeare's Sonnets*, ed. Stephen Booth (New Haven, 1977), p. 27. I cite this edition parenthetically by sonnet and line number in what follows.

his literary self-presentations, finds shame in somewhat unusual places or situations. Montaigne suggests in the early essay 'Of Idleness' that he writes essays after an unsatisfactory, shaming experience of solitary reflection. That is, he turns to reflective writing because in disgrace with his own eyes. The essay writing serves in turn as his attempt to shame himself into a better mode of reflection:

Dernierement que je me retiray chez moy, deliberé autant que je pourroy, ne me mesler d'autre chose que de passer en repos, et à part, ce peu qui me reste de vie: il me sembloit ne pouvoir faire plus grande faveur à mon esprit, que de le laisser on pleine oysiveté . . . Mais je trouve . . . que au rebours, faisant le cheval eschappé, il se donne cent fois plus d'affaire à soy mesmes, qu'il n'en prenoit pour autruy; et m'enfante tant de chimeres et monstres fantasques les uns sur les autres, sans ordre, et sans propos, que pour en contempler à mon aise l'ineptie et l'estrangeté, j'ay commancé de les mettre en rolle, esperant avec le temps luy en faire honte à luy mesmes.

It is not long since I retired my selfe unto mine own house, with full purpose, as much as lay in me, not to trouble my selfe with any businesse, but solitarily and quietly to weare out the remainder of my well-nigh-spent life; where me thought I could doe my spirit no greater favour, than to give him the full scope of idlenesse . . . but I finde . . . [t]hat contrariwise playing the skittish and loose-broken jade, he takes a hundred times more cariere and libertie unto himselfe, than hee did for others; and begets in me so many extravagant *Chimeraes*, and fantasticall monsters, so orderlesse, and without any reason, one hudling upon an other, that at leasure to view the foolishnesse and monstrous strangenesse of them, I have begun to keepe a register of them, hoping, if I live, one day to make him ashamed, and blush at himself.[3]

The act of making thought visible by writing might cause thought to feel shame and thus reform itself, Montaigne suggests, perhaps somewhat facetiously. Nonetheless, it is clear that Montaigne found his mental state during the initial, non-writing period of retirement disturbing.[4] But the shame he feels at his own undisciplined mental processes differs from what Tomkins considers the root affect, which requires the presence of another's gazing eye; if Montaigne has internalized shame as a gazer within himself, he has managed to make shame almost entirely nonsocial, a part of a process of interior reflection. Clearly Montaigne did not tame his galloping thoughts, which continue to bolt off like runaway horses throughout the *Essais* – though he may have cured himself of the discomfort caused by his mental errancy by turning it into a writing programme. Indeed, if Montaigne's essay-writing is curative, it cures him not of mental bolting but of being ashamed of it, and the *Essays* are delightful partly by being so persistently unencumbered by shame. Using both Roy Leake's *Concordance des essais* and machine-searchable etexts,[5] one finds about 90 instances of *honte* in the *Essais*, and a surprising number of them, like the one just cited, are either repudiations of shame, prescriptions for curing it or proposals to use shame productively in a corrective programme aimed at Montaigne himself or at his culture.[6] The first mention of shame in the *Essais* describes both shame's power over a reflective person humiliated in public and Montaigne's relative freedom from that power:

[I]l a esté remarqué par les anciens que Diodorus le Dialecticien mourut sur le champ, espris d'une extreme passion de honte, pour en son eschole et en public ne

---

3 Pierre Villey, V.-L. Saulnier, and Marcel Conche, eds., *Michel de Montaigne: les essais, édition Villey-Saulnier* (Paris, 2004), p. 33. John Florio, trans., *The Essayes of Montaigne: John Florio's Translation* (New York, 1933), p. 24. Page references to these editions are included parenthetically henceforth.

4 See, e.g., Donald Frame, *Montaigne: A Biography* (New York, 1965), pp. 143–55; Géralde Nakam, *Montaigne et son temps: les événements et les essais* (Paris, 1982), pp. 106–10; M. A. Screech, *Montaigne and Melancholy* (Cranbury, NJ, 1984), pp. 65–9.

5 See Roy Leake's *Concordance des essais de Montaigne* (Geneva, 1981), pp. 602–3; for a machine-searchable English translation, see www.gutenberg.org/etext/3600 at Project Gutenberg.

6 By my count, 23 describe how potential shame marks helpful moral boundaries (in general or in specific historical situations), 12 describe the shamefulness of the age Montaigne inhabits, 11 describe shame as immediately productive of its own cure (often through self-violence or some other violent reversal of past behaviour), 8 describe shame as attaching to relations between custom and embodiment, 5 offer remedies for shame (e.g. ways to overcome sexual impotence), 5 document Montaigne's own shameless or shame-free attitudes and 5 register surprise at shame's power over others.

se pouvoir desvelopper d'un argument qu'on luy avoit faict.

Je suis peu en prise de ces violentes passions. J'ay l'apprehension naturellement dure; et l'encrouste et espessis tous les jours par discours.   (I.2.14)

[I]t is noted by our Ancients, that *Diodorus* the Logician, being surprized with an extreme passion or apprehension of shame, fell downe starke dead, because neither in his Schoole, nor in publique, he had beene able to resolve an argument propounded unto him. I am little subject to these violent passions. I have naturally a hard apprehension, which by discourse I daily harden more and more.   (Florio, 9)

Diodorus died of shame on-stage. Before his death, he felt, presumably, 'As an unperfect actor on the stage, / Who with his fear is put besides his part' (Sonnet 23: 1–2). This is a reminder that while the stage may be represented by its critics as shameless, the imminent possibility of extreme shame energizes theatrical performance. According to contemporary psychologists, fear of being shamed by failure in public performance features widely in contemporary anxiety dreams,[7] and Shakespeare's sonnet suggests that it was a prevalent fear in the Renaissance as well.

Given this, the sequence of exposure to others, shame, isolation, reflection, release from shame, re-emergence into social life, is in its very shape a comforting and therapeutic one. It is a way of handling the dangers and fears that lurk in social life by asserting partial control of them in imagination. As Ewan Fernie remarks, 'shame in Shakespeare works as an ethical wake-up call, the dissolution of the anxious subject's phantasmal self automatically revealing the world beyond it.'[8] Moreover, shame, reflection and return in this sequence seem linked, as though inner reflective life were shame's product and as though further communication with others, on altered terms, were reflection's product.[9]

Several recent books about Shakespeare as a reflective author place a remarkable emphasis on Montaigne. Millicent Bell's *Shakespeare's Tragic Skepticism*[10] and Colin McGinn's *Shakespeare's Philosophy*[11] illustrate the connection I want to draw. Let me focus briefly on McGinn, noting

that Bell offers a parallel case.[12] McGinn blandly assumes that Shakespeare's reading of Montaigne was deep and life-long (he sees influential parallels between passages about dreaming in *An Apology for Raymond Sebond* and *A Midsummer Night's Dream*, for instance),[13] and he grounds a claim for Shakespeare's sceptical naturalism on his view of Montaigne's sceptical naturalism. Montaigne is magnificently sceptical and naturalistic, and Montaigne's essays provide passages that richly anticipate a variety of later philosophical positions from Descartes to Hume to Wittgenstein to Thomas Kuhn and Peter Singer. Thus, by assuming that cognate passages (not actual borrowings, but similar thoughts) in Shakespeare participate in an intellectual context supplied by insightful reading of Montaigne, McGinn can plausibly treat Shakespeare as in implicit dialogue with a subsequent philosophic tradition. Montaigne supplies the reflective stance

---

[7] Joanne Davis, Patrick Newman, personal communications. The recurrent I-can't-find-the-classroom dream experienced by many academics before the first day of the new semester is a related phenomenon, perhaps not untouched by wish-fulfilment. For a census of dream themes, see http://psych.ucsc.edu/dreams/Norms/main.html.

[8] Ewan Fernie, *Shame in Shakespeare* (London, 2002), p. 6.

[9] For a discussion of Bernard Williams's and Richard Wollheim's accounts of how shame may be more morally productive than guilt (and, concurrently, of how it is wrong to claim that moderns inhabit a guilt-culture that can be opposed to the shame-culture of the ancients), see Lars Engle, '"I am that I am": Shakespeare's Sonnets and the Economy of Shame', in James Schiffer, ed., *Shakespeare's Sonnets: Critical Essays* (New York, 1999), pp. 185–97. On guilt as a species of shame, see Tomkins, *Affect*, pp. 118 and 138–9.

[10] Millicent Bell, *Shakespeare's Tragic Skepticism* (New Haven, 2002). For Bell's reliance on Montaigne, see her introduction, pp. 12–25; for an instance of her use of Montaigne in locating Hamlet, see p. 31.

[11] Colin McGinn, *Shakespeare's Philosophy: Discovering the Meaning Behind the Plays* (New York, 2006).

[12] I should probably add here that A. D. Nuttall's *Shakespeare the Thinker* (New Haven, 2007) and Tzachi Zamir's *Double Vision: Moral Philosophy and Shakespearean Drama* (Princeton, 2006) do not use Montaigne in this way.

[13] McGinn, *Philosophy*, p. 22. Though McGinn's note refers one to p. 67 in Screech's Montaigne, the reference is in fact to p. 674. For the centrality of Montaigne to McGinn's claims, see his introduction, pp. 6 and 15–16.

and the philosophical claims; Shakespeare has characters who make speeches that are strikingly reminiscent of provocative moments in Montaigne; *et voilà!* Shakespeare emerges as a thinker remarkably prescient with respect to modernity, though also a thinker located at a pre-Cartesian pre-scientific historical moment that more or less guarantees a broad humanism rather than a rigorous search for certainty.

It is easy for me to track this argument, because in a way I have been making it myself for some time. Hugh Grady has also made it, and in Grady's case it is implicitly part of a broadly presentist agenda for the interpretation of Shakespeare's thought that sees Montaigne as a sixteenth-century stand-in for contemporary theorists of resistant consciousness like Habermas and Machiavelli as a sixteenth-century stand-in for recent theorists of interpellative power-knowledge networks like Foucault.[14]

My own tack on this argument differs from McGinn's and also from Grady's in that I see a Shakespeare who resists at least some of the aspects of Montaigne that make twenty-first-century readers so comfortable reading Montaigne. Montaigne anticipates, perhaps not consistently but strikingly, a number of modern or postmodern enlightened attitudes: anti-ethnocentrism, anti-dogmatism, categorical opposition to cruelty, distaste for and amusement at sexual repression and adherence to the idea that many different kinds of lives should be livable in a state of self-approval. All of these, especially the last three, are related to Montaigne's generally liberatory attitude towards shame: Montaigne thinks much shame is unnecessary.

Now, we do not know for sure that Shakespeare read Montaigne deeply. But the comparison I am drawing is helpful whether or not it describes a relation of influence, since it points to general ways of framing both Montaigne and Shakespeare that clearly distinguish their relations to shame and reflection. That distinction will turn out to be important when we look critically at efforts to see Shakespeare as modern in the ways we see Montaigne as modern. Moreover, I myself

think Shakespeare did read Montaigne deeply, and I will thus present contrasts between Shakespeare and Montaigne on shame and reflection as Shakespeare's responses to Montaigne. I see a Shakespeare impressed with and provoked by Montaigne, but deeply suspicious of the very possibility of a sustained Montaignean stance towards the world – a stance of free reflection largely uninterrupted by the continual pressure of negotiation and thereby largely freed from shame imposed by others from without. It is this resistance, a resistance that I connect with Shakespeare's commitment to the necessity of encountering and feeling shame in relation to others, that I explore in what follows.

Montaigne discusses his process of reflection in the late essay 'Of Three Kinds of Commerce' in ways that at least somewhat recall the dialectic of shame and discursive reflection introduced in 'Of Idleness' and discussed above:

> Ce n'est pas estre amy de soy, et moins encore maistre, c'est en estre esclave, de se suivre incessamment, et estre si pris à ses inclinations qu'on n'en puisse fourvoyer, qu'on ne les puisse tordre. Je le dy à cette heure, pour ne me pouvoir facilement despestrer de l'importunité de mon ame, en ce qu'elle ne sçait communément s'amuser sinon où elle s'empeche . . . La plus part des esprits ont besoing de matiere estrangere pour se desgourdir et exercer; le mien en a besoing pour se rassoir plustost et sejourner, << *vitia otii negotio discutienda sunt,* >> car son plus laborieux et principal estude, c'est s'estudier à soy. (III.3.819)

> It is not to bee the friend (lesse the master) but the slave of ones selfe to follow uncessantly, and bee so addicted to his inclinations, as hee cannot stray from them, nor wrest them. This I say now, as being extreamly pestred with

---

[14] Hugh Grady, *Shakespeare, Machiavelli, and Montaigne: Power and Subjectivity from Richard II to Hamlet* (Oxford, 2002); Lars Engle, '*Measure for Measure* and Modernity: The Problem of the Sceptic's Authority', in Hugh Grady, ed., *Shakespeare and Modernity: Early Modern to Millennium* (London, 2000), pp. 85–104; Lars Engle, 'Shakespearean Normativity in *All's Well that Ends Well*', *Shakespeare International Yearbook 4* (Aldershot, 2004), pp. 264–79; Lars Engle, 'Sovereign Cruelty in Montaigne and *King Lear*', in Graham Bradshaw, Thomas Bishop and Peter Holbrook, eds., *Shakespearean International Yearbook 6* (Aldershot, 2006), pp. 119–39.

the importunity of my minde, forsomuch as shee cannot ammuse her selfe, but whereon it is busied . . . Most wits have neede of extravagant stuffe, to un-benumme and exercise themselves: mine hath neede of it, rather to settle and continue it selfe: *Vitia otii negotio discustienda sunt* (SEN. *Ep.* lvi.), *The vices of idlenesse should bee shaken off with businesse:* For, the most laborious care and principall studie of it, is, to studie it selfe.   (Florio, 737)

Like many of Montaigne's reflections on his own reflective habits, this one is both self-deprecating and uncompromisingly self-absorbed. The self-absorption is potentially unwelcoming to readers, and Montaigne gives fair warning of this. His readers, unlike readers of normal books that strive to please or promise benefits, must be odd enough to want to know Montaigne himself:

Ainsi, lecteur, je suis moy-mesmes la matiere de mon livre: ce n'est pas raison que tu employes ton loisir en un subject si frivole et si vain. A Dieu donq, de Montaigne, ce premier de Mars mille cinq cens quatre vingts.
                                        ('Au Lecteur', 3)

Thus gentle Reader my selfe am the groundworke of my booke: It is then no reason thou shouldest employ thy time about so frivolous and vaine a Subject. Therefore farewell. From *Montaigne*, the first of March, 1580.
                                        (Florio, xxvii)

We must go without guarantees or inducements to where he lives. The identification of his name with his place of residence hints at the strong gravity-field of self-preoccupation we enter in reading the *Essais* and at a fairly complete absence of shame at the self-exposure involved. The prefatory valediction ('Therefore farewell') as a whole signals Montaigne's take-it-or-leave-it attitude towards what we might find. But if Montaigne takes our reading the essays lightly, as our whimsical participation in his discursive selfishness, he honours the processes of reflective thought that go into attempts at self-understanding: Montaigne continually asserts the value of self-examination, of a process of productive reflection on what locates him (and thus us) in what and where he is. And it is in this process, rather than the gaze of the other, that shame finds its productive locus for Montaigne, even if the shame attaches to a social act:

Mon ame, de sa complexion, refuit la menterie et hait mesmes à la penser.

J'ay une interne vergongne et un remors piquant, si par fois elle m'eschappe, comme par fois elle m'eschappe, les occasions me surprenant et agitant impremeditéement.

                    (II.17.648; Villey-Saulnier glosses 'vergongne'
                                        as 'honte'.)

My minde of her own complexion detesteth falsehood, and hateth to think on it. I feele an inward bashfulness, and a stinging remorse, if at any time it scape me; as sometimes it doth, if unpremeditated occasions surprise me.   (Florio, 587)

By comparison to the textual self-location insisted on by Montaigne of Montaigne, Shakespeare of New Place might well seem Shakespeare of no place. Shakespeare's alleged return to Stratford, in some ways like Montaigne's retirement to Montaigne, is also deeply different: Shakespeare's retirement seems rather the culmination of a process of socially mobile self-transformation that on the whole Shakespeare seeks *not* to make visible. The same could be said of Shakespeare's treatment of his personal heritage. Montaigne writes essays praising his father's temperament (which he himself in part inherits), physique, athleticism, discretion in conducting love affairs, mode of life and care for Montaigne's early education. Shakespeare buys his shiftless father a coat of arms so that he himself can become at 35 a gentleman born. And so on: it is easy to draw out a systematic contrast between the two, which in the end must involve a contrast not only between two temperaments but also between two genres, essay vs. commercial drama, and two modes of life, leisured self-revealing reflective Montaignean *otium* vs. busy reticent active Shakespearian negotiation. (Obviously this downplays Montaigne's political activity and his estate management, but it is equally obvious that by contrast to Shakespeare's life, Montaigne's is leisured.)[15] One aspect of this contrast may well be a keener

---

[15] On the very substantial non-writerly activity in Montaigne's life, including the parts of his life in which he writes the essays, see George Hoffman, *Montaigne's Career* (Oxford, 1998).

sensitivity on Shakespeare's part to shame, and thus a gravitation towards arts of self-displacement or self-concealment rather than self-exposure.

Given this contrast, it makes sense to examine Shakespeare's representations of leisured detached reflection, using Montaigne as a backdrop, and seeing the two also as having something important in common. Literary history is surely right to see both as pioneers in the literary representation of deep inner selfhood. Both remain huge resources for the self-enhancement of readers and auditors. Clearly their means of exploration, and the kinds of resource they provide, differ. We have no essays by Shakespeare himself, indeed no unequivocally autobiographical documents. His will busily shapes his daughters' future lives, but does not reflect on his own. His prologues and epilogues on the whole speak for the players' will to please and fear of giving offence, not for the author's literary aspirations (unlike Ben Jonson's, the obvious contrastive case). The dedications of *Venus and Adonis* and *The Rape of Lucrece* direct attention away from the unworthy dedicator to the noble dedicatee, fairly ardently in the second case, without offering any grounding details of relationship. It is a *faute-de-mieux* necessity, then, in thinking about Shakespeare on reflection, to do what also seems sensible: that is, to assume that, as a theatre poet, Shakespeare investigated human activities by creating characters and situations that exemplify those activities. That is, Shakespeare reflects on reflection by embodying it.

Shakespearian reflective personae, often satiric, include the speaker of the Sonnets, the courtiers of Navarre in *Love's Labour's Lost*, the exiles, especially Jacques, in *As You Like It*, the stoics in *Julius Caesar*, Hamlet and Horatio and perhaps Polonius in *Hamlet*, several reflective figures in *All's Well* and Prospero and Gonzalo in *The Tempest*. The two of these who have sometimes been thought to embody autobiographical reflection on Shakespeare's part are Prospero and the speaker of the Sonnets. The scanty concordance entries for 'reflection', 'philosophy' and 'meditation' and their cognates demonstrate that fancy words for introspective thinking are not heavily used by Shakespeare. The name

'Plato' does not appear in Shakespeare's works, and the name 'Socrates' appears only in a reference to Xantippe's shrewishness, which may suggest how little interest he takes in the reflective tradition that is so important to Montaigne.[16] The courtiers of Navarre, Shakespeare's first and in some ways his only avowed reflective philosophers, sustain their plan to make themselves into an ascetic academy, 'Still and contemplative in living art' (1.1.14), for about five minutes, until 1.1.131. The reflective passages in *Hamlet* explore obsessively the poor fit between a contemplative temperament and the task of the revenger. We might put this slight comic example and this central tragic one together to say that Shakespeare's dramatic treatments of reflection often illustrate the poor fit between reflection and the task of being enmeshed in the action of a play. They also illustrate an intimate connection between reflection and shame: all of Hamlet's soliloquies are full of shame, and, as Fernie comments, 'the prince is ashamed from the very beginning, but he comes to terms with this only at the end';[17] Berowne and the other courtiers of Navarre are shamed repeatedly out of reflective postures in *Love's Labour's Lost*.

We think that one factor in the increased gravity of reflection in *Hamlet* might be Shakespeare's reading of Montaigne.[18] Jacques in *As You Like It*, written about the same time, offers an interesting case, though one that continues to support the idea that Shakespeare regards detached reflection as somewhat ludicrous. Jacques is not only reflective, but he is resistant or impervious to shame, partly because he has no purposes beyond self-interested

---

[16] See Marvin Spevack, ed., *The Harvard Concordance to Shakespeare* (Cambridge, MA, 1973), pp. 807, 977, 984, 1046 and 1170.

[17] Fernie, *Shame*, p. 112.

[18] See James Shapiro, *A Year in the Life of William Shakespeare: 1599* (New York, 2005), pp. 293–4. Shapiro points out, citing William Corwallis (who read Montaigne in English in the 1590s), that not only was Florio circulating parts of his translation in manuscript but that Florio himself says that 'seven or eight of great wit' had attempted an English translation already and failed to complete one. Florio's comment is on p. xxiii.

reflection. Hazlitt calls him 'the only purely contemplative character in Shakespear... the prince of philosophical idlers; his only passion is thought; he sets no value upon any thing but as it serves as food for reflection.'[19] Jacques is first described moralizing over a weeping, dying deer by a lord attending the banished Duke Senior:

> [H]e lay along
> Under an oak, whose antic root peeps out
> Upon the brook that brawls along this wood,
> To the which place a poor sequestered stag
> That from the hunter's aim had ta'en a hurt
> Did come to languish. And indeed, my lord,
> The wretched animal heaved forth such groans
> That their discharge did stretch his leathern coat
> Almost to bursting, and the big round tears
> Coursed one another down his innocent nose
> In piteous chase.[20]

Jacques 'moralize[s] this spectacle', as the Duke puts it, in terms of inhumanity and cruelty (though he is not reported to use the word 'cruel'); the lord reports that Jacques

> most invectively... pierceth through
> The body of the country, city, court,
> Yea, and of this our life, swearing that we
> Are mere usurpers, tyrants, and what's worse,
> To fright the animals and to kill them up
> In their assigned and native dwelling place.
> (*AYLI*, 2.1.58–63)

Duke Senior asks if they 'left him in this contemplation' (one of Shakespeare's 14 uses of the word, many of them like this one evidently somewhat satiric) and the lord replies 'We did, my lord, weeping and commenting / Upon the sobbing deer' (*AYLI*, 2.1.64–6).

As a number of scholars have noted, this scene is reminiscent of a passage in Montaigne's 'Of Cruelty':[21]

> De moy, je n'ay pas sçeu voir seulement sans desplaisir poursuivre et tuer une beste innocente, qui est sans deffence et de qui nous ne recevons aucune offence. Et, comme il advient communement que le cerf, se sentant hors d'alaine et de force, n'ayant plus autre remede, se rejette et rend à nous mesmes qui le poursuivons, nous demandant mercy par ses larmes,

> quaestuque, cruentus
> Atque imploranti similis,
> ce m'a tousjours semblé un spectacle tres-desplaisant.
> (II.11.432–3)

> As for me, I could never so much as endure, without remorse and griefe, to see a poore, sillie, and innocent beast pursued and killed, which is harmelesse and void of defence, and of whom we receive no offence at all. And as it commonly hapneth, that when the Stag begins to be embost, and finds his strength to faile-him, having no other remedie left him, doth yeeld and bequeath himselfe unto us that pursue him, with teares suing to us for mercie,

> *Questúque cruentus*
> *Atque imploranti similes:*–VIRG. *AEn.* vii. 521
> With blood from throat, and teares from eyes,
> It seems that he for pittie cryes.
> Was ever a grievous spectacle unto me. (Florio, 382)

What has not, I think, been noticed, is that Jacques's own tears over the dying deer might also remind a reader of Florio's version of Montaigne's self-reported susceptibility to tears a few pages earlier in 'Of Cruelty':

> Il n'est rien qui tente mes larmes que les larmes, non vrayes seulement, mais comment que ce soit, ou feintes ou peintes. Les morts, je ne les plains guiere, et les envierois plutost; mais je plains bien fort les mourans... Les executions mesme de la justice, pour raisonnables qu'elles soyent, je ne les puis voir d'une veuë ferme. (II.11.430)

> There is nothing sooner moveth teares in me, than to see others weepe, not only fainedly, but howsoever, whether truly or forcedly. I do not greatly waile for the dead, but rather envie them. Yet doe I much waile and moane the dying... Let any man be executed by law, how deservedly soever, I cannot endure to behold the execution with an unrelenting eye. (Florio, 380)

---

[19] William Hazlitt (1817), quoted in Richard Knowles, ed., *As You Like It: A New Variorum Edition of Shakespeare* (New York, 1977), p. 583.

[20] William Shakespeare, *As You Like It*, in Walter Cohen, Stephen Greenblatt, Jean Howard and Katharine Eisaman Maus, eds., *The Norton Shakespeare: Based on the Oxford Edition*, 2nd edn (New York, 2008), 2.1.30–40. Further references to Shakespeare's plays will be to this edition.

[21] See Knowles, ed., *As You Like It*, p. 74, citing Gervais (1901).

This makes Montaigne sound weepy. But Florio's translation is in fact misleading about Montaigne here. He mistranslates 'il n'est rien qui tente mes larmes' (there is nothing that tempts my tears) as 'there is nothing that sooner moveth teares in me' – making an inclination sound like an habitual action. (He also does not appear to understand 'ou feintes ou peintes', 'whether feigned or painted'). In the previous sentence, Montaigne has made clear that, when others weep, he *would* cry *if* he knew how to cry.

... je me compassionne fort tendrement des afflictions d'autruy, et pleurerois aiseement par compaignie, si, pour occasion que ce soit, je sçavois pleurer.   (II.11.430)

(I feel very tender compassion for the afflictions of others, and would readily weep to keep others company, if, whatever the occasion, I knew how to weep at all.)

Florio, partly because of the way he punctuates, makes it far less clear that Montaigne is by his own account habitually dry-eyed: 'I have a verie feeling and tender compassion of other mens afflictions, and should more easily weep for companie sake, if possiblie for any occasion whatsoever, I could shed teares' (Florio, 380). Though he does more or less translate the final clause, the following sentence shows that he has not really understood it, since Florio's version implies that Montaigne is often moved to tears and gives a strong account of how Montaigne wails and moans for the dying (again a mistranslation of 'je plains bien fort', 'I very strongly pity' or 'I lament strongly'). From Florio's vagueness and misdirection, Shakespeare might well have constructed a Montaigne who was a weeping moralizer like Jacques.

To do this Shakespeare would have to have read Florio's version of 'Of Cruelty' by around 1600. We know he read this essay in Florio's version at some point, since it is closely paraphrased in *The Tempest*. We have rare-word evidence that Florio's translation influenced *Hamlet*, written around 1599, and *Lear*.[22] Florio's translation was not published until 1603, but Florio's preface shows that it had been in preparation for some time – following, he says, upon Lucy Countess of Bedford's reading of a translation of one of the essays commissioned

from Florio by Sir Edward Wotton (Florio, xvi–xvii). A poem encouraging Florio by one of his helpers, Matthew Gwinne, is dated 1599 (xxiv), and the book was entered for publication in 1600. Valentine Sims, who printed a number of Shakespeare's quartos, was Florio's printer, and Edward Blount, who twenty years later would help publish the 1623 Shakespeare folio, was the publisher. In his own preface to the translation, Florio dramatizes his own desperation over the length and macaronic difficulty of the *Essais* by referring to the description of the dying deer in 'Of Cruelty': 'As for mee, I onely say, as this mans [Montaigne's] embossed Hart out of hart (*Lib.* ii. *c.* 11), I sweate, I wept, and I went-on, til now I stand at bay' (Florio, xvii). This suggests that the passage, and perhaps the essay as a whole, were well known. (In the previous sentence Florio also compares himself to a cannibal captive being fattened for a feast, alluding thus to the other essay that we know Shakespeare to have read, 'Of the Cannibals' [Florio, xvii].)

Given that Florio had been writing with Southampton's support at roughly the time of *Venus and Adonis* and *Lucrece*, when Shakespeare seems also to have been close to the young earl, it is quite possible that Shakespeare knew Florio and could have seen some of Florio's translation prior to publication;[23] it is also possible, though it seems less likely, that Shakespeare was one of those like Lucy Countess of Bedford and Lady Anne Harrington to whom Florio will 'repeate in true English what you reade in fine French' (xv).

These possibilities – and they are only that – may seem more persuasive when one notes that

---

22 See, e.g., Bell, *Tragic*, pp. 17–20. See also Leo Salingar, '*King Lear*, Montaigne, and Harsnett', *The Aligarh Journal of English Studies*, 8 (1983), pp. 124–66, *passim* and especially pp. 125–7, where he summarizes rare-word evidence derived from Kenneth Muir. For an account of Montaigne's English impact before and just after the publication of Florio's translation in 1603, see William Hamlin, *Tragedy and Scepticism in Shakespeare's England* (Basingstoke, 2005), pp. 60–1.

23 See Colin Burrow, ed., *The Oxford Shakespeare: Complete Sonnets and Poems* (Oxford, 2002), p. 13. Florio said in the dedication to his 1598 *World of Words* that he had been paid by Southampton for some years.

the last line of Jacques's most famous speech, 'Sans teeth, sans eyes, sans taste, sans every thing,' resembles a line from Florio's translation of the essay that follows 'Of Cruelty,' the 'Apologie for Raymond Sebond': 'as the soules of the gods, sanse tongues, sanse eyes and sanse eares, have each one in themselves a feeling of that which the other feele'.[24] Another reflective philosophizing character in *As You Like It* is the clown Touchstone: William Lloyd long ago invoked Montaigne in comparing Touchstone's mode of reflection to that of Jacques: 'Perhaps Jacques, in his parody of Amiens's song, approaches the critical vein of Touchstone pretty closely, but he is inferior in that mixed vein of self-observation and self-knowledge, which approximates Touchstone at one time to Mr Pepys, and at another to Michel de Montaigne.'[25] Both the character Touchstone and the name 'Touchstone' are invented by Shakespeare. It has not, I think, been noticed before that the name and perhaps some of the character might plausibly be connected to an odd capitalization in Florio's translation of the *Apologie*. It comes at the climax of a characteristic Montaignean avowal of inconstancy and the limitations of reason:

How often change we our phantasies? What I hold and beleeve this day, I beleeve and hold with all my beleefe . . . I am wholy and absolutely given to it: but hath it not been my fortune, not one, but a hundred, nay a thousand times, nay daily, to have embraced some other thing, . . . which upon better advise I have afterward judged false? *A man should at the least become wise, at his owne cost, and learne by others harmes.* If under this colour I have often found my selfe deceived, if my Touch-stone be commonly found false and my balance un-even and unjust; What assurance may I more take of it at this time, then at others? (Florio, 507)

Of course, it is likely enough that the capital T is supplied by Valentine Sims's compositor rather than Florio's manuscript, and thus even possible that influence is working backward, from Shakespeare's stage to a momentary hand-to-upper-case impulse in the printing house that came from remembering 'Touchstone' as a name.

Either Jacques or Touchstone, if seen as an actual version of Montaigne, would be a parodic one – the first sentimental and self-isolating, the second earthy, sceptical and (in his marriage to Audrey) embracing embodiment. When Shakespeare creates reflective figures that seem Montaignean, they often appear in complementary pairs, like Lafeu and Paroles in *All's Well That Ends Well* or Prospero and Gonzalo in *The Tempest*. Paroles, in *All's Well*, offers an extraordinary instance of the relations between shame and reflection.

Paroles throughout the play has presented himself as an exemplar of military virtue and has been accepted as a tutor in honour by Bertram (even though wiser observers, starting with Helena, have seen through him throughout). To expose him, Bertram's friends arrange his capture, bring him blindfolded before Bertram and have his alleged Muscovite captors demand that he describe the Florentine forces and especially the French who fight for them. After Paroles has traduced by name Bertram and the other nobles of the French camp, his blindfold is removed and he finds himself looked at by them.

Interpreter. Come, headsman, off with his head.
Paroles. O Lord, sir! –Let me live, or let me see my death!
Interpreter. That shall you, and take your leave of all your
     friends.
     [*He unmuffles Paroles*]
So, look about you. Know you any here?
                                                (4.3.286–90)

Gazing scornfully at him are Bertram and the Lords Dumaine, whom Paroles has just slandered and betrayed. Paroles, after they have reviled him and left, comments 'Who cannot be crushed by a plot?' (4.3.302), and the soldier who has pretended to interpret Russian responds rather oddly in his attempt to express how thoroughly Paroles is disgraced:

Interpreter. If you could find out a country where but
     women were that had received so much shame, you

[24] Quoted in Knowles, ed., *As You Like It*, p. 137.
[25] Knowles, *As You Like It*, p. 585.

might begin an impudent nation. Fare ye well sir. I am for France too. We shall speak of you there.

Exit (4.3.303–6)

He casts Paroles as a kind of Founder, in Machiavellian terms, of a new world of shamelessness, an 'impudent nation'. Such a view of the shamed Paroles as a potential impious Aeneas might, along the lines of argument I lay out here, count as a recognition of the difference Montaigne's attitudes toward shame and the desirability of repudiating or accepting it could make. Setting aside a variety of kinds of shame could create a new world, though not in this case a very savoury one. A number of critics have felt that *All's Well That Ends Well* and *Othello* register the way Montaigne's essays, and especially 'On Some Verses of Virgil', challenge attitudes towards chastity and other shame-related forms of honour.[26] Paroles, having been shamed and then left alone, of course reflects:

Paroles.   Captain I'll be no more,
  But I will eat and drink and sleep as soft
  As captain shall. Simply the thing I am
  Shall make me live . . .
  Rust, sword; cool, blushes; and Paroles live
  Safest in shame; being fooled, by fool'ry thrive.
  There's place and means for every man alive.

(4.3.308–16)

Paroles recovers from shame by adopting shame as a mode of life, with an evident relief that seems close to the recovery of a true self after being entrapped in a false performance for others (this being one of the standard therapeutic goals of shame-induced reflection).[27] From this viewpoint, Paroles's shame has allowed him to become 'simply the thing I am', an achievement of a Montaignean kind. Two passages from 'On Some Verses of Virgil' illustrate this:

Au reste, je me suis ordonné d'oser dire tout ce que j'ose faire, et me desplais des pensées mesmes impubliables. La pire de mes actions et conditions ne me semble pas si laide comme je trouve laid et lâche de ne l'oser avouer.

(III.5.845)

For my part I am resolved to dare speake whatsoever I dare do: And am displeased with thoughts not to be published. The worst of my actions or condicions seeme not so ugly unto me, as I finde it both ugly and base not to dare to avouch them.

(Florio, 760)

This resolution on Montaigne's part involves a willingness to embrace what others might find unutterably shameful, such as his apparent admission that he has been, or at least in old age is being, scanted by nature in penis size. This avowal comes after Montaigne points out that human beings are so foolish that we may be reasonable in calling both the act and the parts involved in making more human beings 'shameful': 'd'appeller l'action honteuse, et honteuses les parties qui y servent' (III.5.878). Montaigne adds a parenthesis: '(asteure sont les miennes proprement honteuses et peneuses)' '(mine are properly so at this moment)' (III.5.878; Florio, 792). Montaigne says more along these lines a few pages later, though the key passages are in Latin. Speaking of women who look at him reproachfully because he has disappointed them sexually, he writes:

Quand j'en ay veu quelqu'une s'ennuyer de moy, je n'en ay point incontinent accusé sa legereté; j'ay mis en doubte si je n'avois pas raison de m'en prendre à nature plustost. Certes, elle m'a traitté illegitimement et inciviliment,

  Si non longa satis, si non bené mentula crassa:
    Nimirum sapiunt, vidéntque parvam
    Matronae quoque mentulam illibenter.
Et d'une lesion enormissime.

  Chacune de mes pieces me faict esgalement moy que toute autre. Et nulle autre ne me faict plus proprement homme que cette cy. Je dois au publiq universellement mon pourtrait.

(III.5.887)

---

[26] See, e.g., Arthur Kirsch, *Shakespeare and the Experience of Love* (Cambridge, 1981), pp. 121–7; Arthur Kirsch, 'Sexuality and Marriage in Montaigne and *All's Well That Ends Well*', *Montaigne Studies*, 9 (1997), pp. 187–202; Janet Adelman, *Suffocating Mothers: Fantasies of Maternal Origin in Shakespeare's Plays*, Hamlet *to* The Tempest (New York, 1992), p. 282. A preliminary survey by William Hamlin suggests that 'On Some Verses of Virgil' is the most heavily annotated essay in surviving copies of the first two editions of Florio's translation (personal communication).

[27] For a contrasting view of this outcome as non-reflective and thus disgusting, see Fernie, *Shame*, pp. 98–9; he views Paroles's shamelessness as 'the nemesis of the human, as gross and unredeemed animality' (p. 99).

When I have perceived any [female sexual partner] weary of me, I have not presently accused her lightnes: but made question whether I had not more reason to quarrell with nature, for handling me so unlawfully and uncivilly,

> Si non longa satis, si non benè mentula crassa:
> Nimirum sapiunt videntque parvam
> Matronæ quoque mentulam illibenter, – Lus. Priap. penul.
>   1. ibid. viii. 4.

and to my exceeding hurt. Each of my pieces are equally mine, one as another: and no other doth more properly make me a man then this. My whole pourtraiture I universally owe unto the world.   (Florio, 801)

Florio leaves the Latin untranslated, contrary to his normal practice, though for the same reasons he leaves a number of other Latin passages in 'On some verses' untranslated as well. Villey-Saulnier annotates 'Si non longa satis . . . crassa' euphemistically: 'L'idée est: "si elle m'a mal pourvu".' It glosses the next two Latin lines with similar caution: 'L'idée est: "Les matrones elles-mêmes voient sans plaisir de maigres apparences".' (III.5.887n). M. A. Screech translates the Latin non-euphemistically (translating rather than alluding to *mentula*) but also renders Montaigne's comment on his own member an entirely conditional or subjunctive one:

I have asked myself, rather, whether I would be right to rail against Nature.

> Si non longa satis, si non bene mentula crassa,
> [Should my cock be not long enough nor good and
>   thick,]

then Nature has indeed treated me unlawfully and unjustly –

> Nimirium sapient, videntque parvam
> Matronae quoque mentulam illibenter
> [Even good matrons know all too well and do not
>   gladly see a tiny cock]

– and inflicted the most enormous injury.[28]

Admittedly the macaronic passage is hard to sort out, and it all comes in the course of a meditation on the way ageing inflects sexual life that is partly a contrast between Montaigne now and Montaigne then, but I find Donald Frame's version truer to the French:

I have wondered whether I did not have reason rather to blame Nature. Certainly she has treated me unfairly and unkindly –

But if the penis be not long or stout enough . . .
Even the matrons – all too well they know –
Look dimly on a man whose member's small
– and done me the most enormous damage.[29]

Read a bit unsympathetically, by someone more sensitive to exposure and less resigned to the erotic embarrassments of age than Montaigne, this passage could easily be seen as the declaration of someone content to cool his blushes and let his sword rust while he lives safest in shame. Moreover, given that Paroles embraces shame obviously, rather than somehow accommodating himself to shame or in some other less totalizing way revaluing shame, Paroles seems aware that the exposure he has endured might destroy others: 'If my heart were great / 'Twould burst at this', he says, perhaps thinking of victims of shame like Demodocus (4.3.307–8). He also seems unfazed at the threat of being spoken of badly – that is, having endured the shame of exposure, he seems impervious to being discussed in ways that emphasize his guilt (shame seen here as an affect of the eye, guilt of the ear, sensitive to what is spoken to and about one). Thus Paroles counts as among Shakespeare's most Montaignean characters, though in a refracted or parodic way, perhaps to be twinned (like Jacques and Touchstone) with the sceptical, warm-hearted Lafeu. Whether or not Shakespeare is thinking about Montaigne, he creates in Paroles a brilliant exemplar of the full consequences of two essential Montaignean positions: 'C'est une absolue perfection, et comme divine, de scavoyr jouyr loiallement de son estre' (III.13.1115); 'It is an absolute perfection, and as it were divine for a man to know how to enjoy his being loyally' (Florio, 1013); and 'Nostre vie est partie en folie, partie en prudence' (III.5.888); 'Our life consisteth partly in folly, and partly in wisedome' (Florio, 801–2). 'Simply the thing I am / Shall make me live' (4.3.310–11).

---

[28] M. A. Screech, trans., *Michel de Montaigne: The Complete Essays* (Harmondsworth, 1991), p. 1004.
[29] Donald Frame, trans., *The Complete Essays of Montaigne* (Stanford, 1968), p. 677.

This brings me to my final case of Shakespearian reflection, the Sonnets and their relations to Montaigne, shame and embodiment. Peter Holbrook comments that 'there is at least one Shakespearean text – the *Sonnets* – that truly deserves the honorific "Montaignesque"'. This is because 'they are committed to individual authenticity'.[30] They present a Shakespeare undefended and resolutely committed to his own peculiar experiences and passions: for Holbrook, the key claim in the Sonnets is 'No, I am that I am' in 121, a claim he links explicitly to Parolles's 'Simply the thing I am / Shall make me live'.[31] I find this view of the Sonnets attractive, and I feel the same way about Holbrook's general claim that Shakespeare and Montaigne are, like Emerson and Nietzsche, teachers of how to live as oneself instead of someone else. Holbrook follows an appealing variant of the strategy for assimilating Shakespeare to later intellectual traditions by way of Montaigne that I sketched above. But once again, in my view, the Shakespearian texts in question register a quite different attitude towards reflective mental life from Montaigne's. Assuming the Sonnets to be (a) genuinely autobiographical and (b) intentionally made public by Shakespeare (both currently respectable scholarly opinions, though based upon uncertainties),[32] the Sonnets count as a form of authorial self-revelation. This self-revelation, like Montaigne's, asserts the validity and complexity of the private self and opens up areas of selfhood that past traditions of both sonnet-writing and autobiography had left largely unvisited. Holbrook strives to make Shakespeare's Sonnets share, with Montaigne and Emerson and Nietzsche, a commitment to 'cheerfulness' in self-acceptance: 'there is a vital unbudgeable root of self-love under the *Sonnets*, which are the product of an author who, like Montaigne, "hunger[s] to make [him]self known".'[33]

Here I want to pause. I have argued throughout that Shakespeare casts doubt on Montaignean reflection as a self-sustaining activity, and that Montaigne's personal capacity to transform and cast off shame does not seem easy for Shakespeare to emulate in what little he leaves us as autobiographical writing. The Sonnets are intense registers of self-examination, but not of leisured reflection. Much of what they examine is the painful inescapability of social life and specifically the pain of being 'vile esteemed' (121) either by an imagined social audience or by a beloved other or by a judging part of the self. When they treat reflection as an activity, it turns out to be either a rehearsal of the speaker's enmeshment in a mimetically competitive unnourishing social environment, or to be a quasi-comic dead-end. Consider two great reflective sonnets that are alternative versions of one another and appear together.

29

When in disgrace with fortune and men's eyes,
I all alone beweep my outcast state,
And trouble deaf heav'n with my bootless cries,
And look upon myself and curse my fate,
Wishing me like to one more rich in hope,
Featured like him, like him with friends possessed,
Desiring this man's art, and that man's scope,
With what I most enjoy contented least;
Yet in these thoughts myself almost despising,
Haply I think on thee, and then my state
Like to the lark at break of day arising
From sullen earth, sings hymns at heaven's gate;
    For thy sweet love rememb'red such wealth brings,
    That then I scorn to change my state with kings.

30

When to the sessions of sweet silent thought
I summon up remembrance of things past,
I sigh the lack of many a thing I sought,
And with old woes new wail my dear time's waste.

---

[30] Peter Holbrook, 'Introduction', in Peter Holbrook, ed., 'Shakespeare and Montaigne Revisited', *Shakespearean International Yearbook 6* (Aldershot, 2006), p. 11.

[31] Holbrook, 'Introduction', p. 12. For a similar claim about the importance of Sonnet 121, see Engle, '"I am that I am"'.

[32] For the prevailing state of scholarly opinion on these matters, and registration of the uncertainties involved, see Burrow, ed., *Complete Sonnets and Poems*, pp. 94–7; for a discussion of how many unexamined assumptions are involved in standard readings of the Sonnets as a sequence, see Heather Dubrow, '"Incertainties now crown themselves assur'd": The Politics of Plotting Shakespeare's Sonnets', in Schiffer, ed., *Shakespeare's Sonnets*, pp. 113–33, first published in *Shakespeare Quarterly*, 47 (1996), 291–305.

[33] Holbrook, 'Introduction', p. 13.

Then can I drown an eye, unused to flow,
For precious friends hid in death's dateless night,
And weep afresh love's long since cancelled woe,
And moan th' expense of many a vanished sight.
Then can I grieve at grievances foregone,
And heavily from woe to woe tell o'er
The sad account of fore-bemoanèd moan,
Which I new pay as if not paid before.
    But if the while I think on thee, dear friend,
    All losses are restored, and sorrows end.

Most readers would agree that the first of these two sonnets registers a more urgent intellectual and emotional process, imposed by an unspecified condition of 'disgrace', the second something like an intellectual and emotional habit. Colin Burrow notes wryly that the 'When' at the beginning of 30 in effect 'cancel[s] the joyous leap of the *lark at break of day arising*' in that its 'repetition of the first word of the previous sonnet takes us back to the gloomy isolation evoked at its opening'.[34] This accounts, perhaps, for the slightly self-mocking quality of 30, beautiful and moving as many of its much-quoted phrases are: it has a 'here I go again' quality, and its subdued imagery of a judicial audit becomes an explicit account of waste or imbalance in the final quatrain, with its 'sad account of fore-bemoanèd moan, / Which I new pay as if not paid before'. Neither sonnet presents self-examination as dignified or in itself rewarding: the inner turmoil must be stilled, the inner debit cancelled, by thoughts of the friend. And the sequence as a whole registers the relationship with the friend as not only enriching and compensatory but also destabilizing and productive of vicissitudes of self-regard (as is the relationship in the last sonnets with the dark lady): the friend is often reproached for leading the speaker to let down his defences against the world, as in 33–35, which offer a key instance of the sonnet-speaker and the sonnet-addressee

traversing the space between them by shaming one another consecutively. To speak very generally, moving inward in the Sonnets always involves reaching outward for help in a kind of panic at what one finds inside, or, as in 121, pushing back at the world in ringing assertion that one is, at any rate, no worse than everyone else. This is far from both the prevailing mood and the prevailing method in Montaigne's form of reflection. It demonstrates that, while shame may push Shakespeare into reflection, he does not easily emerge from reflection with a new sense of his relation to the world, or with a consistently Emersonian self-acceptance.

I conclude, then, that Montaigne needs to be treated with caution as an analogue or model for Shakespeare's treatment of embodied mental life. The relation between the two thinkers is, I suggest, as rich and complex as are the works of both, and Shakespeare's response to Montaigne needs to be recognized as ambivalent rather than assumed to be celebratory and directly appropriative. Shakespeare seems particularly exercised both by Montaigne's general retreat into contented reflection and by his specific willingness to cast off shame in the process of self-examination and self-exposure. This does not mean that one should not use Montaigne as a way of connecting Shakespeare with later intellectual traditions, or with our own moral and intellectual habits. In fact, as I have suggested above, it means that we can see Shakespeare's reactions to Montaigne as hints – sometimes chastening hints – towards how he might regard our own Montaignean attitudes.

---

34 Burrow, *Complete Sonnets and Poems*, p. 440. Stephen Booth, *Shakespeare's Sonnets*, p. 181 links 30 with 31 rather than 29.

PLAYING THE LAW FOR LAWYERS: WITNESSING, EVIDENCE AND THE LAW OF CONTRACT IN *THE COMEDY OF ERRORS*

BARBARA KREPS

The Comedy of Errors' opening focus on the twins' father Egeon was not suggested by either of the play's two principal sources (Plautus's *Menaechmi* and his *Amphitruo*), but the addition of this new plot element immediately directs audience attention to a number of different kinds of bonds – from the physical restraints visible on the prisoner to the law's theoretical restraints on the Duke; from the history of Egeon's severed family ties to the history behind the severed commercial and social relations between Ephesus and Syracuse now motivating the old man's imprisonment. Though Egeon's plight remains disjoined from the comedy of the twins' mistaken identities until the final scene, the opening view of the bound and imperilled father launches visual and narrative elements decidedly pertinent to the play that follows, for the bonds and obligations of family and commerce – subsequently to find their key metaphor in the chain (which itself appears in interchangeable symbiosis with the rope) – provide the impetus for almost every plot turn.[1] The play's first known audience, assembled at Gray's Inn on Holy Innocents Night (28 December) 1594, had a close professional interest in such questions. *The Comedy of Errors* was perhaps written specifically for that occasion but the surviving evidence of that performance was published almost a century later. The play was long considered an early piece of writing (Shakespeare's presumed lack of experience thus becoming a reason for some to disparage it). But as the twentieth century progressed, the play increasingly found defenders, as well as some textual critics willing to argue that the play was commissioned for the law

students' Christmas revels – a repositioning of its date which would preclude any argument about its being apprentice work.[2] My article has nothing to add to the hypotheses concerning the circumstances of the play's composition. Certainly an audience of lawyers and lawyers-in-training would have had an advantage in catching the legal jokes, as well as the legal implications of the agreements and obligations that bind and limit people, of nuances of promise and performance, of parole agreements and questions of contract. I shall point out later, in fact, how *The Comedy of Errors* specifically reflects for a moment the problematic duality of options open to litigants suing out debt in commercial agreements gone wrong. But if some of the legal jargon is for the initiated, the play's continuing

---

[1] References are to *The Comedy of Errors*, ed. Charles Whitworth (Oxford, 2002). The frequent iterations of 'bond' appear in variant lexical forms (bondsman, bind, band, bound [and bound for]): e.g. Adriana's interrogation of Dromio S. at 4.2.49: 'was he arrested on a band?' In these variant forms 'bond' thus covers a large semantic field, its denotations physical as well as mental. It appears as both intention to do something or to move elsewhere (e.g. 'I am bound to Persia') and as (paradoxically) its opposite, the constriction of movement (as when the arrested Dromio quips with multiple meaning 'Master I am here entered in bond for you').

[2] See, principally, Sidney Thomas, 'The Date of *The Comedy of Errors*', *Shakespeare Quarterly*, 7 (1956), 377–84; Alan Nelson, 'Early Staging in Cambridge', in *A New History of Early English Drama*, ed. John D. Cox and David Scott Kastan (New York, 1997), p. 66; Ros King's update of T. S. Dorsch's (1988) edition of *The Comedy of Errors* for Cambridge University Press (2004) suggests (on p. 33) that there was at the least some ad hoc writing for the Gray's Inn performance.

appeal is clearly also wider: audiences with no special training respond easily to the dialogue and plot
events built on the general public's understanding of the two-sidedness inhering in most social
and commercial agreements. Like most comedies,
Errors generates mirth from situations of distress:
it repeatedly demonstrates that, though the agreements people enter into often seem uncomplicated,
judging people and situations can in practice be a
tricky business, because what appears to be solid
evidence about human relations is sometimes not
as straightforward as it seems.

A lot of *Errors'* romp comes from its self-
consciously egregious play with binary forms –
binary forms of people certainly, but also binary
forms of language and of logic. The twins' plot
begins to take shape when the two Dromios make
separate appearances in 1.2, although the audience's
'view' of the two sets of twins is not completed
until Antipholus of Ephesus appears in Act 3.[3]

Dromio of Ephesus has no way of knowing in
1.2 that the Antipholus he sees is not his master,
while Antipholus of Syracuse is angered by the
contradictions coming from the Dromio he mistakes as his servant. Identity mistakes are the play's
most basic premise, providing much of its comedy
(as in 1.2) through cross-purpose dialogue.

But the play's dualities and contradictions also
include arguing two sides of the same question, as
when Adriana and Luciana debate gender roles in
marriage. The argument between the married and
the unmarried sisters (at its beginning we learn,
appropriately, that 'it is two o'clock' [2.1.7]) rests
on their opposite viewpoints regarding the accept-
ability of social assumptions about the roles available to men and women. Adriana chafes at her
sister's defence of the husband/master's liberty in
marriage ('A man is master of his liberty' [2.1.8])
as well as the sanguinity of her presumption that
women's wills must be 'bridled'. (Adriana objects
that 'none but asses will be bridled so' [14], but
in the two iterations of 'bridle' in lines 13 and 14
the homophone 'bridal' is of course equally heard
and subtended.)

The marriage lecture continues in 2.2, the argument directed this time not to husband and wife

as unequal adversaries, but on the contrary to the
marital partners' state as two-in-one, which Adriana berates her 'husband' for failing to respect:

> how comes it
> That thou art then estrangèd from thyself?
> Thy 'self' I call it, being strange to me
> That, undividable, incorporate,
> Am better than thy dear self's better part.
> Ah, do not tear away thyself from me;
> For know, my love, as easy mayst thou fall
> A drop of water in the breaking gulf,
> And take unmingled thence that drop again
> Without addition or diminishing,
> As take from me thyself, and not me too.
>
> (2.2.122–32)

Antipholus of Syracuse promptly rejoins that Adriana is mistaken, his protest about his connection
with Ephesus calling up another instance of the
play's insistence on the number two: he cannot be
her husband, since 'In Ephesus I am but two hours
old' (2.2.151).[4]

---

3 The idea of look-alike servants is suggested by Mercury's
impersonation of Sosia in Plautus's *Amphitruo*, but in making
the servants to be real blood twins Shakespeare doubles the
number of twins he found in *Menaechmi*. The casting of only
one actor rather than two for each set of twins is one of the
play's possibilities but the choice has obvious staging implications, most particularly in 3.1, where both sets of twins
have parts written for them. Actors have successfully taken
on both roles but such absolute identity has undermined for
some critics the comedy's need to maintain for the audience
an element of discrepancy permitting them to know for sure
which twin is which. The argument goes that it is this level of
audience knowledge, superior relative to that of the characters on stage, that helps generate the humour. For arguments
on both sides see reviews by Alan Pryce-Jones and Howard
Taubman in *Shakespearean Criticism 26* (1995), pp. 152–4; John
R. Ford, 'Looking for *The Comedy of Errors* in Performance',
Shakespeare Bulletin, 24 (2006), 13–14.

4 Within the inexorable logic of time's advance, two o'clock
remains a frequent point of reference in *Errors*. When that
same time is next referred to, it calls conspicuous attention
to the problematics of two/one in a context of debt, and the
temporal relationship leads into another of the play's puns. At
line 58 below, the word 'season' – aurally the same as 'seisin'
and (in the pronunciation of 1594) 'seizing' – appropriately
conflates time, debt, legal problems associated with possession
(the holding of property which, importantly, is not to be
confused with seisin or title) and the law's various kinds of

In Act 3, the unmarried Luciana's propensity for lectures in defence of marriage is sparked by the comportment of the man she takes to be her brother-in-law. Her perception of his 'double wrong' of 'Ill deeds . . . doubled with an evil word' (3.2.17–20) is further doubled not only by the shared sounds of rhyme and alliteration (insistent for the first seventy lines) but also by contrastive pairings such as 'eye/tongue', 'vice/virtue', 'fair/taint', 'sin/saint', 'bed/board', 'deeds/word'. The rhyme, alliteration and pairing create unmissable rhetorical relations within a play so centrally *about* relations, while here and elsewhere in the play frequent punning creates (like the theory of marriage) two-in-one existences, pairs within a single word, eliding the singleness of meaning into the creation of an unstable pair, each element of which achieves with the other an interchangeable identity.

With a plot turning explicitly on twinning and the comedy's success depending on its semination of doubt through the mistaking of signs, the gemini words and ideas that constitute punning are linguistically appropriate. But some of the puns in *Errors* are culture-specific, located within a legal system that has undergone radical transformation in the last four centuries. This is the case, for example, of the pointedly self-conscious economic puns so noticeably extended in the 2.2 'heir/hair', 'fine and recovery' banter between Antipholus and Dromio of Syracuse. This repartee is too tied to the particular legal terms of Tudor property dispositions for most audiences now to be able to follow the jokes in the sequence. But if some of the jokes have lost their oomph, many others remain. Largely thanks to the Dromios, who get most of the self-pointing language play, punning runs rampant throughout. And the puns are particularly suitable to a play in which the logic of the singularity of names (usually conferred as aids to separating and identifying people) is deliberately not only ignored but doubled with respect to Plautus.

The play's wry naming logic also affects the commercial base of this mercantile society. Money is everywhere in evidence but the denominations are uncertain, constantly changing identity.

When it is not just generically 'gold', money is variously called guilders, marks, sixpence, angels, ducats. The money in use in Ephesus is not tied to Ephesus: it is English, Italian, German, Dutch. As this multiplicity of names indicates, money is international, exchangeable, indifferently transferable. That very transferability may be the point too, as Laurie Maguire has suggested, of withholding a given name from the Courtesan.[5] Certainly in a play that depends so consciously on names, her namelessness contrasts with most of the other major characters. Through the only name the play gives her, the Courtesan is thus known principally for the nature of her business, one that is up front about the commodification of sex and its attachment to money, so that she does not necessitate a unique identity any more than does the unnamed merchant who in Act 4 arrests the merchant Angelo. But the legitimacy of marriage in Ephesus is itself hardly above the question of money. Adriana has a strong emotional attachment now to her Antipholus but the point is made several times that their marriage was a political combination originally mixed from Adriana's wealth and the Duke's favour (see 3.2.5–6; 5.1.136–8; 5.1.161–4). Indeed, even

---

'seizing' in consequence of the bankruptcy, debt and theft referred to. Editors note that that both 'season' and 'seisin' are equally heard here, but 'seizing' is also part of the mix. If that is understood, the passage (below) that has seemed problematic to editors is less of a crux:

Dromio of Syracuse. It was two ere I left him, and now the clock strikes one.
Adriana. The hours come back! That did I never hear.
Dromio of Syracuse. O yes, if any hour meet a sergeant, a turns back for very fear.
Adriana. As if time were in debt. How fondly dost thou reason!
Dromio of Syracuse. Time is a very bankrupt, and owes more than he's worth to season.
 Nay, he's a thief too. Have you not heard men say
 That time comes stealing on by night and day?
 If a be in debt and theft, and a sergeant in the way,
 Hath he not reason to turn back an hour in a day?
 (4.2.53–61)

[5] Laurie Maguire argues the significance of the Courtesan's namelessness (at pp. 369–71) in 'The Girls from Ephesus', in *'The Comedy of Errors': Critical Essays*, ed. Robert Miola (New York, 2001), pp. 355–91.

the besotted idealist Antipholus of Syracuse – whose character is so unlike that of his twin – finds the best expression of his love for Luciana in the valuable metals of traditional Petrarchism: 'Spread o'er the silver waves thy golden hairs / And as a bed I'll take them,[6] and there lie' (3.2.48–9).

The play's questions of love and economics converge in the chain. As the truth about this physical object rapidly becomes embroiled in the play's various questions of debt, the chain works concomitantly as a metaphor within a play so much about bonds, an image appropriate indeed to the close connections the plot draws between love, money and truth. Adriana is the first to mention it: 'Sister, you know he promised me a chain', though she would willingly forgo the jewel 'So he would keep fair quarter with his bed' (2.1.107, 109). The next reference to the chain comes from Antipholus of Ephesus, who appears for the first time in 3.1, and his opening lines, urging the goldsmith to provide an alibi for his absence from home, indicate that Adriana apparently has some reason to be jealous: 'My wife is shrewish when I keep not hours. / Say that I lingered with you at your shop / To see the making of her carcanet' (3.1.2–4). His word choice here is apparently innocent of hidden meanings; but a public familiar with Latin might have heard in 'carcanet' some closeness to *carceris*, 'jail' (thus appropriately extending the sisters' earlier debate on liberty and bridles).[7] For those who miss that possible resonance, the chain's connection with jail will in any case certainly become far more direct later in the play when Antipholus is led off in bonds for non-payment of his debt. But that lies in the future. For now the point is that, before the chain ever physically appears, the couple's earliest references invest it with a meaning specific to them. Adriana links its promise to her husband's sexual behaviour and apparently so too does Antipholus; certainly the rapidity with which he is disposed to transfer it from his wife to the Courtesan leaves little doubt that he sees the chain as an indicator of his sexual links with these women. But quite apart from the emotional values attributed to the chain in this ménage, its market value remains its principal point

of interest for the other members of the play whose lives rapidly become entwined by it. For the chain sets off a series of events that link together questions of credit, debt, identity, witnessing and proof.

The chain is of course fundamental in the relations between Antipholus of Ephesus and Angelo, the goldsmith: it is one of the two elements necessary to make their business exchange complete, Angelo's quid for Antipholus's quo (money). The simplest kinds of commercial exchange are frequently this 'my object for your object' agreement and are typified by the immediacy of exchange. But the agreement between Angelo and Antipholus goes beyond material objects literally passing hands, and it involves more than the simple present. Anterior to the materiality of the exchange is a communal idea regulating commercial behaviour, a theory of money rather than money itself: that idea is credit. And credit is not bound by the present; it is implicitly a promise, and the fulfilment of a promise lies in the future. Credit, as its Latin root indicates, is a placement of belief, *credo*, a fiduciary act. In the community this belief is enabled by the perception of one's honour, of giving good-character value to one's word, and it is this community reputation that is spent in credit transactions. The play's merchants understand this well, as Angelo protests the damage to his reputation and signals the equivalence of lost reputation and lost business credit caused by

---

[6] Whitworth here follows Capell's emendation; F1 has 'as a bud Ile take thee and there lie' (TLN 836).

[7] 'Carcanet' is perhaps a strange lexical choice for a jewel everywhere else referred to as a chain. Whitworth glosses it as a 'collar or necklace (usually in gold or silver, and ornamented with precious stones)'. R. A. Foakes's Arden text glosses it as 'a necklace set with jewels': see *The Comedy of Errors* (London, 1962), p. 40 n. 4. This is its meaning in Sonnet 52 and, as the *OED*'s numerous citations illustrate, 'jewelled necklace' was the word's standard significance; but to a public familiar with Latin, *carceris* might have been liminally suggested, while those with French would know that *carcan* is both a choker (a kind of necklace) and a pillory. The *OED* shows that 'carcan' also had brief currency in English during the sixteenth century; its first entry glosses the word as 'an iron collar used for punishment'. Antipholus is the only one to use this word, and he uses it just this once, but the word opens up a series of apposite meanings.

Antipholus's behaviour: 'Consider how it stands upon my credit . . . This touches me in reputation' (4.1.68–71). Angelo's reliance on Antipholus's payment in order to discharge his own bond with the Second Merchant gives just a small glimpse for the nonce of the larger mercantile reality, showing how one defective link ripples through the community's chain of credit, impeding a number of transactions revealed to be only apparently unrelated to the original one in default.

Debet (in the Latin that stands behind 'debt') has two English translations – 's/he owes', and also 's/he must'. The latter lies in the semantic field of 'duty'. Duty, at times counterintuitive and unpleasant, is the social force that brakes desire. The play's opening scene, Shakespeare's complication over Plautus, shows among other things the duty of the Prince to respect the law notwithstanding his personal feelings. Other examples of the clash between id and superego follow in the relations of servants and masters, wives and husbands. Duty – the behaviour that is owed or due – is the substance of Luciana's ironic double-pronged marriage counselling (discussed above) to her sister and her imagined brother-in-law. Emilia (who also delivers a homily on marital duty to Adriana) for her part stands for duty against the entire community in her refusal to relinquish the man who has sought sanctuary in the priory: 'It is a branch and parcel of mine oath, / A charitable duty of my order' (5.1.106–7). Far cruder is the kind of physical obligation without choice often on display in *Errors*, as the shabbily treated Dromios accept their beatings, and transport and account for the money entrusted to them. It is the kind of slapstick that tends to generate audience laughter and, as the butt of it, the Dromios necessarily put up with their condition – though not without comment: as Dromio of Syracuse privately laments, 'Thither I must, although against my will; / For servants must their masters' minds fulfil' (4.1.112–13). (This same Dromio earlier externalized spunkier thoughts of transgressive possibility, however, when he reminded his boss that though he himself may be a 'trusty villain' [1.2.19], some servants would take the money and run.)

Despite the chain's value (two hundred ducats, as we finally learn at 4.4.135), the only commercial bond actually mentioned in the play is the one that emerges in Act 4 naming Angelo as the obligor and the Second Merchant as the obligee:

> *Second Merchant.* (*to Angelo*) You know since Pentecost
>   the sum is due,
> And since I have not much importuned you;
> Nor now I had not, but that I am bound
> To Persia, and want guilders for my voyage.
> Therefore make present satisfaction,
> Or I'll attach you by this officer.
> *Angelo.* Even just the sum that I do owe to you
> Is growing to me by Antipholus,
> And in the instant that I met with you
> He had of me a chain. At five o'clock
> I shall receive the money for the same.
> Pleaseth you walk with me down to his house,
> I will discharge my bond, and thank you too.
>
>   (4.1.1–13)

Unlike this bond, the bargain originally driven between Angelo and Antipholus of Ephesus appears to have been verbal rather than written. Certainly the legal superiority of specialty (i.e. a sealed bond) lay in its estoppel value, since such a document was a non-confutable witness.[8] But aside

---

8 In 4.1 Angelo delivers a note to Antipholus of Ephesus specifying the chain's weight, the quality of its gold and his charge for workmanship. But this is an itemized bill for work already done, not a bond, the legal purpose of which is anticipatory: a bond's function is to preclude (to estop) the possibility of future denial of debt: S. F. C. Milsom, *Historical Foundations of the Common Law*, 2nd edn (London, 1981), p. 258. The temporal difference between a bond and a bill thus concerns the difference between executory debt and executed debt.

On estoppel, see J. B. Thayer, *A Preliminary Treatise on Evidence at Common Law* (Boston, 1898; repr. 1969), chapter 8; W. S. Holdsworth, *A History of English Law*, 17 vols. (Boston, 1938), 9:144–63; Roderick Murphy, *Evidence*, 4th edn (Oxford, 2007), pp. 34–8; William Twining, *Rethinking Evidence*, 2nd edn (Cambridge, 2006), pp. 58–9. On the specific issue of estoppel by deed, see J. H. Baker, *An Introduction to English Legal History*, 3rd edn (London, 1990), pp. 346–7. On bonds see A. W. B. Simpson, *A History of the Common Law of Contract: The Rise of the Action of Assumpsit* (Oxford, 1975), pp. 88–125; Baker, *An Introduction*, pp. 362–71. On parole agreements and covenant, see Simpson, *A History*, pp. 47–52; S. F. C. Milsom, *Historical Foundations*, pp. 292–6.

from the fact that informal contracts were quite normal, Angelo also had every reason to believe Antipholus's word would be as good as his bond (in the community he was 'Of very reverend reputation . . . / Of credit infinite, . . . / His word might bear my wealth at any time' [5.1.5–8]). Moreover, when credit was misplaced or commercial transactions went wrong, the law provided recourse for pursuing the promissory liability of parole agreements.

DEVELOPING LEGAL TUTELAGE OF DEBT AND OBLIGATIONS

In sixteenth-century England, in fact, depending on the circumstances of the issue contested, a plaintiff might try one of two possible courses of action: the older action of debt or the newer remedies that had been spawned by the logic of tort and known as actions 'on the case'. The latter were cases of wrongdoing (or 'trespass', in the sense still heard today in the Lord's Prayer) which included the breach of promise known as *assumpsit* ('he undertook'). Although in theory these two legal options could be heard in either Common Pleas or King's Bench, these two courts did not – particularly in the mid-sixteenth century – judge actions on the case with the same attitudes. If the case was argued locally at nisi prius, the two courts of Common Pleas and King's Bench shared the work (through travelling circuit judges). But litigants who wished to have their cases argued in a specific court at Westminster discovered they might avoid the expense of procuring a writ from Chancery (for cases of trespass argued in Common Pleas), by procuring instead a bill of Middlesex in order to proceed (more cheaply) in King's Bench. The procedural differences and the competition that ensued between the central courts profoundly affected debt litigation in the sixteenth century: on the one hand the older action of debt was favoured by Common Pleas, while actions on the case (and specifically assumpsit) found particular favour in King's Bench.[9]

The early logic of assumpsit grew out of promise, and when problems arose that were appropriate for the attention of the king's courts (rather than the spiritual courts) remedy lay in tort: plaintiffs could seek an action on the case, not for debt (for which there already existed a remedy at law) but for the defendant's wrongdoing ('trespass'). Early in the sixteenth century, the issues contested in actions on the case tended to lie in the existence or not of promissory language and the perceived times of promise; also for a brief time it was important to know if new consideration[10] had been added after the original agreement. Until 1532, a successful plea brought in assumpsit could therefore be awarded damages but not the debt. But in 1532, the justices of King's Bench decided (after some internal wrangling) that the plaintiff in *Pykering* v. *Thurgoode* (aka Throughgood, Thoroughgood) 'could elect whether to bring debt on the contract or *assumpsit* on the breach of promise'.[11] The crux here was the plaintiff's reliance on the unfulfilled promise (Thurgoode's failure to deliver malt), which as a consequence caused Pykering's brewing business to sustain hardship: the nonfeasance had resulted in 'injurious reliance'.[12] Milsom elaborates that 'reliance in a general sense was the

---

9 On procedure by bill and the advantages this gave litigants in King's Bench over proceeding by writ in Common Pleas, see J. H. Baker, *An Introduction to English Legal History*, 4th edn (London, 2002), pp. 41–5. On the conflict between King's Bench and Common Pleas see also Simpson, *A History*, pp. 291–7; David Ibbetson, 'Sixteenth Century Contract Law: Slade's Case in Context', *Oxford Journal of Legal Studies*, 4 (1984), 295–317.

10 The commentary on 'consideration' is vast. Milsom asserts that 'The essence of the common law of contract is the doctrine of consideration' (*Historical Foundations*, p. 356). In one of its simplest formulations, consideration is 'the motive inducing a promisee to act on the promise made to him': S. J. Stoljar, *A History of Contract at Common Law* (Canberra, 1975), p. 37. As pointed out in *Cheshire, Fifoot and Furmston's Law of Contract*, ed. Michael Furmston, 15th edn (Oxford, 2007), the role of promise and the early tutelage of promise by the spiritual courts is part of what makes the history of consideration controversial (p. 8). The courts ruled in the course of the sixteenth century that consideration need not be material (money, land, chattels), but might also be constituted by family relations and ties of friendship.

11 Baker, *An Introduction*, p. 342.

12 Baker, *An Introduction*, pp. 385–6.

original basis of assumpsit'.[13] The nature of the damage resulting from the plaintiff's reliance on the defendant could take several forms. One sort of damage that shows up with some frequency was the plaintiff's 'loss of credit with third parties whom the plaintiff had let down because of the defendant's failure'.[14] But if the allegations of hardship caused by lost credit brought in the 1530s are credible, by the 1590s many have the sulphuric whiff of legal fictions. In particular, Milsom notes the suspicious claims made by the clients who were represented by John Williams of London. Having made various agreements with different people, Williams's clients stand out for bringing suits in assumpsit, all lodging the complaint that 'the various breaches of their various defendants had compelled them all to dishonour some obligation towards John Denne and Richard Fenne; and it was of the injury to their credit with this indignant pair that they all particularly complained'.[15]

Throughout the sixteenth century, areas of overlap in claims on contract debt continued to perplex litigants seeking to identify which of the two actions was more likely to find success; the choice was crucial, because if plaintiffs brought the wrong claim they were in danger of being non-suited. The traditionalist judges of Common Pleas stuck to the principle that assumpsit was not a valid alternative to the action of debt on a contract because, they insisted, one cause could not give rise to two different forms of action. But the admission of damages (at first for malfeasance and then for nonfeasance) opened the way for a profoundly significant legal change – particularly since, as David Ibbetson notes, Common Pleas judges were already 'willing to conform to the King's Bench view in a number of cases which could not logically be distinguished from contractual debt'.[16] On the issue of damages, they concurred with King's Bench in conceding assumpsit when 'the plaintiff had suffered some special damage so that he could not be wholly compensated by the action of debt'.[17] Hence by the 1590s the idea had developed and become entrenched for both courts 'that assumpsit lay on a contract if there had been some extraordinary loss suffered'.[18]

As commentators on the history of contract law now largely agree, the single most important difference between the two actions involved the nature of evidence.[19] Actions of debt allowed 'wager of law', a form of proof that called in eleven oathhelpers (to make up, with the accused, twelve deponents). The defendant's reliance on these witnesses (known as compurgators) did not mean that they were privy to the facts of the case or that they had actually seen the transaction in issue. The 'proof' these men offered, on oath, was of the defendant's credibility, his trustworthiness, their belief that the defendant was telling the truth about the question in issue.[20] If wager of law was successful, the suit ended there. It is clear why plaintiffs should prefer to argue on the case: actions on the case did not permit wager of law. Instead the case went directly to trial, with the verdict decided by the jury. After the 1602 decision in *Slade* v. *Morley* (*Slade's case*), which legal historians consider a benchmark decision in the rival positions on contract debt,[21] assumpsit was to become the appropriate way to plead contractual debt, a victory for jury hearings that has made wager of law now seem both quaint and naive; but few people would argue that the result obtained has been the infallibility of

---

[13] Milsom, *Historical Foundations*, p. 338.

[14] Milsom, *Historical Foundations*, p. 338.

[15] Milsom, *Historical Foundations*, p. 338. The cases Milsom cites were recorded in King's Bench, Easter 1594. The performance of *Errors* later that same year might have drawn on the issue of damaged credit litigated in King's Bench, but no argument is being made here that the connection was direct.

[16] Ibbetson, 'Slade's Case', p. 305.

[17] Ibbetson, 'Slade's Case', p. 306.

[18] Ibbetson, 'Slade's Case', p. 310.

[19] See Baker, *An Introduction*, p. 392; also his 'New Light on Slade's Case', in J. H. Baker, *The Legal Profession and the Common Law* (London, 1986), pp. 393–431; Simpson, *A History*, pp. 297–8. Ibbetson emphatically demurs, however: see 'Slade's Case', particularly pp. 312–13.

[20] D. H. Sacks, 'The Promise and the Contract in Early Modern England: Slade's Case in Perspective', in *Rhetoric and Law in Early Modern Europe*, ed. V. Kahn and L. Hutson (New Haven, 2001), pp. 38–9.

[21] Ibbetson's dissent is based on some straggling decisions afterward: see 'Slade's Case', pp. 310–17.

jury trials in determining truth. Indeed, the strict laws of admissibility that have developed within the modern law of evidence omit much that is true from the jury's consideration before the case comes to trial. (It is worth noting too that, because of these developments, the modern jury trial is antithetical to the premise that originally lay behind compurgation – or at least the community theory on which it was based. Jury selection now depends on members' non-familiarity with the defendant, while the exclusionary principles operating in much of the modern law of evidence specify that hearsay is not admissible.)

EVIDENCE AND *ERRORS*

The legal issues interconnecting witnessing, certainty and proof built into *The Comedy of Errors* derive from the plot's larger premise of the untrustworthy connection between sight and knowledge – untrustworthy, at least for the characters on stage, since of course the audience has to be in on the joke's premise in order for it to work. But the characters themselves also understand how appearances may deceive – at times in fact even usefully deceive. The scene in 1.2 opens with the First Merchant advising Antipholus of Syracuse to hide his identity. Theodore Komisarjevsky, the famous twentieth-century stage director, found in this advice a textual cue for the Syracusan twins to change their clothes on the spot to the fashions of Ephesus, thus enabling the visual mistakes that follow (and helping those in the audience who might need a dollop of realistic explanation as to why the two sets of twins are wearing identical costumes).[22] Luciana's lecture to her presumed brother-in-law also urges him to deceive her sister's sight: 'Muffle your false love with some show of blindness. / Let not my sister read it in your eye' (3.2.8–9). Antipholus of Syracuse, although himself disguised, is paradoxically – as his 'sure uncertainty' indicates – bewildered by his reception now in Ephesus: 'What error drives our eyes and ears amiss? / Until I know this sure uncertainty, / I'll entertain the offered fallacy' (2.2.187–9). Later, in the first throes of his love for Luciana, Antipholus of Syracuse

is obliged to protest what the audience knows to be mistakes of the eye, his mistaken 'I': 'If that I am I, then well I know / Your weeping sister is no wife of mine, / Nor to her bed no homage do I owe' (3.2.41–3). Against the mistakes of sight in Ephesus the seemingly faultless logic of 'I am I' simply is not sufficient evidence of who his 'I' is, and therefore no defence against what others believe about him.

The misperceptions of the first three acts create a web of mistaken identities in which house, wife and chattels (first in the form of the chain, then in the bag of gold kept at home) are transferred from the entitled brother to his twin. The chain's mistaken delivery, with Antipholus of Ephesus's consequent refusal to pay, results in his arrest at Angelo's charge and, as we learn at 4.2.42, 'he is rested on the case' – certainly the appropriate writ in view of the damage to his credit Angelo had sustained as a result of the non-payment.

From Act 4 the visual language takes a legal turn, sight now marshalled, together with speech, to the specific act of witnessing. The most emphatic instance occurs in 4.4 – the scene in which husband and wife finally encounter each other and reciprocally accuse each other. As they exchange their separate accounts of the day's events, each side, convinced of the truth of its version of facts, calls its own witnesses. Indeed, Antipholus of Ephesus – though still officially awaiting the bail that will release him from arrest – manages to conduct the interrogation. Within the ensuing parody of the language and procedure of trial, also noticeable are the reiterations of 'witness' (my italics below):

---

22 Theodore Komisarjevsky's touchstone 1938 production used costume intelligently to nudge audience compliance along. The Syracusans in fact do appear first in distinctive clothing, but upon being informed by the merchant of the danger they are in should they be discovered, they abandon their garb of Syracuse and change onstage into the local garb of Ephesus. See C.'s review for the *Sheffield Daily Telegraph*, 14 April 1938 (reprinted in Miola, *'The Comedy of Errors': Critical Essays*, pp. 477–9).

Antipholus of Ephesus. Did this companion with the saffron face

Revel and feast it at my house today,

Whilst upon me the guilty doors were shut,

And I denied to enter in my house?

Adriana. O husband, God doth know you dined at home,

Where would you had remained until this time,

Free from these slanders and this open shame.

Antipholus of Ephesus. Dined at home? (*To Dromio*) Thou villain, what sayest thou?

Dromio of Ephesus. Sir, sooth to say, you did not dine at home.

Antipholus of Ephesus. Were not my doors locked up, and I shut out?

Dromio of Ephesus. Pardie, your doors were locked, and you shut out.

Antipholus of Ephesus. And did not she herself revile me there?

Dromio of Ephesus. Sans fable, she herself reviled you there.

Antipholus of Ephesus. Did not her kitchen-maid rail, taunt, and scorn me?

Dromio of Ephesus. Certes she did. The kitchen vestal scorned you.

Antipholus of Ephesus. And did not I in rage depart from thence?

Dromio of Ephesus. In verity you did. – My bones bear *witness* . . .

Antipholus of Ephesus. Went'st not thou to her for a purse of ducats?

Adriana. He came to me, and I delivered it.

Luciana. And I am *witness* with her that she did.

Dromio of Ephesus. God and the ropemaker bear me *witness*

That I was sent for nothing but a rope.

(4.4.62–78, 88–92)

On Adriana's side the fact in issue is her husband's madness, evidence of which her witness Dr Pinch finds in both master and bondsman, proof of their insanity lying in 'their pale and deadly looks' (94); and since his expert testimony (to borrow a modern term) convinces all, they are bound and destined (as Malvolio later would be) to 'some dark room' (95).[23] That ocular proof can be highly untrustworthy gets its final comic airing in the last act, where each of the brothers erupts separately onto the stage, to the shock of all present. Adriana

speaks the amazement common to all: 'Ay me, it is my husband! *Witness* you / That he is borne about invisible. / Even now we housed him in the abbey here, / And now he's there' (5.1.186–9).

The audience knows that these people are all mistaken, but it is also clear that they are acting in good faith, telling the truth as far as they know (theirs is not an ethical problem but an epistemological one). But you don't have to be a lawyer to know that some witness testimony is not truthful. And who better than the nameless Courtesan to make that point? The audience itself is the first to hear of the facts of what happened between Antipholus of Ephesus and the Courtesan (thanks to the theatrical truth-convention of the confidence she shares with the audience when left 'alone'): 'A ring he hath of mine worth forty ducats, / And for the same he promised me a chain' (4.3.82–3). At first this simply adds yet another wrinkle to the play's contractual agreements: the chain and the ring represent reciprocal promises with quid pro quo. But this new contractual undertaking has no impact per se on the plot. As becomes clear in the following scene, the real point of her confidence is not about the contract, but about evidence. The audience is in a privileged position to know, when mention of the chain moves the Courtesan to speak later in public, that her story misrepresents what happened: 'your husband all in rage today / Came to my house and took away my ring' (4.4.138–9).

The men assembled at Gray's Inn in 1594 knew very well that the issues contested in parole agreements, once distinctly identified as sounding in debt, were increasingly competing for legal recognition as actions on the case and that the confusing similarity between debt and assumpsit was causing actions of debt to lose time-honoured legal terrain – most particularly as regards the nature of witnessing and ideas as to what constitutes evidence. Shakespeare's play about look-alikes was not, however, suggested by the

---

[23] As they are dragged off, Dromio of Ephesus gets in yet one more pun: 'Master, I am here entered in bond for you' (4.4.126).

juridical conundrum expanding so noticeably by the end of the sixteenth century. Confused identities and epistemological uncertainty were already the building blocks of the plots Shakespeare found in Plautus; as for the law, wrangling over uncertainties was hardly a special purview of Tudor law. That said, the comedy builds upon issues that were acutely meaningful for the early modern legal profession. The particular optics of theatre provide a playful slant on the serious question of evidence – a question which is itself rooted in the very toughest problem of knowledge: how do we know what we think we know? In its representations of uncertain identities, *Errors'* insistence on binaries and doubles calls attention to how a group of apparently reasonable people can be led totally astray by what they deem to be proof. Shakespeare demonstrates, moreover, some precise knowledge of law, since the play shows (through Angelo's decision as to how to proceed at law against his defaulting client) the author's understanding of the two options open to litigants seeking relief for unhonoured debt in the 1590s. As Dromio of Ephesus briefly reminds us, by writing in and calling attention to the damage to Angelo's credit, Shakespeare carefully qualifies the merchant for the surer satisfactions to be obtained at law by an action on the case.

In the legal world itself the dualities – and the uncertainties plaintiffs were obliged to evaluate in consequence of competing legal proceedings – continued; but the appropriate course of litigation was decided at last, almost a decade after the Gray's Inn performance. As was indicated earlier, *Slade's case* was the suit that would eventually determine the victory for assumpsit; it was first heard at nisi prius in the Exeter assizes in the spring of 1596, was removed to the Exchequer Chamber in Michaelmas Term 1597[24] and would not be decided until 1602. Indeed, the disputed grain (the field of wheat and rye) that was to lead to the landmark decision was only sown in November 1594, so that it was literally growing in the field when *The Comedy of Errors* was performed on 28 December 1594. Unlike the play they were watching, the lawyers would have to wait some time before resolving the doubts about how to represent their own set of doubles.

---

[24] Ibbetson, 'Slade's Case', pp. 300–1; Simpson, *A History*, p. 297.

SHAKESPEARE'S NARCISSUS: OMNIPRESENT LOVE IN *VENUS AND ADONIS*

JOHN MCGEE

Love doth approach disguised, / Armèd in arguments
(*Love's Labour's Lost*, 5.2.83–4)

Imagine Narcissus had found his reflection in an object that was animate rather than inanimate. Imagine him with the same 'fixed staring eyes', the same 'wretched rage', the same vanity, destructiveness and self-pity,[1] yet finding himself in the eyes of another person instead of a pool of water. Imagine him then not as a mortal man but an immortal goddess. Do so, and you have the basic idea of Shakespeare's *Venus and Adonis*, a minor Ovidian epic that tells one love-story not found even in Ovid – a story of love itself in love with love itself.

The story of Narcissus is without doubt an important source text for this poem. Venus compares Adonis to Narcissus more than once for failing to respond to her sexual advances. Many critics accept her judgement of the boy as narcissistic. Colin Burrow calls Adonis one of Shakespeare's 'great' narcissists.[2] Coppélia Kahn calls the poem a 'dramatization of narcissism', in which the boy's attempt to 'protect himself against the threat of love actually results in his self-destruction'.[3] Jonathan Bate speaks of Adonis's 'self-consuming absorption',[4] while Kenneth Muir finds in his death a kind of moral – that 'beauty which refuses love is doomed to destruction and decay'.[5] Other critics accept his narcissism with some qualification. Heather Dubrow, for example, sees Venus herself as 'self-centered' in a number of ways, yet for the most part agrees to the validity of the goddess's charge, suspecting 'subterranean motives' of

the boy for his resistance.[6] Anthony Mortimer similarly thinks that Adonis will know no 'other', but appreciates certain reasons why he might not want to know Venus in particular.[7] More recently, Eric Langley has argued for the narcissistic quality of the goddess's gaze but without attempting to relate this to her conduct or character more generally.[8] What I propose to show here is that Venus herself is the true narcissist, and that one of the most important moments of the poem – the goddess's final 'fall' – is virtually incomprehensible until this is recognized. In a briefer, final section, I offer a re-evaluation of the themes of aetiology and metamorphosis.

Let me begin by suggesting why the comparison of Adonis to Narcissus is mistaken.

Critics who favour the comparison of the boy to the infamous self-lover usually point out that he

---

[1] Arthur Golding, trans., *Ovid's Metamorphoses*, ed. Madeleine Forey (Baltimore, 2002), 3.524–604. All references are to this edition.

[2] Colin Burrow, ed., *Complete Sonnets and Poems* (Oxford, 2002), 185n. All references are to this edition.

[3] Coppélia Kahn, 'Self and Eros in *Venus and Adonis*', in Philip C. Kolin, ed., *Venus and Adonis: Critical Essays* (New York, 1997), pp. 181–202; pp. 181–2.

[4] Jonathan Bate, *Shakespeare and Ovid* (Oxford, 1994), p. 61.

[5] Kenneth Muir, *Shakespeare the Professional, and Related Studies* (London, 1973), p. 180.

[6] Heather Dubrow, *Captive Victors: Shakespeare's Narrative Poems and Sonnets* (New York, 1987), pp. 37–44.

[7] Anthony Mortimer, *Variable Passions: A Reading of Shakespeare's 'Venus and Adonis'* (Ithaca, 2000), pp. 31–2.

[8] Eric Langley, '"And died to kiss his shadow": The Narcissistic Gaze in Shakespeare's *Venus and Adonis*', *Forum for Modern Language Studies*, 44 (2008), 12–26.

shares with not only Narcissus but also two other male figures in the *Metamorphoses* the fate of dying not long after having rejected the love of an advancing woman.[9] This similarity does seem suggestive. However, there are at least two major reasons why the comparison is both unacceptable and unwarranted. The first is that it comes from Venus herself. What is problematic about this is not only the fact that the goddess's argument has a definite interest or goal – breaking down the boy's resistance – but the fact that the very futile or self-defeating quality of her arguments generally represents one of the poem's main elements of humour. What is indeed both striking and humorous about the goddess's initial comparison is the very speed with which it is made. The reader is little more than 150 lines into the poem when Venus asks Adonis, accusingly,

> Is thine own heart to thine own face affected?
> Can thy right hand seize upon thy left?
> Then woo thyself, be of thyself rejected:
> Steal thine own freedom, and complain on theft.
> Narcissus so himself himself forsook,
> And died to kiss his shadow in the brook.   (157–62)

At this point Adonis has not yet even spoken – or more accurately, has not been allowed to speak. He made an attempt, but a pugnacious and overpowering Venus immediately stopped his lips and warned him – rather as Tarquin warns Lucrece – that if he should 'chide', his 'lips shall never open' (48; cf. *Lucrece*, 484). Can the argument really tell us anything about him, then? Might it not tell us far more about the goddess herself?

A second reason why the comparison fails is that Adonis as a character is simply insufficiently compelling or memorable to merit it. In many ways, it seems the two characters could hardly be less alike. If what defines Narcissus is passionate desire, what defines Adonis is absence of desire, perhaps the very capacity for desire. If what defines Narcissus is destructiveness, particularly self-destructiveness, what defines Adonis is relative harmlessness. If what defines Narcissus is extreme pathos, what defines Adonis is innocence or naivety. Nor does Adonis share Narcissus's more particular traits such as his self-beguiling gaze or

patently delusional thinking. If the boy is intended as a new Narcissus, moreover, why does the moment when Venus tries to show him his beauty reflected 'in [her] eyeballs' (119) pass without narrative interest or consequence? The reality is that, while there may be good reason to see Adonis as self-protective, there is nothing to suggest he is self-infatuated. Narcissism in the sense of pathetic, destructive, practically solipsistic self-love just does not apply to the boy.

But it does apply to the goddess. Evidence of Venus's narcissism, once searched for, is found to be abundant throughout the poem. The most immediate and compelling evidence for it, however, comes late, after the goddess has come upon the boy's remains and given a long speech describing the significance of his life and death (1075–120). Upon concluding what is a kind of farewell speech to the world, Venus collapses:

> With this she falleth in the place she stood,
>   And stains her face with his congealèd blood.
> She looks upon his lips, and they are pale;
> She takes him by the hand, and that is cold;
> She whispers in his ears a heavy tale,
>   As if they heard the woeful words she told;
>   She lifts the coffer-lids that close his eyes,
>   Where, lo, two lamps burnt out in darkness lies.
>
> Two glasses where herself herself beheld
> A thousand times, and now no more reflect,
> Their virtue lost wherein they late excelled,
> And every beauty robbed of his effect.   (1121–32)

I will return later to the significance of Venus's fall; for now, let me only say that, while it appears to be the climactic moment in the goddess's grief and thus the poem as a whole, there may be a sense in which it is anticlimactic in the extreme. Of these twelve lines of narration, my immediate

---

9 The other two figures are Hermaphroditus and Hippolytus (Ovid, *Met.* 4.317–88 and 15.479–546). Together with Narcissus, they are, as William Keach puts it, 'beautiful young men full of self-love and self-ignorance who come to tragic ends when they refuse to acknowledge the power of sexual love': *Elizabethan Erotic Narratives: Irony and Pathos in the Ovidian Poetry of Shakespeare, Marlowe, and Their Contemporaries* (New Brunswick, 1977), p. 56.

interest is the final four and what they reveal about Venus's peculiar interest in Adonis. Just what did she see in the boy? Herself, apparently. According to these lines, Adonis's 'virtue' was his very reflective capacity, his eyes functioning as mirrors wherein she 'beheld' herself. That she did so a 'thousand' times suggests that the self-admiration had been quite constant, 'thousand' being the preferred term in the poem for innumerably large quantities of objects or acts. The goddess is also revealed to be viewing herself in the exact manner that she had urged the boy to view himself, making that earlier moment conspicuous as foreshadowing, of the particularly self-betraying variety.

What is especially remarkable here, however, is that this is not the first time the reader has encountered such a conspicuous repetition of pronouns. The narrator's 'Two glasses where *herself herself* beheld' (1129) unmistakably recalls Venus's earlier accusation, 'Narcissus so *himself himself* forsook' (161) (emphases added). Verbally reproducing the duplication involved in self-seeing, no doubt these double reflexive pronouns are nicely apposite to the theme of narcissism.[10] Of these two characterizations, the earlier appears blatantly self-interested, while the later objectively descriptive. The effect of this connection is thus strongly and dramatically to suggest that the goddess's accusation against the boy represents not perspicacity but projection. And at least two other passages corroborate this connection.

First, less than forty lines prior to the passage cited above, Venus recollects what life was like when Adonis lived, describing how,

> When he beheld his shadow in the brook
> The fishes spread on it their golden gills.
> When he was by, the birds such pleasure took
> That some would sing, some other in their bills
>   Would bring him mulberries and ripe-red cherries:
>   He fed them with his sight; they him with berries.
>   (1099–104)

The use of the verb 'beheld' here is significant because it anticipates the narrator's usage in 'herself herself beheld' (1129). Even more importantly, Venus's idea that Adonis 'fed [the birds] with his

sight' recalls the narrator's earlier reference to Adonis as the 'object that did feed *her* sight' (822, emphasis added). Once again we have Adonis being compared to Narcissus but the passage upon closer examination appearing to tell us more about Venus herself.

A second instance of corroboration is found in the strange way in which Venus grieves for the boy when she first suspects he has died:

> O, how her eyes and tears did lend and borrow:
> Her eye seen in the tears, tears in her eye,
> Both crystals, where they viewed each other's
>   sorrow ...   (961–3)

Here Venus views herself in her own tears, loving herself, implicitly, the way Ferdinand in *Love's Labour's Lost* hoped his beloved would not: 'But do not love thyself; then thou wilt keep / My tears for glasses, and still make me weep' (4.3.36–7). In addition, one finds another narcissistic echo, 'sorrow' not only ending line 963, but starting 964. In a poem in which narcissism is so prominent a theme, the implication could not be much stronger or clearer.

Nor does this implication seem at odds with the goddess's conduct generally. Every metaphor used to indicate the nature of her desire connotes one-sidedness and self-centredness. Venus is repeatedly compared to a predator (55–8, 63, 547–8, 551) and to a conqueror (80–2, 423–6, 549–52). She is hungry and thirsty for the boy, and actually feeds voraciously on him more than once (55–8, 547–54, 571–2). The moment his resistance weakens, she 'takes all she can' (564). The goddess 'begs', 'entreats', 'petitions' and 'pleads' with the boy. More illustratively, she 'seizes', 'ties', '[en]tangles',

---

[10] There is one more instance of this phenomenon in *Venus* (763), and at least four more in *The Rape of Lucrece* (157, 160, 998, 1566; see also 1196). In every instance it is connected with either self-hatred or self-violence. Venus wants to associate Adonis with self-destructiveness, of course, judging his failure to reproduce himself a crime worse than domestic violence, suicide or filicide (763–6). However, it is she herself who ultimately tries to destroy herself, making these double reflexive pronouns that much more appropriate to her character.

'fastens', 'enfolds', 'binds', 'bands', 'locks', 'hems', '[de]limits', '[en]twines', '[im]prisons', 'engirts', 'embraces', 'presses', 'detains', 'restrains', 'yokes' and 'withholds' the boy – all this before finally locking up his flower in her breast. At one point she tries to sell herself to him like a prostitute (513–14). At another, she states unapologetically that 'Affection is a coal that must be cooled' (387) – this in response to the boy's firm and unambiguous demand to be let go of (379). Her 'love' is also suffocating, insatiable and aroused by resistance itself, Venus wooing according to the principle that 'Foul words and frowns must not repel a lover. / What though the rose have prickles. Yet 'tis plucked' (573–4). A possible exception to this self-centredness might appear to exist in the maternal concern she shows. However, this concern appears only late, there being no specific indications of motherliness in the first two-thirds of the poem, where the actual wooing takes place.[11] Moreover, that desire is itself ambiguous, Venus's final intention being to kiss the boy's flower every minute of every hour (1187–8) – not exactly the mother any of us would want.[12] Rather than qualifying the one-sidedness, what the maternal theme seems to do instead is stress Adonis's immaturity, for there is every indication that the boy is extremely young, indeed, probably prepubescent. Venus herself calls him 'young' (187), 'unripe' (128) and 'tender' (127, 1091) but in her rage wants him anyway. In many of these attributes and others, Venus shares a great deal in common with the 'lustful lord' Tarquin and the only reason this too is not a rape story, one can be sure, is a simple question of sex.

Far more than her selfishness makes Venus narcissistic, however. She appears to share all of Narcissus's most distinctive traits. Narcissus is first defined by his sight. He 'gazes' on his shadow with 'fixed staring eyes' (Ovid, *Met.* 3.524). Those eyes are also called 'ardent' (*Met.* 526), 'greedie' (*Met.* 551) and 'dazled' (*Met.* 602). His sight is directly connected to – and the ostensible cause of – his suffering. The same is true of Venus. Her sight too is called 'fixed' (487), 'glutton[ous]'[13] (399) and 'dazzling' (1064). Multiple passages find her 'gazing' on the boy with a fearful intensity (224, 487–8, 925–7). There are in all dozens of reference to her vision and, on at least two occasions, whole stanzas devoted to the activity of her eyes (816–22, 1031–42). Narcissus is also defined by delusion. He is called a 'foolish noddy' (*Met.* 521), for example. He recognizes early on that he is in love with his own reflection, yet cannot reason his way out of the situation. Venus appears no less deluded; in fact, troubled thinking may well be her pre-eminent characteristic, as will be discussed in greater detail later on. Both Narcissus and Venus are extraordinarily pathetic. Much could be said on this point, but perhaps one comparison will suffice. Having been left by the boy in some 'mistrustful wood', Venus cries, 'Ay me!' and 'Woe, woe!', before beginning a 'wailing note' and 'woeful ditty' that outwears the night (833–41).

---

[11] Is it true that Venus alternates 'throughout' between 'sexual aggression' and 'maternal protectiveness', as Mortimer asserts (*Variable*, 165), or that her love can be 'primarily' characterized as a 'desire to mother the boy', as Wayne A. Rebhorn argues? See 'Mother Venus: Temptation in Shakespeare's *Venus and Adonis*', *Shakespeare Studies*, 11 (1978), 1–19; p. 1. In my view, this argument conflates evidence pointing to her motherly aspect – which is relatively weak – with evidence pointing to Adonis's extreme youth – which is very strong indeed. These two do not necessarily go together. Rather, Venus woos Adonis in explicitly sexual terms despite his young age, telling him, for example, 'The tender spring upon thy tempting lip / Shows thee unripe; yet mayst thou well be tasted' (127–8).

[12] Commenting on this final situation, Katherine Duncan-Jones and H. R. Woudhuysen observe that Venus, 'who has never shown any convincing interest in motherhood earlier in the poem, now possesses a child-like creature which seems to provide her with sexual stimulation rather than maternal fulfillment': *Shakespeare's Poems* (London and New York, 2007), p. 61.

[13] This reference is implicit. Venus speaks of the 'glutton eye' of a lover while instructing Adonis to follow the example of his more amorous horse (399). The reference can be seen as applying to the goddess herself, however, for a number of reasons. First, she is generalizing in a way that is clearly self-justifying. Second, there are many prominent similarities between goddess and steed. Its eye 'glisters fire' (275), for example, just as Venus's eyes are said to be 'fiery' (219). Third, Venus is repeatedly implied to be a glutton. For example, at one point she feeds on the boy 'glutton-like' (548). Finally, as has already been noted, there is a marked tendency in the goddess to betray aspects of her own character when describing the character of others.

This is reminiscent of and may be partly derived from Narcissus crying out 'with piteous voice unto the wood that round about him stands, / . . . "Alas, ye woods, and was there ever any / That loved so cruelly as I?"' (*Met.* 554–7). Finally, and most obviously, Narcissus is self-destructive. As he allows himself to pine unto death, he smites his stomach, beats his breast and strikes his feet against the ground (*Met.* 606, 624). Venus too is self-destructive, and to an even more remarkable degree. Indeed, the fact is not always recognized but much of the final third of the poem takes place either inside or on the person of the goddess, and what one witnesses there is a combination of utter mayhem and catastrophic destruction. The self-punishment begins with Venus beating her heart, making it 'groan' (829). The disastrous internal developments that follow thereafter are compared to a tempest, her 'variable passions . . . consulting for foul weather' (967–72); to a 'mutiny' in which her own parts conduct a rebellion (1045–50); and to an '[earth]quake' that shakes 'earth's foundation' (1045–7). Both Narcissus and Venus are also 'doting', their endeavours are said to be 'in vain', both address the object of their desire as 'fondling', both speak passively of their 'spite'. The similarities are in all too numerous to be listed here.

For all these similarities, there is of course one major difference: Venus goes after a person outside her, and is evidently obsessed not with her own beauty but with the boy's. Moreover, she retains an interest in or commitment to Adonis even after his eye-glasses stop functioning as they once did. What, then, seems to be the precise nature of her narcissism? Just what kind of self-love does she exhibit? I propose that Venus is narcissistic not in the more superficial sense that she is taken with her own face or appearance, but narcissistic in the deeper, more sinister, more all-consuming sense that she can look anywhere and everywhere – at no less than the face of her own ostensible beloved – and see none but herself. To understand this deeper aspect and true quality of her narcissism, one has to consider her concept of the boy – just who she thinks Adonis is.

For Venus, Adonis is not merely an exceptionally handsome young man. He is beauty itself – the very form made flesh – and a creature, therefore, whose existence is fundamental to the stability of the universe. Of course, this gives the poem an allegorical dimension. However, the reason why past attempts to read the poem allegorically have not succeeded is because the allegory is internal, belonging to the storyteller within the story, namely Venus herself. A truly fantastic picture is painted when one takes the statements she makes about the boy and puts them together.

Adonis, according to Venus, is the most beautiful creature in existence. His beauty is such that nature must have produced him from moulds stolen from heaven (730–1). Venus addresses him as the 'the fairest mover on this mortal round' (368) and calls him nature's 'best work' (954). Not only that, he is the source of all beauty in the world. His beauty sets 'gloss on the rose', his breath lends 'smell to the violet' (935–6). The boy's eyes are so bright that they outshine the sun by day and the moon by night (731–2), and such that he is responsible for sight in others (952). Venus actually tells the sun itself, 'There lives a son that sucked an earthly mother / May lend thee light, as thou dost lend to other' (863–4). Adonis is also the panacea. Venus considers the sweat off his hand 'earth's sovereign salve' (28). She suggests that his breath has the power to banish plague (507–10) and that his mere presence brings harmony, taming such wild animals as lions and tigers and wolves (1093–8). Naturally, Adonis is adored by all. His 'full perfection all the world amazes' (634), says Venus. Birds and fishes take great pleasure in seeing the boy (1099–104). The wild animals mentioned above are not only subdued by his presence, but also stop to stare at him and hear him sing (1093–8). The earth itself trips the boy to rob him of a kiss, according to Venus's imagination, and Diana, the goddess of chastity, abandons her vow in hope of the same (721–6). The sun and wind, too, find the boy irresistible, the one peeping beneath the brim of his bonnet and the other blowing off his bonnet to play with his locks, and the two then competing with one another to dry his tears when he weeps (1085–92).

Because beauty is supreme and Adonis represents beauty 'mingled' with the infirmity of mortality (735), his existence carries an apocalyptic dimension as well. Venus appears literally to think that 'the world hath ending with [his] life' (12). Infusing his life with a dreadful prophecy (927), she believes nature would become indifferent to its own existence in the circumstance that he died (953–4). This doom-laden aspect of the goddess's conviction comes out most clearly when, towards the end of the poem, she briefly and mistakenly thinks that Adonis has not in fact been killed by the boar and tells Jove that, of course, his death would have been accompanied by cataclysmic destruction and an all-engulfing darkness:

> 'O Jove,' quoth she, 'How much a fool was I
> To be of such a weak and silly mind
> To wail his death who lives, and must not die
> Till mutual overthrow of mortal kind?
> For he being dead, with him is beauty slain,
> And beauty dead, black chaos comes again.'
>
> (1015–20)

Even this is not the total picture of the goddess's belief, but it is perhaps sufficient to show that we are dealing either with a truly extraordinary young man – and an Adoni-centric universe – or a truly extraordinary degree of hyperbole. Presented in this way, it must be evident which of these is true. In point of fact, many of the most important and intriguing characterizations of the goddess really only begin to make sense once one appreciates the idiosyncrasy. The numerically central line of the poem, 'All is imaginary she doth prove' (597), for example, suggests that Venus's version of reality is wholly fanciful. Similarly, the description of Venus's brain as 'Full of respects, yet naught at all respecting, / In hand with all things, naught at all effecting' (911–12), suggests that her perspective is, while far-reaching, both immaterial and inconsequential. Venus's brain is also called 'drunken' (910) and twice called 'troubled' (1040, 1068). She is implied to have a 'fantastic wit' (850) and 'dire imagination' (975). There are additional references to the 'engine of her thoughts' (367), to her 'vulture thought' (551) and to her 'false bethinking'

(1024). A moment ago we saw Venus implying that she had a 'weak and silly mind' for allowing herself to believe the boy had perished; shortly before this, she had cheered herself up by calling the very possibility of his demise a 'causeless fantasy' (896–7): in both instances the irony could hardly be deeper. Her psychological outlook is additionally characterized as ignorant (925), deeply superstitious (925–8) and extremely fearful (1021–2).

What all of this helps make clear is the significance of the goddess's introductory epithet – 'Sick-thoughted Venus' (5). Many editions of the poem gloss 'sick-thoughted' as 'lovesick', but in the context of her many cerebrum-related representations, this must be seen as not only unhelpful but misleading. 'Lovesick' implies a state of passion that is perhaps unexceptional. 'Sick-thoughted' is in fact very precise and goes with the other opening epithets in both narrative poems, including 'Lust-breathèd Tarquin' (3).[14] Just as the main point about Tarquin is that he is animated by lust,[15] the main point about Venus appears to be that she is mentally ill. Two further comparisons with *Lucrece* are also pertinent here, incidentally. First, Tarquin is characterized as 'brainsick' as he gives himself over to base desire (175). But whereas Tarquin's lust – and accompanying mental affliction – is 'breathed' in the sense of fleeting, Venus's appears to be permanent. Second, Tarquin's harmless and pure victim is called 'holy-thoughted Lucrece' (384), making for a provocative and stark contrast with her feminine counterpart in Venus.

With the goddess's cognitive or ideological disposition in view, is it any wonder that she repeatedly wishes Adonis could not communicate at all, or that she responds to his first significant speech with a stunned, 'What, canst thou talk?' (427)? In representing himself he contradicts her, necessarily. He can perhaps be seen as the reflection that

---

[14] The remaining epithets in the two poems are 'Rose-cheeked Adonis' (3) and 'Lucrece the chaste' (7). All appear to have been very carefully conceived, anticipating much about the character of each in the action that follows.

[15] Credit for this particular formulation, 'animated by lust', goes to Burrow (243n.).

talked back. Then ran off. Then got himself killed. All unfathomable happenings, for credulous, 'hard-believing love' (985). But like Richard II, Venus will hammer out an explanation, and persist in peopling the world with her thought. It is in light of this unbending omnipresence of thought that the goddess's final fall must be examined.

In turning to this incident, what should first be noted is that Venus falls multiple times in the poem. Prior to the collapse cited earlier on in this article and to be looked at more closely now, Venus has taken both herself and the boy to the ground three times (41–3, 545–6, 592–4). On a fourth occasion she has 'flatly falle[n]' down so that the 'silly boy' thinks she is dead (463–7). In each of these instances, the falls are no doubt purposeful – or 'tactical', to use Mortimer's term[16] – 'cunning Love' trying by any means conceivable to keep Adonis close to her. The goddess's final fall needs first, then, to be understood within a pattern of deliberate and calculated falls, one of which resembles a kind of death or suicide.

As mentioned earlier, Venus collapses upon concluding a kind of 'farewell' speech to the world that follows immediately after she discovers the boy's boar-mangled body. Near the beginning of this speech, the goddess's self-punishment culminates in Venus telling her own heart to melt: 'Heavy heart's lead, melt at mine eyes' red fire: / So shall I die by drops of hot desire' (1073–4). She then addresses the world according to its irrecoverable loss in the death of the boy:

Alas, poor world, what treasure hast thou lost,
What face remains alive that's worth the viewing?
What tongue is music now? What canst thou boast
Of things long since, or anything ensuing?
    The flowers are sweet, their colours fresh and trim,
    But true sweet beauty lived and died with him.

Bonnet nor veil henceforth no creature wear,
Nor sun, nor wind will ever strive to kiss you,
Having no fair to lose, you need not fear.
The sun doth scorn you, and the wind doth hiss you.
(1075–84)

The boy is dead, in other words, and there is no more reason to live – for Venus or anyone else. Nature itself will no longer function properly or benignly. The goddess then reminisces on the golden age that was the time when Adonis – the boy she lusted after for an afternoon – lived (1085–104). Finally, she ruminates on how the boar ruined everything (1105–18).

It is at this point that she collapses, making these the immediate context of her fall: a virtual suicide and a doomsday speech. A closer look at the fall may now be taken and a more immediate observation made. Here again are the lines in question:

With this she falleth in the place she stood,
And stains her face with his congealèd blood.

She looks upon his lips, and they are pale;
She takes him by the hand, and that is cold.
(1121–4)

I observe that there is something of a narrative gap here between the stanza describing Venus's fall and the subsequent stanza in which she begins to inspect the boy's corpse. It is clearly *not* the case that the goddess falls on top of Adonis and splashes her face in his blood in order to then examine him. The gap seems in fact so pronounced that it is tempting to ask whether Shakespeare might once have intended to end the poem at this point. However, that is almost certainly not the case. Venus has wanted to see the death of the boy as the death of beauty itself and as having, therefore, universal and catastrophic ramifications. What the gap does is help expose the truly singular and eccentric nature of that belief or the great gulf that exists between reality as the goddess sees it and reality in itself. For, nothing happens. The spotlight stays on the goddess and her activities. No change is seen; the goddess drops but there is no other sign of doom. For Venus herself, this is a tremendous mystery: 'Wonder of time', she exclaims, upon confirming the boy's demise, 'This is my spite, / That, thou being dead, the day should yet be light' (1133–4). It is no accident that these lines form the couplet of the stanza that most clearly makes known her narcissism – the stanza beginning 'Two glasses

---

[16] Mortimer, *Variable*, p. 93.

where herself herself beheld' – for they betray an egocentrism that is truly transcendent. What is the 'wonder' Venus marvels at? The wonder that there is still a world. To the goddess it is incomprehensible that there can be light, the boy's eyes – previously said to light up the world in a way that surpassed the sun – being dark. Taking personal offence at the fact, she identifies the non-death of nature as her own individual 'spite'.

Tempests, earthquakes, mutinies – all that has gone on *inside* the goddess is almost certainly what she has expected to see go on *outside* as well. But chaos remains unmanifest externally. What is the explanation for this? Not, of course, that the goddess's belief about the boy has been mistaken. Rather, nature does not yet seem to have recognized the loss it has suffered. The moment the very possibility of beauty's demise hit her radar screen, Venus began to implode, as she thought appropriate or inevitable. She has done her part in the 'mutual overthrow'. Nature, however, has been slow to react and only now, I think, does it become apparent why the goddess has recently shown such intense feelings of bitterness towards the earth, seeing it as 'foul', 'sluttish', and 'drunken' (983–4): to this point it has proven sluggardly in or unfaithful to the tenet that, when beauty goes, all of nature must go with it.

In falling, then, it may just be that Venus is taking it upon herself to help initiate the dark takeover she sees as inexorable. It is not necessarily that the goddess wants the world destroyed, but she certainly feels that it is a place no creature would ever again want to live in and probably feels that nothing short of total destruction would do justice to the boy's death. Nor is it that she sees herself as capable of destroying the world but, to judge by her many soliloquies in the last part – one to the sun (860–4), two to death (931–54, 997–1008), one to Jove (1015–24), and two more to the world (1075–1120, 1135–64) – this is a goddess who believes all the great powers of reality and the world itself attend her every word and deed. In making her melodramatic fall, then, it may just be that Venus is attempting to shake nature out of its stupor and indicate to it in characteristically theatrical fashion

the absolute immensity of its loss; it may even be that she intends the fall as a distinct signal to nature that *now* is the appointed time for the promised appearance of 'black chaos'. Whatever the precise motive may be, whatever calculations have been made, it is hard not to think that, had she the power or authority – were the fantasy she has harboured true – all would flame and be flooded the instant she hit the ground.

What remains to be done here is to try to reevaluate the poem's conclusion. While many critics consider Venus to be a more sympathetic character in the last part of the poem,[17] I hope to show in a brief way that her behaviour is consistent with what one would expect of a frustrated yet unrepentant self-lover. What seems particularly important to consider is that the anguish Venus shows in the final section is directly related to – and so extreme as to be incomprehensible outside of – her conception of the boy. At the same time, the goddess shows a striking hostility to the world at large. If prior to her final fall Venus addressed the world according to its doom (1075–120), following it she addresses the world according to its surviving wretchedness, in a speech condemning all future participants in love (1135–64). A number of critics have noticed that Love's 'prophecy' on love is bitter, even petulant.[18] A number have noticed that much of it describes what has been already been going on in the life of

---

[17] Dubrow states that 'on the whole our sympathy for Venus increases as the poem progresses' (*Captive*, p. 68). Keach says similarly that towards the end, 'our sympathy [for Venus] deepens' (*Elizabethan*, p. 75). Eugene Cantelupe calls Venus 'a voracious, extravagantly absurd yet immensely comic and sympathetic female', in contrast to Adonis, whom he calls a 'self-indulgent, at times irritatingly obtuse but disarmingly naive male': 'An Iconographical Interpretation of *Venus and Adonis*, Shakespeare's Ovidian Comedy', *Shakespeare Quarterly*, 14 (1963), 141–51; p. 144.

[18] A. D. Cousins calls Venus's prophecy 'anachronistic' and 'wholly negative': *Shakespeare's Sonnets and Narrative Poems* (New York, 1999), p. 22. Dubrow calls it an 'angry prophecy' in which Venus 'mocks the rest of the world' (*Captive*, p. 40). James Schiffer refers to the speech as Venus's 'prophecy-curse': 'Shakespeare's *Venus and Adonis*: A Lacanian Tragicomedy of Desire', in Philip C. Kolin, ed., *Venus and Adonis: Critical Essays* (New York, 1997), pp. 359–76; p. 372.

love.[19] What does not seem to have been noticed is that the speech appears to be exclusively self-referential, its every line not only betraying key aspects of Venus's own character, but also being directly relatable to other parts of the poem. A quick scan of key words here finds 'sorrow', 'jealousy', 'woe', 'false' – terms all distinctly associated with the goddess herself. The main theme of the prophecy is unsteady or 'extreme' behaviour – also distinctly associated with the goddess. To look in slightly more detail at but one pair of lines, Venus prophesies on love that, 'The staring ruffian shall it keep in quiet, / Pluck down the rich, enrich the poor with treasures' (1149–50). While not every detail here can be examined, these lines appear distinctly to refer to the opening scene, where Venus ambushes the boy and plucks him down from his horse. The boy Adonis is referred to as 'rich' at least two times in the poem (552, 724). Venus herself is repeatedly referred to as 'poor' (601, 604, 925, 1057) and the boy as her 'treasure' (552, 1022, 1075). But the goddess, a 'staring ruffian'? Venus is to be thought a contemptible criminal? Yes. This is implied by her numerous yet unsubstantiated perceptions of criminality in others and such self-justifying statements as 'Rich preys make true men thieves' (724). A similar effort can be made with almost every other line of the speech. At this late stage, it is perhaps unsurprising that everything this narcissist says would tell us only about herself, the goddess having undergone no discernible change in attitude or outlook. But what this means is that the speech is less a prophecy on love than a profile of one constitutionally incapable of love; what it means, in other words, is that the speech is an absolute mine for the truest possible characterization of this sweaty, lustful usurper, as Adonis calls her (794). More broadly, what it means is that the poem has no aetiological dimension but a mock one.

As for the fate Venus gives Adonis and herself, it is meant to be unjust and repulsive in the case of the boy and just in the case of the goddess herself. The picture of Venus 'immuring herself' and the boy being locked away in her breast are foreshadowed time and again by references to dark, cavernous, solitary kinds of imprisonment. To cite only the most directly explicit instance of foreshadowing here, Venus resolves at one point

> no longer to restrain [Adonis],
> Bids him farewell, and look well to her heart,
> The which by Cupid's bow, she doth protest,
> He carries thence encagèd in his breast. (579–82)

Being encaged in her breast, next to her 'sick', 'panting' heart (584, 647) – this is what Adonis has to 'look well', that is, look forward, to. But a few lines before this, passing reference has been made to 'beauty under twenty locks' being 'kept' (575). As for Venus's retreat from the world, the process begins long before she yokes her doves to the purpose. That confounded, exasperated withdrawal is unmistakably anticipated in such images as Venus's 'feeling part[s]', being compared to soldiers fleeing a battlefield (892–4); her eyes being compared to a snail,

> whose tender horns being hit,
> Shrinks backward in his shelly cave with pain,
> And, there all smothered up, in shade doth sit,
> Long after fearing to creep forth again (1033–6)

and again the goddess's eyes fleeing 'Into the deep-dark cabins of her head' (1037–8). Earlier in the poem, Venus had at one point referred cynically to 'self-loving nuns' (752). With this in mind, it is interesting to find Venus herself 'weary of the world' and seeking seclusion at the poem's end. Is this one more self-betraying indictment? It is possible that we have here another epithet for the love-lacking goddess herself.

Altogether, then, it would seem a most unfortunate conclusion, both characters ending up as

---

[19] Heather Asals states that Venus's 'prophecy about the laws of love are just those laws that have governed her relationship with Adonis': 'Venus and Adonis: The Education of a Goddess', Studies in English Literature 1500–1900, 13 (1973), 31–51; p. 49. Similarly, Richard Lanham states that the prophecy describes the 'love affair we have already seen': The Motives of Eloquence: Literary Rhetoric in the Renaissance (New Haven, 1976), p. 92. Even Kahn, most of whose criticism is reserved for the boy, sees the speech as 'part curse', with 'her own aborted love affair' as its 'model' ('Self', p. 198).

something like captive losers. But, in fact, Adonis's fate may not be what it appears. Quite simply, he may not end up with Venus – or *in* Venus – at all. For, as James Yoch observes, it is difficult to accept the validity of Venus's perceptions in the last part of the poem.[20] Specifically, the goddess's notion that there is a relationship between the boy and flower she sees cannot be trusted, first because it is a 'comparison' (1172, 1176), one made by an expert at story-telling (845–6) and all that that implies; and second because everything Venus sees at this point is doubly distorted, first by her 'mangling eye' (1065) and second by her 'troubled' brain (1068). Additionally, her face has been bloodied by her fall. Thus, it may be that the boy's true metamorphosis is to go from hunt*ed* to hunt*er*; alternatively, it may be that metamorphosis too is but a mock theme, insofar as Venus's perceptions may have no correspondence with empirical fact. In any case, there can be little doubt that the reader is to feel some solace that the boy's death was relatively swift, that he did not 'wither' either *as* Venus wanted him to or more importantly *where* she wanted him to, that he died in the natural world and not the narcissist's.

At this point it may be useful to return briefly to the passage that describes Venus as having been looking at her own reflection in the boy's eyes for the length of their encounter (1129–32). Evidently, these lines imply something not literal but metaphorical. The point is not that Venus is taken with her own beauty – not, anyhow, in the straightforward sense. Rather, the point has to do with the reality she inhabits. Adonis dies and the world fails to react, much less take notice. Why? Because it does not in fact revolve around him. Venus loves herself and not another, then, in that she relates not

to the particular boy Adonis, but to an elaborately wrought, all-concerning, all-consuming abstraction projected on to him. Hers appears to be a world of ideas in the literal sense.

What seems important to emphasize, in conclusion, is that in the last part of the poem, Venus mourns not so much the death of this individual as the reality he is supposed to embody. Nothing else explains why her display of grief is so frenzied, violent and spectacular, why it far exceeds that shown by the husband and father of the violated and then self-slaughtered Lucrece, by comparison. What the reader witnesses in the final part is an inward reaction to the death of beauty itself. However, that reaction is to be seen as extreme, egocentric and fundamentalist. The emphasis here is on internal as opposed to external goings-on, because the author means to depict the inner workings of the narcissistic mind (and heart), and to show the internal consequences when narcissistic and natural orders of reality conflict. Even more than its sexual reversal of suitor and suited, it is this persistent tension between fantasy and reality, abstraction and actuality that defines the poem and makes it so compelling. None of this is to say that Venus does not remain a major source of comedy throughout, of course. It is to say that there may be a touch of relief in the fact that this self-loving psychopath and would-be agent of Armageddon goes thinking she got what she came for, meaning never again to be seen.

---

[20] 'The Eye of Venus: Shakespeare's Erotic Landscape', *Studies in English Literature 1500–1900*, 20 (1980), 59–71; p. 68.

SURFACE TENSIONS: CEREMONY AND SHAME IN *MUCH ADO ABOUT NOTHING*

ALISON FINDLAY

Beatrice and Benedick 'never meet but there's a skirmish of wit between them' (1.1.60–1), we are warned, and their encounter a few lines later does not disappoint:

Ben. What, my dear Lady Disdain! Are you yet living?
Bea. Is it possible disdain should die while she hath such meet food to feed it as Signor Benedick? Courtesy itself must convert to disdain if you come in her presence.
Ben. Then is courtesy a turn-coat: but it is certain I am loved of all ladies, only you excepted . . .

                                                    (1.1.112–19)[1]

This greeting brilliantly captures the ceremonial idiom central to the social politics of *Much Ado About Nothing*. Both characters overplay deferential formality in their use of titles, 'Lady Disdain' and 'Signor Benedick', while simultaneously flouting the code of politeness in their insults. The satirical effect would be increased by appropriate courteous gestures of greeting: a formal bow from Benedick and an answering curtsey from Beatrice traverse the space between their bodies. Their 'skirmish of wit' immediately establishes Messina as a high-risk environment for face-to-face interactions, something that the tragi-comic extremes of the plot go on to demonstrate.

In the public, courtly environment of Leonato's household, identity is highly dependent on superficial signifiers and interactions. Benedick draws attention to both verbal and non-verbal surfaces in the play, pointedly warning his friends 'The body of your discourse is sometime guarded with fragments, and the guards [decorations] are but slightly

basted on, neither' (1.1.268–70). The lines characters speak are complemented by those drawn by their costumes, gestures, position and movement in the stage space, an elaborate tissue of non-verbal signifiers that Mary E. Hazard refers to as the multiple silent languages of early modern culture.[2] Although such flamboyant surfaces form the social fabric of Messina, as Benedick recognizes, they are insecure: 'slightly basted on', untrustworthy. The play explores how engaging in social discourse is an expression of, or investment of, interest that always involves deep risk to the self: the shame of that interest not being reciprocated. Its plots display a pattern of human interaction outlined by the psychologist Silvan S. Tomkins, who argues that when a subject's interest or joy in a human or non-human object is activated and then inhibited but not completely eradicated, this produces shame as a physiological affect.[3] In Shakespeare's play, Messina's network of ceremonies is designed to mitigate the risks to

---

[1] All Shakespeare quotations are from *William Shakespeare: The Complete Works*, ed. Stanley Wells, Gary Taylor, John Jowett and William Montgomery (Oxford, 1986).
[2] Mary E. Hazard, *Elizabethan Silent Language* (Lincoln, NE, 2000). For more on clothes, see my '*Much Ado About Nothing*', in *Shakespeare: The Comedies*, ed. Richard Dutton and Jean E. Howard (Oxford, 2003), pp. 393–410.
[3] The work of Silvan S. Tomkins is published in *Shame and Its Sisters: A Silvan Tomkins Reader*, ed. Eve Kosovsky Sedgwick and Adam Frank (Durham, 1995), p. 134. It is brilliantly discussed by Elspeth Probyn in *Blush: Faces of Shame* (Minneapolis, 2005), p. 14, a book to which my reading of *Much Ado* is indebted.

identity in everyday encounters and life-changing rites of passage. The early sociological work of Erving Goffman on the importance of ceremony in face-to-face encounters provides a useful model for reading the brittle social fabric of the play. Goffman proposes that 'the self is in part a ceremonial thing, a sacred object which must be treated with proper ritual care and in turn must be presented in a proper light to others.'[4] He argues that everyday interactions, such as the close encounters between Leonato's household and the soldiers, between servants and masters or between Beatrice and Benedick, provide numerous opportunities for minor ceremonial behaviour through deportment, dress, bearing and speech, which limit the risks to identity in the social encounter. The codes of ceremony function like clothing for the naked expressions of interest or enjoyment expressed by the individual. What Beatrice and Benedick do, of course, is to profane the idiom through which proper ceremonial conduct operates in their attempts to discredit each other's identities. In desecrating 'Lady Courtesy' and the established codes of greeting, they set a pattern for the more intensive broken ceremonies of wedding, mourning and betrothal that characterize the play.

The masked ball in Act 2 scene 1 presents an extended series of interpersonal encounters in which the risks of wooing are mediated by the highly structured social ceremony of dance. Alan Brissenden cleverly noted that the units of dialogue in the dance section of Act 2 scene 1 are matched to the movements of actors traversing the space in the formal pattern of a pavane.[5] Here, the dancers' bodies move in a pattern of advance and retreat, whose turns back and forth represent kinaesthetically turns in the conversation. The pavane is a dance of poise in which the partners' movements are symmetrical. Physical balance reflects the delicate status balance in courtship where the subservient female is temporarily elevated as a mistress and the man ceremonially adopts a lower-status position as suitor. Don Pedro claims he has masked his superiority like Jove in Baucis and Philemon's house. Hero, perhaps emboldened by the mask she wears, tartly tells him she may walk away when she

pleases and turns in step with the dance (2.1.78–89). Beatrice and Benedick use their masks as an additional form of ceremonial protection from behind which they can freely demonstrate their fascination with each other and simultaneously shame each other in order to maintain an illusion of high status (2.1.115–40).

The dance also creates an illusion of equality in terms of gender presentation. At the masked ball, there are literally no face-to-face encounters: male characters, no less than females, are recognizable only by an alienated voice (detached from the face as guarantee of authorship), by stance and by costume. The 'sacred' identities of Benedick, Don Pedro, Balthasar and Antonio are fragmented, creating a parallel with the female characters represented by boy actors. Even the evidence of the body is equivocal. When Antonio pretends that he is counterfeiting himself, Ursula tells him 'You could never do him so ill-well unless you were the very man. Here's his dry hand up and down. You are he, you are he' (2.1.106–8). Whatever the age of the actor playing Antonio, the verbal exchange renders corporeal evidence at once conclusive and suspect, as though to prepare the audience for the later events surrounding Hero's supposed infidelity.

The betrothal, wedding and mourning ceremonies that follow are extended sequences of symbolic action, different from interpersonal rituals like greeting and parting or even dancing. They are self-consciously framed as highly charged events that are not enacted by the participants every day. The gaps that open up in the play's formal ceremonies are crux points at which the construction of identity is exposed. Ceremony exists on the surface and in the immediate moment of enactment. Like Austin's speech-act, its full meaning is constituted by the diverse surface elements of which

---

[4] Erving Goffman, *Interaction Ritual: Essays in Face-to-Face Behavior* (Chicago, 1967), p. 91.

[5] Alan Brissenden, *Shakespeare and the Dance* (Basingstoke, 1981), pp. 49–50. He gives the Madam Sicilia pavane in the Bodleian library as a particularly appropriate example. On dancing as a means to enact harmonious social bonding, see also Skiles Howard, *The Politics of Courtly Dancing in Early Modern England* (Amherst, 1998), Chapter 3.

it is made: the form of words spoken, the specific gestures enacted, the textiles and objects that are used. Precise spatial dynamics are also essential to ceremony: the spaces between bodies and how those enacting the ceremony and participating as witnesses or spectators traverse that space, and the place in which all these elements congregate. These material elements, each with its own particular cultural resonance, are orchestrated according to a set pattern or form in order to constitute a ceremony. The coordination of diverse elements for an event weighted with emotional and cultural significance inevitably produces tensions between those surfaces.

The stilted betrothal ceremony of Hero and Claudio emphasizes the formality of gesture and response and the element of risk. Claudio's mistaken jealousy is blazoned in his sulky appearance, including shame at having expressed his interest in Hero only to be ousted in favour of Don Pedro, as he thinks. The fact that his interest (whether financial or romantic or both) remains, even though thwarted, is what produces intense feelings of shame. Claudio refuses to risk a further expression of his interest: Leonato's gesture in offering his daughter is met only with silence until Beatrice prompts Claudio to speak. When Claudio does take the risk of offering himself, another awkward moment follows: his words 'I give away myself for you, and dote on the exchange' (2.1.289–90) are met with silence from Hero. Beatrice retrieves him from the brink of intensified shame by prompting Hero to seal the bargain with words or a kiss (2.1.31–6). The silence and the spaces between Hero's and Claudio's bodies and affections in this first rite of passage are more than a superficial embarrassment. They initiate a pattern in which ceremonial practice is desecrated.

How and why do ceremonies work? When Henry V tries to empty out 'thrice-gorgeous ceremony' as an 'idol' (Henry V, 4.1.237–64) he realizes that, far from being empty terms, such superficial structures order our existence. Henry recognizes 'the deep value of surfaces', to borrow a term from the philosopher of aesthetics, Richard Shusterman.[6] Shusterman's theories help to explain how the representations of ceremony might have worked in performances of Much Ado. He argues that a surface – for example a wedding or a mourning ceremony – is experienced as a unique event in space and time by the participants. Aesthetic naturalism, following Nietzsche, sees the ceremony as a specialized framework through which a sublime moment of presence, the fullness of expression meeting deep human needs, can be briefly realized. However, a ceremony is, by its very nature, a repeated event. Historicist aesthetics proposes that the surface elements of ceremony are constituted by the socio-historical institutional settings; that it reaches beyond the site of enactment to a world elsewhere – a wider community across time and space and, in some cases, to a spiritual entity. A ceremony is thus something of a paradox. The surface is immediate but it invokes the presence of depth – emotionally, spiritually and historically via the weight of tradition. Shusterman uses the metaphor of dramatization to reconcile the opposites of surface immediacy and historical contextualism. By marking off an event or object from its immediate context, the artistic frame of the ceremony, like the performance, intensifies its emotional and sensuous immediacy and simultaneously demarcates it as a particular cultural site in a larger socio-historical framework.[7] Paradoxically, only because it is scripted and inscribed within a tradition and marked off as such, can it offer participants the freedom to access a more intense, immediate experience of human vitality and presence.

A ceremony on stage, however, is not a real ceremony but a fictional representation of an already framed act. It is doubly framed. How do we read such surfaces? They are obviously still spectacular events but do they carry any of the emotional, spiritual and historical charge of their originals when reproduced on stage? According to Shusterman, dramatization should amplify the experience. Drama's power, he argues, derives from its ability to intensify 'our passionate involvement by

---

[6] Richard Shusterman, *Surface and Depth: Dialectics of Criticism and Culture* (Cornell, 2002), p. 1.

[7] Shusterman, *Surface and Depth*, pp. 231–4.

removing other inhibitions to lived intensity'; its artistic form provides 'an indirect route to appreciate the real far more fully or profoundly' by engaging us with a reality 'far greater in its experiential depths of vivid feeling'.[8] Does staging a ceremony create one metatheatrical frame too many and dilute or evacuate its power to engage spectators in an intensely heightened experience? Critical studies have explored how theatre 'empties out' rituals and ceremonies of power but it has also been argued that objects re-presented on stage can function as the materials of memory – carrying traces of their former existence that resonate with the actors and audiences who use or view them in their new theatrical context.[9] I propose that ceremonies in Shakespeare do the same thing, that the surface forms enacted on the stage retain a power, like their originals, to invoke deep cultural, emotional, spiritual resonances for those present. The familiarity of the ceremonial script at such moments creates a diffusion of the individual character, actor or spectator into the communally shared event. Actors or audiences engage via their own anticipated or enacted experiences of these rituals. Such superficial moments in Shakespearian drama are thus specially 'charged' for the temporary community created by the performance. We cannot read the effects for spectator or actor, each of whom has 'that within which passeth show' (*Hamlet*, 1.2.85). However, by paying close attention to the superficial, we can profitably speculate on how the orchestration of immediate circumstances might be the occasion for bringing forth deep effects.

In *Much Ado About Nothing*, the bridal meeting of Hero and Claudio, the mourning ritual and the second betrothal are doubly heightened moments of ceremony where spaces between bodies, material costumes and props are highly charged. However, in each case these ceremonial surfaces are subject to intolerable tensions: all are failures in terms of being disrupted or somehow lacking in authenticity (even if they were enacted beyond the stage). The wedding is a broken nuptial; the audience knows that Hero is not dead when they witness Claudio presenting the epitaph. The

play deliberately upsets any assumed continuum between the customary experience of a ceremony and what happens on stage. Spectators are thus presented with heightened moments of failure rather than fulfilment. The play frustrates the desire for connection in order to replace it with one of shame. This does not lessen the ceremonies' significance. Shusterman reminds us that 'fragmentation and vivid encounters with disagreeable resistance', such as the failed ceremonies encountered in *Much Ado*, can produce a powerfully life-invigorating experience through their exceptional 'power of defiance'.[10] The play's failed ceremonies promote a strategic dialogue between surface and depth, between immediate effects and memories and desires beyond the stage, between actors and spectators.

The wedding ceremony in Act 4 scene 1 brings to a crisis the tensions in representing female identity and exposes these as a source of shame for all. Hero's appearance as a bride is already compromised by Don John's plot and Borachio's narrative of Margaret impersonating Hero at her window by wearing her clothes (3.3.138–56). In Act 3 scene 4, Hero's bedchamber is, effectively, a tiring house for tragedy. The pieces of costume from which the boy actor will create the role of Hero-as-bride, the 'fine, quaint, graceful' (3.4.20–1) wedding gown, the rebato (wired collar or ruff) and the perfumed gloves are itemized. Their immediacy as a series of fragmented parts highlights the process of ceremonially constructing and packaging the bride as pure gift. Hero is prepared as a sacrifice to early modern anxieties about sexuality, anxieties which are phallocentric in origin and whose object is women, but which are shared by all, on- and off-stage.

Ewan Fernie has usefully noted that *Much Ado* dramatizes an 'ethical chasm' between 'different modes of masculine and feminine shame' and, indeed, Claudio and Hero exemplify two classic

---

[8] Shusterman, *Surface and Depth*, p. 237.
[9] For example, Peter Stallybrass and Ann Rosalind-Jones, *Renaissance Clothing and the Materials of Memory* (Cambridge, 2002).
[10] Shusterman, *Surface and Depth*, p. 231.

responses to shame first identified by Helen Lewis.[11] Claudio, although ignorant, is trapped in an aggressive loop in which the subject refuses to accept shame and masks it with anger that ultimately leads to more shame. Hero, although innocent, is trapped in a more passive loop where shame provokes more shame at feeling ashamed, leading to silence and withdrawal. Claudio's response to Hero's supposed infidelity dramatizes anger at social shame. Belief that his expressions of interest have been thwarted and that his fragile attempts to connect with the world (through alliance with Leonato as much as emotionally with Hero) have been mocked, produces a more violent attempt at self-assertion. He declares: 'in the congregation where I should wed, there will I shame her' (3.2.114–15). In lines which bitterly degrade Hero as 'a rich and precious gift' (4.1.28), Claudio inverts the traditional ceremony of gift-giving which should bind him to Leonato and Hero, from a sense that it has already been desecrated:

> There, Leonato, take her back again.
> Give not this rotten orange to your friend.
> She's but the sign and semblance of her honour.
> Behold how like a maid she blushes here!
> O, what authority and show of truth
> Can cunning sin cover itself withal!
> Comes not that blood as modest evidence
> To witness simple virtue? Would you not swear,
> All you that see her, that she were a maid,
> By these exterior shows? But she is none.
> She knows the heat of a luxurious bed.
> Her blush is guiltiness, not modesty. (4.1.31–42)

What Claudio projects onto Hero is his own horror, fear and shame at not being the ideal self: the chosen object of Hero's desire and Leonato's respect. In a culture of self-fashioning, this blow to a young man's attempt to mould an ideal worldly self-image is devastating. As Ewan Fernie observes, 'for Shakespeare, shame is a form of not being, of not being one's ideal self, or else an experience of hideous deformity, of being something horrifically other, *somebody else*' (p. 78). This has further ramifications once Claudio discovers his mistake.

Hero's blush is a mark of shame that has nothing to do with 'guiltiness' of actions, as the audience knows. At an immediate level, Hero, although innocent, can no longer be her ideal self since that self is so dependent on the opinions of others. Vives had advised that it was not enough for a woman to be chaste but to maintain her reputation for chastity. This was accompanied by a very clear prescription on acknowledging shame: 'she can not be chaste that is not ashamed: for that is as a cover and vaylle of hir face . . . No man shulde see it covered with that vayle but he shulde love it; nor none see it naked of that, but he shulde hate it.'[12] Under these rules, the acknowledgement of shame is particular to gender. Hero's blush is a mark of both modesty and guiltiness; it shows she is properly ashamed because she is a maid and doubly shamed because she has been publicly exposed as shameful. In the words of Elspeth Probyn, the blush is a 'metonym for the wider structures of social domination'. It 'stands in for everything that makes me ashamed, including the informative early experiences of class and gender'.[13] As a model maiden, imbued with a sense of shame in order to protect her chastity, Hero has no sense of self that is resilient enough to challenge the accusations. Her relation with her ideal self has broken down because it is so dependent on what others think. This, in itself, may produce further shame: the shame that she is nothing more than the construct of other people, of patriarchal values. She is trapped at the level of surface, trapped in a loop where shame provokes more shame at feeling ashamed and leads to silence and withdrawal. Once misrepresented, she collapses and then vanishes from the stage. She can only be rescued by external factors, by others.

The reactions of Leonato are an extreme example of the contagious nature of shame, something felt keenly by Don Pedro too. Leonato's ideal self

---

[11] Fernie, *Shame in Shakespeare*, p. 87; Helen Lewis, *Shame and Guilt in Neurosis* (New York, 1971).

[12] Juan Luis Vives, *A Very frutful and pleasant boke called the Instruction of a Christen Woman*, trans. Richard Hyrde (London, 1555), fo. 35r, sig. K1r.

[13] Probyn, *Blush*, p. 53.

as a careful father has been shattered by the illusion of Hero's infidelity and he responds with an aggressive assertion of self in lines that are peppered with personal and possessive pronouns (4.1.126–40). Leonato does not simply cast Hero into a pit of ink; he drives her into a vortex or whirlpool of shame. Having declared that 'death is the fairest cover for her shame' (4.1.116), he appears to chastise her for looking up rather than hanging her head (another gestural metonym for shame):

Leonato. Dost thou look up?
Friar. Yea, wherefore should she not?
Leonato. Wherefore? Why, doth not every earthly thing
Cry shame upon her? Could she here deny
The story that is printed in her blood?
Do not live, Hero, do not ope thine eyes.

(4.1.119–24)

The story that is printed in Hero's blood is not that of individual wrongdoing but the legacy of Eve and the burden of prejudice and male anxiety that accompanies it. Because Hero's blood openly acknowledges shame, the story printed there is also that of common mortality, and Leonato's extreme reaction may include an awareness of this and the accompanying shame about the less than ideal human body and human condition. In this sense, Hero's shame is what Probyn calls 'the tip of the iceberg, a visible part of everything that makes us open to shame'.[14]

By virtue of their presence in the theatre as a temporary community (or congregation), actors and spectators are interpellated as participants in the ceremony, witnesses to this doubly framed event. If, as I have suggested, the staged ceremony did retain some of its power to transcend the moment of performance, its emotional and cultural effects would have been considerable: invoking participants' own anticipated or enacted experiences of a highly significant ritual. Claudio's shaming of Hero in a deliberate desecration of the ceremony is all the more shocking because it is anticipated from the first moment of the scene. As the actors enter in the appropriate vestments, take their proper positions, begin to pronounce the 'plain form of marriage' (4.1.1–2) and enact the physical handing over of

the bride, spectators engage with each element in the knowledge of its imminent collapse.

Claudio asks on- and off-stage spectators, 'all you that see her' (4.1.39), to read the blushing face as deceptive, arguing that the corporeal 'exterior show' of maidenhood is just as deceptive as the ceremonially constructed role of bride as pure gift. What do the audience see? As in the earlier example of Antonio's aged hand, the body threatens to expose the deception practised on spectators. If the boy actor does not blush on demand, he may lower his head. In either case, the audience sees neither feminine modesty nor guilt. The blush is a figment of Claudio's fevered imagination and they are invited to collude in his reading of it. The shame of the blush which spectators are prompted to remark is, in fact, designed to include them in a shared guiltiness about their complicity with events on stage. It provokes, I would suggest, shared feelings of shame: shame about the desecration of ceremony, about the misrepresentation of women; shame about their shared, silent assent to a tragic process of shaming. Ewan Fernie argues that 'the audience at a tragedy confronts its own shameful humanity'.[15] I would argue that the audience at *Much Ado* likewise confronts its shame but is then invited, like the characters, to use that shame productively as the play moves beyond tragedy into comic resolution.

Fernie and Probyn propose two positive definitions of shame, both of which are dependent on the subject's acknowledgement of it. For Fernie, welcoming shame is a form of honesty that makes it a redemptive force in spiritual, especially Christian terms: 'we may imagine the shameful self as a gap or hole through which the shamed, enlightened spirit may crawl into God's presence.' In such a reading, Hero's blush is exemplary; she encapsulates what Fernie identifies as a pattern typical of Spenser and Shakespeare: 'a clear commitment to shame, which is exemplified by women but which men must learn to emulate'.[16] Probyn reads the almost

---

[14] Probyn, *Blush*, p. 55.
[15] Fernie, *Shame in Shakespeare*, p. 23.
[16] Fernie, *Shame in Shakespeare*, pp. 34–5, 65.

involuntary acknowledgement of shame in the blush as a radical re-evaluation of the self from a social perspective, arguing that 'through feeling shame, the body inaugurates an alternative way of being in the world'. To analyse this process, she develops Bourdieu's theories of the body and the *habitus* as the embodied history of practices that generates a subject's framework for positioning him- or herself in the world. Shame is, she argues, the body's self-reflexive action, a productive force that 'may reorder the composition of the habitus, which may in turn allow for quite different choices'.[17]

In *Much Ado About Nothing* Hero becomes a focus for others' reactions to shame: both on- and off-stage. Thomas J. Scheff points out that 'acknowledged shame... could be the glue that holds relationships and societies together and unacknowledged shame the force that tears them apart'.[18] Cementing personal and social relationships is a priority in the postwar climate of Messina, a project the play seeks to promote. However, the atmosphere of distrust leads to deflection rather than acknowledgement of shame. Claudio and Don Pedro share shame as a means of avoiding isolation but their accusations of Hero are a clear instance of substituting anger for acknowledgement.[19] To a greater or lesser extent, Benedick and Beatrice, Leonato and Antonio all mask their shame at what has happened to Hero with anger. In addition to their feelings of guilt for wrongdoing in terms of the effects on her, the scene dramatizes their anger as a refusal to recognize their own sense of having fallen short of how they know they should have behaved, in trusting and defending her; what they might have hoped they would do. Immediately after the debacle, spectators probably mask their own shame, choosing instead to share the vengeful, antisocial desire to 'Kill Claudio' (4.1.290).

Claudio's realization of his mistake threatens to perpetuate the antisocial potential of the play by trapping characters in a self-destructive pattern of anger and shame. Borachio vows that he would rather be killed than 'repeat over to my shame' his part in the deception, preferring violent self-mutilation over humble acknowledgement (5.1.232–3). Don Pedro's question 'Runs not this speech like iron through your blood?' and Claudio's reply 'I have drunk poison whiles he uttered it' (5.1.237–8) keenly register the possibility of being consumed by shame and further anger at the discovery that their original anger (a deflection of shame) was misdirected.

Claudio and Don Pedro become agents for the acknowledgement of shame by relinquishing their agency. Both start by admitting only a sin of 'mistaking' (5.1.267) in what appears to be another attempt to avoid or mitigate the tarnish of shame. However, Don Pedro subjects himself 'under any heavy weight' that Leonato will impose and Claudio surrenders himself to Leonato's mercy, welcoming a plan to 'dispose / For henceforth of poor Claudio' (5.1.269, 286–7). Even though Claudio may be relieved at Leonato's leniency, his words still display a humility that effectively releases him from the autonomous position and the reflexive deflection of shame onto anger.

The staged mourning at Leonato's monument is an apparently superficial mechanism to free Claudio from the shame/anger loop by publicly rehearsing his shame in a ceremony. Its significance spreads far beyond the superficial redemption of a single, rather unsympathetic character, however. The shared mourning ceremony is, for all its brevity, an important social device for transforming unacknowledged shame and anger found in Messina's on-stage society and in the temporary community of the audience. The speakers, Claudio and Don Pedro, are accompanied by a group of mourners '*with tapers, all in black*' whose anonymity offers additional points of access to the ceremony. By virtue of their presence in the theatre, off-stage spectators can 'witness' the mourning ceremony

---

[17] Probyn, *Blush*, p. 56.

[18] Thomas J. Scheff, 'Shame and the Social Bond: A Sociological Theory', *Sociological Theory*, 18:1 (2000), 84–99; p. 98.

[19] Helen Lynd first identified the importance of sharing shame in *On Shame and the Search for Identity* (New York, 1958), p. 249.

in the active, participatory sense alongside Claudio, and are thus offered the opportunity to acknowledge their own complicity in the aggressive, exclusive hegemony that appears to grant women no agency. All should be ashamed of a culture in which a woman can be misrepresented and destroyed on her wedding day. The 'solemn hymn' of woe explicitly rehearses the shame of 'those that slew thy virgin knight' with sighs and groans (5.3.14–17). Claudio hints at shame's productive function in the lines 'So the life that died with shame / Lives in death with glorious fame' (5.3.7–8). These words are deliberately vague. They refer most immediately to Hero's life but the references to 'shame', to mortality and the possibility of renewal after death point to a wider, shared acknowledgement, a common shame. Significantly, Don Pedro announces the dawning of a new 'gentle day' after the preying of wolves (5.3.25).

Characters and spectators are propelled towards reconciliation in a final ceremony of betrothal. However, its promises of renewal are deliberately selective. The fact that Claudio must accept the veiled bride given to him by Antonio and 'take her hand / Before this friar and swear to marry her' (5.4.56–7) offers a second chance to complete the wedding ceremony he had desecrated. The betrothal ritual explicitly serves to restore his earlier lack of faith. A benign reading of a youthful Claudio allows us to see that 'through feeling shame, the body inaugurates an alternative way of being in the world'.[20] For Hero, however, there appears to be little alternative way of being. Claudio greets her as 'Another Hero!' (5.4.62), but Don Pedro more accurately and more darkly points out she is 'the former Hero, Hero that is dead' (5.4.65). After her ordeal of shame, the only position available to Hero is her former one. To reveal herself, she must unveil. Here, the play's surface appearances of costume and gesture graphically advertise the tensions under which women continue to live, subjected to shame. In rejecting the image of herself as 'defiled' to assert her innocence as 'a maid' (5.4.63–4), Hero necessarily contravenes the maidenly exhibition of shame prescribed by Vives: 'she

can not be chaste that is not ashamed: for that is as a cover and vaylle of hir face.'[21] Hero's lack of blush, her shamelessness, is potentially shameful. The play thus offers no guarantee that Hero, or any other woman, will not be misread in the future. It uses ceremonies to demonstrate that, for early modern woman, shame is not a transient experience from which she 'may reorder the composition of the habitus, which may in turn allow for quite different choices'.[22] Instead, it is a life sentence to play the part of 'another Hero', another male construction of female identity on the s(h)ame model: 'the former Hero, Hero that is dead!' (5.4.65).

As noted above, shame, according to Tomkins, is positive because it is an expression of our interest: our engagement with the world and with others. Probyn explains that in shame 'the feeling and thinking and social body comes alive' and teaches us 'about our relations to others'.[23] If, as I have argued, the play's ceremonies retain power to engage the audience's interests by recalling or anticipating each person's engagements with rituals and with their own different habitus, then their social purpose is considerable. By invoking and managing the shame of those beyond the stage, the superficial ceremonies in *Much Ado About Nothing* have the power to teach deep social truths about relations to others. To induce shame about the ways woman is constructed from misinterpretations, prejudices, anxieties may not produce immediate, spectacular results. Claudio's repentance is too slight to give confidence that the 'holy rites' (5.4.68) within the chapel will be a marriage of true minds without impediment. Nevertheless, if the aspects of shame represented in the play's ceremonies reinvigorate the social body with new ways of feeling and thinking, then the possibilities for an other Hero, an alternative way of being in the world, can be glimpsed.

---

[20] Probyn, *Blush*, p. 56.
[21] Vives, *A Very frutful and pleasant boke*, fo. 35r, sig. K1r.
[22] Probyn, *Blush*, p. 56.
[23] Probyn, *Blush*, pp. 34–5.

'REMEMBER ME': SHYLOCK ON THE POSTWAR GERMAN STAGE

SABINE SCHÜLTING

The dead are not dead in history. One function of theatre is the invocation of the dead; the dialogue with the dead must not stop until they deliver the future which has been buried with them.[1]

Shylock as Muslim, as the victim of young neo-Nazis, as global player on the international financial market – these are just some impressions from recent productions of *The Merchant of Venice* on the German stage. At first glance, these examples may not be very surprising. Modernized interpretations of Shakespeare's plays, including references to topical cultural or political debates, are the rule rather than the exception in German theatres. However, *The Merchant of Venice* is not just any Shakespearian play but occupies a special place in the German cultural imagination. The conflict between Venetian society and the Jew, Shylock's cruel revenge and his final punishment evoke uncanny associations with German history. So there appears to be a general consensus that German directors should avoid any suspicion of anti-Semitism. More importantly, as one reviewer of a 2008 production remarked, they should by no means show an 'evil' Shylock.[2] And time and again, directors and critics have discussed the question as to whether a German audience is prepared to put up with a play that might incite or reinforce anti-Semitic prejudices.

My article will probe into this conflictual stage history of *The Merchant of Venice* in postwar Germany but, rather than giving a more or less comprehensive overview of recent answers to the challenges posed by the play, I will focus on the relationship between theatre and memory in a number of major German *Merchant*s since 1945, which will include some contemporary productions. Following the suggestion of (East) German director and dramatist Heiner Müller, quoted in the epigraph above, I will argue that German postwar productions and adaptations of *The Merchant of Venice* can be understood as mnemonic practices in which – consciously or unconsciously – German culture faces its problematic history and redefines itself.[3] Indeed, many post-war German *Merchant*s have initiated cultural debates on the legacy of German fascism and fulfilled a crucial function within the discourse of remembrance. At the same time, every German production of the play has entered dangerous territory because it has inevitably commented on the heated debates about the Shoah, the history of anti-Semitism, as well as Jewish life in contemporary Germany. In this context, Shylock can be seen as a figure which has functioned as both the occasion and the medium of cultural remembrance. Frequently, however, Shylock's dialogue with the past has not been a detached analysis

---

[1] Heiner Müller, *Gesammelte Irrtümer 2*, ed. Gregor Edelmann and Renate Ziemer (Frankfurt / Main, 1990), p. 64; my translation.

[2] Anon., 'Der gedemütigte Rächer: Shakespeares *Kaufmann von Venedig* am LTT als Drama eines muslimischen Außenseiters', *Reutlinger General-Anzeiger*, 21 April 2008, www.landestheater-tuebingen.de/main.php/rubrik/spielplan/urubrik/stuecke/stueck_id/224/srubrik/presse/presse_id/206, accessed 2 August 2009.

[3] See Ruth Freifrau von Ledebur, *Der Mythos vom deutschen Shakespeare: Die deutsche Shakespeare Gesellschaft zwischen Politik und Wissenschaft 1918–1945* (Cologne, 2002), p. 262.

of historical events but rather a disconcerting 'invocation of the dead', which has strongly affected the living. In this context, Shakespeare's Jewish money lender has figured as an uncanny revenant which confronts the present with an unresolved past without offering redemption from history.

HAMLET AND SHYLOCK

Shakespeare's Shylock is, of course, not a ghost but a human being with 'hands, organs, dimensions, senses, affections, passions' (3.1.55–6), who laughs if he is tickled, bleeds if he is pricked and dies if he is poisoned. If one looks for ghosts in Shakespeare, *Macbeth* or *Hamlet* are the more obvious plays to study. However, German Shylocks after 1945, like the ghosts in these two tragedies, also confront the living with unexpiated crimes.

In the context of Shakespeare on the post-war German stage, a juxtaposition of Hamlet and Shylock can be of particular interest since the two characters represent two different ways of responding to German history in general and the Shoah in particular. Hamlet has traditionally been *the* Shakespearian hero who since 1800 has fulfilled a crucial function in Germany's self-speculation. In his *Hamlet* essay of 1796, August Wilhelm Schlegel reclaimed Shakespeare for Germany: 'he [i.e. Shakespeare] belongs to no other people, apart from the English, as particularly as to the Germans. He is no stranger to us; we do not have to move a single step out of our character in order to call him all ours.'[4] Schlegel is representative of the German reception of Shakespeare in which the Bard was appropriated as the 'third German classic' – next to Goethe and Schiller – who was, more than others, able to express the German 'spirit', as Friedrich Gundolf (1911) put it. From 1800 onwards, Hamlet functioned as a screen onto which German concepts of national identity were projected. When Hermann Ferdinand Freiligrath wrote in 1844 that 'Germany is Hamlet', he was referring to the unresolvable conflict between reflection and action and between philosophy and revolution which had, according to him, prevented the foundation of a German nation state.

After the Second World War, this explicitly German interpretation of *Hamlet* remained dominant, albeit in a slightly modified form. In *On Truth* (1947), German philosopher Karl Jaspers saw Hamlet as a man on an uncompromising quest for truth, a tragic hero who sought to make sure 'that the age . . . becomes aware of what the King has done'.[5] In other words, German *Hamlet*s of the immediate postwar years drew attention to collective guilt and responsibility. As German writer Martin Walser suggested in 1964, it was in this context that the Danish prince became an 'intimate comrade of that generation which . . . grew up in Germany between 1933 and 1945' and which had to redefine its relation to the father generation.[6] For Walser, Hamlet was a 'figure symbolising the passive thinker and the intellectual who, occasionally, becomes almost pathological in his demand for truth and accountability'.[7] German reunification offered a new political and cultural scenario for rereading *Hamlet* as a 'German' play. In 1989, Heiner Müller produced *Hamlet/Maschine* for the Deutsches Theater in Berlin. The play included Müller's 1977 adaptation of the tragedy in which he had commented on the situation of the intellectual in a socialist society. In 1989, the *Hamlet/Maschine* provided a new foil for the analysis of the political upheaval in Germany after the fall of the Berlin Wall. The intellectual, who finds himself in an in-between state, does not know what to do: the old order has been irretrievably lost, but he cannot savour the new one either.

In 2008 Shakespeare's tragedy once more seemed to offer an allegorical reading of a time out of joint. *Hamlet* became *the* play of the season 2008/9, with

---

[4] August Wilhelm von Schlegel, *Etwas über William Shakespeare bei Gelegenheit Wilhelm Meisters*, in August Wilhelm Schlegel, *Sämtliche Werke*, ed. Eduard Böcking, vol. 7 (Hildesheim, 1971), p. 38; my translation.

[5] Quoted in Franz Loquai, *Hamlet und Deutschland: Zur literarischen Shakespeare-Rezeption im 20. Jahrhundert* (Stuttgart, 1993), p. 12; my translation.

[6] Martin Walser, 'Hamlet als Autor', in Joachim Kaiser, ed., *Hamlet, heute: Essays und Analysen* (Frankfurt / Main, 1965), p. 154; my translation.

[7] Loquai, *Hamlet und Deutschland*, p. 14; my translation.

productions at several major and local German theatres and two academic conferences on the play.[8] The production at the Schaubühne Berlin transferred Hamlet's problem to the more general cultural dilemma of the intellectual in a postmodern society ruled by a cynical and corrupt political system. The Schauspielhaus Stuttgart even held the whole season under the motto 'Generation Hamlet'. The explanation given in the theatre programme read as follows:

It is up to the young Europeans to deal with the ghosts of history that protrude into the future, and to find answers to old and new questions of our existence. 'Generation Hamlet' is an expression that the Munich sociologist Ulrich Beck used to describe this situation: 'The time is out of joint: O cursed spite that ever I was born to set it right.' This could be the motto of the Generation Hamlet which sees itself obliged to redefine and reshape the future of Europe.[9]

In an article published on 27 October 2008 in the influential weekly magazine Der Spiegel, Matthias Matussek took up this motto in order to capture the dilemma of a reunified Germany during a global financial crisis. Shakespeare's Hamlet was referred to as a 'signet text' of the current epoch in which it turns out that 'art can be more important than the leading article in a newspaper because it is more clairvoyant'. For Matussek, 'Generation Hamlet' referred to the 'children of the German reunification', who 'now have to realize that there is something rotten in the system to which they had sworn loyalty'. They have to face the question whether 'to be or not to be'.[10]

My article suggests a shift of perspective from German Hamlets to German Shylocks. Shylock anamorphically distorts the national self-reflection outlined above. He reminds us that two centuries 'after the heyday of German Idealism, and separated from it through the unbridgeable caesura of Auschwitz',[11] the relation between Germany and Shakespeare has to be addressed in a different way. In contrast to Hamlet, the Jewish moneylender is a character who defies identification and who, in the words of the late George Tabori, is 'an embarrassment'.[12] Being both an anti-Semitic

stereotype and the victim of anti-Semitism, he triggers complex affective reactions: aversion and pity, schadenfreude and sympathy. He offers no easy solutions to social and political conflicts, and he does not set the time right. On the contrary, Shylock not only thwarts the attempt to continue the self-congratulatory tradition of the German reception of Shakespeare, but also impedes a form of remembrance represented by Hamlet's self-righteous distancing from the crimes of fathers and uncles. In confronting Shylock, one inevitably becomes guilty, since in German postwar productions of The Merchant of Venice the 'German spirit' turns out to be inextricably intertwined with German anti-Semitism and the Shoah.

SHYLOCK AND CULTURAL REMEMBRANCE

One could argue that the memory of the Shoah is proleptically inscribed in Shakespeare's The Merchant of Venice, in which the Jewish moneylender,

8 The productions of Hamlet included: Hamlet, Thalia Hamburg, dir. Michael Thalheimer; Hamlet, Schaubühne Berlin, dir. Thomas Ostermeier; Hamlet, Gorki Theater Berlin, dir. Tilmann Köhler; Hamlet, Staatstheater Mainz, dir. Barbara-David Brüesch; Die Schock Strategie. Hamlet, Jorinde Dröse's production of Naomi Klein's Hamlet adaptation, Schauspiel Leipzig; and a Hamlet musical with TV-entertainer Harald Schmidt at the Staatstheater Stuttgart, directed by Christian Brey. The conferences were a symposium in Hamburg, organized by the University of Hamburg and the Thalia Theatre in May on the occasion of Michael Thalheimer's production of the play, and the 'autumn conference' of the German Shakespeare Society on Hamlet at the University of Mainz in November.
9 Schauspielhaus Stuttgart, 'Generation Hamlet'; my translation. www.staatstheater.stuttgart.de/schauspiel/konzept/hamlet.php., accessed 2 August 2009.
10 Matthias Matussek, 'Generation Hamlet', Der Spiegel, 44 (27 Oct 2008), pp. 166–7; my translation.
11 Micha Brumlik, Deutscher Geist und Judenhaß: Das Verhältnis des philosophischen Idealismus zum Judentum (Munich, 2000), p. 13; my translation.
12 George Tabori, Ich wollte meine Töchter läge tot zu meinen Füßen und hätte die Juwelen in den Ohren: Improvisationen über Shakespeares Shylock. Dokumentation einer Theaterarbeit, ed. Andrea Welker and Tina Berger (Munich, 1979), p. 11; my translation.

a stereotype of European anti-Semitism, loses his wealth, is forced to give up his religion and to renounce familial ties. From the late 1950s or early 1960s onwards, in West Germany, and in the reunified Germany after 1990, Shakespeare's *The Merchant of Venice* – next to Lessing's *Nathan the Wise* – took on a crucial function for German confrontations with its past, as Anat Feinberg, professor of Hebrew and Jewish Literature at the University for Jewish Studies at Heidelberg, has shown.[13] Focusing on Shylock and Nathan as two opposing stereotypes of Jewishness on postwar German stages, Feinberg differentiates between three stages in postwar German theatre, all of which are characterized by their respective forms of representing Jewish protagonists. The first stage, located in the 1950s, was shaped by a predominance of 'noble Jews' (with Ernst Deutsch's Nathan as a model). The second phase was strongly influenced by Jewish directors who deliberately deconstructed postwar German taboos in order to initiate a more thorough and honest investigation of the past. The third phase began with the broadcasting of the TV series *Holocaust* in 1979. According to Feinberg, this last phase has been characterized by contradictory tendencies: a 'vigorous culture of memory' on the one hand and 'the massive warding off of memory'[14] on the other. A cursory glance at more recent (post-9/11) productions suggests a new phase in which the cultural memory of the Holocaust is frequently discarded in favour of an explicitly presentist perspective and a noticeable shift away from the issue of German anti-Semitism and Shylock's Jewishness. These productions have opened the play to contemporary socio-political debates (such as globalization, migration, terrorism and the problems of multi-ethnic societies), with an increasing interest in the conflicts resulting from the differences between Christians and Muslims within a society shaped by immigration. German postwar productions of *The Merchant* have thus come a long way from the 1960s when the manager of the theatre at Mannheim decided to take *The Merchant of Venice* off the programme because in the face of anti-Semitic demonstrations he was anxious about the consequences of the play. In 1985, the

critic Rolf Hochhuth still demanded, 'Don't play it any more', and director Heinz Hilpert said that he would only put the play on stage when '40 Jews sit in the stalls and laugh about it'.[15]

If, according to German literary theorist Renate Lachmann, cultural remembrance can be described as opening up an intertextual space, every production of *The Merchant of Venice* inscribes itself into the cultural archive, charting it anew, and every staging reconstructs this mnemonic space 'in which previous texts are absorbed through different layers of transformation'.[16] Relevant (inter)texts include the German reception of Shakespeare and the stage history of his plays, debates on Hitler's Germany, the Second World War and the Shoah, German postwar anti-Semitism and the anti-Zionism of the GDR, public discourses of remembrance, as well as current political debates, e.g. on migration and the cultural integration of migrants.[17] Shylock is

---

[13] Cf. Anat Feinberg, 'The Janus-Faced Jew: Nathan and Shylock on the Post-War German Stage', in Leslie Morris and Jack Zipes, ed., *Unlikely History: The Changing German-Jewish Symbiosis 1945–2000* (New York, 2002), p. 234. Between 1948 and the present day, there have been more than 170 professional productions of *The Merchant of Venice* on German stages, with only seven of them being produced in the former GDR.

[14] Aleida Assmann, quoted in Feinberg, 'The Janus-Faced Jew', p. 241.

[15] Cited in Wolfgang Weiß, '"Spielt das Stück nicht mehr!" Über die Schwierigkeiten im Umgang mit einer Komödie', in William Shakespeare, *Der Kaufmann von Venedig*, bilingual edition (Munich, 1995), p. 276; my translation.

[16] Renate Lachmann, *Gedächtnis und Kultur* (Frankfurt/ Main, 1990), p. 36; my translation.

[17] In my research project on the cultural history of *The Merchant of Venice* in Germany, I read the productions and rewritings of *The Merchant of Venice* as moments where different discourses culminate and intersect. I concentrate on those historical moments that mark crucial shifts in Germany's culture of remembrance and examine whether they, in turn, had any repercussions on the contemporary reception of *The Merchant*. These controversies include the public debates on the Frankfurt Auschwitz Trials (1963–5/6); the heated arguments over Rolf Hochhuth's *Der Stellvertreter* (*The Representative*, 1963), a play criticizing Pope Pius XII's role in World War II and Rainer Werner Fassbinder's allegedly anti-Semitic play *Der Müll, die Stadt und der Tod* (*Garbage, the City and Death*, 1975/6); the

the figure in whom all these discourses intersect and through which cultural remembrance is performatively re-enacted in each production.

In what follows, I will discuss these general considerations with regard to three examples that are, to some extent, representative of the major phases of the play's stage history since the 1960s. They show, moreover, a variety of different approaches to the relation between Shakespeare and cultural remembrance.

'MAY THE JEW BE EVIL AGAIN?': FRITZ KORTNER'S SHYLOCK

In 1969, German TV broadcast a production of *The Merchant of Venice* directed by Otto Schenk, which caused controversial debates as to whether 'the Jew may be evil again'.[18] This was the title of a TV panel discussion which was screened in 1969 by the WDR (Westdeutscher Rundfunk, i.e. West German Broadcasting) on the occasion of Schenk's TV *Merchant*. The presence of the Jewish actor Fritz Kortner in the role of Shylock turned Shakespeare's 'Venice' into a clear allegory of fascist Germany. Before the war, Kortner had played Shylock in the Vienna production of 1916, in Max Reinhardt's production of 1924 in Vienna (see Illustration 19), and in Jürgen Fehling's production, which premiered on 27 November 1927 at the Staatliches Schauspielhaus in Berlin.[19] In 1927, Kortner radically opposed Fehling's original plans to portray Shylock as gentle and humane. In his autobiography Kortner comments that in contrast to Fehling's noble intentions he wanted to play a Shylock whose increasing inhumanity would be an obvious reaction to the inhumane attacks from which he was suffering. Kortner managed to convince Fehling and, accordingly, this *Merchant*, Kortner writes, turned out to be 'terribly contemporary. Its reference to the racist fascism, which was now striving for power, electrified both friend and enemy.'[20] Kortner left Germany in 1938 and emigrated to the United States, but returned to Europe in 1949.

When he played Shylock in Otto Schenk's TV version in 1968, he was 76 years old and had already

19. Fritz Kortner (Shylock) in *Der Kaufmann von Venedig*, directed by Max Reinhardt. Theater in der Josefstadt, Vienna (1924).

retired from the stage. His interpretation of the role updated the prewar Berlin production: once more,

student revolts of the 1960s; the so-called *Historikerstreit* (Historians' Quarrel in 1986/7) about the interpretation of Nazi Germany and the legacy of the past; as well as German reunification (1990). For more information, see the project website at www.geisteswissenschaften.fu-berlin.de/en/v/shylock/index.html.

18 'Darf der Jude wieder böse sein?'

19 On Kortner's career as an actor in the Weimar Republic, see Matthias Brand, *Fritz Kortner in der Weimarer Republik: Annäherungsversuche an die Entwicklung eines jüdischen Schauspielers in Deutschland* (Rheinfelden, 1981); and Richard D. Critchfield, *From Shakespeare to Frisch: The Provocative Fritz Kortner* (Heidelberg, 2008).

20 Fritz Kortner, *Aller Tage Abend* (Munich, 1979), p. 297; my translation.

Shylock appeared as a 'traditional' Jew with *tallith* and *kippa*, a thin white beard and tangled hair. He is a deeply religious man whose original benevolence eventually gives way to hatred because he suffers a constant series of anti-Semitic defamations and attacks. In the overall production, which tells the story of Bassanio and Portia as a rather shallow comedy, frequently verging on the folkloric, he is an obvious outsider. Kortner's acting underscores this tension between the love plot and the plot revolving around the pound of flesh. The film shows Shylock as a killjoy, disturbing the sentimental *Heimatfilm*[21] atmosphere and confronting the audience with a past it would rather forget. When in the last scene Shylock not only loses his fortune but is also forced to consent to his own conversion, he raises his eyes towards heaven in mute despair, then draws his *tallith* over his face and asks permission to leave. This is the gesture of prayer, but the scene gets a further meaning when the camera follows his exit through a vacant hallway, its bareness suggesting both the 'disappearance' of the Jews in the genocide of the Shoah, and the absence of both victims and survivors in postwar Germany. To the extent of even visually remembering his prewar Shylocks through costume and acting, Kortner turned the film into a veritable act of cultural memory, establishing a direct link between the increasing anti-Semitism in Germany in the 1920s, the emigration of the Jews in the 1930s, Nazi pogroms and the genocide as well as the problematic relationship between Germany and its small Jewish population after the war.

For many contemporary critics, Kortner's radical breach with the tradition of sentimentalized Shylocks was a provocation. It questioned the postwar consensus based on the collective myth of a successful 'denazification' expressed in the consoling philo-Semitic figure of Lessing's noble Nathan. The production thus tied in with the students' revolts of the late 1960s and their critique of a continuity of Nazi ideology in postwar Germany. It politicized German approaches to *The Merchant of Venice* by reading the play as a study about stereotyping, racist hatred, and the violent reactions of the victims of anti-Semitism. However, many crit-

ics feared that Schenk's interpretation would not only confirm the anti-Semitic prejudices of the older generation but would also encourage the emerging anti-Zionism of leftist groups, which had been reinforced by the Six Day War of 1967.[22] These contentious debates foregrounded the relationship between art and politics in addition to intellectuals' concern about the (uncontrollable) effects of a relatively new mass medium that was associated with the culture industry. They doubted whether the general TV audience was able to understand this sharp analysis of the processes of cultural othering. It was assumed that many spectators would see their anti-Semitic prejudices reconfirmed and *embodied* (rather than *played*) by a Jew.

I do not mean to imply that productions of *The Merchant of Venice* are merely secondary reflections of political controversies. As the debates revolving around the televised *Merchant* show, political, cultural and aesthetic spheres cannot be separated from each other. Each actualization of Shylock on a German stage is the product of complex negotiations, informed by the tensions between aesthetic and medial possibilities and ideological taboos in an intricate web of discourses, practices, art forms and cultural institutions. In contrast to previous studies,[23] I also do not want to propose to celebrate Shakespeare as an opponent of Hitler and a bulwark against violence, terror and racism. Shakespearian drama is not an enclosed cultural space where the 'trust in the values of our culture'[24] can be studied in condensed form. The metamorphoses of Shylock must be understood as an integral part of the cultural debates on German history, hence

---

[21] The *Heimatfilm* is a film genre that was particularly popular in the 1950s. Through its suggestion of an idealized rural world (usually set in the Alps) and a simple dualistic morality it offered escapism from the harsh reality of the postwar situation.
[22] These views were exchanged in the panel discussion mentioned above in which – among others – novelist Günter Grass and director Peter Stein participated.
[23] See, for example, Dietrich Schwanitz, *Das Shylock-Syndrom: Oder die Dramaturgie der Barbarei* (Frankfurt / Main, 1998).
[24] Schwanitz, *Das Shylock-Syndrom*, p. 29; my translation.

as acts of cultural signification which contribute to the self-reflection of a society through cultural remembrance.

ANACHRONOUS IMAGES OF HISTORY: GEORGE TABORI'S *IMPROVISATIONEN ÜBER SHAKESPEARES SHYLOCK*

My second example is George Tabori's 1978 Munich adaptation of *The Merchant of Venice*, which arguably continued the project begun by Kortner but more radically broke with the philo-Semitic tradition of sentimentalized Shylocks.[25] The title of Tabori's play quoted Shylock's lines in 3.1.82–3: *Ich wollte, meine Tochter läge tot zu meinen Füßen und hätte die Juwelen in den Ohren: Improvisationen über Shakespeares Shylock.*[26] Blurring binary oppositions and denying all economic, psychological or sociological explanations of anti-Semitism,[27] it stressed the impossibility of giving merely one reading of Shakespeare's play and, by its resistance to conciliatory conclusions, shocked its audience. In the eighteen scenes, some based on Shakespeare's play,[28] others that explicitly referred to Nazi Germany and the Holocaust, such as 'Concentration Camp Narrative' ('*KZ-Ezählung*') or '*Kristallnacht*',[29] Shylock was played by all thirteen actors in different interpretations or, rather, improvisations. He appeared – among others – as a monstrous caricature of a Jew with a (false) crooked nose, a Jewish prisoner of a concentration camp and a survivor. A 'Ballad of Shylock' from the seventeenth century was juxtaposed with anti-Semitic caricatures in the tradition of the Nazi newspaper *Der Stürmer* and an imitation of Fritz Kortner's Shylock. Tabori's adaptation conjured up disconcerting images from the past, which clashed with audience expectations and violently confronted them with anti-Semitic images of the bloodthirsty and the money-grubbing Jew. The production vividly showed how anti-Semitism was literally inscribed into the bodies of the actors thus constructing them as 'Jewish'.

The production got under the skin, as Anat Feinberg put it. 'Spectators wept (and had to be consoled), expressing anguish and consternation to the troupe.'[30] In the conservative weekly *Die Welt*, one reviewer of the production concluded that only the fact that Tabori was a Jew himself and that his relatives had been killed at Auschwitz protected him from the accusation of anti-Semitism.[31] The critic obviously was not willing (or prepared) to acknowledge that Tabori's production underscored the performative and processual character of staging or adapting the play and, by re-enacting key scenes in several variations (as slapstick, burlesque, tragedy, musical, etc.), self-reflexively foregrounded the process (and the problems) of remembrance and the representation of history. As Judith Butler has shown in *Excitable Speech* (1997), although the repetition of hate speech may re-enact the injury, it can nevertheless reveal how hate speech works. A repetition can show that language is not violent in itself but that it gains its power through a history of repeated citation. The emphasis on the performative nature of any speech act implies that hate speech is also potentially open to new meanings. By offering diverging interpretations of one and the same scene of *The Merchant*, including quotations from anti-Semitic readings of the play and its protagonists, Tabori's adaptation highlighted the violence which is invoked by

---

25 I have discussed Kortner's and Tabori's interpretations and adaptations in more detail in a previous article; see Sabine Schülting, '"I am not bound to please thee with my answers": *The Merchant of Venice* on the Post-War German Stage', in Sonia Massai, ed., *World-Wide Shakespeares: Local Appropriations in Film and Performance* (New York, 2005), pp. 65–71.

26 'I would my daughter were dead at my foot and the jewels in her ear: improvisations on Shakespeare's Shylock.'

27 See Michael Krüger in Tabori, *Ich wollte meine Tochter*, p. 30.

28 'Antonio ist traurig' ('Antonio Is Sad'); 'Bassanio braucht Geld' ('Bassanio Needs Money'); 'Alter Gobbo trifft Jungen Gobbo / Lanzelot' ('Old Gobbo Meets Young Gobbo'), etc.

29 The so-called '*Kristallnacht*' was the night of 9 November 1938, when the Nazis organized a pogrom throughout Germany, burning synagogues, destroying and pillaging Jewish shops and houses, and transporting tens of thousands of Jews to the concentration camps of Dachau, Buchenwald and Sachsenhausen.

30 Feinberg, 'The Janus-Faced Jew', p. 240.

31 See 'Shylock im Souterrain', *Die Welt*, 23 November 1978.

Shakespeare's play as well as the instability of the text as one which can be read in new and potentially liberating ways.

With the multiplication of Shylocks and the merging of various historical moments including Renaissance England, fascist Germany and the postwar situation, time was 'out of joint'. Various mnemonic images were invoked and combined in an irritating collage which did not offer a coherent picture of history. Tabori's *Improvisationen* revolved around the questions of whether it is possible to play *The Merchant of Venice* after the Shoah at all, and whether and how a production can give testimony of the dead. In this project, history remained fragmentary and cultural remembrance was shown to be processual and incomplete. Tabori's Shylocks appeared as anachronic revenants of German and European anti-Semitism.

Ghosts are always 'radically out of time and out of place', Catherine Belsey has argued;[32] or, in the words of Margreta de Grazia, 'ghosts belong less to a temporality than to an "anachronicity" or an "untimeliness".'[33] However, even if one posits a parallel between Shylock and the ghost of Old Hamlet, since they both – *pace* Jacques Derrida[34] – haunt the present and confront it with an unresolved past in order to redirect the future, there is a crucial difference between the respective stage histories of *Hamlet* and *The Merchant of Venice*. The numerous modernizations of *Hamlet*, some of which have been mentioned above, show that for many directors the play is particularly appropriate to discuss the political and cultural tensions of modernity. According to de Grazia, *Hamlet* 'is *timeless* in value precisely because he was found *timely* by each successive age'.[35] In contrast to *Hamlet*, *The Merchant of Venice* is anachronous with the present in that it redirects our gaze back to the past – just like the ghost of Old Hamlet. In postwar Germany, Shylock seems to belong to another time that cannot be repressed or safely stored in archives and history books. Rather than establishing a linear or causal relationship between the past and the present, he disrupts the present and offers uncanny glimpses of a half-forgotten past. In this way, he is comparable to Walter Benjamin's 'Angelus Novus'

(the Angel of History), which for Benjamin figures as a model for the philosophy of history:

A Klee painting named 'Angelus Novus' shows an angel looking as though he is about to move away from something he is fixedly contemplating. His eyes are staring, his mouth is open, his wings are spread. This is how one pictures the angel of history. His face is turned toward the past. Where we perceive a chain of events, he sees one single catastrophe which keeps piling wreckage and hurls it in front of his feet. The angel would like to stay, awaken the dead, and make whole what has been smashed. But a storm is blowing in from Paradise; it has got caught in his wings with such a violence that the angel can no longer close them. The storm irresistibly propels him into the future to which his back is turned, while the pile of debris before him grows skyward. This storm is what we call progress.[36]

Rejecting nineteenth-century positivistic concepts of history, Benjamin stresses that the 'true picture of the past flits by. The past can be seized only as an image which flashes up at the instant when it can be recognized and is never seen again.'[37] The historian, as Benjamin conceives him, resembles this angel of history. He turns his face towards the past and its unrealized potentialities, its unredeemed catastrophes. In this process, the past becomes meaningful for the present not as a linear progress but in a shock-like recognition in which past and present momentarily coalesce.

Like Benjamin's Angelus Novus, Tabori's Shylocks also force us 'to look'; their faces are also 'turned toward the past'. They have literally come to embody the conflict between the present, the future and the demands of an unresolved past. In

---

[32] Catherine Belsey, 'Shakespeare's Ghost Story', paper given at the conference of the German Shakespeare Society in Mainz, 22 November 2008.

[33] Margreta de Grazia, '*Hamlet* before Its Time', *Modern Language Quarterly*, 62 (2001), 373.

[34] Jacques Derrida, *Spectres of Marx*, trans. Peggy Kamuf (London, 2006).

[35] De Grazia, '*Hamlet* before Its Time', p. 355.

[36] Walter Benjamin, 'Theses on the Philosophy of History', in *Illuminations*, trans. Harry Zohn (New York, 1969), pp. 257–8.

[37] Benjamin, 'Theses on the Philosophy of History', p. 255.

this way, they might generate a new understanding of history, thus leading to the recognition of new (political) options for the here and now.[38]

THE TIME IS STILL 'OUT OF JOINT': DIETER DORN'S *KAUFMANN VON VENEDIG*

In 2005, Micha Brumlik, Professor of Education and former director of the Fritz Bauer Institute (Frankfurt / Main) for the Study and Documentation of the History of the Holocaust, suggested that the sixtieth anniversary of the end of the Second World War could mark a caesura. He enquired: 'What lies in wait this side of the threshold? Is it a new time for Germany and the Germans in which they will be at peace with themselves and with their past?'[39] An overview of the productions of *The Merchant of Venice* this side of the threshold shows that the association with the Shoah, which has shaped the German reception of Shakespeare's 'comedy' for six decades, is slowly giving way to a wider range of interpretations. Recent productions frequently tone down the issue of anti-Semitism and concentrate on conflicts in a multi-ethnic society or on the tragedies caused by a globalized financial market.[40] They can be seen as symptoms of a more general trend after reunification, namely the increasing rejection of moralistic and didactic forms of remembrance by (not only) a younger generation as well as the controversial calls for a 'normalization' of Germany's relationship with its past.[41]

This was most obvious in the 2008 production at the Landestheater Tübingen, directed by Clemens Bechtel. It showed Shylock and his daughter as Muslims, thus merging an investigation of anti-Semitic violence with contemporary issues of immigration, cultural integration of Turkish migrants and the conflicts between Islam and Christianity in Western Europe. During the play, two actors quoted key terms of the German discourse of remembrance, such as 'virtual memory' (*virtuelle Erinnerung*), 'year of remembrance' (*Erinnerungsjahr*), or 'stone of remembrance'

(*Erinnerungsstein*), as well as comments by German author and journalist Ralph Giordano on the planned construction of a mosque in Cologne and on 'the parallel Muslim society' in Germany. Giordano's polemic remarks, in particular his provocative association of terrorism with Islam,[42] had caused heated controversies in the media. In this way, the discourse of cultural remembrance was

---

[38] Benjamin's concept of history also challenges more traditional approaches to the reception of Shakespeare in Germany. Rather than writing a teleological history of *The Merchant of Venice* on the German stage, the cultural critic should focus on individual productions as those moments when the past momentarily flashes up. It is a past which must be recollected in and for the present; as a means of taking cognizance of the present. This implies that select productions will have to be '[blasted] out of the homogeneous course of history' (Benjamin, 'Theses on the Philosophy of History', p. 263).

[39] 'Jenseits der Schwelle: Auschwitz im 21. Jahrhundert', *Newsletter* 27 of the Fritz Bauer Institute (2005), p. 12; my translation.

[40] As, for example, in the 2008 production of *The Merchant* by the bremer shakespeare company.

[41] The first phase of the more recent debate can be said to have started in 1986/7 with the so-called *Historikerstreit* (historians' debate), which was provoked by the demand of some historians to 'normalize' and 'historicize' the German attitude towards the Third Reich. In particular, they claimed that the Holocaust had not been unique but could be compared to other genocides, in particular to the Gulag under Stalin. This debate was revived in 1998, when Martin Walser was awarded the Peace Prize of the German Booksellers' Association. In his speech during the ceremony at the Paulskirche in Frankfurt, Walser criticized the 'instrumentalization' of the German past and the ritualization of remembrance by both the media and left intellectuals, which, for them, had become a form of self-congratulatory exculpation. After his speech, Ignaz Bubis, then President of the German Jewish Committee, accused Walser of 'spiritual arson'. The controversy was carried out in the media and focused on sensitive issues such as the German–Jewish relationship and the problem of German national pride. Since then, the debate has been continuing, reaching a new peak in 2002 with the publication of Walser's novel *Tod eines Kritikers*, which was also accused of anti-Semitism, and the verbal attacks on Michel Friedman, then vice-president of the German Jewish Committee, by the liberal politician Jürgen Möllemann and Jarmal Karsli, a former member of the Green party.

[42] Giordano (in)famously maintained that 'not every Muslim is a terrorist but today every terrorist is a Muslim'.

discredited as a mere collection of empty phrases. In addition, the debates on the Shoah on the one hand and on multi-ethnic societies on the other were collapsed into one single narrative around Shylock and his daughter, who appeared as a third-generation kid.

In the 2009 production of the bremer shakespeare company, Shylock also lost his distinctive Jewishness. In Shylock's famous 'Has not a Jew eyes' speech, the word 'Jew' was cut, so that Shylock answered the question as to why Antonio won't stop laughing at him and insulting him with the line 'I am I'. This alteration of the text was certainly an attempt at liberating Shylock from the confines of the past and attributing a more general significance to the figure. However, the word 'Jew' was so obviously missing from the play that the cut identified the production as a more than problematic response to or, rather, an evasion of the past. The Bremen production can be seen as the long-term repercussion of the controversy initiated by Martin Walser's acceptance speech for the Frankfurt Book Fair's prestigious Peace Prize in 1998, in which Walser stated that remembrance of the Shoah was being instrumentalized as a 'moral cudgel'.[43] In the same vein, in a 2003 review article of new German productions of *The Merchant*, German Shakespearian Wilhelm Hortmann expressed his yearning for a *Merchant* that would no longer be obliged to remember the Shoah. Interestingly, his plea for a new phase in the postwar stage history of the play, which he saw suggested in the 2001 Munich production directed by Dieter Dorn, led him back to early twentieth-century German theatre and Max Reinhardt's celebrated *Merchant*. Construing a prewar time of innocence when directors could allegedly still put the Shakespearian 'original' on stage, Hortmann's article is imbued with a nostalgic reminiscence of the 'happy times' when a Jewish director could produce *The Merchant* as 'a colourful fairy tale'.[44]

At second glance, Dieter Dorn's Munich production was not the 'trans-Holocaust' interpretation as Hortmann would have had it, i.e. a play that celebrated the young generation's potential to overcome the inveterate hatred between Antonio

and Shylock through love. The difference between the two generations represented in this production was both highlighted and collapsed. Initially, the gap between them was emphasized through their costumes. While Antonio and Shylock were dressed in black, the younger generation wore lighter colours (see Illustration 20). The trial scene, however, undid this distinction. By donning the black suit of the young doctor, Portia was drawn into the lethal conflict and could remain neither impartial nor innocent. When Shylock exclaimed 'You take my house when you do take the prop / That does sustain my house; you take my life / When you do take the means whereby I live' (4.1.372–4), she became fully aware of the effects of her judgement. Visibly concerned, she asked Antonio what mercy he could render Shylock without being able to rejoice in Antonio's final triumph and the destruction of Shylock. With a frozen face, she enquired whether he was 'contented' (4.1.390), but had to avert her eyes when he just stared at her, unbelieving. She could not help forming part of the group of Venetians – old and young – who thronged around Shylock, as if to leave him no space to breathe.

Portia had also become guilty, and the young generation was shown to be increasingly infected with the distrust and latent aggression of the old. Jessica's and Lorenzo's dialogue in 5.1. thus vacillated between the banter of young lovers and the suppressed hostility of a couple who did not really like each other. There was no happy celebration in Belmont where everybody was taken aback by the blatant bawdiness of Graziano's puns on 'Nerissa's ring' (5.1.307). Venice and Belmont turned out to be inextricably intertwined, a view that was reinforced by the stage design. A huge black cube in the middle of the stage opened up for the Belmont scenes and disclosed the painting of a Renaissance palace, Belmont. But even in the last scene the

---

[43] See footnote 41.

[44] Wilhelm Hortmann, '"Wo, bitte, geht's nach Belmont?" Über ein Dilemma von Inszenierungen des *Kaufmanns von Venedig* nach dem Holocaust', in *Shakespeare Jahrbuch*, 139 (2003), 217; my translation.

20. Rolf Boysen (Shylock) and Sibylle Canonica (Portia) in *Der Kaufmann von Venedig*, directed by Dieter Dorn. Residenztheater, Munich (2001).

massive, rectangular construction hung gloomily over the scene and turned the faded picture of Belmont into the utopian dream of a better world which could not withstand Venice's rough reality, as Hortmann correctly noticed. At the conclusion of the play, when the actors came forward to bow to the audience, the three couples in the middle were framed by the dark and sinister figures of Antonio and Shylock. Their ghostly presence on the scene was disconcerting and seemed to be mutely reminding the audience that the happiness of the young was inextricably intertwined with the hatred and guilt of the old generation, that the present was overshadowed by the violence of the past. In Dorn's *Merchant* there was no 'Generation Hamlet', who could, with a quiet conscience, accuse their fathers and uncles of past crimes, and set the times right.

'DANGEROUS AND REBEL PRINCE': A TELEVISION ADAPTATION OF *HAMLET* IN LATE FRANCOIST SPAIN

JESÚS TRONCH-PÉREZ

On 23 October 1970, Televisión Española broad-cast what had been publicized as one of its impor-tant televised theatre productions: *Hamlet*, directed by Claudio Guerin, and starring Emilio Gutiérrez Caba.[1] Spanish spectators were still living under General Franco's right-wing authoritarian regime, which since the end of the three-year civil war in 1939 had infused the country's cultural life with its fascist-inspired National Catholicism and its repression of dissidence. In such a historical context, a production of *Hamlet* – a play with an 'obvious applicability to political practice in dictatorships'[2] – is bound to raise questions about its relationship with the political tensions of the time: was it appropriated by the dominant ideol-ogy (as when in Soviet-type regimes Hamlet was presented as a 'fighter for social justice, almost a forerunner of socialism'[3])? did it remain apo-litical (also a sort of submission to the authori-ties' imperatives), or did it show the prince as a symbol of the intellectual's endurance or political resistance against a totalitarian state (as also com-mon in the Soviet bloc[4])? How political this 1970 televised *Hamlet* was has not yet been explored in full.[5] In this essay, I will seek to redress this situation by studying external and internal evi-dence for its political uses and effects. Comparing them with how political meanings are generated in other *Hamlet* productions, I will argue that, though not a heavily politicized version, Guerin's *Hamlet* did have a politically critical charge moulded in its artistic features and responding to its historical circumstances.

Research for this essay has been funded by the Research Project FFI2008–01969/FILO 'Shakespeare's presence in Spain in the framework of his reception in the rest of Europe', financed by the Ministerio de Ciencia e Innovación. Illustra-tions are published with the kind permission of Radio Tele-visión Española. My special gratitude to those mentioned in this essay, whom I have interviewed or privately communi-cated with.

1 Enrique del Corral, '*Hamlet*', *ABC*, 18 October 1970, p. 71; M. '*Hamlet*', *Tele-Radio*, 19–25 October 1970, pp. 12–13; Melgar, 'Guerin y su *Hamlet*', *Tele-Radio*, 26 October 1970, p. 9.
2 Wilhelm Hortmann, 'Shakespeare on the Political Stage', in S. Wells and S. Stanton, eds., *Cambridge Companion to Shake-speare on Stage* (Cambridge, 2002), pp. 212–29; p. 224.
3 A. Shurbanov and B. Sokolova, *Painting Shakespeare Red: An East-European Appropriation* (Newark, 2001), p. 152. See also Zdeněk Stříbrný, *Shakespeare and Eastern Europe* (Oxford, 2000); Hortmann, 'Shakespeare'; Irene Rima Makaryk and Joseph G. Price, eds., *Shakespeare in the Worlds of Communism and Socialism* (Toronto, 2006).
4 For instance, J. Burian, '*Hamlet* in Postwar Czech The-atre', in D. Kennedy, ed., *Foreign Shakespeare* (Cambridge, 1993), pp. 195–210; Maik Hamburger, '"Are You a Party in this Business?" Consolidation and Subversion in East Ger-many Productions', *Shakespeare Survey 48* (Cambridge, 1995), pp. 171–84.
5 Apart from contemporary reviews, this version has received very little critical attention, and only in the field of media studies: J. M. Baget Herms's two paragraphs in his *Historia de la televisión en España 1956–1975* (Barcelona, 1993), p. 220; and Rafael Utrera, *Claudio Guerín Hill: Obra audiovisual: Radio, prensa, televisión, cine* (Seville, 1991), partially reprinted

THE CONTEXT

For a number of historians, 1969 marked the beginning of the 'crisis and agony' of Francoism.[6] Even when Spanish society was enjoying a decade of economic boom that made it rank among the industrialized – and democratic – nations, it became more and more agitated with street and university protests, with strikes, with the newly emerged terrorism of the Basque separatist group ETA, and even with some opposition from the Catholic Church.[7] In addition, the internal strife between political 'families' and tendencies in the Francoist cabinet and administration (chiefly among the continuist technocrats and the *aperturistas* – those leaning to greater political openness from within) was accentuated by the issue of 'succession'.[8] The 1947 Law of Succession established Spain as a kingdom, with Franco as Chief of State, and gave him the prerogative to name a successor with the title of King or Regent among any Spaniard of royal blood over thirty years old.[9] Those meeting these requirements were Alfonso XIII's third son and legitimate heir to the crown, Don Juan de Borbón, who in 1943 refused Franco's demand of allegiance to the fascist-inspired Falange and continued to live in exile;[10] his son Don Juan Carlos, who had lived in Spain since 1948 and was educated under Francoist supervision; Don Alfonso de Borbón y Dampierre, eldest grandson of Alfonso XIII;[11] and the Carlist self-proclaimed 'prince' Carlos Hugo de Borbón y Parma, whom Franco discarded as successor in 1962.[12]

By convincing Franco to appoint Don Juan Carlos as his successor, the continuist vice-premier Luis Carrero Blanco and his technocrat ministers had advanced their positions. Although *aperturista* ministers (who rather envisaged a Regency) sought to prevent it, Don Juan Carlos's designation was approved in the Cortes on 22 July and on the following day he vowed loyalty to the regime's principles. This was a crowning step in the institutionalization of the Francoist state, but it did not prevent a growing anxiety over the political future of post-Franco Spain. In August, *aperturista* ministers sought to regain control by exposing the involvement of two technocrat ministers in the financial scandal of the textile corporation Matesa. In October, Franco resolved the crisis by refashioning a homogeneous cabinet in favour of his vice-premier's continuist programme and at the cost of deepening the internal fracture of the political elite. Dramatist Alberto Miralles described a general mood of 'obsessive neurosis' over the succession of power, which was reflected in the themes of a number of contemporary and later plays.[13] To halt the many complications besetting Franco's final years (and in response to the pressure of hard-liners excluded from the new government) the cabinet resorted to drastic repression on all fronts. The new Minister of Information, A. Sánchez Bella, enforced a repressive policy on the media in a clear reaction to the former *aperturista* minister who since 1962 had sought to present a liberal image of Francoist Spain.[14] Yet these measures did not crush

---

in Rafael Utrera, 'Teatro para televisión de Claudio Guerin Hill', in *Cuadernos de Eihceroa*, 2 (2003), pp. 15–60.

[6] Stanley G. Payne, 'Twilight of the Regime, 1969–1973', in *The Franco Regime: 1936–1975* (Madison, 1987), pp. 543–90; Paul Preston, *Franco, Caudillo de España*, trans. Teresa Campodrón and Diana Falcón (Barcelona, 2002), pp. 697–702; Enrique Moradiellos, *La España de Franco: Política y sociedad* (Madrid, 2003), pp. 173–200 and 160.

[7] Rafael Abellá, *La vida cotidiana en España durante el régimen de Franco* (Madrid, 1996), pp. 303–22.

[8] See Payne, *Franco Regime*, pp. 536–42 and 575–81; Moradiellos, *España*, pp. 153–60; L. López Rodó, *La larga marcha hacia la monarquía* (Madrid, 1978), pp. 456–66; J. C. Laviana, ed., *1969: El Franquismo año a año* (Madrid, 2006), pp. 7–18, and *1970: El Franquismo año a año* (Madrid, 2006), pp. 203–7.

[9] *Boletín Oficial del Estado*, no. 208, 27 July 1947, p. 4238.

[10] Pedro Sainz Rodríguez, *Un reinado en la sombra* (Barcelona, 1981), pp. 32–4.

[11] Though Don Alfonso was the eldest grandson of the last Spanish king through the latter's second son, he did not have dynastic rights because his father, a deaf-mute, renounced them for himself and his descendants in 1933, and because his mother was not born of royal descent. He was also a legitimist pretender to the throne of France. See Joaquín Bardavío, *La rama trágica de los borbones* (Barcelona, 1989).

[12] Moradiellos, *España*, p. 154.

[13] *Nuevo teatro español* (Madrid, 1977), p. 50.

[14] Román Gubern, *La censura: función política y ordenamiento jurídico bajo el franquismo (1936–1975)* (Barcelona, 1981), pp. 248–52.

hopes of political change in the near future, for which a more or less clandestine and varied dissidence (ranging from supporters of Don Juan, both within and outside the regime, to Communists) was struggling under the regime's still firm grip.

By January 1970, Televisión Española (TVE), the state-owned corporation created in 1956 that remained the only television broadcaster in Spain until the 1980s, was preparing a production of *Hamlet* directed by Claudio Guerin.[15] Since TVE was opportunistically used by the Francoist authorities for propaganda purposes, cultural control, and filtering of information,[16] one would initially suspect some kind of regime-supporting appropriation of this *Hamlet* and rule out any political intention contrary to the regime. However, if one considers the choice of televised plays, producers and directors had opportunities to adapt titles with a hint of social or political issues unwelcome to Francoism.[17] Censorship was certainly exercised (not in the systematic and regulated way cinema and theatre were) but censors were also erratic (as they were in theatre and cinema).[18]

One clear political effect of this *Hamlet* produced at a time of 'obsessive neurosis' with the succession of power was the initial objections it received in TVE itself. During shooting at the Bronston studios in February 1970,[19] 'some mad censors' feared that the play's plot and its explicit reference to Hamlet's condition as prince would lead to interpretations related to the issue of succession in Spain.[20] This concern is confirmed and expanded by some of the witnesses I have interviewed:[21] an unspecified authority objected to the title of the play and wanted Hamlet to appear as a 'duke' and not a prince. Preposterous as it may sound, Guerin had to resort to a higher authority in order to prevent such an outrage. This objection is in consonance with what Gubern describes as the 'monarchic taboo' in TVE, to which its director general Adolfo Suárez was very sensitive.[22] As Gubern explains, the new Minister of Information, A. Sánchez Bella, had a decisive hand in the cancellation in 1970 of two films by Erich von Stroheim that showed the decadence of European monarchies before the First World War, and two

Lubitsch comedies that satirized old mid-European monarchies.[23] Considering that Sánchez Bella had been appointed by the monarchist vice-premier Luis Carrero Blanco, the artificer of the monarchic succession in the person of prince Don Juan Carlos,[24] this 'taboo' can be understood as one of the measures taken to protect the image of a future monarchy expected to perpetuate the regime.[25] Similar susceptibilities on the part of the authorities are found in Spanish theatre censorship in

---

[15] Melgar, '*Hamlet* en versión de Claudio Guerin', *Tele-Radio* 19-25 January 1970.

[16] J. R. Pérez Ornia, 'Peculiaridades de una televisión gubernamental. I: El modelo', in J. Timoteo Alvárez *et al.*, eds., *Historia de los medios de comunicación en España* (Barcelona, 1989), p. 308.

[17] As privately pointed out by Rafael Utrera and by Carlos Gortari (director of drama programmes in the second channel at that time, and a close friend of Guerin). An immediate example is Guerin's version of Beckett's *Krapp's Last Tape*, aired on 2 February 1969 (Utrera, 'Teatro', p. 37), which countered the official National Catholicism.

[18] For television, Carlos Gortari and Juan Mediavilla (Guerin's assistant director); and for cinema and theatre, scores of examples are given by Gubern's *Un cine*, and Berta Muñoz's *El teatro crítico español durante el franquismo, visto por sus censores* (Madrid, 2005).

[19] Utrera, 'Teatro', p. 49.

[20] Baget Herms, *Historia*, p. 220.

[21] Juan Mediavilla, Emilio Gutiérrez Caba and Carlos Gortari.

[22] Gubern, *La censura*, p. 252. Adolfo Suárez was a monarchist substituting for the former director general, who had allowed TVE to report the Matesa financial scandal, and therefore to attack that vice-premier's side of the cabinet (Baget Herms, *Historia*, p. 203). Juan Mediavilla believes that Guerin resorted to Adolfo Suárez, who used to protect the work of the young 'progressive' creators at TVE.

[23] *La censura*, p. 252. In 1963, when Luis G. Berlanga's black comedy film *El verdugo* (*The Executioner*) was screened at the Venice Film Festival among protests against the regime's execution of two anarchists in August, Sánchez Bella judged it the 'worst libel against Spain' and was irritated by the fact that 'the Communists' had 'scored a tremendous goal against' the regime while the twenty-five members of the Censorship Committee had not noticed such a political attack (Gubern, *Un cine*, pp. 131–8).

[24] Moradiellos, *España*, pp. 153–7.

[25] King Juan Carlos himself revealed that Adolfo Suárez worked hard to cultivate his image when he was director general of TVE – see José Luis Vilallonga, *El rey: conversaciones con Don Juan Carlos I de España* (Barcelona, 1993), p. 99.

relation to allusions to monarchy at that time.[26] All this exemplifies how a critical contemporary situation can charge a *Hamlet* production with political meaning, as was the case of several *Hamlet*s in Poland after the Second World War: in 1956, after the 20th Congress of the Soviet Communist Party where Khrushchev denounced Stalinism, Roman Zawistowski's *Hamlet* became, as Jan Kott put it, 'a political drama par excellence';[27] in 1982, after the imposition of martial law in the previous year, lines such as 'For in the fatness of these pursy times / Virtue itself of vice must pardon beg' (3.4.144–5) created a strong response in the audience of Andrzej Wajda's *Hamlet*.[28]

If Guerin's *Hamlet* resonated with the intrigues of the political elite, its choice also responded to the dynamics of programming in TVE, a staple of which was self-produced drama. In one of the theatre series, 'Gran Teatro', a televised *Hamlet* was broadcast in 1964.[29] The second channel, created for a more cultured audience in 1965, offered 'Teatro de siempre', featuring both classics and modern plays, both national and foreign.[30] Another theatre series was 'Estudio 1', created in 1965 for the first channel with the purpose of popularizing theatre by producing both original TV scripts and titles adapted by renowned writers.[31] Its success and popularity made it the televised theatre show *par excellence* for fifteen years. However, by 1970 the series was in crisis,[32] and television managers decided to invest in great productions of classic authors. Certainly Guerin's *Hamlet*, the eleventh Shakespeare play to be adapted by TVE,[33] was a special case: it was entrusted to a talented, experienced and prestigious director; it was extensively publicized in articles and interviews in different newspapers and magazines as early as nine months before it was aired;[34] shooting lasted three weeks instead of the usual three or four days; and its budget amounted to approximately two million pesetas.[35]

Seville-born Claudio Guerin was one of the 1967 graduate students from the official School of Film that TVE snatched up and that would bring thematic and technical innovations into the medium.[36] Before the 1970 *Hamlet*, Claudio

Guerin had acquired prestige through two shorts, some documentaries he had written and directed, the co-direction of a film and the direction of six plays for TVE, four of them for 'Teatro de siempre' including the successful *Richard III* in 1967 (revived in 1969 in 'Estudio 1') and *El mito de Fausto* in 1968.[37] His productions were ranked among the best ten television programmes of the year,[38] and his premature death in 1973 when he was thirty-five did not prevent him from being widely recognized by critics as the greatest television author in Spain and as a pioneer and visionary director in television production.[39] TVE's choice of Guerin for this and previous projects can be seen as analogous to the regime's capitalization on the exiled 'Communist' but prestigious film-maker Luis Buñuel, who directed *Tristana* in Spain in 1970 to compete, and later be nominated, for the Academy Award for Best Foreign Language Film.

For the script adaptation Claudio Guerin also counted on the poet and dramatist Antonio Gala

---

[26] Muñoz, *El teatro*, p. 268.

[27] Jan Kott, *Shakespeare, Our Contemporary*, trans. Boleslaw Taborski from the 1964 original *Skice o Szekspirze* (London, 1964), p. 53.

[28] Krystyna Kujawinska-Courtney, 'Der polnische Prinz: Rezeption und Appropriation des *Hamlet* in Polen', *Shakespeare-Jahrbuch* (1995), p. 90, quoted in Hartmann, 'Shakespeare', p. 223.

[29] With Julián Mateos in the title role, and directed by Marcos Reyes (Baget Herms, *Historia*, p. 147).

[30] Utrera, 'Teatro', p. 17.

[31] Manuel Palacio, *Historia de la televisión en España* (Barcelona, 2001), p. 146, and Baget Herms, *Historia*, p. 163.

[32] Baget Herms, *Historia*, p. 220.

[33] See Baget Herms, *Historia*, p. 75, 160, 173.

[34] Melgar, '*Hamlet*'; Claudio Guerin Hill, 'Cada hombre tiene su *Hamlet*', *Ya*, 16 March 1970; Vega, Jr, 'Dos jóvenes actores en el eterno drama de duda y amor', *Ama*, February 1970.

[35] Ángel A. Pérez Gómez, '*Hamlet*', *Reseña*, 40 (1970), pp. 606–7. The daily minimum wage at that time was 103 pesetas (Abella, *La vida cotidiana*, p. 309).

[36] Utrera, 'Teatro', p. 15.

[37] Utrera, *Claudio Guerin*, pp. 255–84.

[38] See reviews by J. M. Baget in volumes 68 (1969), 80 (1970), 92 (1971) and 104 (1972) of the journal *Imagen y sonido*.

[39] Palacio, *Historia*, p. 132; and Rafael Utrera, 'Introducción', *Cuadernos de Eihceroa*, 2 (2003), p. 9.

(b. 1936), who had adapted his *Richard III* in 1967.[40] Gala defined their collaboration as himself writing the 'lyrics' and Guerin the 'music',[41] and in the case of *Hamlet* they had different views. Gala saw the political problem of the vacant throne as a consequence of the domestic conflict (like the Atrides of Greek mythology and drama) and was more interested in developing the tragedy of the disillusioned oedipal son.[42] Guerin stated that he wanted to avoid Romantic and philosophical views of the play and to stress Shakespeare's concern with 'the great mechanism', with the conquest of power, with the political fact, as Shakespeare had done in the Richard and Henry cycles.[43] Having a didactic view of television, Guerin added that the ideal way to interpret *Hamlet* was from the present time.[44] Guerin was familiar with Jan Kott's interpretation and even stated that his criticism of the tragedy did not go far enough.[45] Friends and personal acquaintances of Guerin[46] privately confirmed his constant intention of interlarding his productions with political critiques, as it was common for other tolerated 'progressive' artists to try to 'score a goal' against the authorities within possible limits. When I interviewed some of the actors,[47] they denied that Guerin gave instructions as to any specific political interpretation in the Francoist context; but Emilio Gutiérrez Caba observed that it was clear that the play dealt with the struggle for power, and José María Lucena stated that Guerin subtly managed to say what could not be said, as was the case in his adaptation of the politically charged *El mito de Fausto*.

THE FILM

I will now turn to the film itself[48] for evidence from which to explore how Guerin managed to realize his political interpretation of *Hamlet*, alongside the personal or domestic reading expressed by co-adapter Antonio Gala.

Setting is one of the production choices that can easily make the play refer to a political situation. In Soviet Russia, the massive iron grille dividing the stage in a 1950 production and the mobile curtain that controlled the action in Lyubimov's 1971 pro-

duction at the Taganka Theatre in Moscow were clear signs that Denmark/Russia was a prison.[49] For Guerin's televised *Hamlet*, recorded in black and white, studio sets were used. Jaime Queralt designed a late Middle Ages setting, first seen in the costumes and austere decor of the great hall in the first scene (Shakespeare's 1.2) and previously suggested by stills of a medieval castle alternating with the initial Gothic-type credit titles. Gloomy corridors, hallways with Romanesque arched pillars, stairways and crypt, more abstract than realistic, would remind spectators more of Olivier's maze-fortress than of Kozintsev's menacing castle, yet without Olivier's stylized, suggestive and symbolic design.[50] The historical setting and costumes, including a black-clad, blond prince (with perhaps a too conspicuous wig), was a traditional choice in Spanish theatre productions.[51] But it was also a safe way to get authorization from censors

---

[40] Antonio Gala also made television adaptations of *King Lear*, and *Romeo and Juliet* (Díaz, *La televisión*, p. 245).

[41] Utrera, 'Teatro', p. 49.

[42] Utrera, *Claudio Guerin*, p. 260.

[43] Melgar, '*Hamlet*', p. 36.

[44] 'Y desde nuestro tiempo, ése me parece un camino ideal para interpretar esta obra' (Melgar, '*Hamlet*', p. 36). See also Claudio Guerin, 'Cómo veo a Hamlet', *Nuevo Diario*, 25 October 1970, and Carlos Muñiz, '*Hamlet*', *Tele-Radio*, 19 October 1970, p. 14.

[45] Muñiz, '*Hamlet*', p. 14. A Spanish translation of Kott's *Shakespeare, Our Contemporary* was published as *Apuntes sobre Shakespeare* (Barcelona, 1969).

[46] Carlos Gortari, Juan Mediavilla, Rafael Utrera and Antonio Abellán (director of drama programmes on TVE).

[47] Emilio Gutiérrez Caba, Fabio León (Horatio), José María Lucena (Guildenstern) and José Carabias (Player-Queen). Pedro Sempson (Ghost) declined to comment. Fernando Cebrián (King), María Luisa Ponte (Queen) and Alfonso del Real (Polonius) had died before this research project.

[48] I have used a VHS recording of the version aired on TVE's Canal Nostalgia on 12 August 1994, and *Hamlet, príncipe de Dinamarca*, DVD (G.E. on-off, S. L. and RTVE Comercial, 2007).

[49] Anthony Dawson, *Hamlet: Shakespeare in Performance* (Manchester, 1995), pp. 188 and 236.

[50] Bernice W. Kliman, *Hamlet: Film, Television and Audio Performance* (Rutherford, 1988), pp. 25–7.

[51] One exception: Juan Santacana's modern-dress adaptation staged in 1928 in Madrid (Floridor, '*Hamlet*, en pavón', *ABC*, 1 July 1928, p. 44).

since they were susceptible to any allusion to Francoist Spain. Productions using contemporary costumes (such as the Andrzej Wajda's in 1981, with Fortinbras wearing a uniform of the Polish Security Forces[52]) earn political immediacy, although also at some risk: during the Uruguayan dictatorship, director Jaime Yavitz set his 1979 production of *Hamlet* in an unidentified country at war, the stage peopled with ever-watching soldiers, but it proved to be a failure since spectators did not wish to see a reflection of their everyday reality in the theatre.[53]

The traditionalism of the setting contrasts with the innovative filming techniques Guerin ably applied to expressive needs. As Melgar pointed out, Guerin combines camera movements with shifts of locale (as in a musical by Jean-Christoph Averty) in the encounter of Hamlet with his father's ghost (scene 1.5) so that the spectator, like Hamlet, is unsure whether or not the ghost is real.[54] In other places, Guerin alternates introspective shots, abruptly cut while the camera is moving, with still shots brutally slamming into the spectator's eyes. Because of daring filmic choices such as these, Melgar praised Guerin as a brilliant creator in Spanish television.

A significant element of the decor are the effigies of Hamlet's father and uncle attached to columns in a hallway, as well as the empty niche, in the column next to the present king's statue, reserved for the future king. They are aptly deployed to underpin the dialogue (for instance, when Hamlet complains 'So excellent a King, that was to this / Hyperion to a satyr' [1.2.139–40] or when the prince asks his mother 'and what judgement / would step from this to this?' [3.4.70–1] the camera swiftly panning from her late husband's effigy to that of the present king) or to strengthen the significance of certain moments (when, at the beginning of the play, the picture shows a closeup of the effigy of Hamlet's uncle and, as the king starts to deliver his first speech [1.2.1–16], dissolves into a close-up of the speaker). Repeated appearances of these effigies, mainly that of the king, may suggest such common aesthetics in totalitarian regimes, just as the almost omnipresent statues of Claudius in Kozint-

sev's *Hamlet* allude to Stalin.[55] Archaic and dissonant music written by Miguel Angel Tallane and played by Pro Musica Antiqua reinforced an atmosphere of restlessness and things out of joint.

Casting choices can also generate political resonances. The sense of political resistance in Lyubimov's 1971 production in Moscow was enhanced by the protest singer and dissident Vladimir Vysotsky impersonating the prince.[56] In Guerin's *Hamlet*, casting provided a marked difference between generations: Hamlet and Ophelia were enacted by young players (twenty-eight-year-old Emilio Gutiérrez Caba, sixteen-year-old Maribel Martín, respectively) in sharp contrast to the mature age of Fernando Cebrián (forty-one) as king, María Luisa Ponte (fifty-three) as Gertrude and Alfonso del Real (fifty-three) as Polonius. TV critic Melgar judged it a risky decision to entrust the title role to a young actor, and perceived it as intending to stress the intergenerational conflict in the play.[57] Similarly, Peter Kupke's *Hamlet* in Potsdam in 1964, with the prince and Laertes, almost schoolboys, forced into a duel by the adult court, was seen as 'an indictment of power politics crushing innocent, hopeful human beings'.[58] Given that part of the opposition against Francoism emerged with the generational change,[59] a young prince killing the usurper-king could be seen as the younger Spanish generations that would succeed in overthrowing the seventy-seven-year-old dictator.

The individual characterization of the main roles in the tragedy does not lend itself to clear political perceptions. Experienced actor Emilio Gutiérrez Caba embodied the full range of

---

[52] Kujawinska-Courtney, 'Polnische', p. 90.

[53] Juan Carlos Copo, '*Hamlet* a varias voces', in Carlos Sopena, ed., *Hamlet: ensayos psicoanalíticos* (Madrid, 2004), pp. 101–16, p. 103.

[54] 'Guerin', p. 9.

[55] Kliman, *Hamlet*, p. 112.

[56] Stříbrný, *Shakespeare*, pp. 119–20.

[57] Melgar, 'Guerin', p. 9; an issue also observed by Viriato, '*Hamlet* de Gala-Guerin', *Hoja del lunes* (Madrid), 26 October 1970, p. 39.

[58] Hamburger, 'Party', p. 180.

[59] Sainz Rodríguez, *Un reinado*, p. 44.

21. María Luisa Ponte as Gertrude and Fernando Cebrián as Claudius in *Hamlet,* Televisión
Española 1970, directed by Claudio Guerin.

Hamlet's varied and complex personality: medi-
tative, intelligent, sarcastic, with changing moods
and foreboding flashes, and with oedipal intima-
tions when he viciously throws his mother onto
her bed in the closet scene – another choice present
in Olivier's version. Keeping the mercurial aspects
of the character, Gutiérrez Caba's prince is not
a clearly politicized or heroic figure. Fernando
Cebrián played the king as both an insecure, weak
character, deeply regretting his crimes in 3.3, and
an apt personality for keeping up appearances at
court and plotting secret stratagems. The character's insecurity is clearly shown in an added silent
sequence in 4.5 where the queen, Lady Macbeth-
like, infuses courage in her husband by handing
him the staff and sceptre (see Illustration 21) in
order to affirm his royal power in the face of the
threat of Laertes's rebellion.[60]

This characterization responds to Claudio
Guerin's statement that, in order to avoid a
Manichean view of the tragedy, he conceived the
king as a not altogether malign character.[61] While

Claudius in Tocilescu's 1985 production appeared
as a 'short, insignificant-looking', 'vulgar and
aggressive tyrant' in a 'veiled allusion' to Romanian
dictator Ceaușescu,[62] the weak king played by
forty-one-year-old Fernando Cebrián does not
invite analogies with the physical weakness of
the trembling, Parkinson's-affected, seventy-seven-
year-old Franco. By 1970 Franco appeared as both
strict and benevolent, the symbolic old father of the
country.[63] However, both Cebrián and Franco projected an image of fragility and Guerin's embodiment of absolute power as insecure could hint
at the agonistic phase of Francoism, and dissident

---

[60] Laura Campillo privately suggested that the image of a strong
consort would recall Franco's wife, Carmen Polo, who at
that time attempted to exert influence on political affairs
as Franco showed little initiative. See Payne, *Franco Regime,*
pp. 518 and 581.

[61] Melgar, 'Hamlet', p. 36.

[62] Monica Matei-Chesnoiu, *Shakespeare in the Romanian Cultural Memory* (Madison, 2006), p. 208.

[63] Moradiellos, *España,* p. 161; Payne, *Franco Regime,* p. 495.

viewers could relate the Danish king, a fratricide and usurper, to Franco, who usurped power from a democratically elected Republic through a fratricidal war.

Needless to say, the handling of the text can overtly generate political meaning. The script in Guerin's *Hamlet*, as inferred from the video recording, made use of extensive cuts in order to reduce performance time to 112 minutes (without final credit titles), as mandatory in the televised series. Out went episodes and elements traditionally removed: the first scene, Fortinbras's subplot, Reynaldo in 2.1, Hamlet's advice to the players, the dumb-show (though retaining the spoken dialogue of *The Mousetrap*), scene 4.4 including Hamlet's 'How all occasions . . .' soliloquy, Ophelia's first entrance as 'distracted' in 4.5 and Osric's conversation with Hamlet. The tragedy's reference to the 'cess of majesty' in 3.3, a passage that was censored in the 1961 theatre production of *Hamlet*,[64] is also omitted.[65] The removal of the Fortinbras subplot certainly deprives the play of a strong political element but the production can still have political significance, especially in a given historical situation. In his post-Second World War film, Olivier cut Fortinbras and also Rosencrantz and Guildenstern but his ending suggested a 'circular pattern of history doomed to be repeated . . . in line with the dominant political opinion . . . that the rise of fascism, the Second World War and the horrors of the Holocaust, were due to delayed political action' by the allies.[66] The excision of Fortinbras in Guerin's *Hamlet* makes the production incline more to the domestic and human conflict than to political issues, as co-adapter Gala intended, but Guerin's story of the sacrificial prince can be still interpreted, as with Olivier's film, as blaming the opposition's 'delayed political action' for the permanence of oppression. It was only from 1971 that a partly tolerated anti-Francoist opposition began to muster a unified force around specific platforms.[67]

Moreover, the script preserved some elements related to the conflict over the Danish throne and inserted some details which, together with Guerin's visual realization, allowed spectators to see the political undercurrents. Some of the retained features were those stressed in Zawistowski's 'political' *Hamlet* in Cracow (1956) that Jan Kott discussed.[68] Marcellus's remark that 'Something is rotten in the state of Denmark' (1.4.67), though appearing only once and not three times as in the Cracovian *Hamlet*, could immediately recall the Matesa financial scandal that involved two ministers of the cabinet in 1969. Hamlet's Folio-only remark 'Denmark's a prison' (2.2.246), contemporized as 'Spain under Franco is a prison', could well be sensed by dissidents as the new cabinet in 1969 toughened the state's repressive force, especially in the Basque country where emergent ETA terrorism caused the detention of hundreds.

Other retained elements with political resonance are Hamlet's debate on ambition with his schoolfellows (2.2.254–67) and the king's open declaration that Hamlet is 'immediate to our throne' (1.2.109), which would recall Franco's final decision to designate prince Don Juan Carlos as his successor. The very last words in the script 'For he was likely, had he been put on, / To have proved most royally' (5.2.351–2), here spoken by Horatio instead of Fortinbras, could have special significance for some spectators. Someone who would have 'proved a great king' (as the Spanish

64 Berta Muñoz Cáliz, *Expedientes de la censura teatral franquista* (Madrid, 2006), p. 30.

65 Other cuts comprise Polonius's advice to Laertes, all the dialogue of 1.4 until the Ghost's entrance at 1.4.38, two-thirds of 4.7 (from line 8 to 124a), as well as sections of long speeches such as Hamlet's soliloquies (for instance, the 31-line first soliloquy is reduced to 20 lines and the final section of the second soliloquy 2.2.587–605 is excised), or Polonius's exhortations to Ophelia (1.3.122–36).

66 J. Lawrence Guntner, '*Hamlet, Macbeth* and *King Lear* on Film', in R. Jackson, ed., *The Cambridge Companion to Shakespeare on Film* (Cambridge, 2000), p. 119.

67 Moradiellos, *España*, pp. 192–5.

68 *Our Contemporary*, pp. 53–4; *Apuntes*, p. 77. Although Guerin's *Hamlet* does not include the Gravedigger's remark 'the gallows is built stronger than the church' (5.1.47–8) that Kott pointed out, the script's retention of 'the more pity that great folk should have count'nance in this world to drown or hang themselves more than their even Christian' (5.1.26–7) makes clear that the Gravedigger is well aware for whom he digs.

22. An added silent shot with Hamlet (Emilio Gutiérrez Caba) caressing the royal throne, in
Claudio Guerin's *Hamlet* for Televisión Española, 1970.

dialogue can be translated back into English) 'if he had reigned' was Don Juan de Borbón, who in July 1969 proclaimed no connection with his son's appointment as Franco's successor and reaffirmed his preference for a constitutional monarchy in line with Western European systems.[69]

Guerin's production aptly compensated for cuts in the dialogue with visual information in silent sequences. For instance, after the first court scene Hamlet is shown alone in the great hall, approaching the throne, almost caressing it with reverence, and finally sitting down with a smile of satisfaction (Illustration 22). Thus Guerin enhanced the play's political issue of Hamlet's ambition for power.

Laertes's return in 4.5 is presented as a threatening armed rebellion. Hamlet, in his final agony, alone in the hallway, raises his hand towards the effigies of his father, then of his uncle, and then towards the empty niche in the following column reserved for the next king (Illustration 23).

It is tempting to hypothesize that Guerin, in compensation for Gala's removal of the Fortinbras subplot, reinforced his political reading of the play with these telling textual visualizations.

Hamlet's complaints about the king's revelling and the drinking reputation of the Danes (1.4.8–21) are transformed into images of the court at a banquet shown in dissolve while Hamlet delivers his complaints about his mother's frailty (1.2.138–142, 145–50). The licentious behaviour of the monarchs is reinforced as they appear at dinner while Polonius explains the reason for Hamlet's madness (2.2.86–167), and as they giggle behind their bed canopy before they welcome Rosencrantz and Guildenstern (2.2.1–39). Thus the king and queen are shown as pleasure-seeking monarchs united in love and politics. Franco, however, led a relatively austere life, hunting being his only publicly known leisure activity.

The order of scenes and episodes is basically the standard sequence except for a few major

---

[69] See his 'Declaración' on 19 July 1969, reprinted in Sainz Rodríguez, *Un reinado*, p. 344.

23. A dying Hamlet (Emilio Gutiérrez Caba) reaching out towards the empty niche that would have held his effigy as king.

transpositions. The 'solid flesh' soliloquy is delivered after scene 1.3, a common shift in theatre productions (among them Olivier's version); the king's and Laertes's plotting of the duel in 4.7 is shown after Ophelia's burial in 5.1 – a change also present in Olivier's film. The key lines where Hamlet explains his definitive motivation to requite the king 'with his arm' (5.2.64–9) are assigned to Horatio. Thus Hamlet's friend appears as an instigator plotting against the usurper: not only has he revealed the apparition of the late king's ghost to Hamlet but he also incites the prince to action. With this transposition of speech assignments the prince may be perceived as not altogether persuaded to take revenge. Hamlet's added brief reply to Horatio's encouragement, 'For that purpose I came back', does not sound determined enough, as he immediately plunges into his melancholy mood saying 'a man's life's no more than to say "one"' (5.2.75).

But another significant transposition later in this scene shows that he is not an irresolute character:

Hamlet is told that he is slain (line 313) *after* he has already killed the king (lines 321–7). This markedly alters the character of Hamlet: Guerin's prince thrusts the envenomed sword into the king's breast before he is aware of his immediate death, and therefore his revenge is not a reaction to his realization that he will soon die but only to the murder of his mother. Thus this Hamlet's revenge finally appears as a slightly more resolute action than in the received version. Making Hamlet a resolute revenger is common in productions portraying the prince as opposing a tyrannical order, whether it alludes to Stalinist regimes (as in Vlad Magur's 1958 'covertly subversive' *Hamlet* in Romania[70]) or to fascism (as Arshan Burdzhalian's 1942 *Hamlet* in Yerevan, capital of the Soviet Armenia, was reported to be[71]).

---

[70] Matei-Chesnoiu, *Shakespeare*, p. 201.
[71] Mikhail M. Morozov, *Shakespeare on the Soviet Stage* (London, 1947), p. 43; and B. Arutiunian 'Virmenskii teatr', in Vishnevskaia, pp. 342–3 (in Irena M. Makaryk's

The 'To be or not to be' soliloquy is retained in its standard position but also appears before the title and initial credits as a kind of prologue. Guerin chose to film this famous moment in a medium shot ('waist up'), with the actor moving only his lips and eyes and looking slightly to the right of the camera for most of its 110 seconds. The same *mise-en-scène* of a motionless Hamlet is used when the soliloquy is repeated but Guerin then opted for a medium closeup, both long takes edited between a fade-in and fade-out. Since they are the only shots of their kind in the film, the famous soliloquy is presented as a distinct, almost isolated, moment in the play, brutally confronting the spectator.[72] Such an emphasis on Hamlet's key words could make 1970 spectators perceive the initial dilemma as whether 'to suffer' or 'to take arms against' a repressive regime. The prince's meditations that 'the dread of something after death' makes one bear 'Th'oppressor's wrong' (3.1.70) – in Spanish 'la injuria del tirano'– could resonate with anxieties over an uncertain future after Franco's death.

Additions to the playscript, though small in number, can shape the production into a given interpretation. In the *Hamlet* staged in the state-funded playhouse Teatro Español in Madrid in 1949, the translator-adaptor José María Pemán, the foremost dramatist and poet of the early Francoist regime,[73] introduced allusions to Christian beliefs and images in Hamlet's speech that turned him into a 'Romantic, Christian – even Roman Catholic – young prince' sounding familiar to the panegyric rhetoric of Francoism.[74] Guerin and Gala's script contained short, though significant, additions.

A salient non-Shakespearian element is a kind of 'postscript' after the end-title and before the final credits: 'It does not matter what they made of us. The only thing that matters is what we did with what they made of us.' These lines are a modulated translation of Jean-Paul Sartre's statement 'L'important n'est pas ce qu'on fait de nous mais ce que nous faisons nous-même de ce qu'on a fait de nous.'[75] As Benedict O'Donohoe explains, this dictum reflects Sartre's shift from his early subjectivist and individualistic 'We are what we do'

to a dialectical, socially focused and historically determined 'we are what we make of what others make of us', a conceptualization developed in his 1960 *Critique of Dialectical Reason*.[76] This Sartrian epilogue invites the spectator to reinterpret the tragedy in an existentialist perspective, more in tune with Gala's interest in the personal conflict of the play. From this perspective, 'to be' is 'to act', yet not only to act out our inexorable freedom to choose what to do (a free choice that entails a moral reponsibility) but also to act our freedom in the face of given historical circumstances, in the face of 'what others make of us'. As the film emphasizes Hamlet's most philosophical soliloquy, 'To be, or not to be', through its repetition and its distinctive *mise-en-scène*, it offers a Hamlet reflecting on the implications of his freedom as conditioned by what others make of him: the Ghost urging him to revenge, the king spying on him and seeking his death and, towards the end of the tragedy, Horatio prompting him to eliminate the king in 5.2.64–8. Unlike Shakespeare's prince, this Hamlet does not finally give out reasons for his vengeance. In the hands of Antonio Gala and Claudio Guerin, the tragedy of Hamlet is the tragedy of the individual aware of – and perhaps so aware that he attempts to sidestep it – his responsibility to freely choose his actions.

Alongside this existentialist reading, the added Sartrian 'epilogue' could nod to sensitive dissidents who knew that Sartre had been included in the *Index Librorum Prohibitorum* until 1962 for being a Communist (some of his plays were allowed when

---

unpublished paper for Clara Calvo's seminar 'Shakespeare, War and Remembrance' at the 2008 International Shakespeare Conference).

[72] Melgar, 'Guerin', p. 9.

[73] S. Sanz Villanueva, *Historia de la literatura española: el siglo XX (Literatura actual)*, vol. 6/2 (Barcelona, 1984), p. 207.

[74] R. Portillo and M. Salvador, 'Spanish Productions of *Hamlet* in the Twentieth Century', in Ángel-Luis Pujante and Ton Hoenselaars, eds. *Four Hundred Years of Shakespeare in Europe* (Newark and London, 2003), p. 187.

[75] *Saint Genet, comédien et martyr* (Paris, 1952), p. 55.

[76] 'Why Sartre Matters', *Philosophy Now*, 53, at www.philosophynow.org/issue53/53odonohoe.htm, accessed 29 November 2006.

authorities sought to offer a more liberal image of Francoism), and was one of the international intellectuals protesting against the 1970 'Trial of Burgos' against sixteen members of ETA (six of them facing death sentences). Sartre and Herbert Marcuse were the most popular authors among university students.[77]

Further emphasis on the political issue of ambition and struggle for the throne appears in some non-Shakespearian phrases in the king's lines. In a kind of Freudian slip, the king drops 'and to spy . . . ', then interrupts himself, smiles, and continues 'and to gather, / So much as from occasions you may glean' (2.2.15–16); instead of 'give him a further edge' (3.1.26), the king says 'carry on with your enquiry'; instead of 'Madness in great ones . . . ' (3.1.188) he delivers 'Madness in those aspiring to a throne must not unwatched go'. Additions and substitutions such as 'To spy', 'watch' and 'enquire' were precisely the words Jan Kott pointed out as most commonly heard at the politically charged production in Cracow in 1956.[78] As if hinting at a police-state, the film emphasizes the Danish court as a place where everyone is being spied on. One significant moment is seen when Hamlet is *whispering* to Horatio that *The Mousetrap* will enact his uncle's murder: as Rosencrantz slowly walks near, Hamlet interrupts himself after 'Observe my uncle . . . ' (3.2.80), then Hamlet waits for Rosencrantz to pass by, and resumes his instructions to Horatio. Another emphasis on 'spying' is the script's retention of the king's request that Hamlet stay in Elsinore: the prince can more conveniently be under close watch, a task the monarch will entrust to Rosencrantz and Guildenstern. This could remind some 1970 spectators of Franco's interest in having Prince Don Juan Carlos by his side.

Another telling addition appears in the king's letter to the king of England, in which he defines Hamlet as a 'dangerous and rebel prince'. That a royal title was qualified as 'dangerous' and 'rebel' could have various political resonances in 1970. Although the actual Spanish prince, Don Juan Carlos, had vowed loyalty to the principles of the regime's ideology, a dangerous and rebel prince could refer to (1) the constitutional monarchy represented by the not yet crowned Don Juan de Borbón; (2) the Carlist 'prince' Carlos Hugo de Borbón y Parma, who in December 1968 had been expelled from Spain for his political activities akin to socialism and federalism;[79] or (3) Prince Juan Carlos, whom hard-liners suspected of planning, as king, to lead Spain through legal reforms towards democracy.[80] In the latter case, the interpolation proved to be prophetic, since Don Juan Carlos stood 'rebellious' to the regime when, as king, his appointed prime minister, Adolfo Suárez, initiated the legal reforms for a democratic, constitutional monarchy.

At the end of the film, Hamlet's agony takes up 2 minutes and 20 seconds of the production's footage and ends with a close-up of Hamlet lying dead on the floor. This choice reinforces Gala's main interest in the play as a human and personal tragedy. Yet again the political theme of Hamlet's royal ambition is underlined when Horatio, the dissident-instigator, pronounces the film's very last words before the onlooking courtiers ('To have proved most royally'), and just afterwards the camera shows the effigy of Hamlet's uncle, then pans to the empty niche in the column reserved for the next king, after which the shot shows a dissolve of the niche and a close-up of the dead Hamlet (Illustration 24), then returning to the empty niche, on which the end-title *Fin* appears (Illustration 25).

This is the film's last image, the niche representing royal power in a vacuum that symbolizes the discontinuity of the late king's regime and the hope for a different, though uncertain, political future.

---

[77] See Muñoz Cáliz, *El teatro*, pp. 143–5, 278; Laviana, *1970*, p. 9; and Moradiellos, *España*, p. 163.

[78] Kott, *Our Contemporary*, p. 53.

[79] Tusell, *La España*, p. 225, and Laviana, *1969*, p. 60. Carlism is a traditionalist political movement established in support of the claim to the Spanish throne by a branch of the House of Bourbon, initiated with Don Carlos de Borbón y Parma's attempt in 1833 to become king instead of his liberal-supported niece Queen Isabel II.

[80] As he was advised by the political tutor Franco appointed for him, Torcuato Fernández-Miranda (José Luis Villalonga, *El rey*, p. 98).

24. A dissolve of dead Hamlet (Emilio Gutiérrez Caba) and the empty niche representing royal power.

25. 'Fin' (The End) superimposed on the niche reserved for the next king.

RECEPTION

Guerin's *Hamlet* was broadcast in prime time on a Friday evening, sharing the audience with *Estudio Abierto*, a very popular talk show on the second channel. By 1970, only 40 or 51 per cent of Spanish homes owned a TV set.[81] One personal account of TVE, Lorenzo Díaz's comprehensive *La televisión en España, 1949–1995*, does not even mention this *Hamlet* production among the thousands of programmes referred to.[82] This silence well reflects what the witnesses of this televised *Hamlet* I interviewed were all agreed on: that it passed unnoticed by the general audience. While other productions in the 'Estudio 1' series were later revived, Guerin's *Hamlet* did not appear again until 1994 and 1995 in 'Canal Nostalgia' (or 'Canal Clásico'), the classics-theme channel of TVE.[83]

As for reviews, five of them wrote favourable appraisals of the production's ability to bring the classic tragedy closer to the present day and of Guerin's technical virtues but they remained apolitical.[84] Those that touched on political issues could only do so in an ambiguous way, published as they were in censored media. In a pre-review, Pilar Urbano was alert to a political intention of the production alongside its concern with more personal issues: she emphasized that the prince was deprived of the throne, eager to re-establish his alienated rights and that he hesitated and did not carry out his coup d'état ('asesta su golpe de Estado').[85] This was published in the 'progressive' newspaper *Nuevo Diario*. In *Reseña*, Ángel Pérez Gómez observed that the film side-stepped the political issue and reduced the problem to a personal one and that Guerin lacked a serious ideological stance.[86] What Pérez Gómez means by 'ideological' is ambiguous: the text seems to refer to Guerin's lack of commitment to any personal view of the tragedy but it can also hint at the expectation of a more politically charged version. The latter is what readers could at that time infer from the 'progressive' character of the magazine *Reseña*, financed by the Society of Jesus, which redirected itself towards concerns for social justice and human rights after the Second Vatican Council (1962–5). In an interview with

Pérez Gómez, himself a 'progressive' Jesuit, he explained that, given Guerin's political leaning in tune with the clandestine left (like many directors of his generation such as Pilar Miró, Víctor Erice and Elías Querejeta), he found the *Hamlet* production politically tepid. This shows that in 1970 there were viewers willing to interpret *Hamlet* in oppositional terms to their political status quo.

To conclude, Guerin's *Hamlet* fulfils the three requisites Hortmann points out in order for the political potential of a Shakespeare play to be released: (1) the socio-political situation of an authoritarian regime in its twilight and the critical issue of the succession of power; (2) the director's willingness to use the play, as shown in Guerin's published interviews and, as I have tried to show, in his choices of script and *mise-en-scène*; and (3) audiences 'alive to the socio-political climate' – as seen in reviewer Pérez Gómez – and 'primed to catch allusions'[87] – as seen in the censors of TVE intending to re-dub Hamlet as a duke. All in all, Guerin's *Hamlet* is not a politicized film against the Franco regime, which was unthinkable in a production financed by the state-owned TV broadcaster. Nor is it a simplified version, as Jan Kott described the 1956 *Hamlet* in Cracow. Yet Guerin found subtle ways to hint at political issues of his time in order to hammer home his view of the tragedy's concern with the struggle for political power. Guerin's attitude here resembled the

81 Palacio, *Historia*, p. 60, and Moradiellos, *España*, p. 147.
82 (Madrid, 1994).
83 The exact dates are 13 May 1994, 12 August 1994, 4 August 1995 and 17 August 1995, provided by Ascensión Ruiz from the archive services of TVE, e-mail 29 January 2007.
84 Del Corral, '*Hamlet*', p. 71; M., '*Hamlet*', pp. 12–13; Melgar, 'Guerin', p. 9; Viriato, '*Hamlet*', p. 39; José M. Baget Herms, 'Los diez mejores programas de 1970', *Imagen y Sonido*, 92, February 1971.
85 Pilar Urbano, '*Hamlet*: un príncipe en conflicto político y familiar', *Nuevo Diario*, 17 October 1970, p. 11. On the newspaper: José Cabeza and Julio Montero, 'El *Nuevo Diario* de PESA. El fracaso de un intento de apertura (1964–1970)', in Juan Antonio García Galindo et al., eds., *La comunicación social durante el franquismo* (Málaga, 2002), pp. 445–64; p. 452.
86 '*Hamlet*', p. 606.
87 Hortmann. 'Shakespeare', pp. 213–14.

posibilismo some playwrights practised in order to pass censorship.[88]

If three years before Elizabeth I's death Shakespeare's *Hamlet* resonated with the Elizabethans' anxiety over the succession to the throne, five years before Franco's death Guerin's *Hamlet* had elements tapping into Spaniards' concern with their political present and future. A Hamlet 'duke' of Denmark and a Hamlet 'dangerous and rebel prince' bracket the range of resonances Shakespeare's adapted tragedy had in late Francoist Spain.

---

[88] For playwrights' attitudes towards censorship, see Muñoz, *El teatro*, pp. 296–9. I have found confirmation of this comparison in an e-mail exchanged with Professor Rafael Utrera (19 October 2007).

WHAT SHAKESPEARE DID WITH THE QUEEN'S MEN'S *KING LEIR* AND WHEN

MEREDITH SKURA

This article argues against unnecessarily 'scientific' rigour in determining sources. Source study originated in *Quellenforschung*, a study of classical texts that mined an extant work for information about lost sources but ignored the work's own textual and contextual dynamics. Early source studies of Shakespeare similarly focused on a single source and one simple relation between source and play. Like nineteenth-century classical scholars, they insisted on quantifiable evidence and treated echoes as separate phenomena, as if they had had no effect on one another in the original process of being remembered and reused. Source study had no role in interpretation. The only important questions were: exactly how similar is each source line to its proposed Shakespearian echo? How many echoes are there?

Many accounts of sources still proceed this way but I argue instead for a contextual approach that studies each echo in the context of the original source from which it came, the play in which it supposedly landed and the other echoes from that source. My example is the Queen's Men's play, *King Leir* (1585–7?), long recognized as the primary source for Shakespeare's *King Lear* (1604/5). As critics continue to discover, the old play is the origin of many of its lines but the larger relationship between Shakespeare and *Leir* still remains to be examined.[1] The following article collects all the *Leir* echoes together and adds a few, in order to see *what* Shakespeare borrowed from *Leir*. More important, it discusses what such a collection can suggest about *how* and *why* Shakespeare used the borrowings. What part of the play did he echo and why? When? What did he do with borrowed material and how did his use change over time? Of course, not all borrowings are revealing. Many are boringly predictable: Shakespeare read Plutarch's 'Life of Caesar' before writing about Caesar. Other echoes, no doubt, are accidental, like a tune that you hear and find yourself helplessly singing over and over. But in some cases a borrowed line can point beyond its source to the dynamics of the play, to Shakespeare's process of composition and even to general theatrical conditions.

The longing for scientific measurement is understandable. Source studies depend on parallels, and parallel hunting is a dangerous game. E. H. Oliphant warns about a scholar 'who did really excellent work in this field until he went in search of parallels. No sooner did he do so than his notable logical qualities abandoned him, and he, who had shown himself thoroughly capable of rational thought and keen argument, dropped into futilities

---

This article has benefited from Roslyn Knutson's comments on an earlier draft, and from Ian Munroe's comments on a shorter version prepared for the conference on 'Shakespeare and the Queen's Men' in Toronto (October 2006). I want to thank Jayme Yeo for expert assistance with references and preparation of the paper.

[1] Wilfred Perrett's early 'The Story of King Lear', *Palaestra*, 35 (Berlin, 1904), is still the most thorough. Perrett (before the days of LION databases) must have had a memory more like Shakespeare's than ours; he mentioned most *Leir* traces that I have seen mentioned elsewhere and one that I have not. Others have expanded Perrett. They are summarized in Richard Knowles, 'How Shakespeare Knew *King Leir*', *Shakespeare Survey 55* (Cambridge, 2002), pp. 12–35.

hardly to be expected from a schoolboy.'[2] Similar warnings against Fluellen–like looseness in drawing parallels have been made more recently by Richard Levin about all parallels and by Richard Knowles, about linking performances of the anonymous *King Leir* with Shakespeare's *King Lear*.[3] Both critics wisely remind us how easy it is to see parallels where no one else does and how easy it is to overstate one's case.

But it is possible to take caution too far, as I believe Knowles does when he dismisses nearly all previous claims about Shakespearian parallels to *King Leir* (prob. 1605) before that play was printed. Unconvinced about early echoes of the old play, Knowles finds it more plausible 'that Shakespeare never encountered *Leir* until he read it in Stafford's edition of 1605' (p. 27).[4] But what counts as 'plausible' in judging echoes? And must this be an either/or choice? Surely Shakespeare in *Lear* could have – would have – used both memory and the new text if available. The following argument is in part a response to Knowles and to questions that his argument raises.

Evidence for a supposed borrowing is almost never definitive but it is cumulative. Judgement about any one 'parallel' almost always depends on other information about both source and other Shakespearian texts. If we are already certain about some parallels between *Leir* and *Lear*, then other, less certain echoes in *Lear* become more likely. Similarly, already known echoes in *Lear* can help establish uncertain *Leir* echoes in other Shakespearian plays, especially if they come from the same scene as the *Lear* echo. Even without definitive evidence in a particular case we can establish different levels of collective plausibility. Some of the following suggestions may thus be more convincing than others. But even the less 'certain' connections can be useful so long as their ambiguity is recognized and read in the larger context.

The collection of generally accepted echoes of *Leir* in *Lear* is extensive enough to have suggested, at least to some scholars, that Shakespeare acted in the earlier *Leir* or, even more specifically, that he played the role of Perillus in that play.[5] These echoes have been well analysed before and need not

be addressed here. Echo detectors, however, claim soundings in some seventeen other plays, extending from *1 Henry VI* (1590) through *Hamlet* (*c.*1600/1) to *Cymbeline* (*c.*1608/9), and I turn now to look at the whole group.[6]

The first impression from the group is that Shakespeare seems to have been most influenced by only a few scenes among the more than thirty in the old *King Leir* play, the ones about the very 'Shakespearian' topic of family bonds. The scenes can be divided into two groups: those representing the wickedness of the daughters who betray *Leir* and those representing Leir's rescue and redemption by the daughter *he* betrayed. It is as if Shakespeare's memory gravitated towards the emotional centre of the old story, the family's 'holy cords ... too

---

[2] Oliphant, 'How Not to Play the Game of Parallels', *Journal of English and Germanic Philology*, 28 (1929), 1–15; p. 13.

[3] Richard Levin, 'Another Source for "The Alchemist" and Another Look at Source Studies', *English Literary Renaissance*, 28 (1998), 210–30; Knowles, 'How Shakespeare Knew', pp. 12–35.

[4] Knowles finds 'none of these claims of *Leir*'s early influence completely convincing, and most of them vacuous' ('How Shakespeare Knew *King Leir*', p. 19). He concludes that nearly all arguments for *Leir*'s influence either are badly argued or fail to consider alternative explanations. But although 'plausibility' suffices for his own argument (i.e. that Shakespeare came to know *Leir* through print), Knowles asks for certainty in early echoes of *Leir*. (I should say at the outset that some of mine are among the echoes that Knowles dismisses, pp. 20, 24.)

[5] Arguments for Shakespeare's acting with the Queen's Men were made by Karl Wentersdorf, 'Shakespeare's Erste Truppe', *Shakespeare Jahrbuch*, 84–6 (1950), 128; Hardin Craig, 'Motivation in Shakespeare's Choice of Materials', *Shakespeare Survey 4* (Cambridge, 1951), p. 32; Kenneth Muir, *King Lear*, Arden Edition (1952), p. xxxii. These and others are cited by Knowles, who dismisses all of them, claiming that we have 'no firm evidence' ('How Shakespeare Knew *King Leir*', p. 18). Knowles omits Robert Adger Law, '*King John* and *King Leir*', *Texas Studies in Language and Literature*, 1 (1960), 473–6.

[6] For *1 Henry VI*, see Thomas H. McNeal, 'Margaret of Anjou: Romantic Princess and Troubled Queen', *Shakespeare Quarterly*, 9 (1958), 1–10. For *Hamlet*, see W. W. Greg, 'Shakespeare and *King Leir*', *Times Literary Supplement*, 9 March 1940, p. 124. For *Cymbeline*, see Roger Adger Law, 'An Unannotated Analogue to the Imogene Story', *Texas Studies in English*, 7 (1927), 133–5. The *Cymbeline* parallels mentioned by Knowles are dismissed by him (pp. 22, 26–7).

intrince t'unloose', as Kent calls them (*King Lear*, 2.2.74–5). He echoes and redistributes lines about both the 'sinned-against' and the 'sinning' daughters, as if Cordella, Gonorill and Ragan were all facets of a single daughter, bound to their father by mutual sinning and forgiving between them.[7] In fact, Shakespeare's first echoes of *Leir*, in the three *Henry VI* plays, centre on a notably multifaceted, or two-faced, woman who combines good and bad daughters in herself. She is the lovely Margaret of Anjou who turns into the wicked Queen Margaret, nemesis of both Henry VI and Richard III.[8] In Margaret's first scenes, when Suffolk crosses the sea to court her for Henry VI by proxy – and falls in love with her himself – she echoes the innocent Cordella. But later she echoes Gonorill and Ragan and behaves the way they do (McNeal, pp. 8–9).

In other early plays, however, good and bad Leir daughters also exerted independent effects. Consider first the evil Leir sisters. Some lines from *Leir*'s comic bickering between Gonorill and Ragan (scenes 2, 6) and from the bawdy joking between their suitors (scene 5) have left traces in *Lear*.[9] The scenes that most influenced Shakespeare, however, are those showing the sisters' attempted murder of Leir and his friend Perillus (scenes 12, 17, 19, 25).

In the end the murder plot fails but the attempt is particularly horrible because it reveals his daughters' cruelty to the helpless Leir. Gonorill recruits one assassin; then Ragan enlists another and, making clear what she wants without actually saying it, she sends both to the lonely 'thicket' where she has already told Leir to wait for her (scenes 12, 17). When the murderers attack, Leir invokes Queen Ragan's name to save himself, only to discover that his supposed protector is the one who ordered his death. Meanwhile Ragan fears that the murderer will fail and leave her to be discovered. 'Oh God, that I had bin but made a man,' she cries, knowing she could do it better (scene 25).

The *Leir* murder has been claimed as a source for King Richard's heartless order in *Richard III* (1591) that his own brother, Clarence, be killed, as Clarence learns to his horror just before he dies (*Richard III*, 1.4).[10] In addition, the *Leir* murder

seems to have become confusingly mixed into the murder of young Arthur in *King John* (1595/6). It deflected the latter from the model it had until then been following closely, *The Troublesome Reigne*, another Queen's Men's play. In *Troublesome Reigne*, King John does not order Arthur killed, although he would like to. He sends orders to Hubert to 'keep him safe' and wait for further instructions:

> *Hubert de Burgh*, take *Arthur* here to thee;
> Be he thy prisoner. *Hubert, keep him safe*,
> For on his life doth hang thy Sovereign's crown;
> But in his death consist thy Sovereign's bliss;
> *Then Hubert, as thou shortly hear'st from me*,
> So use the prisoner I have given in charge.
> (*Troublesome Reigne*, ix.29–34, italics added in last two lines)

Instructions follow, telling Hubert to 'put out the eyes of *Arthur Plantagenet*' (*Troublesome Reigne*, xii.50). The king's innocence is emphasized when Hubert reads the letter aloud on stage. In contrast, Shakespeare's King John, like *Leir*'s insidiously indirect Ragan, gives Hubert on-stage orders to kill Arthur:

> *K. John.* Death.
> *Hubert.* My lord?
> *K. John.* A grave.   (*King John*, 3.2.66–8)

The murder is clear enough that Pembroke knows about it and reports that Hubert had orders (from

---

7 See Janet Adelman's argument for merging the daughters, 'Introduction' to *Twentieth-Century Views of 'King Lear'* (Englewood Cliffs, NJ, 1977).

8 McNeal, 'Margaret of Anjou', pp. 4–6, 8–10. Knowles dismisses McNeal's argument ('How Shakespeare Knew *King Leir*', pp. 22–3).

9 McNeal finds echoes of these scenes in *Midsummer Night's Dream, Romeo and Juliet* and *Two Gentlemen of Verona*: see 'Margaret of Anjou', pp. 6–7.

10 Such claims, of course, assume that *Leir* is the earlier of the two plays: Perrett, 'The Story of King Lear', pp. 113–14; R. A. Law, '*Richard the Third*, Act 1, Scene 4', *PMLA*, 37 (1912), 117–41. Knowles concedes that 'some similarities of incident between these roughly contemporary plays are highly suggestive', but concludes that 'the details in *R3* may have come from elsewhere than *Leir*' ('How Shakespeare Knew *King Leir*', p. 20).

the king) to 'do the bloody deed' (*King John*, 4.2.69). Yet elsewhere, we hear that John, like the king in *Troublesome Reigne*, is innocent.[11] It is as if Shakespeare were following two conflicting models in *King John* without realizing it. After *King John*, still other traces of the *Leir* murder scene turn up in *Hamlet* and *Cymbeline*. When Shakespeare wrote his own version of Leir's story in *King Lear*, he left the attempted murder out of the Lear plot but it nonetheless lurks behind the similarly shocking cruelty of the blinding scene in Gloucester's plot, where the old man, about to have his eyes torn out, calls for help from his son Edmund and learns that Edmund ordered the attack.

In the context of these *Leir* parallels, other, less certain echoes can be informative. Thomas McNeal, for example, thinks that *Leir*'s Ragan affected later female characters like Lady Macbeth, even though there are no echoes of *Leir* in *Macbeth*. Lady Macbeth says, to explain why she didn't murder Duncan, 'Had he not resembled / My father as he slept, I had done't' (*Macbeth*, 2.2.12–13). The old play about father and daughters helps explain her otherwise extraneous mention of her father, who appears nowhere else in *Macbeth*, even though it has no equivalent line. This woman, Shakespeare implies, wittingly or unwittingly, is not only a child-killer but, by association with Ragan, a potential father-killer (*King Leir*, 17.1318–20).

McNeal also suggests that Ragan left traces, surprisingly, in Beatrice of *Much Ado About Nothing* (1598). Ragan's frustrated cry, 'Oh God, that I had bin but made a man' (*King Leir*, 2371) may lie behind Beatrice's outburst, 'Oh God that I were a man!' (*Much Ado*, 4.1.304) just before she orders Benedick to 'Kill Claudio!' Knowles dismisses this parallel because Beatrice and Ragan seem too different: Ragan's cry marks tragic familial rupture, while Beatrice's marks 'one of the great comic moments in the play'.[12] Knowles's only context here is generic and his judgement depends only on 'similarity': tragedy influences tragedy and comedy, comedy. But other contexts and relationships seem to have been operative for Shakespeare. In both *King Leir* and *Much Ado*, for example, the word 'melt' appears near the wish for manhood, a similarity in local verbal context that is more important here than genre:[13]

Ragan. O God, that I had bin but made a man;
  Or that my strength were equall with my will!
  These foolish men are nothing but meere pity,
  And *melt* as butter doth against the Sun.
          (*King Leir*, 25.2371–4)

Beatrice. O that I were a man!... O God that I were a man!
  ... But manhood is *melted* into courtesies.
          (*Much Ado*, 4.1.304–20)

Exploring the 'unlikely' Ragan echo in the still larger context of Beatrice's character can suggest something new about her complexity – or Shakespeare's.[14]

The second group of influential *Leir* scenes all show the good daughter Cordella after Leir banishes her. They include the *Lear*/*Leir* parallel first noted by scholars, in the scene where father and

---

[11] E.g. from Hubert (*King John*, 4.1. 33–40). See Law, '*King John* and *King Leir*', pp. 474–6. The contradiction in Shakespeare can be explained away if necessary, but the fact remains that Arthur's murder in Shakespeare is closer to *Leir*: (1) King John gives Ragan-like indirect orders to the murderer, and (2) Hubert, like Ragan, is closely related to his victim. Knowles finds the parallels between *Leir* and *John* 'far from conclusive' (22).

[12] Knowles, 'How Shakespeare Knew *King Leir*', p. 23. He cites Eleanor's line in *2 Henry VI* (1.2.63) as a more likely source (Eleanor: 'Were I a man, a duke' [Knowles, p. 23]). But (1) Eleanor's line, unlike Lady Macbeth's and Beatrice's, does not have 'melt' in its local context, (2) Knowles does not provide the 'conclusive' (e.g. p. 22) or 'completely convincing' (p. 19) evidence that he demands from other critics. Eleanor's line existed '*possibly* before *Leir* was written' (italics added, p. 23). The most important point is that, even if Shakespeare was his own source here, McNeal is still correct in arguing for a 'surprising' link between two such different women.

[13] McNeal, 'Shakespeare's Cruel Queens', *Huntington Library Quarterly*, 22 (1958), pp. 47–9. Jacqueline Pearson, '*Much Ado About Nothing* and *King Leir*', *Notes and Queries*, 226 (April, 1981), pp. 128–9, supports McNeal. Knowles disagrees with both critics ('How Shakespeare Knew *King Leir*', p. 23).

[14] Cf. Philip Hobsbaum on Shakespeare's power to recognize affinities 'in works which, to a more superficial gaze, would seem disparate'. Hobsbaum, 'Shakespeare's Handling of His Sources', in *Tradition and Experiment in English Poetry*, ed. Philip Hobsbaum (Totowa, NJ, 1979), pp. 89–125; p. 89.

daughter are finally reunited and compete almost comically with each other in kneeling for forgiveness (scene 24).[15] Shakespeare cut most of the kneeling in *King Lear* itself (*King Lear*, 4.7.57–9), but he included a *Leir*-like excess of it earlier, in his *Richard II* (1595). There he even calls attention to the kneeling, as if in a metadramatic allusion to old-fashioned plays like *Leir*.[16] There the Duke and Duchess of York compete for Bolingbroke's attention, each ostentatiously kneeling to ask that he save (the Duchess) or condemn (the Duke) their son, who is also kneeling. Exasperated, Bolingbroke says wryly, 'Our scene is altered from a serious thing, / And now changed to "The Beggar and the King"' (*Richard II*, 5.3. 90–6, 77–8).[17] True, as Knowles complains, kneeling as an isolated phenomenon is 'an ubiquitous piece of stage business' that in itself 'can hardly show dependence of one particular play on another' (p. 25). But kneeling in the context of *Richard II* is hardly ubiquitous in the period's drama. It is a very special case of kneeling, quite unlike the ordinary sort that was a part of sixteenth-century daily life on-stage and off: (1) there is more than one kneeler, (2) the kneeling is inappropriate because of the characters' rank and social context, (3) the kneeling is made into a competition and, most of all, (4) it is excessive enough that Bolingbroke comments on it.[18]

Two scenes in *Leir* that show Cordella's banishment earlier have also left traces in the plays. Cordella wanders, exiled and destitute (7. 698–706), while, as the audience knows, the disguised Gallian king is crossing the sea and is about to court her (scenes 4, 7). These scenes are first echoed in *1 Henry VI*, as noted above, when French Margaret, like Cordella not yet queen, is seen from English Suffolk's admiring point of view.[19] The courtship scenes are also echoed in *The Merchant of Venice* (1596), when Bassanio courts Portia. She is another multifaceted woman like Margaret,[20] the most desirable of wives – fair, rich and virtuous – but also an 'unruly woman' who demands that Bassanio 'give and hazard all [he has]' (*Merchant*, 2.7.9) to court her, and later threatens adultery or worse if he betrays her. (Bassanio would rather cut off his hand than admit he has lost Portia's ring [*Merchant*, 5.1.177–8]).[21] Echoes of the *Leir* courtship help establish Portia's innocent side or at least suggest that Shakespeare was trying to establish one, although they can seem ironic in her play as they never did in *King Leir*.

---

[15] George Steevens, ed., *Twenty of the Plays of Shakespeare*, 4 vols. (1766), vol. 1, p. 16, cited by Knowles, 'How Shakespeare Knew *King Leir*', who accepts the evidence for similarities between *Leir* and *Lear*, pp. 13–17.

[16] Jacqueline Pearson, 'The Influence of *King Leir* on *Richard II*', *Notes and Queries*, 227 (April, 1982), 113–14. Knowles dismisses the *Leir/R2* parallels as 'commonplace' and 'unremarkable', and emphasizes the differences between the two scenes ('How Shakespeare Knew *King Leir*', p. 24). Knowles also dismisses a parallel (*Richard II*, 5.3. and *Leir*, scene 19) suggested in my *Shakespeare the Actor*, p. 285 (pp. 24–25).

[17] Perrett, 'The Story of King Lear', p. 79. Perrett proposes that *Lear* includes metadramatic comments about the old-fashioned *Leir* play, p. 277. (Regan: 'Good sir, no more; these are unsightly tricks' [*King Lear*, 2.4.159]; Goneril: 'No more; the text is foolish' [*King Lear*, 4.2.37]; and Edmund: 'pat he comes, like the catastrophe of the old / comedy' [*King Lear*, 1.2.141–2]).

[18] Shakespeare's early attention to excessive kneeling may have contributed to the importance of kneeling in later plays such as *Measure for Measure* and *Coriolanus*. For *Coriolanus*, see Pearson, 'Influence of *King Leir* on *Richard II*', p. 11.

[19] Other possible echoes of banished Cordella suggest that her scenes were important to Shakespeare: see Henry VI after his exile (McNeal, 'Margaret', pp. 4–5) and Richard after Bolingbroke's usurpation (Pearson, 'Influence of *King Leir* on *Richard II*', p. 114). Knowles disagrees: 'no weight can be placed on the coincidence that France [i.e. the Gallian king] has a "Palmer's staff" [*King Leir*, 698] and in a different play [*2 Henry VI*, 5.1.97] York tells Henry he is fit for a palmer's staff' ('How Shakespeare Knew *King Leir*', p. 22).

[20] Perrett, 'The Story of King Lear', pp. 110–11; McNeal, 'Margaret', p. 7. Martin Mueller, citing Freud, argues for similarity (1) between *Leir*'s first scene and the 'basic donnee' in *Merchant of Venice*, and (2) between the wicked Leir sisters and Portia's dark side: Mueller, 'From *Leir* to *Lear*', *Philological Quarterly*, 73 (1994), 195–217. Knowles dismisses all claimed connections ('How Shakespeare Knew *King Leir*', pp. 25–6).

[21] Leslie Fiedler argued that Margaret and Portia embody the threatening figure of *The Stranger in Shakespeare* (New York, 1973), pp. 101–6, 112–16, 130–5. The phrase 'unruly woman' is from Karen Newman, 'Portia's Ring: Unruly Women and Structures of Exchange in *The Merchant of Venice*', *Shakespeare Quarterly*, 38 (1987), 19–33, one of many post-Fiedlerian treatments of Portia's ambiguity.

Both Bassanio and the Gallian king must cross the sea for their women, and both liken themselves to Jason voyaging for the golden fleece.[22] Both suitors travel with a comic sidekick, a libertine (Mumford in *Leir*, Gratiano in *Merchant*), whose jokes are like those of the bawdy men courting Leir's two wicked daughters.[23] Portia, meanwhile, is as devoted to her father's will as Cordella is to Leir's, although for both young women it threatens to destroy their happiness and deprive them of a husband.[24] Portia also claims to be as graciously indifferent to Morocco's complexion as Cordella is to the Gallian king's (supposed) poverty (all from scenes 4 and 7).[25]

Later moments in *Merchant* echo the *Leir* forgiveness scenes that affected *King Lear*. Portia's rescue of Antonio when he is about lose a pound of flesh (*Merchant*, 4.1) parallels Cordella's rescue of Leir when he is at the point of starvation (*King Leir*, 24. 2160–80). Both heroines are associated with nurture that rains from heaven:

Leir. Me thinks, I never ate such savory meat:
　It is a pleasant as the blessed *Manna*,
　That *raynd from heaven* among the Israelites.
　　　　　　　　　　　(*King Leir*, 24. 2201–3)

Portia. The quality of mercy is not strained,
　It droppeth as the gentle *rain from heaven*
　Upon the place beneath.　　(*Merchant*, 4.1.181–3)

Lorenzo. Fair ladies [Portia and Nerissa], you drop *manna*
　in the way
　Of starved people.　　(*Merchant*, 5.1.294–5)

Both plays also cite Medea's restoration of Jason's father, Eson, as an analogy for their happy endings, although, again, Shakespeare's echo is far more ironic than the original. These are the only plays to cite Eson until after *Merchant*'s performance in 1596:

Cordella. And may that draught be unto him, as was
　That which *old Eson* dranke, which *did renue*
　His withered age.　　(*King Leir*, 24.2188–90)

Jessica.　　　　In such a night
　Medea gathered the enchanted herbs
　That *did renew old Aeson*.　　(*Merchant*, 5.1.12–14)

Cordella restores Lear; Portia restores Antonio's 'life and living', although she inflicts collateral damage elsewhere. Finally, *Merchant*, like *Leir*, even includes a comic kneeling reunion scene between father and child. Shakespeare assigns it, more appropriately than *Leir* did, to *Merchant*'s clowns: Launcelot Gobbo fools his blind father into thinking he is dead. Then, kneeling, he restores himself to life and asks for a blessing – just to see the old man cry (*Merchant*, 2.2.46).

Why so many echoes in *Merchant*? Some of the individual echoes seem slight enough to attribute to general influence rather than a direct link to *Leir*, which seems so different in any case. But separate lines can become more significant in the context of other aspects of a play besides overt plot and morality. Here each play veers close to fairytale, or fantasy as Freud called it in his essay on the two plays. Cordella begins as a helpless victim of her father's tyranny and ends by saving his life and bringing an army to restore him to the throne. Portia begins by complaining that she is subject to her father's will, 'an unlessoned girl' as she describes herself to Bassanio (*Merchant*, 3.2.159), and she ends

---

[22] Perrett, 'The Story of King Lear', p. 111; McNeal, 'Margaret', p. 7; and Mueller, 'From *Leir* to *Lear*', p. 208. Knowles dismisses the claims, citing several alternative sources ('How Shakespeare Knew *King Leir*', p. 25).

[23] Perrett, 'The Story of King Lear', notes a general similarity between *Leir*'s Mumford and Gratiano in *Merchant*, p. 111. See also an unnoticed but more extensive echo of Mumford nearer *Leir*'s heyday on the stage, in Berowne's similarly 'bad boy' complaint in Shakespeare's *Love's Labour's Lost* (1593/4) (*Love's Labour's Lost*, 1.1.33–109).

[24] *Cordella.* I will professe and vow a maydens life (*King Leir*, 7.624). *Portia.* If I live to be as old as Sibylla I will die as chaste as Diana unless I be obtained by the manner of my father's will (*Merchant*, 1.2.92–3).

[25] *Cordella.* Except my heart could love, and eye could like,
　Better then any that I ever saw,
　His great estate no more should move my mind
　　　　　　　　　　　(*King Leir*, 7.665–9)
For having thee, I shall have all content
　　　　　　　　　　　(*King Leir*, 7.698–706)

Portia. Yourself, renowned Prince, then stood as fair
　As any comer I have looked on yet.
　　　　　　　　　　　(*Merchant*, 2.1.13–21)

by saving the life of Bassiano's paternal benefactor, Antonio. Both plays nod towards their primitive original with their overt romance elements. King Leir's riddling test for his three daughters ('Who loves me most?'), along with the Gallian king's voyage to choose among the same three daughters, are like the folktale courtship imposed by Portia's father, with its three caskets and their three riddles.[26] In both plays a simple fairytale moral marks the correct choice. Cordella's plain speech is better than her sisters' pleasing flattery; plain lead is better than gold, and giving and hazarding are better than getting what you want or deserve.

So far I have been speaking only of *Leir*'s language as a source for Shakespeare. Scholars surrounded by books tend to assume that words and verbal echoes are the gold standard for detecting influence. Knowles would even limit *Leir*'s influence to the printed rather than the spoken word. But words are only one part of theatre and those who worked in a three-dimensional medium would have been influenced by dramatic actions, props, exits and entrances as well. The Queen's Men in particular, as McMillin and Maclean argue, were known for their visual effects and for making language concrete on-stage. *Leir*'s repeated begging in the forgiveness scene, already noted, is the most obvious example of an attention-getting action. In addition, a striking gesture from the murder scene in *Leir* seems to have left its own mark on *Richard III*. In *Leir*, when Leir talks his would-be assassin out of killing him, the latter drops his knife, unable to go on (*King Leir*, 19.1739–40). In *Richard III*, Anne similarly drops her sword in the midst of rebuffing Richard's courtship (*Richard III*, 1.2.186).[27] Richard had offered her the sword and asked her to choose between accepting him and killing him, a gesture as melodramatic as the one in *Leir* – as an actor like Richard would know.

As a final example of staging echoes, consider two dramatic entrance lines from *Leir*, each of which may have helped shape a dramatic entrance in Shakespearian plays. All the lines quoted are spoken by characters making a first entrance in the play – a powerful moment on stage:

Leir. Thus to our griefe the obsequies performed
  Of our *(too late) deceast* and dearest Queen ...
  ... disposing of our princely daughters,
  For whom our care is specially imployd,
  As nature bindeth to advaunce their states,
  In royall marriage with some princely mates:
          (*King Leir*, 1.3–11)

Claudius. Though yet of Hamlet our dear brother's *death*
  The memory be green ...
  ... our sometime sister, now our queen, ...
  Have we ...
  Taken to wife.   (*Hamlet*, 1.2.1–14)[28]

Gallian King. Disswade me not, my Lords, I am resolv'd,
  This next fair wynd to sayle for Brittany,
          ... to see if flying fame
  Be not too prodigall in the wonderous prayse
  Of these *three* Nymphes, the *daughters* of King *Leir*.
          (*King Leir*, 4.343–7)

Baptista. Gentlemen, *importune me no farther*,
  For how *I firmly am resolv'd* you know;
  That is, not to bestow *my youngest daughter*
  Before I have a husband for *the elder*.
          (*Shrew*, 1.1.48–51)

On the basis of verbal similarity alone, the parallels can be debated and Knowles has debated the latter. But when considered in dramatic context, the likeness in each pair is foregrounded: in the first, between two kings each entering soon after a funeral while announcing a somewhat problematic marriage and, in the second, between a suitor's entry line refusing debate about his decision to win one of three daughters and a father's entry line refusing debate about his decision to marry off one daughter before the other. Even at the distance

---

26 Sigmund Freud, 'The Theme of Three Caskets', in *On Creativity and the Unconscious* (New York, 1958), pp. 61–75; Vera M. Jiji, 'The Influence of Unconscious Factors upon Theme and Characterization in *The Merchant of Venice*', *Literature and Psychology*, 26 (1976), pp. 5–15, 10); Mueller, 'From *Leir* to *Lear*', p. 208.

27 Law, '*Leir* and *RIII*', p. 135.

28 Perrett, 'The Story of King Lear'; Mueller, 'From *Leir* to *Lear*', pp. 205–6. Knowles disagrees, citing 'inaccuracies' in arguments about echoes and pointing out other differences between the *Leir* and *Hamlet* scenes ('How Shakespeare Knew *King Leir*', pp. 26–7).

of four hundred years, audiences can see for themselves that the Queen's Men's strength lay in action together with their words. Shakespeare would have known it too and he seems to have learned from both kinds of example.

I end by returning to Shakespeare's most extended use of *Leir*, when he returned to rewrite it all in *King Lear*. Here the relevant context for individual *Leir* echoes extends even beyond the bounds of the old play itself to include other Queen's Men plays. In *King John*, as noted earlier, Shakespeare's echo of *Leir* accompanied wholesale borrowing from Acts 1–3 of *Troublesome Reigne*. In *King Lear* the *Leir* borrowings are paired with material from the Queen's Men's *Selimus*, which had been on stage at about the same time. The latter, if noted at all in discussions of *Lear*, has been categorized as a secondary source, which contributed to the scene in which Gloucester is blinded, as was Bajazet's servant Aga in *Selimus*.[29] But *Lear*'s debt to *Selimus* includes much more than the blinding. In fact it may have been the conjunction between these two Queen's Men's plays that shaped Shakspeare's unique version of the old Leir story.

Selimus is about a bad son's mistreatment of his father as *King Leir* is about a father's mistreatment of his daughter. Selimus is the youngest son of the weak Turkish emperor Bajazet, son of the Bajazeth who was infamously caged by Tamburlaine. *Selimus*'s Prologue promises that we will see the wicked son 'pursue / His wretched father with remorselesse spight' (*Selimus*, Pro. 6–7), and the rest of the play more than fulfils his promise. Selimus crushes everyone in his way to the throne, brothers as well as father, strewing bodies and parts of them as he does so.

Shakespeare may have echoed *Selimus* soon after it was first performed, in *Richard III*, but *Titus Andronicus* (*c.*1593) offers a more striking early parallel to *Selimus*'s violence and its effect on the character Bajazet.[30] The horrible sequence of physical and psychic mutilations that Titus confronts in his play resembles the horror that Bajazet endured. First, the bodies of Bajazet's niece and nephew are brought to him by his 'Bemangled and dismem-

bred' commander (*Selimus*, 1237), who reports that Bajazet's (other bad) son, Acomat, killed them. The emperor is stunned:

Bajazet. How shall I mourne, or which way shall I turne
   To powre my teares ...   (*Selimus*, 1252–3)

So too Titus when he sees his mutilated daughter Lavinia:

Titus.   what shall I do
   Now I behold thy lively body so?
                 (*Titus Andronicus*, 3.1.104–5)

Then when Bajazet sends his beloved servant, Aga, to plead with Acomat, the son tears out Aga's eyes, chops off both his hands and tucks them into Aga's bosom to carry back with him to Bajazet. Now the emperor is beyond stunned:

Aga. Why is my soveraign silent all this while? ...
Bajazet. Bajazet Aga, faine would weepe for thee,
   But cruell sorow drieth up my teares.
                (*Selimus*, 1422–7)

So too Titus, after he sends his self-amputated hand in promised exchange for his two imprisoned sons – and receives only his sons' bleeding heads in return.

Marcus. Now is a time to storm. Why art thou still? ...
Titus. Why? I have not another tear to shed.
        (*Titus Andronicus*, 3.1.262, 265)

Both men cherish the mangled victims:

Bajazet. Come, mournfull *Aga*, come and sit by me ...
   Give me thy arm; though thou hast lost thy hands,
   And liv'st as a poore exile in this light,
   Yet hast thou wonne the heart of *Bajazet*.
           (*Selimus*, 1508, 1511–13)[31]

---

29 The argument for *Selimus* as the source for the blinding scene in *King Lear* has been well made by Inga-Stina Ekeblad, *Notes and Queries*, 4 (May, 1957), 193–4, and Clifford J. Ronan, *Notes and Queries*, n.s., 33 (September, 1986), 360–2.

30 As is so often the case, claims about the relation between two plays can be only as certain as the dates, which are not reliable. I assume here that *Selimus* came first.

31 Assuming that *Selimus* came first, resemblances before *Titus* include the fact that both Selimus and Richard III cheerfully draw up lists of those who must be eliminated on their way

Titus. Gentle Lavinia, let me kiss thy lips
　Or make some sign how I may do thee ease.
　　　　　　　　　(*Titus Andronicus*, 3.1.120–1)

But both also call for revenge:

Belierbey. Farewell deare Emperour and revenge our
　losse ... [*He dies.*]
Bajazet. Avernus jawes and loathsome *Taenarus* ...
　Send out thy furies from thy firie hall.
　　　　　　　　　(*Selimus*, 1242, 1244, 1248)

Titus. Then which way shall I find Revenge's cave?
　　　　　　　　　(*Titus Andronicus*, 31.1.269)

The echoes are not exact, the sequence of Bajazet's responses is rearranged, and – a Shakespearian touch – it is Titus's daughter who is mutilated rather than his servant. But it is difficult to believe that two of the most violent plays of the 1580s and 1590s are not related. After this, Shakespeare does not seem to have returned to *Selimus* until writing *King Lear*.

　　There he confronted the pieties of the Queen's Men's *Leir* with the Marlovian and narcissistic impiety of *Selimus*, using one old play for the *Lear* family story and the other for the Gloucester family history. The Gloucester plot, we know, was partly modelled on the story of the blind king of Paphlagonia in Sidney's *Arcadia*. There the king's good son cares for the father who had rejected him, just as Edgar helps Gloucester. But Sidney accounts for only the second part of the play. The Paphlagonians provided no material for the first part of *King Lear*, in which Edmund announces his villainy and initiates his attack. For these Shakespeare turned to *Selimus*. Edmund's opening soliloquy borrows heavily from Selimus's first speech, in which he announces his godless Machiavellianism and mocks the piety in others:

　　Let *Mahounds* lawes be lockt up in their case,
　　And meaner men and of a baser spirit,
　　In vertuous actions seeke for glorious merit
　　　　　　　　　(*Selimus*, 174–6)

Like Edmund, Selimus rationalizes his behaviour:

　　I wreake not of their foolish ceremonies,

　　But meane to take my fortune as I finde
　　　　　　　　　(*Selimus*, 200–1)

　　I am a Prince, and though your yoonger sonne,
　　Yet are my merits better than both theirs
　　　　　　　　　(*Selimus*, 559–60)

And he sums up his case in words that might serve as Edmund's motto: 'Since he is so unnatural to me, / I will proove as unnatural as he' (*Selimus*, 485–6).[32] In addition to borrowing from Selimus's wicked son for *Lear*'s Edmund, Shakespeare, not surprisingly, also borrows from scenes about the suffering and humiliation of Selimus's father, Bajazet. Comparing Selimus's and another son's wickedness to that of a third son, for example, Bajazet indulges in a painful, Lear-like calculus:

　　But *Coecut* numbreth not my dayes as they;
　　O how much dearer loves he me then they!
　　　　　　　　　(*Selimus*, 957–8)

　Lear. Thy fifty yet doth double five and twenty,
　　And thou art twice her love.
　　　　　　　　　(*King Lear*, 2.2.433–9)

Shakespeare seems also to have noticed smaller details that he later elaborated in *King Lear*. Bajazet's cry, for example,

　　But *thou, like to a craftie Polipus* [i.e. cuttlefish],
　　Doest turne thy hungry jawes upon thy selfe;
　　For what am I *Selimus* but thy selfe?
　　　　　　　　　(*Selimus*, 525–7)[33]

---

to the crown (*Selimus*, 170–97, 299–306, 332–48, 1606–42, 1321–31; *Richard III*, 1.1.32–41, 149–51 161–2). After *Titus* they include: (1) Bajazet, like Richard II, handing over a physical crown that has been already lost (*Selimus*, 1586–91) – something that Marlowe may have noticed before Shakespeare did; (2) *Selimus*'s braggart soldier, Bullthrimble, has been cited as a possible source for Falstaff (*Selimus*, 1220–30); (3) Selimus, like Macbeth, sends soldiers to kill an innocent queen and her children but they, like Duncan's sons, decide to escape in separate directions.

32　Other resemblances between Selimus's and Edmund's attitude might be cited, e.g. Selimus's claim, 'For long inough the gray-beard now hath raign'd, / And liv'd at ease, while others liv'd uneath; /And now its time he should resigne his breath (*Selimus*, 302–4)

33　'Polypus' is a name for 'small fresh-water gelatinous animals', with mouths surrounded by tentacles (*OED*). In the

may have led to Albany's horrified prediction:

> It will come,
> Humanity must perforce *prey on itself*,
> Like *monsters of the deep*.
>
> (*King Lear*, 4.2.48–50)

Part of *King Lear*'s power lies in its presentation of both sides of the conflict between parents and children.[34] The *Leir* play alone was one-sided and piously unambiguous: Leir banishes his innocent daughter and rewards her evil sisters. He errs and Cordella forgives; he is wrong and she is right. *Selimus* alone was equally clear: Selimus wrongs his innocent father; he is wrong and Bajazet is right. In each the moral 'lesson' is obvious. Already in some earlier responses to *Leir* and *Selimus*, Shakespeare had begun to muddy the moral simplicity of the Queen's Men's characters. He blended good and evil daughters in a single figure, first Margaret in *1 Henry VI* and then in Portia. He made Titus, unlike Bajazet, partly responsible for the mutilation of his beloved followers. Far more extensively in *King Lear*, he made both sides sinning and both sinned against, with no one to blame except 'nature'.

Not all the parallels proposed here between Shakespeare's and the Queen's Men's plays will satisfy a soul hot for certainties. But together the mass of plausible connections is impressive. This is especially true given that the Queen's Men's plays, unlike those of Marlowe and Kyd that Shakespeare so often echoed in his early years, do not seem noteworthy enough to have compelled his attention, unless he had been a captive audience as one of the Queen's Men. I suspect, in fact, that some of what Shakespeare borrowed from the Queen's Men's plays – perhaps much – may have been common currency elsewhere as well. We know that not only Shakespeare's but also nearly all drama in the 1580s and 1590s was, as Hardin Craig said half a century ago, a mosaic of pieces produced elsewhere.[35]

But this doesn't mean that the 'parallels' to Queen's Men's plays were not sources of a kind. Even if a Queen's Men's play was not the only possible origin for a line or gesture that came from a common tradition, it may still have been the young Shakespeare's introduction to that tradition, or it might have been the occasion for a repetition that finally caught his ear. Audiences may have identified Marlowe's or Shakespeare's version of a line or bit of business even though it took off from something they had encountered elsewhere.[36] It is not easy to locate specific origins in the echo-chamber of early Elizabethan drama. As we come to understand more about which sources Shakespeare used and how, 'a' source or even a 'primary' source becomes harder to distinguish from the period's dense network of intertextuality and inter-dramatization. I think it is time that we move away from a scientific model that limits proof to a mechanically exact verbal echo, and consider as well other forms of textual connection that are more characteristic of human minds than physical objects.

---

sixteenth century the word seems to have referred to the cuttlefish, which (supposedly) actively lured its human prey. Gascoigne refers to the 'Polipus', who 'draws in . . . ' / The dazled wights whome she (to drowne) doth like' (*Tears of Joy* [1576]). Origins for Shakespeare's monsters of the deep may depend on the same 'cluster of associations which throng up from the nether depths of consciousness' that John Livingstone Lowe cited in his study of sources for the snakes and other creatures in Coleridge's 'Ancient Mariner'. Lowe, *The Road to Xanadu: A Study in the Ways of the Imagination* (1927) (Boston, 1964), p. 68.

[34] See my 'Dragon Fathers and Unnatural Daughters: Generational Conflict in *King Lear* and Its Sources', *Comparative Drama*, 42 (2008), 121–48.

[35] Hardin Craig, 'Motivation', p. 29.

[36] Similar conditions exist among performers today. Recently, one magician accused another magician of plagiarizing 'his' version of an 'old and well-documented trick': Campbell Robertson, 'Dueling Magicians: Whose Trick Is It Anyway?' *New York Times*, 27 September, 2006, B1.

RE-COGNIZING LEONTES

ARTHUR F. KINNEY

Hamlet. My father – methinks I see my father.
Horatio. O where, my lord?
Hamlet. In my mind's eye, Horatio.

As the denouement of *The Winter's Tale* begins to unfold, we learn that, many years before, Paulina commissioned a statue of Hermione, the presumably long-dead queen of Sicilia, that with its presence will help to reconstitute the royal family. It is, the Third Gentleman reveals to the court and to us,

a piece many years in doing and now newly performed by that rare Italian master, Giulio Romano, who, had he himself eternity and could put breath into his work, would beguile Nature of her custom, so perfectly he is her ape. He so near to Hermione hath done Hermione that they say one would speak to her and stand in hope of answer (5.2.93–100).[1]

Nowhere else in this play, which so closely follows the romance of *Pandosto* by Robert Greene that it may well be a tribute to him, does fiction reach out to incorporate an authentic historic person. Why does Shakespeare make such a temporal and generic interruption and why, given this stretch, does he choose a deceased Italian artist who was far better known, in Florence and in Mantua, as a painter, architect, engineer and interior decorator than as a sculptor?

It is quite possible, of course, that Shakespeare and several members of his audience might well have known of Romano's considerable stature in his own country. He was born in Rome around 1492 and at an early age distinguished himself as a leading assistant to Raphael, filling the painter's designs and cartoons; at the death of the famous painter, Romano, at the age of twenty-eight, was chosen to complete his master's work then in progress – a vast fresco of the 'Hall of Constantine' in the Vatican consisting, along with minor matters, of four large subjects: the 'Battle of Constantine', the 'Apparition of the Cross', the 'Baptism of Constantine' and the 'Donation of Rome to the Pope'. In 1524, Romano was invited to Mantua by Duke Federico Gonzaga (both would later appear as characters in Castiglione's *Il Cortegiano*) to pursue Federico's architectural and decorative projects. In time he also drained the marshes, protecting the city of Mantua from the floods of the River Po, a remarkable feat of engineering. As an architect, he restored and decorated the Palazzo del Te, the cathedral of Mantua and a ducal palace. Later, he designed the façade of the church of St Petronius in Bologna. His greatest masterpieces in oil that remain are the 'Martyrdom of St Stephen' in Genoa, the 'Holy Family' in Dresden, the 'Mary and Jesus' now at the Louvre and the 'Madonna della Gatta' in Naples. He died in 1546. How Shakespeare knew of him is unclear; Vasari writes of Romano, whom he admired as a man who was genial, well-bred, temperate and given to fine clothes and a high standard of living, but none of this has a bearing on *The Winter's Tale*. It is far likelier, in fact, that Shakespeare knew Romano in

---

[1] Quotations from *The Winter's Tale* are taken from Frances E. Dolan's edition for The Pelican Shakespeare (New York, 1999).

quite another way, as the engraver whose sketches of sixteen positions of human fornication illustrated an erotic work by Aretino. That book was an underground sensation as it travelled through sixteenth-century England. Yet this only seems to add to the puzzle. Why would Paulina commission a pornographic artist to create a sculpture of the chaste Hermione? I want to propose that it is precisely because of Romano's scurrilous reputation as an illustrator of Aretino that Shakespeare breaks open the fiction of his play by a reference to a notorious artist whose art will have wondrous and curative power. From his initial appearance Leontes has been characterized as a man endowed with, susceptible to and reliant upon his capacious faculty of sight and it is through his sight that Paulina herself engineers the re-establishment of the royal family. As we shall see, Paulina's plan, and Romano's various reputations, have been prepared for from the outset.

II

The *Winter's Tale* is a late play – as intellectual as *Hamlet*, say, but less given to soliloquy while still centring on the actions of seeing, thinking and knowing. We are helped to understand the thoughts and behaviour of Leontes because of the enormous advances in cognitive science, neurology and psycholinguistics in the past thirty years. But such matters take us into Shakespeare, not away from him. He understood human nature much as we do and, in cognitive terms, not much has changed. 'The human brain evolved to its fully modern form well over 100,000 years ago,' Richard F. Thompson and Stephen A. Madigan have recently written; 'No changes in brain structure or organization have occurred for a very long time.'[2] The mind of Leontes, of Shakespeare and of Shakespeare's audiences would have been operationally correlative, and someone as observant of human nature as Shakespeare was quite capable of drawing a character like Leontes that would act and react in ways that current cognitive specialists

are now exploring. He fashions Leontes as a character who depends largely on his own sight – on what he sees, on what he thinks he sees, and on what he recalls in his 'mind's eye' at the time when, the art historian Stuart Clark tells us, the age was characterized by 'ocularcentrism'.

A kind of ocularcentrism was already prevalent in sixteenth – and seventeenth – century European culture... The very opening in Aristotle's *Metaphysics* spoke of love of the senses, 'above all others the sense of sight,' preferred because it 'makes us know and brings to light many differences between things.' Plato's *Timaeus* was equally favorable, describing sight as 'the source of the greatest benefit' to men by 'enabling them to grasp number, time, and philosophy,' 'than which no greater good ever was or will be given by the gods to mortal man [*Metaphysics* 80a; *Timaeus* 46].'[3]

So in *The Arte of Rhetorique* (1553), Thomas Wilson writes that of all man's senses 'the eye sight is most quicke, and conteineth the impression of things more assuredly' (116). In his *Breviary of the Eyes* (1622), the ocularist Richard Banister notes that 'The eye is the sunne of this little work' (sig. B1) that excelled for 'the certainty of the apprehension' (sig. A12v), while Helkiah Crooke sees the body as a castle and the eyes as 'Centinels or Scout-watches in the top of the Towre, whence they may discerne farther off' (*Microcosmographia*, 1616, 530). But sight was not only outward; it was a powerful inward force as well. According to Juan Luis Vives in his essentially Artistotelian *De Anima et Vita* (1538), sight provided 'an image of things imprinted on the mind as in a mirror',[4] announcing a commonplace trope for the next two centuries. 'We were, fair queen', Polixenes tells Hermione of his childhood with Leontes,

2 Richard F. Thompson and Stephen A. Madigan, *Memory: The Key to Consciousness* (Princeton, 2005), p. 212.

3 Stuart Clark, *Vanities of the Eye: Vision in Early Modern European Culture* (Oxford, 2007), p. 9.

4 Quoted in Debora Shuger, 'The "I" of the Beholder: Renaissance Mirrors and the Reflexive Mind', in *Renaissance Culture and the Everyday*, ed. Patricia Fumerton and Simon Hunt (Philadelphia, 1999), p. 33.

Two lads that thought there was no more behind
But such a day tomorrow as today,
And to be boy eternal...
We were as twinned lambs that did frisk i' th' sun,
And bleat one at th' other.   (1.2.63–6, 68–9)

Their fundamental twinship is what he primarily recalls.

Such observations by Shakespeare's contemporaries likewise have antique pedigrees. Lucretius writes that 'What we see with the mind is similar to what we see with the eyes,' but this physical process is accompanied by a mental process: 'The first question is why each person's mind immediately thinks of the very thing that he has formed a desire to think of. Do the images observe our will, so that as soon as we form the wish the images impinge on us, whether our desire be to think of sea, land or sky?' (*On the Nature of Things*, Book IV).[5] Polixenes is, however, quite aware that what we thought we saw then is not necessarily what we know now:

              We knew not
The doctrine of ill-doing, nor dreamed
That any did. Had we pursued that life,
And our weak spirits ne'er been higher reared
With stronger blood, we should have answered heaven
Boldly 'Not guilty', the imposition cleared
Hereditary ours.   (1.2.70–6)

It is otherwise with Leontes, who seems fixated on a boyhood companionship that cannot be severed, a paired presence that should not be broken.

Leontes.   Stay your thanks a while
   And pay them when you part.
Polixenes.   Sir, that's tomorrow.
   I am questioned by my fears of what may chance
   Or breed upon our absence, that may blow
   No sneaping winds at home to make us say,
   'This is put forth too truly'. Besides, I have stayed
   To tire your royalty.
Leontes.   We are tougher, brother,
   Than you can put us to't.
Polixenes.   No longer stay.
Leontes. One sev'night longer.
Polixenes.   Very sooth, tomorrow.
Leontes. We'll part the time between's then, and in that
   I'll no gainsaying.   (1.2.10–20)

Polixenes's position is given linguistic weight although he has no evidence there is trouble at home; he enlists facts to counter the image Leontes has of their unending companionship. Leontes is holding to an image partly insinuated by Polixenes – 'fears', 'breed' and newly combining them. In both their cases as in ours, reality is made by the mind.

Indeed, such reinterpretation, once unmoored from the present conversation may, for Diogenes Laertius, pass through the mind into the imagination and even into 'dream-impressions'.[6] We can make our eyes lie. Polixenes and Hermione talk of the present as the present, under current conditions, which helps to explain why Hermione can find the means to persuade Polixenes to stay a bit longer in Sicilia, while Leontes replaces the present situation with his strong memories of a childhood friendship that did not encounter separation. In *De Memoria*, Aristotle talks of the 'objective thing' being displaced by 'a picture' or 'a likeness' or a 'representation' by which a mental impression and desire are secured. According to their now classical study of *The Way We Think*, Gilles Fauconnier and Mark Turner address Leontes's cognitive situation. 'How we apprehend one thing *as one thing* has come to be regarded as a central problem of cognitive neuroscience, called the "binding problem",' they write; 'We do not ask ourselves how we can see one thing as one thing because we assume that the unity comes from the thing itself, not from our mental work.'[7] The one overriding thing for Leontes is the inseparableness of his friendship with Polixenes, beginning in their shared childhood. It is something he must restore. It is not something which is threatened in his mind at this point by the intervention of Hermione on his behalf, because she has no part in the preservation of his

---

5 My text is from A. A. Lang and D. N. Sedley, *The Hellenic Philosophers: Translations of the Principal Sources, with Philosophical Commentary* (Cambridge, 1987), p. 75

6 Diogenes Laertius, 14F2: Lang and Sedley, *The Hellenic Philosophers*, p. 77.

7 Gilles Fauconnier and Mark Turner, *The Way We Think: Conceptual Blending and the Mind's Hidden Complexities* (New York, 2002), p. 8.

understanding of his relationship with Polixenes. In Shakespeare's dramatization of the first stage of Leontes's epistemology, the king of Sicilia fails to distinguish between what the philosophers of phenomenology call autonomous (the situation) and the heteronomous (the interpreted situation). In his mind's eye, Leontes prolonging the presence of Polixenes at first has nothing at all to do with Hermione.

III

'We do not see what we sense,' Tor Nørretranders tells us; 'We see what we think we sense.'[8] The matter of seeing is really a matter of thinking. 'When we talk of "seeing",' write Paul M. Matthews and Jeffrey McQuain, 'we are not speaking of eyes at all; we are speaking of an activity of the brain. The brain activity in "seeing" occurs specifically in the primary visual cortex, which is found in a thin rim of gray matter at the back of the brain along with the inner surface of each hemisphere. As in other areas of the brain, the neurons in the visual cortex and their organization are highly specialized.'[9] The human retina contains roughly 126 million rods and cones, photoreceptors that sense the wavelength and intensity of light and convert these data into neural impulses, a language that the brain can understand. The retina does not process all of the light it receives; that would be overpowering. Rather, it selects the data it wishes to process, allowing less than 10 per cent to pass through to the brain. Such selectivity helps us to see better and the brain to process more comprehensively. Still, our initial vision has certain limitations. We see, first of all, only what is in front of our eyes; we do not experience vividly objects or actions that are peripheral. We see surfaces, not depths. We see in two, not three dimensions. And we see from a certain perspective – both from a certain distance and from a certain angle.[10] From the start, then, the brain is a selective, not a recording or instructional system. It is stochastic and epigenetic – that is, strongly influenced by the fact that neurons that fire together wire together.[11] Data first enter a short-term memory system which may be reinforced by what is known as a working memory,

and that, when frequently employed, is transferred to a long-term memory. Since the brain's data are not arranged logically but by (repeated) patterns of recognition, Leontes's long-term memory of his association with Polixenes is stubbornly forceful in his memory.

Disruption of this hard-wired long-term memory can be jolting. Horatio refers to this some time before Hamlet talks to him when he tells Bernardo and Marcellus that the sudden appearance of King Hamlet's ghost is 'A mote . . . to trouble the mind's eye' (1.1.112). At the crucial moment of disturbance, when the common belief that 'seeing is believing' is displaced by that of 'looks are deceiving', the mind scrambles to accommodate new information which challenges long-held belief. That sudden disturbance throws Leontes off balance too.

Leontes.   Is he won yet?
Hermione. He'll stay, my lord.[12]
Leontes.   At my request he would not.
              (1.2.87–8)

This sudden reversal throws Leontes's singular perspective of Polixenes into one that is anamorphic. Like the anamorphic portrait of nine-year-old Edward VI hanging in the privy gallery at Whitehall where Shakespeare's company performed, Leontes's mind views Polixenes from two independent viewpoints which cannot be accessed together. He is both an old friend and one who listens to entreaties from Hermione rather than from himself. At such moments, the brain races

---

8 Tor Nørretranders, *The User Illusion: Cutting Consciousness Down to Size*, trans. Jonathan Sydenham (New York, 1998), p. 186. This paragraph is taken from Arthur F. Kinney, *Shakespeare and Cognition* (London, 2006), p. 16.

9 Paul M. Matthews and Jeffrey McQuain, *The Bard on the Brain* (New York, 2003), p. 44.

10 The observations in this paragraph are drawn from Michael S. Gazzaniga, *The Mind's Past* (Berkeley, 1988), p. 86, and Steven Pinker, *How the Mind Works* (New York, 1997), pp. 257, 243.

11 Gerald M. Edelman, *Second Nature: Brain Science and Human Knowledge* (New Haven, 2006), p. 55.

12 Shakespeare customarily resorts to monosyllables to accentuate lines.

to reorganize data which it transmits by replacing the neural pathway worn to rapid use by repetition to form a new pathway to accommodate new sensations from fresh observations. Since Leontes has no instant way of changing his understanding of Polixenes as he did not anticipate his change in behaviour, much as he desired it, he is keenly watchful, perhaps too keenly watchful, for unanticipated clues that will explain this unanticipated situation. What he sees, or what he thinks he sees, or what his mind's eye projects, is a new relationship between Hermione and Polixenes that is consonant with her persuasive powers and inconsonant with past behaviour.

Leontes.   Too hot, too hot!
To mingle friendship far is mingling bloods.
I have *tremor cordis* on me. My heart dances,
But not for joy, not joy. This entertainment
May a free face on, derive a liberty
From heartiness, from bounty, fertile bosom,
And well become the agent. 'T may, I grant.
But to be paddling palms and pinching fingers,
As now they are, and making practiced smiles
As in a looking glass, and then to sigh, as 'twere
The mort o' th' deer – O, that is entertainment
My bosom likes not.   (1.2.109–20)

Such an aside would seem to be out of a current textbook illustration in cognition. Working from the chief concern ('friendship') which overrides all else, and transferring the object of that concern from himself to his wife, Leontes builds on a false premise that can sufficiently explain Polixenes's change of heart. To make synonymous the newly formulated 'mingling' as something which transfers from 'friendship' to 'bloods' reveals the kind of insecurity that can result from something alien and inexplicable. We will never know how this scene was first staged – whether the two were holding hands, paddling palms, pinching fingers, or whether Leontes's strained ability to make sense of what he sees is imposing his mind's eye. But in a sense this does not matter; what matters is that he is collecting evidence he witnesses by sight – his instantaneous perception – with a cluster of associated concerns: *friendship, blood, liberty, heartiness, fertility* all in *seeming smiles*

('practiced smiles') that reflect back on Polixenes and Hermione his own sense of partnership – 'As in a looking glass'. What seems to hold together the scattered thoughts here is that Leontes's boyhood friend – his twinned lamb – has displaced him altogether and that Polixenes's concession to join Hermione (rather than Leontes) is to reconstitute marriage in a way which isolates, diminishes, and defeats Leontes. This entertainment is a new narrative, a new disposition – a new play in which paddling palms and practised smiles are the chief gestures. That an entertainment can be short-lived, may not be a new establishment, suggests Leontes's own uncertainty; and so, it would seem, is the death of the deer, the conclusion to which this passage first builds (the second conclusion, an address to Mamillius, we shall consider shortly). Such a death may figuratively relate to Leontes but it may also find its referent in the death of his association with Hermione or the death of the new remarriage between his wife and his childhood friend. It is customary for a mind jolted out of a long-established idea (or image) to resort to ambiguity rather than to a final and decisive new interpretation.

Such events as Leontes sees, and such images and ideas he has as reactions, are cognitively traumatic. Intense anxiety results in such situations, we are told by cognitive scientists, and the consequence is usually a mixture of fear and anger. What Leontes is doing here is reading the situation as we in turn are reading the situation and reading him. Scholars such as Ellen J. Esrock, author of *The Reader's Eye*, have applied the relatively new studies of the theories of mind to the act of reading. For her, 'men and women should be distinguished in terms of their tendencies to read themselves into texts with accompanying visualization'.[13] For her, imaging can produce new semantic values, while for us they can also disclose Leontes's mental processes. Such imaging as his choice of words reveals concentrates heavily on involving him – on his searching for a role in the new script. The liberty initially enjoyed by the two perceived lovers really

[13] Ellen J. Esrock, *The Reader's Eye: Visual Imaging as Reader Response* (Baltimore, 1994), p. 186.

settles in new rather fixed roles for the three of them. For Esrock, this is one reaction to the traumatic denial of Leontes's long-lived expectations. Another is the need to reassert control. Having lost all bearing through surprise and reversal, Leontes must find a way to right wrongs, to reassert stability. One way is to reposition the people involved. Another is to take charge, to assert unmitigated authority. Esrock's third reaction is voyeurism – the first impulsive reaction Leontes has. And the final reaction is to readdress the situation and its participants in a way that will make the situation more comprehensible (186–93). The frames of reference which lie at the heart of all of our thinking, according to Fauconnier and Turner, need to be changed; Leontes's neural pathways need to be reinstated and redistributed. Leontes will try all four possibilities: he has already repositioned Hermione, Polixenes and himself; he has already had voyeuristic thoughts. Now he will try to readdress the situation to make it more understandable and, when that fails, he will try tyrannical control.

IV

Leontes's necessity to deal with a new conception – a reconception – is not something new for Shakespeare. Hamlet's situation may be one that comes readily to mind, but Shakespeare has also worked out such a situation in more obvious detail with Cressida in the Greek camp following the departure of Diomedes.

Cressida. Good night. I prithee, come.
  Troilus, farewell. One eye yet looks on thee,
  But with my heart the other eye doth see.
  Ah, poor our sex! This fault in us I find,
  The error of our eye directs our mind.
  What error leads must err. O, then conclude
  Minds swayed by eyes are full of turpitude.[14]

Her fundamentally anamorphic attitude towards Diomedes and Troilus is echoed almost at once by Troilus himself in a passage that anticipates Leontes:

Troilus. Sith yet there is a credence in my heart,
  An esperance so obstinately strong,
  That doth invert th'attest of eyes and ears,

As if those organs had deceptious functions,
Created only to calumniate.
Was Cressid here? . . .
This she? No, this is Diomed's Cressida.
If beauty have a soul, this is not she;
If souls guide vows, if vows be sanctimonies,
If sanctimony be the gods' delight,
If there be rule in unity itself,
This was not she. O madness of discourse,
That cause sets up with and against itself;
Bifold authority, where reason can revolt
Without perdition, and loss assume all reason
Without revolt. This is and is not Cressid.

(5.2.122–7, 140–9)

Cressida's attempt to harness both eye and heart, like Troilus's bifold authority of beauty and soul, are unstable alternatives which cannot be reconciled. Such destabilization characterizes Leontes before his sight of Hermione going off-stage with Polixenes. Hermione's betrayal – Leontes's sight of her disappearance with Polixenes paddling palms; the evidence of things *seen* – now turns, in Leontes's mind's eye, to another betrayal that is at first anamorphic.

Leontes.   Mamillius,
  Art thou my boy?
Mamillius.   Ay, my good lord.[15]
Leontes.   I' fecks!
  Why, that's my bawcock. What, hast smutched thy
    nose?
  They say it is a copy out of mine. Come, captain,
  We must be neat – not neat but cleanly, captain.
  And yet the steer, the heifer, and the calf
  Are all called neat. – Still virginaling
  Upon his palm? – How now, you wanton calf?
  Art thou my calf?
Mamillius.   Yes, if you will, my lord. (1.2.120–8)

Mamillius is and is not Leontes's son. Leontes has only Hermione's testimony: 'Women say so, / That will say anything' (1.2.131–2). Yet unlike Cressida and Troilus, Leontes has the presence of mind still to reflect on his own misgivings.

---

[14] *Troilus and Cressida*, ed. Jonathan Crewe (New York, 2000), 5.2.108–14.

[15] This shared line is Shakespeare's appropriate forewarning of the act of blending to follow.

Leontes. No bourn 'twixt his and mine, yet were it true
  To say this boy were like me. Come, sir page,
  Look on me with your welkin eye. Sweet villain!
  Most dear'st! my collop! Can thy dam? – may't be? –
  Affection, this intention stabs the center!
  Thou dost make possible things not so held,
  Communicat'st with dreams – how can this be?
  With what's unreal thou coactive art,
  And fellow'st nothing. Then 'tis very credent
  Thou may'st co-join with something; and thou dost,
  And that beyond commission, and I find it,
  And that to the infection of my brains
  And hard'ning of my brows.   (1.2.135–47)

What Cressida, Troilus and Leontes all face is the need for conceptual realignment, what Fauconnier and Turner term *blending*. Faced with two incompatible frames of reference, the mind attempts to blend them into a new conceptualization. 'Complex blending is always at work in any human thought or action but is often hard to see', they comment. 'The meanings that we take for granted are those where the complexity is best hidden' (25). 'Nearly all important thinking takes place outside of consciousness and is not available on introspection; the mental feats we think of as the most impressive are trivial compared to everyday capacities; the imagination is always at work in ways that consciousness does not apprehend' (33–4). For them, blending occurs in three steps: identity of the differences or oppositions, an integration where possible and an active imagination that will determine the success of an integration that will effectively close the anamorphic view into one acceptable concept (6). Leontes is enabled to blend the thoughts of Hermione as the true mother of Mamillius and himself as father in the comparison of Mamillius and himself:

Leontes.   Looking on the lines
  Of my boy's face, methoughts I did recoil
  Twenty-three years, and saw myself unbreeched,
  In my green velvet coat, my dagger muzzled
  Lest it should bite its master and so prove,
  As ornaments oft do, too dangerous.
  How like, methought, I then was to this kernel,
  This squash, this gentleman. Mine honest friend,
  Will you take eggs for money?   (1.2.154–62)

The mental blending of the boyish appearances of Leontes and Mamillius makes possible the boy's legitimacy: 'So stands this squire / Officed with me' (1.2.171–2). Hermione's response, however, seems to confirm Leontes's suspicions: 'If you would seek us, / We are yours i' th' garden' (1.2.177–8), and although she invites Leontes to join them his doubts are sustained.

Leontes. To your own bents dispose you. You'll be found,
  Be you beneath the sky. I am angling now,
  Though you perceive me not how I give line.
                                          (1.2.179–81)

Reconciled to his son, he is far from reconciled to his wife. 'Go play, boy, play. Thy mother plays, and I / Play too, but so disgraced a part, whose issue / Will hiss me to my grave. Contempt and clamour / Will be my knell. Go play, boy, play' (1.2.187–90). What identity, integration and imagination work for Mamillius will not work for the child Hermione carries in her womb.

V

Leontes's final choice in responding to his sense of marital betrayal is to turn his vengeance on Hermione and Polixenes. His own reputation, his own self-respect, his own ability to rule are weighing in the balance.

Leontes.   Ha' not you seen, Camillo –
  But that's past doubt, you have, or your eye-glass
  Is thicker than a cuckold's horn – or heard –
  For to a vision so apparent rumor
  Cannot be mute – or thought – for cogitation
  Resides not in that man that does not think –
  My wife is slippery?   (1.2.267–73)

His visual awareness – his powers of sight, his mind's eye – is now fused with the thought of adultery. A spiced cup can, Camillo argues, 'work / Maliciously like poison' (1.2.320–1). Leontes argues this with further perceived evidence that avalanches into a widespread finality.

Leontes.   Is whispering nothing?
  Is leaning cheek to cheek? Is meeting noses?
  Kissing with inside lip? Stopping the career

Of laughter with a sigh? – a note infallible
Or breaking honesty! – horsing foot on foot?
Skulking in corners? wishing clocks more swift?
Hours, minutes? noon, midnight? and all eyes
Blind with the pin and web but theirs, theirs only,
That would unseen be wicked? Is this nothing?
Why, then the whole world and all that's in't is nothing,
The covering sky is nothing, Bohemia nothing,
My wife is nothing, nor nothing have these nothings,
If this be nothing.   (1.2.284–96)

Like his predecessor Othello, he is obsessed by the green-eyed monster and, initially, given to more tyrannical acts as king of Sicilia, plotting the death of Polixenes, the imprisonment of Hermione and denying her daughter as his own – for women know who their children's fathers are, but the fathers cannot be sure. Still Leontes is not exempt from punishment himself. Cognizance and consciousness fuse to punish him too; his alert and associative mind returns to Camillo's cup image, and his fractured mind builds on it:

Leontes.   There may be in the cup,
   A spider steeped, and one may drink, depart,
   And yet partake no venom, for his knowledge
   Is not infected; but if one present
   Th' abhorred ingredient to his eye, make known
   How he hath drunk, he cracks his gorge, his sides,
   With violent hefts. I have drunk, and seen the spider.
                            (2.1.39–45)

The earlier need for ocular proof creates it. As Stuart Clark writes, 'The thinking mind, it seems, was more responsible for what was seen than the presence or absence of objects in the visual field' (41).

   Fixated on what his mind's eye reveals to him, Leontes grows more accusatory: 'calumny will sear Virtue itself – these shrugs, these hums and ha's . . . She's an adulteress' (2.1.73–4, 8). In this, Leontes's thinking is representative. 'In the four decades either side of 1600', Clark writes,

the imagination was still essentially an internal sense (an 'inner wit') charged with the perception of absent sense objects, just as the five external senses (the 'outer wits') perceived present ones. By its particular virtue, according to a popular English account of the period, were

apprehended to the 'likenesse[s] and shapes of things of particulars received, though they bee absent'.[16] This made the early modern imagination essentially what it had been for Aristotle, who had declared canonically in *De Anima* that 'visions appear to us even when our eyes are shut'. It was still known as much by the Greek name *phantasia* ('fantasy' or 'fancy' in English) as by the Latin *imaginatio*, and the sensible forms (*species, idola,* or *similitudines*) of external things which it retained and manipulated were still called *phantasmata* (hence, 'phantasies', or 'fantasies').[17]

But for Leontes, visual matters extend to other senses, become *bodily*. The sights in the mind's eye become visceral. The hippocampus, the part of the brain that modulates learning and memory combines thought, imagination and emotion. 'You smell this business with a sense as cold / As is a dead man's nose; but I do see't and feel't' (2.1.151–2).

   Cognitively, reiterations themselves become facts through their pronouncement. Both things present to Leontes's sight – Hermione's overly familiar behaviour – and things absent, such as the flight of Polixenes and Antigonus by night, collude and confirm,

Leontes.   I have said
   She's an adulteress; I have said with whom,
   More, she's a traitor and Camillo is
   A federary with her, and one that knows
   What she should shame to know herself
   But with her most vile principal, that she's
   A bed-swerver, even as bad as those
   That vulgars give bold'st titles – ay, and privy
   To this their late escape.
                  . . . If I mistake
   In those foundations which I build upon,
   The center is not big enough to bear
   A schoolboy's top. Away with her to prison!
                            (2.1.87–95, 100–3)

Like Hamlet, Leontes thinks too precisely on the event, brought to a state then known as melancholy. As the physician Richard Napier writes in his notebook, 'Mind much troubled with false conceits

---

[16] *Batman upon Bartholome* (1582), p. 15.
[17] Clark, *Vanities of the Eye*, p. 42.

and illusions . . . Supposeth that he seeth many things which he seeth not',[18] like Macbeth's daggers of the mind. 'Melancholike folks', according to Levinus Lemnius, 'will hardly be disswaded or brought from theyr opinions, that they once lodge wythin their owne conceipts.'[19] The self-reflective Leontes knows this, too: 'Though I am satisfied and need no more / Than what I know' (2.1.189–90), his impregnable conviction can only be verified and further authorized by the oracle at Delphos. When the potentially counterfactual baby is born to Hermione, Paulina, in presenting Leontes with his new-born daughter, is abruptly dismissed as 'A mankind witch! . . . A most intelligencing bawd' (2.3.67–8). For Edward Reynolds, in *A Treatise of the Passions and Faculties of the Soule of Man* (1640), the imagination could disrupt and falsify public and private vision: 'Those strange yet strong delusions, whereby the mind of melancholy man (in whom this facultie hath the most deepe and piercing operation) have beene peremptorily possessed: Hence, those vanishing and shadowy assurances, hopes, feares, joyes, visions, which the dreames of men (the immediate issues of this facultie) do produce' (25). Such 'blacke thoughts, tremblings, and horrors' were not received 'from without, but by impression and transfusion from within' (25–6). Leontes, however, insists on erasing any distinction between private and public and calls his lords and officers to a public session, declaring: 'Let us be cleared / Of being tyrannous, since we so openly / Proceed in justice' (3.2.4–6). But the singularity of his sight denies the message: 'There is no truth at all i' th' oracle. / The sessions shall proceed. This is mere falsehood' (3.2.138–9). Four lines later, Leontes learns of the death of his unquestioned son Mamillius and this second cognitive jolt returns him at once to reality: 'Apollo's angry, and the heavens themselves / Do strike at my injustice' (3.2.144–5). It is at this juncture that Hermione swoons and the suddenly bereaved Leontes no longer commands but enquires, 'How now there?' (3.2.145). It is Paulina's turn to establish a truth of her own that is also a verdict and condemnation: 'This news is mortal to the queen. Look down / And see what death is doing' (3.2.146–7). In reply,

Leontes comes to a full awareness and demonstrates anew his love for his wife:

Leontes. Take her hence.
Her heart is but o'ercharged; she will recover.
I have too much believed mine own suspicion.
Beseech you, tenderly apply to her
Some remedies for life. (3.2.147–51)

Just as Hermione's behaviour instigated Leontes's doubts and her trial and judgement, so now her behaviour frees him from any cognitive delusions.

Leontes. Apollo, pardon
My great profaneness 'gainst thine oracle!
I'll reconcile me to Polixenes,
New woo my queen, recall the good Camillo,
Whom I proclaim a man of truth, of mercy.
(3.2.151–5)

The outer vision of events destroys entirely Leontes's sight in his mind's eye.

VI

According to Thompson and Madigan, 'The number of *possible* synaptic connections among the neurons in a single human brain may be larger than the total number of atomic particles in the known universe' (231). The actual synaptic connections which allow neural pathways that lead to conceptualization and understanding total roughly one quadrillion, all of them potentially active in our brains all of the time. This staggering figure helps to explain why memories in long-term storage are dropped over time as that part of the brain becomes more and more crowded, and why data stored in the short-term memory may be transferred to the long-term memory. Both neural activity and neural repetition, keeping the chemical and electrical charges frequently in operation, are what result

---

[18] Michael MacDonald, *Mystical Bedlam: Madness, Anxiety, and Healing in Seventeenth-Century England* (Cambridge, 1981), p. 157; quoted Clark, *Vanities of the Eye*, p. 54.
[19] Levinus Lemnius, *The Touchstone of Complexions*, trans. Thomas Newton (1576), p. 151.

in recognition, knowledge and individual understanding. These relatively recent scientific discoveries would not have been available to Leontes or to Shakespeare, but what happens throughout *The Winter's Tale* is notably in agreement with the latest scientific information.

Signals for the brain are organized into patterns – this will explain the sudden substitute pattern of infidelity that Leontes pursues mentally – and what is needed for his recovery is an acceptable pattern more attuned to reality. That recovery begins before the announced losses of Hermione and Mamillius; it begins, in fact, with Hermione herself confronting her mistaken husband at her trial.

Hermione. Sir,[20]
　You speak a language that I understand not,
　My life stands in the level of your dreams,
　Which I'll lay down.[21]
Leontes. 　　　　　Your actions are my dreams.
　You had a bastard by Polixenes,
　And I but dreamed it. As you were past all shame –
　Those of your fact are so – so past all truth,
　Which to deny concerns more than avails; for as
　Thy brat hath been cast out, like to itself,
　No father owning it – which is, indeed,
　More criminal in thee than it – so thou
　Shalt feel our justice, in whose easiest passage
　Look for no less than death.
Hermione. 　　　　　Sir, spare your threats.
　The bug which you would fright me with I seek.
　　　　　　　　　　　　　　(3.2.78–90)

Hermione has made two crucial transferences here. She has realigned Leontes's charges to dreams with which he agrees, and she further claims that such dreams have no power of fear in her. Making Leontes's charges insubstantial – a premise with which he fleetingly agrees – she returns to them as 'The bug', a bugbear or ghost, again making them insubstantial. Since neural pathways seek patterns of knowledge built on analogies, her reference, although she does not know it as we do, is an imagistic response to Leontes's spider in the cup which his own neural connections will make use of. Hermione thus not only confronts and corrects her husband, but she plants a concept which

will help him retranscribe 'dream'. In the following scene, just as 'bug' displaces 'spider', Paulina's scorn – 'O thou tyrant, / Do not repent these things, for they are heavier / Than all thy woes can stir' (3.2.205–7) – replaces Leontes's and cancels it out through reversal, while Leontes's own reply is especially revealing:

Leontes. 　　　　　Thou didst speak but well
　When most the truth, which I receive much better
　Than to be pitied of thee. Prithee, bring me
　To the dead bodies of my queen and son,
　One grave shall be for both. Upon them shall
　The causes of their death appear, unto
　Our shame perpetual. Once a day I'll visit
　The chapel where they lie, and tears shed there
　Shall be my recreation. So long as nature
　Will bear up with this exercise, so long
　I daily vow to use it. Come, and lead me
　To these sorrows. 　　　　　(3.2.230–41)

This is an especially packed speech. His agreement with Paulina's charges, his acceptance of responsibility, his desire to visit the members of his family now pronounced dead and his shame are all clear enough. But what is going on cognitively is more important: he has returned to the blending that first led him astray – the initially anamorphic vision of Hermione and Mamillius together – and secures their innocent relationship in a single grave. But the sudden neurological jolt that caused him to suspect and accuse his wife of infidelity he now replaces with a response to the announced deaths of Mamillius and then Hermione. He will displace that sudden accusation with the slow daily repetition of graveside visitations. Through habit he will establish so strong a neural pathway acknowledging their deaths and his shame that he will prepare a corrective *habitus* of mind that will be tougher than steel. That shall be his recreation (deliberately punning on re-creation).

---

[20] Shortened lines in Shakespeare may denote a special emphasis in the delivery of that line.

[21] This line is essentially ambiguous. Hermione may mean 'that I shall now rehearse', but she may also mean, 'that I will now put aside'. Examining them or not, her key word in this speech is 'dreams'.

Paulina in turn has asked for forgiveness from an unnamed Lord who has admonished her and from Leontes, alert to what she has just said. But she is also alert to what she heard Leontes say. His acknowledgement of the long-term need for healing, in order to prevent sudden shifts of perspective, in order to cure the insecurities and hidden fears that must have first initiated his outburst of jealousy, would seem to be a direction Paulina takes seriously. She will keep Hermione absent from court on the grounds of saving her for a possible reunion with Perdita; she will keep Hermione apart to allow Leontes's mind the long necessary season of recuperation.

VII

Linguistic psychology has long concerned itself with the relationship of cognition to frames of reference. What was established in Leontes's mind at the start of the play is always, even if unconsciously, part of the play's ending, the referential frame any audience would intuitively supply. This is something Leontes shares with Shakespeare's audience at *The Winter's Tale*. Returning to Leontes from a pastoral interlude, we re-establish, out of the universal framing cognizance, the man we left at the point of daily graveside mourning. Daily reiteration has kept long-ago events in the short-term memory and in the working memory and made the conceptualizations that are thus neurally activated now virtually impermeable. By keeping Hermione cognitively alive, he has prepared himself for her actual reappearance. A second preparation comes in the appearance of his long-lost daughter whom he thought dead. Her plan to marry Florizel, allying the kingdoms of Sicilia and Bohemia, establishes a historic blending, a container into which Leontes can pour his reconciliation with his childhood friend Polixenes and the future of both their children.

But we have seen that Leontes has unusual powers of sight and it is through the sight of the statue of Hermione – at first missing from Paulina's gallery as Leontes visits it for the first time along with

his daughter – that 'Her natural posture!' is seen (5.3.23):

Leontes.   O, thus she stood,
  Even with such life of majesty – warm life,
  As now it coldly stands – when I first wooed her!
                                                    (5.3.34–6)

But what he reads is no ideal hope; what he sees is a charged reality of the present: 'Hermione was not so much wrinkled' (5.3.28). Leontes is not told, in this play, that the statue is the work of Giulio Romano – in the fiction of the play that would mean nothing to him as he reads the statue – but to Shakespeare's audience, as they recognize the reference, Romano would signal two quite different possible meanings. According to Vasari, Romano was known as a fine sculptor of tombs and of finely dressed figures on them. J. H. Pafford, in his Arden edition of *The Winter's Tale*, quotes Vasari's comment that Romano was so lifelike in his painting and sculptures that he aroused the jealousy of Jupiter: 'Jupiter saw sculptured and painted statues breathe and earthly buildings made equal to those in heaven by the skill of Julio Romano.'[22] Frederick Kiefer refers to the room of giants in the Palazzo de Te, Mantua, where Romano's painting of Jupiter struggling to the heavens is especially impressive.[23] Romano's reputation, then, for such painted sculptures, scholars believe, had accompanied his reputation in England in the sixteenth century. This is one way Shakespeare's audience could react to the reference to Romano. But there is also Romano's pornographic reputation as well. Shakespeare risks the introduction of both because each viewpoint represents a stage of Leontes's thinking and places the audience in the positions Leontes has been portrayed in through his initial disparate conceptions

---

22 *The Winter's Tale*, ed. by J. H. P. Pafford (London, 1963), p. 150. I am grateful to John Mahon for bringing this passage to my attention.

23 Frederick Kiefer, *Shakespeare's Visual Theatre: Staging the Personified Characters* (Cambridge, 2003), p. 150. I have benefited from Frederick Kiefer and other members of the 2008 International Shakespeare Conference seminar on 'Ocular Encounters in Shakespeare's Late Plays' directed by Maria Delsapio, and from Brandon Shaw, who read an early draft.

of Hermione. What Leontes does at the conclusion of the play is blend his two conceptions of Hermione – the sexual adulteress, the lost wife – in the restored queen. By introducing the person of Romano to his audience, Shakespeare requires of playgoers the same experiences of women and the same act of blending that Leontes undergoes, reinforcing his transformation with its accompanying wonder and suggesting the psychology of Leontes by aligning it with that of the audience. It is one of the resources for the power of this moment of wonder. Indeed, we know that such blending is at the heart of the play because Polixenes has already made a point of this with Perdita: the necessary blending of nature and art, of the two Romanos.

> Polixenes.　　　　nature is made better by no mean
> 　But nature makes that mean. So, over that art
> 　Which you say adds to nature, is an art
> 　That nature makes. You see, sweet maid, we marry
> 　A gentler scion to the wildest stock,
> 　And make conceive a bark of baser kind
> 　By bud of nobler race. This is an art
> 　Which does mend nature – change it rather – but
> 　The art itself is nature.　　　　　　(4.4.89–97)

What neurologists now call blending, Polixenes and Perdita see as hybridity. For Polixenes, it is a matter of nature and, by extension, a matter of social class, so that in the end the marriage of Prince Florizel and Princess Perdita is also a kind of blending.

But the statue of Hermione does not come to life at once. Paulina has learned to avoid sudden jolts to Leontes's cognitive awareness. Rather, she lets him approach the statue slowly, absorbing it both in his sight and in his mind's eye in stages that he himself describes.

> Leontes.　　　　　　O royal piece,
> There's magic in thy majesty, which has
> My evils conjured to remembrance and
> From thy admiring daughter took the spirits,
> Standing like stone with thee. (5.3.38–42)

> Do not draw the curtain. (5.3.59)

> 　　　　　　Let be, let be.
> Would I were dead, but that, methinks, already –
> What was he that did make it? See, my lord,
> Would you not deem it breathed? And that those
> 　veins
> Did verily bear blood? (5.3.61–5)

> The fixture of her eye has motion in't,
> As we are mocked with art. (5.3.67–8)

> 　　　　　O, she's warm!
> If this is magic, let it be an art
> Lawful as eating.　　　　　　　(5.3.109–11)

Because it is sight, not sound, that is important in Leontes's re-cognition and because visual and mental blending of past and present is also crucial to audience perception, it is especially fitting that, when Hermione finally steps forth, she does not speak at all. Neither does Leontes; it is Polixenes and Paulina that must take up the slack. That is because it was never words – it was fully sight – that first caused Leontes's suspicions and fears to arise. The new sight corrects the old one. This is sufficient; it is also total fulfilment in what little is left of the play. Hermione speaks only to Perdita (whom she has never seen); Leontes speaks only to Paulina (for whom he provides a mate as she does for him). Language is not reduced at the conclusion of *The Winter's Tale* because it has never been the focus of attention. The heart of *The Winter's Tale*, like the basis of our brains, of all cognition, is spectacle. We still live in an ocularcentrist world.

SHAKESPEARE PERFORMANCES
IN ENGLAND 2009

CAROL CHILLINGTON RUTTER

18 January 2009. I'm in the Arts Centre at War-wick University, breathing down the necks of the men who are putting up the exhibition that's going to open in two days' time, curated by my col-league, Tony Howard. I'm getting in their way, but I hardly notice, because my whole concen-tration is on the panels they're fixing to the wall. These storyboards are telling of a life – its 'battles, sieges, fortunes', 'disastrous chances...moving accidents...hair-breadth scapes' – that's making a Desdemona of me. Headlined 'A Slave's Son at Stratford', the storyboards remember a date fifty years ago. 7 April 1959. When Paul Robeson kept an appointment at the Shakespeare Memorial Theatre.

He'd been somewhat delayed. In August 1950 the US State Department had ordered Robeson to surrender his passport. Any trip abroad 'would not be in the interests of the United States'. The UK Home Office agreed. The actor, singer, interna-tional political activist for labour, race and social equality, was, a Home Office minute from August 1950 declared, 'a nuisance'. He'd supported the Welsh miners in the 1930s (after he'd first come to London to play *Othello* in 1930); he'd 'played a leading part in the formation of the World Peace Congress' in 1949; given the chance, he would 'play a dangerous part in his capacity of Saviour of the Negro and Oppressed Colonial'. So Robe-son, stripped of his passport, was condemned to internal exile in the US. The FBI and MI5 kept him under surveillance. The House UnAmeri-can Activities Committee (HUAC) interrogated him in 1956. Blacklisted, denied work on stage

or screen, the most extraordinary voice in America was gagged. But not silenced. In 1957, spearheaded in Britain by trades unions, artists and the Left, the 'Let Paul Robeson Sing!' campaign organized an international concert in London and Wales via the transatlantic telephone cable. In November, Glen Byam Shaw, Artistic Director of the SMT, invited Robeson to play Gower in *Pericles*, and later, when the passport was again refused, *Othello*. In June 1958 the US Supreme Court finally ruled that it was unconstitutional to deny a US passport on political grounds. A month later, Robeson flew to Lon-don. He sang to millions on television and radio; became the first lay person – and first non-white – to take the pulpit in St Paul's Cathedral; revisited the USSR; and prepared *Othello*. In December, British newspapers were lining up the stars who would dazzle in the 100th Shakespeare season in Stratford. Charles Laughton would be there to play Bottom in Peter Hall's *A Midsummer Night's Dream*. Laurence Olivier would be there to play Cori-olanus with Edith Evans as Volumnia. An Ameri-can actor new to Shakespeare had been cast as Iago: Sam Wanamaker. The Royal Court's young turk, Tony Richardson, fresh from filming *Look Back in Anger*, would direct. And Paul Robeson would play Othello – the first black actor ever to play the Moor on Shakespeare's 'home' stage.

Fifty years later, whether they consciously knew it or not, that history of struggle served another generation. On the day that the first black Presi-dent of the United States was inaugurated in Wash-ington DC, in the UK, the Ghanaian-born Patrice Naiambana (who's adopted a Sierra Leonean name and the West African tools of the *griot* to address Shakespeare) opened *Othello* at Warwick, the first leg of a Royal Shakespeare Company UK tour that would have Shakespeare's play and Howard's Robeson exhibition travelling together. A couple of weeks later, at the West Yorkshire Playhouse, the Dudley-born son of immigrant Jamaican parents, the UK's best-loved stand-up comic, who'd been hiding from Shakespeare his entire life, stepped (terrified) into Robeson's shoes – and found they fitted. A critic who'd predicted 'a car crash' called Lenny Henry's Northern Broadsides's Othello 'one of the most astonishing debuts in Shakespeare' he'd ever seen – a debut a London audience got to see when the production transferred to the West End for a twelve-week sell-out run.

But the impact of Robeson's legacy on this year's work didn't end there. Its traces were felt in the Baxter Theatre Centre's *Tempest* from Cape Town that brought the legendary John Kani to Stratford; in Propeller's touring *Merchant* and *Dream*; and more distantly, in the various international initiatives that aimed to promote cultural traffic travelling east and west: Sam Mendes's 'Bridge Project' linking Brooklyn to London; and Yukio Ninagawa's Kabuki *Twelfth Night* for London's BITE festival. (Its red-laquered bridges connecting lotus to lily beds in Olivia's garden figured notional bridges connecting this production both to a contemporary Anglo-Japanese audience – an audience Robeson assiduously cultivated – and to a spectacular performance tradition that vanished in England with Irving and Beerbohm Tree.) Wherever I looked this year – at Gugu Mbatha-Raw's Ophelia, Indira Varma's Olivia, or Noma Dumezweni's Paulina; at Gruffudd Glyn's Young Shepherd or Babou Ceesay's Helena; at the ethnic diversity in the audience at the Leicester Curve's *As You Like It*; at the mobilization of children as weird sisters and gunslingers in *Macbeth* at the Royal Exchange Manchester (where the figures for a day's commodities trading, some of it in cotton, remembering Manchester's connection to plantation slavery in the American south, are preserved as a record on the wall); at a whitewashed *Antony and Cleopatra* in Bristol (another city built on the transatlantic slave trade) – I saw Paul Robeson looking back. He's the ghost who haunts this review.

COMEDIES

History may have directed my viewing this year, but Shakespeare's histories were themselves entirely absent from the repertoire, exhausted, perhaps, by last year's (and the year before's) epic cycle at the RSC. But if no history, plenty of comedy: to begin with, a trio of *Twelfth Night*s. All of them saw the play as a sea story – though one was sailing through typhoons and dodging pirates off Kyushu while the second learned the tango in a slightly dotty but terribly English remains-of-the-day seaside resort, Illyria-super-Margate. The third set the play against crumbling masonry somewhere in Albania – but contrived to bring the sea onstage.

Twelfth Night delivers some of the simplest love lines in Shakespeare, as simple as signage, but that turn out be finger-posts marking the entrance to a labyrinth, the tangled knot-garden of the undisclosed human heart: 'My father had a daughter lov'd a man'; 'I was adored once too'; 'Madam, you have done me wrong'; 'Most wonderful!' Michael Grandage's production (the signage said 'Donmar-at-Wyndhams': now there's an oxymoron) built a seaside boardwalk that, if it didn't get to the centre of this play's heart, was at least strolling in the right direction.

Wyndham's is newly restored to its 1899 François Boucher-esque chocolate-boxness, all turquoise and gilt and cherubs trailing ribbons, but that bizarre flourish of ornament was somehow the right frame for a stage that Christopher Oram seemed to have nicked out from under the original Donmar – a theatre that began life as a Covent Garden warehouse and banana ripening shed. His design, an empty expanse of dilapidated floorboards like ship's planking backed by floor-to-ceiling shutters, put us on a tramp steamer headed for the tropics. This visual prompt turned out to be a nice premonition. Grandage's production began in a storm. Orsino (Mark Bonnar) stumbled in clutching a dressing gown as though awaked by the thunder clapping overhead; then Viola

(Victoria Hamilton) pitched up in sea-green like a storm-tossed mermaid stranded above the tide line. In the morning, though, with the sun shafting through the shutters, we were in a distinctly steamy late-Edwardian Illyria (though period here was elastic: some ideas Victorian, some between wars, some 1930s).

With practically no furniture to negotiate, characters walked their stories straight onto the stage. Ron Cook's Toby Belch in damaged white tie and tails trailing crumpled streamers looked like the victim of a Christmas cracker (or perhaps the chintzy prize inside). Was he recovering from last night's drinking? Or weaving his way into today's? Whichever, he made the mistake of trying to stand and talk at the same time, discovering 'What a plague means my niece to take the death of her brother thus?' to have, at that time of the morning, far too many syllables to deal with individually. Alongside his pint-pot Belch, Guy Henry's stick-of-Brighton-rock Sir Andrew was a constant sight gag. But otherwise unencumbered by the usual funny business that hangs like an albatross around this role's neck, he was an Aguecheek of exceptional, if bewildered, dignity. Certainly a dimwit. Certainly no more hopeful a partner to Olivia than a brolly languishing in her umbrella stand. But what a voice! How did that sound get inside that ridiculous body? It was as much a mystery as how the writing gets inside the rock. (I have to admit, though, that I missed the huge fun of the cowards' combat, the Captain Spurios in this production not even measuring swords never mind taking a stab at each other.)

Indira Varma's Olivia was another bundle of contradictions. She may have spun Orsino's messenger some chilly line about 'a cloisteress' and a room awash with 'eye-offending brine', but the sisterly widow's weeds she'd vowed to wear through 'seven years' heat' told a different story. High fashion mourning, this was no nun's habit. It was a dress to take Cinderella (or even better, the widowed Scarlett O'Hara) to the ball – a dress already feeling the heat, already sliding off her shoulders. And by the time she'd met Orsino's latest messager the second time (the rendezvous, her pri-

vate beach; the beachmat she unrolled, suggestive of striptease; herself, arranged on it, *Im*patience de-monumented in 'come hither' position), she looked like a sultry Kate Hepburn with Lauren Bacall hair, leggy in trousers, co-respondents and sleeveless beachwear. Poor Cesario's buttoned-up little sea cadet, frankly terrified, finally perched on the strip of empty beachmat Olivia patted invitingly, as though settling down next to gelignite.

The gulling of Malvolio took place on that same beach. When the interior shutters flew out after Shakespeare's 2.4, a heat-shimmering vista (horizonless, blue, after Magritte) opened up behind, transforming the stage from ship's deck to sun-drenched promenade and discovering the conspirators, laden with beach kit, labouring as if across sand dunes to hide out of sight behind a striped windbreak they assembled only just in time. Derek Jacobi's Malvolio was out of Ishiguro – morning suit; wing collar; watch chain; white hair, crew-cut, spruce as a boar bristle shaving brush – via one of the Gheeraerts. He had the habit of standing like a figure in Tudor portraiture – the aristocrat as servant – or a below-stairs Perkin Warbeck who saw the whole household as impostors. But he spoke – the servant as self-improver – with an over-pointed regard for the formal structure of everyday speech – 'Infirmity, that decays the wise, doth ever make the better fool' – that gave you the sense of a man who spent a great deal of time polishing the individual tines on silver dinner forks. His daylight fantasy caught him dealing with the impostors by new-peopling the world – with midgets. (Jacobi, we remember, has Richard II behind him.) Summoning 'my kinsman Toby', the stern line of vision that tracked his imagined subject into view made Sir Toby a beetle. When he first encountered the forged lettter – Maria had wedged it upright between boards in the decking – he stepped over it with the ostentatious hauteur of, say, the Archbishop of Canterbury high jumping a hurdle. Strode one pace. Froze. Spun round. Froze. Thought. Folded himself in half from the waist. And took the bait. But even hooked, this Malvolio was more royal carp than flounder. Only when he finally attempted the smile – one half of his face

26. *Twelfth Night*, 1.5, Donmar, Wyndham's Theatre, directed by Michael Grandage. Indira Varma
as Olivia, Zubin Varla as Feste, Derek Jacobi as Malvolio.

cracking at a time before the ear-to-ear grin broke
the mask of his so-practised gravity – did he expose
the full ghastliness of the jumped-up pleb turned
aroused seducer, lips curling into lecher's leer. Did
Olivia-in-lust steam? Malvolio released-to-desire
curdled clotted cream.

I've been writing about this *Twelfth Night* as a
series of cameos because that's how it played: a collection of sketches, brilliantly executed and slightly
saucy – like end-of-pier postcards. Here's one: Alex
Waldmann's gormless Sebastian blasted off his unre-
luctant feet by the heat of Olivia's ardour: one
moment, boys' brigade tourist gawping through
Illyria; the next, live lunch on a hungry woman's
plate. And another: Samantha Spiro's tiny, terrific
Maria, in full cry like a beagle, nose down scent-
ing the plot. And another: Malvolio in wrecked
wooing gear. (He'd appeared before Olivia like an
advert for fish fingers, Captain Birdseye in blazer,
cravat, bermudas – yes, *bermudas* – and high yellow knee socks held up with elastic tabs. Now his
humiliation was worse than being caught with his
trousers down. Those *bermudas*. They made him
just an over-grown big girl's blouse in short pants.)

And finally: Victoria Hamilton drop-jawed on 'I
am the man'. (Though by the by, nobody would
have been fooled by this Cesario's disguise. While,
thankfully now matured from those days when she
was giggling her way through a silly Cressida, she's
kept her girlish sparkle but she's not an actor who's
kept a boyish figure. And a second by the by: I've
never been so aware how colourless, nay *invisible*,
Viola can be playing straight-man to the clowns,
even in a production like this one that consciously
cut the fooling.)

But the downside of making the stage, like
Oram's, a kind of everywhere – look! no
furniture! – is that it's nowhere: I never got a sense
of a world where any of the star turns I was watching *mattered*. Except once. At Orsino's in 1.4. It's
that 'all boys together' scene where the languishing Count gives his new likely-lad instructions
for wooing-by-proxy. I've seen it played dozens
of ways. In a fencing school. In Orsino's estate
office. With a sulky Valentine in dress uniform ear-
wigging the conversation. What were Grandage's
'all boys together' doing while their master prepped
the kid? They were in each other's arms. Eyes

staring fixedly past each other. Practising the tango. Now, *that* was a world I wanted to know more about.

A bit of standard business that Jacobi rejected came to mind when I was watching Yukio Ninagawa's Kabuki *Twelfth Night* at the Barbican. Jacobi's Malvolio got to the place in the letter where he's commanded to 'Revolve'. That's regularly a cue for a cliché fish-eye to the audience then a slow twirl. Got it? 'Revolve'. His Malvolio paused. Considered. Then daffed aside such nonsense with a contemptuous flick. Steward he was, but no stooge. His Kabuki counterpart – doubling Malvolio with Feste [*sic*] – couldn't have been so dismissive. His professional life depends on 'revolve'. (Think about it: doubling the clown and the killjoy, the Kabuki actor is going to meet himself on stage.) I'd bet *Survey* readers a dime to a dollar that they don't know what I learned from Ninagawa's programme: that the theatre revolve was invented in Japan around 1758. And what I saw on the Barbican stage was that, in terms of technology, it was the star of Ninagawa's show.

The work this director is undoubtedly best known for in England is Samurai-style productions of *Macbeth* (1980), *Titus Andronicus* and *Coriolanus* (*Shakespeare Survey 60, 61*) all of them plays that lend themselves to displays of martial arts even as the formality of their blood rituals, culturally translated, can be honoured in an aesthetics that shocks the Western eye with its severe beauty. Working for the first time not with his own company (as in those earlier productions) but with Shochiku Grand Kabuki Company, however, Ninagawa was doing, as the slogan on the Barbican programme said, 'something different', and so was the Kabuki company, taking on the English playwright for the first time, and billing their *Twelfth Night* as '*after* William Shakespeare'.

Like my predecessor in this job writing about earlier Ninagawa productions, I have no Japanese. Like him, then, I have no idea how, really, to listen to dialogue that (between men) sounds like it's being fired by two Gatling guns at close range, or (between women) swoops nasally up and down an a-chromatic scale you couldn't find on any West-

ern piano. I don't know how to interpret some of the oddities of Japanese translation of Shakespeare, especially in a tradition like Kabuki that estranges performance not just culturally but by a grammar of the theatre remote from Western conventions that serve us as 'naturalism', where faces are made up like masks in pan white or inscribed with stylized lines; where movement is formal and minutely legible; where *kata* (fixed patterns of performing a role) are handed down from master actor to apprentice as learned theatrical behaviours; and where the *onnagata* – the cross-dressed actor playing the woman – makes transvestism an art that is to the human body what bonsai is to arboriculture. But also like him, I was bowled over by the sensational spectacle I saw on stage, and the sheer technical virtuosity of this all-male company matching itself to the physical demands of this text. *Twelfth Night* could have been a script they commissioned.

For beginners: as the striped curtain was drawn open (like a slow wipe in film), spectators found themselves looking at themselves in a wall-sized mirror that filled the Barbican stage. It was a brilliant initial trope for a play that plays with 'natural perspective[s]', doubles, difference and 'what is not'; but it was brilliant, too, in giving us a sight of ourselves 'othered': a London audience, but half of us in kimonos, native to the 'Illyria' we would be visiting.

Next: the mirror, now back-lit, became translucent. Through it was revealed, stretched the full width of the stage, a cherry tree the size of an English oak in full bloom. Beneath it, three children trussed up so tight in kimonos and wide obis that they stood as stiff as lacquered dolls (but wearing capes strangely topped with Elizabethan ruffs) sang to the tune of the English advent hymn 'O come, o come Emmanuel' accompanied by harpsichord with taiko percussion. (To my ears, this was as bizarre as Barber's 'Adagio for Strings' played continuously as muzak underscore to Ninagawa's *Macbeth*, not least because it put us on the wrong side of Christmas for Twelfth Night.) Orsino (Nakamura Kinnosuke II: like English kings, Kabuki actors, inheriting their titles, get numbered) stood listening, as gorgeous

27. *Twelfth Night*, 1.2, Shochiku Grand Kabuki, Barbican, directed by Yukio Ninagawa. Onoe Kikunosuke as Sebastian, Ichikawa Danshirō as Sea Captain.

as a glittering bird of paradise and as impassive as a kipper.

Once the musicians trooped out, Valentine sped on like an American baseball player stealing third, sliding several feet to arrive in that crouching one-knee-up position from which imperial servants address their master. His story told, the scene went to blackout.

Twelve seconds later (I counted), the lights came up. The cherry tree was gone. Spectators were looking at a near-full-sized junk sailing straight at them, young Sebastian (Onoe Kikunosuke V) heroic in the prow staring steadfastly out to sea. The Captain (Ichikawa Danshirō IV, a man in his fifties, though the stylized make-up that carved weather-beaten creases in his face made him ninety) observed: 'I am sorry you and your twin sister are orphans.' That cued Sebastian to gesture below decks and call out 'Viola, Viola'. Then he himself ducked below hatches as if to summon her – and seconds later (again, I counted) reappeared *as his sister*. Not just nominally changed. *Completely* changed: kimono, wig, head-dress, make-up, posture, hands, gesture. Terrified by the storm she saw coming, Viola immediately retreated below, passing (she must have) her brother on the ship's ladder, for now *he* appeared topside, to be swept overboard by a tsunami-sized wave (that came rolling across the stage: billowing silk manipulated by half a dozen stagehands). We watched him drown – rising on the waves then losing the fight and sinking beneath them – *and so did Viola*, just then appearing at the junk's cabin window. A crash of thunder brought the rigging down. Blackout. Lights up. On a painted backcloth giving a traditional Japanese landscape where Viola hatched her plot with the Captain – exited, and returned *as Cesario*.

The whole performance was simply astonishing, the precision of gesture and pose, the spectacle, the impossible quick changes and doubles, the nuanced stories told in the minute flick of kimono hem or flash of lining. I've never been in a theatre so loud with 'ooooohs' from the audience. And it went on like that. The revolve gave us the exterior of Olivia's house as tea ceremony verandah; her garden as acres of lotus and white oriental lily beds connected by red bridges (the effect doubled by the mirror surface dropped in behind); Orsino's, a tatami room in candlelight as simply gorgeous as a lacquerwork box; the 'night kitchen' of Sir Toby's caterwauling as nippon art deco interior. Exiting that scene in search of more sake to lubricate Toby's voice, Feste (Onoe Kikugorō VII) immediately returned – as Malvolio.

The company's take on the 'drunken tinkers' was hilarious. While as Feste Kikugorō was off, demure Maria (Ichikawa Kamejirō II), her mouth made up in a permanent pout, was finally persuaded to dance, first close-kneed, then getting into the swing of it, losing herself in her fandango so that she didn't hear the woodblock clap that announced an entrance and, stepping sideways, following the horizontal movement of her fan, collided with a thunderous Malvolio. She collapsed, flat. Then as he turned all the attention of his fury on Toby, her kimono-clad self, imitating a silkworm, tried inconspicuously to inch away. But once Malvolio was gone, the worm turned – into a dragon (or perhaps Katisha from *The Mikado*). Striking one outsized pose after another, plotting revenge in hyperbolic semaphore with her fan, she 'did' the love letter, 'did' the writing brush, 'did' the writing, the sword chopping off the steward's head. Toby, captivated, called time – 'To bed' – and sweeping one kimono sleeve around her, concealed her as though behind a screen. The gesture was electrifying. We 'saw' sex! And so did poor Aguecheek hiding behind *his* fan (though peering through its bamboo spokes), saved only when Feste at last returned with the drink.

There was great fun in this production: Malvolio flashing himself to a near-fainting Olivia wearing nothing underneath his canary yellow kimono but a canary yellow loincloth; Aguecheek armed to the teeth with enough kit to equip seven samurai. But mostly there was technical actorly craft that took your breath away: Kikunosuke's Cesario, left alone when the screen slid shut behind Orsino, losing male definition, shrinking, sinking into pensive sitting, head, hands, voice, all Viola; or the reverse, somehow 'girled' by that interview with Olivia, stopping outside the garden, squaring 'her' shoulders, straightening 'her' back, rotating 'her' hips, Viola resuming Cesario. Or Nakamura Tokizō V in the senior *onnagata* role, his Olivia making lust visible (compare Varma's Olivia on her beachmat) by the merest movement of hand to lips – artfully contriving that her sleeve fall back to expose her wrist. In that deliciously reticent gesture she might have been shedding every silken layer to stand stark naked.

Question: if you buy a theatre ticket on the basis of the advance publicity, and it turns out the production has nothing to do with the image the marketing department has sold, are you within your rights to claim your money back? The *Twelfth Night* promised on the 'coming soon' RSC poster was certainly one I wanted to see: five bodies dressed like undertakers crammed together back to back under a single black umbrella, five faces all looking in different directions. What a mass of ideas and contradictions was captured in that image! Pinched and poignant; isolated and overcrowded; fraught with comic possibilities ('he's behind you!'). The image managed to caption a play described by its latest director as 'surely the most achingly sad of all Shakespeare's comedies, tinged with a melancholy sadness and almost Chekhovian in its sense of loss.' So what happened to that advertised *Twelfth Night*? And what accounts for the *Twelfth Night* Greg Doran actually staged, an orientalist fantasy that looked like it might be gearing up for panto season at the Hackney Empire?

I got the measure of Doran's show early on, in that first exchange that saw Miltos Yerolemou's Feste having a hard time jesting his way back into Olivia's (Alexandra Gilbreath) favour. While the actor (out of character) mugged the audience (and patronized Shakespeare) as if to say 'Don't blame me: I didn't write this stuff', his jokes fell one after the other flat on their face under her chilly fish eye. That was supposed to be the joke. But this leaden stuff turned out to be what this graceless, art-of-coarse-acting *Twelfth Night* was made of.

Had Doran heard what Grandage was up to at the Donmar? Had he sent a courier round to the Donmar rehearsal rooms to pick up all the puerile gags that Grandage's production had elbowed? In Doran's show we got fart gags (but *please*, the clue is in the name: it's Belch), urinating in a bucket gags, dropped trouser gags, tart gags, Turkish bathroom towel-flicking gags – and a sad, seedy take on a geriatric Malvolio (played by seventy-something Richard Wilson, a.k.a. television's grumpy old man, Victor Meldrew) as the kind of senior citizen you tell schoolboys to avoid in public lavatories. When he tucked up his coat-tails to reveal his yellow stockings, he exposed drooping grandad's underpants and sagging male tackle – and suggested the kind of dreary, superannuated lechery Poins pities in Doll-pawing Falstaff ('Is it not strange that desire should so many years outlive performance?'). So the gulling here wasn't funny; it was queasy.

It didn't help that Doran set this *Twelfth Night* in 'real' Illyria, on the Albanian coast, but updated to the time of the European Grand Tour and Byron in Ali Pasha mode. Olivia's household appeared to be 'Levant Lunatics', washed-up English colonialist ex-pats stretching their cash by living abroad and employing the natives. James Fleet's (arriviste?) Aguecheek maintained standards in Scotch plaid and velvet, and Cesario (Nancy Carroll) – like her brother (Sam Alexander) – was trussed up in frock-coat and button-fly trousers straight out of *Vanity Fair*. But Richard McCabe's bloated Sir Toby had 'turned Turk' in Ottoman slops, the sartorial equivalent of his slurred speech and wobbling jowls. (This was an actor who used to deliver danger. Remember his snarling Autolycus of the wicked gob-stopper eyes and controlled identity crisis? Now he's more interesting when he's playing drunk than sober.) Maria (Pamela Nomvete) had evidently been sprung from some local harem; and Feste was just back from moonlighting in a touring *Aladdin*. (Can't this actor carry a tune – or were those settings *tuneless*?)

Robert Jones's design gave us a decaying civilization of crumbling sun-bleached surfaces: upstage, the ruined wall of a Greek temple supported by Doric columns. Left, a pair of curling, mini-tsunami-sized waves used in the first five minutes of the show for back projections that brought the sea storm on stage (and, stuck there permanently, made the scene on stage always intractably 'outside'). But what with the relentless blue sky, the Adriatic sun beating down, the jaunty ethnic music, and the need to keep six near-mute 'Arab' extras busy laying out everything from rugs and cushions to washing lines and market stalls, this was an exhibitionist *Twelfth Night* that seemed to be always located in a frantic casbah where the universal fancy dress crushed the point of Malvolio's yellow stockings. Ironically, all the hyperactivity made this the slowest *Night* in living memory. Not even the excellent Gilbreath could pull it together. Playing Olivia as an ageing heroine out of Austen who'd missed the marriage boat back home and gone into genteel exile as her brother's spinster lady-housekeeper, her early wooing scenes with Carroll's earnestly bland

but authentically boyish Cesario (many years her junior) were wonderfully poised. They were equal parts archness and playfulness, arousal like a colt hearing music, then tragic slump ('I pity you'). This was an Olivia who was truly delighted – as well as flabbergasted – to have her languid arrogance ('Is't not well done?') smacked down ('Excellently done [pause, pause, pause] – if God did all'). But Gilbreath was also permitted to indulge her actorly vocal mannerism, a tendency to stretch and over-pronounce individual syllables. (Think of Maggie Thatcher addressing her cabinet as if they were a slightly dim pack of poodles.) And it may be the new performance cliché, but to allow Olivia at the end to look at the twins and growl 'Most wonderful!' as if she's imagining kinky sex is just crass.

Three *As You Like It*s put me more often than I would have liked in Touchstone mode gazing with 'lacklustre eye' at my 'dial' and muttering to myself that 'when I was at home I was in a better place'. Is there a political play hiding out in *As You Like It*? Peter Holland is sure there is – and just as sure that Shakespeare didn't give it legs. At the RSC, Michael Boyd's production on the Courtyard stage seemed determined to play stalking-horse to a play the playwright never wrote.

The programme did a hard-sell on a gritty rural deprivation drama. There were pictures of dead rabbits and game hung out on a pole like washing. There were notes that informed us that Shakespeare's first audiences would have seen a play about a 'ruthless' 'new economy', an impoverished Corin, tenant to a harsh 'Carlot', thrown off his land. Unemployed. Homeless. Hungry. How topical! How like our very own experience of credit crunch, negative equity, repossession – with our own Celia-esque rescue package ('we will mend thy wages') in the form of 'quantitative easing'. Except that after 2.4, this plot line disappears. So was this production about 'them'? Or 'us'? Wanting it both ways, Boyd got neither.

The opening court scenes (the designer was Tom Piper) gave us a blank canvas: a white wooden floor backed with cross-hatched and whitewashed wood panelling, like a Tudor hall screen. To begin with, Elizabethans populated this place. They wore doublets and hose, jackets and farthingales, all of them black on the white ground, Celia (Mariah Gale) and Rosalind (Katy Stephens) in particular given a physical structure, an armature, by their costumes to move, hold themselves and speak this play's precisely structured prose with precision: 'If my uncle thy banished father had banished thy uncle the Duke my father . . . ' But something didn't fit. Touchstone (Richard Katz) in gag bondage trousers, legs buckled together at the knee in a kind of ankle-length straitjacket, was a time-traveller from another century – and a signal. For by the time we got to Arden, the Elizabethan world was coming apart, *literally*. The panels in the screen came out, opening windows onto a place where unidentified men hung around on ladders – and where the carcass of a deer hung by its hooves. (I couldn't believe my eyes! Wasn't it Nigel Playfair in 1919 who finally, over howls of protest, retired the Charlcote stuffed stag that had made obligatory appearanaces in *As You Like It* for fifty years? Who in their right mind would restore that cliché? Or was the dead deer a nudge in the ribs towards a 'topical' eco-critical reading: 'et in Arcadia' etc.?)

Perversely, there was not even the shadow of a tree in this forest, so nothing for a poet to write on (all that white woodwork was clearly off limits for the graffitist). Orlando's verses, scrawled on cardboard (recycled packing boxes from the exiled court's removal?), had to be gaffer taped to the theatre's balconies by stagehands in the interval. Costumes – a bad idea evidently borrowed from *The Taming of the Shrew* last season – turned increasingly (and incomprehensibly) modern. Audrey (Sophie Russell) appeared in Essex-girl bum-warmer and white stilettos (when will the RSC stop playing rustics as idiots?); Celia, in *Last of the Summer Wine* florals; Rosalind, first in what passes in London SW7 as country casuals, then in a frightful strapless retro wedding dress by Next.

Where exactly *was* Arden? Down a rabbit hole? Sometimes. The banished duke ('Ferdinand': Clarence Smith) and his jack-in-the-box co-mates in exile popped up from traps like hobbits; Orlando (Jonjo O'Neill), heading for the green world, dived underground. But Celia arrived tucked up in a sweet little wheeled vehicle. Weather conditions were similarly variable. Sometimes Arden was in Siberia. While Ferdinand philosophized ('sweet are the uses of adversity'), snow fell, and his men – one of them, eyes bandaged, clearly snowblind – wrapped each other's frost-bitten hands. (It's all very well Boyd banging on about the new-model-RSC-as-ensemble, but if you put twenty-one [*sic*] actors on stage to perform *As You* you'd better give them something meaningful to do; otherwise, they'll fill their narrative void space with naff 'character' stories.) For Touchstone, though, Arden was in a drought-dry Warwickshire. His closest encounter with nature was to wrestle to the ground a desiccated tangle of wild clematis. Later, he stood far off, pulling disgusted faces at another bit of rural life: Geoffrey Freshwater's Corin filled the intra-act by expertly skinning and decapitating a (real) rabbit, so that when the second act began with his question 'How like you this shepherd's life?', Touchstone was retching. (And the point of this was? That 'we're' ruining Arden – planet-wrecking killers who make deer sob and Nature weep? Or that visitors had better get used to blood because there are no Waitrose home deliveries in the forest?)

This production marked Boyd's 'return to the rehearsal room for the first time since *The Histories*' (as he wrote in the programme), and I'd like to think he chose the comedy to give women, reined in by the cycle, their heads. (If so, it was a generous gesture. Comedy isn't Boyd's genre. Think back to his unfortunate *Twelfth Night* and misjudged *Much Ado About Nothing*.) What a waste, then, to squander these women, sending Gale's Celia upstage in the wooing scenes to act invisible and making sure Stephens's Ganymede wouldn't be taken seriously by putting her in joke moustache and goatee, the kind that kids graffiti onto the Mona Lisa. How lame to have her Ganymede dropping her trousers on 'what shall I do with my doublet and hose?' to discover a flannel shoved down her y-fronts. And how insulting to these actors to permit Forbes Masson's self-indulgent Jaques – here, not resident melancholic in Arden but posturing narcissist – to suck all the oxygen out of this production.

Masson is an actor with a stunning counter-tenor voice who's served Boyd as in-house troubadour for several seasons – increasingly, it has to be said, bizarrely (witness the flying harpsichord in *Richard II*). But his Jaques – I couldn't work out whether it was the actor or the character – was a monster. He looked like an over-weight Tom Jones fancying himself Lord Byron in opera coat, unbuttoned-to-navel purple shirt, sunken eyes and hair fashioned in a wind tunnel. He was given all Amiens's songs, and, solo, full run of the stage to bait the audience solipsistically with his own lines. 'More?' he taunted us after a verse of 'Under the greenwood tree'; then snidely, 'It will make you melancholy.' The butchery he committed upon the Seven Ages of Man – gurning and grimacing and torturing each image ('schoolboy'; 'lover'; 'soldier'): if you did that to a dead rabbit you'd be had up by the RSPCA. Only in the quiet moments at home between the cousins, or before the wrestling match when they showed the electric quality of their listening, rapt by O'Neill's desperate, desperately rash Orlando, or in Rosalind's 'O coz, coz, coz... how many fathom deep I am in love', uttered heartstoppingly with her heart in her mouth, did you get a glimpse at the performances these actors might have produced. But why give Stephens's Rosalind not the epilogue at the end but a modern Irish ballad – a cultural nod that made nonsense of the previous three hours' re-routing of O'Neill's real Irish voice down the cul de sac of English RP?

News not having reached the metropolis from the provinces warning that *As You Like It* 'might easily be mistaken for a sunny comedy', Thea Sharrock made the easy mistake of directing it at the Globe as a sunny comedy. And at a matinée on the hottest day of the summer when I saw this production, the packed Globe audience: well, they made the mistake of watching it as one.

This show harked back to 'original practices' productions: equal parts, then, fascinating (actors serving as walking archives of 'authentic' Elizabethan fashion) and irritating. (Postmodern behaviours in early modern clothes: they just don't fit, so cut the giggling and shrieking, women, as though you were teenie boppers waiting at the stage door for your own autographs.) When these costumes were allowed to work, they operated on Naomi Frederick's Rosalind and Laura Rogers's Celia as speech platforms and (sometimes) as witty signifiers. At Court, Dominic Rowan's Touchstone wore motley; in Arden, registering himself, the urbanite, as rustic refusenik, he was wall-to-wall velvet, courtier down to his socks. But in Arden, why was Rosalind cross-dressed as Orlando's twin? Had I been Orlando, I think I might have smelled a rat when I realized the kid called Ganymede I'd just met *looked exactly like me*. Here I have an apology to make, to Jack Laskey. I could hardly watch his goggle-eyed, shock-headed Orlando. He was ruined for me by that demented-parrot Biondello he gave at the RSC last year (*Shakespeare Survey 62*). But I'm recovering: I loved Laskey's bit where Orlando, truly if goofily furioso, churned out writing like ticker tape while out of the heavens Nature in sympathy dumped a cloudburst of poetry on Arden.

Unnecessarily, Sharrock's designer, Dick Bird, continued the recent vogue of 'improving' the Globe – fixing a curved lip onto the thrust stage, adding wooden gangways into the yard and a number of pillars to play trees: 'unnecessarily' because this production's best effects were achieved by the simplest means, and actor-, not designer-driven. For example, space was marked out for the wrestling match by a circle roughly chalked on the floor. Later, scuffed, blurred by traffic, it never quite disappeared, and so its traces kept spectators faintly, teasingly in mind of Jaques's remarks about fools and circles and how we – in the Globe's wooden O – were inscribed in one too. And that chalk, tracked on feet into the forest, left prints that showed Arden as a kind of improbable Clapham Junction where if you missed one wooer, no matter, another would roll up shortly. That was the point that Sharrock's production made. Touchstone earnestly wooing a peascod, Silvius (Michael Benz, the star of this show for me, a delicious moping dope who deserved *so much better* than Phoebe) suicidally wooing his executioner, and Orlando uncomprehendingly wooing smoke up a chimney:

this *As You Like It* showed that these were all the same love-baffled, Arden-snared man. And showed too that whether she was Rosalind, Phoebe or Audrey, the woman in love was more fleshified oyster than pearl.

Undoubtedly, though, the *As You Like It* not to have missed this year was Tim Supple's in the Curve's inaugural season. The Curve is brand new: a spanking twenty-first-century design – the clue is in the name – set down among derelict Victorian garment factories in Leicester's St George's district; a building with a mission, to put a theatre at the heart of urban regeneration. And what a theatre! Imagine the Barbican turned inside out, all its workings – props shop, rehearsal room, offices – on display and you've got the Curve. It's a big open box under a cloche of louvred glass where there's no front of house or backstage or wings; where the two auditoria are 'islands' looped by space that serves as foyer, café and scene dock for actors waiting for entrances, who walk onto the stage through giant metal shutters. Putting everything we take for granted in that word 'theatre' up for grabs, the Curve is a kind of Arden.

Supple (fresh from his triumph with Dash Arts' *A Midsummer Night's Dream* (*Shakespeare Survey 60*)) was clearly at home here. In a programme note, he said he aims 'to see and hear Shakespeare in different forms and voices. Different than we are used to and different from each other.' The cast he assembled honoured that aim. Young (but anchored by a couple of veterans, like Louis Mahoney from Attenborough's *Cry Freedom* years ago), they were bright and ethnically diverse. The programme read like a mini-United Nations: names from Armenia, Rwanda, Yemen, the Gambia, Greece; oh, and England. And they looked like their audience. The Leicester crowd on the night I saw this production was just as young and culturally diverse.

Clearly aimed at a new audience, this modern-dress *As You Like It* asked us to re-think Arden-as-England. What, for starters, does 'modern-dress' look like in multi-cultural Britain when in downtown Leicester you can see women in burkahs and saris, denims and – that year's hot winter fashion – leggings topped with short shorts? How do we

today conduct the debates the play stages about the 'native' and the 'usurper', banishment, exile, asylum, a run for your life to a place called 'liberty'? These are real debates in cities all over Britain – and serious politics as against the manufactured 'issues' of Boyd's production. On Supple's stage, we heard cultural debate articulated in the sounds the production made instrumentally and vocally. Ashwin Srinivasan and Nitin Sawhney composed for an ensemble of mandolin, accordion, trumpets, mangkang and pung, and all kinds of accents came out of the speaking – RP, the minority sound.

Anna Fleischle's design gave substance to that debate. On the forestage, flanked by garden chairs, a stylized tree growing citrus the size of grapefruit doubled as estate orchard and Court orangery. Behind it, raked steeply, the stage was boarded with wood planks, guy wires attached to them running up into the flies producing the effect of rows and rows of blighted trees stretching into a horizonless wasteland. Violence was native to this place. Orlando (David Ononokpono), a lad in blue jeans, went for his brother's jugular. He (Ery Nzaramba), in turn, hired the wrestler (Andrew Dennis) as hitman, but wound up under interrogation waterboarded by thugs working for Munir Khairdin's bully-boy Duke, who appeared entirely capable of arranging an 'honour killing' if that's what it took to keep his niece in line. We saw a culture where that was possible. Unlike the men, the girls were culturally marked, owned. They wore saris – and spoke from behind veils (so the moment Tracy Ifeachor's Rosalind fell in love and the cover slipped off, she was shockingly exposed). Only Kevork Malikyan's old-world Touchstone, a dignified fool in a coat that made you think both of orthodox rabbis and Robert Armin in the frontispiece to the *Two Maids of Mortlake*, came from a sweeter place, a place where 'service sweat for duty not for meed'.

So how did they find Arden? A lot like home, really. Justin Avoth's Jaques looked like the mad brother Karamazov, a raddled Jeremiah in mouldering frock-coat sucking a roll-up. But was his railing *self*-directed? (A livid sore on his cheek, perhaps a Kaposi sarcoma, suggested he'd lived the life the Duke imputes to him, a 'libertine'.) Or

28. *As You Like It*, 3.2, Curve, Leicester, directed by Tim Supple. Justin Avoth as Jaques.

was it social protest? (What was Jaques registering when he entered after the deer-killing lugging a bucket of blood and the hacked-off antlers?) Or was it a despairing love letter to life? 'All the world's a stage' was deadpan. Its final words – 'sans . . . sans . . . sans' – were delivered as Orlando arrived with Adam in his arms so that the old body of the exhausted servant became the ultimate illustration of the nothing of 'everything' (a word this Jaques barked with laughter). And yet, while Amiens sang 'Blow, blow thou winter wind', the cynic sat breaking off pieces of bread and feeding the old man. In the silence after, as the houselights went up for the interval, Duke Ferdinand (doubled by Khairdin) wrapped Orlando in a bear hug, that embrace the antidote to toxic violence. After the interval, we saw a world being cured by love.

Earlier, Celia's cry 'to liberty . . . !' had cued a mini-earthquake. Wood planks here, there, under her feet, upstage in a corner, began juddering, then rising, lifted by the guy wires upright, strangely miraculous resurrections, like so many coffin lids ascending into heaven, exposing not a green-world (sentimentality not admitted) but brown earth underneath. In the second act, more wood lifted, transformed into trees jigging in the air. And now they were graffitied with 'I love Rosalind' and strung with poetry, so many dancing scripts, a world alive with love. In this new world, not only had women cast off veils; one of them had put on liberating masculinity, Ifeachor's Rosalind delightfully freed by Ganymede into playful intimacy. But her technical brilliance in the role as an actor was to see what Shakespeare's writing was doing for her and to use every line to tell the story. (Compare Rogers's Celia at the Globe, hitting every pronoun so missing any meaning beyond 'me . . . me . . . me . . . me . . . me'.) The

349

wooings here were full-blooded but also deeply affectionate. (Compare Stephens's frantic physicality, which surely would have sent Orlando seeking the calm comfort of Audrey's goats.) Stavros Demetraki's stubborn, stolid, decent Silvius and Malikyan's courtly Touchstone: these suitors, 'doing' love, really did have the power to change oysters into pearls.

At the end, Supple's Arden looked in two directions. Jaques, still bloodstained, still raging, refused inclusion. His exit line – 'To see no pastime, I' – as he walked into exile left a nasty taste. But only for two heartbeats. Recovering, the Duke motioned to his new-found daughter and niece, who made a different ending: laying out silk beds, lighting wedding lamps, spilling confetti and dancing. Arden's earth still looked scorched. But blooming with silk marriage beds, it promised fertility.

It wasn't so long ago that a reviewer on a national broadsheet could notice with surprise that productions of one of Shakespeare's most 'neglected' comedies (if 'comedy' is what it is) were suddenly thick on the ground: she'd just seen her fifth *Winter's Tale* in four years. This year alone I've seen three. Back in the spring of 2001 that reviewer wondered whether it was 'millennial consciousness', hopes for the dawn of a new golden age, that was giving currency to Shakespeare's *The Winter's Tale* – hopes that didn't survive beyond 9/11. What accounts for the play's currency today? Is it, since that September, our culture's profoundly adjusted attitude to time, history and loss, the daily acknowledgement of life's fragility? Is it a longing for a return to a place we can't recover, the longing contained in a line like the one from *Richard II* that, written on a scrim and back-lit by dozens of hanging candles, hung like an epigram over Sam Mendes's production, 'O call back yesterday, bid time return'?

Mendes's *Winter's Tale* launched The Bridge Project, a three-year collaboration between the Old Vic in London and the Brooklyn Academy of Music in New York. It was a smart choice of play to assemble this first transatlantic cast. Shakespeare's Sicilia and Bohemia are on opposite sides of the globe. Their long-separated kings, raised together as boys, are supposed since to have 'shook hands as over a vast'. Straightforward enough then to make Sicilia England and Bohemia America. Even better, early on, to use the acoustic clash of accents wittily to mark out a cultural territory of mutual incomprehension firmly bedded in the script. When Camillo (Paul Jesson), who'd just been suborned to murder Polixenes (Josh Hamilton), fielded the visitor's baffled questions about his host's sudden change of countenance, and the stiff-upper-lipped voice of English diplomacy tried to end-run Yankee directness (or was 'I dare not know, my lord' pusillanimous evasiveness and 'How, dare not?' just mulish?), the mismatch was hilarious. Our ears were instantly tuned to a pair of nations well and truly separated by a common language.

Mostly, however, Mendes found nothing very much to make of Bohemia-as-America. He drew on easy stereotypes to set the sheepshearing vaguely in late nineteenth-/early twentieth-century *Oklahoma!* mode instead of, say, using what he'd learned from his 1999 film *American Beauty* to locate the Bohemians in a more ironic, dysfunctional place (small town, small time, in-our-time) that might have paralleled the dark domestic ruin in Sicilia. As it was, we got something like a down-home county fair on the Fourth of July with Perdita as best of show. There were plenty of red, white, and blue balloons (an *homage*, perhaps, to Adrian Noble's *Tale* that played opposite Mendes's *Richard III* in the 1992 RSC season), sunbonnets, and slick American musical theatre routines with high kicks and splits and obvious balloon gags. Ethan Hawke's Autolycus was a carpetbagger in a stove-pipe hat twanging a guitar, a refugee from a Coen brothers film whose cracker-barrel delivery occasionally hit an oil slick into a place of dark menace, like some patent medicine man out of Cormac McCarthy. It was a lovely touch to dress Morven Christie's bright, brave Perdita – 'goddess-like prank'd up' – in American Greek revival costume. But in this context of a land peopled with Mark Twains, it was hard to take seriously the royal rantings of the unmasked Polixenes. Quail before the aristo? More likely, they'd have run him out of town on a rail.

Still, bumptious Bohemia gave us necessary respite from a Sicilia where we'd experienced not winter, but *nuclear* winter. Things had started so well. Mendes's Sicilia (designed with beautiful restraint by Anthony Ward and lit gorgeously by Paul Pyant) was a child-full place cast in purple shadows. It was seen first through a scrim as though looking into a child's imagination at the tale we heard coming, magically anticipated in four notes, played over and over, as from a toy music box located somewhere in the heavens (scored by Paul Arditti). Stage right: a child's bed where Leontes (Simon Russell Beale) sat perched with Hermione (Rebecca Hall), relaxed, abundantly pregnant, at his feet. Stage left: a family table, where Polixenes stood, glass in hand, about to speak. Centre stage: a pile of cushions. Everywhere: teddy bears. Down centre: Mamillius in striped pyjamas. (The extraordinary Morven Christie: I *saw*, and afterwards *swore* I saw, a child in the part, my notes even telling me to 'find out who was boy on 3 July'.) Ventriloquizing his teddy – 'Tell's a tale'; 'Merry or sad, shall't be?'; 'A sad tale's best for winter' – Mamillius was the originator of this *Tale*. He remained on-stage, in view, its focus right up to the trial. He leaped into 'uncle' Polixenes's arms when the guest agreed to stay. He hugged his father ('Art thou my boy?') with a big 'Ay!' and submitted to being tucked up in bed by dad to sleep through court business then sat up, wild, as from a nightmare when that father's furious voice ('you lie! you lie!') woke him. He listened, big-eyed, to the adult talk about his mother, a little somnambulist, leaving bed, finding his crayons, colouring in the dark while Camillo and Polixenes whispered; put back to bed by mom who wanted a story, then yanked from her arms, when she's arrested, made to hear his mother denounced as adulteress, traitor, 'bed-swerver', and to watch her exit to prison. The listless little boy who was trundled on in a wheelchair at the top of 2.3 ('How does the boy?') was a desperately sick child, head slack, eyes already dead.

And this little boy was the centre of Leontes's universe. Never before have I seen Shakespeare's rip-tidal opening to this play played not *à trois* but as twin double acts. Leontes and Mamillius were a couple of kids in parallel play with the grown-ups, with Russell Beale clutching child-like at memories of a 'boy eternal' to keep at bay adult 'thoughts' that would 'thick' his 'blood'. Wiping his son's 'smutch'd' nose, he lingered, sought paternity in that face by measuring the little nose against his own (a gesture that he remembered – and that remembered his doubts – when, settling Mamillius back to sleep, holding his hand, singing a lullaby under his breath, he gently touched the boy's nose). This slightly dumpy, greying, unmade-bed-of-a-man whose hair he tugged up into exclamation marks, was somehow *like* his child: guileless. Quizzing Camillo – 'How cam't Camillo, / That he did stay' – his feet trod anxiously like a duck's. Suddenly goggle-eyed ('GOOD?'), one hand flapping to find a pocket to dive into, he was for all the world the astonished child carpeted by the headmaster. But one stung. Infected. Watching Polixenes play with Mamillius, Leontes's face spasmed, like Milton's Satan viewing Paradise. He suddenly stepped between son and guest, warning off the proxy dad with a threatening gesture that, instantly embarrassed, he turned into an awkward 'manly' handshake.

This Leontes was, in short, a staggering oxymoron, weaving between child and man. Words like 'Satisfy?...satisfy?' came out like projectile vomiting (and made us hear Iago). But 'sluic'd in's absence...pond fish'd...Sir Smile', and 'slippery.../ My wife's a hobby-horse' raised snorts of laughter from the audience, not just because these bizarre imaginings were 'Fancies too weak for boys, too green and idle / For girls of nine' but because, sluicing these words around in his mouth, Russell Beale's Leontes was boying himself, the voice the strangled squawk of the grubby kid discovered hiding pornography under the mattress. But then 'No barricado for a belly' reversed this process, heaping decades on his back as though he'd instantly aged as each word dropped octaves into the bottomless crater lake of his misery. He clutched at his genitals – 'bag and baggage' – as if weighing up this apparatus to measure its violation.

Over and over Russell Beale made actorly choices that revealed this divided self – the heart wrecked by the spoiled imagination. When Sinead Cusack's tough Paulina off-loaded the baby into his ambushed hands with her parting shot ('Look to your babe, my lord . . . we are gone'), he instinctively cradled the bundle against his neck, rocking, humming. Two beats later, the time it took thought to defeat instinct, he flipped, shrieking, 'see it instantly consum'd with fire!' Later, stupid with sleeplessness, he managed to find his way into his grown-up black suit coat for the trial – but forgot his shoes. So as Hall's ashen-faced Hermione began, carefully unfolding a paper to read her defence in a voice hollow with prison, he sat there on the far end of the empty table that separated husband and wife, barefoot. We heard the devastation playing out between them ('My life stands in the level of your dreams'; 'Your ACTIONS ARE MY DREAMS!'). But couldn't take our eyes off those absurd, pitiful, *human* naked toes.

Earlier, in 'Inch-thick, knee-deep' we looked inside the cranium Leontes opened up, at the sickening, hard mass of tumour in his mind. 'Tóo hot, tóo hot' registered the man's berserk arithmetic (and Russell Beale's genius). Hermione and Polixenes lounged on the cushions centre stage, their gestures under deep purple light in slow motion demonstrating the actions Leontes had in mind. 'Hot' was acceptable; 'too' was too much. At the end of the trial, though, his insanity was ludicrous, the posturings of a midget. Snapping Apollo's message primly back in its box – here, spirit writing inscribed by a magically automatic quill – he firmly announced, 'There is no truth at all i' th' Oracle', threw defiant arms to the heavens to cock a snook at the gods that invited a lightning bolt, waited, heard only silence, and barked out a huge 'HA!'. Only then from the side did the messenger silently slip in. Mamillius was 'gone'.

Whoever thought of it, it was inspired to stage 'What studied torments, tyrant, hast for me?' as a two-hander. Only Cusack's heart-broken, fearless, fierce Paulina returned to face the fallen king and to batter him with her contempt ('Thy tyranny . . . thy jealousies . . . The sweet'st, dear'st creature's dead!') while he clutched her knees and roared into her skirts – and she fought to get away. Sixteen years later, they'd still be there, still together, suspended in light that offered no perspective, no horizon, a couple of old geezers on a bench out of Beckett, stranded alone as if at a bus stop (she, stiff, standing aloof; he, sitting hunched, as if gnawing his walking stick) waiting for an arrival that would never come. And then it did.

Lines from Anne Michaels's *The Winter Vault* can gloss the end of this *Winter's Tale*: 'For better or worse . . . love is a catastrophe'; 'only real love waits while we journey through our grief . . . It is this waiting we must do for each other . . . as if forgiveness were a rendezvous.' Catastrophe lay in wait at the end of Mendes's *Winter's Tale*. Russell Beale's Leontes couldn't stop remembering: 'Kill'd! She I kill'd.' That sound, hollow, low, boomed distantly out of his heart, the verbal equivalent of arctic ice shifting. But so did rendezvous. Leontes reached out a hand as if – a strange impulse – to touch the face, the nose, of the girl called Perdita who'd just been introduced. But it was Paulina who recognized her, *knew who she was* – and led them all to the final rendezvous, with a statue that, moving, terrified Leontes as though he'd seen a devil. Touched, it released his soul from hell. 'O, she's warm!' produced a voice that thawed Time frozen around the human heart.

There's a question that Leontes asks, wonderingly, of the statue in Paulina's care: 'What fine chisel / Could ever yet cut breath?' It's rhetorical and, in the event of course, comically ironical. The statue is 'only' acting. Watching Russell Beale's Leontes – 'only' acting – I had the feeling that the same chisel was somehow at work on him.

In Mendes's production, the significant property was the bed: actually, Mamillius's bed, but figuratively keeping before spectators' eyes the question 'Who's in bed with Hermione?' In David Farr's *Winter's Tale* on the RSC's Courtyard stage, it was the bookcase. Or rather, two bookcases, two storeys high, wedged floor to ceiling with hundreds of thick tomes. This formal, frock-coated Edwardian Sicilia (designed by Jon Bausor) was a place where stories mattered, where tales were remembered, recorded, published, shelved, returned to; where 'is it true?' could be answered by a turn to

29. *The Winter's Tale*, 5.1, Bridge Project, Old Vic, directed by Sam Mendes. Gary Powell as Cleomenes, Simon Russell Beale as Leontes, Sinead Cusack as Paulina.

the material. (Though I didn't believe for a minute that Greg Hicks's lean, fitful Leontes, found staring at a book at the top of 2.3 – 'Nor night, nor day, no rest' – was actually a reader). At the end of 3.2 (after the trial, after the deaths), a stunning *coup de théâtre* overwhelmed this man's exit from his known court to unknown 'sorrows'. As the big doors upstage swung open onto fog-grey gloom, a windstorm of swirling pages blasted Leontes in the face. Behind him, the bookcases, with the tremendous crash of a world order collapsing, fell into each other, spilling their contents into mountains of twisted covers, split spines, torn paper, writing like tongues ripped from mouths and spewed across a new wilderness. After the interval, it was both a terrific joke and a relief (I'd hung around in the auditorium, anxious to see how the poor stage management would clear away the mess) to see that Bohemia was made out of Sicilia's debris. Piles of

books, the litter of disembowelled volumes (that turned out to be copies of Hansard, so that was okay), half-remembered tales, ballads: these were Bohemia's bricks and mortar – and native language. Instead of satyrs, 4.3 produced an Alice in Wonderland stagger-through by giant-sized (and phallically equipped) hardbacks. And the bear – in Mendes, he might have been borrowed from London zoo, he looked so real – was here a puppet, a bookcase-sized shaggy monster made of curled pages torn from age-browned books, 'like an old tale still'.

This was a more even production than Mendes's – but without the great high of Russell Beale's performance. Hicks's saturnine Leontes admitted no laughter. He was a man of military precision whose life seemed to conduct a perpetual court martial, a man who threw his head back like rifle recoil to fire single words: 'satisfy'; 'slippery'. Where for Russell Beale's Leontes a word

30. *The Winter's Tale*, 3.3, RSC, Courtyard Theatre, directed by David Farr. The Bear.

like 'play' dodged around like a bead of mercury, for this Leontes words were cold metal, high-impact ammunition, single-targeted. But if fastidious, he was also prissy, a man whose codes, but not his heart, were broken. On 'You have mistook', wrinkling his nose as though offended by a stink, he unscrewed his wedding ring from his finger and crushed it into Hermione's bewildered hands. When she kissed him goodbye ('I never wish'd to see you sorry; now / I trust I shall', the gentlest of farewells), he whipped out his handkerchief and pawed at the nastiness she'd left on his cheek.

Kelly Hunter's middle-aged Hermione, a mother who'd clearly longed for her second child and now in high pregnancy was large in spirit, beautifully beside her ungainly self, by turns gracious, laughing, generous, mischievous, moved across the astonishing speech Shakespeare gives her in the opening scene like a giant dragonfly. Brilliant as she was in this first scene, Hunter failed to convince at her trial. She entered as though blinded, hands shading her eyes, by the interrogation lamps that, flipped on, flooded Leontes's court in cold light. She was wrapped in stained sheets yanked from the birth bed – presumably by the midwife who'd attended her, and who'd earlier showed up bloody to the elbows as though she'd been delivering cattle. But this Hermione wasn't a woman, like Rebecca Hall's choked queen, who'd lived those sheets, whose voice had caught the cold of prison, or whose body was wailing its child-parting.

Still, almost everywhere you looked in this production you saw fine acting served up to spectators with wonderful immediacy on the Courtyard's open platform stage. Furniture was swiftly disposed of (like the formal Christmas party table of the opening that turned into Mamillius's bed in 2.1, or a single chair set downstage for the trial). Darrell D'Silva's silver-haired, walrus-moustached, solid but playful Polixenes had the agility of a heavy-weight boxer and the alertness of a politician – or a lover – to every nuance of language. He recoiled as if hit by a cobra on 'He thinks . . . / that you have touch'd his queen / Forbiddenly'. Beside him, John Mackay's fine Camillo, allowed in this production his native Scots accent, was by turns a slightly wheedling Morningside Uriah Heep and a tougher Inspector McLevy. The two of them appeared in Bohemia as dotty ornithologists lost on some Tyrolean holiday (it was the hats at the sheepshearing that gave the location away) where they encountered a Perdita – Samantha Young – who, by the time I saw the production a second time, mid-season, had grown into the part, truly Hermione's daughter. She had all her mother's swiftness and seriousness. In Bohemia, she was an unschooled girl daft with love. In Sicilia, bug-eyed at court opulence, she hid behind her Florizel (Tunji Kasim). (I must say, however, that the thrust stage's invitation to designers – *pace* Tom Piper in the *Histories* last year – to fly set in with actors attached to it is worrying. Poor Perdita had to cling to a tree hanging 30 feet up for a good twenty minutes while Brian Doherty's snaggle-toothed Autolycus did his turn. I'd have needed oxygen. Or probably just gin. Presumably Actors' Equity is keeping an eye on this sort of thing.) Her big brother, Gruffudd Glyn's gormless, warm Welsh-voiced Young Shepherd, was a sartorial jumble sale (orange trainers, braces, knee pads, flap-eared woolly hat). His performance – 'sea . . . land . . . ship . . . bear' – had him lunging like Nureyev from disaster to disaster even as his opposite arm anchored down flying costume. It was he, single-handedly (as Shakespeare, I think, intended in the writing), who turned the oil tanker of this play on a dime towards repair. Near the end, when Sam Troughton's Steward appeared, totally endearing, giddy with wonder and hugging himself in a one-man tango, telling us of the 'lost' that's been 'found', 'joy waded in tears', 'king . . . daughter . . . mother . . . shepherd . . . bear', we saw this cameo as the companion piece to (and resolution of) Glyn's clod-hopping ballet.

But the great performance of this *Winter's Tale* was Noma Dumezweni's Paulina. As an actor, she has the ability to hear on stage everything *for the first time*, to get every piece of news *new*. She can also mesh raw feeling with thought and towering dignity with punishing comic attack. (She has a way of rising to a challenge by straightening her back as though stacking additional vertebrae in her spine.) And she has a voice like warm honey that can harden into sheet ice. This Paulina walked blind into Leontes's sucker punch – 'GOOD QUEEN!' – a verbal blow that caught her on the jaw. But it gave her the measure of the fight she was in and the stakes played for, but also its ludicrous indecency. There was something so foolish about this father who wouldn't recognize the nose on his own face, never mind the 'little print' of the one on his infant daughter's. Dumezweni hit every note Shakespeare gives Paulina in 2.3: diplomatic, manipulating, cajoling, soothing, shrewish, dangerous, lacerating, loving ('Behold my lords . . . '). She swooped diva-like among the helpless courtiers (the whole space of the open stage was this woman's stomping ground), shushing the baby in the Moses basket when she cried (this was a Paulina you

believed *was* the mother of three daughters), but pinning Leontes to his chair and nailing him with mockery ('I'll not call you tyrant . . . weak-hing'd fancy'). Genuinely alarmed at the threats against the baby, hearing them as real, this Paulina took the biggest gamble of her life leaving the child behind. And the mistake she knew she'd made was fixed on her face in the trial scene like a Greek mask. At the end, her whole history with Leontes was retold in a single line. It voiced the deep memory of his original sin, his faithlessness, accusing Hermione of unfaithfulness, reissued now as serious instruction for life in the future: 'It is *requir'd*,' she levelled at Leontes, 'You do awake your faith.' Watching Dumezweni's Paulina, I was sure I was looking at our next great Cleopatra. Directors, take note.

But on the evidence of her Paulina for Headlong Theatre's *Winter's Tale*, they should give Golda Rosheuvel an availability check, too. (It can't have escaped notice, can it, that both these powerful actors have, in the recent past, played sidekicks to white Cleopatras. When are they going to be first casting for a role Shakespeare wrote *black*?) I caught up with Simon Godwin's handsomely spare touring production, which set the play in 1930s Sicily (on a dull-gold tiled floor, like a Renaissance loggia or sand on a shore, designed by Miriam Nabarro), at York's Theatre Royal. Like Mendes's and Farr's, Godwin's production focused on an object: here, a box. It spilled Mamillius's toys in the first scene, and, shut, stored his memory in the last, Perdita gazing at it lingeringly (a box she somehow recognized?) before she finally exited, the last to go. Nine actors played all the parts – sometimes working too hard on disguising themselves: Rosheuvel's Old Shepherd(ess) was principally characterized by a rustic mumble produced as if by dentures that didn't fit. But only sometimes. John Hodgkinson's Antigonus-doubling-Autolycus in a plum voice that out-courtiered the courtiers and in trousers wincingly tight in the crotch produced a 'torture speech' that left Gwynfor Jones's hapless Young Shepherd gurgling with fear. Bryony Hannah's Mamillius/Perdita/Midwife triple reminded me of young Kathryn Hunter: quirky, androgynous, an 'old' child or childlike crone moving with the disjointedness of the infant or geriatric, a screwball ingénue in Bohemia. If for the most part Vince Leigh was an under-powered Leontes, a man of surfaces, at the end he astonished. Reaching out to the statue, he might have been Adam in Michelangelo's Sistine fresco, touching one finger-tip to find 'She's warm!' First tentatively, then hungrily, his groping hands travelled up Hermione's (Amanda Ryan) arm to catch her in an embrace. It was Ryan's laughter that opened this production with Hermione deliciously sprawled on a chaise longue sharing family stories. And it was her wondering recognition of her daughter as her hands scanned Perdita's face, arms, hands, hair, waist, that brought tears to the eyes at the end. But again, it was Paulina who powered this *Tale*. Rosheuvel shoved Leontes to the ground – 'What studied torments . . .' – beat him, cowering, back, then threw herself on him, straddling him, going for his eyes, before being hauled off. She was a Paulina so lost to grief as to be murderous; a one-woman feminist brigade indicting masculinity of every fault from cowardice to tyranny. (If Russell Beale's Leontes made us hear Iago, Rosheuvel's Paulina was Emilia: men in this Sicilia were gulls and dolts, 'As ignorant as dirt'.) With the least means – a flex of naked lightbulbs strung between poles, a trestle table stacked with cheese and wine, accordion music – it was Godwin's *Tale* that produced the most joyous sheepshearing scene. Here was a party, with its local dance in the town piazza where Ferdinand Kingsley's Florizel was simply down-dressed as an Italian waiter in a white apron, that emerged out of the culture that produced it.

Viewing them together, I can see these *Tales* establishing a serious cultural shift in understanding of this play, ideas explored first, I'd say, by Cheek by Jowl (1998) and Propeller (2005). *The Winter's Tale* used to be 'about' Leontes, his failure of self, his crisis of masculinity and erotic dementia that precipitate domestic ruin and international political isolation. It still is about all that – but now seen through the enquiring eyes of the child. All three of these productions began with Mamillius. In Mendes, Mamillius framed the *Tale*, speaking the opening. In Farr, he opened the door into the play, appearing in a crack of light he let through, then running in to hide under the Christmas cracker-laden table as behind him some grown-ups came in to chat. In Godwin, Mamillius was even more preliminary. He was a green summer child running through grass-high fields but also a blue winter boy, dungarees rolled up, standing on a pebbled shore, gazing out to sea: boys who appeared in matched images on the programme, separated by the fold. Mamillius gave us *unsafe* conduct into each of these productions. For audiences today, this play is not just about adult ruin but the consequences of adult ruin, the ruin of childhood.

Watching the Baxter Theatre's *Tempest* brought from Cape Town to the RSC's Courtyard Theatre directed by Janice Honeyman, I couldn't get one of Paulina's lines out of my head. ''Tis time,' she tells the statue, 'descend; be stone no more.' I was thinking of Athol Fugard's *The Island*, a two-hander first performed in Cape Town in 1973 – almost a companion play to this *Tempest*. In Fugard, the prisoner 'Winston' (Ntshona) talks about 'Old Harry', a lifer on Robben Island condemned for defying apartheid by burning his passbook. He spends every day in the quarry working with hammer and chisel, turning out 'Twenty perfect blocks of stone'. 'He's forgotten himself. He's forgotten everything,' says Winston. 'Look into his eyes. They've changed him. They've turned him into stone.' Antony Sher, Prospero in Honeyman's *Tempest*, admits that he didn't know anything about apartheid until he arrived in England from Johannesburg in 1968. Apartheid to him in South Africa was invisible because 'natural', learned 'from your earliest lessons': 'you know, the alphabet goes ABC, one and one make two, black people are an inferior form of life.' 'We did not know what was going on on Robben Island' – although from the beaches at Cape Town 'you can't *not* see it' – 'because we didn't want to know.' Honeyman used *The Tempest* as a history play that called time on apartheid's project of turning men into stone. It was an act of remembering and an act of knowing, acts made all the more urgent (and poignant) by another piece of casting: Caliban was John Kani – the 'John' to whom 'Winston' was talking thirty-six years back on that other island.

This was a pan-African *Tempest*, its sounds, images, languages, masks, puppets, body painting drawn from across the continent 'as though carried on the wind', as the programme put it. In its way, it estranged *The Tempest* as vividly as the Kabuki company did *Twelfth Night*. Xhosa was spoken here. And Swahili.

Across the Courtyard stage a dry, half-fallen tree lay like the skeleton of some prehistoric reptile (designed by Illka Louw), some of its leafless branches reaching up into a tangle that the spirits would use as a climbing frame. Its trunk formed a cave. Around it, curved runways and steps. This was an arid landscape, dusty, thirsty, where Prospero was a fierce, furious and reluctant hermit forgotten on a Libyan-dry desert island. Full-bearded like an Old Testament prophet, draped in a cloak made from skins and tribal weaving freighted with animistic power – hoof-prints, shells – he wielded his staff like a sjambok. Underneath, though (I thought of the Wizard unmasked in Oz), he was just a greying, portly residual European in soiled linen trousers and waistcoat, still pathetically prizing a battered Panama hat. Loving both daughter and surrogate child, Ariel, he was able to show it only to himself as anguish and to them as controlling irascibility.

His tempest was danced by a giant undulating *Inkhanyamba* from Zulu cosmology, part horned snake, part toothed dinosaur, part goofy glow-worm manipulated by half a dozen tribal-spirits-as-puppeteers (Nkosinathi Gaar, Alex Halligey, Thami Mbongo, Omphile Molusi, Chuma Sopotela). Later, the wedding masque congregated garish outsize puppets that would have been at home in the carnivals in Rio or Notting Hill that these ancestors begot. The banquet emerged out of a strange giant armadillo, and Ariel-as-Harpy appeared on hoof-footed stilts, like a monstrous winged gazelle. The story of his imprisonment by Sycorax – here, built from articulated puppets that came apart into threatening components (blue eyes, monstrously nippled breasts) – was acted. A pair of giant, golden, long-nailed hands clamped

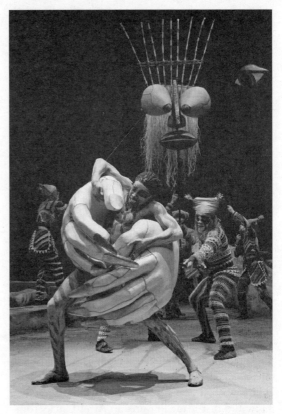

31. *The Tempest*, 1.2, Baxter Theatre, Courtyard Theatre, directed by Janice Honeyman. Atandwa Kani as Ariel, a puppet Sycorax.

around him as his struggling body replayed his torture.

On this island, the spirit and mortal worlds rubbed shoulders. Animals, ancestors and humans wore each other's skins and traded each other's functions. Miranda (Tinarie Van Wyk Loots) was a long-legged simian who hunkered down on her haunches (though, unlike Mariah Gale's autistic Miranda (*Shakespeare Survey 60*) she was fully socialized). When the Europeans stumbled into this drumming, throbbing, humming, eye-assaulting, dervish-dancing place wearing crisp military whites, Napoleon Bonaparte hats and dangling lollipop medals, they weren't 'civilization'. They were another 'tribe' in another 'native costume' – and absurd. But they were also a political insult. The finest 'products' of their imported white supremacist regime were a sodden jester in a big game hunter pith helmet and a glorified bell-hop butler (Trinculo: Wayne Van Rooyen; Stephano: Elton Landrew), here colonial types of inferiority borrowed from the hard-drinking, wisecracking, Afrikaans-speaking Cape Coloured community. In Cape Town, where they were read as satire and political critique, Janet Suzman told me that they brought the house down. In Stratford-upon-Avon, stony-faced audiences didn't – couldn't – get the joke.

So for all the diverting spectacle, the politics of this colonialist *Tempest* were disturbingly ambiguous. There was the matter of voices. Like Trinculo, Atandwa Kani's Ariel had a colonized voice, a voice, working in translation, as tortured into the sounds of English as his body had been in Sycorax's hands. Subjected to Prospero's magic, he was the white man's lackey, doing time as a kind of whipper-in of the spirit world, boss-man running Prospero's spirit gangs. But he was clearly, too, a resistant servant-under-contract who knew Prospero's time was running out. Loose-limbed, dreadlocked, he was nearly naked, his black body white-washed and marked with tribal characters. How did that read? Erasure, an Ariel Uncle Tom-ed by service to the colonialist? Or defiance, black origins surfacing defiantly on the body up through the white man's attempts to white him out? Or something else illegible to Courtyard spectators, a liminal body, in transition? Later, setting Ariel free, Prospero would pour water from a gourd over that body, washing off the white: cleansing it from the leprosy of colonialism – or completing a native initiation rite?

Throughout, Prospero longed to touch this 'chick' – but could never make contact. And black Ariel left him without a backward look. (The sea-sorrow of the colonizer come to self-recognition must be that he never knew what belonged, what was native; and that the monster he made in this place was himself.)

It was impossible not to hear 'This island's mine by Sycorax my mother' as echoing Biko and Mandela – and indeed, Paul Robeson's Emperor Jones. John Kani's Caliban, in the remaining rags of his native dress, was an old 'monster' to match Sher's old supremacist. He stooped on crutches, doubly colonized, subjected not just to Prospero but – insultingly – to the spirits, his ancestral brothers, who were the instruments of his slavery. That voice was rusty with disuse, the vocal equivalent of Old Harry's dead eyes. And it broke across the sounds his Xhosan mouth couldn't make. But for all that, in the stand-off between them, this massively dignified Caliban had history – his, ours – on his side. When Sher's Prospero, grudgingly concluding that 'The rarer action is / In virtue than in vengeance', his forgiveness was *for the white men*. Making to leave the island, Panama hat and rolled-up brolly instead of sjambok in hand – the European gent headed back to the city after a holiday – he was stopped. Caliban had emerged from the cave, hobbling on his crutches, blocking the way. There was a long, hard silence. Then Prospero spoke Shakespeare's last couplet directly to Caliban: 'As you from crimes would pardoned be / Let your indulgence set me free.' Silence. Finally, Caliban stepped aside. Prospero passed. And Caliban laboured to the top of the cave to see him go. Then faced the audience. Dropped the crutches. And stood erect.

This ending for me produced a mass of conflicted emotions. The white man got off impossibly lightly. He demanded pardon – by displacing crime. The black man: how could he simply straighten that body? Wasn't the gesture pure sentimentality? Or was the final stage picture a true representation of black African history, finally prevailing by moral courage and indomitable patience over white supremacism that appears not to have learned very much about itself? Howsoever that might be, ''Tis time'.

In Honeyman's *Tempest* Shakespeare occasionally bumped against *The Lion King*. In Marianne Elliott's *All's Well That Ends Well*, Shakespeare met Tim Burton and the brothers Grimm. This, the most important rethinking of the play since Trevor Nunn's elegiac, Chekhovian production at the RSC in 1981, was a beautifully inventive, eccentric and intelligently wonky *All's Well* – one that honoured the riddling brokenness, the sheer emotional awkwardness of the play. It saw it as a gothic fairytale with, at its heart, a kind of Edward Scis-sorhands as its anti-romantic lead.

On the National Theatre's Olivier stage, Rae Smith designed a world inspired by the 1920s animated silhouette films of Lotte Reiniger and (more recently) the children's book illustrator Jan Pieńkowski, compiled from grotesquely stretched and spiky overlaid cut-outs: black floor, black walls, a door that, opened, framed expressionist pictures backlit on its threshold; a steep, black curving stairway climbing vertiginously towards a black Burton-esque haunted house on the black distant hilltop; bare skeleton trees; a flapping owl in sil-houette (courtesy of back projection) and a huge spider web hung with a giant, prowling (black) arachnid. Oliver Ford Davies's King of France in outsize crown and dressing-up-box robes was part King John (out of Milne as drawn by Shepard), part mad, sick scientist (out of Burton) chancing his young people's lives. His stable of listless wards languishing in his moribund court (Ben Allen, Rob Delaney, Alex Felton, Tom Padley) was a collec-tion of Dickensian goof-ball adolescents (the stu-dent 'naturalist' carrying butterfly net and speci-men jar; the 'philosopher' in wire-rim spectacles juggling books; the 'laboratory chemist' with gog-gles and test tubes; the Wildean 'dandy', wafting a flower), all of them first bemused then horri-fied that their marital future might be settled in a game of pass the parcel. Clare Higgins's Count-ess was a white witch in widow's weeds tuned in to her children's unspoken thoughts; her flunkey was a frock-coated hoop-shaped ancient (Michael Mears) with a face like a funeral and a forward gear aspiring to slow motion who silently portered Bertram's mountain of luggage and (at Court: he doubled his servile twin) just as silently laid out Helena's wedding dress.

All this imaginative business was underpinned with profound thought. Fairytales encrypt (under the alibi of childhood) our hearts' longings and, proposing monsters to stand in for our 'real' fears, narrate our rites of passage into adulthood – fig-ured in that dark gothic pile on the top of the hill. Imagining both the longing and the monsters, Elliott put two wondrously fresh, but painfully cal-low youths at the centre of Shakespeare's story, one of them chasing that suicidal 'girls' own' fairytale of romantic-love-as-cure-all; the other, the just as deadly misguided 'boys' own' fantasy of masculin-ity as pursuit of counterfeit honour.

When we first saw Michelle Terry's Helena, she was a flat-footed, plain-looking Little Dorrit in servant's apron and pumps dazzled by a 'bright particular star' (who, leaving Rousillon, hardly noticed her) and doomed to live in his 'collat-eral light'. (Terry's handling of this soliloquy was a master-class in thinking through Shakespeare's mind-knotting, mind-unpicking writing: utterly simple storytelling, standing motionless, centre-stage, riding the iambic pentameter. And what a voice this actor has: like a cello!) With Parolles, she was intriguingly front-footed ('How might one do, sir, to lose it [virginity] to her own liking?'). On this, Conleth Hill's absurdly vain boor drizzled a smile, flicked his hair, shot her an appraising look – and checked his watch. Charging towards Paris, she wrapped herself in a little red riding hood and took the stairs two at a time. There, armed with nothing but couplets, she promised miracles – but, canny as any streetwise hawker, knew her price ('if I help, what do you promise me?'). Coming home, humil-iated, she was still in the pumpkin-turned-princess white tulle Cinderella dress and diamante slippers she'd been married in (and had her 'official' pho-tograph taken in, framed in that doorway, splashed with confetti; her husband, the moment the flash-bulb popped, turning away). Roaring her grief ('Till I have no wife I have nothing in France'), she shed riding hood and shoes and, leaving them for others to find like a corpse, took the stairs again, a trudging runaway on a pilgrim's progress.

When we first saw George Rainsford's flop-haired Bertram he was rehearsing for Troy – or Narnia. In a long dumbshow induction, alone on-stage in near-dark, he practised thrusts and cuts, slashes and jabs and chops, as though, like Burton's Edward, he had an arsenal of weapons instead of fingers at his hands' ends. (This was a kid you'd want to keep well away from your daughter.) But these stunts – increasingly fantas-tic, increasingly silly – belonged to the nursery, to

32. *All's Well That Ends Well*, 3.5, National Theatre, directed by Marianne Elliott. Full Company with Helena (Michelle Terry) at centre barefoot.

a world of toy soldiers. No wonder this Bertram hero-worshipped Parolles-as-Captain-Spurio! And no wonder, seeing through him, the King of France dressed Bertram at Court as Little Lord Fauntleroy. The significant achievement of this actor was that he managed to let us hear both Bertram the boy-child's blighted frustration, his heart-broken end of monster-quelling dreams ('O my Parolles, *they have married me!*') and Bertram, the arrested adolescent's insufferable arrogance, his lovelessness ('A poor physician's daughter my wife?').

Brilliantly, after the interval, Elliott put these two runaways not on a collision course, but in parallel play, using simultaneous staging, stop-action blocking and freeze-framing to tell the double story of their coming of age. Bertram's war played against back projections of turreted towns in Italy. It spilled his troops down the stairs, all male carnival and testosterone-fuelled strut that turned into myth as the scene braked from real time to slow motion then freeze while the women of the St Jacques hostel – here a soldier's bar – walked among them, pointing out 'such a one' and 'which is he?' to the just-arrived pilgrim. Looking on, Helena saw her 'idolatrous fancy' come true. But his martial heroism glitteringly established, Bertram became the double butt (and double subject) of the double ambush plots that followed. Stage left, the lads (impressively led by Elliot Levey and Tony Jayawardena as the fully grown-up Dumaine brothers) went after Parolles to 'out' the *miles gloriosus*. Stage right, the lasses (as in Burton's suburbia, colour-coded; led by the excellent Janet Henfrey's Widow, a tough old biddy who'd been around the block so many times she could spell any Bertram backward) hunted him to 'out' the boy-lecher.

These ambushes, scenically intercut almost as if Elliott were working on film, weren't, however, uncomplicatedly triumphalist. Helena in pilgrim hood sat head down at a bar table in the background listening to her husband seduce Diana (Hasina Haque) by trashing his marriage ('I was compell'd to her'). Bertram, later pinned to his interrogator's chair by blindfolded Parolles's 'discovery' of him as 'foolish idle boy . . . a whale to virginity', could only choke impotently on his rage: 'I could endure anything before but a cat, and now he's a cat to me.' But he failed to discover himself in this scene of exposure, failed to connect with it the curious fact that the virgin he'd just corrupted – or thought he had – had been dressed as a cat. In a delicious sequence of power reversal – abusing the abuser – Diana and Helena strung up sheets between trees, constructing a 'bedroom' that, lit from inside, would perform the X-rated interior action as shadow play for all to see. Diana, like something imagined by Hugh Hefner in stilettos, fishnets, corset, ears and tail, was a male-fantasy cat all in red who lured Bertram, feather-tickled, to insane arousal. Helena, her twin but in white, had to stand dumbly outside and watch, then, when he was blindfolded, had to slip in and take over. But if these felines on the prowl were gleeful predators, and if the double humiliation of Bertram as soldier and lover offered a satisfyingly devastating critique of masculinity's cherished, self-regarding archetypes, still, no one came off well here. The business of exposure was sordid; the best anyone able to make of it, 'Simply the thing I am / Shall make me live.'

At the end, Elliott didn't feel the need to 'solve' this play. Helena returned to Rousillion a miracle. Her hesitant walk down the stairs was a wonder and a riddle disclosed – and a renaissance: petals fell, covering the stage in blossoms. Lucky Bertram! The comrades who'd discarded him (finding his perversion of a gentlewoman – 'he fleshes his will in the spoil of her honour' – not sport but conduct unbecoming) were able to embrace him again. The mother whose grief was killing her was restored. The king, whose fury had been molten, could forgive. Lucky Bertram, too! Hearing Helena's quiet little comment, 'Oh, my good lord, when I was like this maid / I found you wondrous kind', the penny finally dropped. The lugubrious servant wandered among them with his black-draped box camera capturing happy couples – mother and son, subject and monarch, comrade and comrade. Finally he turned his lens on Helena and Bertram. The white flash of the bulb caught their smile, turned into a black-and-white image. But as the dazzle dispersed, the look on those faces settled into something like panic. Trouble ahead? Or a couple who would find each other 'wondrous kind'?

Last year I saw Cheek by Jowl's brittle *Troilus and Cressida* as a tragedy for grown-ups. This year, Matthew Dunster's production at the Globe lurched between panto and farce, a teen romance for the theatre's 'Young Hearts' season that (from this showing) imagined that kids today have 'no more brain than earwax'. Its Prologue was given to Thersites (Paul Hunter), a randomly characterized cripple in leg iron, shoulder hump and goggles (perhaps wandered in from *Richard III* auditions?) whose ad libs ('Trojan war memorabilia!'; 'Hector's war diaries!') evidently aimed at naturalizing him as hawker and huckster to the otherwise toga-and-sandals Greek camp. Its Epilogue was cut and replaced with a meretricious rewind of the whole story told on fast forward by a grief-or-disease-crazed Pandarus pastiching his 'best' lines. Here, Matthew Kelly wasn't the 'broker lackey' of Troilus's savage indictment. He was an embarrassing pastel-coloured mincing 'dame' with a jelly-roll hairdo that did most of his acting. In between, we got 'Troilus + Cressida' as walking chick-lit: Laura Pyper's Cressida, cute, pert, with purple punk hair; Paul Stocker's Troilus, adenoidal, wearing his heart not only on his sleeve but all the way down his back in heart-shaped tattoos. Young – not to say 'o'er parted' – actors, they did their best to walk the walk but neither was up to the demands of the script, Stocker making little sense of 'I am giddy: expectation whirls me round' and both of them losing their way – stumbling as if into furniture in the dark – in the knotty love duet of 3.2.

It's fine for Dominic Dromgoole (the Globe's Artistic Director) to urge his directors to be bold: 'You have to tell big stories here.' But whose stories? And what are they saying? Cressida on Cressida, Ulysses on Cressida, Diomedes on Helen, Agamemnon and Nestor on intramural politics: these are stories Shakespeare's characters tell of themselves and each other. But in this production, they were cut to shreds to make room for extra-textual stories that Dunster wanted to tell – stories that weren't as good. So we got a war dance to open the show, played out among faux-primitives in body paint and costumes that (evidently) had been picked up on much more recent Mediterranean holidays; a bustling bazaar in the Greek camp (featuring live chickens and a rubber snake whose handler – groan – demanded payment from the Globe groundlings); thin-chested, half-naked boys playing at camp servants then metamorphosing, improbably, into Myrmidons to slaughter Hector; a truly weird lullaby accompanying the lovers' departure to bed and much more muzak drowning out dialogue elsewhere, including, the first time round, a chorus line on 'Love, love, nothing but love' (lifted from Cheek by Jowl, a cheap imitation) then a final reprise that brought the full company in behind Pandarus, now the Alzheimer victim gabbling dementedly, 'Is this the generation of love? . . . Nothing but love'. Anna Fleischle's design – which wrapped the Globe stage in grey canvas that put you in mind both of dust on the Dardan plains and skin flaking from desiccated corpses – provided one stunning effect. An extension (yet another) to the stage curved out, away and down, making what looked like both a battlefield trench and a crumbling wall. Hector, dead, was rolled into the trench. He lay there for the rest of the night, his blood slowly draining away, mute comment on the whole story of a 'war for a placket'. Too bad, then, that from where they were sitting or standing, most of the audience couldn't see him.

And now, a (partial) retraction. This is a play that in the Epistle to one of its Jacobean quartos advertised itself as 'neuer stal'd with the Stage, neuer clapper-clawd with the palmes of the vulger'. It's a play that has no performance history to speak of until the second half of the twentieth century; a play never set at A-level; a play off the tourist's radar. And yet, the Globe's *Troilus and Cressida* was a sell-out. The night I saw the show, twelve hundred people heard at least *something* of this bleaker-than-bleak script. The yard was crammed with look-alike Cressidas who were clearly not just following the ugly twists and turns in the plot but forming (sometimes loud) opinions and relishing both argument and language, much more 'brain than earwax'. They deserved a better production. But at least it was a start.

Some comedy this year performed exploratory surgery on my willing heart; some had me chewing my programme. But for full-throttle, ballsy, smart and utterly play-full comedy, nothing beat Propeller's double bill, this fourteen-strong all-male company's *A Midsummer Night's Dream* and *The Merchant of Venice*. Directed by Edward Hall, designed by Michael Pavelka, it played the Watermill Theatre and UK venues then went on an international tour.

As soon as the skinhead fairies, part manikin, part wind-up doll, swung into view – in white long johns, corsets, whiteface, clown eyebrows, rouged cheeks and lipstick, wearing miniature harmonicas on lanyards around their necks – using every bit of their arctic white camouflage-draped set as gymnastic apparatus – this *Dream* was the property of the anarchists, the upside-down merchants. And they'd play all the parts. Puck (the absurdly over-talented Jon Trenchard: he also composed the show's music) arrived feet first. Out of a magic box: sparkly ruby slippers, red-and-white striped tights, battered (once white) tutu, grubby corset, wicked grin. The box was Puck's theatre. His costume skip – producing a jumble of vaguely Victorian opera cloaks, top hats, gloves, fur swags, frock coats that the fairies used to dress themselves on-stage as their mortal doubles as the story began, 'Now fair Hippolyta . . . !' Also his best joke of the night. Capturing the mortal for the lickerish Fairy Queen, he stuck ass-headed, buck-toothed Bottom, a much more than life-sized Bob Barrett, in that box – confinement enough, you'd

33. *A Midsummer Night's Dream*, 2.1, Propeller, Watermill, directed by Edward Hall. Richard Dempsey as Titania.

imagine. But then lifted the pyramid dome off its top, and put it into Titania's hands (Richard Dempsey, cackling wildly). And collapsed the box. No Bottom! Gone! Our eyes swivelling from box to fairy hands told us he'd been *translated*! Titania had him! Trapped, shrunk, in that miniature prison! And her triumphalist laughter! Oh, poor little weaver: how ravished, *transported* you'd been by the idea of Quince's play. Now, how long the night was going to be for you!

This was a production that perfectly judged the balance between menace and mayhem. Chris Myles's bullet-headed Egeus, hearing that stuff about his designated son-in-law's attentions to Helena, biffed poor Demetrius around the head (Sam Swainsbury, a deliciously frantic caught-with-my-trousers-down look in his eyes). Appearing out from under camouflage on high tennis umpire chairs (another joke on Alice in Wonder-

land perspective), Richard Clothier's black demon king Oberon was (also) just a hen-pecked husband to a grand dame, Vita Sackville West-esque Titania – Dempsey in black lipstick, kohled eyes like holes burnt in a bedsheet, lace gloves, and black ostrich feather stole. In a company where *everyone* 'does' poetry, where *everyone* 'does' sparkling textual clarity, this Titania's 'forgeries of jealousy' speech was miraculous: taunting, elegiac, apocalyptic, seeing horror, uncompromising ('SET YOUR HEART AT REST!'), drawn up to the full height of female imperiousness ('The fairyland buys not the child of me!') – which made her hot-flush swooning over Bottom all the more hilarious. In the wood, the lovers' ding-dong was part all-in wrestling, part Keystone Cops, part four-part harmony on a heartbreaking love lament where the lads came off incredibly badly: it's as though this company, which never attempts female

34. *A Midsummer Night's Dream*, 3.2, Propeller, Watermill, directed by Edward Hall. Babou Ceesay as Helena, Sam Swainsbury as Demetrius, Jack Tarlton as Lysander, John Dougall as Fairy in background.

impersonation or persuasive transvestism, gets a real kick out of dismantling hegemonic masculinity. Richard Frame's prim little Hermia in flounced skirt had given whiffling sounds of demure pleasure when Jack Tarlton's Lysander – in a Simon Legree melodrama cape, a dead giveaway – proposed the runaway. But now she dropped her voice an octave to throw herself at Helena's eyes, Babou Ceesay, twice Frame's size, backing off in terror from the Exocet-terrier. Nothing in this production was more painful than this Helena's abjection: 'Let me go. / You see how simple and how fond I am.' Or more delightful than the sounds that came out of it – produced by the fairies on instruments ranging from insides gutted from a piano to glockenspiel and waterphone. When they heaped into a circle and fell asleep, harmonicas in mouths, their in-out breathing gave the sound of fairies snoring.

After the turn-around (full marks to stagecrew: Nick Chesterfield, Claire Henders, Bridget Fell, Bryony Rutter), the same team came back for *Merchant*. With the camouflage removed, we could see what fairyland was really made of: metal cages. A prison. (And another terrifically theatre-worthy design by Pavelka, with component sections that could be moved around to make corridors, interrogation cells. The skinhead fairies? Those were prison haircuts.) This was *Merchant* set in a space saturated with violence, one that made sense of the stakes Shakespeare's play plays for, that literalized the *lex talionis*. Here, 'Hath not a Jew eyes?' was not seeking wet turn-the-other-cheek sympathy but tough Judaic retribution, making Christians 'see feelingly'. Asking the question, Richard Clothier's lean and hungry Shylock had found Solanio alone, strung him up by his wrists to a

35. *The Merchant of Venice*, 1.1, Propeller, Watermill, directed by Edward Hall. Sam Swainsbury as Solanio, Richard Dempsey as Lorenzo, Bob Barrett as Antonio, Tom Padden as Tubal (deep behind), Babou Ceesay as Prison Governor, Kelsey Brookfield as Portia (deep behind), John Dougall as Gobbo (behind), Richard Clothier as Shylock, Chris Myles as Nerissa (behind).

spar, delivered his homily, then had lunged forward and gouged out an eye, pulping it in his hand. The deafening acoustic in this place was metal on metal: plates, cups, slop buckets banging on bars; whistles, sirens, the terrifying noise of incarceration – and the aspirational sound of reformation: hymns, prayers. A place, then, that understood that Shakespeare's 'trial' isn't confined to Act 4. Trial, in this play, is the repeated, the continuous scenic content.

The daily routine of this prison never let up. Nor the illicit anti-routine: whatever was happening in the foreground, in the background the running action saw drug stashes delivered, bribes paid, favours exchanged. Men's bodies were tribally marked: prison greys the uniform, but underneath, Antonio (Bob Barrett: this merchant a depressive photo-reverse of his loopy Bottom) had a crude cross tattooed upon his heart, and under his

jacket you could just see the fringe of Tubal's (Tom Padden) prayer shawl.

Plenty of Propeller's signature anarchy was stamped on this production. Jonathan Livingstone's rasta rapper Morocco (arms the size of hams; crescent tattoo on one of them) had a West Indian accent you could have poured out of a bucket. (Black) Portia (Kelsey Brookfield) in bustier and pedal pushers turned up her nose at him – the wrong kind of black – while Nerissa (Chris Myles), a raddled, camp vision in wrecked fishnets, lace-up tart's boots, short-shorts, and corset that projected her nipples through the bars of her braces, played the casket lottery like a game of Chase the Lady, complete with focus pulls, trick playing cards and dangling keys. Jon Trenchard's Jessica (flipping his fizz-bang-wallop Puck), in pinny and headscarf, cringed and shrank – and ran away from 'home' in a duffel coat whose hood pulled down discovered, shockingly, her head shaved. All of these performances were 'beyond' gender: they weren't transvestite; they weren't male whores, guys girling it up for the sexual recreation of fellow prisoners. They were actors playing parts that isolated high emotional content. Listening to the letter that Antonio directed to Bassanio in Belmont, a letter that told their 'LOVE', Portia shed tears of rage. Nerissa, learning that Gratiano (Richard Frame) had disposed of her ring, threw furniture – then wrung his balls. And Clothier's Shylock: so thoroughly gutted by the loss of his child that he couldn't say the word 'turquoise'.

At the beginning, kicking the whole thing off, Babou Cessay's big black prison governor had come on in a white linen suit, smoking a fat cigar, languidly asking 'Which is the Merchant here, and which the Jew?' Barrett and Clothier had stepped forward. At the end, he returned, asked the same question. Shylock, condemned to conversion, stared at Antonio. So who *now* was the Jew? Circling round to the beginning, starting all over again, this frequently shocking and dangerous production made us finally see not a *Merchant* set in a prison. But Shakespeare's play as a prison from which we can't escape.

TRAGEDIES

On the back of last year's terrific Tobacco Factory *Hamlet*, I raced down to Bristol for this season's *Antony and Cleopatra*, eager to see how a world 'past the size of dreaming' would conduct its epic rememberings, its global map-redrawing politics, its grand diva trantrums, seductions, oglings and dazzling, sexy, funny show-biz self-promotions crammed onto a stage that's the size of a postage stamp. I could have saved my petrol. Locating the play visually in the 1640s on the eve of the English Civil War, prompting spectators to think of Romans and Egyptians as Roundheads and Cavaliers (Caesar = Cromwell?; Lepidus = Laud?; so Antony = a boozy Wilmot-as-Rochester?), and to see Cleopatra and her 'girls' in Caroline bedroom wear, the director, Andrew Hilton, crossed

our semiotic wires into a knot to stymie even Alexander. For Hilton in the programme, Shakespeare's Egypt 'is neither North Africa nor Middle Eastern'. Perhaps. But neither is it Henrietta Maria's drawing room with a Cleopatra (Lucy Black) more likely to be indoors grooming her King Charles spaniels than out on the public street playing hop-scotch. (When Black ordered 'Lead me to my chamber' I swear I heard Barbara Woodhouse calling 'Walkies!') It's just wrong for Hilton to write that Shakespeare's Egypt was a kind of fanciful 'new imagining', 'not as might be recorded by . . . a historian'. Plenty of history (Herodotus, Plutarch) imagined Egypt, and Shakespeare knew it. And he knew Egypt from Ovid and Virgil and from native sources, as an exotic Other and, perhaps most significantly, black. So when are productions going to stop whiting out Cleopatra? (Lucy Black? Oh, would that she had been!) When are they going to give us what Shakespeare wrote – black Alexandria – and to show us the stakes this play plays for: not just west v. east, male v. female, Rome v. Alexandria and Caesar v. Cleopatra but white v. black, an imperial sweepstakes whose winner will write the future history of the world?

Ranting aside, there were things to admire in this production: Simon Armstrong's battered Enobarbus (much the better drunk – and man – than his master). Dying on a low groan of that master's name – 'O, Antony' – he gave us the sound of a heart breaking. Equally good was a disconcertingly young Lepidus (Paul Brendan, fresh from drama school) who, as 'tried and valiant solider', really did suffer in the comparison with Antony's horse and, as triumvir, was 'girled' by the other two. Most interesting was Byron Mondahl's rolypoly Just William Octavius: hardly the lad to have been doing anything even so vigorous on the playing fields of Philippi as keeping 'His sword e'en like a dancer' when clearly he would have been in the school tuck-shop scoffing cream cakes. But his rage against Antony – 'You have broken / The article of your oath' – was an eruption that escalated petulant schoolboy squabble into high politics. No longer just the fat kid who kept score but a serious player interrogating the failed captain of the First Eleven, he registered betrayal, contempt, the disillusioned end of hero worship. But he was also a Malvolio-in-waiting, a 'kind of Puritan' (and in that costume, looked the part). Though he played along, there was never the chance that Cleopatra's last-but-one seduction would work; and though he wept taking Antony's stained sword into his bread pudding whitely fingers, those tears were a crocodile's. As soon as the public moment was over, he turned away, rubbing the blood off his hands, disgusted.

I'm told that having failed to get a ticket for *Julius Caesar* earlier in the Tobacco Factory's two-play 'Roman Season' I missed the backstory that made richer sense of Mondahl's Octavius as a man literally sickened by Antony's tumbling on the bed of Ptolemy and reeling the street at noon and, worse, his delinquent forgetting of his assassinated 'father', Julius, whose ghost continued to haunt the younger man, legitimating his take-over as a restoration, Caesar for Caesar. Watching Lucy Bailey's *Julius Caesar* on the RSC's Courtyard stage, I came away feeling I was missing the rest of the story. I wanted the sequel. How would Darrell D'Silva's blockish Antony fare in an empire post-Philippi? I couldn't see this sprawling, joyless reveller-turned-brutal-thug sitting whistling to the air in a vacant marketplace in Cydnus. Or fascinated by Cleopatra's delicious pranks. (In Caesar's Rome, D'Silva's Antony spewed last night's soured drink in a corner before heading for the Capitol; in battle, blood-crusted, he tossed the mangled head of an enemy at prissy Octavius (Joseph Arkley), more Hannibal Lector than Hannibal the Great.)

As Boyd's *As You Like It* this season will be remembered as 'the one with the rabbit', Bailey's *Caesar* will be 'the one with the back projections'. The director and her designer (William Dudley) created urban Rome in a series of arresting CGI images thrown up high on the stage's back wall like digital versions of an architectural frieze: Caesar's triumphal arch; his statue, exploding into digital fragments; an orchard of leafless black trees; a wasteland of blighted stumps awaiting crucifixions; the Colosseum festering with tiny humanity like maggots. At stage level, played across six black screens, projections of film footage (digitally multi-plied into an endless sequence) gave the city not as its buildings but its populace. Life-sized, this mob was tumultuous, potentially riotous – and always on the move, inexhaustibly restless. On holiday, it reeled in carnival conga lines. Later, it bristled with weapons, in phalanxes stretching out to the crack of doom. These screens could swivel, turning their flat surfaces into angled walls, making corridors where real people – street revellers, soldiers – entered. When the real replaced the virtual, the momentary effect was a surreal distortion that flummoxed the eye until it adjusted.

This was a brutal Rome, a Rome defined by the savagery of its origins. Not only did the iconic image of Romulus and Remus suckling the wolf mother hang like a caption over the production's opening ten minutes, that opening animated the city's wolfish past. Two lads, filthy, feral, language-less, in loincloths, alone on a dark stage, stalked each other, tumbling like wolf cubs playing at hunting until one sank his teeth into his brother's neck and came away with a face full of blood. Red confetti began to fall, ritualistically mediating history into myth.

When Shakespeare's opening scene began, the Lupercal remembered Rome's bloody origins. Loud with wild animal sounds on horns and braying reeds, it was more than a street party: a savage, orgiastic rite that had men in wolf heads and skins flailing each other with whips and women in leather bustiers, nipples proud as if to invite suckling. Only Sam Troughton's Brutus and John Mackay's Cassius stood apart in this scrum, in linen robes that looked like first thoughts on the toga. Beside them, Greg Hicks's Caesar was a half-naked tribal chieftain who slammed out arrogance ('always I am Caesar') while sucking in flattery ('Caesar says "do this" and it is performed'); a sleek, mercurial Caesar who was master of the half line ('would he were fatter') but also deeply stupid, more Shere Khan in this pack than Mowgli. (No smarter comment was made about this Caesar than Calpurnia's (Noma Dumezweni) 'Your wisdom is consumed in confidence'.)

Subsequently, the assassination, too, remembered Rome's origins. The conspirators

36. *Julius Caesar*, 1.2, RSC, Courtyard Theatre, directed by Lucy Bailey. Greg Hicks as Julius Caesar.

(aspirationally, culinary artists carving a dish for the gods; in the event, butchers wading through an abattoir) had to kill him twenty times before he died. Troughton's Brutus (wild-eyed, last to strike) finally accepted what Hicks's Caesar offered not as a rebuke but an invitation – 'et tu, Brute?' – by cutting Caesar's throat. The funeral remembered these origins too, not just in the bloody hands raised to the crowd to display the bloody weapons that had 'freed' them but in the bloody face D'Silva's Antony presented to that crowd, smeared with Caesar's blood, Romulus's avatar, the animal now as orator.

Seeing this city as a wilderness of wolves, Bailey said plenty about a 'state of (brutish) nature' in a Rome that Thomas Hobbes would have recognized. But not much about what else Shakespeare explores in *Caesar*, the corrective of 'culture'. This is a play that has men constantly thinking about learning; remembering their school-days; poking fun at Cicero (a core author every Elizabethan schoolboy knew); registering what the (Elizabethan) future would remember ('In states unborn and accents yet unknown') about Rome besides the assassination, that it was Rome that taught them the effective use of human speech, persuasion, rhetoric learned to manage political life: the uttering mouth in place of the bloody chops. In Bailey's over-produced staging, Shakespeare's rhetorical play was forgotten (a particular irony, given the constant connections speakers make between eyes and tongues, hands and mouths, the embodied apparatus for making things known). Even where speech was most urgent and muscular, where it conducted thought via emotional and ideological switchbacks (for example, Cassius's question, 'Tell me good Brutus, can you see your face?' or Brutus's reassurance, 'yet see you but our hands . . . / Our hearts you see not'), we didn't hear speech as 'live' discourse. We were looking at actors who had learned speeches and were reciting them, not listening to Romans whose native learning, equipping them rhetorically, allowed them, by speaking, to improvise a new political world order and to utter it into being: 'It must be by his death.' Simply, neither Mackay's Cassius nor Troughton's Brutus was art-ful, was 'cultured' enough for Shakespeare's play, and Bailey, paying more attention to effects than text, gave us less than half a *Caesar*.

Still, that was considerably more of the play than Matthew Dunster gave us of *Macbeth* at the Royal Exchange, Manchester. His notion of 'collaborating with Shakespeare' is to see 'where he [*sic*] would benefit from our contemporary eyes', decide 'we don't need that', and cut whatever's 'no use to us' – in this case, 'all the witchcraft'. Dunster 'just got rid of it'. And plenty more besides: the Porter, most of 'If it were done', the Old Man, 'double double', etc., etc. You'll have recognized him by now. He's the same Dunster of this year's 'I-had-never-even-read – it!-when-I-agreed-to-direct-it' *Troilus and Cressida* at the Globe, working in the same popular trash shock-as-schlock mode, this time in modern dress that might have walked in off the street – or from a modern war zone off the TV. So we got the theatre draped in black camouflage netting. Squaddies in flak jackets. A coke-snorting WAG-ish Lady M (Hilary Maclean) who read her husband's letter as an email off her laptop and wound up behind a glass wall in a psychiatric unit pushing her drip. A Macbeth (the monotoned Nicholas Gleaves) who, in an offhand persuasion scene ('What news?... Hath he ask'd for me?'), might have been wanting clues to the crossword. This Macbeth was armed for the murder by 'metaphysical aid' in the form of the girl group that passed as the weird sisters lugging in a bucket of blood and handing him a bloody knife (Rebecca Callard, Niamh Quinn, Anna Crump Raiswell). But he was so appalled after the murder at the gore reeking his hands that he stripped naked – shrieks from the school parties in the audience – to stand under a shower head that (conveniently) dropped in from above. We got, too, the apparitions as video replays of various murders. We got an extended, gratuitously brutalized domestic slaughter scene at the Macduffs' that started with a harassed Mum (Rebecca Callard), loaded with groceries and too many kids, falling through the door into her kitchen, then proceeded to an ambush by men in pig masks that had one child beaten to a pulp, another drowned in the sink (the taps having been tested by the assassins earlier), the mother's neck snapped and the nanny shot. And at the end, we got Malcolm-as-Obama (John MacMillan), dressing, rehearsing his speech for the cameras while Fleance (Vincent Bernard) slunk in unobserved, lugging the (re-filled) bucket of blood to fuel the next round of atrocity.

So who were the witches? 'Victims of conflict'? 'Children who've been brutalized by war' as Dunster – all pious political correctness – claimed in interview and pictured in the programme? No. They were sensationalist clichés. Three middle-class white girls watching kids' telly from their bunk bed when soldiers burst in (supervised, we'd realize later, by Macbeth), abducting one, raping two, dragging the victims away folded up in the trashed carpet. Afterwards the girls returned, sometimes as invisible spooks handing out props; as buskers in camped-up military dress performing a rock routine to ghetto-blaster that had sister-on-sister simulating the sex attack; as provocative Lolitas dragging a chain-gang of trussed-up Barbie dolls. And what was deadly about all this was that it was utterly desensitized: designer trauma without pain, extravagant violence without hurt, state-of-the-art mindless brutality – images of Abu Ghraib come to mind – without responsibility. (For contrast, see the way Terry Hands used the boy-soldier, Young Siward, in last year's *Macbeth*.) But it wasn't just the witchcraft Dunster dumped. It was the whole universe of meaning that Shakespeare invokes the metaphor of witchcraft to explore in *Macbeth*: conscience, consequence, the 'life to come' that 'we'd jump' if we thought we'd get away with murder, the mind 'full of scorpions', 'restless ecstasy', the 'milk of human kindness' poisoned in a chalice that will 'return / To plague th'inventor'. Dunster has stories he wants to tell – but they aren't Shakespeare's, and he doesn't need Shakespeare to tell them. But then, Shakespeare doesn't need Dunster. And neither, at present, do I.

Pre-empting the edgiest opening in Shakespeare – 'Who's there?' 'Nay answer me' – Michael Grandage's *Hamlet* (his second production in this season's Donmar residency at Wyndham's) opened not with the sound of male nerves rattling, or with words, but with a weird, unearthly music like wind wailing in a nightmare or human voices, post mortem, strung out like vapour trails. And instead of trigger-happy sentries he fixed a long look on a solitary figure seen through a scrim, grey on grey, who stood frozen, gazing up at the shaft of broken light that struggled into Elsinore through the gloom. No doubt but that filmic 'take' was aimed at Jude Law fans, to give them privileged looking at the star they'd come to see. But it worked also to capture the essense of this Hamlet. Law's Prince would be most himself when most alone. And his story would be framed in a sequence of visually stunning shots fixed in memory with the clarity of black-and-white photographs.

Elsinore was a brooding medieval fortress designed, it appeared, by Christopher Oram to be deliberately too big for the Wyndham stage: massive studded gates; black stone battlements climbing three storeys; the only light, what filtered through the crenellations high up. But modern royals lived there, all of them as grimly monochromatic as their surroundings: Gertrude in linen trousers (Penelope Wilton), a rather vacuous organizer of too many dreary November garden parties; Horatio (Matt Ryan), a lank-haired biker in leathers (whom she'd never have invited and who'd clearly turned up at Elsinore only because he'd been sent down from Wittenberg); Polonius (Ron Cook), a tetchy, small-minded spin doctor straight up from Gordon Brown's Whitehall; and Jude Law's Hamlet, a man in rehearsal gear. In a sense, a man always auditioning.

The best moments of this production explored isolation as a function of overcrowding. In the closet scene, (ghost) father and (remarried) mother sat side by side on Gertrude's bed, gazing at their son, who stared back – all of them in separate worlds. Mad, Ophelia (Gugu Mbatha-Raw) threaded through the scrum of courtiers who defensively circled the queen, utterly vacant, in her pyjamas, clutching a little, little funeral posy, her mind elsewhere. While the Prince wittered on, self-absorbed, about their craft ('Speak the speech . . . '), one of the players, self-absorbed, sat doggedly cutting out a yellow paper crown. As voyeur, Polonius was both alone and part of the audience. We watched his death from reverse: he, downstage, looking (like us), through the arras that had dropped in like a great swag curtain, at Hamlet manhandling his mother on her bed. Then, stabbed, hugging the fabric, he brought the whole thing down, tumbling himself into Hamlet's world to die. At the funeral, when Laertes (Alex Waldmann) clambered into the grave and hauled his sister's corpse upright so that her head lolled acquiesence at the abuse of his near-incestuous embrace, the siblings locked into that grotesque show of bewildered love were also utterly apart.

When least expected, the castle breached its own claustrophobia. The monolithic back wall turned out to be sliding doors that could open – but only into a narrow aperture, and only onto another blank black wall just beyond a narrow verge, Elsinore's only 'outside'. It was here that Hamlet sat, barefoot, knotted dysmorphically into a hunch of misery as he wondered whether 'to be or not to be' while snow fell, collecting his thoughts into little frozen piles. It was across this gap he passed, then paused, en route to his mother's closet, almost a ghost.

But if high-definition production images remain like isolated flashbulb memories on my retina, what I didn't get from this production was a sense of continuity, of life that *mattered* 'between' those moments, implicated, connecting them, and legible on stage. Above, I ventured that Grandage had instructed his *Twelfth Night* company 'no gags'; here, it was as if he'd told his *Hamlet* company 'no stories', which is sort of like saying 'no performances' or – in this most theatrically self-inventive of plays, 'no theatre'. (And if 'no stories', then for me, 'no tragedy'.) So it wasn't just that characters were isolated; they were also blanks. (The players were a dead giveaway: mime artists doing 'The Mousetrap' in white-face and white silks, inscrutable, anonymous, absent.) Wilton's Gertrude – a better actor than showed here – had two modes: fraught maternal looking; anguished hand-wringing. (Compare the 'whole history' Penny Downie's Gertrude was able to tell in last year's RSC *Hamlet*.) When she was sane, Mbatha-Raw's Ophelia was a kind of amnesiac, her 'remembrances' just empty pages. And Law for me failed to make good the promise of his enigmatic opening pose, to tell me the story contained in his 'keeping alone'. Last year David Tennant at the RSC gave us Hamlet as brilliant, brain-damaged (with too much thinking), anarchist clown; Jamie Ballard at the Tobacco Factory, Hamlet as grief-gutted orphan, hungry for touch, astonished to learn his part in the thing that was happening to him. Both Hamlets survived on jokes, passports from their pestered intellect into the 'sane' world of public politics and human intimacy. Jude Law's Hamlet never found laughter. Introverted, he kept the heart of his mystery under wraps.

To finish this year's work, two *Othello*s take me back to where this review began, remembering 1959, Paul Robeson and his legacy. Famously, Robeson learned *Othello* in four languages – five, counting Engish. Watching Kathryn Hunter's touring production with Patrice Naiambana for the RSC, I got the feeling she and her Othello wished they didn't have Shakespeare's play in any language at all. This was a production crowded with extra-textual performance narratives, a production driven by the director's training in physical theatre that can be traced back to her work with Theatre de Complicité. (As an actor, Hunter's hallmark is astonishing physical transformation: she's played both King Lear and Kafka's ape.) Here, she mobilized the resources and the rehearsal vocabulary of Complicité, casting five Complicité veterans, including Marcello Magni (as Roderigo and Movement Director). In addition, the production was driven by Naiambana's long-term investigative work on *Othello* – workshops, master-classes, his own one-man show, a practical performance project at the RSC two seasons earlier – that's determined to find an 'alternative' Othello narrative, one that can use the tradition of the African *griot*, the tribal storyteller, to discover a way of 'leaping out of Shakespeare's terror'. (Ben Okri's essay of that title was the production's 'handbook'.) So this was a production that was trying to do two adventurous things: exploring the play physically and creating deliberately provocative images that invited us to react to issues of race, imperialism and anger. The problem was that this invention was then required to be subordinated to a text-prioritizing RSC production where Shakespeare's words constantly got in the actors' way. And disturbingly, the most insistent 'alternative narrative' to emerge was the Clown's.

Hunter set this *Othello* in the 1950s – the last decade, she thought, when the plain face of racism showed itself unashamedly in public – but inconsistently, so the historical and cultural inaccuracies made nonsense of relationships in the play. Othello's army was not only racially integrated; there were women in the ranks, too. (But wait a second: a black man, an African, in charge of a European army in 1955?) The racism the director had in mind was clearly a US import – but the several accents coming out of the play (German, Italian, Greek, English RP and the weirdly shifting tonality Naiambana produced, sometimes 'native' as though imitating Olivier 'doing' the African prince, sometimes Etonian) were all Old World. The soldiers' uniforms were US, World War II; their riot shields, Belfast, 1977; the 'syndrome' compelling them to domestic violence, post-Falklands 'combat trauma'. Iago (Michael Gould, a serious actor left miserably high and dry in this production) was a pill-popping victim of post-traumatic stress whose condition – 'motiveless malignancy'? – was soberly explained by a long programme note, viz. that it's 'imperative' to give 'troubled soldiers' 'counselling even if they don't seek it'.

On the face of it, Liz Cooke produced an elegant, theatrically useful design: a wooden Bridge of Sighs that could be trundled downstage or split at the arch's apex, its halves swung round to suggest the prow of a ship, a promontory in Cyprus, a narrow street in the dark. But whether the space was working as Venice or Cyprus, Hunter's habit was to cut script to make way for choreographed sequences that served as textual proxies. The production's opening sequence, a full company walk-down to Renaissance *a capella* complete with Doge flanked by crucifixes, offered the solemn ritual of the city's annual marriage to the sea. We could have been in 1590. But then two figures peeled off, confident runaways – a black man in tuxedo; a white woman, sultry in hot burnt orange evening dress – and began dancing, weaving erotically around each other to a different acoustic, the sound of an Afrian *mbira*, singing a song they shared as he draped her in a cloth dyed the colour of dried blood. (Was she picking up the language, or instinctively *knowing* the language?) In the Senate, this Desdemona's (Natalia Tena) sexual charge was there – but her speech was cut. She arrived on Cyprus in high, high heels and red, red lipstick like a movie star, the soldiers forming themselves into a human staircase for her to descend like a Busby Berkeley routine from the ship – but her speech was cut. Later she exited speechless to her bridal night in full Venetian rig-out. But then as Cassio (Alex Hassell), played here as a grinning dimwit hunk, breathed into a microphone a 'dolce vita' aubade, the couple crossed the stage again, Desdemona in French knickers, topless, her legs wrapped around Othello's waist, the general's hat on her head, her bridal tiara on his. (Worryingly, performing this foreplay with Othello, she was evidently listening to Cassio: she knew his song in the morning.) Later still, the willow scene was cut, Emilia's (Tamzin Griffin) part axed, to make way for a dream sequence. The bed became a sea of billowing silk. Across it, Brabantio (Hannes Flaschberger) returned to his near-naked daughter as consoling ghost – taking her speech. This production, in short, performed on Tena and Griffin the misogynistic objectification it 'found' in the text.

Worse, it invented a parallel extra-textual racist narrative, performed on the watch in Shakespeare's 2.3 as subalterns' cabaret, with the Clown in charge of the high-jinks. Bandy-legged, woolly-headed, Miltos Yerolemou (credited in the programme as 'Soldier Entertainer/Chorus') was made up in comic black-face like Al Jolson. 'Mammy', 'You made me love you', he crooned to a life-sized, white, wedding-dressed Desdemona doll, a red gash across her face for lips, tits shoved out like bowsprits, manipulated into obscene poses that finally produced a squat, a grunt – a birth! From under her skirts, a Raggedy Andy doll. Then – squat, grunt – a *second* birth: a Golliwog. How did the one black squaddie in the ranks view this performance? What were we to make of Cassio, applauding, wearing his dopey Leave-It-To-Beaver smile? When this carnival broke out into an ugly, noisy fist-fight and Othello entered, slowly taking in the scene, how should we understand his confiscation of the Golliwog (which he carried with him thereafter, a kind of fetish, the doll later a witness to murder), and behind him, Desdemona, coming face to face with her Other, but showing no recognition, no reaction? When the rest cleared off, Iago took this Other on his lap, questioning her, 'what's he then that says I play the villain?' Hitting upon the way 'to turn her virtue into pitch', he poked fingers into the tin of bootblack he'd confiscated from the Clown, first gobbed her lips, then reached up under her skirts, smearing her privates, now exposed as the blackened 'net' that would 'enmesh them all'.

The problem with heaping such extra-textual, anachronistic and over-determining narratives on its head was, of course, that Shakespeare's play had no way of answering back. It didn't have the words to deal with the stuff Hunter was loading into the performance text. So Cassio looked like a closet complicit, Desdemona, a naive chit, and Othello, Rymer's 'Mauritanian booby'. Making Iago's sickness – 'I hate the Moor' – not individual and aberrational but institutional and endemic, drained the appalling power of his text, his destructive project, into a common sewer, diluting tragedy into social docu-drama (and Gould's performance into a cipher). Given what the exhibition out in the foyer was telling spectators about Paul Robeson playing Othello at the very time Hunter was setting this *Othello* – a play, said the actor in 1959, that was Shakespeare's 'gift' to the black man, a play all about his 'dignity' – Hunter's production looked like it didn't believe him. It gave revisionism, a crude anti-homage.

By contrast, Northern Broadsides's *Othello* gave a 'round, unvarnished tale'. If Naiambana has spent his actorly life chasing Shakespeare, the stand-up comic Lenny Henry has spent his life fleeing him, inoculated against the national poet by the national curriculum like millions of others taught as schoolchildren that they didn't look right or sound right for Shakespeare. Making his high-risk debut with Othello, Henry (who'd never done any 'straight' theatre, never mind Shakespeare) attracted even more media attention this year than David Tennant's Hamlet last year. Making it with Northern Broadsides he improved his chances by putting himself in the hands of a company that grabbed the risk with relish, surrounding him with a tight ensemble – twelve actors (compare Hunter's sixteen), ten of them company veterans who share a rehearsal grammar, performance vocabulary, and attitude towards language and voice – and a director – Barrie Rutter – whose chief interest is swift, clear storytelling, where the story is urgent news told right here and right now for the first time in speeches that can't wait to be spoken.

The look of this production was uninsistently Edwardian: long, rust-red twill skirts, high-necked white blouses for the women (and Bianca – Rachel Jane Allen – flashing red leather boots); Venetian maroon soldiers' tunics and bomber jackets blazoned with the lion of St Mark for the men, and berets that put you in mind both of Monty and today's desert rats in Helmand. Ruari Murchison's near-empty black box suggested Venice (heavy, studded double doors between ancient pillars, set off at an angle, skewing the idea of the urban), Cyprus (a wall of shuttered doors filtered the heat, invited voyeurism), and (proleptically) hell. Theatrically, this design cleared open space for high-speed traffic – and for Lenny Henry.

He's a huge man. And one of the stories this *Othello* told was about that bulk: a towering giant whittled, chipped, sniped at, cut down by inches to the paltry size of Iago's (Conrad Nelson) small, ugly mind. This was a story not of race but of loss.

In the Senate, Henry was an Othello who'd lived his 'travailous history'. When he spoke about 'the anthropophagi', the rhythms of that word rumbling up through his chest as though scaling every rib, you knew he'd met them face to face, shared a meal. Slurs – Brabantio's (Barrie Rutter) viciousness: 'To fall in love with what she feared to look on'; 'Against all rules of nature' – passed over his face in a momentary spasm, his hand instinctively flexing around a weapon that wasn't there. Remembering 'my story being done' how Desdemona 'swore . . . 'twas strange . . . strange/ . . . pitiful . . . pitiful' and how 'She wished' and 'yet she wished', the wonder of that falling-in-love story where he was astonished to find himself the subject was captured, savoured in those dazzled repetitions. On Cyprus, bursting into the scene – 'O my fair WARRIOR!' – he scooped his tiny child-bride (Jessica Harris) up in his arms, rocking her high over his head then below his knees like a boat riding waves to illustrate 'If after every tempest come such calm . . .'. He prattled unashamed; he doted; he was a beaming kid tucking Desdemona's little hand into his great fist and falling into the game when – 'Well met at Cyprus' – she gigglingly mocked the military by playing soldier, marching them off goose-stepping – two strides to his one – to the Citadel.

We knew what they didn't, that this 'fertile climate' of 'delight' was already 'plague[d] . . . with flies', an insect-sized anthropophagus in the shape of Nelson's fly-weight Iago. He was everywhere. Busy. Buzzing. Wheedling. Advising in that chirpy northern voice that sounded as honest as Hovis and decent as a flat cap. He straightened Roderigo's lapels (Matt Connor, incorrigibly credulous) then crushed him in a manly hug that so easily could have turned into a strangle. He set up the rowdy, full-voiced 'cannikin clink' drinking game as all-male line dance and confidence trick to comic trombone accompaniment, Cassio (Richard Standing, 'bromance' personified) getting drunker and drunker as he kept losing, helped in draining bigger and bigger cups by Iago's nudging hand. He mopped up afterwards, the camp skivvy as 'moraler' smartly binning 'reputation' along with the rest of the scene's trash before settling down with still brain-fumed Cassio for some straight 'chap talk': 'I'll tell you what you shall do.' Coming out of Nelson's mouth, Shakespeare's prose felt as new as internet chat. He was a guy who used his hands like props, to hook people into his stories; whose comradely ministrations turned men into puppets; whose intimate manhandling of all and sundry – he even embraced Desdemona when she threw herself into his arms ('Am I that name, Iago?') – underscored his distance, cold estrangement from his wife, here, played for once not as middle-aged hag but by Maeve Larkin as young and beautiful – and silently crushed. Their marriage was fully exposed when, busily collecting the raincapes from the new arrivals on Cyprus – ensign as company valet – he ignored only the garment Emilia held outstretched. So she dropped it – and turned away. This was an Iago who revealed his damned double in soliloquy. Sitting alone, cross-legged, speaking straight out, his precise, pointed confession, 'I . . . hate . . . the Moor', twisted his face into a satanic mask, the devil beneath the skin.

Brilliantly, 3.3 was set out as a study in triangulation: a map of the island on one wall, a model of the fortifications on a table; a draughtsman's easel pinned with charts and drawings. While this war office was constructed around her, Desdemona playfully nagged her husband ('Shall't be . . . ? Tomorrow . . . ? Why then . . . ') and finally pummelled his chest 'mamm'ring on' while he laughed and lingeringly kissed her and she, 'obedient', paused, adoring him, before she exited. 'Perdition catch my soul' was addressed to her disappearing skirts – perdition that was already at his elbow, a concerned voice in his ear: 'My noble lord . . . ? . . . No further harm.' Here, Iago's reluctant promptings that made Othello the insistent interrogator was voice-over to the soldierly business of mapping fortification: men at work, building, surveying, deploying defences. How ironic – as every prop of Othello's self-knowledge was yanked out from under him ('Look to your wife'; 'I know our country disposition well'; 'She did deceive her father marrying you') until the big man's knees buckled and his whole weight thudded onto a stool, every grid point of his known world wiped off his map.

The rage Iago released he hadn't calculated. A knife pulled out of nowhere whistled past his ear and stuck in the drawing board as Othello, following his throwing arm, lunged towards him, Iago only just in time twisting out of a clutch that would have killed him, wailing indignation ('Is't come to this?') before slipping his own knives in ('satisfied'; 'I lay with Cassio'; 'a handkerchief'). Blowing all his 'fond love . . . to heaven', Henry's Othello grabbed a fistful of surveyor's chalk, dispersing it in a cloud. The white stayed on his hand – white staining black.

This was a husband Harris's Desdemona could not recognize. Battered by the story of a handkerchief in 3.4, flattened by his roar in 4.2 so that she scrabbled across the floor out of his reach, hiccoughing silently like a terrified child, her small question 'why do you weep?' was a little oasis where the saving of a marriage might have been possible until the further question – 'what ignorant sin have I committed?' – dried Othello's tears into brutal, disgusted incandescent fury: 'Committed? . . . Impudent strumpet!' In the willow scene, undressed to her smock, she sat on the edge of her bed, a bewildered child with turned-in toes, using the song to probe her grief. But her hollow-toned interruption – 'Nay, that's not next' – cracked open knowledge beyond conscious knowing. She was a bride suddenly old.

Unpinning her, Larkin's Emilia failed in the willow scene to achieve understanding. Her thoughts on men and wives and power and palates and revenge and grace, spoken with the authority of first-hand experience (her northern voice the straight-talking female antidote to her husband's) as she stood with Desdemona's bundled-up clothing in her arms, didn't get through. But in her final extraordinary scene, one of the best performances I saw all year, Larkin's Emilia achieved female heroism beyond revenge. Full-throated, declaring divorce – 'Perchance Iago, I will ne'er go home' – she took Othello's vocal power head-on and topped it – 'I care not for thy sword' – fearlessly saving Desdemona's story for truth from slander: 'I will speak as liberal as the north . . . I'LL SPEAK.' Dying for speaking, Emilia lay whispering

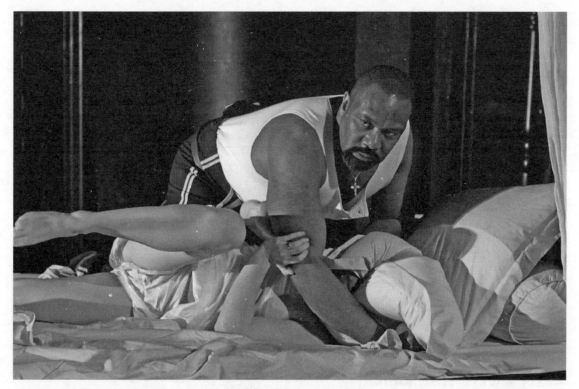

37. *Othello*, 5.2, Northern Broadsides, West Yorkshire Playhouse, directed by Barrie Rutter. Lenny Henry as Othello, Jessica Harris as Desdemona.

'Willow, willow, willow' in Desdemona's ear. Dying wanting someone to speak, Othello kissed his wife, crumpled and rolled in a heap off the bed. Iago's chortle caught in his throat. Cassio slumped. The last word was Lodovico's (Simon Holland Roberts): 'Relate'. Here, relation – the loading of a bed; the story it told – was nothing but loss.

Lenny Henry was nine months old when Paul Robeson played Othello in Stratford. Where has this play come in the fifty years since? One of the things this production showed spectators today is how it explores not (just) race but masculinity, *Othello* emerging here as a series of heart-battering male tragedies: the father's ('O my daugh-ter!'); the officer's ('to deceive so good a comman-der'); the dupe's ('O inhuman dog'!'); the hus-band's ('demand that demi-devil / Why . . . '); even the 'honest' friend's. Nothing is tragically emptier than the wholly evacuated consciousness, as Nelson delivered the line, of Iago's 'What you know you know.' To my mind, Henry's performance with Northern Broadsides shows why 'leaping out of Shakespeare's terror' isn't really an option; why, rather, we need always to be leaping *in*. All of the best work this year – and some of the middling work too – did that. It leaped in to the ques-tions we need Shakespeare's plays continuously to explore.

PROFESSIONAL SHAKESPEARE PRODUCTIONS IN THE BRITISH ISLES, JANUARY–DECEMBER 2008

JAMES SHAW

Most of the productions listed are by professional companies, but some amateur productions are included. The information is taken from *Touchstone* (www.touchstone.bham.ac.uk), a Shakespeare resource maintained by the Shakespeare Institute Library. Touchstone includes a monthly list of current and forthcoming UK Shakespeare productions from listings information. The websites provided for theatre companies were accurate at the time of going to press.

ALL'S WELL THAT ENDS WELL

Theatre Set-up. UK tour June–August.
www.ts-u.co.uk
Director: Wendy McFee

AS YOU LIKE IT

C Company. Bridewell Theatre, London, 22 January–8 February.
www.stbridefoundation.org/bridewelltheatre
Director: Aileen Gonsalves
Part of the Lunchbox Theatre series – 45-minute adaptations for lunchtime.

Watford Palace Theatre. Watford Palace, Watford, 4–26 April.
www.watfordpalacetheatre.co.uk
Director: Brigid Lamour

Guildford Shakespeare Company. Yvonne Arnaud Theatre, Guildford, 17–26 July.
www.guildford-shakespeare-company.co.uk
Director: Sean Aita

Cambridge Shakespeare Festival. Robinson College Gardens, 18 August–6 September.
www.cambridgeshakespeare.com

THE COMEDY OF ERRORS

Forum Theatre Company. Courtyard Theatre, Hoxton, London, 12 February–2 March.
www.thecourtyard.org.uk

Hall Green Little Theatre, 25 February–1 March.
www.hglt.org.uk
All-female version

Guildford Shakespeare Company. Yvonne Arnaud Theatre, Guildford, 19 June–5 July.
www.guildford-shakespeare-company.co.uk
Director: Joanna Read

Cambridge Shakespeare Festival. Robinson College Gardens, 28 July–16 August.
www.cambridgeshakespeare.com

Warhorse Theatreworks. Cockpit Theatre, London, 3–27 September.
www.warhorsetheatreworks.com

Adaptation
The Comedy of Errors – An Identity Affair
Full Tilt Theatre Company. University Theatre, Bath Spa University, Bath, 20–24 May and tour.
www.fulltilt-theatre.com
Adaptor: Gunduz Kalic

376

Beach holiday resort setting with audience members assigned new identities.

HAMLET

Shakespeare at the Tobacco Factory. The Tobacco Factory, Bristol, 20 March–3 May.
www.sattf.org.uk
Director: Jonathan Miller
First guest director at the Tobacco Factory and Jonathan Miller's fourth production of *Hamlet*.

Derby Playhouse Company. Derby Playhouse, Derby, 21 April–31 May.
www.derbyplayhouse.co.uk
Director: Stephen Edwards

Stafford Festival Shakespeare. Stafford Castle, 26 June–12 July.
www.staffordfestivalshakespeare.co.uk
Director: Bill Buckhurst

The Factory. Hoxton Square Bar and Kitchen, Hoxton Square, 13 July and tour.
www.thefactorytheatre.co.uk
Directors: Tim Carroll and Tamara Harvey
The audience decides which actor plays which character, using props supplied by the audience.

Royal Shakespeare Company. Courtyard Theatre, Stratford-upon-Avon, 24 July–15 November; Novello Theatre, London, 3 December–10 January 2009.
www.rsc.org.uk
Director: Gregory Doran
Hamlet: David Tennant
Claudius: Patrick Stewart

Adaptation
Det Lille Turneteater. The Egg, Bath, 4–6 March.
www.detlilleturneteater.dk
Director: Paul Robinson
Cast of two accompanied by two double-bass players.

Frank Theatre Company. Barons Court, London, 18–28 November.

www.franktheatre.co.uk
Director: Amy Son

Humble Boy
Derngate Theatre, Northampton, 11 April–3 May.
Playwright: Charlotte Jones
Director: Richard Beecham

Humble Boy
London Classic Theatre Company. Tour October–November.
www.londonclassictheatre.co.uk
Playwright: Charlotte Jones
Director: Michael Cabot

Rosencrantz and Guildenstern are Dead
Derby Playhouse, Derby, 25 April–31 May.
www.derbyplayhouse.co.uk
Playwright: Tom Stoppard
Director: Karen Louise

Rosencrantz and Guildenstern are Dead
Maddermarket Theatre, Norwich, 16–25 October.
www.maddermarket.co.uk
Playwright: Tom Stoppard
Director: Peter Sowerbutts

Ballet
Northern Ballet. UK tour February–May.
www.northernballettheatre.co.uk
Director: David Nixon
Composer: Philip Feeney

HENRY IV, PART I

Royal Shakespeare Company. Courtyard Theatre, Stratford-upon-Avon, 17 July 2007–14 March 2008; Roundhouse Theatre, London, 3 April–23 May.
www.rsc.org.uk
Director: Michael Boyd
Henry IV: Clive Wood
Falstaff: David Warner

Played as a complete cycle of the first and second tetralogies.

HENRY IV, PART 2

Royal Shakespeare Company. Courtyard Theatre, Stratford-upon-Avon, 25 July 2007–14 March 2008; Roundhouse Theatre, London, 5 April–23 May.
www.rsc.org.uk
Director: Michael Boyd
Henry IV: Clive Wood
Falstaff: David Warner
Played as a complete cycle of the first and second tetralogies

HENRY V

Royal Shakespeare Company. Courtyard Theatre, Stratford-upon-Avon, 25 October 2007–14 March 2008; Roundhouse Theatre, 8 April–23 May.
www.rsc.org.uk
Director: Michael Boyd
Played as a complete cycle of the first and second tetralogies.

Heartbreak Productions. UK tour July–August.
www.heartbreakproductions.co.uk

Adaptation
Henry V, Lion of England
Maverick Theatre Company. February–March.
www.mavericktheatre.co.uk
Playwright: Nick Hennegan

HENRY VI, PART 1

The War Against France
Royal Shakespeare Company. Courtyard Theatre, Stratford-upon-Avon, 6 February–15 March; Roundhouse Theatre, London, 19 April–24 May.
www.rsc.org.uk
Director: Michael Boyd
Played as a complete cycle of the first and second tetralogies.

HENRY VI, PART 2

England's Fall
Royal Shakespeare Company. The Courtyard Theatre, Stratford-upon-Avon, 6 February–15 March; Roundhouse Theatre, London, 22 April–24 May.
www.rsc.org.uk
Director: Michael Boyd
Played as a complete cycle of the first and second tetralogies.

HENRY VI, PART 3

The Chaos
Royal Shakespeare Company. The Courtyard Theatre, Stratford-upon-Avon, 6 February–15 March; Roundhouse Theatre, London, 24 April–24 May.
www.rsc.org.uk
Director: Michael Boyd
Played as a complete cycle of the first and second tetralogies.

KING LEAR

Royal Shakespeare Company. New London Theatre, London, 12 November 2007–12 January 2008.
www.rsc.org.uk
Director: Trevor Nunn
King Lear: Sir Ian McKellen

Shakespeare's Globe. Shakespeare's Globe Theatre, London, 23 April–17 August.
www.shakespeares-globe.org
Director: Dominic Dromgoole
King Lear: David Calder

Liverpool Everyman. Everyman Theatre, Liverpool, 30 October–29 November.
www.everymanplayhouse.com
Director: Rupert Goold
King Lear: Pete Postlethwaite

Opened with a recording of Margaret Thatcher quoting St Francis when taking office in 1979.

Adaptation
I, Lear
The Black Sheep Company. Trafalgar Studios, London, 21 July–16 August.
www.blacksheepcomedy.co.uk
Director: Cal McCrystal
A play about two actors offering a master-class on acting.

Jack Lear
Stephen Joseph Theatre Company. Stephen Joseph Theatre, Scarborough, 16 October–8 November.
Playwright: Ben Benison
Director: Barrie Rutter
Domestic drama involving the fisherman, Jack Lear.

The Cordelia Dream
Royal Shakespeare Company. Wilton's Music Hall, London, 16 December–10 January 2009.
Director: Selina Cartmell
Two-hander drama between an elderly man and his daughter.

LOVE'S LABOUR'S LOST

Cambridge Shakespeare Festival. Fitzwilliam College Gardens, 4–30 August.
www.cambridgeshakespeare.com

Royal Shakespeare Company. Courtyard Theatre, Stratford-upon-Avon, 2 October–15 November.
www.rsc.org.uk
Director: Greg Doran
Berowne: David Tennant

Rose Theatre, Kingston upon Thames, 21 October–15 November.
www.rosetheatrekingston.org
Director: Sir Peter Hall
Don Armado: Peter Bowles

MACBETH

Clwyd Theatr Cymru, Mold, 1–24 May.
www.clwyd-theatr-cymru.co.uk
Director: Terry Hands
Macbeth: Owen Teale
Lady Macbeth: Vivien Parry

Mull Little Theatre. Tour August–October.
www.mulltheatre.com
Director: Alasdair McCrone

Nottingham Playhouse Theatre & Royal Lyceum Edinburgh. Royal Lyceum, Edinburgh, 12 September–11 October; Playhouse, Nottingham, 22 October–15 November.
www.nottinghamplayhouse.co.uk
Director: Lucy Pitman-Wallace

Questor's Theatre Company. Questor's Theatre, London, 31 October–8 November.
www.questors.org.uk
Director: Barrie Adderbroke

Adaptation
Deadkat. The Lion & Unicorn Theatre, London, 7–12 October.
www.dead-kat.org
Puppet adaptation.

Opera
Opera North. UK tour April–June.
www.operanorth.co.uk
Composer: Giuseppe Verdi
Director: Tim Albery

MEASURE FOR MEASURE

Reckless Endeavour. New Players Theatre, London, 23 January–16 February.
www.recklessendeavour.co.uk
Director: Niki Flacks

Creation Theatre Company. The North Wall, Oxford, 19 March–12 April.
www.creationtheatre.co.uk
Director: Charlotte Conquest

Clwyd Theatr Cymru, Mold, 10 April–3 May.
www.clwyd-theatr-cymru.co.uk
Director: Phillip Breen

Hammerpuzzle Theatre Company. The Rondo, Bath, 11–14 June; The Dell, Stratford-upon-Avon, 9 August.
www.hammerpuzzle.co.uk

Centurion Theatre Company. Courtyard Theatre, London, 29 October–23 November.
www.centuriontheatre.co.uk
Director: Michael Sargent

Adaptation
Beyond Measure
Back & Forth in association with York Theatre Royal. Tour September–October.
www.beyondmeasuretheshow.com
Playwright: Bridget Foreman
Director: Juliet Forster
Focuses on Isabella and begins where *Measure for Measure* ends.

THE MERCHANT OF VENICE

Galleon Theatre Company. Greenwich Theatre, London, 12 February–9 March.
www.galleontheatre.co.uk
Director: Bruce Jamieson

Royal Shakespeare Company. Courtyard Theatre, Stratford-upon-Avon, 3 April–27 September.
www.rsc.org.uk
Director: Tim Carroll
Shylock: Angus Wright
Portia: Georgina Rich

Octagon Theatre, Bolton, 18 September–11 October.
www.octagonbolton.co.uk
Director: Mark Babych
Shylock: David Fielder
Portia: Emily Pithon

Adaptation
C Company. Bridewell Theatre, London, 3–20 June.
www.stbridefoundation.org/bridewelltheatre
Part of the Lunchbox Theatre series – 45-minute adaptations for lunchtime.

THE MERRY WIVES OF WINDSOR

Illyria Theatre Company. UK tour May–August.
www.illyria.uk.com
Director: Oliver Gray

Shakespeare's Globe. Shakespeare's Globe Theatre, London, 8 June–5 October.
www.shakespeares-globe.org
Director: Christopher Luscombe
Falstaff: Christopher Benjamin

Adaptation
Falstaff
Welsh National Opera. UK tour March–April.
www.wno.org.uk
Composer: Giuseppe Verdi

Falstaff
Scottish Opera. Scottish tour May–June.
www.scottishopera.org.uk
Composer: Giuseppe Verdi

Falstaff
Pimlico Opera. UK tour October.
www.grangeparkopera.co.uk
Composer: Giuseppe Verdi

A MIDSUMMER NIGHT'S DREAM

Theatre Delicatessen. Theatre Delicatessen, London, 29 January–2 March.
www.theatredelicatessen.co.uk
Director: Frances Loy

Clwyd Theatr Cymru. Anthony Hopkins Theatre, Mold, 7 February–1 March; New Theatre, Cardiff, 4–8 March.

www.clwyd-theatr-cymru.co.uk.
Director: Tim Baker

Royal Shakespeare Company. Courtyard Theatre, Stratford-upon-Avon, 9 May–13 November.
www.rsc.org.uk
Director: Greg Doran
Revival of 2005 production.

Shakespeare's Globe. Shakespeare's Globe Theatre, London, 10 May–4 October.
www.shakespeares-globe.org

Heartbreak Productions. UK tour June–August.
www.heartbreakproductions.co.uk

British Touring Shakespeare Company. UK tour July–August.
http://btsc.homestead.com
Director: Una Buckley

Creation Theatre Company. Headington Hill Park, Oxford, 4 July–13 September.
www.creationtheatre.co.uk
Director: Zoe Seaton

Pentameters Theatre Company. Pentameters Theatre, London, 29 July–23 August.
www.pentameters.co.uk

Antic Disposition. Cochrane Theatre, London, 19–20 September.
www.anticdisposition.co.uk
Directors: Ben Horslen and John Risebero

Footsbarn. Victoria Park, London, 12–30 November.
http://footsbarn.com
Director: Patrick Hayter
Set in a big top tent with on-stage musicians, masks and clowning. Revival of 15-year old show.

Adaptation
Kaos Theatre Company. Contact Theatre, Manchester, 28 February–1 March.

www.kaostheatre.com
Director: Xavier Leret

New Shakespeare Company. Open Air Theatre, Regent's Park, London, 8 July–2 August.
www.openairtheatre.org
Director: Dominic Leclerc
Adaptation for children. Preceded by a modern speech explanation of the plot by Bottom.

Yohangza Theatre Company. Chapter Arts Centre, Cardiff, 30 November–1 December.
Korean company using the costume and characters of Korean folklore.

Ballet
Northern Ballet. Tour March–November.
www.northernballettheatre.co.uk
Composer: Felix Mendelssohn
Director: David Nixon

Opera
Royal Opera Company. Royal Opera House, London, 28 January–11 February.
www.roh.org.uk
Composer: Benjamin Britten

Opera North. Tour May–June.
www.operanorth.co.uk
Composer: Benjamin Britten
Director: Martin Duncan

MUCH ADO ABOUT NOTHING

National Theatre. Olivier Theatre, London, 10 December–29 March 2008.
www.nationaltheatre.org.uk
Director: Nicholas Hytner
Beatrice: Zoe Wanamaker
Benedick: Simon Russell Beale

The Lord Chamberlain's Men. Tour June–August.
www.tlcm.co.uk

The Festival Players. Tour June–August.
www.thefestivalplayers.co.uk

Director: Michael Dyer
All-male production.

Creation Theatre Company. Oxford Castle, Oxford, 13 June–28 November.
www.creationtheatre.co.uk
Director: Charlotte Conquest

Oddsocks Theatre Company. Tour June–August.
www.oddsocks.co.uk

Adaptation
Red Shift. Tour January–April.
www.redshifttheatreco.co.uk
Adaptor and Director: Jonathan Holloway
90-minute version set in war-torn Sarajevo.

Funk It Up About Nothin'
Chicago Shakespeare Company. Musical Theatre@George's Square, Edinburgh, 7–24 August.
Hip-hop influenced.

OTHELLO

Donmar Warehouse. Donmar Warehouse, London, 29 November–23 February 2008.
www.donmarwarehouse.com
Director: Michael Grandage
Othello: Chiwetel Ejiofor
Iago: Ewan McGregor

Anvil Productions. Tour July–August.
www.anvilproductions.co.uk
Director: Anne Jones

Frantic Assembly. Tour September–November.
www.franticassembly.co.uk
Adaptor and Director: Scott Graham and Stephen Hoggett
90 minutes, no interval. Set in a working-class pub.

Adaptation
Phoenix Dance Theatre. Sadler's Wells Theatre, London, 28–29 April.
www.phoenixdancetheatre.co.uk

Choreographer: Jose Limon
Includes *The Moor's Pavane*, based on *Othello*, and set to music by Purcell.

Opera
Otello
Welsh National Opera. Tour September–December.
www.wno.org.uk
Composer: Giuseppe Verdi

RICHARD II

Royal Shakespeare Company. Courtyard Theatre, Stratford-upon-Avon, 7 July 2007–13 March 2008; Roundhouse, London, 1 April–22 May.
www.rsc.org.uk
Director: Michael Boyd
Played as a complete cycle of the first and second tetralogies.

RICHARD III

Instant Classics. Broadway Studio, Catford, 12 February–8 March.
http://broadwaytheatre.org.uk
Director: David Cottis

Royal Shakespeare Company. The Courtyard Theatre, Stratford-upon-Avon, 16 February 2007–16 March 2008; Roundhouse Theatre, London, 26 April–25 May.
www.rsc.org.uk
Director: Michael Boyd
Played as a complete cycle of the first and second tetralogies.

Ludlow Festival. Rougemont Gardens, Exeter, 17 July–9 August.
www.ludlowfestival.co.uk
Director: Ben Crocker
Richard III: John Killoran

The Faction. Brockley Jack Theatre, London, 14 October–8 November.
www.thefaction.org.uk

Director and Richard: Mark Leipacher
Physical theatre with actors on stage throughout.

Adaptation
The Resistible Rise of Arturo Ui
Lyric Hammersmith, London, 14 February–15 March.
www.lyric.co.uk
Playwright: Bertolt Brecht
Translator: Ralph Manheim
Director: David Farr

ROMEO AND JULIET

Northern Broadsides. Tour February–June.
www.northern-broadsides.co.uk
Director: Barrie Rutter

Dundee Rep Ensemble. Dundee Repertory Hall, Dundee, 8–29 March.
www.dundeerep.co.uk
Director: James Brining

Antic Disposition. Jermyn Street Theatre, London, 21 April–17 May; Cochrane Theatre, London, 19–20 September.
www.anticdisposition.co.uk
Directors: Ben Horslen and John Risebero

Shakespeare's Globe Company. Tour May–August.
www.shakespeares-globe.org
Director: Dominic Dromgoole

New Shakespeare Company. Open Air Theatre, Regent's Park, London, 2 June–2 August.
www.openairtheatre.org
Director: Timothy Sheader
Shearder's first production as artistic director of the New Shakespeare Company.

Theatre of Memory. Middle Temple, London, 20 August–13 September.
Director: Tamara Harvey
Juliet: Juliet Rylance

Wales Theatre Company. Tour September–November.

www.walestheatrecompany.com
Director: Michael Bogdanov

Royal Shakespeare Company. Tour October–November; The Courtyard Theatre, Stratford-upon-Avon, 27 November–24 January 2009.
www.rsc.org.uk
Director: Neil Bartlett

Adaptation
Noughts & Crosses
Royal Shakespeare Company. Tour February–April.
www.rsc.org.uk
Book: Malorie Blackman
Director: Dominic Cooke

C Company. Bridewell Theatre, London, 15 July–1 August.
www.stbridefoundation.org/bridewelltheatre
Director: Aileen Gonsalves
Part of the Lunchbox Theatre series – 45-minute adaptations for lunchtime.

Shakespeare's R&J
The Original Theatre Company. Tour July–November.
www.originaltheatre.com
Playwright: Joe Calarco
Director: Alastair Whatley

West Side Story
Sadler's Wells Company. Sadler's Wells, London, 22 July–31 August; New Wimbledon Theatre, 14 October–1 November.
Composer: Leonard Bernstein
Lyrics: Stephen Sondheim
Director: Joey McKneely

Ballet
Russian State Ballet of Siberia. Tour January–March.
Composer: Sergei Prokofiev
Director: Sergei Bobrov

Northern Ballet. Lyceum Theatre, Sheffield, 6–10 May.

www.northernballettheatre.co.uk
Composer: Sergei Prokofiev
Director: Christopher Gable

Independent Ballet of Wales. Tour May–October.
www.welshballet.co.uk
Composer: Hector Berlioz

Scottish Ballet. May–June.
Composer: Hector Berlioz

Royal Ballet. Royal Opera House, London, 26 May–13 June.
www.roh.org.uk
Choreography: Kenneth MacMillan

Romeo and Juliet, On Motifs of Shakespeare
Mark Morris Dance Company. The Barbican, London, 5–8 November.
http://markmorrisdancegroup.org
Composer: Sergei Prokofiev

Opera
Roméo et Juliette
Opera North. Tour May–June.
www.operanorth.co.uk
Composer: Charles Gounod
Director: John Fulljames

I Capuleti e I Montecchi
Opera North. Tour October–November.
www.operanorth.co.uk
Composer: Vincenzo Bellini

THE TAMING OF THE SHREW

Shakespeare at The Tobacco Factory. The Tobacco Factory, Bristol, 7 February–15 March.
www.sattf.org.uk
Director: Andrew Hilton
Petruchio: Leo Wringer
Katherine: Saskia Portway

Royal Shakespeare Company. Courtyard Theatre, Stratford-upon-Avon, 24 April–25 September.
www.rsc.org.uk

Director: Conall Morrison
Katherine: Michelle Gomez
Petruchio: Stephen Boxer

The Pantaloons. Tour May–October.
www.thepantaloons.co.uk
Director: Steve Purcell

Progress Theatre Company. The Reading Abbey Ruins, Reading, 14–26 July.
www.abbeyruins.com
Director: John Goodman

Miracle Theatre Company. Tour September–October.
www.miracletheatre.co.uk

THE TEMPEST

Tara Arts Theatre Company. Tour January–March.
www.tara-arts.com
Director: Jatinder Verma
Prospero/Trinculo: Robert Mountford
A company of 6 actors and played without an interval.

Darker Arts. Rosemary Branch, London, 21 February–20 March.
www.rosemarybranch.co.uk
Director: Helen Tennison

Love and Madness. Riverside Theatre, London, 12–22 March and tour March–April.
www.loveandmadness.org
Director: Jack Shepherd
Prospero: Matthew Sim

Pentameters Theatre. 28 Heath Street, Hampstead, above The Horseshoe Pub, 4–28 June.
www.pentameters.co.uk
Director: Harry Meacher

Chapterhouse Theatre Company. Tour July–August.
www.chapterhouse.org

Adaptation
I'll Be the Devil
Royal Shakespeare Company. Tricycle Theatre, London, 21 February–8 March.
Playwright: Leo Butler
Director: Maria Aberg
Written in response to *The Tempest*.

Knock Against My Heart
Theatre Centre / Nós do Morro. Unicorn Theatre, London, 7–17 October.
Playwright: Oladipo Agboluaje
A retelling drawing on the music, dance and culture of Brazil.

Return to the Forbidden Planet
Pleasure Beach, Globe, Blackpool, 23 May–2 November.
Composer: Bob Carlton

Taming the Tempest
Salisbury Playhouse Company. Playhouse, Salisbury, 25–29 March.
www.salisburyplayhouse.com
Playwright: Mark Powell

Tempest II
Lemi Ponifasio / MAU (New Zealand). Queen Elizabeth Hall, London, 27–28 June.
www.southbankcentre.co.uk
Deviser: Lemi Ponifasio
Dance piece, part of the LIFT Festival 2008.

TIMON OF ATHENS

Shakespeare's Globe. Shakespeare's Globe Theatre, London, 26 July–3 October.
www.shakespeares-globe.org
Director: Lucy Bailey

Adaptation
The Life of Timon
CP Theatre Productions. Putney Arts Theatre, London, 10–15 March.
Director: Caroline Boulton
Timon as a naive but successful actor.

TITUS ANDRONICUS

Richmond Shakespeare Society. Mary Wallace Theatre, Twickenham, 23 February–1 March.
www.richmondshakespeare.org.uk
Director: Jay Wright

TROILUS AND CRESSIDA

Cheek by Jowl at Théâtre Les Gémeaux, Sceaux, March; and at BITE:08, Barbican Theatre, London, 28 May–14 June.
www.cheekbyjowl.com
Director: Declan Donnellan
Prologue delivered by Helen.

TWELFTH NIGHT

Cut to the Chase Company. Queen's Theatre, Hornchurch, 18 April–10 May.
www.queens-theatre.co.uk
Director: Bob Carlton

New Shakespeare Company. Open Air Theatre, Regent's Park, London, 4 June–30 July.
www.openairtheatre.org
Director: Edward Dick
Viola: Natalie Dew
Malvolio: Richard O'Callaghan
Feste: Clive Rowe

Oxford Shakespeare Company. Tour June–August.
www.oxfordshakespearecompany.co.uk
Director: Bill Benkes-Jones

Filter / Royal Shakespeare Company. Tour September–November.
Director: Sean Holmes
Viola and Sebastian: Poppy Miller
Maria and Feste: Gemma Saunders
Shortened version with audience participation such as sharing pizza deliveries to Olivia's household.

Donmar Warehouse. Wyndham's Theatre, London, 5 December–7 March 2009.

www.donmarwarehouse.com
Director: Michael Grandage
Malvolio: Derek Jacobi
Viola: Victoria Hamilton
Sir Toby: Ron Cook

Adaptation
What You Fancy
Phizzical Productions. Rich Mix, London, 4–5 July and tour.
www.phizzical.com
Playwright: Omar Khan
Director: Leylah
Bollywood-influenced production set in modern celebrity-obsessed Britain.

THE TWO GENTLEMEN OF VERONA

Adaptation
Nós do Morro. The Barbican, London, 8–18 October.
www.nosdomorro.com.br
Directors: Gutti Fraga, Fatima Domingues, Johayne Hildefonso, Miwa Yanagizawa
Accompanied by traditional Brazilian song, supplied by a trio of on-stage musicians.

Vakomana Vaviri Ve Zimbabwe
Two Gents Productions. Oval House Theatre, London, 18 November–13 December.
www.twogentsproductions.com
Includes echoes of the Zimbabwean experience of exile, powerful rulers and personal allegiances. Cast of two.

THE WINTER'S TALE

Steam Industry in association with the Courtyard Theatre, Hoxton. Courtyard Theatre, London, 19 December–27 January 2008.
Director: Phil Willmott

Shakespeare at the George. The George Hotel, Huntingdon, Cambridgeshire, 24 June–5 July.

www.atthegeorge.co.uk
Director: John Shippey

Shakespeare's Globe. Tour June–August.
www.shakespeares-globe.org
Director: John Dove
Leontes: John Dougall
Hermione: Sasha Hails

Rain or Shine Theatre Company. Tour July–August.
www.rainorshine.co.uk

POEMS AND SONNETS

The Rape of Lucrece
Tour October–January 2009.
www.therapeoflucrece.co.uk
Adaptor and Performer: Gerard Logan
Director: Gareth Armstrong
One-man show.

Bootless Cries
Supple presents Kryptic Movement. The Egg, Bath, 7–9 March.
Dance inspired by Shakespeare's Sonnets. Part of the Unplugged Shakespeare Season.

MISCELLANEOUS

(in alphabetical order)
Afterlife
National Theatre. Lyttelton Theatre, London, 11 June–16 August.
www.nationaltheatre.org.uk
Playwright: Michael Frayn
Director: Michael Blakemore
Max Reinhardt: Roger Allam
A play about Max Reinhardt.

The Dresser
Watford Palace Theatre, Watford, 4–27 September.
Playwright: Ronald Harwood
Director: Di Trevis

Falstaff
Warehouse Theatre, Croydon and tour June–July.
Director: John Wood

Falstaff: Roger Forbes
One-man show adapted from Robert Nye's novel. Set in the Boar's Head.

The Herbal Bed
Salisbury Playhouse. Salisbury Playhouse, Salisbury, 21 January–23 February.
www.salisburyplayhouse.com
Playwright: Peter Whelan

Shakespeare Party
Footsbarn Theatre. Shakespeare's Globe Theatre, London, 23–25 May.
http://footsbarn.com
A specially created production for Shakespeare's Globe.

Shakespeare Requiem
Leeds Festival Chorus. Leeds Town Hall, Leeds, 29 November 2008 (premiere).
Composer: Judith Bingham

The Shakespeare Suite
Birmingham Royal Ballet. New Theatre, Oxford, 4–5 March and tour.
www.brb.org.uk
Ballet with music by Duke Ellington.

Shakespeare's Saints & Sinners
Creation Theatre Company. St Michael's Tower, Oxford, 26 June–16 August.
www.creationtheatre.co.uk
Director: Heather Davies

Sweet William
Trafalgar Studios 2 Theatre, London, 4–16 February and tour.
Writer/solo performer: Michael Pennington
Personal reminiscences about Shakespeare.

THE YEAR'S CONTRIBUTION TO SHAKESPEARE STUDIES

I. CRITICAL STUDIES
reviewed by JULIE SANDERS

One of this year's finest monographs is Gail Marshall's far-ranging, erudite and engaging *Shakespeare and Victorian Women*. I will return to this excellent book in more detail later in the article, but Marshall commences her study by quoting a remarkable piece by Kathleen Knox, published in 1895, 'in the guise of a letter to her young friend Dorothy' (p. 1). This is where I, too, would like to begin. The premise is that Dorothy has begun to study Shakespeare in a school context and is very uncertain about the whole experience: 'You have recently been moved up into the "Senior Cambridge" form' the 'letter' observes, noting that this obliges Dorothy to undertake a systematic study of a Shakespeare play. It continues (and the Shakespeare scholar's heart sinks) 'you have found the occupation dry, difficult, and uninteresting.' As a result Dorothy wants answers to some pressing questions such as 'why what was meant for a pleasure in one generation should be a pain and grief to another' and 'what there is in Shakespeare to make people rave about him as they do'. 'In short,' Dorothy wonders, 'why should one "learn Shakespeare" at all?' (p. 1). This seems a remarkably contemporary lament, one heard daily in schools and around many breakfast tables, and a large number of publications this year have in part been commissioned with the aim of helping those struggling with the effort to 'learn Shakespeare'. A cluster of companions, handbooks, surveys and guides offer their words and contents to the undergraduate and sixth-form college reader with the aim of making Shakespeare seem accessible, interesting and anything but 'dry' and 'difficult'. It is with this cluster of texts – many of them authored, it should be noted, by the most eminent of Shakespeare scholars, an indication in itself of how seriously the task of engagement is taken both by the academic world and the major publishing houses – that I will commence.

LEARNING SHAKESPEARE: HANDBOOKS, COMPANIONS, AND GUIDES

Palgrave Macmillan's Shakespeare Handbooks series is taking on a confident identity as more volumes boost the catalogue. Aimed primarily at the ambitious school student and the new undergraduate, these books combine a blow-by-blow analysis of the play, including paraphrases of difficult linguistic passages, with a wider overview of key critical and contextual issues, as well as brief reception histories. Sometimes the brevity of the latter can make the decisions for inclusion appear somewhat arbitrary; I felt this in Ros King's selection of 'key productions' in her otherwise excellent study of *The Winter's Tale*. I wanted to know why she considered these 'benchmark' productions, but with little more than a paragraph at her discretion this proved virtually impossible. There was a similar arbitrariness at work in the discussion of screen versions of the play; other than its availability in

DVD/download form, there seemed little reason why King wanted to include the Sher/Doran RSC production here when she had such deep issues with its production decisions. It did seem throughout the volume that the author, ever alert to the performance possibilities in a speech or a certain moment of her focus play, tended to invoke specific productions for the purposes of critique rather than praise. That carping aside, however, King's volume is also the perfect example of the ways in which these short studies can exceed their expectations as student handbooks and become genuine critical interventions. She garners examples from a wide range of visual and aural media, including the internet and radio. I will certainly be using her astute section on Shakespeare in the context of courtly and masquing culture for teaching more than just this specific play. In a few pithy and succinct pages, King manages to convey all the best reasons for recontextualizing Shakespeare within the culture of his time and for seeing his work in dialogue with contemporaries such as Ben Jonson. The comparison between *The Winter's Tale* and *Love Freed From Ignorance and Folly* is richly persuasive in the case it makes that Shakespeare and Jonson may have been working to similar briefs. It was refreshing to see this even in such a single author-focused series as this.

Other volumes in the series that have been published this year are Martin White's engaging response to *A Midsummer Night's Dream* and Jeremy Lopez on *Richard II*. Both these authors have impressive track records in writing about Shakespeare in performance and series editor John Russell Brown has chosen his team with a care that is fully repaid. White's volume includes a detailed and admiring account of Tim Supple's multilingual production that stole so many hearts during the Royal Shakespeare Company's Complete Works Festival at Stratford-upon-Avon (and, indeed, globally) in 2007. In his volume, White achieves the tricky task of selecting and justifying his benchmark productions of *Dream* with aplomb. On the page, his text makes the distinction between discussions of the play that do not require an overall knowledge of its dramaturgic arc

or outcomes (printed in plain text) and italicized sections which require an overall knowledge of the play. There might have been a case for suggesting this could have been a consistent series approach, rather than specific to this volume, but the effect here is wholly positive. White is helpfully attentive to linguistic patterns and issues, which also aids in giving this series multiple potential in teaching contexts.

Jeremy Lopez has an established reputation for thinking about performance conditions and in particular audiences in the early modern period. His handbook on *Richard II* is a clear beneficiary of these skills. Lopez's study features some extended discussions of benchmark productions, including a very interesting response to Mark Rylance's 2003 Globe production in which the then Artistic Director played the title role. The space allotted to these is considerably longer than the brief summaries in the *Winter's Tale* volume, which does suggest considerable variation of practice within the series. I liked Lopez's decision to move backwards in time in these discussions, rather than following the usual forward-projecting teleology. This allowed a more honest approach to those productions which are necessarily only available through the partial archive and not through direct memory and experience, and in turn enabled them to be informed by analysis of productions which fell into the latter category.

Particularly admirable throughout the earlier commentary sections on the play was Lopez's firm intention to open up rather than close down meaning, but also to play early modern and contemporary theatre techniques off against each other in productive ways. The latter approach revealed itself in discussions of boy actors as opposed to adult women performers in the female roles and in extensive considerations of doubling and the creation of meaning that strategy might contribute to. There are, as a result, some enlightening discussions of the queen's role in the play and on-stage. I was very struck by the detailed attention Lopez paid to on-stage spatialities, and the attendant symmetries and contrasts possible, between the queen and her women and the gardeners at 3.4: he suggests that the stage can create the illusion of distance as the queen and her ladies stand in a different space from that inhabited literally and metaphorically by the gardener and his men.

If sometimes neglected or under-noticed moments received fresh focus there were perhaps some surprising absences. John of Gaunt and his much-anthologized 'sceptred isle' speech at 2.1 gets surprisingly short shrift. In fact, the reader almost senses Lopez's frustration with the verbosity of this particular character. Elsewhere though, for example in the discussion of how language and dialect create a sense of geographical shift in 2.4, Lopez brings neglected aspects of the playtext in performance alive in important new ways. There are some lovely points about the ways in which the external world is conveyed on the largely unadorned early modern stage that correlate with work in the book I will discuss next, Kathleen McLuskie's Writers and their Work study of *Macbeth*. Lopez demonstrates with admirable economy how 'Shakespeare depends upon [the] actor playing the Welsh captain to unleash the transformative power of the theatre, turning the bare stage into a landscape of withered trees bloodily overlooked by a pale-faced moon' (p. 37). The ways in which dialect embodies space is beautifully conveyed; Lopez makes a related point about the 3.4 gardener scene, that it introduces a new aural world into the play, the world of the labouring classes. This also invites us as readers to make connections across the Shakespearian and indeed larger early modern repertoire. Playwrights such as Jonson and Brome who were deeply interested and invested in dialect and idiom come to mind as authors who seek to make space through language in a comparable manner. Lopez is a sensitive and astute reader of texts as scripts for performance, frequently inviting us to think about symmetries in stage pictures and to attend to the resonance of silent characters. The deft nature with which he unpacks the rhetorical and poetic effects of this play is equally impressive.

Kathleen McLuskie's volume on *Macbeth* for the Writers and their Work series is similarly far-reaching in it focus and effect. The book is a cogent discussion of the play itself, including in its earlier chapters a close reading of both specific aspects of the play's structure, in particular the witches and the relationship between concepts of past, present and future, and specific speeches. McLuskie is alert, as were the authors in the Handbook series, to the distinct differences between spectatorly and readerly experiences of Shakespeare and the need to account for these differences in analyses of particular plays or themes. She is particularly engaging on the role and function of the off-stage in this play; she suggests the focus it enables on 'Macbeth and his lady' (p. 19), as well as instancing moments when the off-stage offers an important alternative to their world, for example (p. 18) in 1.7 when the servants' handheld props – '*dishes and service*' as the Folio has it – function 'as a purely physical reminder of an alternative off-stage world of feasting and hospitality that frames Macbeth's planned treachery'.

McLuskie is a sharp-eyed, and sharp-eared, reader. Her response to speeches such as 'If it were done' at 1.7 of the play or the second act duet between husband and wife is a brilliant reading of the reduced stichomythia of this carefully orchestrated exchange, one which has, unsurprisingly, attracted the attention of operatic adaptors of the play because of the chromatic and dynamic potential it offers. The volume taken as a whole travels far beyond being just a discussion and analysis of the play, though it has much to recommend it in that regard. McLuskie has an acute sense of the energy and dynamic of her focus play, but she also seizes the opportunity to debate in print provocative and heartfelt ideas about 'the writer and his work' that, as current Director of the University of Birmingham's Shakespeare Institute, she has been presenting at major Shakespeare gatherings in recent years.

In 'The Writer at Work', she provides a (frequently sceptical) survey of recent biographical interventions in the Shakespeare debate, including Michael Wood's BBC television series *In Search of Shakespeare* and Stephen Greenblatt's best-selling but controversial 'imaginative biography' *Will in the World*. All of this will be of interest to students of Shakespeare even if *Macbeth* is not necessarily their set text. In this chapter, McLuskie responds to key questions about Shakespeare's working practice, taking in concepts such as collaboration as well as the value and implications of a 'repertory approach'. In the case of *Macbeth* she notes this releases the play 'from its purely topical connection to historical events' such as the Gunpowder Plot (p. 97). This serves McLuskie's purpose very well, since it is noticeable that this volume eschews, or at least downplays, the usual linking of this play to a Jacobean courtly interest in witchcraft, highlighting the lack of evidence for a court performance and drawing into view its link to other theatrical practices and interests both in the moment of its first performance and during periods of revival such as the 1630s. In the process she is able to offer a confident analysis of the much-debated relationship of Thomas Middleton to this particular playtext. Her discussion of novel modes of 'witchy theatricality' (p. 103) on the stage at the start of the seventeenth century is engagingly lively.

Where her argument really catches fire, though, is in the final two chapters, 'A Lasting Work' (I almost wondered at times if she had been tempted to add an impish question-mark to the chapter heading) and 'The Abstract Work', which is when she gets to the subject of adaptation following on from William Davenant towards reworkings and reconfigurations of *Macbeth* in the twentieth century and up to the present day. McLuskie's point (and it is typically well made) is not to down adaptation studies as a practice or approach to Shakespeare scholarship but to suggest that we need always to consider the cline or spectrum on which these adaptations appear. At what point, she asks, has an adaptation travelled so far from a base knowledge of a Shakespeare text as to be virtually unrelated to its 'source', to be 'abstract', to invoke her own terms? In the process, McLuskie acknowledges the role of educational curricula in establishing the centrality of Shakespeare in the twentieth century and by extension the changing cultural and pedagogic landscape in which we currently find ourselves. She notes the strange context in which Shakespeare is expected to 'represent the transcendent values of tradition' and yet be the impetus for infinite forms of creativity (p. 135), accounting along

the way for interpretations of *Macbeth* such as that in the BBC Shakespeare Retold series that saw the play relocated to a chef's kitchen. In terms of its modernized dialogue and its selective attention to the plot McLuskie appears to consider this as so far 'abstracted' from the Shakespeare text as to be only tangential in its relationship to the play. Some might see this as a reactionary response to Shakespeare adaptations, but, as ever, McLuskie asks us to work a little harder than that in responding to her challenges. We, as critics, need to think further about the kinds of responses, aesthetic and otherwise, occasioned by this form of abstraction and the different sorts of audiences they function for. We have here, then, a primarily student-aimed 'guide' that it would benefit the Shakespearian academic community to take account of in their work, and that is the highest compliment I can pay.

The Cambridge Companion series is now well established as a reliable repository of excellent scholarship and a trusted presence on recommended reading lists in higher education establishments around the globe. The latest contribution to the Shakespeare section of the series is on *Shakespeare's Last Plays* and editor Catherine M. S. Alexander explains in her introduction the rationale behind the choice of 'last' rather than 'late' as the adjective to describe the grouping of plays discussed here. This group includes the late romances *Pericles, Cymbeline, The Winter's Tale, The Tempest* but also the collaborative works *Henry VIII, or All is True* and *The Two Noble Kinsmen* (specifically discussed in a closing chapter by Suzanne Gossett but also touched on throughout whenever contributors broach the issue of collaboration). The different meanings ascribed to 'lastness' (chronology being the driving force in this term) and 'lateness' which has more value-laden judgements embedded within it are the topic of Gordon McMullan's lively starter essay, 'What is a "late play"?'. His argument here continues the discussion begun in his monograph *Shakespeare and the Idea of Late Writing* (Cambridge, 2007; reviewed in *Shakespeare Survey 62*). There is a kind of Foucauldian concern with the 'order of things' in this discussion, and a refreshing willingness to ask how things might be ordered differently, including how we might catalogue early modern playtexts in libraries by paying attention to the observations of repertory studies as a means of renegotiating the terms in which we think about Shakespeare and his plays. Authorship, argues McMullan, is just 'one . . . in a series of intersecting influences' (p. 23). What might have been nice to see in the volume as a whole as it developed was more attention paid to the challenges established by McMullan within the other contributions. Other essay collections this year benefited from a clear exchange of work between the various contributors prior to the final submission of the manuscript. Elsewhere in this volume, we are witness to a more conventional approach to the 'last' plays (perhaps partly dictated by the series style of the 'Companions', it must be acknowledged) with essays devoted to particular plays and the collaborative texts held back for a separate essay at the end.

The gauntlets thrown down by McMullan's essay are largely held back for future consideration, although David Lindley's feisty chapter on the Blackfriars Theatre begins to show us some of the readings possible if the new angles suggested by McMullan are deployed. Lindley takes us through the possible impact of the Blackfriars space and site on particular plays, though he is admirably willing to reject a whole host of clichés and critical givens in the process. Music is one area where he is happy to credit the Blackfriars site with a particular impact on the practices and strategies adopted by plays such as *The Tempest* but Lindley is more hesitant about following the recent party line that has seen the more spectacular elements of the last plays (Jupiter's descent in *Cymbeline*, for example) as a direct product of cross-fertilization with court culture and in particular with the dominant form of court theatre that was the masque. In the process Lindley warns us about the need to be more cautious about assuming that a higher ticket price, and therefore a more wealthy clientele, necessarily means more sophisticated theatrical taste, and he deftly redeploys Martin Butler's work on the influence of Red Bull practices on *Cymbeline* in his Cambridge University Press edition of

the play (2005) to puncture a number of critical bubbles.

The other stand-out essay in the volume in some sense takes an opposite stance to McMullan's company-driven understanding of the cluster of texts known as the late or last plays (the essay in question actually slips between the two terms throughout). Russ McDonald's piece on 'listening to the last plays' is a condensed version of the stylistic analysis conducted in his monograph *Shakespeare's Late Style* (Cambridge, 2006). There is a remarkable body of work here pared down with impressive clarity and flow. McDonald draws attention, among other things, to the function and operation of ellipsis in the late plays and the effects of an increasingly irregular form of blank verse. In some ways there is a connection with McMullan's contribution in that he too is concerned with the 'order of things', although here that concern manifests itself in attention to grammatical detail and complexity, to syntax and to the aesthetic effects of repetition at both a structural and an aural level.

Performance histories of the plays (which are quite varied) are offered, although at times (as with the comparable sections of the Shakespeare Handbooks) I felt we were being given observational rather than analytical summaries. Eugene Giddens in his essay on '*Pericles*: The Afterlife' makes the important point that unlike many of the other texts under consideration in this volume *Pericles* was written for the Globe but it therefore seemed a shame that recent experiments at resurrecting the play in the reconstructed version of the theatre on Bankside did not receive any extended discussion. Having said that, Giddens's essay excels on the printed afterlife of the play, challenging further assumptions and critical clichés in the process. *Pericles* after all was 'the only late play to be published during Shakespeare's lifetime', only suffering a sharp decline in attention in the eighteenth century. I wondered here, as in the essay by Patricia Tatspaugh on *The Winter's Tale*, whether there could have been more space in the volume to consider why the late plays have had particular appeal to more recent decades, both in terms of performance and study. Catherine Alexander, for example, mentions the Kneehigh adaptation of *Cymbeline* in her essay on the play, a production that made a controversial contribution to the aforementioned RSC's Complete Works Festival in 2007, but never begins to get her teeth into questions about why a company like that so associated both with children's theatre and with physical theatre might be drawn to that play at that specific moment in time. This kind of material might have given the volume more of an afterlife of its own, moving the arguments beyond strictly literary study contexts into the realm of performance studies in a fuller and more sustained way. The question of 'afterlife' in the more extended sense of multigeneric adaptations is raised by Virginia Mason Vaughan's essay on *The Tempest*. Choosing for her specific focus 'literary adaptations' she moves from W. H. Auden and H. D.'s poetic responses and Aimé Césaire's dramatic adaptation, *Une tempête*, through to a series of novels including Margaret Laurence's *The Diviners*, Marina Warner's *Indigo* and Gloria Naylor's *Mama Day*. The latter discussion is accompanied by an intriguing denial from the novelist herself – in response to a direct question from Vaughan – that *The Tempest* was ever an influence on her island-set novel with its central character called 'Miranda'. It's a denial that is hard to sustain if one has a knowledge of Naylor's other highly appropriative publications, which include responses to *A Midsummer Night's Dream* in at least two novels and a deeply resonant sequence involving the burning of a copy of the *Complete Works* in another.

There is much to engage the reader in this collection and I am sure this *Companion* will quickly join those student reading lists and find a happy home on university library shelves. The volume could have afforded to be just a little braver perhaps in its overall structure and approach (the radical calls of McMullan are almost forgotten by the end, until Suzanne Gosset picks up on the issue of collaboration in her closing chapter). The absence of any discussion beyond a glancing reference to *Cardenio*, the so-called 'lost' rather than 'last' play, in a year when there has been a major international conference on the theme and when scholars as high

profile as Gary Taylor and Stephen Greenblatt have been performing their own acts of textual resurrection might seem a lost opportunity to some. Conservatism has its place in the world of student textbook publications, I grant, but the 'Companions' do have such a command of the audience that I suspect they can afford to be a little more ambitious.

Kiernan Ryan's *Shakespeare's Comedies* is not a 'handbook' per se but is described on its back cover as being 'essential reading... for students and teachers', which suggests at least an attempt at a survey of this particular genre. Ryan in fact reproduces work on *The Comedy of Errors* and *The Merchant of Venice* from his larger tome on *Shakespeare* (2001) for the same publisher, Macmillan. The publication's sense of audience has impacted on the way in which the work is presented. Ryan himself declares early on his wish to produce a book 'free' of footnotes. In the process he seems to want to cut himself free from the encumbrances (as he regards them) of recent historicist criticism. That is not to say that the book is 'citation free'; Ryan prefers to acknowledge some of his sources in the shape of a 'Works Cited' section at the back of the volume. Interestingly, the scholarship he prefers to acknowledge the influence of is criticism from earlier ages ranging from Dr Johnson and Coleridge, through George Eliot to W. H. Auden. This resurrection of earlier modes of Shakespeare criticism is an interesting project in itself and I, for one, was constantly struck by the pithy teachability of much of the Auden material quoted. My regret, however, was that this rather economic mode of referencing seemed to be achieved at the expense of other forms of more recent Shakespeare scholarship, which, despite his claims, Ryan could be seen to be as influenced by, even as objects to argue against. There is a separate debate to be had perhaps about the precedents set in this plagiarism-haunted era by studies by eminent Shakespearians that choose to disregard the footnote as a form of intellectual acknowledgement – but I am sure Ryan can erect a suitably robust defence that he is a leader in the field who does not need to defer in this way to others in the pack.

My particular bugbear, however, was with the 'Preface' which rather grumpily asserts Ryan's personal dislike and distrust of historicist methodologies and his wish to tackle the plays 'on [their] own terms' (p. xii). A very partial version of those who work at the interface between literature and history is proffered: 'If one is disinclined', says Ryan, 'to immure Shakespeare's drama in its early modern milieu by shackling it to extraneous archival material, and if reducing it to a quarry for cultural historians more interested in maps, make-up, or medicine than in the power of plays is no more appealing than conscripting it to endorse a particular critical theory or procedure, then most of what passes for Shakespeare criticism is of little value' (p. xii). The loaded language here is clear in its dislike – 'shackling', 'extraneous', 'quarry', 'conscripting'; I also regretted the sweeping dismissal of all archival-related considerations of Shakespearian plays as superfluous. But, most of all, what just two years of writing this contribution to *Shakespeare Survey* has taught me is that, while there is some unappealing and unimaginative publishing on Shakespeare (most of which does not usually come near being honoured by a mention in this essay), there is much more that is revealing, insightful, engaging and intellectually challenging. And, dare I suggest – as a practising cultural historian – that some of that work is, indeed, on 'maps, make-up, and medicine' and that an interest in this kind of topic or in the wider early modern milieu in which Shakespeare's plays were realized and performed does not necessarily go hand-in-hand with an inability to appreciate or want to explore the power of drama. In fact, for some of us, the one is a necessary correlative of the other.

Kiernan Ryan might offer the riposte that my own review is highly partial, concentrating as it has on the somewhat Eeyore-ish preface to an otherwise erudite and often thought-provoking book, but I felt throughout that there was a slightly grumpy polemic being allowed to limit the potential in the discussions (the rapid dismissal of the potentiality of film on p. 181 is just one case in point). Shakespeare criticism, like anything else, is a matter of taste and the world of Shakespeare scholarship is broad enough to contain all these different positions. What strikes me as important, though, when introducing students to material (and this is surely the key audience for Ryan's survey volume) is to encourage openness of debate. To be fair, then, the fact that I have spent the last few paragraphs defending the positions attacked by Ryan in his preface suggests he has certainly succeeded in stimulating that debate.

THEOLOGIZING SHAKESPEARE

Several of this year's contributions refer to the 'turn to religion' in recent Shakespeare scholarship and even more have a shared interest in themes of resurrection and redemption as both trope and performative act. The turn to religion informed work that was less concerned with circling around previously held debates as to whether Shakespeare was a Catholic than with locating the man and his works in a newly nuanced understanding of the religious landscapes, material and cultural, of early modern England.

Phebe Jensen's excellent monograph *Religion and Revelry in Shakespeare's Festive World* seeks, for example, to account for 'the post-Reformation Catholic recusant experience' (p. 8). She is interested in the 'relationship, real and conceptual, between Catholicism and festivity' (p. 9) and has spent much time in the archives and commonplace books relating to recusant families to unearth her evidence for those relationships. Her examples include the Petres of East Anglia, the Yorkes in the West Riding and the Blundells of Lancashire. REED is of course a key resource for Jensen in this respect and the impact of that project can be felt across all of the studies that I am analysing in this section. It is RE[E]D (the second E is increasingly, and necessarily, dropped these days as volumes are published on early modern Wales and Scotland) that has identified the strong continuation of medieval forms of drama such as moralities in more far-flung regions of the nation and therefore account for greater contiguities between the early modern and the medieval than previous hardline periodized studies had allowed.

In the process of her study, Jensen identifies households where the performance of festivity and associated rituals became a means of 'creating and sustaining recusant identity' (p. 46), furnishing fascinating individual instances of this, such as the Christmas celebrations at the Yorke household in Nidderdale in 1609–10 which patronized a local group of recusant players sometimes known as the Cholmeley Players which performed a *Saint Christopher* play in preference to *Lear, Pericles* and *The Three English Brothers*, which had been proposed as possible entertainments for the season.

The precise relevance of this to the Shakespearian context appears in the second part of the monograph, where Jensen performs readings of, among others, plays such as *As You Like It* and *The Winter's Tale* (fast becoming the key Shakespearian text in the 'turn to religion' if this year's publications are to be trusted) in the context of this revised understanding of festive culture in a recusant context. Act 5 of *The Winter's Tale* with its statue of a 'blessed lady' that comes to life is, suggests Jensen, 'an assertion of the value of the aesthetics of Catholic devotional practice' (p. 197). This is a more overt and explicit performance of Catholic sympathies than the more embedded references to festivity she locates in *As You Like It*'s Robin Hood references and the subplot of festive misrule in *Twelfth Night*. She also identifies a reconceptualization of ideas of 'holiday' in the *Henry IV* plays (reworking C. L. Barber in the process). This is a carefully researched and enlightening study that paves the way for future research into northern English households and their tangible impact on the dramatic culture of the early modern period.

Shakespeare & the Middle Ages edited by Curtis Perry and John Watkins is both a response to the aforementioned 'religious turn' and a further intervention in the current vibrant (and sometimes highly sensitized) debate about the need for greater rapprochement between scholars of the medieval and the early modern periods. Sometimes that argument has been waged from a position of defiance by those who clearly felt oppressed by a perceived hierarchy in which early modernists had all the status and prestige and medievalists were accordingly undervalued. There is something of this in several of James Simpson's recent trenchant contributions to the discussion, not least his 2004 volume for the Oxford English Literary History, *1350–1547: Reform and Cultural Revolution*, which suggested that in redressing the balance we should value the early modern a little less than we do. As a scholar who runs a department where medieval studies has its own section but where the early modern fights for space in 'modern literature' and 'drama' sections full to bursting with competition, I was fascinated to see such a reputation for tyranny accorded to my area of specialism, but this collection of essays is more about rapprochement and encounter than that rehearsal of previously drawn battle-lines suggests.

In the introductory chapter, the editors take on what they describe as 'the problems of periodicity' and 'the historical problem of teleology' (p. 10) in thinking about Shakespeare and 'the Middle Ages'. They do so with great clarity and I am likely to be using much of this work in my own teaching in future. Perry and Watkins make the crucial point that Shakespeare has been an important filter for our notions of the medieval, and to some extent he has 'invented' popular understandings of the period through the history plays, but they also pose the question of the extent to which Shakespeare was himself 'authored' by the traditions of his preceding age – an age which, they suggest, had for Shakespeare a 'present, binding reality' (p. 13) – in terms of inherited traditions both ethical and artistic.

The collection is divided into three sections to reflect these different approaches to the implicit relationship in the '&' of the title between Shakespeare and the Middle Ages. Part I thinks about 'Texts in Transition', looking at medieval forms in *A Lover's Complaint* (an essay by Christopher Warley), as well as the changing treatment of specific tropes and paradigms, such as those of resurrection in plays ranging from *Much Ado About Nothing* to *Pericles* and *The Winter's Tale* (by Sarah Beckwith, and see later comparisons in this section with an essay by Elizabeth Williamson in the *Shakespeare and Religious Change* collection), ideas of the sacrament and the social contract in *The Merchant of*

Venice (Elizabeth Fowler), and questions of national identity in *King John* (John Watkins).

Part II looks instead at 'Medievalism in Shakespeare's England'. Patrick Cheney considers Shakespeare's intertextual relationship with Chaucer as filtered through the writings of Edmund Spenser. Several of the essays in this section focus on the history plays for the reasons identified in the introduction, that these plays have played such a crucial role in inherited understandings of the period. Brian Walsh suggests that in the Chorus of *Henry V* we can see a self-consciousness about this and about 'historical difference' at the very moment of composition and first performance (p. 157). Curtis Perry seems to pick up James Simpson's challenge to diminish the significance of the 'modern' in the phrase 'early modern' by suggesting that the nationalism often identified in Shakespeare's histories is in part a response to an 'incipient sense of nationhood' in the medieval period (p. 173). In doing so Perry extends his argument beyond the specifically Shakespearian in productive ways.

Part III looks at 'the resources of medieval culture' as deployed by Shakespeare. Michael O'Connell argues for significant links between *King Lear* and morality drama, not only in the figure of the Fool but in performances of penitence as in the Lear–Cordelia reunion in the play. O'Connell is here responding to the persuasive case made by scholars such as Janette Dillon (for example in *The Cambridge Introduction to Early English Drama*, 2006) that Shakespeare and his contemporaries have links with, as well as differences from, medieval dramatic forms and techniques and that we need to keep a balanced view when stressing the innovation and experimentation of early modern theatre and pay due heed to the abiding forms of earlier liturgical and civic theatre.

O'Connell makes the point that this was for Shakespeare and his contemporaries recent theatrical history and therefore a very tangible memory and associational force; in an intriguing observation he notes that all the major Elizabethan playwrights were of an age to have had a knowledge of mystery and morality drama but that Shakespeare's provincial upbringing makes it most likely that he actually witnessed such performances in action through the staging of the Coventry cycles (p. 199). In the process Shakespeare was able to assume a shared knowledge and familiarity in his audiences and to rest assured that they would be able to draw meaning from his allusions. Rebecca Krug's essay also explores morality traditions, and indeed texts, as they re-emerge in *The Merchant of Venice*. In a stand-out essay in the collection, Karen Sawyer Marsalek discusses the reworking of the resurrection paradigm in the figure of Falstaff in *1 Henry IV*. Revisiting the territory already discussed in the volume in Beckwith's essay, she notes that 'the image of a character returning from the dead was a potent and enduring one in early English drama, partly because of the inherent dramatic power of the character's reappearance and partly because the image had a long theatrical history in biblical drama' (p. 217). From the twelfth to the sixteenth centuries, she notes, 'Plays dedicated to Christ's resurrection were a central feature of the English theatrical landscape' (p. 217). Repeating the model of safe allusion offered in McConnell's essay in this volume, Marsalek suggests that Falstaff can therefore parody resurrection because of the expectation of easy audience familiarity with the dramatic trope. He even takes the audience into his confidence in the process (p. 233).

Shakespeare and Religious Change, edited by Kenneth J. E. Graham and Philip D. Collington, is a collection that for obvious reasons has considerable overlaps with Perry and Watkins's volume, in that its focus is 'the relationship between Shakespearean drama and the changing religious culture of post-Reformation England'. Marsalek is also a contributor here, this time analysing the resonant 'lieux de mémoire', to invoke Pierre Nora's much-deployed ideas on the relationship between memory and place, provided by the Blackfriars Theatre for *King Henry VIII*, if indeed it was one of the performance sites for the play in the 1610s, as is suspected by many scholars, including the play's recent Arden 3 editor Gordon McMullan. One of this volume's editors, Kenneth Graham, provides a very helpful introduction that not only sets out the case for the recent 'religious turn' in Shakespeare criticism, but also transports readers on a useful journey through the key texts and moments in that debate. Graham makes the point that the RE[E]D project has been a key player in alerting us to 'the close affiliation between religious institutions, such as the parish, and theatrical production, the complicated relationship between festive and religious culture, and the importance to drama of regional religious variations' (p. 3). This point is borne out by several of the non-Shakespeare-specific essays in this collection, including Alexandra F. Johnston's on 'William Cecil and the Drama of Persuasion', which considers the influence of his Cambridge education and the reformed drama he was exposed to there on Cecil's strand of Protestant humanism, and Mary A. Blackstone's 'The Queen's Men and the Performance of Allegiance, Conformity, and Difference in Elizabethan Norwich', which makes some superb points about performance in an 'intertextual milieu' in a city such as Norwich, a milieu which includes for her sermonizing in cathedrals and churches and speeches attached to progresses and pageants as other 'local performance texts' (see, for example, p. 89).

A number of essays focus in ways complementary to the essays in the Perry and Watkins volume on the residual traces of earlier religious drama in Shakespeare's plays. Elizabeth Williamson, in an essay that can be fruitfully read alongside Sara Beckwith's in *Shakespeare & the Middle Ages*, explores the resurrection tradition in plays such as *Pericles* and *The Winter's Tale* and Jeffrey Knapp limns the link between the Corpus Christi cycles and the history plays in an essay that offers the fascinating statistic that 'of 44 references to Christ's name in Shakespeare's plays, 39 appear in the Lancastrian cycle' (p. 227). Knapp's essay is provocatively matched with Anthony Dawson's oppositional case for a 'secular theatre'. In stark contrast to some of his co-contributors, Dawson takes on the resurgence of religion in Shakespeare studies in a more questioning fashion. For him the early modern theatre remains a predominantly secular domain and form, the doctrinal being in the process refashioned for the purposes of entertainment

and aesthetic effect. He identifies various moments when, he argues, we can see 'the language of religion being taken over for purely theatrical purpose' or when the religious is being made to serve the profane (p. 245). It is the 'purely' in the quoted phrase that is, I think, the key to comprehending Dawson's mindset as opposed to that of fellow contributors such as Tom Bishop, who, in an excellent essay on the ways in which Shakespeare deploys biblical language and allusion in *Othello*, also invokes ideas of profanation. Bishop in a series of impressive close readings suggests a density of biblical intertexts in *Othello* that have been overlooked and which become key to the play's effects. It is wholly separate from his aims and intentions in this essay, but Bishop's discussion of the associative recall involved in the regular mention of foodstuffs in the play drew my thoughts back to Caryl Phillips's remarkable 1998 novelistic response to *Othello* (and *The Merchant of Venice), The Nature of Blood*. Phillips's novel shares absolutely Bishop's notion here that the 'languages of eating, hunger and appetite in the play' are bound up with issues of identity and faith, mobilizing as they do a 'powerful set of religious and cultural discourses' around food, feasting and fasting (p. 202). Bishop describes linguistic encounters of these kinds between the sacred and the dramatic as ongoing acts of 'profanation' in which the former is blunted by the sheer familiarity of the reference. For him this is intrinsic to the tragic genre; that these instances are 'dangerous' uses (p. 211) of language is borne out by the events that unravel in the play. For Dawson – and, usefully, he directly engages with Bishop's essay in making this point – these are instances of the sacred being rendered theatrical, being fashioned into entertainment.

The contrapuntal relationship of the two closing essays in the volume, Knapp's and Dawson's, is a marker of the careful organization and orchestration of this collection. Essays are frequently in dialogue with each other and this makes for a rewarding experience for the reader, encouraged as she is not just to read essays in isolation but to consider them in relationship to near neighbours. Sometimes that dialogue extends beyond the volume to other published work by the contributors. Phebe Jensen, in an essay entitled 'Religion and Festivity in *As You Like It*', reconfigures a section of her monograph which was reviewed earlier and finds links to Catholicism and festive ritual that may be better indicators of ongoing religious practice than mere vestiges of the past.

Sean Benson's *Shakespearean Resurrection: The Art of Almost Raising the Dead* is a book-length study of the previously noted fascination this year with tropes of resurrection and redemption. His introduction notes how 'Shakespeare repeatedly evokes Christ's resurrection from the dead when long-lost characters reunite' (p. 1) and as a result he considers a series of 'recognition' scenes from plays including *Twelfth Night* and *The Comedy of Errors*. Benson too refers to the RE[E]D factor in his stress on how vernacular plays and the space in which touring troupes playing Shakespeare performed frequently coalesced both in private households and civic theatre contexts. Such performances also contributed in his view to a blurring of the semiotics of a particular site, shading between the religious and the secular, and this flowed back into metropolitan theatrical experience in intriguing ways: 'When Hermione is resurrected [in *The Winter's Tale*],' he observes, 'what more fit space is there for her quasi-resurrection from the dead than a church, even a converted one such as Blackfriars?' (p. 7). I thought Benson's awareness of spatial issues was a major strength of his study, as was his flexible understanding of the ways in which liturgical drama's influence might be found and tested in the Shakespearian canon at large. Much of the discussion is genre-led. Benson provides chapter studies of the comedies, including a rich analysis of *The Comedy of Errors* and *Much Ado about Nothing*, and examines 'failed resurrections' in the tragedies, focusing in particular on *Othello* and *Romeo and Juliet*. He argues for *King Lear* as a 'failed miracle play' in ways that connect back with the arguments of Michael O'Connell in *Shakespeare & the Middle Ages*. The closing two chapters focus in on the late plays, with a discussion of the 'limits' of stage resurrection in *Cymbeline* and *Pericles*, followed by a consideration of ideas of 'raising the dead' as they pertain to

The Winter's Tale and *The Tempest*. As a stand-alone monograph this had value enough but read in the context of the wider body of scholarship available on related themes this year there was a sense in which the debate was widened and enhanced by the variety of approaches and interpretations available to the reader.

While Mary Ellen Lamb and Valerie Wayne's *Staging Early Modern Romance: Prose Fiction, Dramatic Romance, and Shakespeare* is not ostensibly religious in theme, there were some intriguing points of overlap and intersection with the body of work I have been discussing so far in this section. Gloria Olchowy's 'The Issue of the Corpus Christi Cycles, or "Religious Romance" in *The Winter's Tale*' makes obvious gestures of connection. She stresses the 'strong genealogical connection between the Corpus Christi cycles and the secular prose romances' that often formed Shakespeare's source material. As well as being highly popular forms, Olchowy notes that they offer up particular versions of motherhood (p. 147). The sustained comparison between Shakespearian romance and prose fiction is a real strength of the group of essays collected here. As well as noting, as the editors do, that prose fiction was a popular form exploited by both print culture and the commercial playhouses, particular light is shed on ideas of generation, adaptation and transition by contributors. Lori Humphrey Newcomb looks at *Pericles*, while Steve Mentz seeks to recover the rivalry implicit in the Lodge–Shakespeare relationship, played out in their versions of Rosalind's narrative in *Rosalind* and *As You Like It* respectively. It was good to see Shakespeare relocated here as a writer operating amid the cut and thrust of the market and competing genres, though there is never a naive attempt at complete homogenization between the different genres under scrutiny. As Mary Ellen Lamb herself notes, 'The social forces that operated on prose romances and plays were not identical – the virtual audience imagined for prose romances was more often gendered – but neither were they entirely separate' (p. 125). Goran Stanivukovic compares *Hamlet* and *Euordanus*; Valerie Wayne considers ideas of citationality in a rich discussion of

Cymbeline's intertexts – I for one was very glad to be introduced to the 1621 text *Westward for Smelts*, a *Decameron*-esque storytelling performed by a group of women returning from selling their smelts at market and subjecting a somewhat wearied waterman (especially if the frontispiece reproduced in the volume is to be believed!) to their tall tales and stories. There are also some excellent essays on non-Shakespearian subject matter, including Lorna Hutson on Philip Massinger's *The Picture* which presents it as a play that emerges at the end of a long line of cultural transmission and transformation.

It may seem that my own discussion has travelled some way from its focus on theology and medieval religious inheritances but it is striking that several of the returns to a consideration of genre this year also embed a concern with the 'religious turn'. One striking example is Valerie Forman's *Tragicomic Redemptions: Global Economies and the Early Modern Stage* which is, as its full title implies, an innovative pairing of economic theory and an interest in genre, with those same themes of resurrection and redemption that defined a number of the contributions to volumes in the sub-field of Shakespeare and religion this year. To simplify somewhat what is quite a subtle and often dense set of arguments in her study, Forman's case is that tragicomedy intersects with economic theory and interests in that it is about 'the *transformation* of losses into profit' often through plotlines of redemption (p. 9). She divides the volume into two parts, the first concentrating on Shakespeare, the second on early modern contemporaries including Massinger and Fletcher (there are useful discussions here of *The Renegado* and *The Island Princess*) and she is admirably upfront about her reasons for this, as well as the fact that the more archival elements of the study (using, for example, East India Company correspondence as a documentary source) tend to cluster in the non-Shakespearian half. For Forman, Shakespeare is the more 'abstract' writer, hence her wish to re-root him in the early modern contexts of trade and economic theory. This is a perfectly valid argument though I sometimes wondered if as a result his texts would have repaid the same kind of documentary approach afforded Fletcher's Spice Islands

play. *Twelfth Night, The Merchant of Venice* and *The Winter's Tale* all receive detailed discussion, but at times I felt the interest in the Shakespearian sections was more towards the redemptive aspects of the argument than the hard finance. The discussion of the role of the piracy subtext in *Twelfth Night* was fresh but was another moment when I thought comparison with other non-Shakespearian dramas could have been fruitful. How does this play sit alongside *The Fair Maid of the West*, for example?

Forman is an intelligent writer and there is much here on genre and in particular on tragicomedy's resistance to closure that will be of interest even for those who occasionally find the economic arguments difficult to follow. The book demonstrates its author's own adventurous nature in a brave conclusion that brings the financial arguments right up to the present day. Such is the speed (or veritable lack of speed) of academic publication that the book was not able to take on the implications of the recent 'credit crunch' and new ideas of profit and loss to the extent that a reader might wish but, through a discussion of the impact of Hurricane Katrina, through the conflicts in Iraq and Afghanistan to the closing discussion of global warming and the issue of sustainable resources, Forman insists her readers connect the past to the present in informed ways. These kinds of closing gesture in monographs on early modern subjects – ones that want to find a connection 'in the moment' as it were – can sometimes seem forced or unpersuasive but here I detected a genuine passion in the argument that was to be admired.

B. J. Sokol's concern in *Shakespeare and Tolerance* is less with religion *per se* than with a particular branch of philosophical ethics. From early on in the monograph he establishes that his definition of 'tolerance' will extend beyond ideas of good will and sympathy. In this study the term applies to actions other than forbearance from harm (p. xiii). In a chapter on jokes and tolerance, he considers whether in the atmosphere of 'new puritanism', where offence is easily and rapidly registered in the mass media (this was the year after all of the so-called 'Twitter storms'), this is not a good time to discuss themes of giving and taking offence. The study is coloured throughout with similar strong statements of opinion, not least on contemporary politics, which sometimes gave me pause, but Sokol does raise important questions en route around the limits of audience toleration in the early modern context. This chapter considers, for example, the ethnic jokes in *The Merchant of Venice* and later chapters focus on racism in *Othello* and misogyny in *The Taming of the Shrew*.

Interestingly, in his chapter on gender and tolerance, Sokol himself handles themes of repentance and redemption in *Love's Labour's Lost* and *The Winter's Tale*. I found especially rich his chapters on national identity and tolerance in which he considered the laws against aliens and the existence in London of Stranger Churches and their impact on plays such as *Sir Thomas More* and *The Comedy of Errors*. Sokol produces a particularly fine reading of the latter and his work is indicative of a recent trend of recuperative readings of this play that have more securely located it in the mainstream canon of read, studied and performed Shakespearian playtexts. I liked how he drew our attention to the ways in which this play 'constantly alludes to commerce, travel, and differing nationalities and places' (p. 70) despite being so physically bounded and carefully located in Ephesus. 'Merchant voyages are planned,' notes Sokol, 'handshake contracts made, credit-worthiness assessed, and actions for debt pursued, just as they would have been in Shakespeare's London' (p. 70). This chapter is able to build on recent consideration of Shakespeare's relationship to the Mountjoy family, with whom he lodged for a time in Silver Street (subject of Charles Nicholls's outstanding biography *The Lodger* published by Penguin in 2007), and also makes some pertinent comments on the significance of dialect and foreign language terms in Shakespearian drama. The final chapter on *The Tempest* strikes another new note by considering what Sokol terms 'geohumoralism' in relation to the play – the idea that climate could produce and condition culture – suggesting that British people suffered, then as now, from a kind of 'latitude envy' of those born in more Mediterranean climes. This is a deep-reaching, if occasionally idiosyncratic,

study which asks us to think again about well-worn topics such as national identity and 'race' from the perspective of tolerance and an informed idea of ethics. If, along with studies such as Valerie Forman's, it contributes to an increased 'ethical turn' in Shakespeare Studies, that could prove very interesting indeed.

Jonathan Gil Harris's rich study *Untimely Matter in the Time of Shakespeare* is, like many of the explicitly theological studies discussed in this section, concerned with residual cultural traces. Reflecting the turn to the object or the artefact as much as the turn to religion in his approach, Harris employs with impressive dexterity a range of recent theoretical material on time (in particular the work of Michel Serres), sites and 'things' (Arjun Appadurai's work, of course, but also much of the layered thinking emerging from memory and trauma studies as well). Alongside discussions of George Herbert's *The Temple* and John Stow's *Survey of London*, plus a chapter on Margaret Cavendish, there is a discussion of Shakespeare's Second Henriad in the context of what Harris terms 'East-West palimpsests'. Most rewarding for me in terms of the Shakespearian content of the volume, however, was the performance-driven consideration of *Macbeth* in Chapter 4 under the title 'The Smell of Gunpowder'. Building on recent advances in the field of 'historical phenomenology' (pioneered in early modern studies not least by Bruce Smith, who is duly acknowledged), Harris explores the 'palimpsests of olfaction' or the way in which smell and the processing of smell provoke acts of remembrance and the specific impact of the smell of squibs and fireworks in an early modern performance of *Macbeth* in the wake of recent parliamentary conspiracies and the contribution this may have made to slippages of time between the present and the past in the watching (and sensing) spectator. In the process, Harris performs a different kind of resurrective effect on his materials and artefacts, Shakespeare's plays included, enabling us to think about them as very much 'live' and in the moment of performance and reception, as well as representing mere vestigial traces or 'stranded objects' from the past.

A final contribution to this year's considerable 'turn to religion' is David N. Beauregard's *Catholic Theology in Shakespeare's Plays* which is interested in the same ideas of residual Catholic culture and practices as Phebe Jensen's book and a number of essays in the Perry and Watkins collection. As well as exploring recent claims about Shakespeare's Catholic family leanings, concluding with others that the biographical record is 'ambiguous at best' (p. 14), the monograph focuses on the handling of specific theological issues in the playtexts. Chapter 1, for example, explores the 'theology of penance' and forms of interiorized repentance as they appear in plays including *All's Well That Ends Well*, *Hamlet* and *Romeo and Juliet*. *All's Well* is also the subject of the second chapter's exploration of the 'theology of grace', and grace is further explored in *The Winter's Tale* later in the volume. The third chapter is a particularly fine analysis of Shakespeare's unusually (in a reformed context) sympathetic treatment of Franciscan monasteries in *Measure for Measure* which places the play in the context of a larger anti-fraternal tradition. Various strategies were employed by reformed drama 'against stage nuns and friars', Beauregard informs us; for example, 'derogatory epithets, sarcastic asides, reversals of attitude, outright rejection of cloistered life, abusive flouting, physical punishment, and many others' (p. 59). For this reader, the account of Duke Vincentio's actions were read too unquestioningly as comprehensible and benign – Beauregard suggests that 'none of his three stratagems – his disguise as a friar, the bed-trick and his substitution of Ragozine's head – is evil in its intention' (p. 69). For all the 'good purposes' intended, there remain some fundamental questions around these actions for me whenever watching this play in performance, but I enjoyed the opportunity to debate with Beauregard's engaged responses to this play and others. The closing chapter on *The Tempest* is an equally thought-provoking analysis of the various references to sin, pardon and grace in that play and again I can imagine deploying these chapters to stimulate discussion in the seminar room in years to come. My review has separated off publications purposely designed for students from the schol-arly monographs and collections discussed here but both, I think, have potential in the end to stimulate students new to Shakespeare or simply grappling with some of the theological and dramatic complexities of his plays.

RESPONDING TO AND PICTURING SHAKESPEARE

I started this review with that striking quotation from Kathleen Knox's 'On the Study of Shakespeare for Girls' with which Gail Marshall begins her study of *Shakespeare and Victorian Women*. It is a mark of Marshall's scholarship that the kind of interest this introductory gambit sparked in this reader is fully sustained throughout her book. Marshall's ostensible subject is the 'enormous variety of ways in which Victorian women read, quoted, responded to, argued with and countered Shakespeare in their work, conversations, letters, education, and performances' (p. 4). This list alone is indicative of the range and depth of Marshall's study. Negotiating as she is the complex and often contradictory Shakespearian legacy as it was invoked and deployed by the Victorians, it helps that Marshall is herself a very fine reader of Shakespeare.

Marshall opts for the idea of 'translation' as the key term with which to account for her subjects' engagements with Shakespeare, man and text. This term, she feels, is more representative of the kinds of 'transactions' she seeks to account for than a phrase like 're-visioning', 'adaptation', or 'appropriation' (pp. 9–10). There is a sudden resurgence of translation studies as a disciplinary sub-field this year and also new ideas of the phrase are being mobilized that it will be interesting to see Shakespeare criticism responding to over the next few years (for one particular intervention in the discussion this year, readers are directed to Roshni Mooneram's work on Creole Shakespeares discussed later in this section).

Marshall's beautifully written book makes the point early on that Victorian girls tended to encounter Shakespeare initially in the home rather than at the theatre so this is largely a 'read'

Shakespeare that we are exploring. Nevertheless, Marshall is able to take us directly into the classroom with some Victorian female students via the extant exercise books of students at Cheltenham's Ladies' College (see, for example, p. 38). We gain a similar intimacy with 'EBB', as Elizabeth Barrett Browning referred to herself, as she explores the fate of Shakespeare's daughter characters in the plays as a means of thinking about her own social position and identity. In terms of 'translation' Shakespeare is most overtly present in EBB's *Sonnets from the Portuguese*. Intriguingly, a popular culture film adaptation of *The Taming of the Shrew*, directed by Gil Junger in 1999 and starring the late Heath Ledger, recognized this meeting point between two poets in its title *10 Things I Hate About You*, deliberately inverting EBB's oft-quoted line: 'How do I love thee? Let me count the ways'. Marshall takes us beyond the surface, however, in tracing the sustained Shakespearian 'presence' in *Sonnets from the Portuguese* as well as other Barrett Browning poems.

Other chapters in Marshall's book focus on the performative presences of Shakespeare in female culture through a consideration of the careers of Helen Faucit and Fanny Kemble and, in the final chapter, of the theatre-work of actresses in the 1890s. Marshall is acutely aware throughout of the complex slippages between private and public space even in the lives of these very public performers. In a particularly fine essay on George Eliot and Shakespeare, Marshall depicts the novelist as both borrowing from and arguing with Shakespeare in her work. What Eliot was resisting in particular was the bardolatry of certain sectors of Victorian society, refusing (again in ways that seem strikingly proto-modern) attempts to understand Shakespeare through his biography (p. 109). Eliot shares much, at least in Marshall's account, with current scholars interested in investigating the cultural appropriations of Shakespeare in the contemporary moment. For Marshall, 'Eliot is not interested in memorializing or preserving Shakespeare, but in exploring what has become of him and his work over time' (p. 126). She was 'interested in the nature of her society's relationship with the playwright'.

Fewer texts this year than in some previous ones engage directly with the idea of translating or adapting Shakespeare, but the idea of 'Shakespeare translated' that haunts Marshall's study is nevertheless implicit in works like Erika Hateley's *Shakespeare in Children's Literature*. The subtitle of this study is the real key to the author's approach, which is to explore the role of 'Gender and Cultural Capital' in numerous (mostly novelistic) responses to Shakespeare aimed at a youth audience. There is a historical overview in early chapters but the book will be a particularly rich treasury for the growing number of modules interested in Shakespeare and childhood as well as Shakespeare and children's literature in its discussions of an impressively wide range of contemporary material that draws in many North American and Australian examples. I thought that Hateley was perhaps unduly dismissive of other recent studies in this field when establishing early on the importance and significance of her own book; the study stands well enough without needing that competitive edge. I also thought that at times her ideological critique of the 'failure' of the majority of her subject texts and authors to get beyond a prescriptive approach to Shakespeare for children, especially for female readers – Hateley's closing wish is for a text which 'knowingly combines feminine autonomy *with* the cultural capital of Shakespeare' (p. 186) – sometimes skewed the close readings in particular ways, but this remains a stimulating and detailed study that will be valued by those working in this vibrant emerging field.

One area where I saw future potential for studies of Shakespeare and youth readership would be in deploying work familiar from corpus linguistics that does actual reader testing to explore for real some of the assumptions about 'implied readers' that Hateley's argument depended on. The linguistic turn in Shakespeare has shown itself at various moments in recent years but the move has never been sustained. The separation between linguistics and literary or performance studies modules that still pertains in many departments in UK and US universities has tended to create discrete debates which only intermittently encounter each other at conferences and in the publishing context.

The work of Lynne Magnusson, Jonathan Hope (even if he does come in for some hard questioning for his claims about Shakespeare and dialect in B. J. Sokol's *Shakespeare and Tolerance*), and others has been key in providing a bridge between those two worlds. However, it is also fitting that Hope should provide the preface to Roshni Mooneram's *From Creole to Standard: Shakespeare, Language and Literature in a Post-colonial Context*. Hope, like other Shakespearians reading this review I suspect, feels that the heart of the book, which is about the development of Mauritian Creole or MC, is 'the encounter between Shakespeare and the MC writer Dev Virahsawmy', who has adapted and translated numerous Shakespeare plays, though not solely with the intention of responding to Shakespeare from a postcolonial subject position but, intriguingly, with policies of language planning in mind. Shakespeare has formed an intrinsic part of Virahsawmy's efforts to standardize MC into a written language and to expand its vocabulary and potential for activities such as metaphorization in the process. Mooneram's book provides us with the necessary background for understanding these counter-cultural moves, though at times the study is written, it must be said, in the very particular discourse of linguistics as a discipline which can occasionally seem unnecessarily excluding to other kinds of audience and readership.

The chapters that will most interest readers of this review, however, are Chapters 4 and 5 which concentrate on Virahsawmy's 'iconoclastic translation' of *The Tempest, Toufann* and other works in response to *Hamlet* and *Much Ado. Toufann* has been re-translated as it were into English and has enjoyed British stage performances, so the act of cultural reclamation could be considered multiple. Mooneram allows us insight into the title – 'toufann' is a Bhojpuri word for 'cyclone' and therefore has specifically rural connotations compared to the more standard 'siklonn' (p. 151) – and to the author's use of code-switching in the text to indicate that 'he sustains admiration for Shakespeare while simultaneously demonstrating that bardolatry does not command his intellectual respect' (p. 159). In the latter respect, there was interesting kinship with Gail Marshall's sense of George Eliot's responses to Shakespeare in a nineteenth-century English context. I was fascinated to see how *Hamlet*, a play so linked in Shakespearian scholars' minds with language, with 'words, words, words' indeed, becomes in Virahsawmy's hands a means for creating new forms and manipulating existing terms in a language planning context. There are unexpected correlations here between the neologisms and coinages of early modern drama in its explosion onto the commercial stages in the late sixteenth century and the rich embrace of linguistic possibility that Virahsawmy's career represents. Shakespeare here is not just material for reconfiguration but a positively enabling figure.

There has been a veritable sub-field this year in terms of studies of adaptations or responses to Shakespeare that look at illustrated responses to the poems and plays. The most impressive of these tomes has to be Stuart Sillars's *The Illustrated Shakespeare, 1709–1875*, lavishly supported by images and a heavyweight publication in every sense. Sillars feels that illustrated Shakespeares have been unduly neglected by scholars; this volume surely puts that right, arguing for illustration 'not so much [as] a transmediation but an alternative form of presentation, reconfiguring the play into its own generic syntax' (p. 16) and it is a marker of this study that it is able to respond with as much depth and clarity to the advances in printing and illustrative technologies as to the Shakespearian readings and responses particular images represent. There is a fascinating early chapter on the 'spatial narratives' in Rowe's Shakespeares, which looks at the deployment of architectural structures in frontispieces and engravings to reflect on the plays themselves. *The Comedy of Errors* is a particular beneficiary of this analysis as Sillars demonstrates how use is made of 'recessive structure as a visual presentation of the play's movement' (p. 47). The later impact of pictorial theatre traditions on the use of tableau effects in illustration is equally well handled. Sillars at all times keeps in play the aesthetic and commercial imperatives behind the images and makes much of key issues such as selection. My only regret was that the conclusion had to hurry over periods of illustration outside the strict remit of the study; does that mean I can hope for a follow-up edition in which Sillars can apply his obvious skills to the work of Eric Gill and Eric Ravilious and other exponents of the 1930s craft revival and interest in woodcut printing, which was so rich in its own engagements with Shakespeare?

The illustrations that accompany Velma Bourgeois Richmond's *Shakespeare as Children's Literature: Edwardian Retellings in Words and Pictures* are not as beautifully reproduced as those in Sillars but it is useful to have the visuals to read alongside the text here as well. Richmond's is a careful study that spends a considerable amount of time establishing the literary and cultural background to the focus of Edwardian versions of Shakespeare for children. There is some fine material in this background detail on the Lambs' highly influential *Tales* and their own wider context in chapbooks and ballad versions as well as on the implicit link between pleasure and pedagogy, or play and learning to use Richmond's terms, in Victorian versions of Shakespeare for children. There are then detailed studies of work by E[dith] Nesbit and others and the accompanying visuals to those texts in print, which were themselves often simplified versions of the Shakespearian plots. There are links to the survey material in Hateley that would provide some interesting cross-referencing. As with the examples in Sillars, too, key questions of emphasis and selection arise. There is more on the idea of 'learning Shakespeare' here, both in the classroom and in the context of home libraries. In a brief conclusion, Richmond brings the story up to date with mention of *The Animated Tales* and other Shakespeare books for children, though this was perhaps too selective in itself, having seemingly no room for the massive contribution that manga and animé traditions have recently made to the field. That quibble aside, this is a carefully considered and well-researched addition to an emergent field.

Richard Meek's *Narrating the Visual in Shakespeare* is not about illustrating Shakespeare but concerns itself with the poet-playwright's references to and engagements with the visual arts. Meek is himself eloquent on the rhetorical traditions which informed this, citing Quintilian and Aristotle at key points in the argument and regularly invoking ekphrasis. The discussion naturally leads to a focus on moments of narration within both poems and plays – and another real strength of this study was its willingness to read these different genres alongside each other, offering essays on *The Rape of Lucrece* and *Venus and Adonis* (which he rightly identifies as invested in various acts of seeing and looking) as well as *Hamlet*, *King Lear* and the ubiquitous (this year at least!) *Winter's Tale*. There is a concentration on absent or 'off-stage' moments that reminded me of Barbara Hardy's *Shakespeare's Storytellers* (London, 1997), which I was glad to see cited in the conclusion to this study. Meek is particularly winning on the fascination of *Hamlet* in these moments of narration – examples would include the Ghost's account of 'his' murder, Hamlet appearing to Ophelia in her closet as she was sewing in a state of considerable emotional distress and Gertrude's poetic narration of Ophelia's own riverine demise – asking what their significance and status is: 'Do they interrupt the action?' he asks, 'Or are they rather an integral part of the play's action?' (p. 82). Meek himself is fairly persuaded of the latter, but the ruminations allow him to look at subsequent readers and interpreters who have focused on these 'off-stage' moments and how the on-stage narration asks the audience or reader to visualize them. Millais's water-logged Ophelia is one obvious example that Meek rightly invokes here. This is a fine, scholarly achievement and an important contribution to a revival of interest in the relationships between visual culture, drama, and indeed rhetoric, in the early modern period.

SMELLING SHAKESPEARE

I began with Gail Marshall's citation of Kathleen Knox's work 'On the Study of Shakespeare for Girls' and it seems fitting to end with that text as well. I want to close, though, not with the imagined 'Dorothy''s resentment of Shakespeare in the classroom but Knox's rather beautiful recommendation of ways to start caring about the process of 'learning' Shakespeare: 'Do not puzzle over words and sentences of Elizabethan English,' she says, 'but read for the story...try to realise Theseus, that most noble Athenian hero and perfect gentleman, and next Shakespeare day in class, I think, some breath of the summer wood and the scent of the geranium will blow on your Clarendon Press edition' (p. 12). I suspect that several of this year's contributors will baulk at the idea of reading only for the story (let alone this version of Theseus); Kathleen McLuskie's implicit criticism of the reworking of Shakespeare from this kind of standpoint in her volume on *Macbeth* is only one case in point. Similarly, Russ McDonald in his brilliant essay on Shakespeare's linguistic and semantic 'late style' in Catherine Alexander's *Cambridge Companion to Shakespeare's Last Plays* might well have taken a sharp intake of breath at the suggestion that we should not puzzle over the 'words and sentences of Elizabethan English'. Shakespeare in school is of course a very different beast from Shakespeare in the academy, although some of the best of this year's work has traversed an all-important contact zone between those two phenomena. Nevertheless, I cannot resist wishing you (and me) just a little of that 'breath of the summer wood' and the 'scent of geranium' in Shakespearian encounters to come.

BIBLIOGRAPHY

Alexander, Catherine (ed.), *The Cambridge Companion to Shakespeare's Last Plays* (Cambridge, 2009)

Beauregard, David N., *Catholic Theology in Shakespeare's Plays* (Newark, NJ, 2008)

Benson, Sean, *Shakespearean Resurrection: The Art of Almost Raising the Dead* (Pittsburgh, 2009)

Forman, Valerie, *Tragicomic Redemptions: Global Economics and the Early Modern Stage* (Philadelphia, 2009)

Graham, Kenneth J. E., and Philip D. Collington (eds.), *Shakespeare and Religious Change* (Basingstoke and New York, 2009)

Harris, Jonathan Gil, *Untimely Matter in the Time of Shakespeare* (Philadelphia, 2009)

Hateley, Erika, *Shakespeare in Children's Literature* (London, 2009)

Jensen, Phebe, *Religion and Revelry in Shakespeare's Festive World* (Cambridge, 2008)

King, Ros, *The Shakespeare Handbooks: The Winter's Tale* (Basingstoke and New York, 2009)

Lamb, Mary Ellen and Valerie Wayne (eds.), *Staging Early Modern Romance: Prose Fiction, Dramatic Romance and Shakespeare* (London, 2009)

Lopez, Jeremy, *The Shakespeare Handbooks: Richard II* (Basingstoke and New York, 2009)

McLuskie, Kathleen E., *William Shakespeare: Macbeth* [Writers and their Work] (Plymouth, 2009)

Marshall, Gail, *Shakespeare and Victorian Women* (Cambridge, 2009)

Meek, Richard, *Narrating the Visual in Shakespeare* (Ashgate, 2009)

Mooneram, Roshni, *From Creole to Standard: Shakespeare, Language, and Literature in a Post-colonial Context* (Amsterdam, 2009)

Perry, Curtis and John Watkins (eds.), *Shakespeare & the Middle Ages* (Oxford, 2009)

Richmond, Velma Bourgois, *Shakespeare as Children's Literature: Edwardian Retellings in Words and Pictures* (Jefferson, NC and London, 2008)

Ryan, Kiernan, *Shakespeare's Comedies* (Basingstoke and New York, 2009)

Sillars, Stuart, *The Illustrated Shakespeare, 1709–1875* (Cambridge, 2009)

Sokol, B. J., *Shakespeare and Tolerance* (Cambridge, 2008)

White, Martin, *The Shakespeare Handbooks: A Midsummer Night's Dream* (Basingstoke and New York, 2009)

2. SHAKESPEARE IN PERFORMANCE
reviewed by PASCALE AEBISCHER

Not too many weeks ago, I received a large parcel containing Richard Dutton's *The Oxford Handbook of Early Modern Drama* in pristine condition. It is a measure of the sheer size of the book and the demands it puts on its reader that my copy is now sadly dirtied and dog-eared: the book is a treasure I have learned to cherish as I have carried it from graduate student to colleague and back, finding information in it that was relevant to the research of so many. I have also been busy updating my reading lists for students, often supplementing and sometimes replacing references to Cox and Kastan's *New History of Early English Drama* (New York, 1997) with new references to the *Oxford Handbook*, which explicitly (and rightly) sets itself up as the successor to the Cox–Kastan *History*. The *Oxford Handbook* will have an impact on the field not only because this is a strikingly handsome and well-illustrated volume, but because it manages to square two circles. Firstly, it brings, thanks to a stunning opening chapter by William Ingram, an awareness of theoretical concerns to a field that has, in recent years, been fiercely empirical and openly resistant to theory, and it does so without in any way deflecting its contributors from their passionate attention to historical evidence and detail. Secondly, it succeeds in making narrative sense and can, despite its bulk, be read cover-to-cover. Each chapter tackles individual pieces of the larger puzzle in ways that highlight the moment where conflicting accounts can be constructed from the same evidence or where there simply is not sufficient evidence to compose a narrative. The result is a remarkably readable collection which brings together established scholars, some of the younger voices that have made theatre history such an exciting field of late and new scholars whose work is receiving its first major airing in this volume.

The brief Dutton gave his authors is simple: they were to 'concentrate on issues of particular interest or concern, to engage with the research frontiers' rather than provide a survey of the available literature. What many of the best essays here do is to follow that brief *and* to prop up work on the research frontiers with a survey of literature, rendering the contributions valuable both for the novice researcher and for experts. The first part of the volume, which is concerned with theatre companies, is split up roughly into ten-year segments and company types. We get started with a chapter on 'Adult Playing Companies to 1583' by W. R. Streitberger, who explores various explanations for the establishment of the theatres in the London of the 1570s and challenges E. K.

Chambers's reconstruction of the workings of the Lord Chamberlain's 'department'. Streitberger explains how the changes to the Revels Office in 1572 and the drive to reduce costs contributed to creating a lively commercial environment that benefited celebrity entertainers and their companies, allowing them to generate income that then benefited the court, for whom fashionable entertainments were now cheap. This makes for fascinating reading which resonates uncomfortably with current developments in the funding of Universities and the Arts in the UK. The multiple conflicting narratives and unresolved questions of Streitberger's account are typical of the essays in this section: Sally-Beth MacLean, who finishes her chapter with 'We simply don't know, but we can begin to ask such questions', is only the most striking example of an unwillingness to commit to answers, coupled with an urge to find out more, which is characteristic of the collection. One thing we ought to concentrate on, according to Roslyn Knutson, is the way in which the repertories of different companies may have interconnected. Knutson provides some brilliant examples about the eight Plantagenet plays performed between 1591 and 1598, arguing that companies may have used links to the repertoires of their rivals as a marketing strategy. For the authors working on theatre companies, the companies and their repertories are much more important as organizing principles than authors. Boys' companies, in particular, are credited not only with producing coherent bodies of work with a recognizable set of homoerotic jokes (Mary Bly) but also with developing artistic strategies tailored to indoor venues that were to leave an enduring legacy (Michael Shapiro). There is perhaps no clearer statement to signal the sidelining of Shakespeare in this section – and indeed, most of the volume – than James J. Marino's assertion that 'Shakespeare had begun to be replaced even before the Globe had, and was already collaborating with the man who would replace him as his company's inhouse playwright. If the Age of Shakespeare had ended, no one much noticed. If the Era of Fletcher had begun, it was far too politic to call undue attention to itself.' This is, on the whole, a book that is resolutely *not* about Shakespeare.

After such a vigorously revisionist opening, the volume sags a little in its second section, which is dedicated to the London Playhouses. Essays on the Theatre and the Globe cover familiar territory and the latter is oddly Shakespeare-centric, recalling William Ingram's ire, at the beginning of the collection, against theatre historians who have 'an unconscious Bardic teleology in their premises'. I much enjoyed David Kathman's work on Inn-Yard Playhouses, which left me wanting to know more not just about these inns but also about Mrs Johanna Harrison, who ran the Bull between 1584 and 1589. Ralph Alan Cohen, on the other hand, writing from the vantage point of his involvement in the reconstruction of the Blackfriars Playhouse in Staunton, Virginia, vividly evokes what it might have meant to have actors playing around stage sitters, to have the stage framed by coloured silks, satins and feathers, and to have the audience's attention diffused to such an extent by act breaks, music and other distractions as to create an opportunity for critical detachment and self-awareness. I was also captivated by Mark Bayer's description of the Red Bull Playhouse and its audience, which deserves the respect and attention he gives it as he challenges its reputation for low-brow entertainment, pointing out that, towards the end of James's reign, Christopher Beeston often transferred plays and personnel between the private Cockpit/Phoenix and the Red Bull.

The inclusiveness of the *Oxford Handbook* signalled by Bayer's work is carried on in the section on 'Other Playing Spaces', where we find chapters on Universities and Inns of Court (Alan H. Nelson), Touring (Peter Greenfield) and Court Theatre (John H. Astington) that supplement the equivalent chapters in the Cox/Kastan *New History*. But we also find more unusual material: Anne Lancashire introduces us to 'London Street Theater' (a portmanteau term which covers everything from Lord Mayor's Shows and Royal Entries to Maying entertainments) and Suzanne Westfall writes eloquently about Household Entertainments. Her essay, which is based on the material

that has become available through REED, demands that we appreciate the paradoxical nature of the aristocratic household and pay greater attention to amateur theatricals and the salons of aristocratic women such as Mary Sidney Herbert, Elizabeth Cary and Margaret Cavendish. Alan H. Nelson, too, calls attention to amateur theatricals: for him, the Orgel/Goldberg school of masque criticism, with its insistence on the solemnity of masquing and its symbolism of royal power 'rather miss[es] . . . the general sense of fun and pleasure which both rehearsals and performance must have generated'.

Fun and how to control it is a keynote in the next section, which is concerned with Social Practices. This is where we find out about patrons of the theatre who have hitherto escaped scrutiny because of their lack of national importance, but whose connections to the theatre Alan Somerset has uncovered thanks, once more, to REED, which is also central to Kathleen E. McLuskie's examination of the Lady Elizabeth's Men, whose touring of plays created commercial relations between London and the provinces. I was particularly intrigued by McLuskie's account of Thomas Puckering, who in 1620 bought a play performance as if it were any other luxury good. Richard Dutton himself contributes an essay to this section in which he highlights the value of court performances to the companies invited to present their work there: we must not underestimate the importance of court patronage to the principal London companies long before King James explicitly extended royal patronage to them. While companies sought the social and political rewards associated with court patronage, financial rewards were important to the theatre entrepreneurs investigated by S. P. Cerasano, who insists on the radical difference between investors promoting entertainment as a trade and the patronage described by Somerset and Dutton. Entertainment was also a trade for the women involved in the theatre and whose off-stage work as seamstresses, gatherers or inheritors of playhouse shares is part of the larger economic phenomenon of the gendered division of labour critiqued by Natasha Korda. The volume concludes with a section on theatrical practices, where we find Tiffany Stern and Alan C. Dessen revisiting their work on actors' parts and stage directions and Lucy Munro considering various musical styles and evolving fashions in indoor and public theatres. Some of the essays in this last section seem somewhat out of place in this book because of their difference in method and tone. The essay I'd like to single out here is by R. B. Graves, whose meticulous work on lighting in the theatres, in which he remarks on the 'warm, but by no means brilliant, artificial light' of an indoor performance in winter, to some extent contradicts the statements about the brilliance of indoor performances in earlier chapters. This will to contest the work of others and to identify the detail that will make a difference to how we understand early modern theatre is the dominant characteristic of *The Oxford Handbook*.

The sense of open-endedness and debate in the *Oxford Handbook* is shared by the other two publications in the history of the early modern theatre this year, which both approach the subject from the vantage point of modern reconstructions of early modern theatres and performance practices. Martin White's *The Chamber of Demonstrations: Reconstructing the Jacobean Indoor Playhouse* is a 'book' on DVD, which is accompanied by a website (www.chamberofdemonstrations.com). Using the Wickham Theatre at the University of Bristol as a generic Jacobean private theatre, White's experiments with candlelit performances are the practical counterpart to Graves's theoretical calculations and tend to confirm Graves's statement about the lack of brilliance of the artificial light prevalent in indoor theatres. What makes White's DVD a quite wonderful teaching tool which will feature in my lectures and seminars from now on are the scenes from Jacobean and Caroline plays (none by Shakespeare, it is worth noting) which are performed to a professional standard by candlelit actors in period costumes and make-up. The performances are filmed from four different angles, corresponding to four distinct audience positions, allowing the viewer to switch from one angle to another in order to see how the same scene can appear quite different for a spectator facing the stage or looking down on it from a gallery at its side. The scenes are well selected in that they are all intrinsically interesting and ask for different types of lighting: White for instance includes the 'dead hand' scene from *The Duchess of Malfi* to show the contrast between the 'darkness' of the first half and the 'light' of the second half (which translates into more and then less murky) and the murder of Bergetto in *'Tis Pity* to illustrate how lanterns may have been used. Other scenes are chosen for their use of the upper level, of a concealed space or of stage location and are both informative and entertaining. My favourite is the scene of Alonzo's murder in *The Changeling*, which is both sombre and hilarious, with some splendid acting and – dare I say it, in the context of a supposed reconstruction of early modern performance practices – inspired directing, presumably by White himself.

The clash between modern and early modern theatre practices is perceptible not only in the fact that the scenes were clearly well-rehearsed and directed, but also in the documentary-style sections on make-up and costuming which can be found in the 'Backstage' section of the DVD. Here, White draws on the expertise of Farah Karim-Cooper and Jenny Tiramani, who are both drafted in from Shakespeare's Globe to bring their practical knowledge about make-up and costuming to bear on the project. Seeing an actress being made up and dressed is surprisingly effective in conveying the sheer cumbersomeness of early modern dress and the peculiar red-and-white beauty described in Petrarchan poetry. The rub, obviously, is that we are seeing a woman, not a boy, being readied in this way – an awareness which is registered when Tiramani touches on how similar the process would have been for a man. In a project that is so deeply concerned with the reconstruction of early modern performance practices, choosing to illustrate period make-up and costume on a woman seems a peculiar choice, especially since a male actor was available to play the Duchess of Malfi in one scene. The DVD thus courts contradiction, as is also obvious from its section on 'History and Reconstruction', which confronts head-on what is perhaps the greatest problem faced by White's project: the very real possibility that the Wickham Theatre may not be a reconstruction of a Jacobean theatre after all, since the Worcester College drawings it is based on may date from the 1660s rather than the 1630s. This theory is explored at length in an excellent filmed interview with Gordon Higgott at the Worcester College library in Oxford, which conveys a wonderful 'hands-on' feel of research and thinking as a process rather than a result. The interview is complemented by another interview with Andrew Gurr, who describes the playhouse design as a Jacobean concept (if not a Jacobean execution), an 'illustrated essay' by Martin White, which explains specific details of staging and provides a good overview of the material covered by the DVD, and a helpful section on the Sheldonian theatre in Oxford, which White compares with the Worcester College designs. Meanwhile the website contains several helpful essays by Higgott and White and provides links to updated research and bibliographies. Not all of these worked when I played around with the site and DVD, but that's a minor caveat about what is in many ways a splendid and innovative project.

Several of the key players in White's *Chamber of Demonstrations* appear again in *Shakespeare's Globe: A Theatrical Experiment*, which is the Shakespearian paper counterpart to White's Jacobean DVD. Christie Carson and Farah Karim-Cooper's aim, in their collection of essays by theatre historians, educators and practitioners involved in the reconstruction of 'Shakespeare's Globe', is to bridge the gap between these various communities and create a dialogue between the scholars who designed the building, the artists who perform and the educators who teach in it. If the dialogue does not always happen or if it sometimes looks like people shouting at each other from either side of the Niagara Falls, that is not for want of the editors trying to guide our responses through multiple forewords, introductions and conclusions that try to negotiate between the scepticism of the scholars and the artists' sometimes metaphysical claims about the building and its 'sacred geometry'. There is,

at several points, an unproductive tension between the statements by the academics whose job it is to argue in writing about details of historical evidence and the artists who earn their living entertaining present-day audiences in a reconstructed theatre which, as has so often been observed, has something of the quality of a living museum about it. It is in the nature of actors, directors and musicians to want to feel a sense of communion with the audience and to crave a positive response from them, and it is unreasonable to expect them to want to try out things which they intuitively know won't 'work' for their audiences. What is so impressive about the practitioners who have shaped the first ten years of the theatre – Mark Rylance, Claire van Kampen, Jenny Tiramani and Tim Carroll – is that they have attempted to do this in their own way and that, against the odds, they have succeeded in experimenting with 'Original Practices' (or 'OP') in ways that have been powerfully suggestive of what an early modern performance might have looked like in some specific respects. Their important contribution to knowledge, it seems to me, would perhaps have been better served by a DVD of the type created by Martin White, in which they might have been able to communicate in a medium suited to their work. Instead, a discourse of authenticity, a dose of 'Globolatry' and peculiar assumptions about scholars sitting in the upper galleries, statements about how the reconstruction of a Jacobean world could 'pull the audience towards it' or comments about the 'spirit' of the building to distract from their achievements. Juxtaposing Jenny Tiramani's contribution to White's *Chamber of Demonstrations* and her chapter in *Shakespeare's Globe* drives home this point: the visuals that support her explanations on the DVD and that make her work so appealing are absent from the book, rendering her comments less engrossing because the materiality of her work is lost in translation.

The contributions by the scholars did not help bridge the gap for me, either. Set side by side with the enthusiasm and lively anecdotal approach of the practitioners, they often appeared rather dry and curmudgeonly (a sin I myself might be accused of here). Alan Dessen mercilessly punctures the 'near mystical expectations linked to the construction of the new Globe in the 1990s (a version of 'if you build it he will come')'. David Lindley persuasively argues that no present-day audience can fully grasp the exact implications and shock value for an early modern audience of seeing Ophelia singing and playing on a lute with her hair down: this can only be achieved in the study, not the theatre in which Claire van Kampen and her team so carefully and painstakingly tried to educate their audience into understanding early music. Even Farah Karim-Cooper appears bizarrely ungenerous at one point, when she notes that 'What has remained inevitably frustrating', in her practical work on make-up at Shakespeare's Globe, 'is that for obvious reasons there were key elements missing from the experiments: the white lead ingredient and boy actors'. Again, I might not have been arrested by this comment, had it not been juxtaposed with the dedication of practitioners who often went to the very limits of reasonable discomfort in order to explore early modern staging practices. Wishing that it were possible to put white lead on anyone's face, whether a boy or an adult, is really a bridge too far in this context.

In the book's final section consisting of a handful of essays on Globe Education and Research, the tensions ease off a little as the collection introduces us to a part of the operations at Shakespeare's Globe which deserves greater recognition: the work of Globe Education and, within that department, the 'Read Not Dead' project dedicated to staging readings of all the extant non-Shakespeare plays. This project, as Patrick Spottiswoode and James Wallace explain, has already had a tangible impact not only on performance practice (all the 'Jacobethan' plays performed at the RSC were first performed as part of 'Read Not Dead'), but also on the production of Globe Quartos. There is something raw and fresh – and, dare I say, 'authentic' – about the ways in which the 'Read Not Dead' performances are cobbled together in record time from the individual study of actors. My only wish is that the 'Read Not Dead' team would also replicate the touring practices of early modern companies to save my having to travel to London to see one of their performances. Finally, with these essays and Gordon McMullan's Afterword, the volume struck the right note, as McMullan combined measured scepticism with practical suggestions about how scholars might use Shakespeare's Globe to help them work out technical aspects of early modern staging practices. Here, the 'productive tension' billed by the editors did end up being 'productive', but it felt like too little, too late.

One thing that does come across very clearly in *Shakespeare's Globe* is the practitioners' shared feeling that the building of the Globe has had a sensible impact on their practice. This comes out particularly clearly in Mark Rylance's observation about how the space of Shakespeare's Globe effectively fractured any attempt at naturalistic acting and the creating of a unified character by forcing him to 'become a storyteller as well as a part inside the story'. *Shakespeare and Character: Theory, History, Performance, and Theatrical Persons*, a collection of essays edited by Paul Yachnin and Jessica Slights, continues this reflection. It, too, questions the possibility of thinking in terms of 'character' and 'personhood' and ends up affirming the importance of thinking in terms of character. Reacting against the now widespread distrust of character criticism by scholars and performers alike, the editors call for a 'new character criticism' which recognizes 'character' as a valid analytic category. Not all of the methodologies the volume's contributors use to reassert the importance of character criticism struck me as helpful or accessible: for example, both I and a graduate student to whom I lent the book gave up on the overly complex conceptualization, by a film scholar, of character as an effect of the stroboluminescent display of minute transparent gelatine pixels. I suspect that this essay is one of several that were included not so much because of their authors' expertise in Shakespearian character studies but rather to showcase the work of the Canadian Shakespeare and Performance Research Team. Other essays, however, are strong and do not deserve to get lost in the eclectic mix of this collection.

One strand common to several essays is a concern with the 'humanity' of characters and the ways in which that humanity exceeds the words on the page. Michael Bristol, in an essay that concentrates on Shylock's question 'Hath not a Jew eyes?', reminds us of the stress Shakespeare lays on the vulnerability of human beings and insists that we do not diminish the 'fatness' of characters for the sake of historical enquiry. For Bristol, engaging with the characters as people whose actions and world we understand has an important ethical dimension because 'it corresponds to the imperative of respect for our human vulnerability to loss and grief'. William Dodd is also concerned with preserving the characters' 'fatness': he wants us to take account of each character's 'discourse biography – the unique history of interactions that accrues to its character and is more than the sum of its social determinations'. When Burbage's Othello asserted that he knew his 'cue to fight', he was carrying the theatrical baggage of his recent performance as Hamlet, the character famous for *not* fighting. The character of Burbage's Othello was thus the effect of both the dialogue and the actor's recent performance biography.

Dodd's focus on an actor's previous roles as a contributing factor in the creation of character is a particularly productive way of approaching this topic and is returned to in several of the essays in the section on performance which forms the heart of the collection. It is here that *Shakespeare and Character* succeeds in creating the constructive dialogue between scholars and theatre practitioners which proved to be so elusive in *Shakespeare's Globe*. This is to a large extent due to the fact that the dialogue seems to have taken place in real life rather than merely on the page. Paul Yachnin and Myrna Wyatt Selkirk's essay on *The Winter's Tale* is based on their collaborative teaching of a practical class which resulted in a staging of the play. For them, character arises out of the actors' relationship with their audience, whose 'ethical spectatorship' is made possible by the metatheatricality of Shakespeare's play. Andrew Hartley, too, sees the audience as a crucial participant in the creation of character. His experience as a dramaturg stands him in good stead as he discusses a production of *The Comedy of Errors* in which both twins were played by the same pop-

ular actor. The character in performance, Hartley insists, is vitally dependent on the actor's body and the memories the actor brings to the performance through her/his 'performative habitus'. Spectators who are familiar with the performative habitus of an actor bring to the performance their own nostalgic memories of earlier performances by that actor. The spectators' sense of their own past selves thus informs their reading of the character in performance. A different way of saying a similar thing about the spectator's participation in the creation of character is explored by Sarah Werner's reflection on a series of productions of *King Lear* whose Cordelia entered armed in Act 4. Werner reassesses the ambiguous '*Cor.*' speech headings in the Folio text and the representation of warrior women in a range of early modern plays. Her essay is a welcome reminder of how powerful a signifier costume can be, contributing to the construction of character. Werner also alerts us to the fact that the ways in which a piece of equipment such as armour on a woman is read today may differ significantly from its meanings for an early modern spectator.

If *Shakespeare and Character* often seems to showcase the work of a specific group of scholars, this is yet more obviously the case with *Shakespeare and European Politics*, a collection of twenty essays edited by Dirk Delabastita, Jozef De Vos and Paul Franssen. The essays are based on a conference held in Utrecht in December 2003 and are distributed into four sections that impose some order on the wide spread of topics under consideration. Although the volume remains difficult to navigate, its virtue is that it does bring to our attention the work of continental scholars whose research sheds new light on the reception of Shakespeare in continental Europe and beyond: as Dennis Kennedy notes, 'continental history created a Shakespeare considerably different from that seen in his homeland'.

This is particularly true of Germany, which seems to have a contorted relationship with Shakespeare that is explored in a string of essays that might have been served better by being confined to a separate volume. At the end of the eighteenth century, Joep Leerssen tells us, Shakespeare was hailed for his 'original genius' and appropriated as a national poet before making way for a medievalist revival that saw *Beowulf* valued as the oldest German epic. Re-instituted as a key figure of the bourgeois performance tradition in the nineteenth century, Shakespeare ended up being the only 'enemy dramatist' whose plays could be performed in Germany right to the end of the Second World War (Andreas Höfele). In the mid-twentieth century, leading theatre practitioners in Germany swore an oath to Shakespeare alongside Goethe and Schiller, vowing to resist 'Directorial Licence' or *Regiewillkür* (Wilhelm Hortmann). Meanwhile, on the other side of the Iron Curtain, Shakespeare was 'liberated' by Bertholt Brecht and Heiner Müller's socialist adaptations, becoming a means of opposing East German *Kulturpolitik* (Lawrence Guntner). Bizarrely, as Andreas Höfele points out in my favourite essay in the collection, Shakespeare was also used by the BBC in 1945 to 're-educate' Germans into becoming peaceful and prosperous members of the European order by projecting Britishness onto them. In forty-five-minute radio broadcasts, the BBC offered its German listeners 'a little touch of Shakespeare for the night', paying respect to the German Shakespeare tradition while appealing to the audience to adopt the 'non-purist integrative liberalism of the English' and of Shakespeare. Today, 'hybrid' Shakespeares that are far removed from postwar re-educational agendas dominate German stages: this is the birth of a new aesthetic paradigm which Wilhelm Hortmann finds 'difficult to critique', unsure as he is of whether hybridization, in this case, is ennobling or degrading Shakespeare.

Germany, however, is not the volume's official focus. As becomes clear from the introduction that belabours the relevance of the book to current affairs, the actual concern of the editors is to showcase the relevance of Shakespeare to contemporary European politics and the post-9/11 world (dis)order. Terence Hawkes sticks most closely to this brief with one of his signature turns in a chapter which juxtaposes the opening of the Folger Shakespeare Library in Washington with the inauguration of the Royal Shakespeare Theatre in Stratford-upon-Avon, teasing out the implications of these inaugural events of 23 April 1932 (or 23/4, as he prefers to call it), for the Prince of Wales, for the creation of the state of Israel and for our own post-9/11 world. Hawkes is aware that his way of using 23/4 and 9/11 as lenses through which to reread Shakespeare's *Henry IV* and its concern with the concept of 'home' may appear scandalous to some, but he makes an excellent case for the 'presentist' agenda and sets the stage for a number of essays which tackle the political implications of performing Shakespeare at key historical junctures for specific European audiences. Of these, I particularly enjoyed Isabelle Schwartz-Gastine's discussion of the 1933 staging of *Coriolanus* at the Comédie Française, which outlines the correspondences between the staging of the play and the contemporary political scene that led to audiences being so vocal that performances had to be interrupted. It turns out that the audience's ire was not directed at Coriolanus but rather at the tribunes: the audience appears to have consisted mainly of fascist sympathizers who opposed Édouard Daladier's left-wing government. The events of 1933 explain why, in France, *Coriolanus* was for decades associated with right-wing politics until Gabriel Garran 'rescued' the play in his 1976 professional staging in which the plebeians were portrayed as responsible citizens opposed to the patricians' war-mongering, giving the production a Marxist twist. Fascist appropriations of Shakespeare are also at the heart of Zoltán Márkus's analysis of stagings of *The Merchant of Venice* in London, Berlin and Budapest during the Second World War. While the London production catered to anti-Semitic sentiments that were only different in degree, not kind, from the crass Nazi propaganda in the Berlin staging, in Budapest Shylock was portrayed in such a positive light that the production was banned after only a handful of performances. State censorship and control over the arts were less rigorous in wartime Hungary than in Germany, allowing for dissident voices to emerge, if only briefly. In the light of this, it does not come as a surprise that, as Veronika Schandl shows, Hungarian audiences in 1985 applauded István Paál's production of

Measure for Measure, which highlighted the parallels between Vincentio's prison-like Vienna and Hungary near the end of the Cold War.

While some of the productions discussed in *Shakespeare and European Politics* seem very alien from a present-day Anglo-American vantage point, they are no more remote than some of the silent films discussed by Judith Buchanan in *Shakespeare on Silent Film: An Excellent Dumb Discourse*. Covering the forty surviving European and American silent Shakespeare films as well as lost films that are reconstituted through an analysis of scripts, catalogue descriptions and reviews, Buchanan succeeds in combining detail with scope and vivid writing with scholarly thoroughness. What makes the book such a joy to read is Buchanan's determination to accept and judge these films on their own merits without trying to rescue them from their 'roguish marginality'. There is something infectious about her affection for the once-famous actors that flicker across our screens at inadequate projection speeds: her description of these 'figures marooned in time, earnestly (and sometimes skittishly) playing to a world that has moved on without them' is moving and her attempt to make her reader view them as they once were, 'the lords of time, occupying the moment with touching confidence', laudable – especially once we come to realize how precarious the survival of these films is, threatened as they have been with loss, destruction, gradual decomposition or even spontaneous combustion. No wonder, then, that this book is, in some ways, a plea for readers to view the handful of commercially available silent films and seek out surviving archival prints, whose location and availability are noted in a filmography in which the notation 'presumed lost' recurs all too often. To motivate us to seek out these films, the book is generously illustrated with a mix of familiar and unfamiliar material that hints at treasures that still wait to be uncovered.

One thing that is lost to us is the experience of the live lectures that accompanied screenings of silent Shakespeares between 1895 and 1913/14. But Buchanan does a good job of piecing together surviving evidence to give us a sense of what such lectures might have involved. What is particularly important here is the context of the films' original reception: as Buchanan argues, these films were conceived for an audience more familiar with Shakespeare's text than we are today and – thanks, in part, to nineteenth-century spectacular staging practices – accustomed to expecting Shakespearian tableaux that evoked the dialogue of an entire scene. She is careful, however, not to lump all the audiences and films together. Instead, the book is structured roughly chronologically to trace the development of the genre from the late nineteenth-century magic lantern show (an intriguing and apparently under-researched chapter in the history of Shakespeare in performance) to the 'transitional period' of 1907–13, when American and European film industries attempted to appeal to the cultural elite. Her chapter on the Vitagraph Company of America and its aggressive marketing strategies, which saw the logo of the company reappear in all sorts of unlikely contexts, is a highlight of the book. 'Authorship' of Shakespeare on film is here clearly defined as corporate rather than individual, and brand recognition seems to have triumphed over the naturalism intrinsic to the medium in an effort to convey to the audience Vitagraph's 'assurance of quality, cultural prestige and wholesome values'. With a fine eye for the incongruous detail, Buchanan spots sleeping senators and parodic harpists who undermine the high seriousness of scenes in *Julius Caesar* and *King Lear*, apparently in an attempt at controlling the unintentional comedy courted by moments of pathos in silent film. While this section contains some of Buchanan's freshest material, I suspect that many readers will – to their own detriment – skip ahead to her chapters on silent films of *Hamlet* and on the Weimar film stars Asta Nielsen and Emil Jannings. In the former, Buchanan compares Forbes-Robertson's and Ruggeri's *Hamlet*s, contrasting the Englishman's gentlemanly respect for Shakespeare's inaudible words with the Italian's reliance on pantomimic codes. In the latter, she reconsiders what is perhaps the most widely viewed silent film, Asta Nielsen's performance in *Hamlet*, contrasting the actress's natural preference for the physical expression of emotion that made her a star of silent film with

Forbes-Robertson's unease with that medium. Framed, as it is, by Buchanan's knowledgeable discussion of other silent *Hamlet*s and cross-gender performances, this discussion of Nielsen's performance (and the analysis of Emil Jannings's *Othello* with which it is coupled) offers more than yet another reading of a famous performance and gives us a sense of why Nielsen's strikingly modern androgyny and intellectual energy appealed to American audiences in the 1920s. This is a book, then, which not only unearths films that have never been discussed before (and makes me want to watch them), but which also sheds new light on much-discussed material. This is a book we will be using for many years.

One of the issues Buchanan's study raises is that of adaptation and the limits of what we may consider to be 'Shakespeare'. Buchanan's answer is to assert that 'the drama's identity is not . . . exclusively dependent on the specificity of its words'; silent Shakespeare may be silent, but it is still Shakespeare. Buchanan leaves the matter at that, but M. J. Kidnie is not willing to let the problem rest quite so easily. *Shakespeare and the Problem of Adaptation* is dedicated to questioning the felt need, in Shakespearian performance studies, to distinguish between 'text' and 'performance' or 'the work' and its 'adaptation'. Kidnie draws not only on recent debates in textual studies and adaptation theory but also on the near-defunct terminology of 1980s pragmatic criticism and reader-response theory to describe the 'work' not as a stable object but rather as an ongoing dynamic process. The Shakespearian work, she argues, is produced through text(s), performance(s) and various users – whether readers or audiences – who, at various historical moments, apply their notions of the Shakespearian 'work' to its time-bound incarnations. For her, the text does not take precedence over the performance but both are 'in their different ways, instances of the work'. Like several of the contributors to *Shakespeare and Character*, who had seen the creation of character as the result of a collaborative engagement by actors and audiences alike, Kidnie thus sees the Shakespearian work not as the *origin* of editions and stagings but as their *consequence*.

Understanding the Shakespearian work as a process, Kidnie argues, allows us to focus productively on moments at which the notion of the Shakespearian 'work' comes under pressure. *Shakespeare and the Problem of Adaptation* leads the way in examining some recent 'border skirmishes about Shakespeare's works' that reveal cultural politics in operation, as competing groups assert their right to define what 'authentic' Shakespeare may be. I would love to see Kidnie perform an analysis of *Shakespeare's Globe* and the competing claim to authenticity in that volume; *Shakespeare and the Problem of Adaptation* speaks to so many of the unresolved paradoxes of the 'Globe experiment' and its involvement of theatre practitioners, academics and teachers who vie for the right to define Shakespearian authenticity in the reconstructed theatre. What Kidnie offers us instead is just as rich and relevant, though the practical application of her theoretical framework does reveal some of its limitations: if everything that users don't recognize as 'the work' is categorized as 'adaptation', we can end up with absurdly reductive spoofs such as the Reduced Shakespeare Company's six-line *Hamlet* being categorized as 'the work' while serious engagements with the Shakespearian text, such as we find in Djanet Sears's *Harlem Duet*, are relegated to the category of 'adaptation'. But it is precisely this desire to police the boundaries of the work which this – in my view – miscategorization provokes which is of interest to Kidnie. She has thought-provoking things to say, for example, about how casting Dame Judi Dench in Gregory Doran's *All's Well That Ends Well* in 2003 coded that production as authentically the joint 'work' of Shakespeare and the RSC at a troubled moment in its history: what made that casting such a master-stroke is the way in which it conflated the authority of the character of the Countess with Dench's authority and her links to the legacy of Peter Hall. Character, as the contributors to *Shakespeare and Character* would agree, here once more emerges as much, much more than the words on the page, as it draws on the actor's well-known views on the company's policies to give authority and 'the illusion of authenticity' to a new version of both the play and the company performing it.

One area in which Shakespearian authority and the notion of what constitutes his 'work' is insistently contested is that of television, which Kidnie describes as a 'neglected medium'. In the BBC's 2005 *Shakespeare Re-Told* series, she suggests, the BBC sought to create 'something like a convincing "Shakespeare effect" that is available to be read by viewers as consistent with the work'. Marketing the series as both 'new' and 'classic' drama, the BBC sought to situate the series within the audience's horizon of expectations in such a way as to attract as large a spectrum of viewers as possible, though for some viewers it seems that the loss of Shakespeare's language proved to be an insurmountable barrier to 'work recognition'. These viewers, presumably, would not have recognized Buchanan's *Shakespeare on Silent Film* as a book about Shakespeare, either, and they will probably also not go out in throngs to buy *Shakespeare on Film, Television and Radio: The Researcher's Guide*, which works hard to interest us not only in long-forgotten television Shakespeares, but also in the yet more under-researched field of audio Shakespeares. Brought to us by Luke McKernan, Olwen Terris and Eve-Marie Oesterlen, the team responsible for the AHRC-funded online database of Shakespeare performances on film, television and radio (http://bufvc.ac.uk/shakespeare/), this guide is designed to be easily navigable and to complement the online resource with a 'collection of essays, archive documents, recommendations of notable productions and some essential reference tools'. Amongst the essays, I found Olwen Terris's account of Shakespeare and the television commercial and the reflections on radio drama by Eve-Marie Oesterlen and Susanne Greenhalgh particularly useful. A little gem, for me, was Oesterlen's observations on the advantages of audio Shakespeare when it came to broadcasting *Othello* for a 1930s audience ('colour-blind' casting indeed!) and Greenhalgh's introduction to thriller and western Shakespeare spin-offs. Audio Shakespeares, as Christie Carson shows, are ever more at home on the internet, where we

also find the National Theatre's *Stagework* site (www.stagework.org/stageworks/index.html) and the RSC's *Exploring Shakespeare* site (www.rsc.org.uk/exploringshakespeare), to which Mike Flood Page draws our attention. While *Stagework* provides access to 'a vast and growing archive of behind-the-scenes video of more than a dozen new productions' at the National, *Exploring Shakespeare* is focused on the RSC's production process of three plays. Primarily aimed at the school market, these sites are having an impact on a new generation of students whose approach to Shakespeare is more performance-oriented than has hitherto been the case.

The articles provide an informative backdrop for the core of the book, which consists of a series of historical documents commenting on the possibility of performing Shakespeare in modern media, personal recommendations of specific performances by well-known scholars, a reference guide and two quirky little sections of trivia about Shakespeare in the media. Quite a few of these entries have amusement value: it's fun to know that Douglas Lanier enjoys *Theatre of Blood*, the camp horror film about a frustrated thespian, or that Godard's bizarre *King Lear* has found a fan in Peter Holland. But I'm not sure that this is where I'll go when I want to figure out which films to watch, nor does finding out that Pinter read the part of Lord Abergavenny for the 1951 broadcast of *Henry VIII* add much to my store of useful knowledge. On the other hand, the list of further reading (which is not exhaustive but a good starting-point), the guidelines about how to cite films and broadcasts of Shakespeare, and especially the notes on and lists of archives, libraries and distributors are excellent research aids that will make accessing rare materials much more straightforward in future. This guide is above all a call for more research on neglected media and I expect it to be widely used by students and researchers alike.

Looking back over the year's publications on Shakespeare in performance, what strikes me is how little they are actually concerned with Shakespeare or, at the very least, Shakespeare's plays in their traditional manifestations. Theatre historians, with a very few exceptions, are busy researching the King's Men's rivals, provincial performances, civic drama, women's contributions to the theatre, Jacobean indoor playhouses and original staging practices, and are doing this not to illuminate Shakespeare (the 'unconscious Bardic teleology' Ingram is rightly wary of), but out of a genuine interest in finding out more about the early modern theatre in itself. Shakespeare may well have been a driving force behind the 'Shakespeare's Globe' project but, as Patrick Spottiswoode admits, that name itself is contested by some of the people involved, who find the presence of Shakespeare's name 'misleading' and are worried about how this 'might encourage the project to become too Shakespeare-centric'. The repertoire of the theatre under Dominic Dromgoole, we are told, will focus on Shakespeare but the work of Globe Education and the researchers associated with the theatre will continue to explore the work of his contemporaries. Even work on Shakespeare in present-day performance is often more concerned with the margins than with mainstream British Shakespeare. North American performers and venues are key to the arguments in *Shakespeare and Character* and, in *Shakespeare and European Politics*, the Shakespeare we encounter is alien and often at not one, but two removes (e.g. French adaptations that are adapted into Spanish). The films Buchanan is so passionate about do not employ Shakespeare's language at all, and when Kidnie talks about *All's Well* at the RSC, she is less interested in the play than in the politics of casting Dame Judi Dench. Kidnie's interest in 'border skirmishes' around definitions of

Shakespeare's work is, in fact, representative of the larger trend: the study of Shakespeare in performance, in 2008–9, has been focused on the borders of 'Shakespeare' and has not only stretched those borders but quite frequently stepped over them without looking back in regret. The days of Bardic teleologies may genuinely be over.

Thanks to Jennifer Barnes and to the *Review of English Studies* for permission to rework some of the material that went into my joint review, with Jennifer Barnes, of *Shakespeare and the Problem of Adaptation*, published in *Review of English Studies*, 60 (2009), 647–8. Thanks also to Chris Richards for sharing his views about *Shakespeare and Character*.

BOOKS REVIEWED

Buchanan, Judith, *Shakespeare on Silent Film: An Excellent Dumb Discourse* (Cambridge, 2009)

Carson, Christie and Farah Karim-Cooper, eds., *Shakespeare's Globe: A Theatrical Experiment* (Cambridge, 2008)

Delabastita, Dirk, Jozef De Vos and Paul Franssen, eds., with a Foreword by Ton Hoenselaars, *Shakespeare and European Politics* (Newark, DE, 2008)

Dutton, Richard, ed., *The Oxford Handbook of Early Modern Theatre* (Oxford, 2009)

Kidnie, Margaret Jane, *Shakespeare and the Problem of Adaptation* (London, 2009)

Terris, Olwen, Eve-Marie Oesterlen and Luke McKernan, eds., *Shakespeare on Film, Television and Radio: The Researcher's Guide* (London, 2009)

White, Martin, *The Chamber of Demonstrations: Reconstructing the Jacobean Indoor Playhouse* (Bristol, 2009)

Yachnin, Paul and Jessica Slights, eds., *Shakespeare and Character: Theory, History, Performance, and Theatrical Persons* (Basingstoke, 2009)

3. EDITIONS AND TEXTUAL STUDIES
reviewed by ERIC RASMUSSEN

This has not been a good year for the texts of *Romeo and Juliet*. Apparently, though, the worst is not so long as we can say 'this is the worst'. I was ready to pronounce an edition prepared by two relatively inexperienced editors, in which I found forty-one substantive errors (see below), the worst edition under review. And yet, that

distinction belongs, utterly surprisingly, to the work of a veteran editor: Jay Halio's new parallel-texts edition of *Romeo and Juliet* contains an astounding 108 errors in the text of the play.

With thanks to Arthur Evenchik, as always, and to James Mardock.

The experience of reading Halio's edition is an emotionally variegated one for a critic concerned with textual accuracy. I laughed at the howlers (e.g. instead of calling for a mattock as he enters the tomb, Friar Laurence requests a 'hammock', Q1 5.2.21; his poison resides not in the infant rind of a weak flower but in its 'instant rind', Q1 2.2.23); I cried at the invented words (e.g. at Q1 1.1.222 'with beauty' unaccountably becomes 'with heaven's beauty'; 'rest' at Q2 4.5.6 becomes 'sleep'); and I got angry at variants appearing in lines which are identical in Q1 and Q2 (e.g. whereas both Q1 and Q2 read 'I lent him' at 2.2.81, Halio's text of Q1 reads 'I gave him'; both Q1 and Q2 read 'poison' at 4.3.20 but Halio's Q1 reads 'potion'). All told, I found seventeen lines with invented words,[1] twenty-one lines with omitted words,[2] twenty transpositions,[3] ten instances in which a different preposition is substituted for the one in the copy-text,[4] an omitted line (at Q2 2.4.127 add 'him than he was when you sought him; I'), and thirty-nine further assorted textual errors.[5] A parallel-text edition of Q1 and Q2 has obvious potential utility, but the unfortunate textual editing throughout renders this one all but useless.

Lynette Hunter and Peter Lichtenfels spent many years preparing a new edition of *Romeo and Juliet* for Arden 3 but have since withdrawn from the series. Not wanting their extensive textual work to have been for naught, Hunter and Lichtenfels have included their edited text – with collations and notes, fully formatted in Arden 3 style – on a DVD included with their book, *Negotiating Shakespeare's Language in 'Romeo and Juliet': Reading Strategies from Criticism, Editing and the Theatre*. The authors have an odd habit of referring to themselves in the third person by their individual specialties (Hunter is 'the bibliographer' and Lichtenfels 'the director'), a curious preference for the passive voice ('When the bibliographer of the appended electronic edition watched the final performances of Q2 directed in California in 1998, considerable shock was experienced'), and a weakness for interminable sentences ('Despite all of the training in historical materialism and the theories of subjec-

tivity and discourse, all the previously hard-won theoretical battles and risky writing, the textual notes, like evolutionary theory, can trap one into progressivist concepts of literature and language').

---

[1] Invented words appear: at Q1 2.2.81, for 'I gave him' read 'I lent him'; Q1 2.4.105, for 'Here comes goodly gear' read 'Here's goodly gear'; Q1 3.3.88, for 'Stand up, and' read 'Stand, and'; Q1 3.5.149, for 'for the hate' read 'for hate'; Q1 4.1.81, for 'in a tomb' read 'in tomb'; Q1 4.4.1, for 'Set them all' read 'Set all'; Q1 5.3.18 SD, for *Boy within whistles* read *Boy whistles*; Q1 5.3.275, for 'early to give' read 'early give'; Q1 5.3.301, for 'shall be no statue' read 'shall no statue'; Q2 1.1.71, for 'Part, you fools' read 'Part, fools'; Q2 1.1.139, for 'to the clouds' read 'to clouds'; Q2 3.1.14, for 'soon to be moved' read 'soon moved'; Q2 3.1.122, for 'spirit that hath' read 'spirit hath'; Q2 3.2.138, for 'Hie you to' read 'Hie to'; Q2 4.4.16, for 'fetch in drier' read 'fetch drier'.

[2] Words are omitted: at Q1 1.5.61, for 'I hold no sin' read 'I hold it for no sin'; Q1 2.1.25, for 'there stand' read 'there to stand'; Q1 2.4.31, for 'very good whore' read 'a very good whore'; Q1 2.5.6, for 'Doth from' read 'Doth hurry from'; Q1 3.3.62, for 'when wise' read 'when that wise'; Q1 3.3.155, for 'in readiness' read 'in a readiness'; Q1 3.4.34, for 'so very late' read 'so very, very late'; Q1 5.1.77, for 'put in' read 'put it in'; Q2 1.2.83, for 'the Montagues' read 'the house of Montagues'; Q2 1.3.53, for 'as young' read 'as a young'; Q2 2.2.189, for 'friar's cell' read 'friar's close cell'; Q2 2.4.83, for 'is most' read 'is a most'; Q2 2.4.189, for 'I take it' read 'as I take it'; Q2 2.5.70, for 'hie you' read 'hie you hence'; Q2 3.2.63, for 'should see' read 'should live to see'; Q2 3.2.72, for 'did, alas' read 'did, it did, alas'; Q2 3.3.51, for 'with word' read 'with that word'; Q2 3.5.241, for 'know remedy' read 'know his remedy'; Q2 4.1.78, for 'From the' read 'From off the'; Q2 4.1.116, for 'he and' read 'he and I'; Q2 5.3.160, for 'Come' read 'Come, go'.

[3] Words and phrases are transposed: at Q1 1.3.17, for 'she shall' read 'shall she'; Q1 1.3.20, for 'at night she shall be fourteen' read 'at night shall she be fourteen'; Q1 1.4.12, for 'But being' read 'Being but'; Q1 2.2.57, for 'fill up' read 'upfill'; Q1 2.4.93, for 'is this not better' read 'is not this better'; Q1 3.5.45, for 'so I will number' read 'so will I number'; Q1 3.5.89, for 'I would soon' read 'I soon would'; Q1 3.5.242, for 'If all else fails' read 'If all fail else'; Q1 5.3.41, for 'So thou shalt' read 'So shalt thou'; Q2 1.3.17, for 'she shall' read 'shall she'; Q2 1.3.20, for 'she shall' read 'shall she'; Q2 2.2.162, for 'I would' read 'would I'; Q2 3.3.6, for 'yet I' read 'I yet'; Q2 3.3.16, for 'wide and broad' read 'broad and wide'; Q2 4.1.27, for 'more of' read 'of more'; Q2 4.5.8, for 'must needs' read 'needs must'; Q2 4.5.39, for 'hath he' read 'he hath'; Q2 5.1.38, for 'I late' read 'late I'; Q2 5.3.14, for 'will I' read 'I will'; Q2 5.3.124, for 'my good' read 'good my'.

All of this makes the task of reading their introduction to this edition a chore.

But the editors' prose style, it turns out, is the least of this edition's worries. Although they thank Richard Proudfoot 'for his advice given when this project was part of the Arden 3 Shakespeare series', Hunter and Lichtenfels apparently thought they could go it alone, without the oversight of a rigorous general editor. If so, they were very wrong. Three separate lines of the play are omitted (1.1.125, 'I, measuring his affections by my own'; 2.5.123, 'By playing it to me with so sour a face'; 3.3.150, 'Which heavy sorrow makes them apt unto'), for which the puckish might find abundant compensation in the accidental addition of nine lines: 3.1.76–9, 3.2.57 and 3.3.93–6 are all repeated, set both at the foot of one page and at the top of the next. There are invented words (e.g. at 1.1.29 for 'well known thou' read 'well thou'; 4.1.49 for 'next to be' read 'next be'), omitted words,[6] omitted or added letters that create different words (e.g. 1.1.128, for 'fed' read 'fled'; 1.1.187, for 'top' read 'to'; 1.3.103, for 'lay' read 'lady'), and two dozen further errors.[7]

Fortunately, no such outrages have been visited upon *Richard III* in the new Arden 3. James R. Siemon, aided by a crack team of general editors (Richard Proudfoot, George Walton Williams and David Scott Kastan), has produced a nearly perfect edition of the play. The lone textual slip I found is a stage direction that somehow evaded modernization: '*He sheweth him a paper*' (5.3.302 SD).[8] This supremely engaging edition opens with a retelling of the scene in Jasper Fforde's novel *The Eyre Affair* in which *Richard III* is performed as an interactive cult ritual, à la *Rocky Horror Picture Show*. (To an audience chanting, 'When is the winter of our discontent?' a volunteer in their midst responds, '*Now* is the winter of our discontent'.) While establishing the play's cultural currency, Siemon's allusion to the novel also provides a fitting introduction to an edition that encourages users to weigh in on its assertions: 'As far as I know, [Richard III's] limp begins with Shakespeare. Readers are invited to correct this claim.' Siemon has a knack for making provocative statements that

implicitly challenge readers to search for counter-examples – e.g. 'Richard is the only character to

---

[4] New prepositions are substituted for copy-text prepositions: at Q1 2.4.146, for 'for supper' read 'to supper'; Q1 5.3.299, for 'in pure gold' read 'of pure gold'; Q2 Prologue 3, for 'into' read 'to'; Q2 1.2. 8, for 'to' read 'in'; Q2 1.3.82, for 'by' read 'with'; Q2 1.4.71, for 'of' read 'on'; Q2 1.5.20, for 'by' read 'with'; Q2 3.2.7, for 'into' read 'to'; Q2 3.3.173, for 'to' read 'on'; Q2 3.5.17, for 'me to ta'en' read 'me be ta'en'.

[5] Further errata: Q1 1.1.94, for 'these' read 'those'; Q1 1.2.67, for 'daughter' read 'daughters'; Q1 1.2.98, for 'began' read 'begun'; Q1 1.4.41, for 'them' read 'thee'; Q1 1.5.145, for 'even no' read 'even now'; Q1 2.2.109, for 'inconstant' read 'unconstant'; Q1 2.6.37, for 'joined you both' read 'joined ye both'; Q1 3.1.48, for 'slave would' read 'slave will'; Q1 3.1.88 SD, for '*thrust*' read '*thrusts*' and for '*flees*' read '*flies*'; Q1 3.3.17, for 'Verona's' read 'Verona'; Q1 3.5.110, for 'found the out' read 'found thee out'; Q1 3.5.140, for 'she thanks thee' read 'she thanks ye'; Q1 3.5.177, for 'you are too hot' read 'ye are too hot'; Q1 4.1.92, for 'the Nurse' read 'thy Nurse'; Q1 5.3.83, for 'thou has prized' read 'thou hast prized'; Q1 5.3.121 SH, for 'LAYRENCE' read 'LAURENCE'; Q1 5.3.265, for 'privy to their marriage' read 'privy to the marriage'; Q2 1.1.127, for 'drew' read 'drive'; Q2 1.1.138, for 'morning' read 'morning's'; Q2 1.2.90, for 'untainted' read 'unattainted'; Q2 1.2.90, for 'they' read 'thy'; Q2 1.2.95, for 'those' read 'these'; Q2 1.3.65, for 'disposition' read 'dispositions'; Q2 2.1.5, for 'the' read 'this'; Q2 2.2.74, for 'you' read 'thee'; Q2 2.3.74, for 'my' read 'mine'; Q2 2.3.77, for 'ere' read 'e'er'; Q2 2.6.7, for 'dares' read 'dare'; Q2 3.2.48, for 'make' read 'makes'; Q2 3.3.17, for 'Verona's' read 'Verona'; Q2 3.5.53, for 'time' read 'times'; Q2 4.1.42, for 'thee' read 'ye'; Q2 4.2.27, for 'bonds' read 'bounds'; Q2 4.4.23, for 'lo' read 'so'; Q2 5.1.24, for 'defy' read 'deny'; Q2 5.3.44, for 'intent' read 'intents'; Q2 5.3.215, for 'a father' read 'thy father'.

[6] Words are omitted: at 1.4.30, for 'blush me' read 'blush for me'; 1.5.1, for 'not take' read 'not to take'; 2.4.157, for 'a gross' read 'a very gross'; 3.1.21, for 'is full' read 'is as full'; 3.1.148, for 'blood spilled' read 'blood is spilled'; 3.3.150, for 'find time' read 'find a time'; 4.5.91, for 'madam' read 'and madam'; 5.1.52, for 'sell him' read 'sell it him'; 5.3.98, for 'do thee' read 'do to thee'.

[7] At 1.1.181, for 'though' read 'thou'; 1.2.100, for 'shall' read 'will'; 1.3.30, for 'than' read 'then'; 1.3.38, for 'should' read 'could'; 1.4.51, for 'has' read 'hath'; 1.4.57, for 'spinner's' read 'spinners''; 1.4.77, for 'sometimes' read 'sometime'; 1.4.84, for 'ears' read 'ear'; 1.5.38, for 'older' read 'elder'; 2.1.8, for 'thought' read 'thou'; 2.3.38, for 'thy' read 'his'; 2.3.72, for 'does' read 'doth'; 2.4.179, for 'convey to' read 'convey in'; 3.1.35, for 'heels' read 'heel'; 3.1.118, for 'has' read 'hath'; 3.1.128, for 'ways' read 'way'; 3.4.8, for 'time' read 'times'; 3.5.58, for 'eyes' read 'eye'; 3.5.134, for 'wind' read 'winds';

open a Shakespeare play with a soliloquy'; 'In 1597, it was probably the longest single play ever printed in English'. In fact, however, Siemon is invariably right. Still, while I find plausible his confident remark that *Richard III* 'is easily the most performed of Shakespeare's histories', I would have appreciated some quantitative data, especially in light of Al Pacino's infamous claim (in *Looking for Richard*) that *Richard III* is Shakespeare's most popular play.

Siemon departs from the recent trend of version-based editing and incorporates a substantial number of Q variants into his F-based text. Though 'purists may argue that any emendation from an alternative basic text constitutes "conflation"', Siemon counters that 'instead of textual purity perhaps we need a richer sense of early playtexts in their various manifestations as raw material for acting companies, or even as "literary" works potentially imagined for readers'. At times, his discussion of the texts relies heavily on the possibilities and limitations of imagination: 'There is no reason to think . . . It is easy to imagine . . . but difficult to conceive . . . It is difficult to imagine . . .' (pages 456–7). But Siemon's imagination only rarely lets him down. Noting that the quarto was set by forms, he surmises that the printer's copy must have been 'legible enough to be precisely cast off'. However, the compositors' accuracy may also owe something to the fact that 98 per cent of the play is in verse, making the space requirements easier to estimate than they would be for a text with a greater quantity of prose. Siemon observes that 'the estimation of space works out so well that there is just room to conclude the final page (M3v) with "FINIS" and a small ornament'. This is in contrast to the 'large blank space' following *Richard III* in the Folio, 'a luxury perhaps not to be indulged in the much less expensive quarto edition'. Quite possibly, though, the quarto printers were striving for the luxury of keeping the actual final page, signature M4, completely blank, so that it could be folded over the title-page of an otherwise unprotected book.[9] Finally, Siemon is not always careful to distinguish between the printer of a quarto and its publisher. Hence we find the apparently contradictory claims that 'Q2 (1598) to

Q5 (1612) were printed by Thomas Creede' and that Q3 was 'printed in 1602 by Andrew Wise'. Actually, Creede was the printer, Wise the publisher. But these are the most minor of flaws in an otherwise remarkably fine edition.

Adele Davidson's *Shakespeare in Shorthand: The Textual Mystery of 'King Lear'*, a long-overdue reappraisal of the role that shorthand transcriptions may have played in the transmission of Shakespeare's texts, calls attention to connections between the then-emerging art of 'stenography' and early modern publishers of play quartos. The seven editions of shorthand transcriptions of sermons preached by Thomas Playfere, for instance, were the only texts Andrew Wise published before 1600, apart from Shakespearian play quartos (Q1, Q2 and Q3 *Richard II*, Q1 and Q2 *Richard III*, Q1 and Q2 *1 Henry IV*) and one work by Nashe. Henry Chettle, wearing his other hat as a stationer, also played a role in publishing shorthand sermons. Davidson cites John Jowett's observation that 'the only book naming Chettle on the imprint, a sermon preached by Henry Smith, was, according to the title-page, taken by charactery'. (Shakespeare twice alludes in his plays to 'charactery', which became a generic word for shorthand.)

Davidson notes that the inventor of early modern shorthand, John Willis, either echoes or anticipates Hamlet's famous soliloquy. In *The Art of Stenographie* (1602), Willis defines the word 'axiom' as 'an Enunciation or Sentence pronouncing anything *to be, or not to be*'. The ornamental frame used on the title-page of *The Art of Stenographie* did not appear in any other book until a fragment was used on the title-page of Q1 *Pericles* (1609). These links to Shakespeare are interesting coincidences but of

---

4.3.11, for 'our' read 'your'; 4.5.113, for 'I will' read 'will I'; 5.1.49, for 'his' read 'this'; 5.3.141, for 'the sepulchre' read 'this sepulchre'; 5.3.219, for 'I will' read 'will I'.

8 At 5.5.4 'long-usurped' probably requires a syllabic è. And the truly finicky might point out that a full stop is omitted from the SD at 1.1.41.

9 See H. R. Woudhuysen, 'Early Play Texts; Forms and Formes', in *In Arden: Editing Shakespeare*, ed. Ann Thompson and Gordon McMullan (London, 2003), pp. 48–61.

course they don't prove anything. More compelling is the connection Davidson makes between the publication of *The Art of Stenographie* in 1602 and the wave of 'bad' quarto editions that began in 1602–3 with Q1 *Merry Wives of Windsor* and Q1 *Hamlet*. Davidson points out that Willis's handbook offers techniques for paraphrasing. In one example, he reduces a six-line passage from *The Faerie Queene* – a flowery evocation of Phoebus's awakening – to a five-word description: 'At last the sunne arose.' This has obvious application to the short quartos of Shakespeare's plays, which often appear to paraphrase longer Folio passages.

Davidson itemizes in considerable detail the ways in which peculiar features of Q1 *Lear* conform to contemporaneous published rules for abbreviated writing. The pattern of dropped initial 'h's in the quarto ('owle' for 'howl', 'Obidicut' for 'Hoberdicut'), for instance, has been explained by previous scholars as a result of actors' dropping their 'h's in performance, but Davidson points to Willis's rule for dropping the aspirate when making a shorthand transcription. Although she cites literally hundreds of such examples, Davidson acknowledges that it is, in fact, 'difficult to speculate on the kinds of processes that may have led the printer's copy for Q to contain elements of abbreviated writing'. She is content merely to note that 'the similarities between the textual anomalies of Q *Lear* and the writing practices advocated in *The Art of Stenographie* suggest that the play bears the stigmata of stenographic transmission'. This understated conclusion notwithstanding, Davidson makes a significant contribution by presenting evidence that early modern shorthand writers were not necessarily seeking to profit financially from publishing others' work. Instead, they may simply have been displaying their technical skill in recording words as they were spoken. The outdated paradigm of the pirate-actor as the agent for the short Shakespearian quartos may thus be plausibly supplanted by that of a shorthand writer showing off his technique.

Paul Menzer has had the exceptionally good idea of constructing a book (loosely) around an observation I once made:

The present study is less concerned with authorial agency, however, than with revisions that respond to theatrical exigency. As Eric Rasmussen notes, 'the emphasis on agency has for too long deflected our attention from an equally important issue – the motivating factors behind the revision of scripts.'

Menzer's *The 'Hamlets': Cues, Qs, and Remembered Texts* explores textual variation specifically as it relates to cue lines. He finds, for example, that Corambis's Q1 cues (both given and received) 'accord with those of Polonius in Q2/F at a rate of nearly double that of other roles' and suggests that the agent behind Q1 may have had access to Corambis's manuscript part. Moreover, the fact that the cue lines remain 'remarkably stable' between Q2 and F may indicate that, despite the changes made to the text of the play over time by a variety of agents and for a variety of reasons, a conscious effort was made not to disrupt the cue lines.

The preparation of parts becomes a verb ('to part') in Menzer's discussion ('we do not know precisely whose job it was to part a playwright's complete script'), and he is chiefly interested in the manuscript that would have been used for this activity. Building upon Tiffany Stern's work, Menzer suggests that, since plays often went into rehearsal before they had been officially licensed, parts would have been transcribed from an early, unlicensed manuscript. This hypothesis accords nicely with Henry Herbert's famous instruction, as Master of the Revels, for the players to 'purge their parts' after he had censored the book of the play.

Menzer usefully expands the range of manuscript possibilities beyond the overused and ill-defined categories of 'foul papers' and 'promptbooks'. He argues that the manuscript behind Q2 *Hamlet* had 'a primary, functional, utilitarian purpose', which was to serve 'as copy text for a scribe to prepare the two dozen or so parts'. Moreover, he argues that the primary function of the manuscript behind the F text was 'to provide the prompter with a serial record of *Hamlet*'s speeches and a clear index of the cue lines'. This manuscript evolved over a decade. 'As Shakespeare and the players worked the play up from their parts, they cut, added, revised, and created a new backstage script over the years'. For Menzer, the notion that this 'backstage script' was intended to provide cue lines rather than directions for stage action explains a curious feature of the F text: 'the paucity of stage directions that has puzzled some scholars'. No such paucity, however, has been discerned by scholars such as Harold Jenkins, who found Folio *Hamlet*'s stage directions to be 'fuller and more systematic' than those in Q2.

There are only a few slips in this thought-provoking study. The authorship of *The Isle of Dogs* is assigned to Day rather than to Jonson and Nashe. More importantly, Menzer mistakenly claims that the Q1 title-page asserts an 'impossibility' when it records that 'his Highnesse ser-uants' had performed *Hamlet* by 1603. Menzer writes that 'only on May 19, 1603, had the Lord Chamberlain's Men received the royal patent', whereas 'Valentine Simmes printed and offered Q1 *Hamlet* for sale in late May or June of 1603'. This claim is based on a faulty reconstruction of the printing of Q1 with no basis in empirical fact.

WORKS REVIEWED

Davidson, Adele, *Shakespeare in Shorthand: The Textual Mystery of 'King Lear'* (Newark, DE, 2009)

Halio, Jay L., ed., *Romeo and Juliet: Parallel Texts of Quarto 1 (1597) and Quarto 2 (1599)* (Newark, DE, 2008)

Hunter, Lynette, and Peter Lichtenfels, *Negotiating Shakespeare's Language in 'Romeo and Juliet': Reading Strategies from Criticism, Editing and the Theatre. Accompanied by a scholarly edition of the play on DVD* (Aldershot, 2009)

Menzer, Paul. *The Hamlets: Cues, Qs, and Remembered Texts* (Newark, DE, 2008)

Shakespeare, William. *King Richard III*, ed. James Siemon, Arden 3 (London, 2009)

INDEX

NOTE: locators in italics denote illustrations.

INDEX

INDEX